PREACHING THROUGH
THE CHRISTIAN YEAR

PREACHING THROUGH THE CHRISTIAN YEAR

Year C

A Comprehensive Commentary on the Lectionary

Fred B. Craddock
John H. Hayes
Carl R. Holladay
Gene M. Tucker

Trinity Press International   Valley Forge, Pennsylvania

First Edition 1994

Trinity Press International
P.O. Box 851
Valley Forge, PA 19482-0851

Cover design by Brian Preuss

Library of Congress Cataloging-in-Publication Data

Preaching through the Christian year. Year C / Fred B. Craddock . . .
  [et al.].
   p. cm.
  Includes index.
  ISBN 1-56338-100-1 (v. 3)
  1. Bible—Homiletical use. 2. Bible—Commentaries. 3. Common lectionary
(1992) 4. Lectionary preaching. I. Craddock, Fred B.
BS534.5.P7272 1992
251—dc20   CIP

Printed in the United States of America on acid-free paper.

94 95 96 97 98 99   6 5 4 3 2 1

Contents

TRINITY SUNDAY

PROPERS AFTER PENTECOST

Introduction

The Consultation on Common Texts issued the *Common Lectionary* in 1983, inviting the churches to use it and then offer suggestions for amendments and modifications. That trial period is now ended, and in December 1991 a final draft of the calendar and table of readings was completed. No further changes in this lectionary are anticipated. The present volume—the second of three to appear in a series—is based on the newly revised *Common Lectionary: The Lectionary Proposed by the Consultation on Texts* (1992).

The now finalized *Common Lectionary* more fully converses with the lectionaries of the Episcopal, Lutheran, and Roman Catholic churches than did the 1983 edition. Readers will notice the influence of these three traditions in both calendar and readings. For example, Holy Saturday with its appropriate readings is offered for those who observe liturgically the Saturday between Good Friday and Easter. At some points, this greater inclusiveness has meant embracing the selected texts in the Roman, Lutheran, or Episcopal lectionaries. In other instances, the texts of these three traditions are offered as alternate readings. In every case, it has been our decision to comment on all the texts, hoping to make this commentary useful to as wide an audience as possible and as helpful to as many pulpits as possible.

In 1989, the New Revised Standard Version of the Bible was published. The present work follows the NRSV as its primary translation. In addition, two other widely used translations, the New English Bible and the Jerusalem Bible, have been used in their new revisions. Other translations are also quoted occasionally.

This commentary series will treat all the readings for each year in a single volume. Having in one volume a full year's calendar, table of readings, and commentary gives the preacher and others who work with the liturgy a clearer sense of continuity and greater ease of reference within a year and of cross reference among the three years. A commentary is a reference book, most at home on a study desk.

As an aid for focus and direction, each of the volumes in the series will provide a brief introduction to the readings for each service.

We think it important that the reader understand the perspectives and convictions that will inform our work throughout the three volumes. We offer these under the following three headings.

The Scripture. There is no substitute for direct exposure to the biblical text, both for the preacher in preparation and for the listener in worship. The Scriptures are therefore not only studied privately but also read aloud as an act of worship in and of itself and not solely as prelude to a sermon. The sermon is an interpretation of Scripture in the sense that the preacher seeks to bring the text forward into the present in order to effect a new hearing of the Word. In this sense, the text has its future and its fulfillment in preaching. In fact, the Bible itself is the record of the continual rehearing and reinterpreting of its own traditions in new settings and for new generations of believers. New settings and new circumstances are properly as well as inescapably integral to a hearing of God's Word in and through the text. Whatever else may be said to characterize God's Word, it is always appropriate to the hearers. But the desire to be immediately relevant should not abbreviate study of the text or divorce the sermon from the biblical tradition. Such sermons are orphaned, released without memory into the world. It is the task of the preacher and teacher to see that the principle of fidelity to Scripture is not abandoned in the life and worship of the church. The endeavor to understand a text in its historical, literary, and theological contexts does create, to be sure, a sense of distance between the Bible and the congregation. The preacher may grow impatient during this period of feeling a long way from a sermon. But this time of study can be most fruitful. By holding text and parishioners apart for a while, the preacher can hear each more clearly and exegete each more honestly. Then, when the two intersect in the sermon, neither the text nor the congregation is consumed by the other. Because the Bible is an ancient book, it invites the preacher back into its world in order to understand; because the Bible is the church's Scripture, it moves forward into our world and addresses us here and now.

The Lectionary. Ever-increasing numbers of preachers are using a lectionary as a guide for preaching and worship. The intent of lectionaries is to provide for the church over a given period of time (usually three years) large units of Scripture arranged according to the seasons of the Christian year and selected because they carry the central message of the Bible. Lectionaries are not designed to limit one's message or restrict the freedom of the pulpit. On the contrary, churches that use a lectionary usually hear more Scripture in worship than those that do not. And ministers who preach from the lectionary find themselves stretched into areas of the canon into which they would not have gone had they kept to the path of personal preference. Other values of the lectionary are well known: the readings provide a common ground for discussions in ministerial peer groups; family worship can more easily join public worship through shared readings; ministers and worship committees can work with common biblical texts to prepare services that have movement and integrity; and the lectionary encourages more disciplined study and advance preparation. All these and other values are increased if churches share a common lectionary. A common lectionary could conceivably generate a communitywide Christian conversation.

However, to the nonlectionary preacher also we offer this commentary as a helpful tool in sermon preparation. An index of Scriptures on which comments are made is provided in each volume. By means of this index, any preacher or teacher will find easy access to commentary on hundreds of biblical texts.

This Book. This volume is not designed as a substitute for work with the biblical text; on the contrary, its intent is to encourage such work. Neither is it our desire to relieve the preacher of regular visits to concordances, lexicons, and commentaries; rather, it is our hope that the comments on the texts here will be sufficiently germinal to give direction and purpose to those visits to major reference works. Our commentary is an effort to be faithful to the text and to begin moving the text toward the pulpit. There are no sermons as such here, nor could there be. No one can preach long distance. Only the one who preaches can do an exegesis of the listeners and mix into sermon preparation enough local soil so as to effect an indigenous hearing of the Word. But we hope we have contributed to that end. The reader will notice that, although each of us has been aware of the other readings for each service, there has been no attempt to offer a collaborated commentary on all texts or a homogenized interpretation as though there were not four texts but one. It is assumed that the season of the year, the needs of the listeners, the preacher's own abilities, as well as the overall unity of the message of the Scriptures will prompt the preacher to find among the four readings the word for the day. Sometimes the four texts will join arm in arm; sometimes they will debate with one another; sometimes one will lead while the others follow, albeit at times reluctantly. Such is the wealth of the biblical witness.

A final word about our comments. The lections from the Psalter have been treated in the same manner as the other readings, even though some Protestant churches often omit the reading of the psalm or replace it with a hymn. We have chosen to regard the psalm as an equal among the texts, primarily for three reasons. First, there is growing interest in the use of psalms in public worship, and comments about them may help make that use more informed. Second, the psalms were a major source for worship and preaching in the early church, and they continue to inspire and inform Christian witness today. And third, comments on the psalms may make this volume helpful to preachers in those traditions that have maintained from earliest times the use of psalms in Christian services.

A brief word about the relation of this commentary to our earlier work, *Preaching the New Common Lectionary*. From the comments above, it is already apparent why those volumes could not be given a new introduction and offered again to you. Changes in appointed texts, revised translations of the Bible, additions to the liturgical calendar, and attention to texts appearing in Lutheran, Episcopal, and Roman Catholic lectionaries necessitated much new writing. The new writing in turn called for a reappraisal of the comments on texts that remained unchanged, prompting additions, deletions, and modifications. The result is a new, larger, and, we hope, improved commentary to aid those who preach and teach.

> Fred B. Craddock (Gospels)
> John H. Hayes (Psalms)
> Carl R. Holladay (Epistle and Acts)
> Gene M. Tucker (Old Testament)

First Sunday of Advent

Jeremiah 33:14–16;
Psalm 25:1–10;
1 Thessalonians 3:9–13;
Luke 21:25–36

The year opens with promises and prayers, promises of the coming reign of God and prayers that the people of God will be ready for that reign. The texts set a tone of hopeful expectation, but not without trepidation in view of the awesome events to come. The Old Testament reading is an announcement that the ancient promise of a Davidic messiah will be fulfilled and Jerusalem will dwell secure. The responsorial psalm is a prayer for help and forgiveness, reaffirming the righteousness and faithfulness of God already expressed in the reading from Jeremiah 33. In the epistolary reading, Paul's prayer that he be allowed to join the faithful in Thessalonica becomes a petition that they be ready for the coming of the Lord. The Gospel lection sets the season of Advent into an eschatological framework: the signs in the heavens indicate that the kingdom of God is near.

Jeremiah 33:14–16

These verses from Jeremiah are located in the context of a series of announcements of salvation. The chapter begins with an introduction that attributes the words that follow to Jeremiah, "while he was still confined in the court of the guard" (33:1), during the Babylonian siege of Jerusalem. However, there are numerous allusions in the chapter to the circumstances of the Babylonian Exile or even later. References to the city and nation as already destroyed (33:7, 10, 12) are followed by these unconditional promises of restoration. Moreover, the fact that our reading is part of a section (33:14–26) not found in the ancient Greek version of Jeremiah is further indication that it comes from a period later than that of the prophet Jeremiah.

Verses 14–16 in fact contain an exact quotation of lines already found in Jeremiah 23:5–6. They apparently are quoted here to provide a text for the explanation and interpretation that follow in Jeremiah 33:17–26, in the same way that preachers cite a biblical text as the foundation for a sermon. Thus, in the context of our reading, an earlier promise concerning the line of David is called to the attention of a new and later group of hearers who are assured that the hope will one day be fulfilled. The major addition to the text from Jeremiah 23:5–6 is the line "when I will fulfill the promise I made to the house of Israel and the house of Judah" (v. 14). Those to whom these lines were addressed must have lived in a time when there was no king in the line of David on the throne in Jerusalem, but it is not clear whether the "righteous Branch" was expected in the near or distant future.

These verses reach to the heart of the Old Testament messianic expectations, assuming the promise, recorded in 2 Samuel 7, of a perpetual kingship in the line of David. The "messiah" (or "anointed one") was the title applied to each new monarch. The Davidic monarchy and the assurance that it would be permanent were gifts of divine grace intended to guarantee the peace and security of the people of God (2 Sam. 7:10–13). Because the people experienced rulers who were less than just and righteous, the promise of a "righteous Branch" was heard through the prophets and was reiterated after the Babylonians brought an end to the Davidic dynasty.

In Jeremiah 33:14–16 it is the Lord who will fulfill the promise and "cause a righteous Branch to spring up for David." Divine intervention is expected, but through a human figure. The language that characterizes this figure occurs also in Isaiah 11:1 (cf. also Isa. 4:2). In Zechariah 3:8 and 6:12, "branch" may refer to a particular individual in the time of that prophet.

Most important here are the functions of the one whom the Lord will "cause . . . to spring up." "He shall execute justice and righteousness in the land. . . . Judah will be saved and Jerusalem will live in safety" (vv. 15–16). This language has become such a part of our abstract religious vocabulary that we must remind ourselves of its concreteness. Justice and righteousness—the most familiar pair of terms from the Old Testament prophets—refer to fair and equitable relationships among people, impartial law courts, the protection of the weak from the strong (justice), and the personal characteristics (righteousness) that make such conditions possible. To "save" Judah and cause Jerusalem to "live in safety" do not refer in the first instance to religious experiences or practices, but to specific political circumstances: Judah will be free of foreign domination and Jerusalem from fear of invasion.

The functions, then, of the righteous Branch are in the realm of what we would call governmental, political concerns, both domestic and foreign. If the Old Testament lesson has a contribution to make to the beginning of Advent, it is to keep before us God's concern for such matters. The reign of God comes not only beyond time and this world, but also in history and in this world. The righteous Branch, the anointed one of God, comes in human form into a human world. That is not just an ancient Israelite hope, but the Christian expectation at Advent as well.

Psalm 25:1–10

Two general features should be noted about this psalm. First, like a few other psalms (Pss. 9/10, 34, 37, 111, 112, 119, 145), this one is an alphabetic poem, sometimes called an acrostic. This means that the psalm flows through the alphabet with each successive verse commencing with the next letter of the Hebrew alphabet. Second, the composition is a lament of an individual; that is, it was originally written to be used in worship services in which an individual's needs were the focus of attention.

The psalm moves back and forth between the individual's petitions to the Deity (vv. 1–7, 16–22), the priest or worship leader's address to the worshiper (vv. 8–10, 12–14), and the worshiper's statement to the priest/worship leader (v. 15). Thus the psalm contains three types of material: petitionary prayer, confession, and priestly proclamation. The lection for today is comprised of two of the psalm's components: a prayer or petition addressed to the

Deity (vv. 1–7) and theological proclamation probably addressed by the priest to the wor-shiper (vv. 8–10).

Two verbs are of fundamental importance in verses 1–7—"wait" and "remember"—and give expression to two of the basic Christian sentiments and postures of Advent—waiting and remembering. Advent is a time of waiting, or expectation, of looking to the future; but it is also a time for remembrance, for recollection, for reflection.

The term "wait" appears in verses 3 and 5. In the former, it appears in a petitionary in-tercession on behalf of a group—"those who wait for you." In the latter, it appears in a confes-sional statement expressing trust. Intercession and confession may thus be seen as two ways of waiting.

In the melody of the waiting there lies, however, a dissonant chord. The time of waiting is not simply the idle passing of the hour; it is a time of misery and trouble. Noted, in verses 16–19, the cacophony of unharmonious notes: loneliness, affliction, a troubled heart, dis-tresses, sin, innumerable foes, and violent hatred. The psalmist waits for God when all the evidence suggests that the waiting may be long and the pain and misery deep. Mere en-durance, however, is not the goal of waiting. Note the counterbalance of requests over against the terms depicting misery: "turn," "be gracious," "relieve," "bring me out," "consider," "for-give," "guard," "deliver," and "do not let me be put to shame." Quite a list of Christmas re-quests for so early in Advent! But isn't that part of what Advent and redemption are all about—recognizing and confessing the nature of the status quo and wanting and requesting a new status of being.

The psalmist also speaks about remembering. Three times the verb occurs in verses 6–7. (The first occurrence, the NRSV translates "be mindful.") The request for remembrance here takes two forms: remembering and remembering not. The psalmist requests that God remem-ber mercy and steadfast love, those divine qualities that predispose the Deity toward human redemption. These are seen as the qualities possessed by God "from of old." On the other hand, there is the request to "remember not"—that is, forget—the human past with its youth-ful sins (inadvertent errors and wayward faults) and more adult transgressions (more deliber-ate and premeditated wrongs). In Advent, with its backward glance and future focus, there is stress on those eternal characteristics of goodness attributed to God and at the same time the human need to be burdened no longer by the past with its accumulated failures.

The final plea to remember is in verse 7b, where the psalmist asks that God should, on the basis of divine love and goodness, "remember me." Remember me, not my past, just me, as I am, waiting and remembering.

1 Thessalonians 3:9–13

Even though the season of Advent is frequently observed as a time of preparation for Christmas, and thus as a time when we direct our thoughts toward the advent, or com-ing, of the incarnate Lord in his birth, it includes much more than this. It becomes a time when we reflect on the Lord's coming in its many dimensions: his historical coming in his birth, his eschatological coming at the end of time, his existential coming into our own present. The first of these, Christ's coming in the incarnation, is not referred to in today's epistolary reading. It focuses instead, like the other epistolary readings in Years A & B for the First Sunday of Advent (Rom. 13:11–14; 1 Cor. 1:3–9), on the future "coming of our Lord Jesus" (v. 13).

But the existential dimension is here as well, for the passage speaks of those things that are central to our appropriation of the Christ-event. It speaks of a God who can actually direct travel plans and bring them to fulfillment (v. 11), an apostle bound to his church by love (v. 12), a Lord who can so enrich Christian love that it reaches both inward and outward (v. 12). It also speaks of a Lord who makes our hearts firm and our lives holy and blameless in preparation for the Lord's coming (v. 13).

When Paul wrote these words, he had established the Thessalonian church just a few months earlier (cf. Acts 17:1–9). Much of the earlier part of the letter is spent recalling his founding visit and reflecting on his ministry among the people (cf. esp. 2:1–16). As one reads this epistle, it becomes clear that this young, fledgling church still occupies his thoughts and prayers. Even though he is now engaged in evangelistic activity in Corinth, his heart and mind still return to Thessalonica. He has tried to visit them but has been hindered from doing so (2:17–20). He recalls the success of the gospel among them, speaking of them as his "glory and joy" (2:20). He is obviously buoyed by the steadfastness of their faith in the face of persecution and resistance (2:13–16), but he is understandably anxious about their welfare. His anxiety is that of the minister who frets over new converts who have been left behind in a struggling mission church, knowing that their faith is fragile at best. Like a "gentle . . . nurse tenderly caring for her own children" (2:7), he is both thankful and joyful for them, but constantly prays that he may see them "face to face" (v. 10) to shore up their faith.

Here we are at the very center of the Lord's coming as it is understood existentially: the minister praying for the members of the church—thankful, joyful, triumphant, yet eager to see them, concerned about their welfare, eager to teach them more and supply what is lacking, hoping that their love for one another will hold them together and that they will be presentable on the day of the Lord.

In another sense as well, this passage illustrates the existential dimension of the Lord's coming. Here we see faith taking root—and taking shape. The Thessalonians have received the word of God not as homiletical verbiage, but "as what it really is, God's word, which is also at work in you believers" (2:13). God has come to them through the proclaimed Word. Yet it still energizes them. God's presence remains a powerful force at work within their midst confirming them in their faith. And it is the community of faith bound to one another in love that becomes the locus of God's activity (v. 12). The apostle's heart is knit to theirs in love, and even in his absence his love for them grows rather than wanes. His hope is that their love for one another will increase even as his does for them, but their form of community is not to be narcissistic, turning in on itself and its own needs exclusively. Instead, he prays that their love will abound to "the whole human race" (JB; cf. Gal. 6:10). The church that genuinely experiences the coming of Christ into its own midst most fully embodies this presence when it extends its love beyond itself and lives for others. The church thus becomes a reenactment of the Christ-story—love for others.

For all this, however, the eschatological dimension is the most explicit motif in the passage. As is well known, the Second Coming of the Lord is a prominent concern in this epistle (cf. 2:19; 4:14–15; 5:2, 23; also 2 Thess. 1:7–10; 2:1, 8). The prayer for their hearts to be made firm so that they might stand before God "holy and faultless" (REB) is reminiscent of other early Christian teaching that insisted on sober preparation for the advent of Christ (cf. 5:23; James 5:8). One exegetical point worth noticing is whether "all his saints" (v. 13) refers to Christians or angels (cf. Zech. 14:5). In either case, the thrust of Paul's remarks is clear: Christians are urged to prepare themselves for the final coming of the Lord.

As we have seen, even though today's passage is anchored in Paul's very personal reflections about the Thessalonian church, and in this sense is quite historically concrete, it enables us to think about the Lord's coming in both an eschatological and existential sense. For homiletical appropriation, it may be possible to explore the nature of Christian community as seen in this passage and the ways this best represents the type of preparation called for by the Advent Season. Alternatively, one may explore the eschatological theme, reminding the church of the ways that past and future are interlocked in the Christ-event.

Luke 21:25–36

One can hardly imagine a more appropriate way to begin the Advent Season than to focus on texts that announce God's fulfilling the promise to bring justice, righteousness, and redemption. The means will be through a righteous branch of David (Jeremiah); the coming of our Lord Jesus (Paul); the Son of man coming in a cloud (Luke). What may seem less appropriate, however, is the Gospel lection that proclaims the apocalyptic end of all things and the coming of the kingdom of God. Nothing is here of virgin and child, of shepherds and heavenly choirs, but rather the shaking of heaven and earth in perplexity, fear, and foreboding.

In each of the three cycles of the lectionary, Advent is begun with a Gospel reading from the apocalyptic discourse of Jesus. These texts impress upon the preacher and the whole church that the coming of the Lord includes much more than the Christmas story; that Advent is God's doing, apart from all human calculation or designing; and that Advent is of such significance that the entire cosmos reverberates with the signs and circumstances of these events. That God comes to us is certain, however uncertain the when and how. It is that certainty, not the uncertainties, which moves us to repentance in our waiting.

Luke 21:25–36 is a portion of the larger unit, 21:5–38, which is itself set within 19:47–21:38, the teaching of Jesus in the temple. Whereas Matthew (24:1–3) and Mark (13:1–4) locate this apocalyptic discourse outside the temple on the Mount of Olives and address it to the disciples, Luke places it within the temple and addresses it to all the people (21:37–38). Our lection for today contains part of Jesus' answer to the twin questions of verse 7: When and with what signs will these things take place?

Luke's dependence on the Markan apocalypse (13:5–37) is quite evident. Within Luke 21:25–36 one notices, in addition to the expected rephrasing at points, the omission of Mark's verses 27 and 32 and the addition of Luke's own verse 28 and an entirely different ending to the discourse. The structure of Luke 21:25–36 is as follows:

Verses 25–28—the coming of the Son of man

29–31—the parable of the fig tree

32–33—the time of the coming of the Son of man

34–36—the ending of the discourse

If one places these four units within the whole discourse, Luke's sequencing of events seems rather clear. The followers of Jesus will have a time of witnessing (v. 13), in response to which there will be severe persecution, religious and political (vv. 12–19). As a consequence, Jerusalem will be destroyed before the eyes of the nations (vv. 20–24). When the time of the nations has been fulfilled, the Son of man will come in a cloud with power and glory, attended by signs in the heavens (vv. 25–28). This event will affect the whole earth and bring distress to all nations, but the faithful are to take heart and raise their heads: redemption is near. As surely as one can discern the approach of summer by the leafing of the fig tree, so these signs will announce that the kingdom of God is near (vv. 29–31). And when? Within this generation, says Luke (vv. 32–33). With this statement as to the time, Luke joins many other early Christians in the belief that they were living in the period between God's punishment of Jerusalem by the Gentiles (nations) and God's judgment of the nations by the Son of man whose appearing will bring redemption to the faithful.

Two additions by Luke to Mark's apocalypse deserve comment, especially in the Advent Season. The first is verse 28, which assures the followers of Christ that the final shaking of heaven and earth will not be for them an occasion for fear and distress. On the contrary, the day of judgment is the day of grace: "Stand up and raise your heads, because your redemption is drawing near." The second addition, verses 34–36, concludes the discourse with a moral admonition. Grace does not mean an automatic exemption from the distress coming upon all peoples of the earth. Rather, let this word about what will be have a sanctifying influence, producing a prayerful watchfulness and a freedom from indulgence and anxiety about things. As for the dulled and dissipated spirit, it is ensnared, not released, by the advent of God.

Second Sunday of Advent

Baruch 5:1–9 or Malachi 3:1–4;
Luke 1:68–79;
Philippians 1:3–11;
Luke 3:1–6

All the readings for this day focus upon the coming acts of God to save. The dominant mood is one of joyful expectation, but not without some reference to the dark background that precedes the coming salvation. Baruch 5:1–9 expresses promises to Jerusalem and the calls for her to change from sorrow to joy. Malachi's messenger of the covenant brings good news to Jerusalem, but also a period of purifying judgment. Used as the responsorial psalm, Zechariah's canticle in Luke 1:68–79 affirms the coming of the messiah and looks to the culmination of God's promise of salvation and peace. The epistolary reading, Paul's warm and joyful thanksgiving for the community at Philippi, looks toward the "day of Christ." Luke 3:1–6 reports the call of John the Baptist, characterizes his message as a baptism of repentance for the forgiveness of sins, and cites the announcement of salvation from Isaiah 40:3–5.

Baruch 5:1–9

The Book of Baruch is one of the least known of the books of the Bible, and in fact there are those who dispute its standing as part of the Christian Scriptures. Protestant Christians, following the lead of the Reformers, include it among the Apocrypha because it was not part of the Hebrew Scriptures. Although no Hebrew text of the book has come to light, at least some of the work must have originated in Hebrew. The style in the first chapters is distinctly Hebraic, but that is less obvious in the concluding sections, including our reading for the day.

Although the book purports to come from Jeremiah's scribe Baruch (see Jer. 32:12; 36:4; 51:59) at the time of the Babylonian conquests of Judah and Jerusalem, it must stem from a later period and from another unnamed person or persons. Among other sources, the work depends upon Isaiah 40–55 (ca. 539 BC) and Daniel 9 (167–64 BC). Consequently, it could have been written no earlier than the middle of the second century BC. Some commentators date it to the time following the fall of Jerusalem to the Romans in AD 70, but that probably is too late. Although not historically accurate, the assumption that the words are addressed to the defeated people of God, now scattered and exiled from the Holy City, is important for understanding the message of our lection.

7

The book as a whole, as most commentators have noticed, consists of two distinct parts, each with two sections. The first part (1:1–3:8) is in prose and contains an introduction (1:1–14) and Israel's confession of guilt (1:15–3:8). The second part (3:9–5:9) is in poetry, containing a poem in praise of God's wisdom (3:9–4:4) and announcements of salvation concerning the restoration of Jerusalem (4:5–5:9).

As part of a unit that begins in Baruch 4:30, the reading for the day is addressed to Jerusalem, understood both literally and metaphorically. On the one hand, the city is the actual holy place, the site of the temple, the home of the exiles. On the other hand, Jerusalem is personified, seen to be grieving like a widow for her sons, a lonely woman for her daughters (Bar. 4:16). She is told to remove her mourning garb and put on "the beauty of the glory from God" (5:1), to stand up and look toward the east to see her children gathered (5:5). As a bereaved woman, she represents the suffering, defeated people of God, and her joy celebrates that of her returning children.

It is not surprising that the early church fathers attributed quotations from this book to the prophet Jeremiah. Although there are none of the usual messenger or oracle formulas ("thus says the Lord," "says the Lord"), the language of this chapter is prophetic both in form and in content. It consists of a series of announcements of salvation. The pattern is an admonition or instruction to the Holy City followed by reasons (introduced by "for") to follow the admonition. Thus, in 5:1–2 Jerusalem is to replace mourning garments with the symbols of God's righteousness, glory, and splendor, "for" (5:3–4) God will show the city's splendor everywhere and perpetually chant her name, "Peace of righteousness and glory of godliness." And in 5:5 Jerusalem is told to stand up and see her children returning, "for" God is bringing them back (5:6), "for" God is preparing a safe and smooth way for their return (5:7–8), and "for" God will lead Israel in the light of his glory and with his mercy and righteousness (5:9).

The attentive reader will not miss the similarity of many of these words of salvation and assurance to those in Isaiah 40 and following. Compare 5:1–2 with Isaiah 61:3; 5:4 with Isaiah 60:14; 5:5 with Isaiah 49:18; and 5:7 with Isaiah 42:16ff. In this respect the Old Testament reading anticipates the citation of Isaiah 40:3–5 in the Gospel lection.

The message of the chapter is clear and unambiguous: A mourning and dispirited city and people will have cause for celebration because God is about to act to bring those people home. The God of mercy and righteousness will not leave God's people scattered and in exile. It is possible that such a message, proclaimed and heard in the season of Advent, can evoke hope and expectation in the hearts of those who wait for the coming of Jesus.

Malachi 3:1–4

"**M**alachi" probably is not a proper name but a title that comes from the passage before us, in which the Hebrew term means "my messenger." The book is thus anonymous, the words of an unnamed prophet or prophets of the postexilic period, following the return of the Judeans from Babylon. The existence of the second temple is taken for granted, and the regular offering of sacrifices there seems to have been resumed for some time. These facts indicate that the prophet was active after Haggai and Zechariah, who are concerned with the rebuilding of the temple about 520 BC, but earlier than Ezra or Nehemiah, around 400 BC. Malachi's interpretation of correct sacrifices does not seem to be aware of the details of the law instituted by Ezra.

The book thus comes from the heart of the Persian period, perhaps the middle of the fifth century BC. Judah and Jerusalem would have been under a "governor" (Mal. 1:8) doubtless appointed by the Persians. There is no evidence of external threats, and apart from a concern with intermarriage and criticism of neighboring Edom (Mal. 1:2–5), the book has little interest in affairs outside Judah.

The Book of Malachi gives us not a word about the prophet. That is not so surprising when we remember that as a rule Old Testament prophets give us remarkably little direct information about themselves. When they do speak of their backgrounds or experiences, they do so in order to present the message of God, which is central. The person who stands behind this book is like earlier prophets in that he courageously speaks in the name of the Lord, and his words often concern the immediate future. However, many of his themes and interests are priestly, and he seems to have been identified with a particular priestly group, the Levites (Mal. 2:4–9), but not uncritically (Mal. 3:3).

There are seven units in the book, each one in the form of a dialogue or disputation between the Lord, or the prophet on behalf of the Lord, and the group addressed. Sometimes the words of the opponents are quoted, thus indicating the problem addressed by the revelation. This pattern gives the book an argumentative character.

In our reading for the day, which in important respects stands at the center of the book's theology, the prophetic and the priestly dimensions come together. Malachi 3:1–4 includes most of the book's fourth unit (2:17–3:5) and should be understood in that context.

The disputation is addressed to those who have "wearied the LORD" (2:17) with particular words. They either have said that God delights in those who do evil or have asked where the God of justice could be found. The prophet's opponents are objecting to a real position, arguing—like Job—that it is not always the righteous who prosper, as Malachi 3:10–12 asserts. The problem is a particularly acute one for those who believe that there is or should be direct and immediate retribution or reward based on obedience to the law of God.

Our reading, then, is a response to the question of the justice of God. Its reaction is to affirm that there will come a time, and soon, when justice will be established. First the Lord will send a messenger to prepare the way for God's own appearance in the temple. It is not always easy here to distinguish between what the messenger is expected to do and what the Lord will do. The sequence of events, however, is transparent. The Lord will send a messenger, the messenger of the covenant, to prepare the way. The day of his coming—probably that of the messenger—will be a fearful one, for he will refine and purify "the descendants of Levi," that is, the levitical priests (cf. Isa. 6:5–7). The priests will then offer the right offerings, which will be pleasing to the Lord. Next (3:5), the Lord himself will come near for judgment, establishing justice by punishing the unrighteous, that is, those who "do evil" (2:17). The list of evildoers includes mainly those who oppress the weak (the hired workers, the widow, the orphan, and the foreigner), but also sorcerers, adulterers, and those who swear falsely.

Thus the prophet answers the question of the opponents, "Where is the God of justice?" (2:17). That God is coming; indeed, God's messenger has already been sent. First there will be purification of worship, and then God will establish justice.

As an Advent lesson, this text articulates the hope and proclaims the good news that God will act to save. Its mood and tone, however, are not those of joyful expectation. Rather, some of the themes of the Gospel reading's account of John the Baptist are emphasized. Preparation for the coming of God includes responding to a call for repentance, or experiencing a time of purification. Furthermore, the good news of God's justice for the weak may entail judgment on the strong, and it is those who stand so near the center of worship—in this case the priests—who require purification.

Luke 1:68-79

The psalm for today is one of the inspired songs that fill Luke 1–2. This song, or eulogy, often called the Benedictus (the Latin translation of the opening word), is a burst of praise by Zechariah on the occasion of the circumcision of his son John (the Baptist). The use of this passage as today's psalm is especially appropriate because John is the focus of the Gospel reading for not only this Sunday but also for both the second and third Sundays of Advent each year.

Luke, who alone among the Evangelists narrates the birth and circumcision of John as well as of Jesus, interweaves the two stories: first the announcement and anticipation of John's birth (1:5–25) and then that of Jesus (1:26–57). John's story continues in 1:57–80. This account consists of three parts: the birth, the circumcision, and the naming of John (vv. 57–66); the inspired prophecy of Zechariah (vv. 67–79); and a brief statement of summary that serves as a transition to his public life (v. 80). Our present concern is the prophetic song itself (vv. 68–79).

The introduction to the song makes two important statements: first, Zechariah is filled with the Holy Spirit; and second, what he says is identified as prophecy. In this characterization Zechariah joins Elizabeth (1:41–45), Mary (1:46–55), and Simeon (2:27–32), as well as Jesus, the apostles, and early Christian prophets. In fact, for Luke a primary role of the Holy Spirit is inspiring speech, and this speech, defined as prophetic, joins the Christian movement with Judaism, where God also worked through prophetic words. The Benedictus itself falls into two units: verses 68–75 and 76–79. The first unit praises God not for sending John but for raising up "a mighty savior for us"; that is, Jesus. Full of Old Testament allusions, these verses are distinctly Jewish, similar to canonical psalms that praise God as deliverer (Pss. 34; 67; 103; 113). The Dead Sea Scrolls contain similar psalms of praise and thanksgiving. Israel's eschatological hopes will be fulfilled, promises will be kept, the covenant with Abraham will be remembered, and all enemies will be overthrown.

The second unit (vv. 76–79) speaks of John, but even here the focus is on Jesus, for John "will go before the Lord to prepare his ways" (v. 76). This song provides a concise summary of what John will do and what Jesus will do, drawing heavily on Malachi 3:1–2; 4:5–6 and on Isaiah 9:2; 42:7. However, we must keep in mind that throughout the passage, the true object of praise is God: "Blessed be the Lord God of Israel" (v. 68). In the ministry of John, God comes to us. That advent prepares us for the fuller advent in Jesus of Nazareth.

Philippians 1:3-11

Paul typically opens his letters with a prayer, usually a thanksgiving (Rom. 1:8–17; 1 Cor. 1:4–9; Col. 1:3–14; 1 Thess. 1:2–10; 2:13–16; 3:9–10; 2 Thess. 1:3–4; Philem. 4–7), sometimes a blessing (2 Cor. 1:3–7; Eph. 1:3–23). It is important to remember that the letters were intended to be read before Christians assembled in house churches, and thus these opening prayers would have had a liturgical function. As one would expect, they are crafted with the hearers in mind, and they speak to the concrete situation of those addressed. Consequently, these opening prayers typically introduce motifs or themes that are later dealt with in the letter itself. In this sense, they serve as a table of contents for the rest of the letter.

This opening prayer of thanksgiving is no exception. As is well known, this letter was written partially in response to a generous gift from the Philippian church (4:15–18). Behind several phrases in the prayer we detect references to the generosity of the Philippians and their financial participation in Paul's ministry. Their "sharing in the gospel from the first day until now" (v. 5) had occurred not only because they had suffered, like Paul, for the sake of the gospel (1:29–30), but also because they had become financial partners with him (4:15). Their partnership with him existed at both a spiritual and financial level. The "good work" that God had started within them (v. 6) may be a reference to this mission effort they had supported so loyally. What becomes clear throughout the prayer is that Paul regarded this church as full participants in his own ministry. They had become "sharers in God's grace" with Paul in his "imprisonment and in the defense and confirmation of the gospel" (v. 7). In one sense, the chains he had worn he had worn alone, and his work of defending and establishing the gospel (cf. NJB, v. 7) he had done alone. But in another sense, he had done none of this alone. The Philippians, through their solidarity with him, had shared in these activities. They became coparticipants in Paul's ministry (cf. 1:19).

It is this level of genuine partnership that existed between Paul and his supporting church that accounts for the intimate tone of this prayer. Every time he thought of them he became thankful. Every time he prayed for them, it was an occasion of joy. His bond with them is one of genuine affection: "You have a permanent place in my heart, and God knows how much I miss you all, loving you as Christ Jesus loves you" (vv. 7b–8, JB). These are the affections generated by a long-standing relationship. Paul is not writing to a church he has only recently established, but to a church he has known for years. He has received their money (4:15–19), their emissary Epaphroditus (2:25–30), their prayers (1:19), and their concern (4:10, 14).

This passage has been chosen for today's lection because of its twofold mention of the "day of (Jesus) Christ" (vv. 6 and 10). The opening prayers of Paul's letters typically moved toward an eschatological climax. Early Christians, of course, expected the return of Christ in their lifetime. Paul speaks his sentiments, and theirs, when he later writes, "The Lord is near" (4:5; cf. 3:20). This provides the overarching perspective in which the prayer is cast. Paul sees the work of God begun within the Philippian church as reaching its fulfillment "at the day of Jesus Christ" (v. 6). In turn, it is his hope that they may be found "pure and blameless" at the day of Christ (v. 10). In both instances, Paul is insisting that they adopt the right perspective on the future, realizing first that any Christian understanding of the future must be defined with respect to Christ. It is no longer the "day of the Lord" in the Old Testament sense of a time when Yahweh would vindicate the cause of Israel. Rather, it is a future radically redefined by the Christ-event.

Basic to this Christian understanding of the future is the realization that it is not fully realized yet. In fact, it is conceivable that some in the Philippian church, or perhaps outside opponents, had already laid claim to the future coming of Christ. One plausible reconstruction of the situation behind chapter 3 is that Paul is combating an overrealized eschatology by insisting that resurrection is still a future attainment. If so, his opening prayer reaffirms his insistence that our task is to live with an eye to the future, not as if we had already laid claim on it.

It is precisely this conviction that we have not yet realized fully the potential for Christian existence that prompts his prayer in their behalf toward the end of our passage. First, he prays that their love for one another will continue to increase (v. 9; cf. 1 Thess. 3:12). Later passages in the letter suggest that the Philippians still had something to learn about harmonious fellowship (2:1–13; 4:2–3). Second, he prays that their capacity for mutual commitment to one another will be reinforced "with knowledge and full insight" (v. 9). His hope is that they would never stop improving their knowledge and deepening their perception (cf. v. 9, JB; cf. Rom. 15:14; Col. 1:9; Philem. 6). Third, he prays that a fellowship of love refined with discerning knowledge will give them the capacity to "determine what is best" (v. 10) or "to learn by experience what things really matter" (REB). The fellowship he envisions is both loving and discerning, informed by both the heart and the head. It is not insensitive, but neither is it naive. It is only through such tough-mindedness that they will emerge before the last day "pure and blameless." Fourth, he is convinced that out of such fellowship will spring "the harvest of righteousness that comes through Jesus Christ" (v. 11; cf. Heb. 12:11; James 3:18; also Prov. 3:9; 11:30; Gal. 5:22).

Luke 3:1–6

On this Second Sunday of Advent, all four writers of the Scripture texts look to the day of the Lord, each having in mind an advent of God. Their understandings of the coming of the Lord differ, but they are of one mind in the conviction that there is no advent without preparation. In that faith, the father of John the Baptist praises God, the prophet looks to the coming of God's messenger who will purify Israel, the apostle ministers in anticipation, and the Evangelist introduces John, the voice crying in the wilderness. John, the son of Zechariah who prepares the way for Jesus, is himself of unusual birth and a gift from God (Luke 1:5–25, 57–80), for Luke understands that not only the Lord's coming but also the preparation for that coming are the initiatives of a gracious God.

In beginning the Gospel with the ministry of John, Luke joins the other three Evangelists. Even the Fourth Gospel, which opens with a hymn to the eternal Word (1:1–18), twice interrupts the hymn to comment about the Baptist (vv. 6–8, 15), even though the narrative proper will begin with the witness of John's ministry (v. 19). However, the most elaborate introduction of John the Baptist is given by Luke, who interweaves the accounts of the annunciations and of the births of John and Jesus. Having done that, Luke needs, at 3:1–6, only to identify him as the son of Zechariah (v. 2).

More important to Luke at this point is the placing in proper context the ministry of this obscure prophet from the hill country of Judea. Luke does so in two ways:

First, he provides the historical context. Multiple chronological indicators are listed (vv. 1–2), the most precise of which is the fifteenth year of Tiberius Caesar, which would be sometime between AD 26 and AD 28, depending on method of calculation. The others in the list are political and religious rulers of lesser rank but whose positions enabled them to have more direct influence upon the careers of John and Jesus. Although unusually elaborate here, this method of beginning a chronicle of events was not uncommon for the time, and, for Luke, was probably patterned after the introduction to the books of Old Testament prophets (Jer. 1:1–3; Ezek. 1:1–3; Hos. 1:1; Isa. 1:1). Such detail is in keeping with Luke's own announced intention, after careful investigation, of writing an orderly account (1:1–4). Of more importance, this setting of the story in the Gospel in the larger religious and political arena is congenial to and expressive of Luke's theology. On its way from Jerusalem to Rome, as Luke unfolds the account in Acts, the Gospel will not only encounter the poor, lame, halt, and blind, but also the synagogue rulers, high priests, governors, kings, treasurers, city officials, leading women, philosophers of Athens, captains of ships, imperial guards, and finally the emperor himself.

The second context Luke provides is that of salvation history, the tradition of God's dealing with the covenant community. John's ministry is the fulfillment of prophecy. Luke omits Mark's insertion of Malachi 3:1 into the Isaiah passage (Mark 1:2), reserving it until later (7:27), but he extends the quotation from Isaiah beyond Mark's use of only one verse (40:3). By citing Isaiah 40:3–5, Luke is able not only to testify to the universality of the gospel ("all flesh shall see the salvation of God") but also to point out that God's embrace of all nations has been in the tradition all along.

After the manner of earlier prophetic calls, "the word of God came to John" (v. 2). In all the region about the Jordan, John preached what Luke was soon to designate "the good news" (3:18). For this Evangelist, the gospel is the gift of repentance and the forgiveness of sins, to Israel and to all nations (24:47). John's greatness lay in his making that announcement which was to be heard around the world.

Our Gospel for today begins, then, with a list of names and titles—how preachers hate lists!—but does it matter? Perhaps Luke was a history buff, but is it important to anyone else? The answer is yes. Luke, by setting the preparation for the advent of Jesus Christ in the context of world history and the universal purpose of God, says that the gospel belongs to all people. The gospel is not the church's possession to be subsequently carried to others. The gospel is for the world before it is ever uttered, by John, by Jesus, or by the church. This is God's gift to God's creation.

Third Sunday of Advent

Zephaniah 3:14–20;
Isaiah 12:2–6;
Philippians 4:4–7;
Luke 3:7–18

Preparation for Christmas continues in the readings for the day with a dominant mood of joyful expectation. Like the Old Testament lection for last week, Zephaniah 3:14–20 pictures a joyful Jerusalem, one that sees salvation on the horizon because God is in her midst. The responsorial psalm from Isaiah 12 consists of songs of thanksgiving for Zion's deliverance. In the epistolary text, Paul calls for his readers to rejoice in the Lord, who is at hand. The apocalyptic dimensions of the Lord's advent are stressed in the Gospel as it summarizes the preaching of John the Baptist, concluding with the note that he "proclaimed the good news to the people" (Luke 3:18).

Zephaniah 3:14–20

According to the first verse of the book, Zephaniah was active during the reign of Josiah of Judah, that is, 640–609 BC. This was the era of Assyrian hegemony over the small states in Syria and Palestine, including Judah, but also the time of Josiah's revolt against Assyrian control and his reformation of religious practices (2 Kings 22–23). The reform, generally associated with the Book of Deuteronomy, opposed pagan influence in Judah's religion and included the centralization of all worship in Jerusalem. Most of the Book of Zephaniah contains indictments of corrupt religious practices and announcements of judgment, even against the city of Jerusalem (3:1–13).

Our reading for the day thus stands in sharp contrast to most of the book in which it is located. Its message, style, and apparent historical situation are different. The concluding verse, for example, appears to assume that the people of God are scattered away from Jerusalem and now are about to return. Consequently, these lines in Zephaniah 3:14–20 probably were added to the book, either during the Babylonian Exile or the postexilic period. The community of faith that supplemented the book would not have done so to deny the validity of the previous announcements of disaster; to the contrary, they affirmed that Zephaniah's view of the future was right. Yahweh had indeed punished the people, as the prophet said he would, but now Yahweh is about to redeem them. Forgiveness follows judgment; celebration of salvation comes after separation and suffering.

Broadly speaking, the passage consists of two major parts of unequal length. The first part (v. 14) is a series of imperatives addressed to Jerusalem and calling for the Holy City to rejoice. The remainder of the passage is the second part (vv. 15–20), which gives the reasons for the celebration. A speaker in the prophetic mode first assures the addressee—Jerusalem, but also its inhabitants—concerning the past and the present: the Lord has removed the judgments, cast out her enemies, and is present with her, even joining the celebration and renewing his love for her (vv. 15–17). The reasons for celebration continue as the speaker quotes the words of Yahweh (vv. 18–20). These are promises concerning the future. In addition to reiterating some of the themes already introduced, the promises affirm that Yahweh will put an end to oppression, save the lame and the outcast, return the people to their homeland, and restore both their reputation and their fortunes.

Several expressions and themes call for special comment. The older translations "daughter of Zion" and "daughter of Jerusalem" (v. 14, RSV) are misleading. "Daughter Zion" (NRSV) or "Miss Zion" more accurately convey the sense of the original, namely, the personification of the city as a young woman. The language in verse 15 echoes that of the psalms of the enthronement of Yahweh as king (e.g., Pss. 47; 24:7–10; 68; 93; 97).

This text is also the last of the Old Testament readings for the Easter Vigil, on which occasion its joyful exuberance—both in mood and contents—appropriately anticipates the celebration of Easter. It is equally appropriate during Advent as the church looks to the birth of its Lord. Furthermore, the dual use of the passage stresses that the links between Christmas and Easter are eschatological. Both the birth and the resurrection of Jesus herald the coming of the messianic age, the establishment of the reign of God. The simple reading of this passage during Advent can contribute to the establishment of the mood and atmosphere of celebration called for by the occasion. But there is more. The church would do well to respond to these calls to Jerusalem, and for the reasons given: God reigns, and will reign fully. The light of that future reign already begins to shine on our time and on our places. Because such a future is assured, our lives can be lived as the celebration of hope.

Isaiah 12:2–6

The responsorial psalm is among that large number of hymns and other Old Testament cultic songs found outside the Book of Psalms. One finds such songs frequently not only in the narrative books (e.g., Exod. 15:1–18, 21) but in the prophetic books as well (e.g., Amos 4:13; 5:8–9; 9:5–6). This fact, which should not be surprising, is due mainly to two factors. First, the authors of the books or the prophets would have been so steeped in the language of worship that they would have used such poetry where appropriate. Second, because the books subsequently were read in the context of worship, psalms would have been added, as one finds in a modern publication of the lectionary texts with all the readings for the particular days printed in the order of their use.

The location of Isaiah 12 within the book is by no means accidental. Broadly speaking, it concludes the first major section of the work, chapters 1–12. For the most part, the prophetic addresses and reports in this collection stem from the early period of the prophet's activity. Isaiah 13:1 clearly signals a new block of material—mainly oracles against foreign nations, different in terms of both form and content from the section concluded by Isaiah 12. More important for our understanding of the reading for the day is the fact that it directly follows a collection of prophecies concerning the Lord's savings acts for Jerusalem and Judah, acts that focus upon the descendants of David. These materials include 9:1–7 and 11:1–9, as well as 11:10–16, all of which herald the new age of peace and justice under "a shoot . . . from the stump of Jesse" (11:1).

It is very unlikely that the prophet Isaiah wrote chapter 12. It was added as the sayings of the prophet were being collected and saved as a book. The chapter serves as a fitting response on the part of the community of faith to the reading of the promises of salvation. It is even possible that the juxtaposition of the hymn of thanksgiving with the word of God through the prophet reflects liturgical practice in the Second Temple, during the postexilic period.

Although the lection begins with verse 2, all of chapter 12 should be interpreted as a whole. It is not obvious whether the chapter contains a single song or two brief ones, along with liturgical instructions for their use. In any case, the chapter contains two distinct parts, verses 1–3 and 4–6. (Verse 3 is to be taken with what precedes, not—as the NRSV divisions suggest—with what follows.) Each of the parts begins with the instruction "You will say in that day." Although it is not clear in English translation, the lines are different. In the original, verse 1a is second person singular and verse 4a is second person plural. Both are calls to give thanks, in verse 1 to an individual and in verse 4 to the community. The first section, then, is a thanksgiving song of an individual, and the second, a communal hymn of thanksgiving and praise. As indicated in verse 1, the background of songs of thanksgiving is deliverance from trouble and the celebration of that deliverance.

The patterns and motifs of the chapter are familiar from the Psalter. Expressions of thanksgiving, trust, or praise are followed by their reasons, introduced by "for" (vv. 1, 2, 5, 6). Confidence is expressed in the Lord as the individual's strength, song, and salvation (v. 2, using the language of the Song of Moses, Exod. 15:2). Songs of thanksgiving are prayers in which one calls to the Lord (v. 4). One sings for joy because the Holy One of Israel is both great and is among the worshipers (v. 6).

Three of the chapter's motifs call for particular attention in the season of Advent. First, there is the emphasis upon the future and the hope for divine intervention in human events. The introductory phrases, "in that day" (vv. 1, 4), make the songs of thanksgiving into promises: there will come a time when the people of God will experience salvation and will sing. Moreover, because the coming of that day is assured, even the present can be a time of joy. Second, because of its reference to Zion, the city of David, and its location in relation to chapter 11, the hope expressed here concerns the messianic age. Finally, though it is "royal Zion" who sings for joy (v. 6), the message of hope is by no means for a single city or a small circle. Giving thanks to the Lord means making "known his deeds among the nations" (v. 4), proclaiming his name "in all the earth" (v. 5). Zion is the center; but when God is in its midst, the good news cannot be contained but must reach out to all the world.

Philippians 4:4–7

"Rejoice in the Lord always; again I will say, Rejoice!" These opening words from today's epistolary lection capture the essential mood of joy that characterizes the traditional designation of this day as "Gaudete Sunday," derived from the Latin *gaudete*, the term for "rejoice" used in the Vulgate rendering of verse 4. The use of rose-colored vestments, or of a rose-colored candle in the Advent wreath, in connection with Advent symbolizes the shift from penance to joy that occurs as we move toward the celebration of Christmas. We also find this theme of joy expressed in various liturgical texts used for this Sunday. For example, joy is the fundamental note struck in the words spoken in connection with the lighting of the third candle of the Advent wreath: "We light this candle as a symbol of joy. May the joyful promise of your presence, O God, make us rejoice in our hope of salvation. O come, O come Emmanuel!" A similar note is struck in the O Antiphon for Advent 3: "O come, thou Day-spring from on high; And cheer us by thy drawing nigh; Disperse the gloomy clouds of night; And death's dark shadow put to flight" (Don E. Saliers, *From Hope to Joy* [Nashville: Abingdon Press, 1984], 52–53).

But what qualifies this reading as an Advent passage is Paul's declaration "The Lord is near" (v. 5). Here, the fundamental exegetical problem the homilist will have to struggle with is whether the statement is temporal or spatial. Ordinarily, it is understood eschatologically and thus taken to mean "The Lord is coming soon." This sense would conform to Paul's earlier remarks about "the day of Jesus Christ" (1:6, 10) and his eagerly awaiting the coming Savior (3:20–21), as well as other frequent New Testament references to an imminent Parousia (Rom. 13:12; 1 Cor. 16:22; Heb. 10:37 [Hab. 2:3]; James 5:8; 1 Pet. 4:7; Rev. 22:20). The language, however, is reminiscent of Psalm 145:18, "The LORD is near to all who call on him, to all who call on him in truth" (cf. also Ps. 119:151). If Paul is echoing the psalmist's sentiment, he may simply be reassuring the Philippians in the same sense: the Lord is always close by, especially to those who call upon him in anxious distress. What is striking is that, like the psalmist, Paul links his reassurance of the proximity of the Lord to an injunction to prayer. A similar connection is seen in Psalm 119:137–152, where the psalmist finds hope in being delivered from his enemies because the Lord is nearer to him than his enemies can ever get.

Given the prominence of the eschatological motif in Philippians, and in early Christian thought generally, a strong case can be made for the eschatological sense here. It may be, however, that Paul affirms the Lord's nearness in both senses. He may be combining the psalmist's reassurance of the Lord's existential nearness with early Christian expectation of the Lord's imminent return. If the eschatological sense is in view here, what is especially striking is the type of response Paul calls for. Rather than facing the future with gloom and despair, or even with penitence, we are called to rejoice at the prospect of the Lord's coming. These are words worth hearing—and proclaiming—because preaching on the Lord's coming can easily degenerate to shouts and threats. To be sure, Advent encompasses both threat and promise, but not threat alone.

Today's passage is instructive for the reassuring way it calls us to face both the present and the future. With a series of straightforward imperatives, it calls us to rejoice (cf. 1:4; 2:18; 1 Thess. 5:16), to be gentle and forbearing (cf. Titus 3:2; James 5:8–9; Wisd. of Sol. 2:19), not to be anxious (Matt. 6:25–34; Luke 12:22–32; 1 Pet. 5:7), to be thankful yet bold in supplicating God (1 Thess. 5:17–18; Col. 4:2; also Rom. 12:12; Eph. 6:18; Acts 2:42; 1 Tim. 2:1). In the admonition that follows (vv. 8–9), we are urged to fill our minds with noble thoughts (2 Pet. 1:5–8), and to hold fast to the tradition as we have learned and seen it in its most faithful witnesses (3:17; 1 Cor. 4:16–17; 11:1; Gal. 4:12; 1 Tim. 1:16; 4:12; Titus 2:7; Heb. 13:7; 1 Pet. 5:3). We are assured that if we live this way rather than being filled with fits of frenzy, we will experience the peace of God even though it surpasses our capacity to understand (v. 7; also cf. 4:9; also John 14:27; Col. 3:15; also Rom. 15:33; 16:20; 1 Cor. 14:33; 2 Cor. 13:11; 1 Thess. 5:23; 2 Thess. 3:16; Heb. 13:20).

"Rejoice! . . . The Lord is near!" In one breath Paul exclaims, "Rejoice!" and in another he affirms, "The Lord is near." Read in the context of the Third Sunday of Advent, these words remind us of that fundamentally optimistic strand that runs through the celebration of Advent—joy that the Lord has come, joyous expectation that the Lord will come.

Luke 3:7–18

Before we can celebrate Zephaniah's comforting word that God is "in your midst" and Paul's joyful announcement that "the Lord is at hand," we must first pass through the desert where an austere preacher of severe earnestness prepares the way for Christ's coming. John insists there is no other route to Advent. His message is a call to repentance with actions that demonstrate one's altered life. Because our Gospel this year is Luke, we can expect often to encounter one of his favorite words, "repentance." But repentance is also appropriate for Advent as we come clean and come empty to receive the gift of God.

Luke 3:7–18 continues the Gospel reading of last week and may be divided easily into three units. The first unit consists of verses 7–9, a general description of John's preaching. These verses have no parallel in Mark, but are in Matthew 3:7–10 in almost precisely the same words except for the introductory descriptions of audiences. Apparently Matthew and Luke here follow a common source. Unlike Matthew, however, who addresses John's words to Pharisees and Sadducees, Luke says John's message was to the multitudes. In harsh and vivid terms, John portrays his listeners as fleeing from "the wrath to come" (Rom. 5:9; 1 Thess. 1:10), as snakes scurrying before a spreading fire. John's call is for a moment of truth, a call to abandon all devices used to maintain an illusion of innocence. "We have Abraham as our ancestor" is neither a valid claim for exemption nor an acceptable excuse for failure. Life and deeds, not ancestry, count before the God whose ax is raised over the fruitless tree.

The second unit, verses 10–14, has no parallel in Matthew or Mark. These verses make it clear that John is not simply a loud evangelist whose screamings do little more than create fear and reduce a pathetic crowd to a pool of guilt. Three groups—the crowds, the tax collectors, and the soldiers—ask in turn, "What should we do?" This, says Luke, is the same question asked by the crowds at Pentecost in response to Peter's preaching (Acts 2:37). The answers John gave to the seekers address the inequities and injustices of that society: food and clothing are to be shared with those who have none; taxes are not to be based on the insatiable greed of the powerful; and the military must stop victimizing the public by threat, intimidation, and blackmail. Just as Luke concluded the apocalyptic discourse of Jesus with a strong admonition (21:34–36), so here he makes it clear that a religion void of moral and ethical earnestness is exactly that, void.

The third unit, verses 15–18, has a briefer parallel in Mark 1:7–8, but again is closer to Matthew 3:11–12. However, only Luke introduces the question which, he said, was in the hearts of many, Is John the Christ? It is a concern that all the Gospel writers feel obliged to address at some point, but none more elaborately than Luke (1:5–80; 3:15–18; 9:18–22; Acts 18:24–28; 19:1–7) nor more directly than John (1:19–28; 1:29–37; 3:22–30; 5:33–36). Luke's response to the question here is twofold: Christ is mightier, before whom John is but an unworthy menial house servant; and their baptisms are of very different natures and purposes. John's baptism in water is a purging in that it is a baptism of repentance and forgiveness, but the one to come will baptize with the Holy Spirit and with fire (v. 16). Mark has only "with the Holy Spirit" and clearly has in mind the gift of the Holy Spirit, which was the hallmark of early Christianity. Luke also understood the gift of the Holy Spirit as an identifying mark of the church (24:49; Acts 1:8; 2:38; 10:47, and others) and not of the Baptist movement (Acts 18:24–28; 19:1–7). However, here "Spirit and fire" can also mean "wind and fire," which were symbols not only for the Holy Spirit (Acts 2:1–4) but for judgment as well. In fact, the present context seems to give this meaning to the baptism of wind and fire: winnowing is an act of the wind to separate wheat and chaff, and the fate of chaff is the fire (vv. 17–18).

Even with this understanding, however, one should not get preoccupied with the burning of chaff. The primary purpose is to save the grain. The listeners knew this (and still do) and hence were in great expectation; the preacher understood this (and still does), and hence the message was called "good news" (v. 18).

Fourth Sunday of Advent

Micah 5:2–5a;
Luke 1:47–55 or Psalm 80:1–7;
Hebrews 10:5–10;
Luke 1:39–45 (46–55)

On the last Sunday before Christmas our expectations are heightened especially by the scene in the Gospel lection, as the two pregnant women, Elizabeth and Mary, marvel at the meaning of the birth of Mary's child. The stage is being set for the fulfillment of the ancient promises as Elizabeth blesses Mary for believing that the promise would come true (Luke 1:45) and Mary affirms that God is remembering what he said "to our ancestors, to Abraham and to his descendants forever" (Luke 1:55). In this context, the Old Testament reading supplies one of the details of that promise, that the one who will be ruler in Israel will come from Bethlehem. The psalm, the community's cry to the "Shepherd of Israel" for help in time of trouble, may be understood on this occasion as the prayer to which the coming of Jesus is the response. Hebrews 10:5–10 then indicates the purpose of the incarnation.

Micah 5:2–5a

The prophet Micah was active in the eighth century BC and was a contemporary of Isaiah of Jerusalem, Amos, and Hosea. He was a Judean whose theological perspective closely paralleled that of Isaiah. Both prophets believed that the dynasty of David was God's means of care for the people and that the city of Jerusalem was God's holy place. Micah's message stressed judgment upon the people because of social injustice, especially in high places (see Mic. 3:9–12).

On the other hand, the message of the *book* of Micah is more complicated: God will indeed judge the people and punish them with military defeat and exile; but later, as an act of grace, the Lord will bring them back and establish a reign of perpetual peace, with its center in Jerusalem and its leader a king in the line of David. The most vivid statement of that promise is Micah 4:1–5, which is virtually identical to Isaiah 2:2–5. This message with salvation as the last word is the result of the history of the book's use and growth through the centuries after the time of the original prophet. Consequently, the book as we have it is the product of generations who heard the word of God in ever new circumstances.

It is not certain whether our reading for the day comes from the time of Micah or later. Because of the reference to the Assyrians in 5:5–6 one must keep open the possibility that the unit as a whole is from Micah in the eighth century. In that case the promise would be the prophetic response to the Assyrian invasions of Israel and Judah and the siege of Jerusalem. On the other hand, the announcement of coming salvation may stem from a time when there was little room for hope, the postexilic period in Judah. The slightly veiled promise of a Davidic ruler would then have been heard by people who no longer had their own king but lived under Persian rule.

Micah 5:2–5a (vv. 1–4a in Hebrew) are best understood as part of the immediate unit, verses 1–6. The lectionary doubtless means by verse 5a only the first line of the verse, although it is not even a complete sentence. The unit follows a pattern familiar in the surrounding sections of the book, moving from a description of the present trouble to an announcement of salvation. The present trouble is characterized as a siege of Jerusalem and the abuse of its ruler (v. 1). Salvation is coming first (vv. 2–4) through a new ruler who will care for the people "in the strength of the Lord" so that their security is assured. Second (vv. 5–6), peace will be established when "seven shepherds and eight installed as rulers" are raised up to deliver the land from the Assyrian threat.

The heart of the promise is the expectation of a new ruler in Jerusalem from Bethlehem. Although the promise certainly is messianic—that is, it expects an anointed leader—there is no explicit reference to the promise to the dynasty of David, as in 2 Samuel 7. However, the new ruler, like David, comes from Bethlehem (1 Sam. 17:12). As in the stories of the elevation of David, we hear of the irony that the one who will be "great to the ends of the earth" (v. 4) comes from the one that is so little among even the clans of Judah (v. 2). The divine destiny of the anticipated ruler is expressed in the phrase "whose origin is from of old, from ancient days" (v. 2). The reference in verse 3 to the birth of the ruler—"when she who is in labor has brought forth"—echoes Isaiah 7:14. But before this one can come, the people must be given up to their enemies and then return—probably an allusion to the Exile and the return from Babylon.

It is the role of the new ruler that most closely expresses both the Old Testament understanding of the function of the Davidic kings and the New Testament hope at the time of the birth of Jesus. The one who comes is sent by God, rules in the Lord's strength, and fulfills God's purpose. That purpose is the care and feeding of the flock and the establishment of peace to the ends of the earth. Just as the kings were seen as God's means of care for the people, so Matthew 2:6 can apply this passage to the birth of Jesus.

Luke 1:47–55

This alternate psalm for the Fourth Sunday of Advent is a song of praise to God who remembers the poor and lowly and delivers them from the proud and oppressive. This psalm is not found among the songs of David but is the song of Mary, mother of Jesus. When the angel announced to Mary that she would bear the Christ Child, she was told that her kinswoman Elizabeth, barren and advanced in years, was now in her sixth month of pregnancy (1:36). So Mary went to the hill country of Judea to the home of Elizabeth and Zechariah, and after greetings were exchanged Mary burst into song.

It is important first of all to note that the song is Mary's, not Elizabeth's, as one would expect. The Magnificat is based largely on the song of Hannah in 1 Samuel 2. The story of Hannah and Elkanah, parents of Samuel (1 Sam. 1–2), should be reviewed in preparation for understanding Luke 1:47–55. Hannah, distressed that she was barren, tarried in the temple after a festival, weeping and praying for a child. The priest Eli thought she was drunk. She made known her prayer, promising that if God gave her a son she would give the child to God. Her prayer was answered and she named the child Samuel. When she brought the child to the temple as a gift to God, she sang a Magnificat. The story so parallels that of Elizabeth and Zechariah that one would expect Elizabeth to sing as did Hannah. Both women were older; Hannah was assured of a child while at the temple just as Zechariah was; both sons, Samuel in the one case and John in the other, were given to God under special vows, and they lived as set apart for God. A few late manuscripts are so attracted to the similarities between the two families that they have replaced Mary's name with that of Elizabeth in Luke 1:46. But that "And Mary said" is the reliable reading is very well established. However, it does not fit for a young virgin to sing Hannah's song. The tradition of God granting a son to elderly childless couples is well established: Abraham and Sarah were given Isaac; Manoah and his wife were given Samson; and Elkanah and Hannah, Samuel. In that tradition of God blessing the barren, John now comes, and to that history he belongs. But when a song from that tradition is sung by a young virgin, the tradition is interrupted, the old is new, and the familiar is strange. God is doing a new thing. Had Elizabeth sung Hannah's song, it would have been said that God continues to be gracious to the barren, as of old. But when the virgin Mary sings, it must be said that God's grace is not as of old, but new and strange and surprising and beyond understanding. This child will not be as Isaac or Samson or Samuel, but will be the Son of God.

And what is it that Mary sings? Her song opens with joy and praise that God has favored a handmaiden of low estate. But only briefly does she speak of herself. She sees God's grace and goodness toward her as but a single instance of the way of God in the world. God blesses the poor and oppressed and hungry; and in the final eschatological reversal, God will bring down the proud and rich oppressors and exalt those who have been disfranchised, disregarded, and dismissed. The most remarkable quality of the song is that the justice God will bring to pass is spoken of in the past tense: has shown strength, has scattered the proud, has brought down the powerful, has lifted up the lowly, has filled the hungry, and has sent the rich away empty. Why the past tense? According to the latest news reports, these things have not yet occurred.

Of course, these conditions are not yet, but one of the ways the faithful express trust in God is to speak of the future with such confidence that it is described as already here. Such faith is prerequisite to being a participant in efforts to achieve that future. To celebrate the future as a memory, to praise God for having already done what lies before us to do: this is the way of the people of God. Without this song of praise, the noblest efforts to effect justice in society become arrogant projects—messianic moves by one group against another, competing for camera time. God's people parade before they march, for history teaches us that without the parade, the march may soon become lockstep, and perhaps even goosestep. Who, then, will remain to say, "My soul magnifies the Lord"?

Psalm 80:1–7

Psalm 80 is a community lament composed for use when the people had suffered humiliation, probably at the hands of a foreign enemy. As such, it is a request for revival, renewal, restoration.

In the psalm, two images are used for the Divine and simultaneously two images for the people. In verses 1–2, God is depicted as shepherd; in verses 8–18 as a vine grower. Israel is thus God's sheep and God's vineyard. The two professions, shepherding and viticulturist, require of the shepherd and vineyard keeper great concern and tender care. The shepherd must direct the flock, look for its pasture, defend it from its predators, care for its injured and sick members, ensure the succor and nurture of its young, and search for and return its wayward members. The vineyard keeper must prune the vines in season, fertilize the plants, weed the fields, and protect the crops from marauders and plunderers.

This psalm accuses God of failure on both accounts. As a shepherd God has not cared for the sheep. As a vineyard keeper God has functioned foolishly so that the vineyard is left without protection, to be used as public property and a haven for wild beasts. The appeal to God throughout the psalm requests a favorable response in which the troubled people would be redeemed and God would be shown to be a concerned shepherd and a competent viticulturist. That is, the psalm is a supplication for a return to normal in the divine-Israel relationship.

Two expressions in verses 1–7 need elucidation for the average reader. The description of God as "You who are enthroned upon the cherubim" (v. 1) draws upon the imagery of early Israelite warfare. The ark was originally conceived as a movable throne upon which the Deity sat. The presence of the ark in battle represented the presence of the Divine. The cherubim were mythological flying guardian figures that were artistically represented on the ark (for this view of the ark, see the story in 1 Sam. 4). (Another interpretation of the ark, which had probably disappeared before much of the Old Testament was written, saw it as a container for the law; see Deut. 10:1–5.) The reference to Yahweh as the one enthroned on the cherubim was a way of recalling the times of bygone warfare and better days and a means of reminding the Deity of divine militancy, now neglected. "To let the face shine" was a metaphorical way of saying "to show favor" or "to be favorably disposed toward." So the refrain in verses 3, 7, and 19 contains parallel requests: "restore us" and "let your face shine."

How may this psalm be related to Advent? First, its sentiments lie on the before, the preside of Advent. The people described their conditions as desperate: God is angry with their prayers (v. 4), tears are their constant companion (v. 5), and they are the butt of their enemies' jokes (v. 6). The personal, interpersonal, and divine-personal relationships are all askew. They had yet to take the road to Bethlehem. Second, they nonetheless look forward with pleas for redemption and restoration, and hope and expectation are the hallmarks of Advent.

Hebrews 10:5–10

Unlike the three previous epistolary readings, which spoke of Christ's second coming, today's epistolary reading, with its opening phrase "when Christ came into the world" (v. 5), shifts the emphasis to his first coming. The focus is not so much on his birth per se as it is on his coming into the world seen as a single event. The phrase has a Johannine ring to it (cf. John 1:9; 6:14; 11:27; 12:46; 16:28; 18:37).

Our passage is striking for the way the words of Psalm 40:6–8 are attributed to Christ himself. They are introduced here as words that "he said." In what sense he said them remains unclear. It is possible that during his ministry Jesus quoted these words from the psalmist and interpreted his own mission in light of them. Yet nowhere in the Gospel tradition do we find Jesus quoting Psalm 40, even though he does share the prophetic conviction expressed in our passage that genuine obedience of the heart is more valuable than offering sacrifices (Matt. 9:13; 12:7; cf. 1 Sam. 15:22; Isa. 1:11; Hos. 6:6; Amos 5:21–24; Pss. 50:7–11; 51:16–17; Prov. 15:8).

The phrase "I have come to do your will, O God" (v. 7) is strongly reminiscent of the Gospel of John (4:34; 5:30; 6:38–39), but it also reminds us of Jesus' words in Gethsemane (Mark 14:36 and parallels).

In at least two senses, then, does Psalm 40:6–8 "speak for" Christ. First, it expresses Christ's conviction that a life obedient to the will of God is fundamentally more pleasing to God than offering various types of sacrificial offerings. Second, it defines the purpose of Christ's coming specifically in terms of doing the will of God.

An additional connection between Psalm 40 and the work of Christ, as understood by the author of Hebrews, is found in the phrase "a body you have prepared for me" (v. 5). This is the wording found in the Greek version of Psalm 40. The Hebrew text reads instead, "you have given me an open ear," or literally, "ears you have dug for me." In the context, the sense of the latter is clear. God has given the psalmist open ears through which to hear, and consequently do, the will of God, and this God prefers to the offering of sacrifices. In the Greek version, however, the meaning shifts slightly, probably by extending one part of the body to the whole. The sense is still clear: "In contrast to sacrificial offerings, you have given me a body, that is, my whole life, to offer as a sacrifice." Obviously, the Greek version lent itself to Christian interpretation, given the author's emphasis on the "offering of the body of Jesus Christ once for all" (v. 10; also 7:27). For his purposes, our author is able to use Psalm 40 to show that the single offering of the body of Jesus far surpasses the multiple offerings of animal sacrifices that were offered "according to the law" (v. 8). More important, it provides scriptural basis for showing that a single sacrifice of a body duly prepared by God and thoroughly committed to doing God's will represents the truest fulfillment of God's original intention. Thus God "abolishes the first in order to establish the second" (v. 9).

In its liturgical setting, today's epistolary passage is significant not only because of its explicit use of incarnational language, but because it links the incarnation with the atoning death of Christ. If the words of the Magnificat in today's Gospel reading focus our attention on Christ's birth, the epistolary reading carries us forward to Christ's death. As we all know, we are scarcely able to celebrate one moment in the life of Christ in isolation from the rest of his life. We know how the story ends. And so did the Gospel writers who, after all, wrote the Gospels from the passion backward. It was the ending that enabled them to make sense of the beginning. As our text states, it was the atoning death of Christ through which we were sanctified (v. 10; cf. 10:14, 29; 13:12; also 1 Thess. 4:3; Eph. 5:2). And yet, his death provides us the vantage point from which to view the work of Christ in both directions—backward to his birth and forward to his coming again. In this respect, our text extends our reflections to include the whole sweep of the paschal mystery. (Cf. *From Ashes to Fire* [Nashville: Abingdon Press, 1979], 11–27.)

A final word about the limits of the passage. Beginning the passage with the word *consequently* (v. 5, NRSV) may seem too abrupt to some. One solution is that adopted for Annunciation (March 25), where the same epistolary reading is used. Start the reading with verse 4, which helps establish the context and provides a slightly smoother opening.

Luke 1:39–45 (46–55)

The discussion below attends to the entirety of Luke 1:39–55, but the preacher may want to deal with the narrative without the song of Mary (vv. 46–55). If the sermon focuses on the song, the preacher is referred to the fuller discussion above, where Luke 1:47–55 appears as the psalm for today.

If there are Sundays when the church senses that the Scripture readings are distant from one another, today is not one of them. Micah 5 anticipates the birth of a great ruler in the small village of Bethlehem; Hebrews 10 explores the meaning of Christ coming into the world; and Luke 1 helps us, through Mary's joy and excitement, to stand expectantly at hope's window. Even Psalm 80 resonates with Bethlehem, David, and the Christ in its address to God as shepherd of Israel.

If there are Sundays when the church senses that the Scripture readings are distant from the life and mood of the congregation, today is not one of them. As music and song fill the Advent Season, so has Luke chosen to sing rather than explain or prove or exhort in our Gospel lection. That the story has been cast as song reminds us of the importance of the nonsemantic quality of language and of the affective force of its form.

Luke 1-2, although of a piece in images and themes with the remainder of the Gospel, has its own structure and focus. The two largest blocks of material announce the promised births of John and Jesus (1:5-38) and narrate the birth stories themselves (1:57-2:20). These two large units are joined by the moving account of the mother of John being visited by the mother of Jesus (1:39-56). This small story of Mary's visit to the Judean hill country home of Elizabeth states in its own way the twin themes of the narratives surrounding it: prenatal and natal signs point to the greatness of both John and Jesus, but the signs are equally clear that Jesus is the greater of the two.

Our Gospel lection, Luke 1:39-45 (46-55), consists of two parts—the first being Elizabeth's song with a brief narrative introduction (vv. 39-45), and the second, Mary's song, commonly called the "Magnificat," so named because Magnificat is the first word of the song in the Vulgate (vv. 46-55). The narrative introduction to Elizabeth's song (vv. 39-41) locates the scene in an unnamed city in the Judean hills. It tells of Mary greeting her kinswoman Elizabeth (v. 40), and of the babe in Elizabeth's womb leaping at the sound of the voice of Mary, "mother of my Lord" (v. 41). Luke is here undoubtedly recalling both a historical reference and a theological point. The historical reference is to Rebekah, in whose womb Esau and Jacob struggled, the message being, as in Elizabeth's case, "the elder shall serve the younger" (Gen. 25:21-23). The theological point is that prenatal activity, preceding as it does all works or merit, accents the sovereign will and purpose of God. The content of Elizabeth's song is a eulogizing of Mary, pronouncing upon her the blessing of God. This blessing of Mary is not mere sentiment or a burst of emotion, as Luke later records from "a woman in the crowd" (11:27-28). Here Elizabeth is inspired by the Holy Spirit and blesses Mary on two grounds: she has been chosen to be the mother of the Lord, and she believed and accepted the word spoken to her from God (vv. 26-38).

The second part of our lection, Mary's song, praises God for the favor bestowed upon a handmaiden of low estate (vv. 46-50) and then proclaims the triumph of God's purposes for all people everywhere (vv. 51-55). Although the Magnificat is a mosaic of biblical texts, it draws primarily upon Hannah's song in 1 Samuel 2:1-10. The preacher would do well to read again that moving story of God's gift of Samuel to Hannah and Hannah's gift of Samuel to God. In movement, Mary's song makes an easy transition from the remarkable act of God to and through Mary to the remarkable act of God by which all the oppressed, poor, and hungry of the world will be blessed. This triumph of God's favor is presented in the form of an eschatological reversal in which the powerful and rich will exchange places with the powerless and poor. And so confident is the singer's faith that God's justice and grace will prevail that the expression of hope is cast in the past tense. Mary sings as though what *shall* be is already true. In this trust, God's servants continue to sing.

Christmas, First Proper
(Christmas Eve/Day)

Isaiah 9:2–7;
Psalm 96;
Titus 2:11–14;
Luke 2:1–14 (15–20)

The texts for all the Christmas services are the same every year, but the story never grows old. The Lucan account of the birth of Jesus, the shepherds, and the angels concludes with Mary pondering all these things in her heart and the shepherds glorifying and praising God for what they had heard and seen. Isaiah 9:2–7 sings of good news that accompanies the birth of one to sit on the throne in Jerusalem, and the responsorial psalm is an exuberant song of praise for God's reign. The epistolary text speaks of living between the times, between the appearance of the glory of God in the incarnation and the return of the Lord.

Isaiah 9:2–7

This poem, so distinctive in many ways, closely resembles the thanksgiving songs in the Book of Psalms (e.g., Pss. 18:5–20; 32:3–5). There is an account of trouble and the deliverance from it, and a thanksgiving service in celebration of that deliverance. But the song also is similar in important respects to prophetic announcements of the future. Although it concerns events that have happened and are happening, it concludes by announcing the implications of those events for the future. In effect, the deliverance from trouble is a sign of what God intends for the future.

Although many commentators in the late nineteenth and early twentieth centuries took the present passage to be a postexilic addition to the Book of Isaiah, it is now widely accepted that it comes from Isaiah in the eighth century BC. The precise date is difficult to establish. There doubtless are historical allusions within the poem itself, but they are obscure. Isaiah 9:1 refers to the territories taken by Tiglath-pileser in 733–732; but this verse probably was added when the book was compiled, and in any case the poem speaks of events after the Assyrian invasion. Some scholars have seen the poem as part of the coronation ritual for a particular Judean king, most commonly identified as Hezekiah in 725 BC. However, it is more likely that the prophetic hymn was composed to celebrate the birth of a new crown prince some time after 732. The sign of God's deliverance is the birth of a new descendant of David.

26

In terms of literary and grammatical structure, the poem has two major parts. Verses 2–3 present an account of release from trouble and the accompanying celebration. Verses 4–7 give three reasons for that celebration, each introduced by "for." Those reasons are the deliverance from an oppressor (v. 4), the destruction of the gear of battle (v. 5), and the birth of the special child (vv. 6–7). Most of the verbs are properly translated as present or past tenses, but the final lines in verse 7 are future.

One may also analyze and interpret this passage as a series of graphic images, each with its accompanying moods and tones. First there are the contrasting images of darkness and light (v. 2). Darkness is a metaphor for depression and death. The NEB makes that explicit in the final line: "dwellers in a land as dark as death" (cf. Ps. 23:4). Light symbolizes life and joy.

Second, in the language and attitude of prayer the prophet sketches a scene of celebration. One can almost see and hear the festivities. People shout and sing to their God as if it were the thanksgiving festival at the end of a good harvest or the spontaneous expressions of joy when a war has ended with victory.

Third, contrasting images again come to the fore—the harsh pictures of the instruments of war and oppression and a gathering lighted by a fire in which those instruments are burned. The mood of joy and celebration from the previous images continues. What begins as the immediate deliverance from a particular oppressor—doubtless the heel of Assyria—becomes a vision of perpetual peace: war boots and bloody uniforms are burned.

Fourth, there is the image of a messenger emerging from the royal palace with the good news that a son—a crown prince—has been born. This birth announcement image is the central scene of the poem. Like the symbolic action reports in the immediate context in the Book of Isaiah (7:10–16; 8:1–4), the birth of a baby is a sign of God's saving activity in behalf of the people of God.

Finally, and with no dramatic transition, the scene moves to the throne room of the king and directs our attention even beyond it. The newborn baby is now seen as the righteous and just king, sitting on the throne of David. This son of David will administer justice, establish righteousness, and inaugurate a reign of peace, all of which corresponds to the will of God and thus will extend forever.

One way for the preacher to proclaim the good news of this passage is simply to present these graphic images to the congregation. Good news is preached not only by what is said but also by establishing a mood of celebration, and these scenes do just that. Or one could explore the specific contents of the passage. Those would be God's deliverance from oppression, the establishment of peace, and the reign of justice and righteousness. Any or all of these would carry forward the message of Christmas.

Psalm 96

The three psalms selected for the Christmas propers all reflect common themes—the triumph and reign of God as king and judge. These, like other so-called enthronement psalms (such as Pss. 47, 93, and 99), appear to have been originally used in the fall festival that coincided with the beginning of the new agricultural year and thus with the New Year season. Part of the festival seems to have emphasized God's re-creation of the world and the reestablishment of world order. Such themes are appropriate for Christmas as the time when God began the reestablishment of his rule. Psalm 96 falls into two halves, each with an introductory section (vv. 1–3, 7–9) and main body (4–6, 10–13). This does not suggest, however, that the work is made up of two independent compositions; it simply suggests the artistry of the poet. The two introits call upon the whole earth and all its people to acknowledge and praise God.

The first main section (vv. 4–6) praises the incomparability of Yahweh, who stands without peer in the universe. Of all the gods, only Yahweh is to be feared. Other gods are merely idols, but Yahweh is the creator of the heavens. (On the gods of other nations and a parody on idols, see Isa. 40:18–20; 44:9–22.) God's creatorship and the world as divine creation testify to the fact that Yahweh, the God of Israel, is the only divine power with whom people must deal.

Verse 10a seems to contain a shout of the fall festival that is best translated "Yahweh has become king" (the NRSV reads "The LORD is king!"). As such, it is the proclamation of the gospel, the good news that the universe is and remains under divine control.

Divine dominion and divine judgment are depicted as the consequence of God's rule (in vv. 10b–13). The dominion is affirmed in the assertion that the world is established and shall never be moved. Such an affirmation gives expression to the belief that the world has a security about it and that one can dwell and live in the world in confidence. Stability and with it predictability are implied by the stress on the establishment and immovability of the world and existence.

Judgment is, however, seen as an aspect of the Divine's relationship to the world. Like the kings in the ancient oriental world, so also Yahweh was viewed as a supreme judge. In this psalm, judgment is seen as a source of and reason for joy. The rationale for this is to be found in what is said about divine judgment. God is said to judge with equity (v. 10c), with righteousness (v. 13a), and with truth (v. 13b). Such divine judgment may be seen as standing over against or far surpassing human judgment, with its inequities, favoritisms, and partial truth.

The whole of the natural order—that is, all established creation—rejoices and greets the coming of the king in judgment—the heavens, the earth, the sea, the field (cultivated land), the forest (the uncultivated land). In the coming of God, the world can rejoice and in divine judgment find joy. The appropriate response is to bring an offering—make a gift—and to worship (vv. 8–9).

Titus 2:11–14

If Christmas is a time to celebrate the faith, it is also a time to affirm the faith. This epistolary text, traditionally read at Christmas, presents us with such a bold affirmation of faith. It begins with the emphatic declaration: "For the grace of God has appeared, bringing salvation to all" (v. 11). The reference point is a definite moment in the past, as seen in the use of the aorist tense ("has appeared"). The chief exegetical question is whether the birth and nativity of Christ are the locus of the "appearing" or whether his whole life is telescoped into a single event. Even if it is the latter, when read in the context of a Christmas service these words will naturally remind us of the very dawn of the grace of God as it was seen and experienced in the birth of Christ.

Wrapped in this bold faith-claim is one of the central elements of the Christmas faith that celebrates divine grace manifested in human form—God's grace openly revealed. Although this passage does not explicitly link the manifestation of God's grace with the person of Jesus, it is a central Christian conviction to do so. Almost invariably, New Testament writers see Jesus Christ as the locus of God's grace (cf. John 1:14–17; 1 Cor. 1:4; 2 Tim. 1:9–10). By participating in time and history, Christ entered the realm of the visible and knowable, as suggested by the word "appearing," which has the connotation of "showing forth." It was an event in the public domain, out in the open for all to witness. Another way of stressing this is in terms of "the revelation of the mystery that was kept secret for long ages but is now disclosed" (Rom. 16:25–26).

Because this text is read alongside Luke's account of the birth of Jesus, it is worth noting that Luke's birth and infancy narrative dramatically highlights God's revelation in Christ as a publicly displayed event. Numerous characters cross the stage of Luke's account: Elizabeth and Zechariah, Mary and Joseph, angels named and unnamed, shepherds, Anna and Simeon, teachers in the temple. In various ways, they all witness the "appearance of God's grace." His account is punctuated with announcements, revelations, prayers, songs, and prophecies—all serving as arrows pointing to this central event. His narrative is so carefully and thoughtfully constructed that both our audial and visual senses are activated. We would have to be both deaf and blind not to see God's grace appearing before us.

There is another central feature of the opening words of today's text—salvation for everyone (cf. 1 Tim. 2:4; 4:10). This, too, echoes Luke's birth and infancy story, which speaks frequently of salvation promised by God and realized in Christ (Luke 1:47, 69, 71, 77; 2:11, 30). Luke's account also stresses from the very outset that God's salvation will be universal in scope, serving as "a light for revelation to the Gentiles and for glory to your people Israel" (2:32; cf. 3:6).

Both of these ideas—the revelation of God's grace and universal salvation—are captured especially well by the REB rendering of verse 11: "For the grace of God has dawned upon the world with healing for all mankind." (Even greater universality would be achieved by rendering the last phrase as "for all humankind.") With the metaphor of "dawning," the REB translators have opened up interesting possibilities for interpretation. It anticipates the later reference to the future appearing of the "glory (or splendor) of our great God and Savior, Jesus Christ" (v. 13). One could interpret our passage as encompassing the whole sweep of salvation-history from the dawning of God's revelation in the incarnation to its even more splendid manifestation radiated in the Second Coming. This imagery of light shining in darkness could be reinforced even further by examining crucial passages in Paul and John (cf. 2 Cor. 4:4–6; John 1:1–18). The Christian view of time and history envisioned in our passage runs not from dawn to dusk, but from dawn to even more brilliant splendor.

We have selected only two motifs from the passage that might be pursued homiletically or devotionally. Obviously, there is much more embedded in this unusually rich text. One of the most conspicuous strands in the text encompasses the ethical demands required by the appearance of God's grace. Clearly, this text sees a direct link between the incarnation and the moral life, which is etched in both negative and positive terms. Typical of the Pastoral Epistles, there is unabashed praise of "good works" (Titus 3:8, 14; cf. Heb. 10:24; 1 Pet. 3:13). Also, as the text unfolds, it moves from Christ's first coming to his Second Coming, speaking of the latter as our "blessed hope" (v. 13). Here, again, we see the two central themes of Advent combined in a single text. Finally, the text speaks of the redemptive work of Christ "who gave himself for us" (cf. Matt. 20:28 and parallels; Rom. 3:26; 2 Cor. 5:15; Gal. 1:4; 2:20; Eph. 5:2, 25; 1 Tim. 2:6; 1 Pet. 1:18–19; also Ps. 130:8) and in doing so formed "for himself a people of his own" (Exod. 4:22; 19:5–6; Deut. 7:6; 14:2; 32:9; Ezek. 37:23).

Luke 2:1–14 (15–20)

Before looking into the Gospel lesson for today, let us pause a moment to reflect on what it means to preach on Christmas Day. Many ministers find it difficult to preach at Christmas. This is especially true of those in traditions in which the sermon is the centerpiece of Sunday morning, all else serving in satellite roles. At Christmas, however, the sermon and every other element of worship become but a part of the rich tapestry of celebration. Some preachers thus feel minimized and confess an ego problem. Others feel the wealth of the season makes even a good sermon seem poor indeed. Who is capable of rising to an occasion on which the most beautiful texts of the Bible are read, texts that can make our sermons turn pale and stammer? Nor is it uncommon for a minister to be burdened by the heavy pathos that haunts the edge of Christmas. The luxury of the season points up in sharpest relief the conditions of human misery everywhere. Frustrated by the futility of laying a heavy load of guilt on the parishioners Christmas morning, the pastor may prefer delivering a plate of food to delivering a sermon.

Then there are those whose very definition of preaching is exhorting, filling the air with ought, must, and should. Then comes Christmas when the angels and the children combine choirs to go caroling. There is nothing here for the common scold. But most of all, the familiarity of the songs and texts clips the wings of a preacher, sending some in covert searches for something novel, even if it is inappropriate, irrelevant, and has no substance. But the familiar, rather than deadening, can be the preacher's delight. To say that the texts and message are familiar is to say that they already belong to the listeners, and there is power, enjoyment, and an occasional "amen" when people hear what they already know. This means it is their sermon, not solely the pastor's. Sometimes we need to preach *for* rather than *to* the church. Now to our familiar text, Luke 2:1–20.

Luke's story of Jesus' birth consists of three units: verses 1–7, the birth itself; verses 8–14, the annunciation to the shepherds; verses 15–20, the visit of the shepherds to Bethlehem. The Gospel reading for today embraces the first two units with the third optional. The alternate reading for the Second Proper for Christmas offers units 2 and 3, with unit 1 optional. Perhaps it would be most helpful to provide comments here on the entire narrative (vv. 1–20) and leave to the preacher the option of using one, two, or all three units, regardless of whether the First Proper for Christmas or the Second Proper for Christmas is followed.

Luke 2:1–7 contains three elements: prophecy, history, and symbolism. Prophecy, fulfilled in Jesus, is not a thesis for Luke to establish but is rather a way of telling the story, of weaving old and new together as one fabric. Without referring directly to Micah 5:2, Luke uses all the elements of that prophecy: Bethlehem, house of David, the Davidic messiah. Similarly, Isaiah 1:3 and Jeremiah 14:8 provide the manger and the image of God lodging for the night. No characteristic of Luke-Acts is more pronounced than the author's insistence on the continuity of Judaism and Christianity. The Hebrew and Christian Scriptures tell one story, not two. God is not starting over with Christians, having failed with Jews. What God said to Abraham is coming to pass: In your seed all nations shall be blessed. The story is marked by rejection and resistance, to be sure, but God is faithful to the promise. For Luke, every Gentile believer can properly say, "Abraham and Sarah are my father and mother."

The second element here is secular history. "A decree went out from Emperor Augustus" (v. 1). Historians have had difficulty with Luke's report of the census under Quirinius (v. 2). Has Luke misplaced the census that came later after Archelaus was deposed as ruler of Judea and the country placed under the governor of Syria? The debates fill the commentaries, but regardless of the reliability of Luke's sources, his purpose is clear—to tie sacred to secular history. As God used Cyrus, king of Persia, to effect the divine purpose (Isa. 45), so God uses Emperor Augustus. The coming of Christ is not hidden in a corner; Rome is joined to Bethlehem. The world is God's, and the gospel is for God's world. The good news does not belong to the church, which may decide to share it with the world. Rather, Mary's baby is God's yes to the world, which includes us.

And the third element is symbolism. Why give attention to Jesus as a baby, wrapped, as any baby would be, in swaddling cloths, lying in a manger crib? Why not, like Mark, go straight to his ministry? Luke paints the whole picture in this small scene. God's Son, vulnerable as every infant is vulnerable, subject to all the conditions under which we all live, fully identified with every human being's need for love, lies here unnoticed, without trumpet or drum roll and without a place to lay his head. Jesus lived from crib to cross, but the teller of the story wrote from cross to crib.

Because verses 8–14 constitute an annunciation, it might be helpful to review the literary pattern common to such stories (cf. comments on Luke 1:26–38, Fourth Sunday of Advent, Year B). The annunciation here parallels the angel's visits to Zechariah and to Mary, the three accounts providing the central structure for Luke's Nativity. That commentaries on this text will refer to analogous stories of the births of emperors and kings, replete with heavenly messengers, signs, and widespread hope for peace and prosperity, should be informative to the preacher but not disconcerting. These stories from secular literature are informative in that Luke is a first-century writer, telling his story in a mode familiar enough to be a vehicle for communication. A modern reader is aided in grasping how Luke's first readers understood his Gospel. But these parallel stories should not be disconcerting. Analogies neither prove nor disprove a writer's claim, but they serve to clarify. If a story is such as to be totally without analogy, then who could understand it? Besides, Luke's theology welcomes similar accounts from other cultures. Luke's God is universally available, never without witness among the nations (Acts 14:17). Even pagan poets said, "In him we live and move and have our being" and "For we too are his offspring" (Acts 17:28). People everywhere hope and rejoice that the birth of a new leader will bring heaven's blessing of peace and joy. Luke's witness is that they brought their hopes to Bethlehem and did not go away empty.

The annunciation is to shepherds in the field. We are not sure whether the shepherds are for Luke a continuation of the focus on David, who was a shepherd of Bethlehem (1 Sam. 16), or a symbol of the poor of the earth, who are in Luke the special objects of the grace of God (4:18; 14:13, 21). Both interpretations could be correct. David is a very important figure for Luke, not only in the stories and songs related to the birth of Jesus (1:27, 32, 69; 2:4, 11) but also in the sermons related to the birth of the church (Acts 2:25–35). In Acts, David is presented as a prophet who spoke of Jesus' resurrection and enthronement at God's right hand (2 Sam. 7:12–16; Pss. 110:1; 132:11). As to the second interpretation, shepherds were not only poor but of poor reputation, treated religiously and socially almost as nonpersons. They qualify easily as the least likely to have God's favor on them, and God's favor on the least likely is a theme throughout the Bible. Israel was the least likely, as was David, and Mary, and Paul, and even Jesus himself. This text certainly provides an opportunity to deal with Jesus' birth through Luke's eyes, quite apart from Matthew, who places Jesus' birth among the wise, powerful, and rich. Matthew will speak to the church later, on Epiphany Sunday.

The heavenly host praised God and spoke of peace on earth. Peace (shalom), a quality of wholeness in life, made possible by a balance of all the forces within and without that affect us, was always the desire of Israel. The eschatological hope (Isa. 9:6; Zech. 9:9–10) was, says Luke, fulfilled in this one who would "guide our feet into the way of peace" (Luke 1:79). This peace is too immense to be confined to an inner experience, but it is also too personal to be left to the affairs of nations. The preacher will want to give careful attention to the translation of verse 14. Some ancient manuscripts read, "on earth peace, good will among people," a phrase without contingency or condition. The best texts, however, make "good will" a condition for having peace. The phrase may read "among people of good will," "among those whom he favors" (NRSV), or "to all in whom he delights" (REB). One must wrestle here not only with texts and translations but with one's own theology.

A brief word about the sign given the shepherds (v. 12). In a field now radiant with heaven, the shepherds are told that the sign is a baby, wrapped as all newborn were, and lying in a feed bin for animals. In other words, the sign was as common as the shepherds themselves. Notice Luke's reversal: earth is not looking to heaven for a sign, but heaven looks to earth. The extraordinary points to the ordinary and says, "See, God is among you."

The third unit of the birth narrative (vv. 15–20) tells simply of the shepherds' visit to Bethlehem, and in this visit units 2 and 1 are joined; this is to say, the message of the angel to the shepherds (vv. 8–14) is confirmed by the manger scene (vv. 1–7). Just as the annunciations by the angel to Zechariah and to Mary proved true, so it is here. Strikingly, verses 1–7 tell a painfully simple story of political power, economic pressure, and the birth of a child away from home. There are no angels, no heavenly host, no revelations. On the other hand, verses 8–14 are filled with the extraordinary and the heavenly. In the shepherds' visit, heaven and earth meet, each witnessing to the other. But is it not strange that the holy family, the principal characters in the drama, get the good news of what their ordeal really means through the witness of others?

When the annunciation to Mary was confirmed, she praised God. When the annunciation to Zechariah was confirmed, he praised God. Not unexpectedly, therefore, Luke concludes this narrative with the shepherds returning, "glorifying and praising God."

Christmas, Second Proper
(Additional Lessons for Christmas Day)

Isaiah 62:6–12;
Psalm 97;
Titus 3:4–7;
Luke 2:(1–7) 8–20

A note that reverberates through the lessons for today is that of proclamation, the making known of the good news embodied in the birth of the Christ Child. The reading from Isaiah recalls weary but alert sentries who herald the coming news of salvation. The psalm affirms that God has become king and that God's kingship is proclaimed by heaven and earth. The reading from Titus testifies to the experience of responding to the good news. The Gospel reading—Luke's birth story—focuses on the proclamation of good news first heard by the shepherds at Bethlehem. This good news leads the shepherds to praise God, people to wonder, and Mary to ponder.

Isaiah 62:6–12

Many of the Old Testament readings for the season concern the dramatic transformation of Jerusalem, the Holy City, into the center for the people of God in a new era of salvation. The motif is taken up in various ways, but usually as part of a prophetic announcement of salvation that ultimately affects not only all peoples but even nature itself. Even texts that are more explicitly messianic have Jerusalem and Zion in the background, as the center from which God will reign through the descendant of David.

The Old Testament text for this occasion likewise looks to the restoration and elevation of Jerusalem, but the angle of vision is somewhat different and the range a bit more limited. Instead of announcing that salvation is coming, the reading begins with prayers for restoration. Only in the final verses does it turn confidently to the future, but even those lines serve to remind Yahweh of the promises he has made. The perspective from which these words emerge, therefore, is quite sober. The prophetic poet knows that the present reality of Jerusalem is far from that anticipated in the ancient promises concerning the city. The city and its people are in trouble, and it is time to pray for deliverance.

Isaiah 62, as part of the collection of material identified as Third Isaiah (Isaiah 56–66), does indeed come from a troubled time, especially for the city of Jerusalem. Precise dates for the units in these chapters are difficult to establish, mainly because they do not come from a single prophet. Rather, Isaiah 56–66 is a collection of prophetic and liturgical materials from the postexilic era, many of them depending upon and extending the message of Second Isaiah (Isaiah 40–55). Many of the sections, including the one before us now, appear to assume the situation in the first decades after the exiles began to return from Babylon to Judah, that is, 538–516 BC.

Most of our evidence for the circumstances of Judah and Jerusalem in those years comes from Ezra 1–6, Haggai, and Zechariah 1–8. Haggai and Zechariah, like Isaiah 62, are concerned with the restoration of Jerusalem, and the rebuilding of the temple in particular. Serious construction work on the new building began in 520 BC, and it was completed in 516 BC. During this period—in fact, for the two centuries from 538 to 333 BC—Judah was a province of the Persian Empire. In the first years after the return, the former exiles found the city and the temple in ruins, experienced conflicts among themselves and with those who had remained in the land, and faced threats from the outside, including from former enemies such as the Edomites. They also faced more than one crisis of faith when the new life in the Holy City fell far short of what the prophets had given them to expect.

Although a central motif in Isaiah 62 is prayer to God for the salvation of the city, it is not easy to identify the various speakers and addressees in the passage. Is the "I" of verse 1 a prophetic voice that will not be silenced, or Yahweh himself who affirms that he will now speak up? The initial speaker probably is a prophetic one, for in verse 6 that same voice speaks first to Jerusalem, appointing sentries for her walls, and then commissions them to remind Yahweh of his promises concerning the city, giving him no rest until he fulfills them. The image of "sentinels" is indebted to a tradition such as the one found in Ezekiel 33; but in that case the prophet was to warn the people, and here the prophetic sentries are to be in continuous prayer to Yahweh.

In the concluding section (vv. 10–12), the prophetic figure now addresses the people of Jerusalem, exhorting them to prepare "the way for the people," that is, for all who will come to the Holy City. The image of a highway is familiar from Second Isaiah, but there it involved God's transformation of the dry wilderness trails into a level road with water along the way. Here those who stayed in Jerusalem and those who have already returned are urged to go out and "build up" the road and "clear it of stones" (v. 10). They are to work hard in behalf of other returnees.

The good news is that the Lord himself is coming to Zion, bringing "salvation," "reward," and "recompense" (v. 11). Throughout the entire chapter it is clear that God is asked for—and will grant—a renewal of the covenant with Jerusalem and its inhabitants. In that covenant the people themselves will be renewed. The new relationship is like a marriage (vv. 4–5). Moreover, the transformation will be effected by giving the city, the land (v. 6), and the people themselves new names that embody the new reality: "Holy People," "The Redeemed of the Lord," "Sought Out," and "A City Not Forsaken" (v. 12).

Psalm 97

As in Psalm 96, the kingship of God and divine judgment are the focal concerns of this psalm. Like other enthronement psalms (see Ps. 93), this one opens with the affirmation "Yahweh reigns," or perhaps better, "Yahweh has become king." It was once used as part of the autumn ritual in ancient Jerusalem when Yahweh's rule as king was annually celebrated.

The three stanzas into which the NRSV divides the psalm can provide a structure for a reading of the hymn. In the first stanza (vv. 1–5), the coming of God as king is described. The metaphorical imagery used in the psalm has many parallels to other biblical texts. For example, its references to fire, smoke, and lightning recall the account of Yahweh's appearance on Mt. Sinai in Exodus 19:16–18 and Deuteronomy 4:11; 5:22. The use of thunderstorm imagery is reminiscent of Psalm 29. The same type of imagery could also be used in ancient Israel when the prophets spoke of the coming day and visitation of God (see Joel 2:1–2; Zeph. 1:14–16).

The God who comes is one who dwells in clouds and darkness (v. 2). This presentation of the Deity as one who dwells in darkness (see 1 Kings 8:12) has given rise to speaking of the Deity as the *Deus Absconditus* (the Hidden God). This psalm, like Advent and Christ, proclaims the self-revelation of the hidden God. Just as clouds and darkness are associated with the Divine, so also are righteousness and justice. The one revealed is thus not a capricious god but one upon whom people can rely. As justice and righteousness are the foundation of God's throne, so proper order and right conditions should be the product of God's appearance. One could argue that the text implies that social transformation attends the divine coming. The focus, however, in verses 1–5 is a stress on the events occurring in the natural realm: fire destroying divine opponents, lightning causing the world to tremble, and mountains melting like wax. (All such descriptions were understood metaphorically; probably no ancient Hebrew really believed that mountains melted like wax!)

The second stanza (vv. 6–9) speaks of the reordering of life or the reaction of humans to the coming of God as king. The negative consequence involves the submission of the gods and the shame of those who worship idols. The positive consequence is the rejoicing of Zion and the other Judean towns (the daughters of Judah). One can see in this depiction the recurring motif that might be called the "reversal of fate." Judah and Jerusalem, who had suffered from foreign oppressors and the worshipers of idols, would find their condition reversed because they were worshipers of the true god.

One should note that there is a certain assurance or smugness about this portion of the psalm. The judgments of God (v. 8c) are assumed to result in the salvation and blessing of Zion. This would suggest that this psalm derives from the official cult and from worship that gave expression to Judah's confidence in its divine protection. Judgment would be her source of joy.

The third stanza (vv. 10–12) infuses a moral coloration to the psalm and moderates the self-assurance of verses 6–9. These verses may be seen as the explication of the identity of those who can rejoice at the judgment of the king: those who hate evil, the saints or loyal servants, the righteous, and those upright in heart. For such the coming of God is always good news; the visit of the king is a time to rejoice and give thanks.

Titus 3:4–7

It is easy to see why this passage has earned a place in the Christmas service. Within a few short verses, the whole drama of salvation-history is unfolded. The text begins by referring to the dawning of God's kindness in the world and ends with the faithful looking forward to eternal life. In the very heart of the passage, we are reminded that "God saved us" (v. 5), which is, after all, what brings us to celebrate Christmas. Just as the Lukan birth story reminds us that Christ is our Savior (Luke 2:11), so does this passage prompt us to recall the saving work of God and Christ (vv. 4 and 6).

Before looking at certain features of the text, we should consider whether this is the best way to delimit the text. On the front end, the preacher should decide whether the thought actually begins in verse 3 (NIV, REB) or verse 4 (NJB). If verse 3 is included in the text, it sharpens the contrast between what we once were and what we now are. On the tail end, a good case can be made for concluding the text with verse 8a: "The saying is sure" (NRSV). The summarizing force of this verse is more clearly brought out in REB: "That is a saying you may trust" (cf. NJB; also NIV).

It is also worth noting that in the latest edition of the Greek New Testament (Nestle-Aland, 26th ed.), verses 4–7 are treated as a self-contained unit and are printed strophically—a recognition that this text might embody an ancient baptismal liturgy. This would explain the grand sweep of the text, for a baptismal setting would provide the appropriate context for rehearsing in summary form the work of God from the first appearance of God's kindness to our inheritance of eternal life. It would also account for the prominence of certain motifs, such as the "water of rebirth and renewal by the Holy Spirit" (v. 5).

Given the liturgical context in which the lection is read, it is certainly defensible to begin with verse 4, because this keeps the saving work of God at the center of our attention. But a good case can be made for concluding the lection emphatically with verse 8a. Christmas is a time for us to be reminded that "this is doctrine that you can rely on" (NJB).

Even though the text is not a nativity text in the sense that it mentions the birth of Christ, it does recall themes we celebrate at Christmas.

First, *the appearance of "the goodness and loving kindness of God our Savior"* (v. 4). The phrase echoes the Old Testament (Ps. 31:19; cf. Wisd. of Sol. 1:6) as well as Paul's emphasis on God's kindness (Rom. 2:4; 11:22; cf. Eph. 2:7), but the word rendered "loving kindness" in NRSV is actually *philanthropia*, which might be rendered more correctly as "love for humanity." Thus the text actually speaks of the appearance, or revealing, of God's kindness and love for humanity. Both are directed toward our salvation, for they emanate from "God our Savior" (cf. 1 Tim. 1:1; 2:3; 4:10; Titus 1:3; 2:10). In this respect, the epistolary lection echoes a central theme of the Lukan birth story: it is God who is to be glorified and praised for beginning the work of salvation in a manger (Luke 2:14, 20).

Second, *salvation by grace* (v. 5). Just as Israel was reminded that it was not their own righteousness that enabled them to possess the land (Deut. 9:5), so are we reminded that we are not saved by our own doing, even by our own righteous doing (cf. Eph. 2:8–9; 2 Tim. 1:9). The voice we hear is Paul's: our salvation comes as a display of God's mercy and grace (Rom. 3:24; 5:1). Also Pauline is the notion of "washing" (1 Cor. 6:11; cf. Eph. 5:26; Heb. 10:22; 2 Pet. 1:9), even if the metaphor of rebirth is not (cf. John 3:5; 1 Pet. 1:3). Through salvation comes "renewal by the Holy Spirit," or perhaps "the renewing power of the Holy Spirit" (Rom. 12:2; 2 Cor. 5:17; Col. 3:10).

Third, *"Jesus Christ our Savior"* (v. 6). It is worth noticing here that our text envisions Jesus as the one through whom the Holy Spirit is mediated to us (cf. John 15:26). Obviously, Jesus as "Savior" connects this text with the Lukan birth story (cf. Luke 2:11; also Phil. 3:20; 2 Tim. 1:10; Titus 1:4; 2:11, 13; 2 Pet. 1:11).

Fourth, *ourselves as "heirs in hope of eternal life"* (v. 7, NJB). As much as our minds return to Bethlehem in the celebration of Christmas, we nevertheless find ourselves looking forward and living "in hope." It was, after all, in an atmosphere of hopeful anticipation that the nativity of Jesus occurred, and his birth directs us to the God who brings the future into the present each time we celebrate his birth.

Once we begin to grasp the fullness of the claims made in this text, our faith begins to be affirmed and reaffirmed. Our confidence grows that this is a "sure saying," and we can exhort our congregations as we read and celebrate the Christmas story, either in narrative form from Luke or in the form of a baptismal liturgy from Titus: "These are words you may trust" (v. 8a, NEB).

Luke 2:(1–7) 8–20

In the discussion of the Gospel reading for the First Proper for Christmas, the entire birth narrative in Luke 2:1–20 was treated. The reader is referred to that discussion if this alternate proper is used for the sermon.

Christmas, Third Proper
(Additional Lessons for Christmas Day)

Isaiah 52:7–10;
Psalm 98;
Hebrews 1:1–4 (5–12);
John 1:1–14

Today's readings combine to produce a symphony of various compositions centering upon the theme of redemptive good news. In the Old Testament reading, Deutero-Isaiah, the anonymous prophet of the Exile, extols the glory of the messenger who brings good news to Zion. The psalm calls for the singing of a new melody making known the victorious triumph of Israel's God. The Epistle lesson proclaims both the unique and the fulfilling quality of the coming of Christ. In the Gospel reading, the redemptive word that becomes flesh in Jesus is identified with the word that existed with God from the beginning.

Isaiah 52:7–10

Second Isaiah, the prophet of the end of the Babylonian Exile (539 BC), again both establishes the mood for our celebration and articulates the goods news of the day. In fact, the contents of the reading concern the proclamation of good news to people in trouble. Although this very familiar poem is hymnic in tone and substance, and it alludes to cultic matters, it is not itself a hymn. By the time we reach its conclusion in verse 10, it is clear that it is a particular kind of announcement of salvation, one concerning the triumph of Yahweh.

The prophet, although actually in Babylon, describes a scene in distant Jerusalem. It is a powerful and captivating portrayal of a messenger arriving at the city with good news. The report of the message is overloaded with terms indicating just how positive the news is: "good news," "peace," "salvation" (v. 7). The actual contents of the messenger's proclamation is, however, a single line: "Your God reigns." It is the triumph of God as king that amounts to such good news.

Then (v. 8) attention shifts to the sentries (or "sentinels," NRSV) on the walls of the city, shouting out that Yahweh is returning to Zion (see Isa. 40:9–10). Either the prophet himself or the sentries on the walls call for the city in ruins to sing for joy (v. 9). Here the hymnic language closely resembles a hymn of praise, typically beginning with a call to praise and then citing reasons for that praise. The reasons, introduced by "for" (*ki*), are that Yahweh has comforted his people (see Isa. 40:1) and redeemed Jerusalem. Finally (v. 10), those reasons for praise are extended to include the entire world. The Lord has displayed power and authority before "all the nations," so that all can see "the salvation of our God."

These four verses set before us a festival of sights and sounds, alternating from one to the other. First there is the sight of the messenger arriving with good news, seen as in a prophetic vision (v. 7a), and then as we look we hear the messenger's news (v. 7b). Next we hear the sentries on the city wall singing (v. 8a), and then are shown the reasons for their joy (v. 8b). Note the mixture of images: the city stands in ruins, but there are walls with sentries stationed on them. This picture is followed by the sounds of the song of praise (v. 9) and concluded with the most dramatic sight of all, the Lord's saving power revealed to the entire world.

A number of the words and expressions in the passage call for comment. The traditional reading, "Him who brings good tidings" (v. 7, RSV), is a somewhat awkward translation of a single Hebrew word and is more accurately read "Herald" (NEB, NJPSV) or "messenger who announces peace" (NRSV). The Hebrew *shalom* (v. 7) is read variously "peace" (NRSV), "happiness" (NJPSV), and "prosperity" (NEB). In this context it does not refer so much to the absence of war as to well-being. The word translated "salvation" in the NRSV (vv. 7, 10) could be taken as "deliverance" (NEB) or "victory" (NJPSV). In any case, it characterizes the concrete activity of Yahweh in behalf of God's people.

The central themes of the passage concern the kingship of Yahweh, Yahweh's return to Zion, and the revelation of his saving power before all the world. As is usually the case in Second Isaiah, the themes are closely related to one another. Yahweh's reign is the good news; Yahweh manifests that reign by returning to Zion; in returning to Zion and redeeming the people the divine king displays authority and power.

The kingship of Yahweh is an ancient tradition, celebrated in the temple in Jerusalem. The three psalms for Christmas (Pss. 96, 97, 98) all come from such celebrations, as do a great many others (e.g., Pss. 47, 93). The expression translated here "your God reigns" (v. 7) is better read "your God is—or has become—King."

That God returns to Zion raises questions about the presence and absence of God, and the meaning of holy places. The particular motif here is known also in Ezekiel and elsewhere. With the destruction and the Exile, Yahweh was believed to have abandoned the Holy City, and even the chosen people. With the release from captivity and the return, the divine presence comes back. The announcement in this passage, then, is addressed to persons who have experienced the absence of God. Behind this understanding, moreover, stands a deep sense of Zion as a holy place, a location where God is more present than elsewhere. Various biblical traditions attempt to understand the meaning of such beliefs. In the Book of Deuteronomy, Jerusalem is the place where Yahweh chooses for his "name" to dwell, that is, the place where he is known and addressed. In Priestly and other traditions, the temple in Zion is the site of God's holiness (e.g., Isaiah 6).

Is this a scandal of particularity, that the God who transcends all places should be present in a special way—and even "return"—to a particular place? Here that particular presence is for worldwide visibility, for revelation, and what is revealed is God's saving activity. That, it appears, is not unlike the event celebrated on this day in the Christian year, the incarnation.

Psalm 98

Psalm 98, like Psalms 96 and 97, proclaims the enthronement and kingship of God. Various motifs are found in all these psalms: Yahweh as king, the judgment of the world, the stabilization of the created world, and the universal rule of God. As a hymn, the psalm is celebrative, oriented to confessional praise, and speaks about, rather than to, the Deity.

Verses 1–3 call upon the people to sing to Yahweh a new song to celebrate God's victory. What victory is the text concerned with? Different answers have been given to this question: (1) the redemption from Egypt, (2) the return of the Jews from exile, (3) some victory in warfare, (4) the creation of the world, or (5) the annual celebration of God's creation of the world. The latter seems the most likely possibility. Such an interpretation assumes that every year at the fall Feast of Tabernacles, the people led by the king celebrated Yahweh's rule as king over history, the nations, and creation. Because this was the time of the new year, the festival celebrated the creation of the world, and it was assumed that Yahweh re-created the world and reestablished the orders of creation at this time. (If the idea that God annually created the world sounds unusual, we should compare it with the fact that we sing every Christmas that Christ was born today!). As creator, God thus ruled as king and judge over the whole of creation. The victory would thus be God's triumph over chaos or disorder and his establishment of cosmos or order in the universe. In many ancient cultures, it was assumed that the creation of order involved the victory of the creator god over the powers of disorder and chaos (see Ps. 89:9–10). Every year, order had to be reestablished, the hostile powers subdued, and a new beginning made. What God did in victory is related both to Israel and to the nations (the Gentiles) and thus has a universal quality about it.

Verses 4–6 call for the whole earth to praise and sing to Yahweh, with various musical instruments, because Yahweh is the universal king. Interpreters of the Bible used to assume that the idea that God ruled over the whole world developed late in Israelite thought. One can assume, however, that this was a very old idea and that God's kingship was celebrated in the Jerusalem temple from the time of Solomon. It is true that Yahweh did not actually rule over the whole world; that is, Yahweh's worshipers were not found universally nor did Yahweh's people rule the whole world. This did not prevent this fact from being proclaimed in the cult. In a sense, one might say that such proclamations were "predictions" or yet to be realized in fact.

The final verses of the psalm (vv. 7–9) talk about the roaring of the sea and the world, floods clapping their hands and hills singing for joy before Yahweh. Here we are obviously in the realm of metaphorical speech. But it is speech that is right at home in the talk about creation of the world. Thus it is a call for the natural and human world to accept the fact that Yahweh is judge; that is, that Yahweh establishes and upholds order in the world of the universe.

The problem of the particular (the elect, the chosen people of God, the Jews) versus the universal (the outsiders, the nonelect, the Gentiles) in religion has always plagued believers. The early church had to struggle with the universalization of its faith and the inclusion of Gentiles. Such psalms as Psalm 98 demonstrate that the Old Testament itself already had strong universal interests and inclinations incorporated within its pages—a universalism that dares to challenge any totally exclusivistic reading of the work of God in the world.

The call to praise and sing in this psalm suggests that ancient Israel realized that certain times and ideas are best celebrated in joyful sound and song. The Christmas Season should itself be seen as such a time—a time for caroling more than a time for preaching; a season of the heart more than the head; a time for those sentiments awakened by song and celebration rather than by syllogism and cogitation.

Hebrews 1:1–4 (5–12)

This epistolary lection consists of two parts: (1) the prologue (vv. 1–4), and (2) the scriptural argument for Christ's superiority to angels (vv. 5–12). The thought unit actually runs through verse 14, but concluding with verse 12 gives the lection an emphatic ending. Set in the liturgical setting of Christmas, this text commends itself as an elevated meditation on Christ. The sheer richness and variety of traditions and images that cluster here suggest an advanced level of christological reflection, if not in time at least in thought. It looks as though the author has thought long and hard about Christ both as person and event. Besides ransacking his mind for appropriate images to capture the significance of the Christ-event, the author has also perused the Old Testament. There he has found a string of passages that attest the preeminence of Christ, especially as a heavenly being far superior to angels.

For him, Christ is the hinge of history, standing between two eras. At one time God's revelation occurred in many forms and was spoken through many persons. But now, these many voices and sounds of God's revelation have become fused into a single voice. No longer is God's word delivered in scattered and fragmented ways. It comes to us in and through one figure— Jesus Christ. Our text thus draws a sharp line between then and now, between the way it was and the way it is. It directs our attention to "the last days" (v. 2), the eschatological age where a new realm has set in. At Christmas, our minds are positioned at the borderline between BC and AD, and here we celebrate the birth of Christ as the event that "turned the ages." The author of Hebrews, no less than the Gospel writers, looks back on the course of history and sees that with the coming of Christ history turned a corner.

If we think of this meditation on Christ as a suitable Christmas text, we should consider some of the separate claims being made here.

First, *Christ as the son who has been appointed heir of all things.* To be a son is to be an heir (cf. Matt. 21:38; Gal. 4:7), but here the legacy is "all things." This echoes the sentiments of Psalm 2, the royal psalm that speaks of the crowning of the king as God's son and God's promise to make the nations his heritage and the ends of the earth his possession (Ps. 2:7–8). In similar fashion, God's legacy to Christ is universal dominion of all things.

Second, *Christ as the agent of creation.* As the prologue of John's Gospel asserts in today's Gospel reading (John 1:3), the creation of the world cannot be thought of apart from Christ. The more early Christians began to think of the preexistence of Christ, the more they regarded him as active agent and divine assistant in the creation of the world (1 Cor. 8:6; Col. 1:16; cf. Rev. 3:14). Here we see Christ supplanting Wisdom who, in the Jewish wisdom tradition, was seen as the One through whom God created the world (Wisd. of Sol. 9:1).

Third, *Christ as the sustainer of the universe by his powerful word.* Closely related to our confession of Christ as creator is the conviction that through him the universe is upheld, or stays on its course. It should be noted that the means of sustenance is his "powerful word," or his powerful command (NJB). This doubtless presupposes the ancients' understanding of divine utterances as dynamic forces capable of holding the world together. In a slightly different vein, Christ is confessed in the Colossian hymn as the One in whom "all things hold together," cosmic glue as it were (Col. 1:17). The important point here is that just as the author cannot conceive of the creation of the world apart from Christ, neither can he conceive of the ongoing of the world, heaven and earth alike, apart from Christ.

Fourth, *Christ is a reflection of the glory of God*. Reflection here is not thought of in the sense of a shadow, but rather as a shaft of light emanating from a dazzlingly brilliant source. In fact, the term "glory" is best understood as "brilliance" or "splendor." The image of light is fundamental to understanding the term. Most likely, the story of God's revelation to Moses at Sinai informs the image (cf. Exod. 24:16; cf. 2 Cor. 3:7–11, 18; also 4:4). Again, the role assigned to Wisdom in the Jewish wisdom tradition appears to be transferred here to Christ (cf. Wisd. of Sol. 7:25).

Fifth, *Christ as the very stamp of his nature, or "the impress of God's own being"* (NJB). Once again, Alexandrian philosophical traditions supply the metaphor, for our text insists that Christ is an exact replica of God's innermost nature, or substance (cf. Col. 1:15; also John 14:9). The ancients debated whether the imprint of a seal on wax could ever be as pristine and original as the seal itself, but this is not the thought in view here. Rather, the claim being made is that Christ in every sense bears the very stamp of God's own nature.

Sixth, *Christ as the exalted high priest who has made purification for sins*. Unlike the other images that tend to be abstract, this one is quite personal, recalling the person of the high priest. Being seated at the right hand of God was one of the ways Christians pictured the exalted Christ after his resurrection (Heb. 8:1; 10:12; 12:2). The language is provided by Psalm 110:1. Christ as the high priest who officiates "once for all" in behalf of us is, of course, a prominent theme in the epistle (cf. Heb. 9:12, 26).

Any of these christological claims is staggering enough in its own right, but the power of this passage stems from the fact that so many such claims are clustered together. Little wonder that Christ is said to be superior to angels! In no sense is he just another heavenly being— some angel, even an archangel, whom God has chosen from the heavenly hosts. He is rather in another category altogether. He is the Son of God, with all that entails.

John 1:1–14

The Gospel of John does not have nativity songs as does Luke, but John does have a hymn to Christ (1:1–18). The Gospel of John does not have a birth story, but John does proclaim that the Word became flesh and dwelt among us (1:14). The Gospel of John does not say that the one conceived by the Holy Spirit would be the Son of God, but John does say that the One who became flesh was with God from the beginning, and what God was, he was (1:1). The Gospel of John does not say that God's Son was wrapped in swaddling cloths, lying in a manger, but John does say that the revelation of God in Jesus was concealed, if not hidden, veiled in flesh (1:14). John 1:1–14 is, then, an appropriate text for Christmas.

The verses selected for today (1:1–14) are a portion of a unit only slightly larger, 1:1–18, commonly referred to as the prologue. The prologue is clearly a distinct literary unit, having a clear beginning and ending, being poetic in nature in contrast to the prose narrative that follows (1:19ff.), and focusing on a single subject, the Word of God. Because of its unusual literary form and because its presentation of Christ as the Word (Logos) appears nowhere else in the Gospel, some have suggested that 1:1–18 was not an original part of this Gospel. The issue is not a vital one for the preacher, because the theological perspective of the prologue is fully congenial with the remainder of the book. In fact, the entire Gospel is in a sense an elaboration upon 1:18: "No one has ever seen God. It is God the only Son, who is close to the Father's heart, who has made him known."

John 1:1–18 consists of three stanzas with two insertions about John the Baptist (vv. 6–8, 15). (For comments on these verses, see the Third Sunday of Advent, Year B.) The first stanza, verses 1–5, relates God to all creation through the Word; the second, verses 9–13, relates God to human life through the Word; and the third, verses 14–18, provides the divine offer of grace and truth through the Word. It is not abortive of meaning to conclude at verse 14 as does this lection, for verse 14 is John's "Christmas story" in capsule; but because verses 14–18 are the affirmation of faith (among *us*, *we* have seen, *we* have all received) concluding the hymn, the sermon properly should embrace the whole of the prologue.

A preacher may recoil at the thought of a single sermon on the entire text, and properly so. Its scope is immense: all creation, Israel, the Baptist movement, the church, preexistence of the Word, and salvation through the revelation of the Word. In addition, the passage is not only hymnic but polemic, contending with the synagogue and the followers of the Baptist (vv. 6–8, 15, 17). But for the occasion of Christmas, one would do well to step back and see the whole of it. Sometimes enabling listeners to sense the size and grandeur of a text is of more value than detailed application to their lives.

Let us, then, allow the Fourth Evangelist to tell us the good news. A fundamental human hunger is to know God. "Show us the Father, and we will be satisfied" (14:8) In fact, to know God is life eternal (17:3). But no one has ever seen God (1:18), and even though God is the creator and sustainer of all life and available to obedient faith (1:1–12), knowledge of God does not come by observation or by the accumulation of proofs. However, because God is gracious toward the world (3:16), the darkness of ignorance and death are dispelled by the coming of the Son as revealer (1:18). In order to tell this story, John borrows a category familiar to Jewish and Greek culture—Word, or Logos (the feminine synonym often interchanged with Logos is Sophia, Wisdom). The Word, or Wisdom, through which God created and sustains the world (Gen. 1:3; Ps. 33:47; Heb. 1:3) came to be personified in late Judaism as a separate being (Prov. 8; Wisd. of Sol. 7; Sir. 24). In Sirach, for example, this Wisdom through whom God created the world asked of God permission to come dwell on earth. Permission was granted, but the earth was evil, foolish, and inhospitable. And so God made Wisdom to become a book, the Book of Moses, to dwell in the tents of Jacob (Sir. 24). But for the Evangelist, the eternal Wisdom, or Word, becomes not a book, but flesh—a person, Jesus of Nazareth.

Not all who met Jesus experienced God, nor do they today, but to all who do, God gives "power to become children of God" (1:12).

First Sunday After Christmas Day

The following readings are used on the First Sunday After Christmas unless the readings for the Epiphany of the Lord are preferred.

1 Samuel 2:18–20, 26;
Psalm 148;
Colossians 3:12–17;
Luke 2:41–52

The First Sunday After Christmas is traditionally associated with the childhood and family of Jesus. The Lucan account of the boy Jesus with his parents in Jerusalem at the time of Passover sets that theme. The reading from 1 Samuel 2 is the story of another precocious boy, Samuel, and it includes the lines quoted in the Gospel lection. Psalm 148 is a hymn of praise, primarily for God's creation, but it also calls on all peoples to praise God who "has raised up a horn for his people." The passage from Colossians calls attention to those virtues especially important in family life, providing a catalog of Christian virtues.

1 Samuel 2:18–20, 26

We may better understand the story of the young Samuel by locating it in its literary context. Two themes are intertwined in the first three chapters of 1 Samuel: the fall of the priestly house of Eli and the divine election of Samuel. Two episodes in the Samuel story precede the reading for the day: the account of his birth to Hannah in her old age, and the report of his consecration to serve the Lord, thus fulfilling Hannah's vow. The song of Hannah (1 Sam. 2:1–10) is presented as part of the service of dedication. First Samuel 2:26 most likely originally followed 2:18–20, as our lection has it, but was separated from the earlier verses by the insertion of the account of the sons of the old priest Eli (2:22–25). Thus Samuel, young but faithful and maturing, stands in sharp contrast to the corrupt priests who would logically expect to succeed their father.

The atmosphere of the story is archaic and cultic. Its setting is the sanctuary at Shiloh, the home of the ark of the covenant and probably at the time the major center for worship among the tribes of Israel. Samuel himself slept near the ark, in or very close to the holy place (1 Sam. 3:3). When the old priest Eli gives his blessing to Elkanah and Hannah we know that the words will be powerful and effective, as indeed they are (vv. 20–21). From the time when

44

he first came to Shiloh Samuel carried out priestly functions; we are expressly told more than once that he ministered to the Lord (1 Sam. 2:11, 18; 3:1). The "linen ephod" and perhaps also the "little robe" (2:18–19) would have been priestly garb.

The little boy Samuel is a child of destiny. As the contrasts between him and the sons of Eli already indicate, he and not they will succeed their venerable father as chief priest in Israel. The mantle of prophecy will also fall upon him, for he will hear the call of God and throughout his lifetime will communicate the word of the Lord to the people. Moreover, as political leader he will be the bridge between the era of the judges and that of the kings, anointing both Saul and David. There had not been one like him in Israel since the time of Moses.

But even children of destiny have parents. Here, of course, his mother Hannah stands out. Although she had "loaned him" to the Lord (1 Sam. 1:28; 2:20, RSV) in fulfillment of her vow, she continued to be his mother. One cannot help but be touched by the account of the mother who sees her young son but rarely, each year bringing him "a little robe." He is, after all, a growing boy, and last year's robe will soon be too short.

So it is a story of growth and development, and of preparation for destiny. That growth takes place, so this account suggests, in the context of both family and worshipping community. The piety of the family—their regular pilgrimage for the sacrifice—is noted in a matter-of-fact tone as only normal. But especially important was a mother willing to gain her son by giving him up. Thus the boy "continued to grow both in stature and in favor with the LORD and with the people" (v. 26).

Psalm 148

Psalms 146–150 constitute a small collection of hymns of praise. All begin and conclude with the cultic shout "Hallelujah" that calls upon the community to "praise Yahweh," "praise the Lord."

Psalm 148 consists of two types of genres: two extended calls to praise (vv. 1–4, 7–12) and two statements giving the reason or rationale for praise (vv. 5–6, 13–14).

The psalm is an exuberant summons for the whole of creation to join in shouting out and celebrating the name and glory of Yahweh. Practically no aspect of creation is omitted in the call to praise: angels, heavenly hosts, sun and moon, shining stars, highest heavens, waters above the heavens, sea monsters and all deeps, fire and hail, snow and frost, stormy wind, mountains and hills, fruit trees and all cedars, wild animals and all cattle, creeping things and flying birds, kings, princes, rulers, young men and women, old and young. What a chorus!

In spite of its tone, Psalm 148 should not be faulted for a Pollyanna perspective on life. There are times when unbounded jubilation should reign and carry us to the limits of celebration, to the borders of insanity, and to the heights of a self-transcendence. Few are the times when the whole world is a chorus and the music of the spheres invades every nook and cranny of existence. Their scarcity should only endear their occurrence. It is only in such moments that we can spiritually and sensually realize the truth that modern ecology has taught us. We are all—from shining star to slithering snake—in this together, and we need to sing, at least occasionally, the same song and join in a common medley.

The psalm offers two reasons undergirding such praise. The first (in vv. 5–6) declares that Yahweh is the creator of all, who has established everything and set a law that cannot pass away (NRSV margin). The created order is divine handiwork in which every part serves its function within a created natural order (see Jer. 5:22–24; 31:35–36). The second (in vv. 13–14) alludes to the rule of the Davidic monarch, the horn raised up for the people of Israel. (On the horn as the symbol of strength and royalty, see 1 Sam. 2:10; Pss. 75:4–5; 89:17, 24; 92:10; 112:9; 132:17; Lam. 2:3, 17.) The psalm thus anchors praise in the divine rule in the universe and the messianic rule over the chosen people.

Colossians 3:12–17

Properly observed, Christmas sets us thinking about the difference Christ's coming has made in our own lives. Not only does it enrich and reorient our personal commitment, but as a celebration in which the entire church participates it deepens our fellowship with one another. Today's epistolary text, read the First Sunday After Christmas, addresses us at both the personal and corporate level. Even though our text is a miscellany of instructions and admonitions, it calls for a quality of life together that mutually edifies and enriches our fellowship with one another. Throughout the text, we are called to be a community of faith living responsibly before one another and genuinely sensitive to one another's needs.

Any division of the passage is somewhat arbitrary, but there appears to be a break with verse 16, where the instructions more directly relate to worship. Thus we may divide the text into two parts. In verses 12–15, we are given a profile of the new life that is ours in Christ. In verses 16–17, we are told how our worship may be enriched.

A profile of the new life in Christ (vv. 12–15). This positive portrait provides the counterpart to the preceding section that sketches the negative portrait of the life we left behind (3:5–11). Several features are worth noting.

1. It is God's action that provides us our new status. We are addressed as "God's chosen ones, holy and beloved" (v. 12). God took the initiative in calling us. Like Israel, we are God's elect (Rom. 8:33; 9:11; 11:5, 7, 28; 1 Cor. 1:27, 28; 1 Thess. 1:4; 1 Pet. 2:9). Consequently, we share God's holy character; we are "God's own" (NEB). But this was not a cold, impersonal summons. It was rather an expression of God's own love. As God's beloved, we are the objects of God's love (cf. Eph. 5:1). As was the case with Israel, election is a concrete manifestation of divine love (Hos. 11:1).

2. Given our new status, we are to be clothed with a new character. We are called to wear a new wardrobe. The charge to "clothe" ourselves with certain virtues recalls earlier instructions to put away, or strip off, old forms of behavior (3:8–9). Several virtues are singled out: compassion, kindness, humility, meekness, patience, forbearance, and a forgiving spirit (cf. Eph. 4:31–32). The first four are aptly paraphrased by C. F. D. Moule: "ready sympathy, a generous spirit, a humble disposition, willingness to make concessions."

These are the qualities of life that make for genuine community, yet our text recognizes that even among God's chosen there will arise disputes and complaints. In words reminiscent of Jesus himself, we are urged to be forbearing and willing to forgive (Matt. 6:14; 18:21–35; cf. also 2 Cor. 2:7; Eph. 4:32). Nor are we asked to muster the power to forgive from within ourselves, but our willingness to forgive should be based in the prior action of the Lord himself who has generously forgiven us (v. 13).

What binds all the others together, indeed what makes them possible, is love (cf. Rom. 13:8–10; 1 Cor. 13:13; 14:1). If the clothing metaphor is continued here, we are actually being instructed to put on love as the final article of clothing—the overcoat, as it were, that keeps all the other pieces in place. Or love is possibly envisioned here as the belt that secures all the other garments. In any case, our capacity to love is seen as a response to God's own love for us (v. 12).

3. The peace of Christ should be the ruling force within us. The word for "rule" in verse 15 may be more literally rendered "umpire." Hence, "Let Christ's peace be arbiter in your decisions" (REB). It is presupposed that first we have been called into the one body of Christ, and as such share a common life (Rom. 12:5; Eph. 1:23; 2:16; 4:4). Here we might recall the song of the heavenly host proclaiming "peace on earth" (Luke 2:14). With Christ as the bearer of this peace within our midst, we have a means of resolving, or umpiring, disputes and conflicts, and thus becoming the place where God's shalom receives concrete manifestation.

The character of Christian worship (vv. 16–17). This is by no means a complete catalog of Christian worship, but several important elements are mentioned.

1. "Let the Word of Christ, in all its richness, find a home with you" (NJB). As the church, we are charged to allow the word of Christ, the gospel, to dwell within us and thus provide the ordering principle for us as God's people. One obvious source to which we turn is Scripture with its manifold witness to Christ, but there are other sources. We also listen to the historical witness of the church's tradition as it is mediated to us through faithful witness. In addition, there is the word of Christ that comes to us in prayer and service.

2. "Teach each other, and advise each other, in all wisdom" (NJB). True community is achieved through mutual edification (Eph. 4:29). More is implied here than the mere transmission of knowledge, although this is obviously essential. We are told to teach each other "in all wisdom." The teaching called for here should be accompanied with a level of understanding that is truly instructive for ordering our lives.

3. "With psalms and hymns and spiritual songs, sing from the heart in gratitude to God" (REB). Worship is envisioned here not only as adoration to God but also as a way of instructing each other (1 Cor. 14:26; cf. Matt. 26:30; Acts 16:25; Eph. 5:19–20; Heb 2:12; James 5:13).

4. "Giving thanks to God the Father" (v. 17). The text has already urged us to "be thankful" (v. 15), but here our thanksgiving is rendered to God through Christ (cf. 1:12; Eph. 5:20; 1 Thess. 5:18).

As a final reminder, we are urged to "do everything in the name of the Lord Jesus" (v. 17). This sets the horizon within which the new life is lived and in which the community worships.

Luke 2:41–52

All the lections for today move us beyond Christmas, not only chronologically but practically; it is time now for internalizing the meaning of Christ's coming and for expressing that meaning in personal and social life. This is especially true of Luke 2:41–52, which offers a childhood experience of Jesus as a model of growth toward others and toward God.

Luke's story of Jesus as a twelve-year-old is so normal and natural, so free of miracles, fulfilled prophecies, or special revelations, that some scholars think the narrative may have once circulated independent of the birth stories. Perhaps so, but even if the story were told in circles that did not know the virgin birth stories, Luke certainly knew them but saw no need to bring the language of this event—"his parents," "your father and I"—into harmony with the virgin birth. The fact is, even for Luke and Matthew, the birth stories were not used in the remainder of their Gospels to argue the true identity of Jesus.

What Luke is doing with this story is to present both home and temple as formative institutions in the development of Jesus. The family of Jesus is a model of Jewish piety. At every point in Jesus' life, the law of Moses has been kept: circumcision (2:21), Mary's purification and Jesus' dedication (2:22–40), and now the family's annual pilgrimage to Jerusalem for Passover (2:41). Jesus, being at the age for Bar Mitzvah, accompanies them (2:42). His lingering behind in the temple is not in any way a denial of filial piety but an indirect testimony to the deep faith of the family and the fulfillment of the act of giving the child Jesus to the Lord (2:22–23). Jesus now claims for himself that special relation to God that was symbolized in his dedication as an infant. Up to this point all signs of Jesus' unusual nature or mission have been to or through others: the angel, Mary, Elizabeth, shepherds, Simeon, and Anna, but now he claims it for himself (2:49). To be sure, not too much should be made of the temple scene; Jesus sits among the teachers as a child of unusual understanding (2:47). There is no reason at this point to impute to Jesus full and clear knowledge of his future mission. A sense of Luke's purpose in this story is provided not by reading Jesus' future into this present scene but by reading Luke's model for the story in 1 Samuel 2. The boy Samuel was given to God by his mother Hannah and in time he was taken to the temple (tabernacle) to live. It was in the temple that he came to an awareness of his special mission. And of the boy Samuel it was said that he "continued to grow both in stature and in favor with the LORD and with the people" (1 Sam. 2:26).

In summary, three statements can be made in reflection on this vignette for Jesus' boyhood, the only record about Jesus between infancy and manhood. First, Luke wants it understood that Jesus was nurtured in a context of obedience and worship. He was from birth to death the true Israelite, unwavering in his observance of the demands of home, synagogue, and temple. Second, at age twelve there were in him vague stirrings of his own uniqueness. The circle of his awareness and sense of obligation is beginning to widen beyond the home in Nazareth. Third, Jesus' move toward God is not without its tensions in the family. Even though Jesus returned home with Mary and Joseph and was obedient to them (2:51), three expressions in the story register the tension: "'Child, why have you treated us like this?'" (v. 48); "'Look, your father and I have been searching for you in great anxiety'" (v. 48); "But they did not understand what he said to them" (v. 50). Even so, the tension here does not approach that reported by Mark (3:31–35) on the occasion of Jesus' mother and brothers coming for him, having heard that he was beside himself (3:21). The truth that Mark states explicitly and Luke certainly implies in today's lection is clear: family loves and loyalties have their life and place under the higher love and loyalty to God.

January 1
(Holy Name of Jesus: Solemnity of Mary, Mother of God)

Numbers 6:22–27;
Psalm 8;
Galatians 4:4–7 or Philippians 2:5–11;
Luke 2:15–21

Celebrating the beginning of the new year on January 1 goes back to the mid–first century BC, when Julius Caesar restructured the civil calendar. Before then, March 1 marked the beginning of the new year. From the outset, it was a festive celebration that easily gave way to excesses of various kinds. In response, the Roman church called on Christians to open the new year with prayer, fasting, and penitential devotions. Another way to provide an alternative to raucous festivals was to designate January 1 as a time for honoring Mary, the Mother of God. The way had been paved by the Eastern church, where the tradition of paying special devotion to Mary was already well established. In the Roman calendar the day was designated *Natale Sanctae Mariae,* the Feast of Saint Mary.

Even though the particular emphasis given to January 1 has shifted through the centuries, in modern times, and especially in the Roman church, this day has received a dual emphasis. First, it is a tie to recall the naming of Jesus, hence the designation the "Holy Name of Jesus." This aspect of its celebration is closely related to the custom, going back at least to the sixth century, of celebrating the Feast of the Circumcision of the Lord on this day. Second, it is an occasion for commemorating Mary, hence the designation the "Solemnity of Mary, the Mother of God."

The readings selected for this day echo these themes. The Old Testament reading is chosen because of its emphasis on the bestowal of the divine name on the people Israel. Psalm 8 begins and ends with praise of the name of God. The epistolary readings (Gal. 4:4–7 and Phil. 2:5–11) in different ways pick up on both themes of the day. The Galatians passage embodies a pre-Pauline tradition in which Christ is confessed as one "born of woman, born under the law," whereas the Philippians reading lays stress on the exalted name that God bestowed on the risen Lord. The Gospel text, of course, combines both themes: the central role of Mary as the one who pondered the divine mystery in her heart and the circumcision of Jesus as the occasion when he received the holy name.

49

Numbers 6:22–27

Within the Pentateuch as a whole, Numbers 6:22–27 is part of the laws given through Moses at Mt. Sinai. The section of which it is a part began with Exodus 19 and will end in Numbers 10. In terms of literary source, this unit, like most of the laws from Sinai from Exodus 25 to Numbers 10, comes from the Priestly Writer (sixth century BC). Specifically, the stress on the priesthood of the sons of Aaron (6:23) reveals that writer's point of view. However, in the great body of legislation this passage stands out for its poetic style, suggesting that the blessing itself is much older than the source in which it is found. Its style and content clearly reflect its repeated cultic use, doubtless by the priests in the Jerusalem temple.

The unit consists of the Aaronic blessing surrounded by a brief narrative framework. The narrative (6:22) simply but significantly indicates that what follows is a divine speech to Moses. Remarkably, the benediction as a prayer for God's blessing was itself a gift from God. In the speech God instructs Moses to tell Aaron and his sons—that is, all future priests in the line, down to the writer's day—to bless the people of Israel, gives them the words of the blessing, and then (6:27) states the meaning of the act of blessing.

The blessing contains three sentences, each with two parts and each one longer than the one before. Every sentence begins with the divine name, Yahweh, followed by verbal forms that indicate wish or hope, for example, "[May] the LORD bless you . . ." They are then prayers for the well-being of those addressed. Because the form of address is second person singular, the blessing may apply equally to individuals or collectively to the group as a whole. The contents concern God's protection (v. 24), gracious care (v. 25), and gift of peace. "Peace" (shalom) is a comprehensive term, a fitting greeting, that includes wholeness. Priests are to pronounce the blessing, but, as verse 27 expressly states, the Lord is the one who blesses.

What does it mean that by pronouncing the blessing the sons of Aaron thus put the divine name upon Israel? One hardly need stress the importance of names in the Old Testament. Abram and Sarai were given with the covenant new names (Gen. 17). After struggling through the night, Jacob was given the new name Israel, but the one with whom he struggled would not reveal his name, for in the name is power (Gen. 32:27–29). Yahweh was to be worshiped at the place where he will choose "to put his name . . ." (Deut. 12:5). To "put the name" of the Lord over the people of Israel is to indicate that they are known, and know themselves by that name. They are thereby identified with this God, and this God with them.

Psalm 8

This hymn was composed in praise of God the creator, whose name and handiwork pervade all the earth. This is made evident in the prologue and epilogue verses (vv. 1a, 9). The second person speech—direct address to God—that appears throughout the psalm is unusual in hymns that are normally human speech to a human audience intent on instilling and enriching faith. (Ps. 104 supplies another example of such a second person hymn.) The hymn could have been spoken in worship by the Judean king who, it appears, may have referred to himself circumlocutionarily as "son of man" (v. 4b; see also Pss. 80:17;

144:3), although the NRSV universalizes this reference by translating "mortals" (see NRSV marginal note *g*).

Two aspects of human existence are highlighted in this psalm. There is, first, the human sense of insignificance when confronted with the awesome reality of the created order. Whoever penned verses 3–4 must have viewed the heavens on some clear, crystal, Palestinian night and wondered, like many of us who have beheld the earth as televised from some silently sailing spaceship, where humans—invisible from such heights—fit into the scheme of things. This is the feeling in the psalm that viewed matters from the human side looking upward.

A second set of anthropological affirmations center on humankind's high status in the created order—"a little less than God" with "dominion over." Humans are thus the intermediates between the heavenly and the nonhuman world. The positions in this psalm should be compared with Genesis 1, the Priestly account of creation. In the latter, humans are made, unlike any other part of the earthly order, in the image of God (1:26) and are granted dominion over the other orders of creation—fish, fowl, and land animals (1:28). As a little lower than God, humans are thus affirmed as related and akin to the divine order. The other side of this affirmation is seen in the role of humans as supreme in the world of creation. Domesticated animals, wild beasts of the field, fowl of the air, and fish in the sea are all seen as subservient and subordinate to the human world. Such a claim and understanding allowed the Israelites, with a sad conscience nonetheless, to slaughter and consume other living beings, only returning the blood (symbolizing life) in sacrifice or burial to God as an apology for killing (see Lev. 17:1–13).

In this psalm there is only a tinge of that anthropological ambivalence that has occupied the thought of philosophers, the concern with humanity's double quality of greatness and depravity. (For the Yahwist, the first human was viewed as a divinely animated clod—Genesis 3—that preserves the twofold quality of human existence.) There is a little of that ambivalence one sees, for example, in the description of humankind by the French philosopher-mathematician Blaise Pascal (1623–62): "What a chimera then is man! What a novelty! What a monster, what a chaos, what a contradiction, what a prodigy! Judge of all things, feeble earthworm, depository of truth, a sink of uncertainty and error, the glory and the shame of the universe."

The elevated, exalted state of man in this psalm and its employment of the phrase "son of man" made it possible for the early church to use this text in expounding an understanding of Jesus, who as "Son of Man" reigns over God's order (see Matt. 21:16; 1 Cor. 15:27; Heb. 2:6–9) and bears the name that is above all names (Phil. 2:9).

Galatians 4:4–7

"**B**orn of a woman, born under the law." These few words are as close as Paul comes to providing a birth and infancy narrative of Jesus. Yet for all their remarkable compactness, they capture the essence of Luke's birth narrative. "Born of a woman" naturally applies to Mary's giving birth to the Son of God, and it is this phrase that especially commends this epistolary lection for the celebration of New Year's Day as the "Solemnity of Mary, Mother of God." Some scholars believe that the phrase is pre-Pauline and thus stems from the very earliest stages of primitive Christianity. If it is part of a creedal statement, we can see that quite early on Mary was the object of early Christian confession.

If "born of a woman" underscores the humanity of Jesus, "born under the law" underscores his Jewishness. For Paul, this had special significance, for he is concerned to show that precisely because Jesus lived under the Mosaic law he was able to redeem us from the bondage of the law. What Paul says here in shorthand Luke portrays in narrative form: Jesus is circumcised according to the prescription of the law (Luke 2:21) and brought to the temple for the rite of consecration (Luke 2:22–38). He is the son of parents loyally devoted to life according to the law of Moses (Luke 2:39–51). Just as the first phrase links the epistolary text with the celebration of Mary as the Mother of God, so does this second phrase link directly with the circumcision and naming of Jesus (Luke 2:21).

Homiletically, these two motifs might be explored by showing how the devotion of Mary, as depicted in the Gospel reading, related to the devotion of Jesus. Both have in common their loyalty to the law of God. We are told that she and Joseph were scrupulously loyal, preforming "everything required by the law of the Lord" (Luke 2:39). In the same breath, Jesus is portrayed in terms reminiscent of Samuel, the faithful servant of God (1 Sam. 3:19). It would be possible to trace the Lukan portrait of Mary, especially noting her favorable status (in contrast to the Markan portrait) as among those "who hear the word of God and do it" (Luke 8:19–21).

Like mother, like son.

Philippians 2:5–11

If one chooses the Holy Name of Jesus as the focus of attention on New Year's Day, this will be the more appropriate epistolary text because it draws our attention to God's bestowal of the divine name on Jesus.

If this epistolary text is chosen, it provides a strong counterpart to the Gospel reading (Luke 2:15–21), where the name given to the Son of God, according to the angel's prescription, is "Jesus" (Luke 1:31). By contrast, in the epistolary reading the "name that is above every name" (v. 9) is "Lord" (cf. 1 Thess. 1:1). This is the name bestowed on Jesus because of his resurrection (Rom. 1:4) or, in the words of our passage, because "God also highly exalted him" (v. 9). To be sure, it is the "name of Jesus" before which the universe bows in submission, but the heart of the confession is that "Jesus Christ is Lord." We can begin to see the true significance of this ascription if we remember that in the Greek Old Testament Yahweh was commonly designated as Lord. Thus, for Christians to give Jesus this title was to ascribe him a status normally reserved for Israel's God, Yahweh.

The sequel to this part of the Christ-hymn is well worth exploring in a New Year's Day setting, because it spells out the implications of confessing and submitting to the divine name of Jesus Christ the Lord (cf. 2:12–13). Submission to the name implies submissive obedience that is worked out in salvation. It is not, however, the work that we do but the work that God does within us that brings about such obedience. We are reminded that "fear and trembling" accompany God's saving work within us—not that we become feckless and craven before a vindictive, bloodthirsty God, but that we respect the exalted status and universal dominion of the One we confess as Lord. Such a perspective creates within us a healthy respect for the numinous and holy that prevents us from confessing the name of Jesus blithely and unthinkingly. This day is, after all, a celebration of the *Holy* Name of Jesus. It may be well to call the church to recover this sacred dimension as it launches into a new year.

Luke 2:15–21

The tradition that calls for this special service on January 1 carries with it a double focus, either one of which may be central to the liturgy and sermon for any given year of the lectionary. Primary attention may be given to Mary, or it may be given to the child upon the occasion of circumcision and naming. In either case, it means for the preacher a return to the Lucan text treated earlier as the Gospel (along with John 1:1–14) for the season of Christmas. Only verse 21 is added to the earlier reading. This return will be no strain either on the familiar text or on the preacher's imagination if the special focus of this service is kept in mind. We will here discuss Luke 2:15–21, with attention first upon Mary and then upon the eight-day-old child, leaving to the preacher the choice of accent. For the recovery of the whole narrative (Luke 2:1–20), the reader may want to review the comments on the Christmas lection.

In Luke 2:15–20, Mary is in the unusual position of hearing from strange visitors, the shepherds, the testimony about her son's significance in God's gracious purpose for "all the people" (v. 10). The shepherds receive from heaven's messenger the good news of a Savior; the shepherds hear the angelic choir; the shepherds are given a sign for confirmation. Mary, the child's mother, hears all this, not directly, but through their testimony—not that there is anything wrong with hearing it the way the whole world receives it (24:47–48; Acts 1:8). But his young mother, in pain, away from home, uncomfortably housed in a stable, would surely have been cheered and encouraged by a brief return of the angel who visited her nine months earlier. Nine months is a long time; in fact, plenty of time to doubt one's own experience, plenty of time to wonder about the adequacy of one's answers to inquiring relatives and friends.

But our quiet wish for Mary is not her own wish. She keeps these things in her heart, pondering, remembering (v. 19). The witness of the shepherds confirms what Gabriel had said (1:26–38) and what her kinswoman Elizabeth had told her (1:39–45). Soon Simeon would add to this testimony, as would Anna, and the child himself at age twelve, causing Mary to ponder further the meaning of all this (2:22–51). Mary was not, however, only a ponderer: She believed God's word and was obedient to it (1:38, 45); she had strong confidence and hope in God (1:46–55); and she became a disciple of her firstborn, joining his other followers in Jerusalem as they prayerfully waited for the Holy Spirit he had promised (Acts 1:5, 14). No fear of an excessive adoration of Mary should blind us to Luke's portrayal of her as a true disciple.

Verse 21 provides the second perspective in today's lesson, the naming of Jesus. Luke, who alone among the Evangelists records this moment in Jesus' life, conveys three messages in the one sentence devoted to it. First, there is the name itself. Jesus is a form of the name Joshua, which means "salvation from Jehovah." Luke has already called Jesus "Savior" (2:11), but it is Matthew who states more directly the choice of the name: "you are to name him Jesus, for he will save his people from their sins" (1:31).

Luke's second point is that the naming of Jesus both fulfills and confirms the word of God delivered by the angel (1:31). To say the word was fulfilled is to acknowledge a pattern of promise/fulfillment very important to Luke both in the Gospel (4:16–21; 24:44) and in Acts (2:17–36). More consistently in Luke than in any other New Testament writer, the theme of continuity between the Old Testament and the New is developed. To say that the word of God was confirmed is to say that the event of naming the child Jesus confirmed the divine revelation. The same was true in the case of John. The name was given to Zechariah in a revelation (1:13), and so the child was called John, much to the surprise of relatives and neighbors (1:57–63). Both John and Jesus are of families who hear, believe, and obey the word of God.

And finally, Luke wants it understood that there was nothing about Jesus and his followers that violated the law of Moses. In chapter 2 alone, Luke cites repeated observances of the law: circumcision, dedication at the temple, purification of the mother, journey to Jerusalem at age twelve for the Passover. Luke's Jesus worships regularly in the synagogue (4:16), and following his death, the disciples continue to worship God in the temple (24:53). Jesus and his disciples do not represent a breach of ancient law and covenant but rather continuation and fulfillment of God's gracious purpose as revealed in the law, the prophets, and the writings (24:27, 44–47).

January 1
(When Observed as New Year's Eve or Day)

Ecclesiastes 3:1–13;
Psalm 8;
Revelation 21:1–6a;
Matthew 25:31–46

All the texts for the day focus attention on time and the passing of time. The Old Testament reading is highly appropriate for a new year, emphasizing the rhythms of time and meditating on the human response to the passing of time. The psalm calls forth praise apropos of a new beginning and identifies the place of that time-bound human being in God's order. The Epistle reading envisions a new and eternal heaven and earth and a new and eternal Jerusalem. The newness of a new year that gives us the taste of beginning again, of leaving behind, also raises the yearning for the totally and permanently new. The Gospel text preserves for us the association, so common in Judaism, of the new year with judgment.

Ecclesiastes 3:1–13

Read as a whole and in its literary context, this is not a cheerful text. The author, Qohelet, begins his book with the declaration that "all is vanity" (1:2) and throughout the work reflects on the futility of all human endeavor. In the text set before us at the beginning of the year, Qohelet meditates on the meaning of time and the times, and is drawn to a somber conclusion.

The lection consists of two major parts, each with its subdivisions. The first part is the poem on times and seasons (vv. 1–8). Verse 1 is an introduction that states the general thesis: "For everything there is a season, and a time for every matter [or "experience," NJPSV] under heaven." Verses 2–8 then develop that thesis in detail by means of fourteen opposites. These in turn begin with the most comprehensive opposites of all, at least with regard to human life: "a time to be born, and a time to die" (v. 2). All the other opposites have to do with human activities or experiences, and a progression of thought is difficult to discern: hostility and violence along with their opposites frame verses 3–8; killing—as in warfare or executions—and healing (v. 3a); love and hate, war and peace (v. 8). The other pairs concern a wide range of human activities, including construction (v. 4), speaking (v. 7), and acts of affection (v. 5b), as well as the extremes of human emotions and their expression (v. 4). The point is conveyed

55

not only by the contents but also by the style and mood, the steady rhythm and the repetitious pattern suggesting the thesis itself: Everything has its regular time, and time moves on.

The lines of the poem on time—apart from their present context—can be heard in many different ways. They can affirm an orderly creation, not only in terms of space but of time as well. The lesson of that understanding, common in Old Testament wisdom literature, would be patience: Endure whatever you face, for its time will end. War and peace, love and hate all have their time. And the wisdom teachers stressed the importance of study and learning in order to know the right time for each thing:

> To make an apt answer is a joy to anyone,
>   and a word in season, how good it is! (Proverbs 15:23)

The wise person has good timing, whether in knowing when to speak or in when to plant particular crops. Or one could take the rhythm of time as a gift, as in Yahweh's promise to Noah following the flood:

> As long as the earth endures,
>   seedtime and harvest, cold and heat,
> summer and winter, day and night,
>   shall not cease. (Genesis 8:22)

But none of these is the conclusion that Qohelet draws from the poem on time, which he probably did not write but is quoting from the wisdom tradition. His response is presented in the second part of our reading, verses 9–13, and probably continues through verse 15. That response has three movements. In verse 9 the author poses a rhetorical question that at first glance appears discontinuous with the poem: "What gain have the workers from their toil?" Answer: None. Second (vv. 10–11), as often in his reflections, the Preacher cites his experiences—"I have seen . . ."—of human life ("business . . . to be busy with") that have led him to conclusions about God. God has, he agrees, "made everything suitable for its time" and has put a sense of time ("past and future," NRSV or "eternity," RSV) in the human mind. But that leads to frustration, because it is impossible for human beings to comprehend God's ways. Third (vv. 12–13), given that situation, Qohelet offers his advice. Human beings should "be happy and enjoy themselves as long as they live," for the capacity to eat and drink and have pleasure in their work is a gift of God. In the verses that follow our reading (vv. 14–15) there is a note of awe in the presence of God's design and knowledge of all times, but there is resentment as well that, although what God does endures forever, human times come to an end.

Reflection on the times, the appropriate times for human activities, has led the Preacher to meditate on time itself and has brought him face to face with human limits. Finally, it is not the difficulty of knowing the right time to do something that produces the frustration and resentment, but the fact that all human times come to an end, that there is the inevitable "time to die" (v. 2). This awareness of death as the final human boundary is the key to the Book of Ecclesiastes. That "time" which God has appointed for all—both the righteous and the wicked, and for the animals—is the day of death (see 3:16–22). "Again I saw that under the sun the race is not to the swift, nor the battle to the strong, nor bread to the wise, nor riches to the intelligent, nor favor to the skillful; but time and chance happen to them all" (9:11).

Awareness of human finitude leads our author to frustration, but it also focuses his attention on life as a gift of God. The advice in 3:12–13 is repeated frequently throughout the book. In spite of the presence of evil, "whoever is joined with all the living has hope, for a living dog is better than a dead lion. The living know that they will die, but the dead know nothing" (9:4–5). Make the most of your life, especially before you grow old and weak, and "desire fails," and finally "the silver cord is snapped, and the golden bowl is broken at the fountain . . . and the dust returns to the earth as it was" (12:5–7).

The beginning of a new year is the best time to meditate on time and the times. So first we can follow the example—if not the advice—of Qohelet and reflect on the times and the limits of human life under God. His is a sober realism that is bracing if not refreshing, and it encourages us to acknowledge the limits of our knowledge and of our lives. No one can count on an infinite supply of New Years. It is certainly possible to hear the Preacher's specific advice in view of that sad reality as stressing physical pleasure: eat and drink and enjoy yourself. But it does call attention to the importance of living in the present tense. To take time seriously is threatening, but to do so can also emphasize that every day of every new year and every moment of every day is precious.

Psalm 8

The contents and emphasis of this lection are almost completely the opposite of Ecclesiastes 3:1–13. The latter presents humanity almost at the mercy of divine determinism. Psalm 8, however, stresses the exalted position of humanity in God's created order, although it too can speak of the human sense of insignificance when confronted with the created universe. Both of these emphases, the greatness and glory of humanity and yet its sense of insignificance when viewed in light of the divine might and majesty and the vastness of the universe, can be combined in a sermon, and the minister can have the two lections dialogue with each other, recognizing the truth in both positions.

Although it is true that Psalm 8 sees humanity in a more exalted status than practically any other biblical text, nonetheless, the focus of the psalm is praise of a God who created the world and conferred on humanity a position of honor and responsibility exceeding that of any other created being. (Note that Eccles. 3:19 declares that humans have no real advantage over animals in that both end up suffering the same fate—death.) This praise of God as the purpose of the psalm can be seen (1) in its hymnic quality, (2) in the fact that it is a hymn directly addressed to the Deity, which is a very rare feature of biblical hymns (for another example, see Ps. 104), and (3) in the use of identical praises in the prelude and the postlude. Thus, what the psalm has to say about both the insignificance and the status of humanity is a way of praising the Deity.

Verses 1b–2 present innumerable problems both to the translator and the exegete, although the sense of the text seems to be that babes and infants recognize and testify to the greatness of God (see Matt. 21:16) and that their testimony puts at rest any enemy or avenger. Babes see the truth that others miss; they have not yet adopted adult perspectives and prejudices.

Verses 3–4 give expression to that universal feeling of humanity's inconsequential status when confronted with the broad sweep of the night skies dotted with the moon and the stars. (One should note that in antiquity, when pollution as so much less and artificial light was nil, the skies at night must have been even more splendid and awesome than they appear today.) Confronted with the lighted canopy of the heavens, humans almost naturally sense their littleness and wonder why God could be concerned for something so small. If the ancients felt this way, now much more insignificant do we moderns feel, who have seen the earth from outer space and are aware of the vastness of the regions beyond our solar system! (With a universe so large, does it ultimately matter if we ordered English peas and instead were served green beans?)

Over against the sense of human insignificance, Psalm 8 affirms the high status of human existence. Humans are created only a little lower than God, who has placed the whole of creation under human dominion. The works of God's hands are placed beneath the feet of humankind. Humanity thus serves as God's vice-regent over the whole of creation. In preaching from Psalm 8, and especially when combined with Ecclesiastes 3:1–13, the preacher could focus on the paradoxical nature and situation of humans in the world. Opposite poles—human lowliness and human heights—are held in tension because both reflect realities of the true situation. Humankind, this mortal creation of insignificance, overshadowed by the vastness of the sky's canopy, nonetheless holds dominion over the whole of the divine creation and shares in the divine dignity.

Revelation 21:1–6a

This text also serves as the epistolary lesson for the Fifth Sunday of Easter for this year as well as for All Saints Day in Year B. The reader may want to consult our remarks on this text in these other liturgical settings.

The use of this text in such varied liturgical settings provides an excellent example of how a single passage will be read and heard differently in different contexts. On All Saints Day, it serves as a reminder of the heavenly hope to which God's people aspire and for which they have lived and died. In the post-Easter season, it serves as one of several semicontinuous readings from the Johannine Apocalypse. Bracketed by texts from the same canonical writing on preceding and succeeding Sundays, it will be heard as part of the continuous revelation of John. In its post-Easter setting, its triumphant note will be especially apparent. But heard in the context of New Year's, the same text is bound to evoke yet other responses.

What strikes us first is the recurrent refrain of the new—new heaven, new earth, new Jerusalem—all finally culminating in the bold declaration by the enthroned God: "See, I am making all things new" (v. 5). We are hearing again the voice of Yahweh, who spoke to the disconsolate exiles, urging them: "Do not remember the former things, or consider the things of old," declaring instead, "I am about to do a new thing" (Isa. 43:18–19a). If they felt locked into the slavery of exile and alienation, they are now reminded that God can break through the old and inaugurate the new. Things need not remain as they have been. Dramatic change is possible when God decides to let "new" shatter "old."

Similar sentiments are echoed when Paul declares Christ to be the arena of new creation (2 Cor. 5:17). He too calls attention to this new reality, inviting us to open our eyes: "Everything old has passed away; see, everything has become new!" If Yahweh had broken through Israel's fixation on the past by reminding them of the divine capacity for renewing, Christ now becomes for Paul (and us) the agent of divine renewal. Through him the old era gives way to the new. In this new age, moral renewal is possible: we can now walk in "newness of life" (Rom. 6:4). Conforming our will to the will of God results in a "renewing of the mind" (Rom. 12:2), which doubtless entails both a renewal of the intellect as well as the will. How we think changes along with how we act—and why we act the way we do. What ultimately matters is not how well religious acts are performed, but whether they are indicative of genuinely moral and spiritual renewal—whether they are expressive of the "new creation" (Gal. 6:15).

To be sure, the vision of the Seer in today's text is an eschatological vision, one of several visions with which the Book of Revelation closes. The collapse of the old order is seen in the passing of heaven and earth, or the world as we know it (v. 1). The vanishing of the earthly order is often depicted in apocalyptic thought as earth, mountains, and sky fleeing away (cf. 6:14; 16:20; 20:11; 2 Pet. 3:7; also Ps. 114:3, 7). Into this cosmic vacuum there descends a new order, the heavenly city of Jerusalem (cf. 3:12; Gal. 4:26; Heb. 11:16; 12:22). With its descent comes the presence of God, radically new in the way it redefines the people of God. The new presence enables the new relationship of which the prophets spoke (Jer. 31:13; Isa. 8:8, 10). To dwell with God is to know God in a radically different way. The pressures, anxieties, and pains of the old order are no more (v. 4).

Even if the vision is eschatological, it is not any less compelling. Is it not the vision of what can be that often forces us to question what is and what has been? It was the future that beckoned the exiles to forget the old and look to the new. It was the Christ-event that shattered the old with the utterly new. It is the hope of a future totally defined by God that shatters our reliance on the past and moves us along toward a new time, a new day.

Matthew 25:31–46

The Gospel reading for today prompts the observance of New Year by reflecting on rather than forgetting the past. The "new" in our text is the new age, the time of final reward and punishment, launched by the coming of the Son of Man, who pronounces judgment entirely on the basis of past behavior toward persons in need.

Before looking at this lection, let us locate it in the scheme of Matthew's Gospel. Jesus' apocalyptic speech delivered from the Mount of Olives details the end of the temple, Jerusalem, and this present age, and envisions the coming of the Son of Man (24:1–36). This discourse is followed by a stern call to vigilance in view of the uncertain time of that certain event (vv. 37–44). The call to vigilance is followed by three parables concerning behavior during a possible delay in the Lord's coming: the parable of the slave supervisor (24:45–51, "My master is delayed"), the parable of the ten maidens (25:1–13, "As the bridegroom was delayed"), and the parable of the talents (25:14–30, "After a long time"). At this point Matthew places our reading, as if to say, "But when the Lord does come, late or soon, it will be as follows." With 25:31–46, an account without parallel in the other Gospels, Matthew concludes the public ministry of Jesus.

Matthew 25:31–46 is not a parable but a prophetic vision not unlike the throne scene of Revelation 20:11–15, in which the final judgment occurs. The enthronement of the Son of Man occurs elsewhere in Matthew 19:28, but the uses of Psalm 110:1 (the Lord seated at the right hand of God) are many and varied in the New Testament. In fact, the image in Psalm 110:1 lies at the base of the early Christian confession "Jesus is Lord" (Rom. 10:9; Phil. 2:11), which replaced "Jesus is the Messiah" as the church moved into cultures where a messiah was not expected.

There is no question but that for Matthew the one enthroned in power and glory is Jesus, but the passage draws upon titles from Jewish literature that Christians applied to Jesus. Daniel 7:13–14 provides a scene of one like a son of man coming with the clouds of heaven to be presented before the Ancient of Days, who grants to this one dominion, glory, and kingdom. The image is, as in Matthew, that of a cosmic ruler. The term "Son of Man" shifts to "king" (Zech. 9:9; Ps. 89:18, 27) at verse 34 as well as to "son of God" (implied in "my Father," v. 34). In addition, there is a variation of the picture of the shepherd dividing sheep and goats from Ezekiel 34. But regardless of the various sources for the imagery, for Matthew the scene is that of the Parousia, the coming of Jesus as Lord and judge of all people, Jews and Gentiles, church and nonchurch alike.

Several features of the judgment are most striking. First, there is the Lord's identification with the poor, lonely, hungry, sick, and imprisoned (vv. 35–36, 40, 42–43, 45). At Matthew 10:40–42 and 18:5 in the instructions about giving the cup of water and practicing hospitality, Jesus says such activity is ultimately toward himself and toward God. But there is nothing there or elsewhere in the Gospels that approaches the complete identification expressed in "I was hungry . . . , I was thirsty . . . , I was a stranger." Nor is there any indication that the text refers only to the poor and neglected within the church; before him are gathered "all the nations" (v. 32).

A second striking feature of the vision is that judgment is not based on heroic deeds or extraordinary feats but on the simple duties, the occasions for expressing care for other persons that present themselves every day. In fact, some students of Matthew have expressed concern over the absence of major Christian themes such as faith, grace, mercy, and forgiveness. That those matters are important to Jesus and to Matthew is beyond question; they are well documented elsewhere, as in 20:1–16, but not every parable or vision emphasizes every truth. To do so would blur all truth. However, it should be said that the Christian's concern for faith and grace should not replace attention to fundamental human obligations that, as this vision reminds us, are a primary concern of him who is Lord of all people of the earth. One does not cease to be a member of the human race once one joins the church.

A third and final unusual feature of the judgment is that both the blessed and the damned are surprised. Those banished to eternal punishment apparently miscalculated on what it takes to gain eternal bliss. And those rewarded had attended to the needs of others with such naturalness and grace that they were surprised that their behavior received heaven's attention. Saints are always surprised to hear their deeds recounted.

Second Sunday After Christmas Day

Jeremiah 31:7–14 or Sirach 24:1–12;
Psalm 147:12–20 or Wisdom of Solomon 10:15–21;
Ephesians 1:3–14;
John 1:(1–9) 10–18

The early church proclaimed that, in the coming of the Christ, the Old Testament prophecies and predictions were fulfilled. The Old Testament lesson from Jeremiah speaks of the redemption to come, when the scattered of Israel would be gathered from the farthest corners of the earth and when merriment, gladness, and feasting would signal the new status of affairs. The reading from Sirach describes the Divine Wisdom, which like the Word in the prologue to the Gospel of John, is said to have existed with God from the beginning and to have become implanted like a tree in Israel. The psalm praises God for his great gifts but above all for the fact that God has not dealt with any other nation as with his own people. The reading from The Wisdom of Solomon, with its emphasis upon the holy people and divine wisdom, is a fitting response to either Old Testament lection and anticipates the Gospel lesson. The Epistle contributes its melody to the theme of the incarnation and the dwelling of God among human beings.

Jeremiah 31:7–14

Jeremiah 31:7–14, which has few direct links with the other lessons for the day, is appropriate for the occasion because it expresses the mood and spirit of the continuing celebration of Christmas. The passage is filled with announcements of salvation—that the Lord has saved, gathered, consoled, and ransomed a people from sorrow to joy.

Because it is so similar to the perspective of Isaiah 40–55 and Isaiah 35, many commentators have taken this passage, along with most of the other materials in Jeremiah 30–31—the so-called book of consolation—as additions to the book from the time of the Babylonian Exile. In that case, the song of gladness anticipates release from Babylon and return to Judah. However, the references to "Jacob," "Israel," "Ephraim," and the "remnant of Israel" could very well mean the inhabitants of the Northern Kingdom who had been carried off by the Assyrians. In that case, Jeremiah here announces the return of those captives, and "the land of the north" (v. 8) would have been the far reaches of the Assyrian Empire in the seventh century BC. In either case, the reading presumes that its hearers are in trouble, exiled from their homeland.

Although the passage is hymnic in tone and in some of its contents, it is part of a prophetic announcement. The call to sing and praise (v. 7) is like the beginning of many hymns, and there are allusions to a ceremony of praise and thanksgiving (vv. 12, 13); but the unit is framed by messenger formulas and oracle formulas that mark it as prophetic address. Throughout, the prophet quotes the words of Yahweh concerning the future. Thus the text is a prophetic announcement of salvation concerning the return of exiles. It is good news that God has "ransomed" and "redeemed" (v. 11) people from captivity.

The context of this reading contains both joy and sorrow concerning the Northern Kingdom. The immediately preceding section (Jer. 31:1–6) is a distinct unit, another prophetic announcement of salvation. The prophet announces not only the return of those exiled from Samaria, but also the reunification of all the tribes at Zion. The passage that follows (Jer. 31:15–22) is the poignant lament of Rachel, mother of Benjamin and Joseph, for her children; that is; for the tribes descended from them.

The passage itself consists of two parts that likely arose as two separate prophetic speeches, verses 7–9 and verses 10–14. The addressees of the first part are not specified, but the prophet hears God announcing that those who are scattered will be returned. Even the ones least able to travel—the blind, the lame, pregnant women, and women in labor (v. 8)—will make the journey. The language of care and concern is particularly strong, as seen in Yahweh's affirmation that he is Israel's "father" (v. 9; see also Deut. 32:6 and Hosea 11).

In verses 10–14, the prophet addresses the (foreign) nations with a summons to hear. They are to hear the news that the one who scattered Israel will gather them, and Israel will come and sing in Zion (v. 12). Mourning will be turned into joy (v. 13), and celebrations will break out. Faces will shine in the presence of the Lord's goodness, and food will be abundant (v. 12). The prophet's point of view is Jerusalem, and even the temple on Mt. Zion. He seems to envision a reunion of the long-divided people in the Holy City.

The central motif of our reading is the redemption of a lost people. In verse 11, redemption and ransom are used as synonymous expressions. Both refer to the practice of reclaiming a possession or a person left in pledge for a debt or from slavery. The people are assumed to be owned by another, a foreign nation. Only Yahweh can ransom or redeem them, although there is no reference to a price paid. Yahweh, like a loving father (v. 9) will reclaim his firstborn. The view is a corporate one, with the firstborn standing for the people. What is their response? They have only to return when released and join in the joyful celebration of their reunion.

Sirach 24:1–12

Few biblical books give us more information about its author than The Wisdom of Jesus the Son of Sirach, also called the Book of Ecclesiasticus. The writer, Ben Sirach, was a wisdom teacher who conducted a school in Jerusalem in the early second century BC. On the basis of information that he gives us, as well as the report by his grandson, who translated the book into Greek (see the prologue), the original composition of the book can be dated shortly before 180 BC. This places the author and his audience in the Hellenistic period, before the Maccabean wars, but in a time when there must have been conflict between Jewish and Greek ideas and religious practices. The somewhat polemical tone at points, insisting that divine wisdom belongs to his people in Jerusalem (24:8–12), should be read in the light of that conflict.

Ecclesiasticus is wisdom literature, similar in both style and point of view to the Book of Proverbs. It includes a great many sayings like those in Proverbs 10–31, and a number of more extended discourses similar to the ones in Proverbs 1–9, Ecclesiastes, and Job. Although sayings and discourses on similar topics are grouped together, attempts to discern the organization of the composition have been less than satisfactory. The author considers wisdom in many different ways—as practical knowledge gained from experience and tradition, and as an abstract and universal phenomenon.

The reading for the day is selected from an extended discourse on the nature of wisdom that includes 24:1–25:11. The immediate context is Sirach 24:1–22, in which personified wisdom herself is the speaker.

Wisdom's speech, rich in allusions to Old Testament traditions, gives an account of the relationship between wisdom and the world in general and Israel in particular. It combines history of salvation motifs with attention to nature and creation, as Ben Sirach frequently does throughout the book.

Verses 1–2 introduce the speech itself and the speaker, personified wisdom. Such personification of wisdom, always as a female figure, is well-known in both earlier and later literature (Prov. 8:22–36; Wis. of Sol. 6:12–20; 8:1ff.). Here she intends to praise herself. She is pictured as standing before and addressing two audiences at once: "her people," that is, Israel; and "the assembly of the Most High." That assembly is mentioned elsewhere in the Old Testament as well as in other ancient Near Eastern literature. The scene pictured is the divine throne room, with the lesser deities or messengers in the presence of God (Isa. 6; Ps. 89:6–7; 1 Kings 22:19–23).

Wisdom's speech itself recalls her cosmic origins (vv. 3–6), her special relationship to Israel (vv. 7–12), her growth like every good plant (vv. 13–17), and concludes with an appeal to follow her (vv. 18–22).

Particularly important when this passage is considered along with the prologue to John is the language of verse 3. That wisdom "came forth from the mouth of the Most High" suggests a parallel to the word (Greek *logos*) of God present before creation. Elsewhere in the book, God is said to have accomplished by his words what is attributed here to wisdom (42:15). The background of this passage certainly is to be found in the accounts of creation in both Genesis 1 and 2, where God creates by word. The "mist" is an allusion to Genesis 2:6. A more fully developed view of personified wisdom as God's activity in the world is found in Wisdom of Solomon 7:22–8:1. In that same book, the identification of wisdom and the word of God is quite explicit (9:1–2).

Verses 13–17 give a virtual catalog of good plants as analogies for the growth and development of wisdom in the good soil of the people of Israel. This series of metaphors picks up on the motif of planting in verse 12 and sets the stage for wisdom's call to "eat your fill of my fruits" in verse 19.

Whereas verses 3–6 emphasize the cosmic presence of wisdom, verses 7–12 affirm that she found her true home among a particular people, Israel, and in a specific place, Jerusalem. The point of that claim is not reached until after wisdom's speech is concluded: "All this is the book of the covenant of the Most High God, the law that Moses commanded us" (24:23). That is, wisdom and the law amount to the same thing. Thus the major concern of the passage is divine revelation. How is God present and known in the world by human beings? God is known in and through wisdom present in creation, and specifically through the revealed law. Through faithfulness to the law of Moses one knows God.

Psalm 147:12–20

Psalm 147 gives the impression of being two (vv. 1–11 and 12–20) or even three (vv. 1–6, 7–11, and 12–20) self-contained units. The ancient Greek translation, the so-called Septuagint, considers the work two separate psalms (vv. 1–11 = Ps. 146; vv. 12–20 = Ps. 147 in the enumeration of the Greek versions as well as the Catholic Vulgate) and associated both with the postexilic prophets Haggai and Zechariah, whose preaching aided in the reconstructing of the temple.

Two themes dominate the psalm throughout: God's power in the world of nature and God's support and care for the chosen people. The pervasiveness of these themes throughout the psalm would suggest that we are dealing with one composition, not a combination of more than one psalm.

Verses 12–20 open with a call to praise, which is then followed, as in most hymns in the Psalter, with the reasons why God is worthy of praise—in this case, by Jerusalem/Zion. The reasons offered are a complex of matters related both to Jerusalem—the elect, the chosen, the particular—and to the larger world—the earth, the nations, and the universe.

First, this portion of the psalm celebrates Yahweh's particular care of the Holy City. The city's protection is ensured and its population increased (v. 13). Within the region, well-being is to be found and foodstuffs abound (v. 14). All of this is what one would assume to be expected; that is, these reflect what should have been the normal state of existence. Here the normal is thus seen as a blessing. For Jerusalem, the most fought-over city in the world, for matters to be ordinary and normal could be seen as extraordinary and abnormal.

Second, the psalm speaks of the created orders, the world of nature, as responsive to and shaped by the word of Yahweh (vv. 15–18). The sending of the word is depicted as a command to which the earth responds (v. 15). The snow, ice, and frost of winter, which too are the work of God, melt before the word and spirit (wind) of God and produce water for the earth (vv. 16–18).

Finally, the word is made known to the chosen people and becomes embodied in the statutes and ordinances given to Israel (v. 19). That is, the law, or Torah, is an incarnation of the special will of God and is given only to Israel. "He has not dealt thus with any other nation; they do not know his ordinances" (v. 20).

In Psalm 147, the word comes as a creative command, as a transforming power, as a special incarnation, and as a unique gift to Israel. Christmas and the prologue to the Fourth Gospel also speak of the divine word and supplement the views of this psalm.

Wisdom of Solomon 10:15–21

The Wisdom of Solomon was composed in Greek, probably in the Egyptian city of Alexandria, by a pious Jewish intellectual living in the Diaspora. Its date is uncertain, although the late first century BC has been suggested by many scholars. More philosophical than most of the other wisdom books, it finds its closest parallels in Proverbs 1–9, especially chapter 8.

In The Wisdom of Solomon 10:1–11:4, the examples of eight lives are treated—seven positively and one negatively—to illustrate how wisdom, understood as a female cosmic figure, brought salvation and the good life: Adam (10:1–2), Cain (10:3), Noah (10:4), Abraham (10:5), Lot (10:6–8), Jacob (10:9–12), Joseph (10:13–14), and Moses (10:15–11:4). The last of these biographical vignettes provides the context for this lection.

In this version of the Exodus, it is Wisdom who plays the role of redeemer and guide for the Israelite people. She delivers from oppression, enters the soul of Moses, and performs the task of leading the people from bondage and through the wilderness. Wisdom tends to assume the place occupied by the Deity in the Exodus account of the events. Verse 20, with its reference to "O Lord," suggests that Wisdom and God, however, are not completely identified in this text.

That this book may have been intended for apologetic purposes in defense of Judaism in an alien Hellenistic climate is indicated by two factors. First, Israel is described in extraordinarily glowing terms: a blameless race, a holy people, and the righteous. Second, none of Israel's faults—murmuring, and so forth—that characterize the Exodus account are even referred to in this particular section.

Wisdom in this text, like the Word (Logos) in John's prologue, is the guiding, unifying principle emanating from and doing the work of God.

Ephesians 1:3–14

Besides serving as the epistolary lection for the Second Sunday After Christmas Day in all three years, this text is also used as the Epistle reading for Proper 10 [15] in Year B. Related portions of the passage also serve as epistolary lessons at other times during the liturgical year: Ephesians 1:11–23 for All Saints Day in Year C, and Ephesians 1:15–23 for Ascension of the Lord in all three years as well as for Proper 29 [34], Christ the King or Reign of Christ Sunday in Year A. The reader may want to consult our remarks in these other liturgical settings.

Today's epistolary lection comprises Paul's opening hymn of blessing (vv. 3–14), which is followed by a prayer of intercession for his readers (vv. 15–23). Naturally, it should be read in the overall context of chapter 1, but as it stands, today's text may be considered as the first part of a two-part prayer, each part having a different focus.

This magnificent eulogy directed to God reminds us of similar prayers of blessing offered in celebration of what God has done in our behalf (2 Cor. 1:3–7; 1 Pet. 1:3–9). It should be noted that the prayer of blessing (Berakah) was a well-established form of Jewish prayer, one still in use in Jewish communities of faith and thus found in various modern Jewish prayer books. In such prayers, God is the object of praise, and the normal pattern is to list the various ways God has acted for the benefit of the one offering the eulogy. The prayer shows us a grateful worshiper so overcome by what God has done through Christ that this meditation of blessing stretches the very bounds of liturgical fervor. The language is exalted because the religious experience prompting it is so profoundly deep.

The opening line of the prayer serves as a summary of the entire prayer: God has "blessed us in Christ with every spiritual blessing in the heavenly places" (v. 3). As the blessings cascade in prayerful utterance, we are reminded of how many, and how rich, those blessings are: being chosen as part of Christ's legacy even before the beginning of time (v. 4); being incorporated into God's family as adopted children (v. 5); being redeemed from slavery and forgiven of our sins through Christ's death (v. 7); being made privy to the divine mystery of God's will (v. 9); receiving an inheritance beyond our wildest imagination (v. 11); living lives full of genuine hope (v. 12); having the reassuring presence of God's own Spirit (v. 13).

These are not the words of an unreflective soul. Neither are they the meaningless utterances of some undirected ecstasy. There is ecstasy here, but it is ecstasy that stems from profound religious experience with a clear organizing center—what God has done in Christ.

From the standpoint of this prayer, it is impossible to think of either beginnings or endings apart from Christ. Nor for that matter does this prayer envision what happens in between apart from Christ. It is, above all, a meditation on Christ, and about Christ, but one prompted by Christ. As we pray this prayer we are invited to think of Christ in the most lavish terms, with the language of worship, praise, and love.

And yet the subject of these various actions is God. This is also a prayer about what God has done—for me, the worshiper, but also for all of humankind. The God who is praised here is not a reclining God, resting on an elbow, surveying the universe in quiet, dispassionate leisure. God is rather seen as One who actively reflects on history and human destiny, and does so aggressively, charting purposes and intents even before the beginning of time. But this God also thinks about the welfare of all creation, especially those who are destined to be a part of God's redemptive history. For them—for us—God has a special place and special calling, one that eventually reaches to the very presence of God—"the heavenly places." Such a prayer gives worshipers a sense of purpose not only because it sketches time and history in purposeful terms but also because it invites us into the story as fully participating characters.

What we have, then, in today's epistolary text is a prayer that looks both forward as well as upward—and thus moves us in the very directions to which the celebration of Christmas calls us.

John 1: (1–9) 10–18

All of today's readings proclaim God's visiting us with favor, but the prologue to John's Gospel is of central importance to Christian history, Christian doctrine, and the understanding of the life of faith. The Gospel lesson for Christmas, Third Proper (second additional lesson), was John 1:1–14, and the preacher is referred to those comments for use here, especially if that lection was not treated in a Christmas service. We will here add to the earlier discussion only comments on verses 14–18, which constitute a unit that concludes the prologue as a literary piece distinct from the narrative beginning at verse 19.

Before proceeding, however, the preacher will want to decide whether to treat verses 1–9 as optional. If John 1:1–14 was used at Christmas, avoiding some repetition would justify exercising such an option. Omitting verses 1–9 would also allow for moving away from the pre-incarnational work of God's Word (vv. 1–5) and the preparatory work of John the Baptist (vv. 6–8) in order to focus on the incarnation of the Word and its benefits for the world. Or more simply, one might use only verses 10–18 in order to attend to a more manageable portion of Scripture. Some preachers avoid John 1:1–18 altogether because its theological and philosophical sweep of thought is so intimidatingly immense. As stated above, we refer the reader to the earlier treatment of verses 1–14 and here focus only on verses 14–18.

Verses 14–18 make the following three statements:

1. "And the Word *became flesh*" is a christological affirmation of a radical nature with far-reaching implications for our thinking about God, life in the world, and what it means to be Christian. Analogies about changing clothes, as in the stories of a king who wears peasant clothing in order to move among his subjects freely, are not adequate for clarifying John 1:14. The church has always had members who wanted to protect their Christ from John 1:14 with phrases such as "seemed to be," "appeared," and "in many ways was like" flesh. Whatever else

John 1:14 means, it does state without question the depth, the intensity, and the pursuit of God's love for the world.

2. John 1:14–18 is a confessional statement. Notice the use of "us" and "we." The eyes of faith have seen God's glory in Jesus of Nazareth, but not everyone has. At the time of this Gospel, the Baptist sect (v. 15) and the synagogue (v. 17) were viable religious groups, and they did not see the glory. Faith hears, sees, and testifies, but faith is not arrogant or imperialistic, as though its view were so obvious as to be embraced by all but the very obstinate. Faith involves a searching (Rabbi, where do you live? 1:38), a response to an offer (Come and see. 1:39), a hunger (14:8), a willingness to obey (7:17). Nothing about Jesus Christ is so publicly apparent as to rob faith of its risk, its choice, and its courage. Faith exists among alternatives.

3. The observation above in no way means that faith must be tentative and quiet about its central affirmation that the God whom no one has seen (v. 18) is both known and available in Jesus Christ. Jesus reveals God (v. 18) and makes God available to us (v. 14) in gracious ways (v. 16). Believing in Jesus is not simply adding another belief to one's belief in God; it is also having one's belief in God modified, clarified, and informed by what is seen in the person and work of Jesus. Jesus' statement "Whoever has seen me has seen the Father" (14:9) does not simply tell us what Jesus is like but what God is like, and to know God is life eternal (17:4).

Epiphany

Isaiah 60:1–6;
Psalm 72:1–7, 10–14;
Ephesians 3:1–12;
Matthew 2:1–12

I n the West, as early as the fourth century, Epiphany has been the festival commemorating
the visit of the Wise Men to the baby Jesus. The account of that visit in Matthew 2:1–12
is thus the center of attention on this day. Because the visit of the Magi is regarded as the
first appearance of Jesus to the Gentiles, Ephesians 3:1–12, which reflects upon the mission
to the Gentiles, is a fitting epistolary reading. The responsorial psalm actually anticipates the
themes of kingship in Matthew 2:1–12. This ancient Israelite prayer for God's blessings upon
the king is now heard over this new "King of the Jews" (Matt. 2:2). Isaiah 60:1–6 doubtless
appears here because of its reference to gold and frankincense (v. 6), but it contributes more
than that through its mood of celebration and its cry, "Arise, shine; for your light has come,"
which describes the appearance of the Lord.

Isaiah 60:1–6

I saiah 60:1–6 begins a distinct section (chaps. 60–62) in the literature associated with
Third Isaiah (Isa. 56–66). Verses from the concluding unit of the section (Isa. 62:6–12)
are among the lections for Christmas (Proper 2). These three chapters contain poetic
proclamations of salvation that must come from early in the postexilic period, but some
decades later than the time of Second Isaiah (Isa. 40–55). The Exile is over, and perhaps the
temple has been built (Isa. 60:7), but the people live in relative poverty.

The tone of the passage is set by the imperatives in verses 1 and 4: "Arise, shine," and
"Lift up your eyes and look around. . . ." Who is the speaker, and to whom are the words
addressed? In view of the contents, and considering the verses that follow our reading, the
speaker is a prophetic voice speaking about God's self-manifestation. In the original historical context, the addressee is probably Jerusalem; the name occurs in verse 1 in the Septuagint
(cf. NEB). The city, with its inhabitants, is the location of the divine revelation.

In verses 1–3 the prophet skillfully employs metaphors of light and darkness to proclaim the
epiphany of the Lord. The language is powerful and evocative, but restrained. There are limits
to what can be said about the appearance of God. Jerusalem is to arise and shine because its
"light" has come. In the next poetic line, "glory of the LORD" parallels "light." The appearance
of the Lord's glory is like that of light in the darkness, like the rising of the sun at dawn. The

images of darkness borrow from the language of Isaiah 9:2: "The people who walked in darkness have seen a great light. . . ." Here those upon whom the light shines will themselves shine—with reflected light—so that "nations" will stream to the source of the light.

It is noteworthy that the prophet describes neither a specific event nor the vision of the Lord. Rather, the appearance of God is like the dawn, bringing an overwhelming light. Moreover, the epiphany is of "the glory" of the Lord. This is not unlike Ezekiel's experience of the presence of the Lord. After describing the vision in detail, he summarizes: "This was the appearance of the likeness of the glory of the LORD" (Ezek. 1:28).

In verses 4–6 the prophet calls for the people—presumably of Jerusalem—to look at what is happening, and what will happen. Their sons and daughters shall come, along with the wealth of the nations. When they see what is happening they will "be radiant" and rejoice (v. 5). The stream of the exiles and of the tribute from all over the world will testify that the Lord has looked favorably on the people of the Holy City. The wealth from west and east is not for the people of Israel, but is tribute to their God.

To what can one compare the appearance of God, the epiphany of the Lord? The more ancient traditions of the Old Testament spoke more directly of the awesome theophany accompanied by dramatic upheavals or transformations in nature. In our text it is the glory of the Lord that appears like the sunrise. That appearance corresponds to the appearance of salvation and is followed by celebration and the procession of all the nations to stand in the light. Finally, we should not miss the point that the ones to whom the light has come, the ones who can see it and celebrate its appearance, are those who are in the darkness.

Psalm 72:1–7, 10–14

Epiphany celebrates Jesus' manifestation to the world. Psalm 72, a part of the ancient Hebrew enthronement of the Davidic kings, was a communal prayer at the coronation requesting that the Davidic messiah (the newly crowned king) would be the object of universal adoration and praise. Thus the central motif of Epiphany finds some of its counterparts and foreshadowings in the royal rituals of ancient Judah.

The ideology and expectations that surrounded the Davidic king ruling in Jerusalem are practically all represented in this psalm. They find embodiment in the form of petitions requesting God's blessing upon the ruler. Among these features are the following: (1) the king was considered the representative of God's justice and righteousness; he was the channel through which these flowed to the people (vv. 1–2); (2) he was the source of prosperity and blessing for the people (vv. 3, 6–7); (3) the king was especially responsible for defending the weak and disenfranchised members of society—the widows, the poor, the oppressed, the fatherless (vv. 4, 12–14); (4) he was promised a universal rule extending from one end of the earth to the other, that is, a rule with worldwide dominion (vv. 9–11); and (5) although only alluded to in verse 1b of this psalm, the king was also the divine son of God, a status to which the king was elevated on the day of his coronation (see Ps. 2:7).

In line with the concerns of Epiphany, we will note in our discussion of this text only those verses concerned with the king's or the messiah's dominion (remembering that the ruling Judean monarch was the anointed, or the messiah). The claims and requests that were made on behalf of the Judean king are very similar to those known from other major Near Eastern powers. Both the Egyptian pharaohs and the Mesopotamian kings claimed the right to rule over the entire world and saw their positions as god-ordained and divinely upheld. All seem to have drawn on what was a common court style and rhetoric. It is quite clear, however, that the prophets, for example, took such forms of expression seriously, and the expectations associated with the earthly Davidic king were projected into the future in the people's depiction of the coming messiah. What was proclaimed as reality in the royal cult was preached by some prophets as a future vision.

Some means that were used to give expression to the expectations of the king's universal rule were mythologically based; others were anchored in more realistic geography. The expressions "sea to sea" and "from the River to the ends of the earth" (v.8) could be classified as mythological, being based on a particular view of the world that conceived of the earth as surrounded by seas. The references to Tarshish and the isles and the rulers of Sheba and Seba (v. 10) were ways of talking about western and eastern extremes of the known world at the time. All of these expressions, both the mythological and the more realistic, were ways of saying "everywhere." Rulers from throughout the known world were to accept the rule of the Judean king and show such submission by bringing gifts and paying tribute. Actual enemies, it was hoped, would bow down and offer obeisance by licking the dust, that is, by falling on their faces.

The ancient royal theology threw a richly embroidered purple robe over the shoulders of the Judean ruler and in so doing anticipated the expected universal rule of the messiah.

Ephesians 3:1–12

This epistolary lection is traditionally read at Epiphany because it carries through the theme of the manifestation of Christ to the nations as part of the eternal purpose of God. With its special emphasis on the inclusion of the Gentiles as full-fledged members of the people of God, it echoes the theme of the universality of God's sovereignty found in each of the other readings (Isa. 60:3; Ps. 72:8–11; Matt. 2:1–12).

In form, these verses actually constitute Paul's prayer in behalf of his Gentile readers; or, more accurately, an interruption of Paul's prayer. In verse 1, Paul the prisoner begins a prayer "for the sake of you Gentiles," but the mere mention of the term "Gentiles" leads to a digression. The next twelve verses unfold Paul's apostolic vocation as a mission directed to the Gentiles and one for carrying out the original intention of God. After an elaborate expansion of this theme, the prayer resumes in verse 14.

As is well known, the Epistle to the Ephesians is widely regarded as pseudo-Pauline, yet there are many genuine Pauline reminiscences in this passage. The setting presupposed is imprisonment, though we do not know where or when (cf. 4:1; Phil. 1:7, 12–14; Philem. 1, 9–13; Col. 4:18; 2 Tim. 1:8; 2:9). He is depicted as a steward of God's grace entrusted with divine mysteries that have been revealed to him. It is clear that the historical Paul thought of himself and his apostleship in such terms (1 Cor. 4:1; 9:17; cf. Col. 1:25). To view this trust as divinely bestowed by God's grace also reflects Paul's own outlook (Rom. 15:15–16; 1 Cor. 3:10; Gal. 2:9; cf. Eph. 3:7–8; Col. 1:25). In addition, to speak of the gospel as "this mystery" formerly hidden but now revealed (v. 5) recalls genuine Pauline sentiments (Rom. 16:25; 1 Cor. 2:1, 6–16). We also hear other Pauline echoes, such as his insistence on being the "very least of all the saints" (v. 8; cf. 1 Cor. 15:9–10; also 1 Tim. 1:15). This suggests that the words and sentiments of our text are Paul's even if they come to us indirectly.

But in the liturgical context of Epiphany, the authorship of this passage is less a concern than how it speaks to us about Christ's manifestation. Several features of the passage are worth noting in this regard.

We should notice, first of all, that the gospel of Christ is presented here as a "mystery." Paul speaks here of the "mystery of Christ" (v. 4; cf. Col. 4:3), noting that he had received it by revelation (v. 3; Gal. 1:12). The specific content of this mystery is given in verse 6: how "the Gentiles have become fellow heirs, members of the same body, and sharers in the promise in Christ Jesus through the gospel." What has been "hidden for ages" (v. 9) is God's intention that the "boundless riches of Christ" (v. 8) be preached to both Jews and Gentiles. The language of manifestation, or "epiphany," is even more explicit in Colossians 1:26: "the mystery that has been hidden throughout the ages and generations has now been revealed to his saints."

In this respect, we notice a slight shift in the way "mystery" is used, as compared with the undisputed Pauline letters. There it is used in a more general, undefined sense (1 Cor. 2:1, 6–16; Rom. 16:25), whereas in Ephesians and Colossians it has specific reference to the inclusion of the Gentiles within the plan of God (Eph. 1:9, 3:9; Col. 1:26–27; 2:2). Thus, by this stage of development of the Pauline tradition, the manifestation of God to the nations is seen as part of the "divine economy" (*oikonomia*; cf. 1:10; 3:2–3, 9).

Second, Christ is to be seen as the turning point in the divine drama, the moment of revelation when God's eternal purpose became fully known. Underlying our passage is a twofold scheme: something previously hidden has now been revealed (cf. v. 5). There is the recognition that a dramatic shift has occurred in the history of salvation and that Christ is the hinge on which history has turned. It is in this regard that our text surfaces some of the central themes of Epiphany, for this is the time when we recognize that darkness gives way to light, hiddenness to openness, mystery to revelation, ignorance to knowledge. Our text affirms that the mystery of Christ "in former generations . . . was not made known to humankind:" (v. 5), and this reminds us that the coming of Christ was a watershed in the divine economy. We stand this side of the apostles and prophets to whom the Spirit revealed this mystery, and now it is possible for everyone to see what was invisible to previous generations (v. 9).

Third, the scope of God's manifestation through Christ as depicted in our passage is cosmic. We have already noted that it is universal, including both Jews and Gentiles. But more than that, today's text affirms that God's mystery has now been unveiled "to the rulers and authorities in the heavenly places" (v. 10; cf. 1:21; 2:2; 6:12; also Rom. 8:38; 1 Cor. 15:24; Col. 1:13, 16; 2:10, 15; Pet. 3:22; Heb. 2:5). The light that has shone through Christ has shone not only on earth but has lit up the heavens as well. If the Gospel reading for today focuses on God's manifestation on earth, the epistolary reading extends this revelation into the heavens.

This text already points us in the direction of mission, for Epiphany often begins a period when the church reflects on its mission, not only in the sense of proclaiming the gospel to the nations but also in the sense of working for peace and justice within the social order. This perspective should provide numerous homiletical possibilities as our text directs us to think about the manifestation of Christ to the nations.

Matthew 2:1–12

Epiphany provides the preacher the occasion for sharing some of the grandest texts of the Bible, for this is the season to declare the manifestation of the divine Son. The revelation is no longer a baby in a manger, no longer a whisper in Bethlehem, but a voice from heaven at Jesus' baptism and the dazzling light of the Transfiguration. Epiphany begins, however, with an even earlier announcement of the glory of the Son of God, the visit of the Magi to Bethlehem (Matt. 2:1–12).

Matthew 2:1–12 is not a birth story. Matthew's birth account is in 1:18–25, and to that story 2:1–12 is not directly tied. "In the time of King Herod, after Jesus was born in Bethlehem of Judea" is a chronological introduction to the cycle of four stories extending through 2:23. These texts are properly treated quite apart from Luke's nativity; trying to conflate Matthew and Luke is more confusing than helpful. The move to Matthew means a shift in the writer's purposes and the theological statements. The shift is dramatic: exit shepherds, enter Wise Men; exit stables, enter palace; exit poverty, enter wealth; exit angels, enter dreams; exit Mary's lullaby, enter Rachel's wail.

Our text, then, is better understood as an announcement story. The emphases in the story are three. First, Christ appears not for Israel alone but for the world. The Wise Men, neither named nor numbered, are probably astrologers and represent for Matthew the fulfillment of Isaiah 60:1–6, which prophesies the pilgrimage of the rulers of the nations to Jerusalem to worship Israel's God, bringing gifts of gold and frankincense. The appearance of the light of God's glory initiates the era of universal worship. In addition, Numbers 24:17 speaks of a star arising out of Jacob, as does the Testament of Levi (18:3). Likewise, Hellenistic literature was not without its stories of heavenly configurations announcing events of great importance. There were available to Matthew and his readers quite sufficient resources for making his declaration that Christ is for the world, to be worshiped by all nations. This Gospel, known for its Jewishness, must not be misunderstood: statements of the universality of the Gospel are frequent (4:15–16; 25:31–46; 28:18–20). In fact, there is not a Gospel that will provide a supporting text for those who want to be exclusive with reference to race, nationality, or sex.

A second emphasis in Matthew 2:1–12 is that Jesus Christ is the true king of Israel. To develop this theme, Matthew uses Bethlehem (Mic. 5:2) and David (2 Sam. 5:2) materials from the Hebrew Scriptures. One might wonder why the Davidic theme would be developed when it was potentially so troublesome, creating messianic expectations that would obstruct the purposes of Jesus' ministry (22:41–46). However, Matthew wants to establish not only that Jesus is the royal shepherd of Israel (10:6; 15:24), but that his life and work were sufficiently witnessed in Israel's Scriptures to make rejection of him inexcusable.

A third and final emphasis in today's Gospel lesson is the hostility to Jesus and the gospel by the political and religious establishment. The tension is posed early in the account by the references to Herod the king and Jesus the king. To develop this theme, Matthew uses the account of the children (Exod. 2). Stories of old rulers being threatened by the birth of heirs to the throne were common in Matthew's day, but clearly the direct antecedent was the Moses story. This image of a tyrant, jealous and intimidated, screaming death warrants and releasing the sword of government against the innocent to preserve entrenched power, stabs awake the reader and abruptly ends a quiet Lukan Christmas. But Matthew must speak the truth: good news has its enemies. One has but to love to arouse hatred, but to speak the truth to strengthen the network of lies and deception. It is no mystery why One who gave himself to loving the poor and neglected of the earth would be killed; there are institutions and persons who have other plans for the poor and neglected. Of course, no one wants a hassle, much less a clash, but what will Jesus' followers say and do? The fearful whisper, "Tell the Wise Men to be quiet about the Child."

Baptism of the Lord
(First Sunday After the Epiphany)

Isaiah 43:1–7;
Psalm 29;
Acts 8:14–17;
Luke 3:15–17, 21–22

The Lucan account of the baptism of Jesus, with the descent of the Holy Spirit and the voice from heaven, is the obvious focus of attention on the day that commemorates the baptism of the Lord, but the other readings have important contributions to make as well. The lection from Isaiah 43:1–7 is a highly appropriate reading for the day, with its references to naming and to water. God has called the servant of the Lord by name and thus claimed him. Psalm 29 is a hymn praising the power of the voice of God and thus anticipates the voice from heaven in Luke 3:22. The passage from Acts echoes the motifs of the word of God and the Holy Spirit.

Isaiah 43:1–7

These verses comprise either one oracle of salvation with two parts (vv. 1–4, 5–7) or two oracles of salvation. Second Isaiah, the prophet of the end of the Babylonian Exile, frequently speaks in the language of such oracles. The salvation oracle contains a message from God to a human audience. Its background very likely is liturgical, the divine message communicated by a priest in response to the prayers of individuals or people. Its liturgical pattern would closely resemble the confession followed by either words of absolution or reassurance as in Christian worship.

Here, however, the voice that speaks on behalf of God clearly is a prophetic one, as indicated by the introductory messenger formula in verse 1, "thus says the LORD," commonly used by the prophets from Amos in the eighth century BC to Second Isaiah in the sixth century. The words are addressed to Israel, the people as a whole. The expressions "he who created you" and "he who formed you" define both speaker and addressee, both God and people. God is creator, and Israel is what God has created. Thus Second Isaiah applies to Yahweh's forming of Israel as a people—probably presuming the story that now runs from Genesis through Joshua—the language of Genesis 1.

The decisive expression in the oracle of salvation is its beginning, "Do not fear" (vv. 1, 5). Such an expression presumes that the hearers are fearful and that they have expressed their fear, often in the language of prayer. Each command to fear not is followed by a motive clause, introduced by "for," giving the reasons why Israel is not to be afraid. In verse 1, this prophetic poet—speaking for God—has drawn together the major old themes of Israel's story, linking creation with redemption. The words here are rich with meaning. "I have redeemed you" gives a past reasons why Israel need not be afraid: Yahweh brought Israel out of Egypt. But the sentence also looks to the present and the future. As the remainder of the passage makes clear, Israel is not to fear because the Lord is redeeming her out of Babylon. The intimacy of Yahweh's redemption of Israel is emphasized by the synonymous expression "I have called you by name, you are mine." To name is to identify, that is, to give an identity to Israel. That Israel is the one who belongs to Yahweh.

But balancing the language of intimacy between God and people is the language of transcendence: "For I am the LORD your God, the Holy One of Israel, your Saviour" (v. 3). So a central concern of this unit is to reassure Israel by making it clear who Israel is and who God is.

More clearly on the surface of the text is the message that rings on very page of Isaiah 40–55: the exile is over, and Israel will go home. The Lord is willing to pay whatever ransom (v. 3) it takes, even the nations of Egypt, Ethiopia, and Seba. God is calling for the exiles from the four corners of the world—east, west, north, and south, from the ends of the earth—to return to the land.

Psalm 29

The accounts of Jesus' baptism in the waters of the Jordan report that a heavenly voice spoke on the occasion. Psalm 29 has been selected for reading on the celebration of Jesus' baptism because it too speaks of waters and a heavenly voice.

This hymn celebrates the manifestation of divine authority and power as these are revealed in the lightning and thunder of a storm that sweeps into Palestine from the Mediterranean Sea (v. 3), passes through Lebanon (vv. 5–6), and moves into the desert of the south (vv. 7–8).

A number of surface features about this psalm are noteworthy. First, the sevenfold repetition of the term "voice" gives the psalm a staccato quality (see Rev. 10:3). Second, the voice of God creates disturbances and manifests its power over the waters (v. 3), trees (v. 5), mountains (v. 6), the desert (v. 8), and animals (v. 9, which can be translated "makes the hinds to calf and brings ewes to early birth"). Practically the whole of the natural order becomes involved. Third, neither humans nor the chosen community of Israel play any real role in the psalm and are mentioned only at the end of the composition. Fourth, the psalm moves from the heavenly world of the sons of gods to the world of humanity via the imagery of the storm. One might say the psalm moves from *Gloria in Excelsis* to *Pax in Terris*, from "Glory to God in the Highest" to "Peace on Earth" (see Luke 2:14). Fifth, a polytheistic, mythological worldview is assumed throughout the text. The "sons of gods" ("heavenly beings" in the NRSV) are called upon to praise God (Yahweh) in the heavenly realm. Yahweh sits enthroned upon the waters, the turbulent powers of chaos that threaten world order.

The whole of the psalm supports the assertion that God is in charge. The thunder, lightning, and storm are manifestations of God's voice speaking from the cosmic abode of the Divine. In spite of the turbulence in the world of nature, God is enthroned as king (v. 10). In fact, the rainstorm only demonstrates the fact; it does not challenge it.

Acts 8:14–17

I n this tiny vignette we are told how the Samaritans received the gift of the Holy Spirit at the hands of the apostles Peter and John. It is set within chapter 8 of Acts, which records the spread of the gospel into the regions of Samaria, just as the risen Lord had predicted (Acts 1:8). We are told that the death of Stephen had precipitated an intensive wave of persecution against the church in Jerusalem (8:1). Although many fled for safety to the surrounding regions of Judea and Samaria, the apostles remained in Jerusalem.

The leading role in evangelizing Samaria was played by Philip the evangelist, one of the seven men chosen by the apostles to assist them in caring for the needy (6:1–6). Like the others, he was commended because of his good reputation, but also because he possessed a full measure of the Spirit and wisdom (6:3). His preaching in the regions of Samaria was well received, as "the crowds with one accord listened eagerly to what was said by Philip" (8:6). Along with his preaching, he performed signs and wonders, including exorcisms and healing the paralyzed and lame (8:7). So impressive were the signs he performed that even Simon Magus, the self-promoting Jewish magician who had dazzled the Samaritans with his magical feats, believed and was baptized. Even though later in the narrative Simon's faith proves to be fraudulent, at this point he serves as living proof of the effectiveness of Philip's preaching.

What puzzles us about today's lection is that Phillip's preaching, for all its power and effect, was deficient in one critical respect: it was not accompanied by the gift of the Holy Spirit. Elsewhere in Acts, when converts are baptized they ordinarily receive the Holy Spirit at the same time or shortly thereafter (Acts 2:38; 10:47; 11:15). Here, however, we are told that the Samaritans "had only been baptized in the name of the Lord Jesus" (v. 16). This reminds us of how the twelve disciples were later described as having heard only of the baptism of John (19:1–7), but who, as soon as they were baptized "in the name of the Lord Jesus" (19:5), received the Holy Spirit through the laying on of Paul's hands (19:6).

The Acts narrative makes clear that "baptism in the name of the Lord Jesus" and the reception of the Holy Spirit through the laying on of hands are two distinct acts, and they may be separated by a considerable space of time. In today's text, the Spirit is bestowed by Peter and John, the two apostles who have played the leading role up to this point in the story (Acts 3:1, 11; 4:13, 19). In one sense, their action here diminishes the role of Philip, for it makes clear that bestowing the Spirit in this manner did not lie within his power. Yet their action legitimates his preaching among the Samaritans by linking it with the apostolic circle who had been with the risen Lord. In this way, the spread of the gospel beyond Jerusalem receives the apostolic imprint even though it is being carried out by lesser figures such as Philip.

In spite of these wrinkles in the text, some important points emerge.

First, as is the case elsewhere in Acts, baptism and the laying on of hands are closely associated. Like the baptism of Jesus, the bestowal and reception of the Spirit were crucial in signifying that the presence of God had been conferred. Both in the case of Jesus as well as that of the disciples who later believed in Christ as the Son of God, receiving God's Spirit is what gave baptism its true significance. Even as Jesus was acknowledged as the Son of God, believers became children of God and thereby came into possession of God's very own Spirit.

Second, the conferral of the Spirit occurs in response to prayer (v. 15). Here the Holy Spirit is not something God bestows automatically or even something the believer receives as a free bonus. Instead, it comes in response to earnest, fervent prayer. In this respect, today's epistolary lection is resonant with today's Gospel reading, which depicts the descent of the Spirit occurring while Jesus was praying (Luke 3:21–22). To be sure, in Acts this is not a consistent pattern, for at other times the Holy Spirit descends in the act of preaching (10:44; 11:15; cf. 19:6).

Celebrating the baptism of Jesus enables us to see more clearly the meaning of becoming God's child, because among other things, it provides a special occasion for us to ponder the significance of the prophetic proclamation "The Spirit of the Lord GOD is upon me" (Isa. 61:1).

Luke 3:15–17, 21–22

A traditional subject for Epiphany is the baptism of Jesus as presented by one of the Gospels. However, when Luke is the Gospel, the subject more correctly is on events surrounding Jesus' baptism; for, as we will see, the baptism itself is noticeably subordinated to the heavenly attestation to Jesus as God's Son, the opening of the heavens, and the descent of the Holy Spirit, to which both Isaiah 61 and Acts 8 testify. In fact, the psalm for today (Ps. 29) praises God's glory through flood, wind, and fire, elements that serve in biblical language as symbols for the Holy Spirit.

The Gospel lection is in two parts: Luke 3:15–17 and 21–22. Verses 15–17 deal with John the Baptist, but it is not his person that is central here. Even though verse 15 expresses the general public interest in John, Luke actually removes John from the scene prior to the account of Jesus' baptism (vv. 18–20). Neither John nor the Jordan River appear in Luke's story of the baptism. Luke's interest in John at this point is in his witness to the larger and vastly different ministry of the One coming after him. Even though John does not identify that greater one as Jesus—that identification is in the Fourth Gospel—the reader makes that association naturally enough. The greatness of the One to come is pointed out in the contrast between water baptism and baptism with the Holy Spirit and fire. Because of the overlay of Christian interpretation, both by the writer and the reader, it is difficult to know what John understood by "Holy Spirit and fire." Because "spirit" can also be translated "wind," and because the elaboration in verse 17 is about the wind separating wheat and chaff, perhaps the central thrust of John's message concerns the coming judgment. That is, whereas John's ministry involved a purging by water, the One to come will purge with wind and fire. But even if that is John's understanding, wind and fire are for Luke symbols of the Holy Spirit (Acts 2:2–3), and the Holy Spirit is for Luke and other early Christians the promised gift of Christ to the believers (Acts 1:5, 8; 2:38).

Verses 21–22 focus not upon Jesus giving the Holy Spirit to others but upon his receiving it at baptism. As mentioned earlier, Luke subordinates the baptism itself to other concerns. John is already in prison (vv. 18–20), Jesus comes among all the people (v. 21), and the baptism is set in a subordinate clause, along with prayer (v. 21). This minimal attention to Jesus' baptism may be due in part to some early Christian difficulty with, if not embarrassment over, the fact that Jesus was baptized. Matthew 3:13–15 addresses that problem, as did later Christian writings that turned the baptismal scene into a spectacle with bright lights, fire on the surface of the water, and a heavenly voice explaining the divinity of Christ. But Luke's scant attention to the baptism itself is also motivated by a desire to give major attention to the epiphany qualities of the occasion. The opened heavens signaled the launching of a new age. The heavenly voice addresses Jesus, as in Mark 1:9–11, not the people, as in Matthew 3:13–17. However, the descent of the Holy Spirit has a public dimension in that it comes "in bodily form" as a dove.

The voice from heaven, in identifying Jesus, combines Psalm 2:7, used at the coronation of Israel's king as God's son, and Isaiah 42:1, a description of the servant of God. Jesus is the

Servant King or the Sovereign Servant. The use of Isaiah 42:1 indicates that the coming of the Holy Spirit is not to make Jesus the Son of God—Luke affirmed that in the birth story—but to empower the Servant for his task. This view is confirmed in 4:16–30, where Luke clearly states that the Holy Spirit was an anointing for public ministry. Some manuscripts of Luke 3:22 use the remainder of Psalm 2:7, "today I have begotten you," opening the door to an adoptionist view of Christ as Son of God.

The preacher will want to notice the reference to prayer in verse 21. The prayer life of Jesus is a matter of importance for Luke (5:11; 6:12; 9:18; 9:28–29; 11:1; 22:32, 39, 46; 23:34, 46), but not the prayer life of Jesus alone. Just as Jesus was in prayer when the Holy Spirit descended, so the church, awaiting the promised power of the Spirit, was (Acts 1:8, 14) and should continue to be constant in prayer.

Second Sunday After the Epiphany

Isaiah 62:1–5;
Psalm 36:5–10;
1 Corinthians 12:1–11;
John 2:1–11

The dramatic manifestation of the power of God is the dominant theme in the readings for this day. The Gospel lections for the season call attention to the beginning of the ministry of Jesus. The account of the miracle at the wedding in Cana in John 2:1–11 is, according to the Fourth Gospel, the first of Jesus' signs, when he "revealed his glory" (v. 11). In this context the lection from 1 Corinthians 12:1–11 calls attention to the manifestation of God through the gifts of the Spirit. In Isaiah 62:1–5 the brightness of a vindicated Jerusalem reveals God's grace. Psalm 36:5–10 is a hymn of praise for God's steadfast love, faithfulness, righteousness, and judgment, the one in whose light "we see light" (v. 9).

Isaiah 62:1–5

A striking number of the Old Testament readings for this season are taken from the coherent section of proclamations in Isaiah 60–62. (For discussion of the unit as a whole, see the commentaries for Epiphany and for Christmas, Second Proper.) Unlike Second Isaiah, who announces the release of the Babylonian exiles and their return to Judah, Third Isaiah in these chapters proclaims the restoration of the people in general and the city of Jerusalem in particular. He sees no single dramatic political event on the horizon, but an inner transformation of the people.

The passage is a prophetic speech, basically a proclamation of salvation to Zion and, by implication, Zion's people. But it begins with what almost amounts to a vow by the prophet himself: he will not keep silent; he will not rest until Zion is vindicated. These lines, which parallel verses 6–7, suggest a note of lament and petition to God. The prophet, like many before him, has assumed an intercessory role on behalf of the people.

The imagery for Zion's vindication and salvation has been encountered frequently in Third Isaiah. It is the image of light, as in Isaiah 60:1–3 (see the commentary on the texts for Epiphany). The brightness of this vindication will be seen by "the nations," by "all the kings" (v. 2). Royal metaphors continue with the picture of Zion held like a "crown," a "royal diadem," (v. 3) in the hand of God.

All of that concerns the revelation of the transformation that God has effected. The transformation itself is the subject of the remainder of the passage; it is characterized as God's gift of a new name (vv. 2b, 4–5). Though developed poetically, the proclamation concerning a new name is similar to the earlier prophetic reports of symbolic actions. There is the account of an action or the divine instructions to perform one, followed by the interpretation of its meaning. There are numerous such accounts, and it is striking how many of them concern names (Isa. 7–8; Hos. 1:2–9). The prophet promises a new name from the mouth of God (v. 2b), gives new names as reversals of past conditions (v. 4), and gives a metaphorical explanation of the meaning of the names (v. 5).

The names, old and new, symbolize the nature and reality of Yahweh's relationship—past and future—to Zion and Zion's children. Formerly they were Forsaken, their land Desolate. Could there be a more powerful statement of the absence of God? For the prophet and his original hearers, the Exile was accepted as divine judgment, the time when Yahweh turned aside from them. But now they will be called My Delight is in Her (in Hebrew, *hephzibah*) and the land Married (in Hebrew, *beulah*). This symbolic naming to indicate new realities of relationship is seen also in Hosea 1–3, especially 1:6–9 and 2:16–17. The Book of Ezekiel concludes with a new name for Zion, "The LORD is There" (48:35; see also Jer. 33:16).

The re-naming of Zion and the land means that Jerusalem's children will return and claim her, like a young husband takes a wife. Moreover, it signifies that God will rejoice over his people as a bridegroom over a bride (v. 5). Such intimate metaphors were possible within the framework of a conventional relationship between God and people in which the initiative was God's. The new names thus announce and confirm a new election of the people. It makes a difference what one is called, especially if the name is given by God.

Psalm 36:5–10

These hymnic verses of Psalm 36 are sandwiched between a description (addressed to a human audience) of the wicked person (vv. 1–4) and a plea for protection against evildoers (vv. 11–12, actually begun already in v. 10). Thus we have a psalm with most of the features of an individual lament.

Before examining verses 5–10, which celebrate the epiphanies of God and their accompanying blessing, a side glance should be given to the opening and closing sections. The description of the evildoer in verses 1–4 may be seen as a negative contrast to the description of divine benevolence in verses 5–10 and as a counterpart to how the worshiper would like to be viewed. In most cultures, portraits of the villainous character serve an educational and moral function just as much as the descriptions of the hero type. Such typologies allow a person to engage in self-assessment and character imitation. (Note that in Western movies, one of America's basic forms of morality plays, the villain as well as the hero is a character figure.) According to the psalm description, the evildoer is one who has no fear of God, believes that one's iniquity will not be found out, speaks deceitfully and without normal restraints, and even while awaiting slumber upon the bed plots schemes. In other words, the evil person is one who fundamentally considers him/herself to be an exception to the rule. What applies to others is irrelevant to his/her case, and anything can thus be excused. Arrogance, the self-assurance of one's existence as an exception to the rule, and evil frequently go hand in hand (see v. 10).

The closing petition (vv. 10–12) has the worshiper requesting divine protection so as not to become the object of abuse or the casualty of someone else's arrogance and wickedness. To fall prey to such a state is to be at the mercy of another, to lose one's freedom and dignity (v. 12). The hymnlike section at the heart of this psalm testifies, in direct address to

God, to the benevolence and protection of the Divine. In expressing this sentiment, the psalm writer compares God's qualities to features of the natural world—the heavens, the clouds, a mountain, the great deep (the cavernous, watery deeps beneath the earth). Yet the one who receives such benefactions is placed in the same category as an undomesticated animal: "you save humans and animals alike" (v. 6c). What may initially strike us as odd in such a comparison or classification might not appear so if we give it some thought. The beast receives its blessings, its food, its livelihood without setting out to please God or anybody; it makes no effort to measure up to any standard; it simply drinks in the benefits that come its way from the created order controlled by God. The writer is suggesting something similar is the case with humans.

Verses 7–8 extol the extravagance of God's benefits bestowed in the temple, the place of worship. Not only is God like a protective bird under whose wings one can find shelter, but also God's house, the temple, is a place of abundance. What is said in verse 8 should be seen against the background of temple services and sacrifices. Many of the sacrifices were consumed by the worshiper who offered them. After the priest had received his share of the sacrifice (his salary!), and after the fat and other portions were burned on the altar, the remainder went to the worshiper who cooked and consumed it in the company of family, friends, and others. The sacrifice, or the animal's meat, had to be eaten on the day of or, at the latest, on the day following the sacrifice (see Lev. 7:11–18). Sacrificial worship was thus very much like a family or communal barbecue. It was a period of conspicuous consumption when the normal drive to conserve food was countermanded. Thus the psalmist can praise the pleasure, the hedonism of those times, in the house of God when food abounded and drink flowed in abundance (see 1 Sam. 1:1–18).

1 Corinthians 12:1–11

With today's epistolary lection, we begin the semicontinuous reading of 1 Corinthians 12–15 that takes us through the Eighth Sunday After the Epiphany. We should remember that the Epistle lessons for the Sundays after the Epiphany in all three years are supplied, for the most part, by First and Second Corinthians. Thus, at this time of the liturgical year we are allowed to look at the way one early Christian community appropriated the Christian gospel in a very concrete setting.

Today's lection introduces a three-chapter unit in the epistle (chaps. 12–14) that deals with the question of "spiritual gifts" (v. 1), or perhaps "spiritual persons." The opening words, "Now concerning . . . ," suggest that the Corinthian church had inquired of Paul about this topic, and in what follows we have his response to their question. It is well known that the question of "spiritual gifts" was of special concern to this church. At least, the topic is addressed more fully in the Corinthian letters than in any other New Testament writing.

Early on in the letter, Paul reassures the church that they were not deficient in this regard (1:7). From what we can gather, some members of the church were experiencing the Spirit in highly visible ways, with the result that other members who were not similarly endowed with the Spirit felt that their faith was severely lacking. Paul's concern is pastoral: he seeks to reassure the whole church in its faith and to relate each of the members, regardless of one's particular form of spiritual endowment, to the rest of the members in ways that edify the whole church.

In the opening section of today's lection (vv. 1–3), Paul reminds his readers of their former pagan status, when they worshiped "idols that could not speak" (cf. Hab. 2:18–19; Ps. 115:4–5; 3 Macc. 4:16; Acts 17:29). Regardless of their previous motivations, they were "enticed and led astray" by these false gods. In their new life in Christ, they are now reminded that there are proper bounds within which the Holy Spirit works. It is simply not enough to claim that we are speaking "by the Spirit." Rather, we must ask what the Spirit prompts us to say. If it is "Let Jesus be cursed!," we can be assured that God's Spirit is not responsible for such an imprecation. But if it is "Jesus is Lord," we can be just as assured that God's Spirit is the ultimate motivation.

We are not sure what actual situation, if any, is reflected here. Possibly, some Christians, in moments of ecstasy, were actually calling down curses on Jesus—a conceivable scenario if certain Corinthian "gnostics" were disparaging the human figure Jesus and devoting themselves instead to the "spiritual Christ" (cf. 1 John 4:2–3). Their curse would then mean: "The historical, or the fleshly, Jesus be cursed." Another possibility is that behind these words we hear the accusations from the Jewish synagogue charging that a crucified Jesus is accursed under the law (Deut. 21:22–23). Or it may be that Paul is stating a theoretical possibility and not reflecting an actual situation at all.

The important point to note is that it is not enough simply to claim to be speaking "by the Spirit." We must ask what is said "by the Spirit." In this case, Paul insists that the Christian confession "Jesus is Lord" serves as the fundamental criterion for weighing spiritual utterances (cf. Matt. 7:21; Luke 6:46; John 13:13; Rom. 10:9; 2 Cor. 4:5; Phil. 2:11; Col. 2:6).

In the second section of today's lection, Paul turns to a discussion of spiritual gifts. It should be noted that he prefers to use the term *charismata*, because it conveys the idea that they are bestowed as a gift of grace (*charis*; cf. Rom. 12:6; also Heb. 2:4). The fundamental point he makes in this section is that there is a diversity of gifts. They are referred to in different ways: "varieties of gifts . . . varieties of services . . . varieties of activities" (vv. 4–6). Yet, for all their variety, in every case they have a single source—the same Spirit, the same Lord, the same God. His conviction is summarized in verse 11: "All these are activated by one and the same Spirit, who allots to each one individually just as the Spirit chooses."

These words are well worth hearing, for Paul insists here that diversity of gifts, services, and activities is part and parcel of Christian community. As will become clear later in these chapters as he discusses the gift of tongues, some in the church were elevating one gift to a position of supreme importance above all the rest. According to them, there was one supreme gift to which everyone had to aspire. Not many, but one. For them, all should seek the same gift. For Paul, each should recognize his or her individual gift and use if for the good of all. The Pauline word for us is that functional diversity is a given. Moreover, it is God-given. We should not think of diversity as an obstacle to be overcome but as a resource to be used.

Besides affirming the value of diversity, Paul instructs us about the proper use of these gifts: they are "for the common good" (v. 7; cf. 1 Cor. 6:12; 10:23; 14:26). Here he attacks the robust individualism within the church. The Spirit gives us gifts, not for the sole benefit of personal enrichment, but so we can enrich the faith of others. As we will see later, this becomes an important criterion for judging the worth of particular gifts. Do they contribute to community, or do they destroy community by establishing tiny cells of spirituality wholly unrelated to one another, and in the end, insensitive to one another?

The various gifts are mentioned in verses 8–10. To determine precisely what each gift entailed and how they differed from one another, the preacher will need to consult concordances and commentaries. It is worth noting, however, that tongues are mentioned last, no doubt for a reason. As Paul surveyed this situation, he thought the gift of tongues least commendable because it contributed least to corporate solidarity.

John 2:1–11

The lections for this Second Sunday After the Epiphany join in announcing the manifestations of God among us and do so with festive spirit and with gifts in abundance. This is especially true of the story of the wedding in Cana, recorded only in the Gospel of John.

That John 2:1–11 is an Epiphany text is evident both by direct statement and by symbolic clue. The direct statement occurs in verse 11, "revealed his glory," and the symbolic clue is the opening phrase in verse 1, "On the third day." If one tries to understand the third day as a chronological reference, the calculation is confused by the use of "the next day" to mark each of the three preceding events (1:29, 35, 43). However, as a resurrection symbol, the third day is appropriate to signal a revelation event. In fact, the next account in John, the cleansing of the temple (2:13–22), is also a "third day" story (vv. 20–21) in that the temple cleansing is, in this Gospel, a death-resurrection sign. Given the favorable reception accorded Jesus in Galilee and the rejection in Jerusalem, it is not coincidental that the wedding is set in Galilee and the "funeral" (2:13–22) in Jerusalem.

Approaches to the Cana story in terms of its sources are not very fruitful. The Dionysius cult in Syria had stories of gods turning water into wine, and Philo of Alexandria characterized the Logos as giving the people wine instead of water. However, whether the Evangelist was aware of such background stories is unclear; and even if he were, interpreting a text on the basis of sources is of limited value. More pertinent is the question, What is John saying about Jesus in the Cana wedding story?

It seems clear that John is not attempting to prove a miracle was performed, as, for example, Matthew attempts to prove the resurrection (28:1–15). Were that John's purpose, surely more details would be provided. Who issued invitations to the wedding? Why was the family of Jesus there? What gave Jesus' mother (never called by her name in this Gospel) reasons to believe that Jesus could relieve the wine shortage? Did she expect a miracle or a purchase? Or did she expect him and his friends to leave and thereby relieve the short supply? From where did the servants get approximately one hundred fifty gallons (six jars holding eighteen to twenty-seven gallons each) of water, a major task in itself? If proving a miracle were John's purpose, surely more witnesses to the miracle would have testified to its having occurred. But neither the servants nor the wine steward knew what happened. Who, then, believed the sign? Jesus' disciples (v. 11).

Let us, then, allow the Evangelist to make his point. First of all, the writer wants it understood that Jesus performed his signs according to God's will (5:19, 30; 7:6; 8:25) and not in response to any person's wish or need. Although his mother is an unwitting helper in this first sign, Jesus does not act at her bidding. He distanced himself from her (v. 4), indicating that his ministry would be according to "his hour" (v. 4), a recurring theme in this Gospel. When his brothers urged him to go up to Jerusalem, he said it was not his hour, and then he went (7:1–9). When Martha and Mary sent word to Jesus about their brother's illness, he tarried two days before going (11:1–7). In John's Gospel, Jesus speaks and acts not in response to any claims of kinship, friendship, or even need, but at his own initiative as God's will is revealed to him. This pattern may seem to be without compassion, but something more than compassion is involved. In the Cana story as well as in those involving his brothers and his friends, Jesus meets the need, but he does more. Compassion alone might provide wine, but sovereign grace does more: it reveals God in what is done and confirms the disciples' faith in Jesus.

Second, the Evangelist is saying that a sign is not a miracle to amaze or an offer of proof for his teaching. The sign was a window through which God was revealed. To attend to the miraculous and to miss the revelation would be no more than curiosity wallowing in the unusual.

And, finally, a sign is not evident to all and bears an uncertain relation to faith. At Cana, Jesus manifested his glory, and those who believed were already his disciples (v. 11). On other occasions it is said, "Many believed in his name because they saw the signs that he was doing" (2:23), but obviously being present was not sufficient to generate faith. In fact, Jesus said to Thomas, "Have you believed because you have seen me? Blessed are those who have not seen and yet have come to believe" (20:29).

Third Sunday After the Epiphany

Nehemiah 8:1–3, 5–6, 8–10;
Psalm 19
1 Corinthians 12:12–31a;
Luke 4:14–21

Thematic connections among the elections for this day are not easy to discern, and it is not necessary to impose them upon the readings. Each passage has enough to say in itself, and any one offers rich possibilities for the preacher. The Old Testament text and the responsorial psalm concentrate upon the law—the book of the law read by Ezra to the people, the law of Moses, the divine instructions for life. The Lucan account of Jesus in the synagogue in Nazareth continues this season's interest in the youth and early ministry of Jesus. The epistolary text from 1 Corinthians 12:12–31a is Paul's classical statement of the church as many members but one body in Christ.

Nehemiah 8:1–3, 5–6, 8–10

Our Old Testament reading contains the essential elements of the report (Neh. 7:73b–8:18) of Ezra's reading of the book of the law to the people assembled in Jerusalem after the return from the Exile. Important as the report is in itself, it is only part of a larger account of ceremonies in Jerusalem. After the law was read, the people engaged in prayers of confession and fasting, and then renewed the ancient covenant with their Lord (Neh. 9–10).

The account is filled with ritual and ceremonial allusions. The people are assembled in the square before the Water Gate, part of the newly rebuilt walls of Jerusalem. Ezra is identified as a priest (v. 2). The date ("the first day of the seventh month") probably refers to the calendar of religious events. The position and posture of Ezra and the people indicate a solemn occasion: He stood on or at a wooden pulpit or platform, surrounded by others (v. 4), opened the book where all could see him do it (v. 5), pronounced a blessing or invocation, and all responded by saying "Amen, amen," lifting up their hands in prayer and prostrating themselves (v. 6). Then he read clearly, and the Levites "gave the sense" (v. 8). Finally, Ezra declared the day to be one of sacred celebration (vv. 9–10).

The ceremony must be distinguished from the rituals of the temple. It included all the people who could understand—men, women, and young people—and it did not take place in the sacred precincts. The patterns of speech and action suggest that although we may have the report of an event that took place once, the ceremonies were not invented for the occasion but depended upon more ancient tradition. Compare this reading with one reported in 2 Kings 22. Certainly this activity of reading, teaching, and responding to the law is like that of the later synagogue, and some of the practices are doubtless older. When one considers the broader framework that leads to the renewal of the covenant, one can compare the events with accounts such as that in Joshua 24, in which Joshua led the people in the renewal of the Sinai covenant. In any case, religious services that concentrated upon the reading and interpretation of the Scriptures came to be central in the synagogue and from there formed the basis for Christian services of the Word.

The most important theme here concerns the reading and interpretation of the book of the law. It is not possible to know what book or books Ezra actually read. The author of the Books of Chronicles-Ezra-Nehemiah uses the expression to refer to the Torah, or the Pentateuch. There is no suggestion that all these books were read: Ezra read "from it" (v. 3), and the time given would limit how much could be read. Clearly, in the time of the author—if not already in the time of Ezra—it was widely held that the Torah was scared Scripture, soon to be fully recognized as canon.

Given the degree of reverence for the book of the law, it is all the more remarkable how the book is treated. Notice that it was "read . . . clearly," and then the Levites "gave the sense" and "gave instruction in what was read" (v. 8, with NEB). It is not enough to hold it in reverence or even just to read it publicly. It also must be explained and taught. The role of the Levites here is not unlike that reflected in the Book of Deuteronomy, in which ancient laws are presented, explained, and reinterpreted, and then laid upon the hearts of the people. The meaning of the ancient Scripture must be made plain in a new time.

Psalm 19

Psalm 19 is concerned with two major topics: the world of creation, the heavens and the sun especially (vv. 1–6); and the way of the law, or Torah (vv. 7–10). In conjunction with the account of Ezra's reading of the law in the Old Testament lection, the second part of the psalm draws attention.

In spite of its complexity, the psalm can be seen as a unity. The nature portion, verses 1–6, declares that creation, without normal words, voice, or speech, points to divine will and control and thus prompts expressions of praise. The law portion, verses 7–10, focuses on the written law formulated in words that elicit attitudes of praise. Verses 11–14 are a prayer that one might be aware of sins, faults, and errors in order to live a life that is without great transgressions. The final plea, in verse 14, requests that not only the words but also the unspoken meditations of the heart be acceptable to God. Thus the psalm moves from describing the unarticulatable expressions of nature, which proclaim God's work and fill the whole expansive realm of creation, down to the inarticulated meditations of the heart. Thus the thought of the psalm moves from the outer reaches of the natural world to the inner recesses of the human personality, the human heart.

Verses 7–9 contain a series of six affirmations in praise of the law that follow a common pattern. The first line of each of the affirmations begins with a different synonym for the law, which is followed by a declaration and a participial construction defining a function of the law. The following are the synonyms: law, decrees, precepts, commandment, fear, and ordinances. The adjectival declarations are these: perfect, sure, right, clear, pure, true and righteous. The functions of the law are given as: reviving the soul (or renewing life), making wise the simple (educating the unlearned or simpleton), rejoicing the heart, enlightening the eyes (we would say "restoring strength"; see 1 Sam. 14:24–30), enduring forever.

Verse 10 is an adulation of the law stated in the form of a "more . . . than" saying. Here the law is compared to two items and their distinctive qualities: more desired than gold (in ancient as in modern times, the most coveted of metals) and sweeter than honey or the honeycomb (the ancients' primary source of sweetening).

A twofold function of the law is affirmed in verse 11. Negatively, the law functions to warn and thus to aid one in right living (v. 11a). Laws such as the Ten Commandments functioned not to tell one what to do but as signposts at the periphery of experience warning that one should not go beyond a certain point. The law thus served to define the boundaries within which one could operate and live safely. It served as a canopy under which one could live. It functioned to provide a reading on one's location in the larger world of experience. Positively, the keeping of the law is related to rewards (v. 11b). Rewards should be seen here not as something presented by God like trophies for winning a race but as the results or consequences inherent in obedience to Torah itself. Law's shaping of life and the shape of life produced are its rewards. Obedience to Torah means that one has experienced what is promised in the declarations of verses 7–9.

Verses 12–14 constituted the petition proper embodying the requests of the worshiper. Because it is difficult for one to be certain when errors occur and hard to avoid the pitfalls of self-delusion, the worshiper asks to be kept from certain fallacies. Two types of conditions or sins are singled out: (1) hidden faults that are not obvious to the undiscerning eye; those personality factors and unseen attitudes that can corrode character or shape the personality in distorted ways; and (2) presumptuous sins, acts that one may commit thinking they are some bold adventure in courage, some venting of a true, primeval drive, or some daring experiment in being one's own person. Hidden faults and presumptuous sins are the two extremes by which one may step beyond the law and the goals of Torah.

The final request (v. 14) likewise employs extremes: doing (words) and thinking (meditation of the heart) are ways of speaking about a totality.

In preaching from the Old Testament, and from such psalms as Psalm 19, the Christian preacher should be attuned to the values inherent in the law and expound the positive qualities of life lived according to Torah.

1 Corinthians 12:12–31a

In the previous section, Paul has stressed the common source of the various manifestations of the Spirit in the church. He now turns to discuss *the paradox of the one and the many* as it is experienced in Christ.

First, *the one* (vv. 12–13). For Paul, it was axiomatic that there was one body, the church (Rom. 12:5; 1 Cor. 10:17; Eph. 1:23; 4:4; Col. 3:15). But besides being one in number, the church also exhibits another level of oneness. The one Spirit, viewed here both as the agent of baptism and the source of spiritual sustenance, brings about a kind of unity that eliminates ethnic and social differences. Thus Jews and Greeks, slaves and free, share a common initiation by the Spirit through which they achieve a level of oneness: they become one body (Gal. 3:28; Rom. 10:12; Col. 3:11). In this respect, the church is like a human body. It has many parts, but they function as part of a single entity (cf. v. 27; Rom. 12:4).

Second, *the many* (vv. 14–30). In this section, the other side of the paradox is discussed: "the body does not consist of one member but of many" (v. 14). Unity does not exclude diversity.

The two may exist together, but they must be properly understood. To help explain the nature of the "many," Paul cites the well-known example of the human body, an analogy used by Greco-Roman authors to illustrate the nature of the state.

As used here, this example enables Paul to make two points. (1) The human body has many parts with many different functions. It is absurd to think that there could be only one part with a single function. Thus, "there are many members, yet one body" (v. 20). (2) The parts are interdependent. They are many, but not in the sense that there are many pebbles in a box. Rather, they are organically related. The pain one part experiences is experienced by the other parts. They form an ecology of suffering and rejoicing (v. 26).

By this point, Paul has established, largely through his analogy of the human body, that the one can encompass the many; in fact, that it is impossible to speak of one body in any meaningful sense unless we grant the existence of its many parts. Oneness does not mean sameness. Unity does not mean uniformity.

Having elaborated on the one and the many, Paul now applies his remarks to the church: "Now you are the body of Christ and individually members of it" (v. 27). He does not say: "You are a body of Christians," as if the church were merely a group with a common identity. Rather, his claim here appears to be metaphysical, not metaphorical, even though this point is hotly disputed among commentators. If Paul here is making a fundamental claim about the nature of corporate Christian existence, he is asserting that the risen Lord finds concrete, living manifestation among us, the church. Whether the best way to conceive of this is to think of the church as the extension of the exalted body of Christ is debated. Even this may not be emphatic enough to account for Paul's bold claim here. But however we conceive of this claim, we should see the church as the Body of Christ in some real rather than metaphorical sense.

Accordingly, God has constituted the church with a variety of gifts, services, ministries, offices, and functions. These are elaborated in verses 28–30. As applied to the church, Paul's earlier point now receives concrete application. There is one church, but it cannot exist if there is only one part with a single function. Then it becomes grotesque. We can speak of oneness only if we recognize diversity.

The overall direction of Paul's remarks in this chapter is clear. There is not one spiritual gift to be sought as the *summum bonum* of Christian existence. There are many gifts, each with its own form and function, uniquely able to contribute to the whole.

These words of Paul, when taken seriously, keep the church from developing a cookie-cutter mentality. The missionary thinks everyone in the church should become a missionary; likewise, the teacher, church musician, and so forth. We all live with the tyranny of the specialties, each of us looking at the whole through the lens of our particular gift, wondering why everyone does not aspire to it as we do. But should every person in the church be a teacher? Paul thinks not. His is not a monochrome vision of the church.

Luke 4:14–21

Luke 4:14–21 joins Nehemiah 8 and Psalm 19 in affirming the revelation of God in the Word that is read in the assembly of believers. The act of reading and hearing the Word of revelation provides a theme most appropriate for Epiphany.

Our Gospel lection consists of two parts: verses 14–15 and 16–21. Verses 14–15 function in three ways: (1) they provide a transition both in terms of location and of activity from Jesus' wilderness temptation to the launching of the Galilean ministry; (2) they continue the attention on the power of the Spirit in Jesus' ministry in Galilean synagogues before focusing upon one of the synagogues in particular, the one in Nazareth; and (3) they set the general context of Jesus' ministry in Galilean synagogues. It is important also to receive the report of Jesus' rejection in Nazareth and the attempt on his life (vv. 28–29) against the backdrop of wide reputation (v. 14) and most favorable reception (v. 15).

The second part of our Gospel, verses 16–21, poses for the preacher a small problem. These verses are in fact a portion of a unit extending through verse 30. However, verses 21–30 (v. 21 is an overlap) constitute next Sunday's reading. The preacher is thus faced with the task of treating a single narrative on two separate occasions. Is this problem insurmountable, or is a violation of the text inevitable? No. There are two characteristics in the text that offer some justification for the division: first, verses 16–21 record the first movement of the synagogue service, Jesus reading the Scripture, whereas verses 22–30 provide Jesus' sermon on the text and the congregation's response. The division is somewhat natural. Second, verses 16–21 tell of a positive response to Jesus, whereas verses 22–30 report a very negative response. The contrast is so sharp that some scholars have suggested that Luke is here conflating two stories from the tradition. We can, therefore, confine ourselves to verses 16–21, and it will be important not to steal from verses 22–30, thereby robbing next Sunday's message of its punch.

Clearly, the event Luke here describes is the same as the one recorded in Mark 6:1–6 and Matthew 13:54–58, although the accounts differ so much that one must conclude that Luke is following a different source. More important, however, is the different purpose to which Luke puts the story. Both Mark and Matthew place the rejection in Nazareth (actually only Luke names the town) well into Jesus' ministry, whereas Luke locates it at the beginning, prefaced with only a general comment about Jesus coming into Galilee, teaching in the synagogues (vv. 14–15). In fact, Luke sacrifices chronology in the service of another purpose, for even though Jesus goes to Capernaum later (4:31–37), our story assumes he has been there and his ministry is widely known (v. 23). Although admittedly awkward, this placing of the Nazareth event first is Luke's way of making it programmatic, a preview of all of Jesus' ministry that will now unfold. Perhaps it will sharpen our focus if we press the impact of verses 16–21 into a series of brief summary statements.

1. Jesus' ministry is in the power of God's Spirit, both in his movement and his activity (3:22; 4:1–2, 14, 18). Luke's model here is probably Elijah, whose itinerary as well as power came from the Spirit (1 Kings 18:7–16).

2. All of Jesus' ministry was inside, not outside, the bosom of Judaism and the traditions of his people. Here Jesus affirms by his faithfulness the sabbath, the Scriptures, and the synagogue. He is, according to Luke, a reformer and not an opponent of his heritage.

3. By reading Isaiah 61:1–2, Jesus has not only announced fulfillment of prophecy (v. 21) but has defined what "messiah" means. Isaiah 61 is a servant song, and if "anointed me" is taken literally ("christened," "made me the Christ or Messiah"), then the Christ is God's servant to turn the hopes of the poor, imprisoned, and oppressed into reality. The messiah will bring the amnesty, the liberation, and the restoration of the year of jubilee (Lev. 25:8–12).

4. The "someday" of hope is now the "today" of fulfillment (v. 21). For Luke's church and for us, it is still "today," and preaching that turns "today" into another vague and distant "someday" has not listened carefully to the text.

Fourth Sunday After the Epiphany

Jeremiah 1:4–10;
Psalm 71:1–6;
1 Corinthians 13:1–13;
Luke 4:21–30

The Gospel reading continues the account of the first events in the ministry of Jesus with the semicontinuous readings from Luke. Jeremiah's report of his vocation is good preparation for the Lucan emphasis upon the parallels between the role of Jesus and that of the Old Testament prophets: gracious words came out of his mouth, and no prophet is honored in his own country. Psalm 71:1–6 is an individual's prayer for deliverance. It responds in particular to the election of the prophet "from [his] mother's womb" (v. 6 and Jer. 1:5), but it supports the theme of conflict with opponents in the Gospel lection. First Corinthians 13 reminds us that the gift of love is even greater than that of prophecy or tongues.

Jeremiah 1:4–10

It is appropriate that we consider the vocation reports of the prophets—Jeremiah today and Isaiah next Sunday—in the context of the beginning of the ministry of Jesus. We are encouraged to reflect not only on the prophetic aspects of that ministry but, like the first disciples, also upon our own response to God's vocation.

The calls of prophets and other servants of God are very private matters. That is especially true of Jeremiah, who reveals throughout his work so much of his personal turmoil. It is all the more remarkable, therefore, to learn that Jeremiah's report of his call has a great many features in common with other Old Testament vocation reports. These include the reports of the calls of Moses (Exod. 3:1–4:17), Gideon (Judg. 6:11–24), Isaiah (Isa. 6:1–13), and Ezekiel (Ezek. 1–3). All these report an encounter with God, a commission to do the Lord's will or speak the Lord's word, and a ritual act or sign symbolizing the designated role. In all cases except Ezekiel, the one who is called objects to the vocation and then is reassured. We may conclude from the persistence of this feature in vocation reports that resistance is not linked so much to individual personalities as it is to the very experience of standing in the presence of the Holy One and being called as God's servant. It goes with the office, even verifying that one is called by God, to feel unworthy or inadequate.

Some of the vocation reports (Isa. 6; Ezek. 1–3; cf. 1 Kings 22:19–22) give accounts of the Lord's heavenly throne. Jeremiah's report, like those of Gideon and Moses, focuses rather upon the encounter with the word of God, as verse 4 explicitly states. The pattern of the report is that of a dialogue between Yahweh and the prophet. The initial divine speech (v. 5), remarkably, announces past events. Even before Jeremiah was formed in the womb he was known by Yahweh, consecrated, and appointed "a prophet to the nations." Jeremiah's response (v. 6) is an objection that he does not know how to speak, that he is too young. Yahweh then reacts (v. 7) to both the objections, but one more than the other. Yahweh simply tells the prophet not to say that he is only a youth; but to the question of speaking ability, Yahweh announces that he will command Jeremiah to speak, and what to speak. Then Yahweh responds with the promise of deliverance to an objection that had not been voiced—fear of opposition: "Do not be afraid of them." This allusion indicates that the purpose of the account was to respond to opposition from the people. Prophets reported their vocations in order to establish their authority to speak.

At this point the dialogue is over and the ritual of ordination begins. As befits designation for the prophetic role (see Isa. 6:5–7; Ezek. 2:8–3:3), Yahweh touches Jeremiah's mouth and gives him the message he is to deliver (vv. 9–10). It is a message of both judgment and salvation.

One of the most important aspects of this report concerns the meaning and authority of the prophetic word. In the first place, it is clearly indicated from beginning to end that the words of the prophet are to be those the Lord gives him. That self-understanding persists not only in Jeremiah but in all other Old Testament prophets: they are messengers bearing revelations from their God. Second, it is equally clear that the prophetic words are not idle talk but powerful. To have the words of God in one's mouth is to be set "over nations . . . to pluck up and to pull down" (v. 10). As in Genesis 1, when God speaks, it is so. No wonder that one called by God to speak such a word would be reluctant to take on the task. Have the church and our culture completely lost the sense of such words as powerful? Which words, if any and by whom, do we consider to be effective?

Psalm 71:1–6

Psalm 71 is a complex lament in which a description of trouble (vv. 7–11) occurs along with various appeals for help (vv. 2–4, 12–13, 17–18), statements of trust and confidence (vv. 1, 16, 19–21), and vows to perform certain actions in the future (vv. 14–15, 22–24).

The first six verses have been selected to accompany the other readings for the day because of the parallels between these verses and statements in the call of Jeremiah. Psalm 71 seems to be a prayer of an aged man, perhaps a king, at a time of sickness or approaching death. The person's youth is reflected upon as a time that inaugurated a lifelong devotion and fidelity to Yahweh.

The psalm opens with a statement of confidence and trust (v. 1a) but quickly shifts to a request (v. 1b). Throughout verses 1–6, this same interweaving of trust and appeal for cure occurs. The enemies of the person are the wicked, the unjust, and the cruel. As bargaining power to secure help in old age (v. 9), appeal is made to the fidelity that has characterized life since birth. Like Jeremiah and Paul, the psalmist is willing to affirm a special status or at least a special relationship with God from birth.

1 Corinthians 13:1–13

Ordinarily, this chapter is read as a poetic hymn to love and as such is all too easily removed from its immediate context. Some scholars argue that it breaks the train of thought introduced in chapter 12 and consequently should be treated as an excursus with no thematic relation to what precedes or what follows. But a strong case can be made for seeing it as intrinsic to the discussion of spiritual gifts introduced in chapter 12 and continued in chapter 14.

How then does it function? A clue is provided by the earlier discussion of eating sacrificial meats in chapters 8–10. There Paul introduces the topic about which the church had inquired (chap. 8), but midway in the discussion he presents two examples for the church— one positive (his own apostolic behavior, chap. 9), the other negative (Israel, 10:1–22)—and finally resumes the discussion (10:23–11:1).

The discussion in chapters 12–14 unfolds in similar fashion. First he introduces the topic of "spiritual gifts" about which the church has inquired (chap. 12). He then provides his own apostolic behavior as an example for the church (chap. 13). After this, he returns to the discussion of spiritual gifts and contrasts the gift of tongues with the gift of prophecy (chap. 14). Read this way, chapter 13 is to be seen primarily as a discussion of Paul's own apostolic behavior.

Accordingly, it divides into three parts. In part one (vv. 1–3), he characterizes various aspects of his own apostolic behavior. Note that he consistently uses the first person singular and that each of the items relates directly to his own apostolic behavior: speaking in tongues (14:6, 18); prophecy (14:6; cf. 14:37); mysteries (2:1, 7; 4:1; 14:2; 15:51; Rom. 11:25; 16:25); knowledge (8:1–2); faith to remove mountains, that is power to work miracles (Matt. 17:20; 2 Cor. 12:11–13); giving up his possessions (1 Cor. 4:11; 2 Cor. 6:10); handing over his body for the glory of his ministry (2 Cor. 4:7–12; Gal. 6:14; note, however, the important textual variant here, "hand over my body to be burned"). Each of these is best understood in direct reference to Paul's own behavior. Paul insists that if any of these apostolic acts is not motivated by *agape*, it is of no value, least of all to himself. *Agape* serves as the fundamental mainspring of his apostolic work.

In part two (vv. 4–7), Paul characterizes *agape*. The contrast between *agape* and *eros* is well known, and there is an abundant literature on the significance of *agape* in antiquity. What each of these characteristics stresses is the self-giving, sacrificial dimension of *agape*, and this fits well with Paul's earlier insistence that *agape* builds up, whereas *gnosis* puffs up. Love, as Paul understands it, translates into a form of life that does not insist on its own way, is not egocentric but self-giving. This was the way of Christ (Phil. 2:4–11), the expected norm of Christian behavior (1 Cor. 10:24), and the earmark of Paul's apostleship (1 Cor. 10:33).

In part three (vv. 8–13), Paul presents *agape* as the supreme eschatological reality that "never ends" (v. 8). By contrast, the other gifts of the Spirit, such as tongues, knowledge, and prophesying, are partial and temporary. But *agape* transcends time: "It is the future eternal light shining in the present. It therefore needs no change of form. It is that which continues" (Barth). When set against "the complete" (v. 10, probably a reference to the end time), love endures, because it represents the dimension of God that reaches from the future into the present through the Christ-event (cf. Rom. 8:39).

But how does this relate to the Corinthians' situation. Paul urges them to "pursue love" (1 Cor. 14:1), convinced that their task is to translate the eschatological reality of love into a congregational life-style that fosters corporate edification instead of individual self-interest (1 Cor. 14:5, 26).

One of the main tasks the preacher faces in dealing with this all too familiar text is to make it concrete. Preaching on 1 Corinthians 13 can all too easily become an exercise for poetic soaring rather than an occasion for addressing pressing problems in the church. Though the preacher will find it all too tempting to ascend into the clouds, it will be far better—and harder—to keep one's feet firmly on the ground of congregational realities and human needs. For it was here—on the ground—where God's love finally became manifest and where it has to be translated into human form in the ongoing, daily existence of church life and practice.

Luke 4:21–30

All the readings for today declare that we are fully known of God, even from the womb. In that understanding is great comfort, for being known of God does not mean that one is known or accepted by one's contemporaries. In fact, being known of God in the sense of being chosen for special service sometimes stirs hostility in others, even in those whom one may seek to serve. Although this is the testimony of Jeremiah, the psalmist, and Paul, it is especially true of Jesus in Luke's record of his visit to Nazareth. Epiphany, the celebration of the manifestation of Christ to the world, has its darker side.

The reader is urged to review the comments on verses 14–21, last Sunday's Gospel lection. There is nothing in those verses to justify the opinion of some that verse 22 should be taken as a negative response to Jesus. Those who chart the congregation's reaction to Jesus as moving from favor (v. 22a), to disfavor (v. 22b), to violence (v. 28) are presuming to read a mood of doubt in the words "Is not this Joseph's son?" A better case can be made that there was a radical shift from favor to violence. But whether there is doubt or injured pride in the congregation, Jesus understands them as expecting a demonstration for the hometown folk of the extraordinary work being reported from Capernaum. Jesus also understands that proximity and familiarity tend to be blinding privileges. Luke reports as much on other occasions. The people of Nineveh and the queen of the South will judge the generation that did not heed one greater than Jonah and Solomon (11:29–32), and those who appeal to enter the kingdom on the grounds that Jesus taught in their streets and ate in their homes will be turned away (13:26–27). In fact, the woman in a crowd who declared a blessing on Jesus' mother was corrected: "Blessed rather are those who hear the word of God and obey it!" (11:27–28). The warning to the church in these statements is quite clear.

Jesus' response to the congregation's expectation makes it evident that the problem is far deeper than simply blind familiarity. If the citizens of Nazareth assume certain privileges for themselves, that error is joined to a more serious one—a possessiveness that resents Jesus taking God's favor to others beyond Nazareth, especially to Capernaum, a town very likely having a heavy non-Jewish population. Such is the clear implication of the two stories Jesus told. Many widows in Israel were suffering under the prolonged drought. Elijah brought relief to one, a foreigner in Sidon (1 Kings 17:1–18:1). With many lepers suffering in Israel, Elisha healed but one, a Syrian (2 Kings 5:1–14). These two stories were, of course, in their own Scriptures and quite familiar. Perhaps this accounts in part for the intensity of their hostility; anger and violence are the last defense of those who are made to face the truth embedded in their own tradition. Such truths will not go away even after the one who pointed to them has been removed. Those at war with themselves and what they know to be true often make casualties even of those who seek their good. It is a common theme in Luke that the quarrel is not really between Jesus and Judaism or between the church and the synagogue. The tension lies between the synagogue and its own Scriptures.

The synagogue, now a mob, attempted to stone Jesus. The law permitted that stoning could be either by throwing stones at a person or by throwing a person against the stones (v. 29). Jesus' escape, not described in detail (v. 30), is reminiscent of the elusive Elijah and anticipates the escapes of Peter (Acts 12:6–11) and Paul (Acts 16:25–28).

The event in Nazareth foreshadows Israel's rejection of Jesus and the taking of the message to Gentiles. However, it is important to notice that here Jesus does not go elsewhere because he is rejected; he is rejected because he goes elsewhere. Luke's point is that Israel should have understood. Readers of Luke's Gospel expect Christ to go to the nations, having heard a certain word in the matter as early as Simeon's prayer over the infant (2:29–32). But Israel, says Luke, knew of God's grace toward the nations as early as the covenant with Abraham (Gen. 22:18; Acts 3:25). The tragic difference between knowing and really knowing has not departed from God's people, even to this day.

Fifth Sunday After the Epiphany

Isaiah 6:1–8 (9–13);
Psalm 138;
1 Corinthians 15:1–11;
Luke 5:1–11

As the semicontinuous readings from the Gospel of Luke and from 1 Corinthians continue in this season, the lections do not always present a single or even dominant theme for the preacher. However, a motif present in one way or another in most of these readings is concern with the power and authority of the word. In Isaiah 6 the prophet reports his call and the harsh words he is to proclaim. The responsorial psalm is a song of thanksgiving from the temple, the location of Isaiah's vision. First Corinthians 15:1–11 is Paul's summary of the gospel that he had preached and through which God works. In Luke 5:1–11 the people crowded to hear from Jesus "the word of God" (v. 1), he taught them from the boat, and at the "word" of Jesus Simon let down the nets again. Moreover, the Gospel account of the call and response of the apostles parallels in significant ways the vocation of Isaiah and his response.

Isaiah 6:1–8 (9–13)

Like the Old Testament lesson for the previous Sunday (Jer. 1:4–10), Isaiah 6 is the report of a prophet's vocation. While Jeremiah's account concentrates upon the encounter with the word of Yahweh, Isaiah 6 closely parallels Ezekiel 1–3. Both are reports of visions of the Lord's heavenly throne. Similar also is the scene described by Micaiah ben Imlah in 1 Kings 22:19–22: "I saw the LORD sitting on his throne, and all the host of heaven beside him." Neither Isaiah nor Ezekiel sees God directly, but both have the sense of being on the outskirts of the heavenly throne room and hearing the deliberations going on there. Such Old Testament imagery is indebted to ancient Near Eastern traditions concerning the heavenly court. In those polytheistic traditions, the court includes the chief god and the other deities; in the Old Testament, God holds court with his messengers (see also Job 1:6–12).

The date formula that begins Isaiah's report also sets the mood. "The year that King Uzziah died" would have been 742 BC, but that king's death signaled the end of an era of relative independence for Judah. During most of Isaiah's lifetime, his nation lived under the threat of Assyrian domination. The prophet was active for some forty years, from the date given here until at least 701 BC.

The date formula, however, is mainly a preface to the description of the vision of Yahweh as king on a throne (vv. 1–4). That the "hem of his robe" ("train" in the RSV) filled the temple suggests that the prophet stands at the entrance to the sacred precincts, and probably that the ark of the covenant was understood as the symbolic throne of Yahweh. Other aspects of temple worship are the antiphonal hymn of praise sung by the seraphim and the fact that the "house"—that is, the temple—was filled with smoke, probably from offerings. The seraphim who attend the Lord must cover both their "feet" (a euphemism for their nakedness) and their faces because no one can see God directly and live.

Isaiah responds to the scene with a cry of woe (v. 5) similar to a confession of sin and an expression of mourning for both himself and his people. Confronted with the presence of the Lord, he knows that he is unclean, although by the priestly criteria he would have been judged ritually clean before he approached the temple. In reaction to his confession, one of the seraphim performs a ritual of purification combining word and deed. He touches Isaiah's mouth with a coal from the altar and pronounces that his guilt is removed and his sin forgiven. This ritual parallels those in the vocation reports of both Jeremiah and Ezekiel in that all of them concern the mouth of the ones called to speak for God.

The vision report reaches a climax when the prophet overhears Yahweh asking the heavenly court whom he shall send, and the prophet steps forward (v. 8). The remainder of the chapter consists of the Lord's terrible commission to the prophet to bring a word of total judgment, interrupted only by the prophet's unsuccessful prayer of intercession.

Viewed in the context of other vocation reports, the purpose of this account becomes clear. The authority of the prophets to speak frequently was challenged (see Amos 7:10–17), especially if their message was one of judgment. Because prophets had no "official" standing comparable to that of, for example, priests, their right to speak in the name of the Lord was open to question. The vocation reports were their responses. Because of a call from God, the prophet was not only entitled to speak but compelled to do so. In the case of Isaiah 6, the prophet specifically justifies his harsh message by reporting his vocation.

A great many features of this passage cry out for proclamation. There is first of all the emphasis upon the sacred, including its cultic dimensions. One should therefore not drive a wedge between the prophetic and the priestly. It is in the temple that Isaiah experiences the awe-inspiring presence of the Lord, is aware of his uncleanness, and is purified. The holiness of God—the radical difference between the Divine and the human—is a persistent theme in the words of Isaiah. Second, there is the call itself and the prophet's response. God does not address Isaiah directly, but the one purified by the divine messenger is able to hear the call and accept the commission. Note the sequence: Encounter with the presence of God, confession, purification, overhearing, and then acceptance of the commission. Third, there is the theme of the effectiveness of the word of God and of the word of God through human expression. As with Jeremiah, the prophet is empowered with words that will prevent repentance and will bring judgment. Are there any modern words that have—or are believed to have—such power?

Psalm 138

This psalm may be subdivided into three parts. Verses 1–3 thank and praise God; verses 4–6 extol the grace and glory of God and their impact on the rulers of the world; and verses 7–8 express trust in God.

The general tone of the psalm clearly identifies it as a thanksgiving. It differs, however, from most thanksgiving psalms in two ways: (1) there is no description of the trouble or the distress from which the person was rescued (see v. 3, which refers to an appeal to God at an earlier time of distress), and (2) the psalm is addressed directly to the Deity throughout (v. 8a is possibly an exception), whereas most thanksgivings are addressed to a human audience.

The person offering thanks in the original usage of this psalm was probably the king. This is suggested by the references to the kings of the earth in verse 4 who hear the words of Yahweh's mouth, perhaps words spoken by the Judean king. Also, the king was especially the man of God's right hand (v. 7; see Ps. 110:1).

Several elements in the psalm call for elucidation:

1. The reference to "before the gods" (v. 1) could mean one of several things. Ancient translations read "before the angels," "before kings," or "before judges." If the reference is to pagan gods, then the worshiper could be saying no more than, "I sing your praise in an alien culture." If the reference is to heavenly beings (see Pss. 29:1; 82:1), then the phrase could denote worship before the heavenly council of God.

2. To bow down toward the temple does not imply that the worshiper is in some foreign land or away from Jerusalem. This could be a reference to worship or activity at the temple gate, near the main altar, or in the temple courtyard.

3. The lowly may not refer to a class—the poor, the downtrodden, or others in similar conditions—but could be a self-designation, even of a king—the lowly over against the Divine.

4. The verb translated "to perceive" in verse 6b may mean, on the basis of an Arabic parallel, "to humble." Thus "the haughty he humbles from afar."

The statement of trust in verses 7–8 gives expression to a serene confidence—almost. Verse 8c still resorts to petition even after the statement of assurance. Note that the psalm does not assume that life will be free of distress and problems but only that God will preserve one through them all. Trouble and enemies are the givens in life; grace and preservation to endure and overcome them are the sustaining gifts.

1 Corinthians 15:1–11

Because this passage served as one option for the epistolary reading for Easter, Year B, we provided there some basic observations about its overall structure and some of its prominent motifs. We will not repeat those observations here.

One of the chief difficulties we face in preaching on this text during the season of Epiphany is our tendency to think of it almost exclusively as an Easter text, suitable for proclamation only in that liturgical context. But even if we hear more loudly the claim that "he was raised on the third day" (v. 4), we do well to remember that in one sense every Sunday is a celebration of the Easter faith.

But there is another approach to preaching this text in the context of Epiphany. In some traditions, the period after the Epiphany has been a time when the church has thought about mission in ways that are all too humanistic in their orientation. Today's text seriously challenges this stress on human agency and reminds us of the dramatic initiative God takes in confronting us with the claims of the gospel.

We first observe that by referring to the gospel as what the church has received (vv. 1 and 3), Paul readily acknowledges that his gospel preceded him in time, that it was something he inherited from his predecessors in the faith. He did not create it; he received it as a gift of grace (vv. 10–11). Standing within the succession of faithful witnesses beginning with Cephas and the Twelve (vv. 5–8), Paul sees himself as a faithful tradent who transmits the sacred message. He is all too aware of the distance that stretches between himself and the sacred tradition he had received, and it is a distance he understands and respects (1 Cor. 7:10, 12, 25, 40; 9:14; 11:23; 14:37; 1 Thess. 2:13).

Thinking of the passage this way reminds us that even though the gospel may have become our own story, it is not something we create. It was here before we were and possesses its own existence apart from us. As the dialectical theologians have reminded us, the word of God precedes us and comes from beyond us. For all its immediacy, the gospel is not our own. We can receive it and in turn transmit it, but only God sees fit to give it to us in the first place.

This same emphasis is seen in verses 5–8, where Paul rehearses the "appearances" of the risen Lord to the succession of witnesses. Quite often, the questions we bring to this part of the text arise from our concern with historicity. We find ourselves asking about the nature of the risen Lord's body, the form in which the disciples saw him or experienced him. From there, we tend to ask about modes of validation and verification. Although these questions are legitimate in their own right, they are not the only questions worth asking. Of central importance here is the fundamental truth-claim being made: the disciples did not discover the Easter faith; it was revealed to them. It came to them from without, not from within, and it continued to be revealed beyond Easter morning into Paul's own time. This suggests that it can neither be measured nor contained by time and history in any ordinary sense. Put simply, this text proclaims a basic Christian truth: the Easter faith creates disciples; disciples do not create the Easter faith.

Also worth observing is how Paul conceives the gospel as providing us a place to stand, as that "in which also [we] stand, through which [we] are being saved" (vv. 1–2). When we acknowledge the gospel as that which anchors our own existential identity, we acknowledge its prior claim on us. The faith of the gospel is the Christian's compass, and we are continually encouraged to establish our angle of vision toward life from its perspective (Rom. 11:20; 1 Cor. 10:12; 16:13; 2 Cor. 1:24; 1 Thess. 3:8). It becomes the window through which we look at life. By finding our center of gravity within the gospel, we experience there God's saving power that both gives us salvation and leads us to salvation (Rom. 1:16; 10:9; 1 Cor. 1:18, 24). When Paul says, "By the grace of God I am what I am" (v. 10), he is not merely telling us who he is but also where he stands.

Approached this way, today's epistolary text enables us to bear witness to the gospel as the gift God bestows, the revelation God unfolds, and the work God does.

Luke 5:1–11

Today is one of those extraordinary Sundays on which all the readings speak with a single voice. Isaiah has the vision of God, is struck by his own unworthiness, but nevertheless is sent to preach. Paul sees the risen Lord, realizes he is unfit to be called an apostle because he persecuted the church, but by God's grace he works harder than any of the others. And in Luke 5:1–11, Simon Peter gets a glimpse of the power and knowledge of Christ, falls before him in the profound grip of his own sinfulness, but even so, is called by Christ to become a fisher of men.

Our text, Luke's version of the call of the first disciples, is clearly an Epiphany story. Both Matthew and Mark tell of Jesus preaching from a boat in order to get away from a pressing crowd (Matt. 13:1–2; Mark 4:1), and they both record the call of the first disciples from the life of fishing on the Sea of Galilee (Gennesaret in Luke). However, Mark (1:16–20) and Matthew after him (4:18–22) place the event early, making it all the more remarkable, because the backdrop for their call consists only of a general statement about Jesus coming into Galilee preaching. In Luke, however, the call comes after Jesus' ministry in Nazareth (4:16–30), an exorcism in a synagogue in Capernaum (4:31–37), healing Simon's mother-in-law (4:38–39), many healings and exorcisms in that city (4:40–41), preaching tours (4:42–44), and such a growing popularity (4:37) that the crowds were pressing against him (5:1). This location of the story allows Luke to say two things about Jesus calling disciples.

1. His own success made helpers necessary, a fact that became even more evident later in the sending out of the seventy (10:1–2). The work of Jesus is thus prophetic of the church's successful spread of the gospel as Luke reports in Acts, a fact that also required the enlisting of more workers (Acts 11:19–26).

2. The disciples Jesus calls are responding to a Jesus who has demonstrated power to which they are witnesses. They follow a transcendent and compelling Christ in Luke, not a new preacher of an approaching kingdom, as in Mark and Matthew.

In this sense, then, Luke's account is closer to that of John (21:1–23), which is a resurrection appearance narrative and therefore, not surprisingly, an Epiphany narrative. In John also the story focuses on Simon Peter, even though other disciples are present. In Luke 5:1–11, Simon Peter appears for the first time in this Gospel, even though he is mentioned by name in the earlier account of Jesus healing his mother-in-law (4:38–39). The story so thoroughly centers on Simon that his partners are unnamed and unnumbered until the end of the story. James and John are then named (v. 10), but not Andrew, Peter's brother. The remarkable catch of fish recalls the stories of miraculous provisions in the Elijah-Elisha stories (1 Kings 17; 2 Kings 4:1–7, 38–41, 42–44), the prophets who have already proven to be a favorite resource for Luke (4:22–30). Luke's comfort with miracle stories—quite unlike Paul—is well known. However, even he is aware of the ambiguous role of miracles in the generation of faith and in their power to prompt discipleship (11:14–19). He also knows that non-Christians can work wonders (11:19; Acts 8:9–11). However, for Luke, the power of God not only characterized the ministry of Jesus but also was essential in the mission and witness of the church (Acts 1:8; 4:33).

Before the demonstrated power and knowledge of Jesus, however, the response of Peter is not one of powerlessness or ignorance. (Why could we not do it? Why did we not know where the fish were?) Simon's skill as a fisherman is not the issue; rather, it is Simon's sin as a human being unworthy to be in the presence of the Lord. His sin does not disqualify him, however; for the same power that caused him to fall on his knees now lifts Simon into Jesus' service—but not as a better fisherman; rather, as one who will be "catching people" (v. 10). The word translated "catch" meant "to take alive in the sense of rescuing from death." The prominence to which Simon Peter later rose surely never erased from his memory·the day he knelt in a smelly fishing boat at the feet of Jesus.

Sixth Sunday After the Epiphany

Jeremiah 17:5–10;
Psalm 1;
1 Corinthians 15:12–20;
Luke 6:17–26

The readings from Luke and 1 Corinthians continue, each raising different issues. Luke 6:17–26 begins the Sermon on the Plain with a series of blessings and woes, in part parallel to the Beatitudes (Matt. 5:3ff.). Both the Old Testament lection and the responsorial psalm use the same kind of expressions as in Luke to stress the contrast between the righteous and the unrighteous, between weal and woe. First Corinthians 15:12–20 turns our attention to Paul's argument concerning belief in the resurrection. It does to some extent suggest some of the eschatological tone of the Gospel reading.

Jeremiah 17:5–10

The authorship and historical circumstances of Jeremiah 17:5–10 are uncertain. The chapter as a whole does not develop a consistent theme but includes a variety of materials, some of which (vv. 14–18 in particular) correspond to Jeremiah's thought and language. The concern with the heart in verses 9–10 is consistent with Jeremiah's perspective. The wisdom sayings of verses 5–8 are unusual in Jeremiah, but there is nothing in them that is explicitly contrary to the prophet's views.

Our reading contains two major parts, verses 5–8 and 9–10. The first part begins with an introductory messenger formula, "Thus says the LORD," but what follows is neither prophetic address nor divine speech; the Lord is spoken of in the third person. What follows the introduction is a neatly balanced and concise wisdom speech, extended sayings giving the two sides of a coin. The first (vv. 5–6) points out that "those who trust in mere mortals," who turn away from the Lord, are cursed, and then compares them to a shrub in the desert. The second (vv. 7–8) gives the antithesis. Those who trust in the Lord are blessed, like a tree planted by the water. The parallels of this section to Psalm 1—both in form and contents—are strong and obvious. The view of most scholars that Psalm 1 is later than and dependent upon this passage is probably correct.

The second section (vv. 9–10) also contains two parts: the first, a proverbial-like saying on the human heart as "devious" and incomprehensible; the second, a divine speech in which Yahweh affirms that he knows the heart and gives to everyone according to his or her ways.

A number of themes or issues present themselves for homiletical reflection:

1. As in other Old Testament prophetic and wisdom literature from the time of Jeremiah onward, the focus is upon the inner life of the individual. God is concerned with the heart—the thoughts and beliefs of the person. Note, however, that the passage concludes by pointing out that the Lord looks also "to the fruit of their doings" (v. 10), to what emerges from that inner life.

2. Perhaps the key word in this text is "trust" (vv. 5, 7). This trust does not mean belief in propositions, but commitment, devotion. The verb must have an object, and that is the decisive point—to trust in what is human or to trust in God, that is the question.

3. The passage raises the question of divine retribution, as does the reading from Luke. *Does* God give to all people according to what they have done? One who preaches on such texts is obligated in the first instance to let the text have its say. Here that would include reflection in the context of verses 5–8 as well, which suggests that those who trust in what is human and those who trust in God have their reward. To do the one is to live an arid life; to do the other is to live the abundant life. Having examined the perspective of the text, then one might reflect on the extent to which the viewpoint corresponds to experience and to the rest of the biblical canon.

Psalm 1

Psalm 1, which opens the Psalter, might just as well be an introduction to the Pentateuch, for it focuses on legal piety and Torah observance. The psalm opens in beatitude form, although the actual content of the psalm expands such a form beyond its bounds and becomes a poem of admonition.

The psalm profiles two types of persons—the righteous and the wicked—and thus reflects a pattern frequently found in the Old Testament. Obviously, the intention of the text was to encourage emulation of the righteous and to discourage imitation of the wicked. As such, the psalm is a sharp call for commitment to a certain pattern of life, a pattern based on study and meditation on the Torah and observance of its commandments.

In such depictions of opposite attitudes to life there is no neutral ground; there are no neutral corners. The two ways lead in two different directions, and one cannot walk in both paths. The decision for Torah is the decision to take upon oneself the shield and protection, the ordering and regulation, of the Torah. To refuse Torah is to choose chaos, impermanence, the lack of a mooring for life.

In depicting the righteous person, the psalm does so in a series of negative characteristics (v. 1). The righteous person does not follow the counsel of the wicked, does not take the path of sinners or join the company of the insolent. The positive description (v. 2) describes the righteous as making the law a fundamental concern of life, an object of meditation day and night.

Verse 3 may be read as the promise conditional upon the Torah piety described in verse 2. The righteous person becomes like a tree—fruitful, productive, predictable.

The description of the wicked, on the other hand, presents them as unstable, insecure, open to the whims and winds of the moment, carrying in themselves no weight of character (v. 4). Thus sinners, or the wicked, will be unable to stand in judgment; that is, they will be either unable to serve as judges and participants in legal suits or else cannot survive the judgment of their (righteous) peers.

Finally, the two ways are summarized. The way of the righteous God knows (cherishes, upholds, aids), but the way of the wicked is on its own—doomed, perishing, headed for chaos.

1 Corinthians 15:12–20

There can be no doubt that in rehearsing the outlines of the early Christian kerygma in last week's epistolary reading, Paul is operating at the most elementary level. But he begins at ground level purposely: the Easter faith is the fundamental axiom of Christian preaching. There the story begins and from there it moves both backward and forward.

Today's text succinctly states the most basic Christian assumption: "Now if Christ is proclaimed as raised from the dead . . ." (v. 12). Even though this is an "if clause," its content is assumed to be real. With this claim, we are at the fulcrum of the Christian faith, for on this everything else turns.

We are told that some in the church were saying, "there is no resurrection of the dead" (v. 12). Paul may have been astonished that some were denying such a cardinal Pharisaic principle, but he doesn't for a moment take it lightly. What precisely they found incredible is not at all clear, but there are several possibilities.

First, they may have simply claimed that *there is no life after death*—a position advocated in both Jewish and non-Jewish traditions. Sadducees were the most notable example of the former (cf. Matt. 22:23–33 and parallels), the Epicureans of the latter.

A second possibility is that they said that *there is no resurrection of the body*. One well-established position in Greco-Roman thought held that the soul is imprisoned in the body and longs for escape. If the body is thus seen as a tomb, to think of a raised or revivified body is not an especially pleasant prospect. It is one thing to be entombed for a lifetime, but who wants eternal entombment? If some held to this more philosophically informed view of the body, it is not surprising that they would have found it difficult to believe in a resurrection of the physical body (cf. v. 35).

As a third option, they may have claimed that *there is no future resurrection*. There is evidence that some early Christians believed "that the resurrection has already taken place" (2 Tim. 2:18), which probably means that they conceived of resurrection not so much as a future event but as a present reality—a form of existence that could be experienced here and now in the present. This view is known to have existed in certain Gnostic circles in the second century, and some form of it may have occurred as early as the New Testament period (cf. 1 Cor. 4:8–9).

Whether any of these views was held by Paul's readers is hard to say, but he pushes them to think through the implications of their position. Arguing in the form of *reductio ad absurdum*, he insists that if they are right three things must follow:

1. Christ has not been raised (vv. 13, 16). His logic here is straightforward: it is impossible to deny resurrection in principle and affirm the resurrection of Christ in particular. Here he contends that they cannot have it both ways: they cannot affirm the resurrection of one individual (Christ) and deny the resurrection of every other individual (all humanity). This sounds, of course, like they had no doubts about Christ's resurrection, only about their own, as if they regarded Christ as a special case. But for Paul Christ's resurrection and that of everyone else stand or fall together.

2. Paul's preaching is in vain (v. 14–15). Because the Easter faith was the cornerstone of Paul's gospel, to deny the possibility of resurrection would not only undercut his preaching but render him a false witness "misrepresenting God." Their position threatens his personal integrity.

3. The church's faith is in vain (v. 14). Here Paul appeals to their own experience of the Easter faith as something they regard as a given. He says, in effect: "You are a community of the Easter faith. Your very being is predicated on belief in the resurrection of Christ. Your own experience attests to this. You cannot deny what you know and have experienced. To disallow resurrection in principle is to call into question your own existence." To do so, he insists, means that "your faith is futile and you are still in your sins" (v. 17). Moreover, they would have to despair over their fellow Christians who had already died with false hopes.

This line of reasoning, where Paul appeals to their own experience, may appear odd, even unconvincing, to us because it seems to beg the question. Yet for Paul, Christian existence had such palpable, undeniable concreteness that it could function as the fulcrum of his argument.

Paul finds it so incredible to grant their point that he concludes with a strong reaffirmation of faith: "But in fact Christ has been raised from the dead, the first fruits of those who have died" (v. 20). Here we are near the heart of the gospel he preaches (Rom. 8:11; 1 Cor. 6:14; 2 Cor. 4:4; Gal. 1:1). By identifying Christ as the "first fruits" (15:23; Col. 1:18; Acts 3:15; 26:23; 1 Thess. 4:13), he asserts the continuity between Christ's own resurrection and our own.

The force of today's epistolary text is clear: our destiny is indissolubly linked with the destiny of Christ. At the heart of Christian faith is a claim so central that our identity as a community of the Easter faith depends on it.

Luke 6:17–26

The texts for today join in describing the conditions of those living under God's favor (blessing) and those under God's disfavor (curse or woe). On the lips of members of the faith community addressing one another, a blessing is a celebration of someone's pleasant and happy circumstance, and a curse or woe is a lament over someone's plight. However, when spoken by God or by one who speaks for God, blessings and woes are more than descriptive; they are pronouncements that declare in effect that those conditions will prevail. On the lips of Jesus Christ, therefore, the blessings and the woes of our Gospel lection can be taken as the "official" proclamation of the way life will be among the people of God. In other words, as an Epiphany text, Luke 6:17–26 does more than suggest how to be happy, not sad. In fact, the passage does not contain exhortations, as though these are conditions that are the result of effort, and the preacher will want to guard against slipping into phrases such as "We ought to be hungry now" or "Let us not laugh now lest we later weep and mourn." Blessings and woes are to be heard with the assurance that they are God's word to us, and God will implement them.

It is a bit difficult to follow the sequence of events in Luke here, given the changes from Mark's order and from Matthew's location of the sermon which we know in that Gospel as the Sermon on the Mount. Luke's order of calling the Twelve (6:12–16) and healing the crowds (6:17–19) is a reversal of Mark (3:7–19). Luke also shifts the scene from the sea (Mark 3:7) to a level place (6:17). Although the sermon beginning at verse 20 is later in Luke than in Matthew, there are similarities in location. Matthew places his version of the sermon after the call of four disciples and a general statement about Jesus' ministry (4:18–25), whereas Luke sets his version after the call of twelve disciples and a general statement about Jesus' ministry (6:12–19). Luke's sermon is but one-fourth the length of Matthew's, but it is clear that, given the differences appropriate to their own views and reader needs, both writers are working with much the same material.

What accents in this text, far more familiar to the church in its Matthean parallel, impress themselves upon the reader? First, there seems to be a theological use of geography. The mountain is the place for prayer to God and for choosing those "whom he named apostles" (v. 13), a designation for the Twelve that is very important to Luke. Being selected on the mountain and in prayer, they are a special group, as Acts 1 bears out. Having chosen the twelve leaders (a new Israel?), Jesus now moves to the plain below with all the people. With them he identifies, as he did at his baptism (3:21). Only after coming off the mountain to the people and having healed them all (v. 19) does Jesus preach this "inaugural" sermon on life in the kingdom.

The sermon opens with four beatitudes and four woes reminiscent of the blessings and curses set before Israel (Deut. 11:26, 28). Luke's beatitudes are not only briefer than Matthew's (5:3–11); they also pronounce favor upon persons who are entirely different. All four beatitudes bless the deprived: the poor, the hungry, those who weep, and those despised and rejected. This is not surprising, given Luke's special attention to the poor, the captive, the oppressed, the wounded, the lame, the halt, and the blind (4:18–19; 14:12–14). The four woes are pronounced on those whose lives are the very opposite of the blessed: the rich, the full, the laughing, and the socially accepted. This contrast, combined with that of setting *now* over against the future, puts the entire passage in an eschatological frame of reference. As Luke stated as early as the "Magnificat" (1:46–55), the arrival of the kingdom in its fullness will be marked by a complete reversal in the fortunes of the rich and poor, the powerful and the powerless, the full and the empty.

To say that Luke here contrasts present and future is not to say that he is urging disciples to sit and wait for that blessed future. Christ's presence has already launched the reign of God's love and care. As Jesus said in the synagogue at Nazareth, "*Today* this scripture has been fulfilled" (4:21). The Messiah who will come *has come*, and it continues to be "today" among the followers of Jesus.

Seventh Sunday After the Epiphany

Genesis 45:3–11, 15;
Psalm 37:1–11, 39–40;
1 Corinthians 15:35–38, 42–50;
Luke 6:27–38

The Old Testament text doubtless was selected because it reinforces the main concerns of the Gospel lection from Luke 6:27–38, in which Jesus teaches that one should love one's enemies. Joseph, in his forgiveness of his brothers, becomes an example of such love, of lending without thought of return. Psalm 37:1–11, 39–40 responds to a major theme of the reading from Genesis, God's providential care. The confident tone in the psalm may be heard to support Paul's faith in the resurrection expressed in 1 Corinthians 15:35–38, 42–50.

Genesis 45:3–11, 15

Genesis 45:1–15, from which our reading is taken, is a key episode in the Joseph story (Gen. 37, 39–50). In fact, this account of Joseph's revelation of his identity to his brothers is the climax of the narrative, the point at which the main tensions of the plot are resolved and the purpose of the events disclosed. That purpose is not easy to understand without considering this episode in its larger context.

The Joseph story, although similar in some respects to the other narratives in Genesis, is quite distinctive. The fact that it is a long, highly developed story, with a coherent plot from beginning to end, has led many scholars to compare it to the modern short story or novella. There is serious interest in human personalities and emotions, and such subtle points as the awareness that foreigners may need to communicate through translators, carefully constructed subplots, and literary techniques such as foreshadowing. Moreover, unlike most of the other narratives in Genesis, this account shows the differences between the characters in their youth and their maturity. One needs only to compare the Joseph of our passage with the one of Genesis 37. A spoiled brat has become a generous, compassionate, and mature man. The reader can also sense that the brothers are bent with age and with the effects of their struggles, and that they still bear the effects of their crime against Joseph.

Although the story as a whole is a unity, it bears the marks of the combination of the older pentateuchal sources, J and E. Careful reading of our passage will reveal some evidence of the combination. It is not clear, for example, whether Joseph's display of emotion was private or heard by the Egyptians. Also, he twice tells the brothers who he is, and—perhaps indicating that something has dropped out of the narrative—he asks if his father is still alive (v. 3) but proceeds to give instructions to bring him to Egypt without hearing the answer.

The brothers, jealous of Joseph, had sold him into slavery, where he had not only survived but prospered. His special talents and skills had taken him, as he says, to the second highest office in Egypt. (The language of 45:8 and elsewhere indicates that the narrator sees him as the Grand Vizer.) The entire region, including Egypt, is suffering the period of famine foreseen by Joseph, so the brothers come looking for food. The tension had been allowed to grow: how will the conflict be resolved? Our text shows the answer and also makes it clear that the plot—the development of the story—had actually been taking place on a different level.

The passage before us—except for verses 3b and 14–15—is a speech by Joseph. It is filled with the emotion of the reunion. When Joseph says who he is, the brothers are "dumbfounded" (NEB) by fear and unbelief. Will Joseph, who now is so powerful, repay them with what they did to him? The brothers quickly learn what we, the readers, know already—that he will forgive them. But significantly, Joseph gives what amounts to a theological explanation for his attitude and his actions: "God sent me before you to preserve life. . . . God sent me before you to preserve for you a remnant on earth" (vv. 5, 7). That is the point of the narrative as a whole, expressed somewhat more comprehensively in Genesis 50:20: "Even though you intended to do harm to me, God intended it for good, in order to preserve a numerous people, as he is doing today."

Thus the movement of events, so transparent on the human level, is the expression of a gracious divine purpose, which only in the end becomes plain. The two main themes of the passage then come together. One who understands and has confidence in God's providential care is able to love even enemies. Who knows, God may be in the process of using the wrath of human beings to praise him?

Psalm 37:1–11, 39–40

Psalm 37, which reads in many ways like a miniature version of the Book of Proverbs, contains numerous parallels to the Gospel lesson from Luke. Both are collections of sayings that admonish and invite one to try to follow a certain life-style.

Several assumptions may be seen as foundational pillars undergirding the teachings of the psalm.

1. The world and life are assumed to be reasonably well ordered and to make sense if understood in proper perspective. This seems reflected in the well-ordered form of the poem itself—an alphabetic composition.

2. A strong and necessary interrelationship is presumed to exist between actions and results, between deeds and consequences. That is, a particular type of pattern or action is assumed to lead to predictable results.

3. What appears to contradict this view of the world and behavior, such as the success of the wicked or the triumph of the unrighteous, is only a temporary state, an illusory condition that will soon pass.

4. When the world and human society do not seem to conform to the pattern, in that temporary disruption of the normal state of affairs, one should remain faithful and endure the momentary absence of proper conditions.

5. Ultimately, the good, the right, the proper will be rewarded—"the meek shall inherit the land" (v. 11*a*) and prosperity will be the reward of the diligent.

Various ways of speaking of the human situation and of the proper conduct of life are found in these opening verses of the psalm. Verses 1–2 contain two prohibitions followed by the motivation or reason, in this case the reason one should not act a certain way. Verses 8–9 contain two imperatives followed by the reason one should act a particular way. Verses 10–11 contrasts two consequences of behavior patterns.

Let us look at some of the practical advice offered in this psalm. First, throughout the psalm one is warned against jealousy and the agitation of life that comes from being obsessed with the success of others. "Do not fret" occurs several times (vv. 1, 7, 8). The resentment of others that underlies jealousy and anger is seen as self-defeating and as ultimately a denial of faith in God's justice. Fretting tends only to produce evil (v. 8*b*). Second, being jealous, especially of the wicked and wrongdoers, is bad because their success is doomed and their fate foretold. Third, the best attitude in life is one that trusts in God, does good, and waits patiently. Fourth, those who are not given to anger, not overcome by wrath, and not "torn-up" over others' status—that is, the meek—will possess the land and enjoy its fruits.

This psalm must have offered encouragement and provided sound advice to those in ancient Judah who may have doubted the value of their commitments in the light of the success of the wrongdoers. At the same time, it held out hope for a change for the better and affirmed the age-old conviction that sowing and harvesting are intimately related in spite of all evidence to the contrary.

The final verses of the psalm (vv. 39–40) affirm that God saves the righteous from trouble and the wicked, and serves as a sure refuge in times of uncertainty.

1 Corinthians 15:35–38, 42–50

In what form will we experience resurrection life? It is a question Christians have asked in every age, and one they continue to ask for it addresses one of the central mysteries of the faith. The question could hardly be ignored in chapter 15, Paul's most extensive and systematic treatment of the question of the resurrection of the dead.

The question is posed here on the lips of an imaginary interlocutor. The style of Paul's treatment is diatribal, which suggests that it is an objection or question Paul wants to address rather than an actual question being raised in the Corinthian church—not that it is merely a hypothetical question, however. As phrased in our text, the question runs, "How are the dead raised? With what kind of body do they come?" (v. 35).

The background that gives rise to this set of questions is probably one that drew a sharp distinction between the body and the soul. In Greek thought, it was common to believe in the immortality of the soul. The soul could easily be conceived as having an eternal existence, without beginning or end in time. As such, it could come to inhabit the body, and in some instances it was felt that this cycle could occur several times, or become reincarnated in different bodily forms. The physical body was thus viewed as a temporal dwelling with little significance in comparison with the eternal soul. Because the body consisted of physical matter, like the rest of earthly existence, it was difficult for many Greeks, and some Jews, to conceive of its being resurrected. Once the living body becomes a corpse, how can we speak of its being raised? Should we envision life being breathed back into the corpse so that the person is revivified and literally lifted up into the heavens? These are questions many Greeks would ask about the Christian teaching of resurrection.

In the first part of today's epistolary lection, Paul addresses these questions by citing an example from nature, a common form of illustration in diatribal teaching. For him, the process of sowing a grain of wheat into the ground and eventually emerging as a stalk of wheat perfectly illustrated the Christian understanding of resurrection. This metaphor may have even originated with Jesus himself (John 12:24). The grain of wheat provided a helpful image in at least three respects.

First, it illustrated that in nature we see one form of existence (seed) transformed into another form of existence (plant). In appearance, form, and substance, each form differs radically from the other, and yet there is continuity between the two forms. Even in its transformed state, the stalk of wheat is still the same entity as the grain of wheat. In spite of the different forms, the stalk and the grain are a single organism.

Second, the change between the forms is brought about by a "death." Before the transformation can occur, the seed must be buried in the ground. There it has the germ of life within it, but this life is only potential. It does not, and cannot, blossom forth into full life until it "dies." The grain of wheat thus shows how something living, by dying, can be transformed from one mode of existence into another mode of existence. So understood, death is not the end of life, but a point of transition from one form of live into another.

Third, it is a process under the control of God (v. 38). It was a common assumption in antiquity that the cycles of nature occurred under divine auspices, however differently God may have been viewed. In our text, of course, it is the Genesis creation story that informs Paul's own view (Gen. 1:11–12). The important point is this: in nature various forms of life do not undergo change willy-nilly, but occur according to a divinely ordered pattern.

In the second part of today's lection (vv. 42–50), Paul uses the metaphor of the grain of wheat to illustrate how our form of existence is transformed in the resurrection. It may help to summarize his remarks by noting the ways he envisions the two different modes of existence:

it is sown:	it is raised:
perishable	imperishable
in dishonor	in glory
in weakness	in power
a physical body	a spiritual body
a man of dust	a man from heaven

As with the grain of wheat, so can our own existence be conceived as having two different forms: the one we experience this side of death; the other we experience the other side of death. They are radically different because they are of a different order. Yet there is continuity as we move from one form of existence to the other.

But how can we be assured that this is the case? Because, Paul insists, Christ himself has already experienced this change. Here Paul draws on the creation story again as he contrasts "the first man, Adam" with Christ, "the last Adam" (v. 45). They differ in one crucial respect: the first Adam "became a living being," whereas Christ became a "life-giving spirit" (v. 45). The man Adam experienced life at one level, primarily as a recipient of biological life. Christ, the second Adam, through the resurrection came to experience life at a completely different level. As a recipient of resurrection life, or life with a capital "L," he became Life-giver. His existence as exalted Lord is already imperishable, in glory, in power, fully spiritual, and heavenly. As full possessor of resurrection life, this transformed mode of existence, it is fully his to give and ours to receive.

According to our text today, then, resurrection is not at all "unnatural," for it involves a process we witness in nature's own cycle of life. Just as the grain of wheat is a parable of our own life and destiny, so Christ is the first to illustrate its full truth.

Luke 6:27–38

The Gospel lesson continues the teaching of Jesus in the sermon on a level place (6:17), Luke's parallel to Matthew's sermon on the mount (chaps. 5–7). Verses 27–38 follow immediately the blessings and the woes with which the sermon begins (vv. 20–26). Matthew's version of verses 27–38 presents the content in a different order (5:39–42, 44–48; 7:12; 7:1–2). This difference in order—the shifts from plural you, to singular, to plural again (vv. 27–28, 29–30, 32–36)—and the packing of many instructions on diverse and very weighty matters into a very brief span persuade the reader that Luke (and Matthew) draw upon a compilation of teachings rather than a single sermon delivered on a single occasion.

The most noticeable differences between Luke 6:27–38 and the Matthean parallels are two. First, Luke's "he [God] is kind to the ungrateful and the wicked" (v. 35) expresses Matthew's "he [God] makes his sun rise on the evil and on the good, and sends rain on the righteous and on the unrighteous" (5:45). Although in different images, both affirm the radical nature of grace that finds its reason in God and not in the merits of its recipients. Both Matthew and Luke elaborate this theme in parables that portray not only God's graciousness but the offense that is felt by those who regard impartiality as unjust. To the offended in Matthew's parable of vineyard workers, grace says, "Are you envious because I am generous?" (20:15), and to the offended in Luke's parable of the prodigal, grace says, "We had to celebrate and rejoice, because this brother of yours was dead and has come to life; he was lost and has been found" (15:32). The second noticeable difference between Luke and Matthew is that Luke's "Be merciful, just as your Father is merciful" (v. 36) is in Matthew, "Be perfect, therefore, as your heavenly Father is perfect" (5:48). But again, the difference is more apparent than real. If one is not misled into thinking of Matthew's "perfect" as moral flawlessness but rather lets the context provide understanding, then the two statements make the same affirmation about God and offer the same admonition. Of course, lesser differences occur, such as Luke's preference for the term "sinners" (vv. 32–34) while Matthew speaks of tax collectors and Gentiles (5:46–47).

Luke 6:27–38 consists of three units, as the paragraphing in major English translations reflects: verses 27–31, 32–36, 37–38. The first unit lays down the general principle that kingdom people do not reciprocate, do not draw their behavior from that of those who would victimize them. Following the statement of principle are numerous examples of forms of mistreatment: hating, cursing, abusing, striking, stealing, begging. The important point to notice here is that these teachings assume that the readers/listeners are victims, not victimizers. Jesus offered no instruction to followers who would strike, steal, hate, curse, and abuse others, because such is not kingdom behavior. But to those who are vulnerable and likely recipients of the world's abuse, Jesus gave teachings on how not to be a victim: take charge of your life and the situation by taking the initiative in loving, caring, giving. This unit concludes with Luke's version of the Golden Rule (v. 31), found not only here and in Matthew (7:12) but also in Homer, Seneca,

Tobit, 2 Enoch, Philo, and elsewhere. For a principle to be widely embraced and widely stated does not make it any less valid or binding.

The second unit (vv. 32–36) repeats the principle of the first unit; that is, one is not to reciprocate in responding to others. However, the principle was first applied in relation to those who violate us, and here it is applied in relation to those who treat us favorably. In other words, just as one's behavior is not determined by the enemy, neither is it determined by the friend. Christian behavior and attitude are prompted by the God we worship, who does not hate in response to hatred or love in response to love. God does not react; God acts in love and grace toward all, and such is the way of those who are children of the Most High (v. 35).

It follows, then, in the third unit (vv. 37–38), that the children of God do not judge or condemn, but rather give and forgive. One will notice, however, a bit more justice, a bit more reward and punishment, in this unit than in the first two. But even the balanced fairness of "the measure you give will be the measure you get back" (v. 38) is broken by the image of abundant generosity poured out upon those who give. The phrase "into your lap" (v. 38) refers to the large pocket formed by the fold in a robe above the belt. Even this huge pocket will not contain the pressed-down, shaken-together, running-over blessings that come to those who give generously to others.

God is full of grace, and the final work of grace is to make us gracious, too.

Eighth Sunday After the Epiphany

Sirach 27:4–7 or Isaiah 55:10–13;
Psalm 92:1–4, 12–15;
1 Corinthians 15:51–58;
Luke 6:39–49

Both of the Old Testament readings have links with the psalm and with the Gospel lection, but at different points. Both Sirach 27:4–7 and Luke 6:43–45 consider the relationship between a tree and its fruit, although the point of the metaphor is different in each case. The proclamation in Isaiah 55:10–13 that God's word will be effective relates to Luke 6:46–49: those who hear the words of Jesus and acts on them will be like a house with a sound foundation. The imagery of trees and fruitfulness appears in Psalm 92. The continuation of the readings from 1 Corinthians concludes with Paul's thankful affirmations concerning resurrection.

Sirach 27:4–7

For information concerning the authorship, historical circumstances, and the perspective of the Book of Sirach (or Ecclesiasticus), and some observations about wisdom literature in general, see the comments on Sirach 24:1–12 under the readings for the Second Sunday After Christmas Day in this volume.

It is always wise for the preacher to consult more than one modern translation of the assigned or chosen texts. That is especially important when preaching or even reading in worship proverbial literature such as Ecclesiasticus 27:4–7. The original sense of sayings often is particularly difficult to capture in another language because they are so pithy or even enigmatic that the meaning sometimes seems to lie between the lines. Moreover, they make extensive use of images, similes, and metaphors from the original culture, and the translators will have to decide whether to translate the words or to find equivalent images or ideas. The New English Bible and the Jerusalem Bible are both more clear and accurate translations of today's text than is the NRSV.

The broader context of Ecclesiasticus 27:4–7 contains teachings and advice about behavior in society. The passage is surrounded more immediately (26:28–27:29) by teachings about good and bad character, how character is tested by circumstances and how one may recognize it in oneself and others. The poetic instruction immediately before our reading (26:9–27:3) meditates on the temptations that business presents for a person, and urges steadfast and zealous piety as the way to avoid dishonesty and its effects.

Sirach 27:4–7 itself is an artistically composed wisdom speech that employs three comparative sayings (vv. 4–6) to support the concluding instruction (v. 7). Each of the sayings states a conclusion about something that can be observed: the shaken sieve, the potter's kiln, the fruit of a tree. Each then applies its general conclusion to an aspect of human thought or discourse. The first (v. 4) concerns "thoughts" (RSV) or "talk" (JB); the second (v. 5) deals with "reasoning" (RSV), "debate" (NEB), or "conversation" (NRSV, JB); and the third (v. 6) relates a person's "speech" to the "cultivation of his mind" (NRSV) or to one's "character" (NEB).

The concluding instruction (v. 7) gives direct advice and draws a general conclusion. Ben Sirach advises against praising a man until you have heard him "speak" (NRSV, "reason" in RSV), or "in discussion" (NEB). The general conclusion provides the reason for the advice, "for this is the way people are tested" (NRSV). On the surface the instruction is advice for evaluating one's associates, but it also means to encourage a certain behavior. One should work on the ability to reason, to carry on thoughtful discussion, for that is a test of character.

In preaching on this text one may want to stress the importance of the mind, human reasoning, and rational communication. There may be a tendency to treat such considerations as strictly individualistic. However, not only civilization but any humane society is founded upon the use of reason, careful communication, and even lively debate. It is through the use of such capacities that prejudices and preconceptions are challenged. By thoughtful conversation persons know and appreciate one another.

Isaiah 55:10–13

This text concludes the section of the Book of Isaiah (chaps. 40–55) attributed to Second Isaiah, the prophet of the end of the Exile. In some respects the passage parallels the beginning of the work (40:1–11). Both stress the power of the word of God, and both proclaim the good news that God will bring the people out of exile and return them to their land. The words would have been spoken originally in 539 BC, the year before the end of the Babylonian Empire. The first audience was the community in exile.

Our assigned reading is part of the longer discourse that includes all of chapter 55. (Isaiah 55:1–11 is one of the texts assigned for reading during the Easter Vigil.) In language resembling that of a hymn, the chapter consists of admonitions to listen to and believe in the word of God and celebrations of the Lord's word and works. God's grace to the exiles includes food that will satisfy both physical and spiritual needs. The one who seeks the Lord finds life.

Isaiah 55:10–13 consists of two parts, closely related but distinct in terms of both form and contents. In the first part (vv. 10–11), Yahweh is the speaker, continuing the previous discourse. In the second part (vv. 12–13), the prophet is the speaker.

Verses 10–11 give reasons for following the exhortations of verses 6–7: "Seek the LORD. . . ." The "For" of verse 10 parallels those of verses 8 and 9. This third reason is in the form of an extended comparison between water from heaven—rain and snow—with its effects (v. 10) and the word of the Lord (v. 11). Just as the rain and snow bring about growth, seeds, and bread, so the word of the Lord is effective, accomplishing what the Lord intends. God accomplishes his will through the word, as in Genesis 1 and as in the prophetic announcements.

Verses 12–13 begin with another "For," which may give yet another set of reasons for seeking the Lord. The verses contain proclamations of salvation concerning the exiles and their future. When they go out—from Babylon—in joy and are led in peace, nature itself will join in the celebration. Second Isaiah's poetry is rich in the imagery of creation because of his sense of the cosmic scope of God's work. The thornbush and the brier will be replaced by the cypress and the myrtle. The only point not clear in the concluding verse is the antecedent of the "it" that will be the memorial and sign. It could refer to the people or to the saving event itself, the going out in joy and peace. Salvation, or those saved, will be a perpetual sign, calling to mind the Lord of Israel.

The purpose of this passage is the proclamation of good news. It means to evoke in the hearers and readers confidence in God's word and the joyful celebration of hope.

Psalm 92:1–4, 12–15

This psalm, as the superscription suggests, was used in early Jewish worship services as the sabbath psalm. Seven psalms, which actually offer a summary of the basic tenets of Judaism, were sung by the Levites at the main temple services during the week: Psalms 24 (Sunday), 48 (Monday), 82 (Tuesday), 94 (Wednesday), 81 (Thursday), 93 (Friday), and 92 (Saturday). In Psalm 92, the Israelite name for God, Yahweh, occurs seven times (given as the LORD in the NRSV; vv. 1, 4, 5, 8, 9, 13, and 15). This can hardly be coincidental in a psalm intended for use on the seventh day of the week!

The ancient rabbis even suggested that Adam was the author of this psalm and that he sang it on the first sabbath in the Garden of Eden.

This psalm is a thanksgiving that offers thanks for redemption from enemies (vv. 10–11). The first eleven verses are addressed directly to the Deity, whereas verses 12–15, proclamation or preaching, are addressed by the worshiper to a human audience.

Verses 1–4 declare that it is good to offer praise to God, morning and evening. This may be a way of saying that it is good to offer praise "all the time." Or it may reflect the fact that daily sacrifices were offered in the temple in the morning and evening—when music would have accompanied the ritual (v. 3).

Verses 12–15 declare that the righteous, the faithful, are securely planted, firmly anchored, and will flourish and bear fruit even into old age. God is a rock upon whom life's house may be built with secure confidence, and the passing of time does not diminish the care and the products of life. Note the verbs that describe the faithful in verses 12–15: flourish, grow, produce, are always green. In the imagery of the psalm, the faithful do not plant their house: they are planted in God's house; that is, they are a constant feature in temple worship.

Like the reading from Luke, Psalm 92 stresses the reliability, the trustworthiness of God. "The LORD is upright; . . . and there is no unrighteousness in him" (v. 15).

1 Corinthians 15:51–58

This final section of Paul's exposition on the resurrection, or what might be called the Pauline apocalypse, is introduced with the solemn declaration "Listen! I will tell you a mystery!" (v. 51). Against the background of Jewish apocalyptic, this would mean that Paul, one of the "stewards of God's mysteries" (1 Cor. 4:1), is now unveiling the secret of the end time. With an eye to the future, Paul now adopts the stance of the apocalyptic seer (cf. Rev. 1:1–3).

The essence of the Pauline apocalypse is this: "We will not all die, but we will all be changed" (v. 51). At the end time, both the dead and the living will undergo transformation (1 Thess. 4:15–17). Throughout this section, both groups are in view, and it is possible to interpret his remarks accordingly.

For example, verse 53 may be describing the way each group experiences the final transformation. Thus, "this perishable body must put on imperishability" means that those who have already died and whose bodies have experienced corruption will be clothed with a transformed, incorruptible nature suitable for resurrected existence. And, "this mortal body puts on immortality" means that those who are still alive yet destined eventually to die because of their mortal nature will be clothed with an immortal nature suitable for eternal life with God.

In similar fashion, the biblical quotation in verse 55, "Where, O death, is your victory? Where, O death, is your sting?" would appear to state the victory cry of both groups, the dead and the living. To be sure, it is a rough paraphrase and reinterpretation of Hosea 13:14, which reads in Hebrew, "O Death, where are your plagues? O Sheol, where is your destruction?" and in the Septuagint, "Death, where is your judgment? Hades, where is your sting?" In the prophetic context, Hosea's words are words of judgment, warning Israel of impending punishment.

These prophetic words are appropriated by Paul as words of reassurance to both the dead and the living. As in the Old Testament quotation, the questions are addressed to Death personified. Those who have died in Christ, assured that even in death their corruptible nature will be clothed with a new, incorruptible existence, can finally hurl these words at Death, "Where is your victory?" It looked as if Death had won, but in the end time Death has no hold on the dead in Christ. In similar fashion, those who are still alive, who have not yet experienced the sting of death, can also claim victory over Death. Through the resurrection, they are able to bypass death and twit Death, asking, "Where is your sting?" So, it is the dead in Christ who finally shout, "Where, O death, is your victory?" and those who are alive in Christ who shout, "Where, O death, is your sting?" The paraphrase of Isaiah 25:8, "Death has been swallowed up in victory" (v. 54), becomes the ultimate cry of vindication of Christians both dead and alive.

We should note that in this Pauline apocalypse, the transformation to resurrected life is instantaneous: It occurs "in a moment, in the twinkling of an eye, at the last trumpet" (v. 52). Part of this vivid imagery is supplied by the Old Testament, where trumpets were used to summon Israel to worship (Num. 10:1–10; Lev. 23:24; 2 Chron. 7:6; Sirach 50:16), but also to put them on military alert (Num. 10:9; Amos 3:6). Israel was also accustomed to reminders that trumpets would herald the impending punishment to come upon them (Isa. 18:3; Hos. 8:1; Jer. 4:5; 6:1), or that the Day of Yahweh would be ushered in with the sound of trumpets (Joel 2:1; Zeph. 1:16).

The Christian Parousia is envisioned here as the gathering of the elect of God for the Day of Yahweh, but the crucial difference is that God "gives us the victory through our Lord Jesus Christ" (v. 57; 1 John 5:14). What has been accomplished in the work of Christ is that the three mortal enemies—death, sin, and the law—have finally been vanquished (Rom. 7:13, 25).

It is significant that the Pauline apocalypse concludes with a call to steadfast diligence (v. 58). Thinking about the resurrection can all too easily turn into ill-focused musing about the Eschaton. The temptation is to disengage from life and its demands, to lay down our tools and sit with folded arms, gazing expectantly into the heavens. For Paul, this is not an option. The proper way to prepare for the end is to be engaged in productive work for the Lord (cf. Col. 1:23).

Luke 6:39–49

With this lesson we conclude Luke's sermon "on a level place" (6:17). Upon a first reading of verses 39–49, three statements can be made. First, we apparently are dealing with isolated sayings of Jesus that Luke has chosen to put together in this place. That they are isolated is supported by a lack of internal unity in the subject matter and by the fact that Matthew has this material located in a number of settings. Verse 39 is in Matthew 15:14, verse 40 in Matthew 10:24–25, verses 41–42 in Matthew 7:3–5, verses 43–45 in Matthew 7:16–20 and 12:33–35, verse 46 in Matthew 7:21, and verses 47–49 in Matthew 7:24–27. Second, this difference in the location of a saying of Jesus alters the meaning of the saying. For example, the statement that a disciple is not above but rather is like the teacher (v. 40) is in Matthew a warning to the disciples that they can expect the same mistreatment and persecution Jesus received (10:24–25), whereas in Luke's setting, the statement refers to the fact that disciples become like their teachers. If one learns from blind, hypocritical, and judgmental teachers, then one becomes such a person. In other words, choose carefully your teachers. And third, Luke's reason for joining these isolated sayings to form the sermon's conclusion is not evident to the reader. Perhaps some clarity will come from further investigation.

It is helpful in such passages as verses 39–49 to discern lines of thought within the material that will permit division into subunits. Here the yield of four segments seems natural and fruitful: 39–40, 41–42, 43–45, 46–49. Verses 39–40 warn of the kind of leadership that presumes to instruct and guide others in matters that the leader has not personally understood, believed, or embraced, and disciples of such leaders cannot expect to be any different or any better. Like teacher, like pupil. Verses 41–42 use the tragicomical scene of a person with a log in the eye attempting to improve the condition of another whose eye has a speck in it in order to address the problem of moral superiority found in those without the faculty of self-criticism. It is not an uncommon trait in helpers of all kinds to be deceived by the altruism of their efforts to attend to the needs of others ("Friend, let me take out the speck in your eye"). Looking always to others, not self, can be a beautiful veil protecting one from honest soul-searching. Verses 43–45 underscore the inseparable union of what one is and what one does. More specifically, the union is between what one is and what one says: "For it is out of the abundance of the heart that the mouth speaks" (v. 45). One's words, sooner or later, will reveal character just as surely and naturally as the appearance of fruit announces the kind of tree bearing it. And verses 46–49 concludes the entire sermon by joining confession and obedience. The confession of Jesus as Lord (v. 46) was and is, of course, appropriate. Paul's writings show this to have been one of the earliest forms of the Christian confession of faith (Rom. 10:9; Phil. 2:9–11). However, this confession unaccompanied by the obedience implied in such a confession is shallow emotional exuberance that will not hold firm against the inevitable storms that assail the faithful. Luke's storm is the rising of a stream, quite different from Matthew's wind, rain, and flood (7:24–27). Commentators suggest the differences may reflect the differences in climate and weather in the locales of the two writers.

Do these verses reveal an organizing theme, a theme not imposed upon the material but one prompted by the content? Preachers need to be alert to the integrity of a passage, not only to understand it better but also in order to present it to the listeners with clarity. One would not be far afield to identify as an organizing theme Luke's joining of character and influence. The culture in which the New Testament was written looked favorably upon imitation of one's teacher as a primary mode of learning, and modeling behavior by the teacher as a primary responsibility of the vocation. Many Christian texts support Luke here (Acts 20:17–35; 1 Cor. 4:15–17; 11:1; Phil. 3:17; Titus 2:7), as do most congregations. This is not to say imperfections in leaders disqualify them. On the contrary, Luke's point is that blindness to one's own imperfections is the disqualifying factor. The demand is neither for laxity nor rigidity but for honesty in the effort to be obedient to Jesus as Lord.

Ninth Sunday After the Epiphany

1 Kings 8:22–23, 41–43;
Psalm 96:1–9;
Galatians 1:1–12
Luke 7:1–10

Except for the Epistle, all the readings for the day have in common the theme of welcoming outsiders—foreigners—into the faith. Continuing the readings from Luke for the season, the Gospel lection is the story of the healing of the centurion's servant, in which Jesus is heard to marvel at the Roman soldier's faith: ". . . not even in Israel have I found such faith" (v. 9). The Old Testament lesson's selections from the account of Solomon's dedication of the temple conclude with the prayer on behalf of the "foreigner" who will come to that temple. The responsorial psalm is a song of praise, including the invitation to the "families of the peoples" to praise the Lord and to come into his courts (vv. 7–8). The epistolary text is the opening paragraphs from the letter to the Galatians, in which Paul rebukes the hearers for deserting him and the gospel he proclaims, which gospel he received from God.

1 Kings 8:22–23, 41–43

First Kings 8, as the account of Solomon's dedication of the temple in Jerusalem, lies near the heart of what later generations considered most important about Solomon. Foremost among his many building projects was the magnificent temple. The verses assigned for reading on this day come from the king's dedicatory prayer. The prayer had been preceded by the account of the assembly and the installation of the ark of the covenant in the new building (vv. 1–13), and Solomon's address to the assembly (vv. 14–21). After the prayer (vv. 22–53), the king addresses the people again with a sermon (vv. 54–61) and then concludes the ceremony with sacrifices and a feast (vv. 62–66).

Virtually all of the chapter bears the marks of the theology and style of the Book of Deuteronomy and thus stems from the Deuteronomistic Historians who were responsible for collecting and editing the account of Israel's history from the time of Moses to the Babylonian Exile (Deuteronomy through 2 Kings). Although there are numerous older written and oral sources in the work, and there probably was a pre-exilic edition of it, the work as a whole was completed shortly after the last event it reports (2 Kings 25:27–30), during the Babylonian Exile (ca. 560 BC). Consequently, the report of the dedication of the temple was composed for a people who had lost their land and Holy City, and knew that the magnificent temple of Solomon lay in ruins.

Solomon's prayer of dedication is a series of four prayers of petition. The first (vv. 23–26) is a prayer that God confirm the promise to David that one of his sons would always sit on the throne in Jerusalem. The second (vv. 27–30) and fourth (vv. 52–53) are general requests that God hear and respond, and the third (vv. 31–51) contains a series of petitions concerning seven possible future situations.

Our assigned verses contain the narrative beginning and the initial lines of the first prayer (vv. 22–23), and the fifth of the petitions concerning future circumstances (vv. 41–43), the one that expects "foreigners" to come to the temple.

The first verse (v. 22) of the reading, as well as its larger context, invites reflection on prayer, particularly public prayer. Some of the liturgical features are obvious here, and others are not. It is assumed that Israel's kings performed important priestly functions and were a special link between Yahweh and the people. As the temple is dedicated, Solomon is said to be standing before the altar and in the presence of the assembled people, but the precise location is difficult to identify. (The parallel account in 2 Chron. 6:13 has him in the courtyard of the temple on an elevated platform.) The posture of prayer is standing with hands outstretched "to heaven" (cf. Exod. 9:29; Isa. 1:15). In view of the fact that gods, like kings, in the ancient Near East generally are pictured as sitting on thrones, the posture of supplication is to stand with outstretched arms. Note, however, that when the prayers are concluded, Solomon is said to have been kneeling before the altar (8:54).

The initial lines of the prayer itself (v. 23) invite reflection on several matters central to the biblical faith. First, Yahweh, God of Israel, is addressed as incomparable ("no God like you"). This is not an assertion of monotheism, although it comes close. Rather, it parallels the view of the First Commandment ("You shall have no other gods before me," Exod. 20:3). Devotion to their God, rather than the abstract question of the number of the gods, is the central concern for ancient Israel. Second, Israel's God is trustworthy and loyal, "keeping covenant" and "steadfast love" to those who are faithful. These two expressions are virtually synonymous, emphasizing the stability of God's relationship with the covenant people.

The petition in verses 41–43 indicates that ancient Israel's concerns reached beyond boundaries of nation and culture. It is an intercessory prayer on behalf of any "foreigner" who comes to pray in the temple. If Yahweh is incomparable, other peoples will hear and come to worship him. Solomon asks that their prayers be heard. Although stressing the importance of the temple, the petition acknowledges that God's true dwelling place is "in heaven" (v. 43). The goal is that the Lord's "name"—who he is and what he has done—be known to all peoples (v. 43). The Lord does not actually dwell in the temple, but it is called by his name, and is the place where he chooses to "put his name" (Deut. 12:5).

Psalm 96:1–9

This psalm was discussed earlier as one of the readings for Christmas, Proper 1.

Galatians 1:1–12

Because today's epistolary lesson opens the letter to the Galatians, a few introductory remarks are in order.

At least two sets of issues emerge in Galatians—one theological, the other personal. As we will see, they are closely related. Theologically, the fundamental question is soteriological: on what basis are we accepted by God—by faithfully keeping the law or by faithfully hearing the gospel (3:2)? The practical issue had to do with the terms on which Gentiles could be admitted into membership as the people of God—generally, whether they had to live "subject to the law" (4:21; cf. 2:16–21; 3:2–4:7), and specifically, whether they had to undergo circumcision as the required initiation rite (5:2–12; 6:12–15; cf. 2:3, 12). For Paul, it was a question of freedom versus slavery (4:1–11, 21–32; 5:1).

The personal issue centered on the legitimacy of Paul's apostleship. He had been seriously challenged by those who opposed this theological position and who argued for salvation *through* Torah as opposed to salvation *apart from* Torah. For them, Paul's gospel had unduly relaxed the requirements of God. They saw his message of freedom from the law as mere concession to human weakness. In their eyes, Paul's gospel offered an easy solution to the pain of circumcision by simply doing away with it. Construed one way, this was a "people-pleasing" approach calculated to gain popular appeal (1:10). The decisive question, then, was where and how Paul received the authority to preach a message so radically challenging to a well-established interpretation of Torah and an equally well-established way of being religious based on this interpretation.

The fusion of these two issues within the churches of Galatia prompted one of the most severely polemical letters from the hand of Paul. Not only his gospel but his personal integrity was on the line, and at every turn we can see the blood vessels in Paul's enraged eyes. The tone of the letter is bombastic (1:6; 3:1, 3) sarcastic (2:2, 6, 9; 5:12, 15), even desperate (4:11, 19–20). Even in those rare moments when he seeks to be pastoral and conciliatory, his encouragement gives way to stern words of warning and rebuke (5:13–15; 6:11–16). It is a letter written in white-hot heat.

In today's epistolary lection we have the opening words of this letter. The text easily divides into three sections: the opening greeting (vv. 1–5), a solemn warning (vv. 6–10), and a reaffirmation of the divine origin of his gospel (vv. 11–12).

The Greeting (vv. 1–5). Compared with other Pauline greetings, this one is colder and more abrupt. Nothing commendable is said of the Galatians. There is, however, the traditional prayer of grace and peace in their behalf (cf. Rom. 1:7; 1 Cor. 1:3; 2 Cor. 1:2; Eph. 1:2; Phil. 1:2; Col. 1:2).

Even in these opening words, the two central issues of the letter emerge: the source of Paul's apostolic authority (v. 1) and the work of Christ as the sole basis of our deliverance (vv. 3–4). Paul insists that his apostleship is neither humanly initiated nor humanly validated—it is not "by any human authority or human act" (v. 1, REB). On this note, his defense begins (1:11). What he preached he "received . . . through a revelation of Jesus Christ" (1:12), and his prophetic call to preach resulted from the divine intervention of God, who had raised Christ from the dead (v. 1).

The essence of his gospel is stated in the form of a kerygmatic summary (v. 4), which aligns him with well-established orthodox Christianity. It is a move reminiscent of Romans 1:1–6, where he commends himself to an unknown audience by introducing his theological position in thoroughly acceptable terms. Three important elements should be noted: (1) the vicarious death of Christ "who gave himself for our sins" (cf. 2:20; 2 Cor. 5:15; Eph. 5:2, 25; Titus 2:14; 1 Tim. 2:6; also Matt. 20:28); (2) our deliverance "from the present evil age," elsewhere seen to be under the dominion of satanic forces (2 Cor. 4:4; Acts 26:18; also Gal. 4:8–9) and a competing threat against Christian existence (Rom. 12:2; Eph. 5:16; 1 John 5:19); and (3) God as the approving agent of the gospel (cf. Heb. 10:10) to whom all glory is due (Rom. 11:36; Eph. 3:21; Phil. 4:20; 1 Tim. 1:17; 2 Tim. 4:18; Heb. 13:21; 1 Pet. 4:11; 2 Pet. 3:18; Jude 25; Rev. 1:6; 4:11).

The Warning (vv. 6–10). Instead of the usual prayer of thanksgiving offered on behalf of his readers (cf. Rom. 1:8–17; 1 Cor. 1:4–9; Phil. 1:3–11), the opening greeting here is followed by this stern warning. By the absence of an opening pastoral prayer, we already sense the severely strained relations between Paul and the Galatians. For him to dispense with the opening prayer marks the extreme urgency of the situation.

The source of Paul's astonishment is not only the Galatians' fickleness in changing loyalties but the speed with which they have deserted the ranks. He can attribute it only to a combination of their stupidity and the beguiling tactics of the competition (3:1–3). He stresses that it is a desertion of their divine vocation—a "deserting [of] the one who called you in the grace of Christ" (v. 6; cf. 5:8). It is God whom they have abandoned.

What had seduced them was a "different gospel" (v. 6), which suggests that the competing message was also Christian (2 Cor. 11:4; cf. 1 Tim. 6:3). On second thought, Paul is only willing to concede that there is one saving gospel, which his opponents are distorting (cf. 5:10; 2 Cor. 11:4; Acts 15:1, 24). So convinced is he that his gospel stands in direct continuity with the apostolic tradition, he issues an anathema on his opponents (cf. 1 Cor. 16:22; also 12:3; Acts 23:14; Rom. 9:3). Indeed, it is a double anathema, repeated for emphasis (cf. 5:3; 2 Cor. 13:2; 1 Thess. 3:4; 4:6). The Galatians are in sharp contrast to other Pauline churches who sought steadfastly to adhere to the apostolic tradition (1 Cor. 11:2; 15:1–3; 1 Thess. 2:13; 4:1–2; 2 Thess. 2:15; 3:6).

The second section concludes on the note on which the opening greeting began—whether Paul's gospel was merely a ploy for human acceptance. Here, as elsewhere, he insists that his motivation is not to curry human favor (1 Thess. 2:4). Had he wished to play the game of gaining acceptance from his peers and living according to human standards, he would never have forsaken the race for religious one-upmanship to become a slave of Christ (cf. Phil. 3:4–11). Paul stoutly denies preaching with an eye always on the opinion polls and a finger on the popular pulse.

The Divine Origin of Paul's Gospel (vv. 11–12). Because Paul was not one of the original circle of Jesus' disciples, he was vulnerable to the charge that he preached a gospel "of human origin." Doubtless, this meant that it was a message he had devised himself rather than one traceable to God's revelation. He emphatically denies this charge, insisting that his gospel was ultimately traceable to Jesus Christ himself. Even though he would be the first to admit that the gospel must be transmitted and preserved by human beings, Paul would still insist that a humanly conceived message can never be ultimately salvific.

Luke 7:1–10

Luke 7:1–10 opens a section in the Gospel (7:1–8:3) sometimes referred to as "the little insertion," which consists of six units inserted into the Markan framework. Some of this material is found also in Matthew. This is true of 7:1–10, the healing of the centurion's slave, which appears in both Matthew (8:5–13) and John (4:46–53). Both Matthew and Luke place the story after Jesus' great sermon (on the mount in Matthew, on the plain in Luke), and John joins the two of them in locating the incident in Capernaum. The Matthean and Lucan accounts contain more than sixty identical words, but even so, differences are noticeable and significant. The two most important are Luke's use of intermediaries in the centurion's appeal to Jesus and Matthew's insertion of a saying of Jesus (vv. 11–12) that Luke places elsewhere (13:28–30). The preacher may find it helpful to read Matthew's and John's accounts in order to hold in sharper focus the accents peculiar to Luke.

The centurion, a Roman military officer, represents the believing Gentile living within Jewish territory. Luke's practice of relating parallel events from the life of Jesus and the life of the church is continued here. Luke 7:1–10 has its parallel in Acts 10: "In Caesarea there was a man named Cornelius, a centurion of the Italian Cohort, as it was called. He was a devout man who feared God with all his household; he gave alms generously to the people and prayed constantly to God" (vv. 1–2). The story in Luke 7:1–10, therefore, not only foreshadows the mission to the Gentiles that unfolds in Acts but also gives authoritative precedent for that mission from the ministry of Jesus himself. And all of it unfolds what Luke presented at the outset of Jesus' ministry in Nazareth (4:16–30).

Luke paints a most favorable portrait of the centurion. He is deeply concerned for an ailing slave (v. 2) and believes Jesus can heal him (vv. 3, 7, 10). However, rather than approach Jesus directly, the centurion sends two sets of intermediaries. The first, Jewish elders, appeal to Jesus on the ground that the centurion is worthy, loving the Jews and building a synagogue for them (vv. 3–5). The officer might have been a proselyte-at-the-gate, a Gentile who believed in and worshiped Israel's God but who had not submitted to the rites whereby a Gentile became a Jew. The second set of intermediaries, friends of the centurion, brought word to Jesus that the man felt himself unworthy to receive Jesus in his home (vv. 6–7a). Regarded worthy by others, regarded unworthy by himself; not a bad combination of credentials. Joined to this quality was the centurion's confidence that a word from Jesus had performative power. As a soldier in the Roman army, he knew the authority of a command given and received (vv. 7b–8). Jesus praises his faith (v. 9), and the slave is healed by the word of Jesus (v. 10).

Matthew inserts into the story a saying of Jesus that prophesies a mass influx of Gentiles and the rejection of many in Israel (8:11–12). Luke does not. Even though Jesus says the centurion's faith is not matched in Israel (v. 9), still it is important that Jesus' blessing of a Gentile came through the intercession of Jewish elders. Acts makes it clear that Luke understood the shift from a Jewish to a Gentile majority in the church, but his two volumes also make it clear that Luke understood God to be a "both-and" and not an "either-or" God.

And so begins the story of faith among those "afar off," not only geographically but also racially—and not only racially but also temporally, for later generations who would not be able to see Jesus would be able to receive his blessing through his word (v. 7; John 20:29).

Last Sunday After the Epiphany
(Transfiguration Sunday)

Exodus 34:29–35;
Psalm 99;
2 Corinthians 3:12–4:2;
Luke 9:28–36 (37–43a)

On the day that commemorates the transfiguration of the physical appearance of Jesus, the Gospel lection that reports the event is the center of attention, but all the assigned readings contribute directly to the same theme. Exodus 34:29–35 is the account of the change in the appearance of Moses' face after he had been on Mt. Sinai in the presence of God. The responsorial psalm, a hymn to the kingship of Yahweh, celebrates the holiness of God and alludes to Moses, Aaron, the pillar of cloud, and the holy mountain. Second Corinthians 3:12–4:2 includes Paul's interpretation of the report of Moses' shining face and the veil.

Exodus 34:29–35

Our Old Testament reading is part of a section of the Book of Exodus (chaps. 32–34) concerning the renewal of the covenant following the rebellion of the people of Israel and the breaking of the original tablets of the law. In many respects the report is parallel to Exodus 19–24, the account of the initial covenant. Consequently, some commentators have seen duplicate traditions or sources concerning the same event, but the matter is disputed. The immediate context of Exodus 34:29–35 is the return of Moses from Mt. Sinai with the words of the covenant written upon new tablets (34:28).

However one resolves the question of the relationship of Exodus 32–34 to Exodus 19–24, the passage before us contains a distinct and special tradition primarily concerned with Moses. On the surface it appears to be a relatively simple and direct account of the awesome shining face, its effect upon the people, and the solution of the problem with Moses' veil. Upon closer examination, however, the complexities of the story begin to appear. When and why did Moses wear the veil? He put it on because the people were afraid to come near him, but he put it on only after he had finished talking with them (v. 33). Does the text mean to describe an event that happened once, or a continuing activity? Verses 29–33 are correctly translated in the past tense, for they recount what happened once, following Moses' forty days and forty nights on Mt. Sinai with God. Verses 34–35, on the other hand, are properly translated in the present tense, indicating that Moses would take off the veil when he would go in to speak with God, and put it on when he came out to speak to the people. These last verses suggest the tradition not of the revelation on Sinai but of the tabernacle. Thus it appears that the passage is the combination of at least two traditions.

One of the more interesting interpretations of this account is found in the Vulgate, in which the Hebrew verb meaning "to shine" was incorrectly taken to mean "had horns." That is the source of many representations—including Michelangelo's—of Moses with horns.

At one level, a major concern of the account is the figure of Moses, and Moses contrasted with the people of Israel, including Aaron. Moses is the only one who can approach God. He it is who acts as intermediary between God and people. Having interceded on their behalf, he now receives the law and communicates it to the people. Their fear of his changed countenance contrasts with his freedom to talk directly with God. However, even traditions such as this that glorify Moses know the limits. Moses remained a fully human mediator, not even aware that his appearance had been changed (v. 29).

At another and deeper level, the concern of this text is the holiness of God and its effects, a point not even rejected in Paul's treatment of this passage in 2 Corinthians 3. Moses' face shone "because he had been talking with God" (v. 29). The rays of light are reflections of the glory of God. In the Old Testament view, it is terrifying and dangerous to be in the presence of God. Is it still possible that one who approaches God, who encounters the Holy One, will be transformed so that others can see the effects of that encounter?

Psalm 99

Psalm 99, like Psalms 96–98, which were readings for Christmas Day, is an enthronement psalm. These psalms were probably used in ancient times as part of the celebration of Yahweh's annual reenthronement in the Jerusalem temple at the fall festival (the Feast of Booths or Tabernacles). This particular psalm stresses factors or figures drawn from Israelite history more than do the other enthronement psalms. As a rule, the enthronement psalms focused on the themes of creation rather than the narratives of history.

The liturgical character of this psalm and its employment in worship are evident in the complexity of the psalm. The speaker and addressee change rather frequently. Hymnic speech about God occurs in verses 1–2 and 6–7. Liturgical directions or admonitions are found in verses 5a and 9. A cultic shout—"Holy is he"—appears in verses 3b and 5b. (Verse 9b may have once also had this form.) Direct address to God appears in verses 3a, 4, and 8. One perhaps should envision the component parts of this psalm as having been spoken by different participants in a dramatic ritual in the temple. The entire congregation or certain Levitical choirs sang the hymnic parts (vv. 1–2 and 6–7), another group or choir addressed the Deity directly (vv. 3a, 4, and 8), priestly participants or Levites encouraged the congregation (vv. 5a and 9), and the congregation probably joined in the worship with a responsive "Holy is he" (vv. 3b, 5b, and 9b; see Isa. 6:3 for the threefold acclamation "holy, holy, holy").

Some expressions in this psalm would need explanation when preaching on it.

1. "Enthroned upon the cherubim" (v. 1b) is a description of God that is dependent on old mythological concepts that were incorporated into early Israelite theology and iconography. The cherubim were composite guardian beings associated apparently with the winds or storm clouds and also were associated with the ark (see 1 Sam. 4:4). They seemed initially to

have been conceived as part of the heavenly "transportation" for the Deity. Cherubim were found in the Holy of Holies in the Jerusalem temple as well as engraved on the temple walls (see 1 Kings 6:23–29; 8:6–7), and God could be understood as enthroned on these figures.

2. The "footstool" of God (in v. 5a) is probably synonymous with the "holy mountain" of verse 9a. The "footstool," however, may also have been identified with the ark (see Ps. 132:6–7). If God sat enthroned on or over the cherubim, then the ark that rested between the cherubim may have been considered his footstool.

Two emphases dominate the affirmations and celebrations of this psalm. First, Yahweh reigns as king over the created order and the peoples of the earth (vv. 1–4). As king, Yahweh is the embodiment and defender of justice and right order in the world. Divine rulership is exercised in Zion, and it is from here that God rules over the world. Second, God is one who responds to intercession, forgiving Israel's sins and avenging their wrongs (vv. 6–8). Moses, Aaron, and Samuel are seen as intercessors (see Num. 14:13; 16:46; 1 Sam. 12:1–25; Jer. 15:1) whose intercession in the past was successful. God did respond to them and forgive. Verse 8c, which the NRSV translates as "but an avenger of their wrongdoings," seems to suggest that God punished the people before forgiving them. The phrase may be understood and translated differently, as in the NEB ("forgave all their misdeeds and held them innocent") or the NJPSV ("exacted retribution for their misdeeds").

The surface parallels between Psalm 99 and the transfiguration story are the mountain imagery, the historical figures from the past, and the awesome holiness that pervades the materials.

2 Corinthians 3:12–4:2

Today's epistolary lection is the latter part of Paul's midrashic exposition of the giving of the law to Moses at Sinai (cf. 2 Cor. 3:1–11). With its focus on Moses as the one through whom God's revelatory light shone and its contrast between the fading splendor of the Mosaic revelation and the permanent splendor of the new covenant of Christ, it is an excellent text for the Last Sunday After the Epiphany, when we celebrate the Transfiguration of the Lord. Although Paul makes no direct reference to the Gospel account of Christ's transfiguration, which is rehearsed in today's Gospel reading (Luke 9:28–36; cf. Mark 9:2–8; Matt. 17:1–8), his exposition may be said to reflect the faith expressed in the divine voice, "This is my Son, my Chosen; listen to him!" (Luke 9:35).

It is also fitting that today's Old Testament reading is Exodus 34:29–35, for this is the biblical text that informs Paul's midrashic exposition. To make any sense of Paul's remarks, it will be necessary for the preacher to have this text from Exodus firmly in mind.

The central image from the Exodus text that informs Paul's exposition is that of the veil. Moses' encounter with God in receiving the law on Sinai was such a numinous experience that his face glistened (Exod. 34:29). So blinding was his appearance that he was required to wear a veil when he appeared before the people. But when he returned to God's presence, he removed the veil from his face, thus enabling him to encounter God "face to face."

For Paul, the image of the veil illustrates something else, and something more far-reaching. Just as Moses' face was veiled so that Israel would not be blinded by the dazzling light that shone through his face, so had Moses' message become similarly veiled to Israel. Israel had *seen* Moses through a veil, but so had they *read* Moses through a veil. The true form of his face had escaped their view, but so had the true meaning of the words he had received from Yahweh.

It is important to notice that in Paul's exposition in 2 Corinthians 3, he shifts his use of the image of the veil. He first speaks of the veil that hides the message of Moses, but then speaks of the veil that covers Israel's mind (v. 15). He appears to be saying that God's message given in the law through Moses was not in itself inscrutable or incomprehensible. Rather, the minds and hearts of the Israelites had become hardened (v. 14; John 12:40; Rom. 11:25; also Mark 3:5; 6:52; 8:17; Eph. 4:18). The real fault lay not with the law but with the Israelites' inner faculties of perception, for there is where the light of God's revelation had been shut off.

Paul insists that things had reached an impasse: the word of God as revealed through Moses to the people of Israel had become short-circuited. What had been intended to give life had only produced death (v. 6). What had begun as a relationship of splendor had dimmed to a flickering light (v. 10). What had been meant to speak to the needs of living, human hearts had been reduced to lifeless letters coldly inscribed on stone (vv. 3–6).

This impasse was broken through Christ, whose appearance on earth effectively removed the veil (v. 14). Here, the Synoptic account of the Transfiguration symbolizes this dramatic shift, for in the Gospel narratives we see the old way of knowing God through the law (Moses) and the prophets (Elijah) give way to the dazzling brightness of the transfigured Son of God, upon whom the divine voice bestows its blessing. Once Moses' face glistened before God on Sinai, but on this Christian mountain of revelation, the glistening face of Christ now becomes the focus of attention. The transfigured face of Moses pales beside the transfigured Christ. For Paul, Moses' reentry to God, where the veil is removed (Exod. 34:29, 35), becomes the prototype for our "turning to the Lord" (v. 16). The image behind verse 16 of our text is Moses' reentering the sacred place where he encounters God directly, but in its indefinite form it now encompasses our own encounter with God. What is different in the Christian experience, however, is that we confront the "Lord [who] is the Spirit" (v. 17), and in this encounter we find freedom (v. 17; cf. John 8:36; Rom. 6:18, 22; 8:2; 1 Cor. 7:23; Gal. 5:1).

As a result, our view of God now takes place "with unveiled faces" (v. 18), and through the transfigured face of Christ we gaze at the "glory of the Lord" (v. 18). So dazzling is this experience of God that it has a transforming effect on us, for we find ourselves "being transformed into the same image from one degree of glory to another" (v. 18; cf. Phil. 3:21; also 1 Cor. 15:43, 49, 53; Rom. 8:29; 12:2; 1 John 3:2). Our experience of knowing God, which Christ has made possible, quite literally becomes a spiritual metamorphosis, because it "comes from the Lord, the Spirit" (v. 18).

The impact of this new way of knowing and seeing God was empowering: "We do not lose heart" (4:1; cf. Gal. 6:9). As he says in verse 12, "we act with great boldness." Because of the directness of his encounter with God, his position before God is one of genuine confidence. But there was another effect: it was also sobering. Such an unmediated, pristine encounter with God prevented him from playing fast and loose with God's word (2 Cor. 2:17; 1 Thess. 2:3). All underhanded dealings are excluded when one confronts the living God this directly. No behind-the-scenes negotiating is permitted, for now the proclamation is public and out in the open. These last words are doubtless directed against Paul's opponents in the Corinthian church who had accused him of double-dealing in his apostolic work. But for Paul, the manifestation of God through Christ meant that his own behavior became open to public scrutiny.

For Paul, the light that had shone through Christ did not cease to shine in the earthly ministry of Jesus. It continued to reveal the nature of Christ to the world, and in so doing, exposed the true nature of Christian ministry (2 Cor. 5:12; also 1 Cor. 4:5).

Luke 9:28–36 (37–43*a*)

The season of Epiphany, which began with the visit of the Wise Men, concludes with the Transfiguration of Jesus. The Transfiguration and its companion story, the baptism of Jesus (Luke 3:21–22), are the foundation for the Christian celebration of the revelation of the Son of God to the world.

Quite clearly, Luke follows Mark (9:2–8) in this account, as does Matthew (17:1–8). Like Mark also, both Luke and Matthew locate the transfiguration story immediately after the confession of Simon Peter and the introduction of the passion into the teaching of Jesus (Luke 9:18–27; Mark 8:27–9:1; Matt. 16:13–28). As we will notice shortly, this location of the account is significant, as are also the points at which Luke modifies the story as received from Mark.

Hardly any passage in the Gospels has prompted interpretations as widely divergent as has this one. Some scholars confine themselves to questions of historicity and debate whether it occurred on Mt. Tabor or Mt. Hermon. Others understand the experience as a mystical vision that Jesus had, one in which three of his friends were involved. From time to time the theory that the Transfiguration is a displaced resurrection story is seriously entertained, as is the view that this is an artistic expression of the Christian confession that Jesus is Lord and Son of God. Whatever may be the historical event or circumstance prompting the Gospel accounts, two observations can be made with certainty. First, the story as it comes to us has been told after the manner of the theophany recorded in Exodus 24:12–18. The two events share many details: the mountain, the cloud, six days (Luke has eight), Moses, the voice, the glory. In addition, Matthew and Luke describe the face of Jesus as shining like the face of Moses after being in the presence of God (Exod. 34:29–35). Second, the location of the Transfiguration immediately after the first prediction of the passion of Jesus is significant for its interpretation. Just as Jesus, after submitting to the baptism of preparation, received heaven's confirmation as the Son of God, so here, he, after stating his commitment that would lead to Golgotha, is again confirmed as Son of God. The one who will be crucified is not just another martyr in a lost cause; for a moment he is seen by three of his disciples and the reader as the church saw him after the resurrection.

However, our Gospel lection for today is not simply the Transfiguration, but the Transfiguration according to Luke. The Lucan accents are important. Instead of "six days later" (Mark 9:2), Luke says "about eight days" (9:28). Possibly Luke is tying the story to the resurrection, which occurred on the eighth day, the day after the sabbath, or he may be reflecting the use of this account in Christian worship, which was held on the eighth day. In verse 29 Luke says that the experience occurred while Jesus was praying. Luke had said earlier (v. 18) that Jesus was praying when he asked the questions that led to Peter's confession and the first teaching about his coming death. And even earlier, after Jesus' baptism, Luke says that it was while Jesus was in prayer that he received the Holy Spirit and the voice of divine approval (3:21–22). The major events and critical moments in the life of Jesus were, according to Luke, marked by prayer.

Luke's only extended addition to Mark's account occurs in verses 31–33. Luke alone reports the content of the conversation among Jesus, Moses, and Elijah: they "were speaking of his departure [exodus], which he was about to accomplish at Jerusalem" (v. 31). That the law and the prophets testify to Jesus' suffering, death, and resurrection is an important theme in Luke (24:25–27, 44–46). The three disciples were not privy to this conversation because they were heavy with sleep (v. 32), but they awoke to see the two with Jesus and to see Jesus' glory. They also experienced the overshadowing cloud and heard the voice say, "This is my Son, my Chosen; listen to him!" (vv. 34–35). In other words, for Jesus, the experience not only gave heaven's confirmation of who he was but also confirmed that his passion was according to God's purpose revealed in the law and the prophets. The "exodus" of Jesus would launch a new exodus for the people of God. For the disciples, the experience permitted them to see who the Jesus on the way to death really was, and to know that he, regardless of what suffering, denial, and humiliation was to come, was Lord, taking precedence over the law and the prophets.

The disciples were silent about these things "in those days" (v. 36), not needing Mark's command that they tell no one (Mark 9:9). And that is understandable; the silence following extraordinary experiences makes more powerful the words that eventually break that silence.

If the preacher wants to extend the message to include verses 37–43, the larger text permits a look at the effects of recent critical events on the disciples. Jesus had announced his approaching death at 9:22 and at 9:51 will turn toward Jerusalem. The Transfiguration had been experienced by but only three, and they had kept silent (9:36). What is the condition of the disciples in this atmosphere of coming suffering and death? In 9:1–6, Jesus had given them power over demons and disease, and they had ministered effectively. But now they are powerless before a demon-possessed child. Has Jesus' announcement robbed them of faith and commitment? Or had their previous success made them arrogant, failing to sustain their ministry with prayer? Whatever their condition, Jesus himself has not diminished in power and purpose. He has chosen in the will of God to go to Jerusalem, but he has not accepted the role of victim. In the presence of faithless followers he continues to meet a need with power and grace.

Ash Wednesday

Joel 2:1–2, 12–17 or Isaiah 58:1–12;
Psalm 51:1–17;
2 Corinthians 5:20*b*–6:10;
Matthew 6:1–6, 16–21

The texts for Ash Wednesday initiate the season of Lent with calls to confession and repentance, prayers for forgiveness, and admonitions to engage in fasting. They also caution people not to display their acts of contrition before others, but only before God. The Old Testament reading from Joel has a call to repentance at its center. The responsorial psalm, one of the penitential psalms, is a confession of sin with the goal of restoration to the joy of salvation. The epistolary reading is likewise a call to be reconciled to God. The Gospel text sounds the warning about doing alms or fasting in order to impress others with one's righteousness.

Joel 2:1–2, 12–17

It is appropriate that verses from the Book of Joel lead the church on a solemn occasion that initiates a season of penitence, fasting, and self-examination, for the book developed and was used in similar liturgical contexts in ancient Israel. The book as a whole certainly is a prophetic one, and these verses in particular reflect that fact. However, there are priestly and liturgical dimensions as well. In fact, many commentators rightly have called Joel a cultic prophet, and the book a prophetic liturgy.

The verses before us today contain that merging of prophetic and priestly sensibilities and perspectives on the relationship between God and people. The prophetic dimension, although more detailed in chapter 1 and in 2:3–11, sets the tone at the outset. In Joel 1 and 2:3–11, it is present in the descriptions of the approaching judgment upon the land. In our reading, the prophetic perspective is apparent in the announcement that the day of the Lord is coming (v. 1). Thus, although the prophet's explicit message is a call to prayer, fasting, and repentance, that message assumes the announcement of impending divine judgment.

The expectation of the day of the Lord in Joel is almost, but not quite, an apocalyptic expectation. Joel 2:1–2 is closely paralleled by Zephaniah 1:15 and stands in a long prophetic tradition. One of the clearest articulations of that tradition is also one of its oldest, Amos 5:18:

> Alas for you who desire the day of the LORD!
> Why do you want the day of the LORD?
> It is darkness, not light.

Clearly, Amos announces the reversal of a contemporary (eighth-century) hope. The tradition behind the hope for the day of the Lord probably was the holy war, the time when Yahweh would act against his enemies. For Amos and other early prophets (cf. Isa. 2:9–11), the people of Israel had become Yahweh's enemies. That is no less true for Joel, who emphasizes that Yahweh, marching at the head of his army, is ready to destroy his enemies, the people of Israel (v. 11).

Thus the threat of the end, if not of history at least of the covenant people, provides the urgency for Joel's call. The cry is both an alarm—the trumpet (v. 1) announces the approach of the enemy, "a great and powerful army" (v. 2)—and a summons to assemble for a service of worship. What are the people to do in the shadow of the day of the Lord, before the threat of divine wrath? They must assemble to fast and pray.

The priestly–liturgical dimensions of Joel are present in the instructions for the service of worship. Speaking for Yahweh, the prophet calls for the people to "return" (vv. 12, 13) to the Lord, instructs them to fast, weep, and mourn, and then spells out the details of the assembly, including the duties of the priests (vv. 14–17). The religious ceremony in view here is one that is well known from elsewhere in the Old Testament, especially from the psalms of lament or complaint. An individual who was ill or otherwise in trouble called for a priest who would gather the person's primary group—family and neighbors—for a service of prayer. At the center of such services were the psalms of individual lament or complaint. Likewise, when the people were threatened by drought, famine, or enemy invasion, they gathered to plead with God. The prayers they offered (see Psalms 44, 74, 89; Lamentations 5) included invocations of the divine name, confessions, affirmations of confidence in God, and, above all, petitions for divine favor. Other texts that reflect such services are Judges 20:26–28; 1 Kings 8:33–36, 44–45; Jonah 3:5–10, and Isaiah 63:7–64:11.

Joel, like the other texts, emphasizes the corporate, communal dimension of the prayer service. After all, it was the entire community that was in trouble. Thus everyone is to participate, men and women, from elders to nursing infants. Even the new bride and bridegroom are to join in (v. 16).

The people's public behavior is an important part of the time of prayer. Joel instructs them to fast, weep, and mourn. These actions are known elsewhere in the Old Testament as expressions of grief, as rituals of sorrow following death (1 Sam. 31:13; Judith 16:24). Their purpose here is twofold: to convince God that the people know the seriousness of the threat and to demonstrate the sincerity of their repentance. Contemporary Christians, taking seriously New Testament texts such as our Gospel reading for today, often disparage such outward displays of piety, and often rightly so. However, such rituals have their value, for habits of the body may even shape the habits of the heart. One's feelings may be trained by such rituals, even to experience genuine repentance. But lest the point be missed, Joel enjoins his hearers, "rend your hearts and not your clothing" (v. 13).

At the center of the text is the call for the people to return to the Lord their God. This "return" is the directing of their full devotion to the God of Israel, and it is also repentance. Remarkably, there is no mention of the sin or sins for which the community is to repent. The fundamental concern is with orientation in the right direction. On the one hand, the urgency comes from awareness of the impending day of the Lord, the possibility of a judgment that would end the community's life. But on the other hand, the call to repent is based on the conviction that God "is gracious and merciful, slow to anger, and abounding in steadfast love" (v. 13). Indeed, Joel urges all his hearers to repent, for God is one who "repents of evil" (v. 13, RSV); that is, the Lord is both able and willing to be affected by the people.

Isaiah 58:1–12

This reading is concerned with the definition of genuine piety and the relationship between religious practices and the moral life. Isaiah 58 considers the question in terms of fasts and fast days, and thus is a highly appropriate reading for the day that initiates a season of fasting.

Our passage is part of the so-called Third Isaiah (Isaiah 56–66) and very likely stems from the years soon after the return of the exiles from Babylon. The reading reflects some of the religious practices that developed during the Exile and afterwards, and also indicates some of the divisions that were emerging in the newly reconstituted community of faith in Judah. The mood of disappointment and frustration with the new life in Jerusalem is similar to that reported in Haggai 2:1–9 and Zechariah 7.

The reading is part of a composite unit of literature (Isaiah 58) concerned with the general topic of cultic activity. Verses 1–12 concern fasts; verses 13–15 turn to the issue of proper observance of the sabbath.

In some ways, the form of the passage is similar to the prophetic torah, or instruction, in Micah 6:6–8 (see also Amos 5:21–24 and Isa. 1:10–17), with a question from the laity answered by a religious specialist. But the dialogue here is more like a dispute than a request and an answer. It is clear that the addressees are the people in general, but the role of the speaker is not so obvious. Generally, the speaker assumes prophetic authority; that is, he presumes to speak on behalf of God. It is quite possible that the setting for such a discourse was the sort of community of worship and teaching that later became the synagogue.

The initial address (vv. 1–2) appears to be a divine speech to a prophetic figure. God instructs the hearer to speak with a voice like a trumpet indicting God's people for their rebellion, for their sin.

Next (v. 3ab), our speaker quotes the words of the people. They complain to God because their fasts have not been effective. The assumption is that fasts are a form of prayer, probably of penitence. Fasts in ancient Israel, along with the use of sackcloth and ashes (v. 5), generally were associated with rituals of mourning, but they were also used as part of petition and intercession (2 Sam. 12:16, 22). Public fasts became important in the exilic and postexilic periods, and several such days were known (Zechariah 7). The rituals for the Day of Atonement must have included fasts (Lev. 16:29–31; 23:27–32; Num. 29:7).

Then (vv. 3c–4), the speaker responds on behalf of God with an indictment of the people for their attitudes and their behavior on fast days. The meaning of the "rebellion" and "sins" of verse 1 is made plain. Business as usual, and oppressive business at that, continues on such days (v. 3c). People are contentious when—verse 4 implies—the public fast should be a reverent expression of solidarity before God.

To this point the author has said, in effect, that fasts are not effective because the participants do not take them seriously. In verses 5–7, however, the prophetic figure begins to question the very idea of fasts (v. 5) and then to state what kind of "fast" would evoke the desired response from God (vv. 6–7). In a series of rhetorical questions, each expecting the answer "yes," an answer is spelled out in four points: "loose the bonds of injustice," "undo the thongs of the yoke," "let the oppressed go free," "break every yoke" (v. 6).

It turns out that these four metaphors refer to one activity—to care for the poor, to set them free from oppression, from the bonds of their poverty. Verse 7 states the point in very practical terms. Those complaining should see that those in need have food ("share your bread"), housing ("bring the homeless poor into your house"), and clothing ("when you see the naked, to cover them"). The final line of the verse is best read, "And not to ignore your own kin" (JPS), that is, your fellow Judeans. This catalogue of social responsibilities is similar to that in Zechariah 7:8–10 and is an echo of Isaiah 1:10–17, which advocates justice and righteousness, especially for widows and orphans, as the necessary prerequisite for genuine worship.

Verses 8–9a promise that when these conditions are fulfilled, the people will live in the light of God's presence, and the Lord will indeed hear their prayers. It is possible to take this promise as a form of works righteousness, that good works will earn salvation. Good works would then only replace fasting as means of earning God's favor. Doubtless many heard—and many will continue to hear—these words in that way. However, the more fundamental meaning is that those who attend to justice and righteousness thereby live in the presence of the just and righteous God; they are part of God's people. Moreover, when the people attend to the needs of the hungry, the homeless, and the naked, they have their own reward: the solidarity of the community is strengthened, their "light" breaks forth, their "healing" springs up, and their "righteousness" is active.

Psalm 51:1–17

Of the seven penitential psalms (6, 32, 38, 51, 102, 130, 143), Psalm 51 is by far the one most characterized by personal intensity and depth of feeling. It is the penitential psalm par excellence, the Miserere of the Psalter.

Because the words of this psalm are so well known and ingrained into the Ash Wednesday ritual, we will here focus on some of the conceptual frameworks that lie behind the surface words of the text.

First, verses 1–2 assume that sin/iniquity has a staining, polluting, contaminating quality about it. Sin can be seen as dirt that taints and discolors the human and the human personality. All of us are aware of the general sense of shame, inferiority, and feeling of being wrongly different that so often comes our way. Sometimes we speak of feeling filthy, or we feel that way even though we do not talk about it. In priestly theology in the Old Testament, it was assumed that human sin as well as life's impurities dirtied or polluted the temple (Lev. 15:31). Sin sacrifices and the blood ritual associated with them purged the temple and the altar from the pollution that became attached to them. "Washing" and "cleansing" are thus appropriate images to associate with sin/dirt/filth.

Verses 3–4 manifest the assumption that sin is fundamentally a theological matter. Sin violates God, is an affront to the Deity. In addition to their moral and ethical dimensions, sins are acts against God, disruptions in the human-creator relationship.

Verse 5 assumes that sin is a universal, human condition that pervades the whole of life. Conception and birth are here related to sin. Perhaps behind this view lies the fact that in the Old Testament sexual intercourse rendered the man and woman unclean (filthy, dirty) for a day (Lev. 15:18) and a woman was unclean for days after giving birth, forty days if the child was a male, eighty days if it was a female (Lev. 12:1–5). The view that life was tainted by sin was shared by most of the ancient world. A three-thousand-year-old Sumerian proverb written centuries before Psalm 51, for example, declares:

> Never has a sinless child been born to its mother,
> a sinless youth has not existed from of old.

Even if these texts affirm no more than the utter guilt, the total misalignment of life, they are sharp testimony to the pervasiveness of sin.

The plea for help in verses 6–12 makes its requests in a torrent of practically synonymous appeals. Two aspects are noticeable. (1) On the one hand, there is the plea that the stain, the pollution, the sense of being marked be removed. "Purge," "wash," "hide," "blot out"—these are words from the realm of ritual bathing, of cultic cleansing, of material substance, of dirt removal. One might say that these give expression to the hope for surface cleansing, for the type of salvation that makes possible facing life again unmarked. (We must remember that in much of Christendom we have given up those earthy, materialistic acts that signify change and newness; we have thrown out ritualization, with its substance, stuff, and feeling, and substituted cognition, with its conceptualization, sanitation, and synthesized sentiments.) (2) On the other hand, there is the recognition that matters must be changed, altered, reformed, reshaped, and even re-created from the center out. The secret heart, the bones, the spirit, all these must be reshaped. A cleansing of the old and the creation of the new are the sources of joy and gladness, and both are needed.

2 Corinthians 5:20b–6:10

Even though there is a chapter break in today's lection, it does not coincide with the most natural shift between thought units. Today's lection may be seen as comprising two parts: 5:20b–6:2 and 6:3–10.

In the first part, a direct appeal is made to the readers (and to us). We are urged, "Be reconciled to God" (5:20), and cautioned "not to accept the grace of God in vain" (6:1). A note of urgency concludes the appeal: "Now is the acceptable time; . . . now is the day of salvation!" (6:2).

Here we are being confronted with the eschatological urgency of the gospel. Through the gospel comes God's appeal. As we listen to the minister and messenger of reconciliation tell the story of God's love and Christ's death, we hear God calling us directly. It is a summons related by God's ambassador, but it comes from God. This is why we cannot blithely ignore it. As the quotation from Isaiah 49:8 suggests, God has lent an open ear to us and come to our rescue (6:2). Because God has acted decisively, so must we.

At this point, the emphasis shifts. The remainder of the passage deals with Paul's apostolic ministry (6:3–10). The tone is apologetic, and we get the clear sense that he is defending his ministry, both its form and content. This is consistent with the epistle as a whole, much of which is Paul's defense against various charges. But what he insists on here is that neither he, nor his colleagues, nor their form of ministry have stood as obstacles to the gospel. This of course suggests that in the mind of some they had. Perhaps his manner of life had appeared too boorish. Perhaps his manner of speaking had not sounded "apostolic" enough. In any case, his apostolic credentials appear to have been called into question, and verses 3–10 provide us an insight as to the kind of apostolic credentials Paul thought worthwhile.

His remarks here pertain primarily to apostolic ministry. In verse 3, he speaks of "our ministry." But even though he is talking about "servants of God" in a restricted sense (v. 4), his remarks have a wider import. In fact, they provide us with useful reflections about what, in Paul's mind, really counts when it comes to certifying or authenticating service done in the name of God. On Ash Wednesday, at the beginning of Lent, as we consider the themes of penance and death, we do well to reflect on what actually qualifies any of us to live as "servants of God" for the sake of the gospel.

We should notice the way Paul commends himself, or authenticates his ministry of service. As we look more closely at verses 4b–10, what otherwise appears to be a long and cluttered list of vicissitudes and virtues turns out to have a certain pattern. In fact, we can organize and summarize his remarks under three headings.

1. *Authentication through hardship* (vv. 4b–5). Under the heading "great endurance," Paul includes a series of nine hardships, which can be arranged in three groups of three. Some of these have clear reference to experiences in his own life that we find mentioned elsewhere, whereas others are quite general. Commentaries will supply the details on the precise significance of each. The general point we can make is this: for Paul, the place to begin talking about meaningful service in the name of God is with hardship and difficulty. The discussion must begin "from below" for Paul, not with experiences "from above" or with a list of triumphs. Being an authentic servant of God, before it means anything else, means knowing and experiencing the difficulties of human existence. We should note that here he speaks not of authentication after endurance, but through endurance.

2. *Authentication through moral character* (vv. 6–7). We tend to describe the next set of qualities as "virtues," and surely they are in one sense. But they are more than this. Eight items are listed, the last of which is "the power of God," which in a way summarizes all of them. Elsewhere, these are spoken of as "fruit of the Spirit" (Gal. 5:22–23). Again, commentaries can supply detailed treatment of each one. But the general point we should note is that service in the name of God is also authenticated by our active participation in the very nature and character of God as we experience it through God's own Spirit. We become servants of God when the effects of God's power are visible within the contours of our own life and service.

3. *Authentication through paradox* (vv. 8–10). There is some question whether "paradox" aptly describes this final set of remarks. They are unlike the first two groups because in each case they join opposites. Perhaps they are better called "antitheses." They are not arranged in a uniform pattern. For example, verse 8a is in chiastic form: honor (a) and dishonor (b) are set over against ill repute (b) and good repute (a). The form of the final list is "as . . . and yet." What is striking about this section is that genuine servanthood is seen as a dual existence. It is neither wholly vicious nor wholly virtuous. It is rather life where opposites converge within us. But more than that, it is the capacity to affirm while being denied. In each case, Paul's own apostolic identity is severely called into question. He is regarded as an impostor, unknown, dying. What he sees himself to be is being radically denied. In face of such denial, his is a stance of radical affirmation. What emerges then, as a criterion for authentic servanthood, is the capacity for radical affirmation in the face of radical denial.

In the context of Ash Wednesday, this epistolary lection enables us to reflect soberly on the meaning of service in the name of God—the form it takes and the way to tell if it is real or fake.

Matthew 6:1–6, 16–21

Today is Ash Wednesday, the beginning of Lent, a day of profound meaning for some, a day only casually marked by others, and a day viewed with suspicion among those Christians who feel the key to genuine spirituality is the minimizing of all rites and ceremonies. It is appropriate to look to Matthew for instruction at this time, for he knew as well as anyone in the New Testament both the depth and the emptiness of what he calls "practicing your piety" (6:1). He understood and felt keenly the difference between altars that served as stations on one's pilgrimage and cold stones that stood along the road to nowhere.

Our lesson today consists of an introductory warning about practicing piety (6:1) followed by instruction in the practice of true piety in these areas: alms (vv. 2–4), prayer (vv. 5–6), and fasting (vv. 16–21). The warning does not concern whether or not these acts are to be done but before whom—human spectators or God. The instructions in these acts of devotion are catechetical and formulaic, certain phrases being repeated in each case: "whenever you give alms" (pray, fast); "not be like the hypocrites"; "be seen by others"; "your Father who sees in secret"; "they have received their reward"; "your Father . . . will reward you." Matthew chose to insert (vv. 7–15) here the Lord's Prayer with attendant comments. One can easily see the balanced threefold nature of the passage without the insertion. Therefore, it is well to consider verses 7–15 separately, even though they do deal with the subject of prayer introduced at verse 5. The passage assumes that these three acts are well-established practices in Matthew's church and that they have been observed long enough to become, for some, empty and void of meaning except as displays of religion.

In three very clear ways the church reflected in Matthew 6 is in continuity with Judaism.

First, both communities (church and synagogue) held in high regard these three acts of devotion. Jewish writings speak of alms, prayer, and fasting as indications that one has grown beyond the minimal requirements of the law, as acts of special merit and of such favor in God's eyes as to atone for other breaches of the law.

Second, both communities contained practitioners who missed the point of the acts but did see benefit for themselves in public displays of religion. It was a practice in some synagogues to announce in the assembly the names of donors to the alms box and the amounts given. Some Christians will recognize parallels in their own churches. All the possibilities for competition, improper motivation, and the dehumanization of the recipients are too obvious to require comment.

And third, both communities had prophetic calls for reform. Jesus' voice here joins those of Isaiah 58:5ff., Jeremiah 14:12, Zechariah 7:5ff., and Joel 2:12 in seeking to keep alive in the community of faith the faculty and voice of self-criticism. Without it, hypocrisy and idolatry move in quickly. It is important to see these parallels in the two faith communities lest one be seduced into making false contrasts and false dichotomies. For example, one certainly wants to avoid giving the impression that Judaism as a whole was hypocritical, whereas Christianity was as a whole genuine; or that Judaism was an "outward" religion, whereas Christianity was "inward." On the contrary, the text presents Jesus instructing his church on precisely these same "outward" rites: alms, prayer, fasting.

Students of this text do not agree on the immediate background for these saying of Jesus. Did the synagogue practices in Matthew's community involve trumpets, masked faces, and playing to the crowds, or has Matthew portrayed those and all such public displays of religion in the language and images of the Greco-Roman theater of that time? Because "hypocrite" means "actor," one can easily see how trumpets, masked or disfigured faces, and applauding audiences could have been drawn from the analogy of theatrics.

Whatever the source of Matthew's analogy, the point being made in these sayings of Jesus is clear: God is the proper audience for all our acts of devotion. And because God is in secret and sees in secret, no display is necessary. In the final analysis, it is God with whom we deal in all our work and worship. If the clear assurance that God sees is not in itself payment in full, then our piety will go in search of additional recognition, with occasional applause. Again, it should be understood that the call for correction of abuses is not a call for the cessation of these acts of devotion. Sometimes a sincere but simplistic call for reform would attempt to cure hypocrisy by passivity. But it is a flawed logic that says if we do not attend worship service we are the true worshipers, if we do not pray our spirits are in tune with God, if we do not fast we honestly care, and if we do not give any money we have sincerely given our hearts. Is there not, after all, such a thing as reverse hypocrisy?

First Sunday in Lent

Deuteronomy 26:1–11;
Psalm 91:1–2, 9–16;
Romans 10:8b–13;
Luke 4:1–13

Because Lent commemorates the forty days of Jesus' temptation and fasting in the wilderness, the Lucan account of that period comes to the fore. The Gospel lection stresses that the response of Jesus to the temptations was faith in God and the confession of that faith. The other readings for the day carry forward these themes. Deuteronomy 26:1–11 presents the instructions for the celebration of the festival of the first fruits, including the recital of a confession of faith. The responsorial psalm is a meditation on God's care for those who trust in the Lord, and the epistolary text is a classical Pauline statement that justification follows belief and salvation follows confession.

Deuteronomy 26:1–11

The journey of the church from Ash Wednesday to Easter includes a review of the history of ancient Israel by means of the Old Testament readings. Today's text, with its summary of the saving events from the patriarchs to the entrance into the promised land, is the appropriate beginning. On subsequent Sundays the lections call attention to the covenant with Abraham, the call of Moses, the first Passover in the land in the time of Joshua, and Deutero-Isaiah's proclamation of release from captivity and a new way through the wilderness.

As is the case throughout the Book of Deuteronomy, except for the verses at the beginning and end, this passage is presented as part of the long speech of Moses just before his death. The circumstances are the last stop in the wilderness before the people enter the land of Canaan. The instructions envisage and actually presuppose the circumstances of the people of Israel centuries after the time of Moses. Although there are doubtless genuinely ancient traditions behind our text, the Book of Deuteronomy originated in the seventh century BC.

Deuteronomy 26 comes at the end of a long series of laws, ordinances, and instructions of various kinds, all of them intended to be valid for the members of the community of God's people throughout all time. Chapter 25 is a collection of such instructions having to do mainly with responsibilities to others in the society. The unit that immediately follows our text (Deut. 26:12–16) concerns tithes. Chapter 27 begins the instructions for a covenant ceremony to be carried out once the Israelites enter the land.

The style of the Book of Deuteronomy is quite distinctive. Although it is identified as a law book, and it contains numerous legal sentences and instructions, the form and style on the whole are more hortatory and parenetic than legal. That is, a great many of the individual sections and paragraphs of the book are like short sermons on the law or on the events of the history of salvation. The style is the second person of direct address, urging the hearers to obedience and faithfulness. Often an old law known from tradition is cited, then explained, frequently even reinterpreted for a new situation, and then laid upon the hearts of the listeners. It seems clear that the speakers and writers who actually developed the Book of Deuteronomy stood in a situation centuries removed from the saving events and the revelation of the law. In that respect, their situation parallels that of contemporary preachers and their congregations.

Deuteronomy 26:1–11, however, is not in the form of a sermon but is structured as an ordinance—the instructions for the feast, or ceremony, of the first fruits. The faithful Israelite is given the liturgical actions to perform and the words to say. The instructions open with the indication that the ceremony is to begin "when you have come into the land that the LORD your God is giving you for an inheritance to possess, and possess it, and settle in it" (v. 1). The liturgy actually reaches from the farmer's field to the sanctuary. The Israelite is to take some of the first fruits, put them in a basket, and take them "to the place that the LORD your God will choose as a dwelling for his name," that is, Jerusalem. There is some conflict in the instructions at this point. Whereas in verse 4 the priest takes the basket and places it before the altar, in verse 10 the worshiper is told to set it down "before the LORD your God." It is possible that this slight discrepancy reflects stages in the oral or literary development of the instructions.

Words are at the heart of the ritual. Notice that they are uttered not by the priest but by each individual worshiper. There are two speeches. Although they are words addressed to God, they are not in the form of prayers. The first (v. 3b), a declaration made to the priest but addressed to the Lord, is a simple statement that the participant is here in the land promised to the patriarchs. Its point is the one emphasized throughout the passage, namely, that the land is God's gift. The second (vv. 5–10a) is one of the central passages in Deuteronomy, a confession of faith frequently identified as the little historical credo.

The credo is a summary of the central themes of the Pentateuch: the promise to the patriarchs (the "wandering Aramean" was Jacob), the exodus from Egypt (here spelled out in some detail), and the entrance into the land ("a land flowing with milk and honey"). Note that all the events are the work of the Lord in behalf of the people. The acquisition of the land in particular should not be described as "conquest," as if Israel could have taken something not granted by God. These are the historic events central to the entire nation's confession. However, the words of the individual there at the altar with a gift for the Lord do not end at that point. Rather, the concluding line turns from confession to a personal prayer of thanksgiving. The Lord has done all that, "so now I bring the first of the fruit of the ground that you, O LORD, have given me" (v. 10a).

Given the fact that the ritual occasion is a thanksgiving service for a harvest, the contents of the confession are remarkable. One might have expected praise and thanksgiving for the God of creation who makes the land fertile and thus cares for the people. The focus of attention is, however, upon the actions of God in history, and especially the actions that brought the people into a particular territory and gave it to them.

The deuteronomic preachers have a great deal to teach us, both about style and contents. In terms of style, they constantly keep the hearers and their immediate situations in view. They appeal to the heart, they plead, they work to evoke a response of faithfulness. In terms of contents, their themes concern, as here, the action of God and the response of human be-ings. A favorite term in the book is "remember," as in "do this in remembrance of me." Those who remember what God has done to bring them into a blessed land will respond with deeds and words of thanksgiving.

The season of Lent is a time for such remembrance and response.

Psalm 91:1–2, 9–16

The use of this psalm in the description of the temptations of Jesus by both Matthew (4:6) and Luke (4:10–11), who probably wrote independently, indicates that the early church in the very beginning employed this text when talking about the nature and shape of Jesus' ministry.

Psalm 91 oozes with religious assurance, with divine promises and pledges. It expresses elements of faith ready-made for overconfidence and pious extravagances.

In some respects, the psalm is an enigma for scholars. In what context did it originate? Who is being spoken to and about in the psalm? A breakdown of the psalm may help answer these questions. Verses 1–8 seem to me to be a brief sermonette addressed to a "you" but spo-ken in reasonably general terms. The thrust of these verses is to assure the worshiper of divine care and preservation in the face of a forthcoming situation of grave danger. In verses 9–13, the address to the worshiper becomes a little more personal, a little more directly assuring. Reading these verses, one gets the feeling of a particular "you," an actual human person being spoken to. Verses 14–16 shift from human-human speech to divine-human speech. In God's address, the "you" has become a "he" (RSV; "those" in NRSV); the person earlier spoken to has become the person spoken about.

One way of interpreting this psalm is to see it as originally used in a worship service in which the king was the central figure (see Psalms 20–21). The king was perhaps facing the dangers of a forthcoming war. (If not a king going to war, then perhaps the context was a situa-tion in which an ordinary person was confronting a major but dangerous undertaking—a long journey, a dangerous job, military service. At any rate, the psalm was to launch one forth with confidence and chutzpah.)

The verses for this lection contain the positive words addressed to the worshiper, perhaps by the priest (vv. 9–13), but also by God himself, the words probably delivered as divine address by the priest (vv. 14–16). The basis of confidence is expounded in verse 9 (compare vv. 1–2, which describe the person who seeks refuge and shelter in God), namely, the worshiper's will-ingness to seek refuge with and take recourse in God. The consequences of such protection are stated negatively and then positively. Negatively, the person will not fall victim to any evil or scourge (two general terms, the first perhaps denoting evil in the sense of moral wrong and the latter signifying amoral ill fortune). Positively, the worshiper is assured that God's angels (or messengers; the Hebrew and Greek words mean both) will be guards who will watch over even such small matters as the foot stumbling against a stone. Playing off the imagery of the foot, the writer declares that the worshiper can tread on snakes and trample beasts underfoot.

The divine speech that finishes off the psalm uses language that is both calming and con-soling. There is no longer reference to snakes, thousands dying on every hand, pestilence in the night, and "things that go 'bump' in the dark." There is, however, the repetition of the causal relationship, as in verses 1–2 and 9: "Because he hath set his love upon me" (KJV). These final verses are dominated by a focus on the divine: in God's speech, the first person pronoun or suffix occurs twelve times in Hebrew. The divine "I" hovers over the sentiments of the psalm and is the source of the promises of protection.

Romans 10:8b–13

Today's text overlaps with the epistolary lection for Proper 14 [19] in Year A (Rom. 10:5–15). The reader may want to consult our remarks there.

It makes a smoother introduction to begin this epistolary lection with the words "The word is near you" (v. 8b), but we should look at the larger context. It should be noted that Paul here is contrasting "righteousness that comes from the law" (v. 5; "legal righteousness," NEB) with "righteousness that comes from faith" (v. 6). The background to his exposition is provided by Deuteronomy 30:11–14, which emphasizes the nearness and accessibility of God's covenant with Israel. What God requires through the covenant is not remote. It is neither in the heaven nor beyond the sea, as if Israel had to go find it. Rather, "the word is very near to you; it is in your mouth and in your heart for you to observe" (Deut. 30:14). In establishing a covenant with Israel, Yahweh had graciously reached out in their direction, had drawn near to them, had indeed come to be within them—on their lips and in their hearts (cf. Jer. 31:31–34).

Drawing on these words from Deuteronomy, Paul reads them in light of the Christ-event. Just as Israel was reassured that the covenant was not remote and far away, so Paul insists that Christ is to be sought neither in the heavens nor in the abyss of Hades. It is not as if we must go in search of Christ to find him. He may be physically absent, but he is nevertheless fully present—here. And how is this so? Through the "word of faith that we proclaim" (v. 8). It is through this proclaimed word, the gospel, that the "word is near you, on your lips and in your heart" (v. 8). Here Paul is insisting that Christ as mediated to us through the preached Word is as near, as much within us, as was the covenant Yahweh made with Israel.

It is difficult to think of anything nearer or more existentially present than the very words on our lips or the convictions of our hearts. What is said and what is believed define who we are. Here, what is said is the Christian confession—"Jesus is Lord" (1 Cor. 12:3; 2 Cor. 4:5; Phil. 2:11; Col. 2:6)—and what is believed is the Easter faith: God raised Christ from the dead (Rom. 4:24; 1 Pet. 1:21). It is on the basis of this conviction and this confession that we are justified, or saved.

It follows rather naturally that salvation should be universally available. After all, every human being has convictions in the heart that are uttered with the lips. Consequently, Paul cites Isaiah 28:16 to show that all who believe will find their faith coming to fruition. They will not be put to shame. They will not be disappointed. This applies to everyone—Jew and Gentile alike. Because there is only one Lord—that is, Jesus Christ (Acts 10:36; Phil. 2:9–11)—there can be no two ways of salvation. Everyone is justified on the same grounds and in the same way—through faith. We should recognize that the Lord's bounty is extensive enough to accommodate everyone who is willing to yield in faith. Thus, "everyone who calls on the name of the Lord shall be saved" (v. 13; cf. Joel 2:32).

We should note the repeated insistence that everyone has access to God in faith. If we see ourselves as the elect of God, it is only too easy to conclude that we have a monopoly on God's riches. But God draws near through the preached Word to everyone, and those who respond by calling on the name of the Lord for help and hope will not be disappointed—they will be saved.

From this midrashic exposition of Deuteronomy 30:11–14, and its use of other Old Testament passages, we can make the following observations:

First, salvation is not so much a matter of our drawing near to Christ, as if to seek him out and find him at the end of a long search. It is rather that Christ has drawn near to us through the gospel. This means that the presence of God as mediated through Christ has become both universalized and localized. It is no longer necessary for us to go find Christ in a sacred place (cf. John 4), for now the Word of God has become portable. Christ becomes present whenever and wherever the gospel is preached. Salvation is to be found here and now—within us—because God has drawn near.

Second, salvation belongs to the faithful—all the faithful, not to a select group who regard themselves as the most faithful or the only faithful. The basis on which all of humanity comes to know God is now common to us all. We can be assured that our faith, if it is genuine, will not come to nought. We can also be assured that God's riches are bountiful enough to go around. We may believe that God is exclusively ours or that we relate to God in a uniquely close relationship, but the fact is that everyone who calls out to God for help, even as we do, can and will be heard.

Luke 4:1–13

The forty days of Lent (except Sundays) bring immediately to mind the forty days of Jesus' struggle and testing in the wilderness, a story that had its antecedents in Moses' forty days without food on the mountain (Exod. 34:28; Deut. 9:9), Elijah's forty days in flight to the mountain of God (1 Kings 19:4–8), and, of course, the forty years of Israel's struggle in the wilderness. In fact, this last reference to the wilderness trials of Israel, especially as recited in Deuteronomy, is clearly the immediate background for the Gospel lesson today. Not only does Deuteronomy provide the Old Testament reading, but the Epistle draws upon Deuteronomy 30, and in Luke 4:1–13 Jesus quotes from Deuteronomy three times.

Because the temptation of Jesus is recorded in all three Synoptics, the preacher would do well to spend some time getting into focus the story as Luke tells it. Evidently Luke owes little to Mark's brief account (1:12–13) but holds much in common with Matthew (4:1–11). However, even there noticeable differences appear. Matthew, following Mark, joins the temptation directly to the baptism. Paul, in describing Israel's wilderness experience, moves directly from "baptism" in the Red Sea to temptations and tests of loyalty (1 Cor. 10:1–10). Luke, however, places the genealogy of Jesus between the baptism and the temptation accounts. This pattern may have been suggested by the fact that Moses' call and ministry are separated by a genealogy in Exodus 6:14–25. The break is not disruptive, however, because the baptism, the genealogy, and the temptation all affirm Jesus as Son of God (3:22, 38; 4:3, 9). In Luke, Jesus' not eating "during those days" (v. 2) is not formalized into a forty-day fast as in Matthew (4:2). In Luke, the devil's showing Jesus all the kingdoms of the world is stated temporally ("in an instant," v. 5), whereas the reference is spatial in Matthew ("to a very high mountain," 4:8). Luke's second and third temptations are reversed from Matthew's order. Because the temple was given so much importance in Luke's story of Jesus and the early church (Luke 2:41–52; 24:53; Acts 2:46; 3:1; 22:17), the temple temptation may have been made the story's climax. Finally, it is worth noting that Luke, although quite comfortable with angels, has none here, as Mark and Matthew do (Mark 1:13; Matt. 4:11). Instead, the devil simply leaves until an opportune time arrives for renewing the struggle, a time that did present itself through Judas (22:3).

Now that we have Luke's telling of it more clearly before us, what emphases present themselves for consideration?

First, it should be said that Luke's Jesus, though less dramatically than Mark's, opposes and is opposed by strong forces of evil. In whatever images or concepts the power of evil may be presented, it is the testimony of experience as well as Scripture that there is in the world opposition to love, health, wholeness, and peace. It does not go away by closing the eyes and smiling. In fact, it is those called of God and committed to the way of God in the world who experience most forcefully the struggle with evil. If Jesus wrestled, why should any of his followers think that believing makes them exempt from the fray?

Second, notice Luke's accent on the Holy Spirit. Jesus was born of the Spirit (1:35); he received the Spirit at baptism (3:22); he was full of the Holy Spirit (4:1); he was led by the Spirit (4:1); and following his temptations, Jesus went into Galilee to minister in the power of the Spirit (4:18). This Spirit was not Jesus' alone but was promised to and is experienced by the church (Luke 24:49; Acts 1:8; 2:1–4, 38). Resisting evil and ministering to human need are not left to willpower and psychic strategies; the effective presence of God is offered and available.

Third, Jesus is the victor in the time of testing by joining to the presence of the Spirit the appropriate use of Scripture (4:4, 8, 12). Scripture can be used inappropriately, to oppose obedience to God and to undermine the purposes of God, as the devil demonstrates by quoting Psalm 91:11–12. But the fact that even the grossest errors may be blessed by some misused biblical text should not cause the people of God to shun the use of Scripture to enlighten, inform, and discipline faith. It is important for Luke and Luke's church that the story of Jesus—from birth, through death and resurrection, to the proclamation of good news to the nations—is "according to the Scriptures" (24:27, 44–49). The church, armed with the Spirit and with the Scriptures, will not be overcome by evil but will overcome evil with good.

Second Sunday in Lent

Genesis 15:1–12, 17–18;
Psalm 27;
Philippians 3:17–4:1;
Luke 13:31–35 or Luke 9:28–36

The readings for the Second Sunday in Lent stress promise and expectation. The account of the covenant with Abraham in Genesis 15 presents God's promise of a child to the childless, and Abraham responds with faithful trust in the God who makes the promise. The responsorial psalm is filled with assurance and confident trust in God. The epistolary reading calls attention to the cross and reminds the church that it awaits its savior. The words of Jesus to Herod in Luke 13:31–35 spark anticipation of the events commemorated during Holy Week.

Luke's account of the transfiguration (Luke 9:28–36) points forward to Jesus' departure and thus not only to the events of Holy Week but also to Jesus' glorification.

Genesis 15:1–12, 17–18

The literary and theological context of Genesis 15 is the story of the patriarchs (Genesis 12–50), in which the dominant motifs are the promises God gives the ancestors and the covenants God makes with them. Covenants are, in effect, promissory oaths, in which one party vows to do something in the future for the other party. Our text is but one of the accounts of the covenant with Abraham. At the heart of this covenant is God's promise to Abraham to be with the patriarch, to give him a son, and through that son descendants as numerous as the stars in the sky. Those descendants will in turn inherit the land in which Abraham is only a resident alien. A close parallel to this covenant appears in Genesis 17, and the contents of the covenantal promise had already been presented with the initial call of Abraham in Genesis 12:1–3. Similar if not identical promises and covenants will define the stories of the other patriarchs, Isaac and Jacob.

The identification of Genesis 15 with one or more of the pentateuchal sources has long been a matter of dispute. In addition to the parallels to other material in the Abraham story, evidence for a complex history of transmission is seen in the duplicates, repetitions, and slight inconsistencies within the chapter itself. Some commentators see here the beginning of the Elohistic source, and others mainly the work of the Yahwist. If E material is present, it is only in bits and pieces, and hardly in the form of a complete story. It is likely that the tensions within the account reflect the history of its oral transmission rather than the combination of literary sources. In any case, the chapter comes from the older literary strata of the Pentateuch.

Consider the structure and contents of the passage. It is a narrative, an account of the Lord's encounter with Abraham for the purpose of establishing a covenant. It is not at all clear how much of the activity is understood to have occurred within a "vision" (v. 1), as a dream while Abraham slept (v. 12), or as a divine audition (vv. 1, 4) like those of the prophets. Only two characters appear, the Lord and Abraham, and much of the story recounts the dialogue between them. There are two rather distinct units, verses 1–6 and 7–18.

The first section of the dialogue (vv. 1–6) deals with the promise of descendants to Abraham. The Lord speaks first with a word of assurance (v. 1), and Abraham responds with an expression of his fear and concern about his childlessness (vv. 2–3). The Lord's next speech (vv. 4–5) is a specific promise concerning the patriarch's descendants. Abraham's response is belief, which the Lord "reckoned . . . to him as righteousness" (v. 6).

The next series of dialogues (vv. 7–21) concerns the covenant itself, its contents and the ritual for concluding it. The Lord speaks (v. 7), identifying himself in terms of past actions (bringing Abraham out of Ur) and future promises (the gift of the land). As in his response to the initial encounter, Abraham raises a question that suggests uncertainty if not doubt (v. 8). The Lord then instructs the patriarch to bring certain animals (v. 9). Abraham does so, cuts them up and lays them out in a specific ritual pattern, and then falls into a deep sleep (vv. 10–12). In the dark a "smoking fire pot and a flaming torch passed between these pieces," and the Lord concluded the covenant with Abraham, promising to his descendants the land from "the river of Egypt to the great river, the river Euphrates" (vv. 17–18).

A number of points require some explanation. The structure of verses 1–6 is similar to the oracle of salvation found in prophetic literature and probably rooted in cultic practice. Verses 3–4 presuppose an ancient practice whereby a slave could be the heir of one who had no natural children. The animals of verses 9–10 are not sacrifices, but part of a covenant ritual. Covenants are like oaths in that they are conditional self-curses. The practice of cutting up the animals and passing between their halves is a symbolic representation of the covenant curse, calling down upon the participants such a fate if they do not abide by the stipulations. Such practice is probably behind the idiom "to cut a covenant." The "smoking fire pot" (better, "oven") and "flaming torch" that passed between the pieces is a representation of the presence of the Lord.

Under the general theme of promises for the future, the main motifs that call for homiletical reflection seem to correspond to the two parts of the passage. Verses 7–18 stress the covenant, its establishment through solemn—even fearful—ritual, and its contents, the promise to Abraham of descendants who will later possess the land. As in virtually all divine-human covenants in the Old Testament, the initiative is God's. The promise comes without precondition, but it does call for response. Note also what is concrete and what is not. God's future has a concrete and specific place in view, and particular people. But Abraham himself has only the hope and the signs of its eventual fulfillment in the form of ritual and, later on, the first of his descendants.

The issue of the first section (vv. 1–6), as stated in its concluding verse, is faith. A problem—fear, anxiety, doubt?—is assumed at the very outset, else there would be no need for reassurance. Moreover, Abraham at first challenges God, finding the promise difficult to accept, for he is childless (v. 2). When the Lord responds with the specific promise of descendants as numerous as the stars, "he believed the LORD; and the LORD reckoned it to him as righteousness" (v. 6). "Belief" here does not refer to a single act or experience, but to a continuous response. Nor does it mean agreement to certain ideas or propositions. Rather, this belief, or faith, is trust and commitment to the God of the covenant, the acceptance of the promise. To have that faith "reckoned" as "righteousness" should be understood in the context of the covenant relationship. "Righteousness," frequently linked in prophetic literature to "justice," concerns being in accord with the covenant stipulations and expectations. There is no indication of what in particular Abraham did that God took to be faith. The account at that point reports no words at all. Could that be the point? Could faith be found in the silent acceptance of the divine promise? On the other hand, both before (v. 2) and after (v. 8) being accounted faithful, Abraham is heard to express to God his doubts and questions.

Psalm 27

The unity of this psalm can be seen in the following outline: (a) an affirmation of confidence addressed by the worshiper (the king?) to a human audience prior to the offering of sacrifices (verses 1–6), (b) a petitionary prayer addressed to God probably in conjunction with the offering of sacrifice (verses 7–12), (c) a confessional statement by the worshiper to a human audience perhaps to the cultic personnel in charge of the ritual (verse 13; note the confessional counterpart in verse 10), and (d) the response of the cultic official to the worshiper (verse 14). All of these components fit together nicely as the component parts in a worship service.

The first stanza, verses 1–3, is an affirmation of confidence, of trust, of confession, of certitude. In spite of the speaker's assertion of his confidence in God's support, spoken to his peers, perhaps by the king to his subjects, a sense of fear and insecurity permeates the material. This is only natural for if fear and fright are not real then neither are confidence and trust. The vocabulary of opposition—evildoers, adversaries, foes, a host, war—is balanced by descriptive assertions about God—my light, my salvation, the stronghold of my life. The speaker's confidence lies not in personal character traits like courage and fortitude but in the assurance of divine support and aid. The sense of confidence is not equivalent to arrogance, as is even clearer when the psalm turns to petition in verse 7. The affirmations of confidence are like islands situated in the sea of life's terrors—safe but always threatened.

The psalmist's opponents are described in metaphorical fashion, as is common in the psalms. The goal of the evildoers in the second line of verse 2 is described as "to devour my flesh." This may refer to slander (so the NRSV) or be terminology borrowed from the way one would speak of wild animals and thus denote the enemies as beasts. Adversaries and foes are general terms but verse 3 utilizes military terminology. If this psalm were originally written for the use of the king, then the situation of distress could have been a potential military engagement. At any rate, the speaker is certain of overcoming fear as well as his opposition.

In the second stanza, verses 4–6, the emphasis shifts to focus on expectations associated with entry into the temple. The temple is seen as the source of refuge from the enemy and of communion with the Deity.

Verse 4, with its reference to dwelling in the house of the Lord (= the temple) forever, unless this is to be taken entirely metaphorically, could suggest that the psalm was used by some temple functionary or official. Probably this would not mean a priest since priests did not live in the temple precincts. The priests at the Jerusalem temple served only during the major festival celebrations and for two additional weeks in the year on a rotation basis. It is not impossible that the person speaking was guilty of manslaughter and was seeking the security of asylum in the sanctuary (see Exod. 21:12–14).

The single-minded desire of the psalmist—"that I may dwell in the house of the Lord all the days of my life"—had two goals in mind. The first was to behold the beauty of God and the second was to inquire in his temple (verse 4). The expression "to behold the beauty of the Lord" may have its roots in the ancient practice of carrying statues of the gods in parades so the worshipers could see the deities unveiled. Probably in this text it means to experience the gracious presence of God or to experience the Divine in a state of worshipful ecstasy. "To inquire in the temple" would imply that the worshiper wished either to receive a response from God or to contemplate (note the word's connection with the term "temple") the Divine in an atmosphere of religious intensity.

The consequences of his appearance in the temple are described as twofold. (1) God will protect him from his enemies (v. 5). Three images are employed to convey this expectation: being hidden in a shelter (the word refers to the special booth lived in at the festival of tabernacles), being concealed under the cover of a tent, and being placed on a high rock. The first two images draw on the idea of gaining the asylum and protection from a host while in his company. (2) The worshiper eventually expects to be victorious over the enemy and to celebrate his success with sacrifices of joy, which would involve feasting and celebrating, and singing before the Lord.

In versus 7–12, the worshiper addresses God directly. In the early portion of the psalm, the speaker addressed a human audience. The person-to-person address, in verses 1–6, is characterized by confidence and reliance. In fact, it might be said to contain a slight air of braggadocio. The address to the Deity is radically different. It is a lament pleading with the Deity for support and for divine presence.

The lament opens with a request for a hearing and for a favorable response from the Deity (v. 7). The psalmist reminds God that the worshiper is now doing what has been the divine invitation, namely seeking the face of God (v. 8). "To seek the face of" could here refer not only to worship but also to a direct appeal to the Deity which would result in a divine decision communicated to the worshiper, probably through the cultic personnel in charge of the ritual. "To turn one's face from" or "to hide one's face" was to give a negative response. (See the priestly benediction in Num. 6:24–26 where "to make the face shine" is an expression of favor.)

The same request as found in verses 7–9a, but expressed in different words, appears in verse 9bc. Here the request is formulated in terms of the impact on the worshiper: "Turn not your servant away . . . cast me not off, forsake me not." Whereas the worshiper had earlier bragged of having the presence of God which made him confident even though beset by an army, he now pleads not to experience the absence of God, not to be forced to endure the divine forsakenness.

Verse 10 is an interesting verse. Its reference to the Lord in the third person seems to disrupt the prayer that is expressed directly to God in verses 7–9 and in verses 11–12. The verse could be seen as a confessional statement made by the worshiper in the midst of a service but addressed to the cultic leader assuring the human audience that his faith is still strong and that solid confidence still lays beneath the surface fear of being abandoned. The reference to having been forsaken by both parents can be understood in various ways (see Job 19:13–14; Ps. 38:11): (a) it may have been merely a metaphorical expression intending to indicate how all alone and isolated one felt, (b) the person could have been an abandoned child, perhaps one given to the temple (see v. 4), and (c) as one considered guilty, the person may have been deserted even by his own kith and kin. As such, one would have been abandoned even by those—the family—whose support should endure regardless of the conditions. However one interprets the specifics of the claim, its general intent is clear: the worshiper claims to be totally forsaken with only God as a hope for support.

In verses 11–12, the tone of the prayer shifts to very specific requests. Earlier the psalmist spoke of dwelling in the house of God, of beholding the beauty of God, and of inquiring in the temple (v. 4). All of these reflect a desire for mystical and extraordinary experiences. The threefold petitions in verses 11–12 are much more down to earth. (1) The worshiper prays to be taught, to be instructed in the way of the Lord. To place oneself in the posture of a pupil, to renew the status of a learner is an act of humility. To pray to be taught is the expression of a willingness to make a new beginning, to start afresh. (2) There is a second request: that one be led on a level path. The request may be nothing more than the hope that henceforth life will be more predictable, more normal, less filled with the canyons and crags of uncertainty and turmoil. Or it may be a request for life to assume a new shape and a new form. To pray to be led on a level path suggests a commitment to follow the straight and narrow. A willingness to be led implies a willingness to walk. These first two requests are made "because of my enemies"—so that the enemies would have no real grounds to accuse or so they could not attack from ambush. (3) The third request expresses a negative desire—not to be given up to the greed or will of one's opponents. The person may have been charged with a crime or slandered about (note the reference to false witnesses in v. 12) and thus requests that God support his cause (perhaps by giving a verdict in his favor; see Deut. 17:8–13).

The concluding verses of the psalm are to be understood as a final confession made by the worshiper (v. 13) and an oracle of encouragement addressed to the worshiper by the priestly functionary (v. 14) who presided at the ritual when this psalm was utilized. The worshiper's confession is life-affirming. In spite of the distress of the hour, he is convinced that he will see the goodness of God, that is, experience divine blessing as long as he lives. "In the land of the living" is a circumlocution to avoid making a reference directly or indirectly to one's death when it is not imminent. The priestly word is upbeat. Wait, be strong, take courage. The Greek translator here has the text say, "Be manly."

Philippians 3:17–4:1

We may think it presumptuous for Paul to instruct his readers to imitate himself and others whose way of life conforms to his own. But it was accepted practice for Greek and Roman moralists to urge their readers to follow a certain course of action and then offer them examples of the behavior they wanted to promote. It was quite acceptable for a teacher to offer himself as a model for his students, for parents to offer themselves as models for their children, or for the elderly to serve as examples for the young.

Today's epistolary lection conforms to this well-accepted form of moral instruction. First, we have the exhortation or appeal (v. 17), and it is specifically a call to imitation. Then we have a negative depiction of a way of life to be avoided—an earthly mind-set (vv. 18–19)—followed by a positive portrait of the way of life Paul himself exemplified—heavenly citizenship (vv. 20–21). Finally, there is an endearing call to steadfastness (4:1).

As to the call for imitation, this is a note frequently sounded in Pauline paraenesis (1 Cor. 4:16; 11:1; 1 Thess. 1:6; 2 Thess. 3:7–9; also Gal. 4:12). Even further, we find repeated instances in early Christian teaching where the faithful serve as role models (1 Thess. 1:7; 2:14; 2 Thess. 3:9; 1 Tim. 4:12; Titus 2:7; Heb. 6:12; 13:7). In some cases, the object of imitation is God (Eph. 5:1) or Christ (1 Cor. 11:1; 1 Pet. 2:21; perhaps Phil. 2:5–11).

Viewed one way, imitation as a form of ethical praxis appears hollow and thoughtless. After all, what is there to be gained by rote behavioral simulation? Does this not transfer the center and motivation for moral renewal from ourselves to someone else? And yet, as little as we admire mindless copying of mannerisms and life-style, we all recognize the intrinsic worth of an exemplary life. Martin Luther King Jr. regarded Gandhi's life and teaching as exemplary, yet King's appropriation of Gandhi's philosophy of nonviolence and radical love for peace was by no means rote. Imitation as a form of exhortation simply recognizes a fundamental human truth—the capacity for one human life to form and influence other human lives. This no one can deny.

Having issued the call for imitation, Paul sketches the negative side. Those who have brought him to tears are the "enemies of the cross of Christ" (v. 18). We can tell very little about who these enemies actually were because his description of them employs fairly stock phrases used to pillory opponents. They are bent on destruction (cf. 2 Cor. 11:15; 2 Pet. 2:1). They have no capacity for restraint or moderation, because they give in to their own appetites, probably for food but possibly for sex (Rom. 16:18; 2 Tim. 3:4). They are self-indulgent. The "shame" in which they glory may be a euphemism for circumcision. The language is supplied by Hosea 4:7. In a word, they have an earthly mind-set (Col. 3:2).

In sharp contrast to this is the outlook defined by the transcendent reality of the risen Lord (vv. 20–21). The life to which Paul has committed himself is impelled by a view of the city of God of which he is a heavenly citizen (cf. Eph. 2:6; Col. 3:1; Heb. 11:10; 12:22; 13:14; Rev. 21:2). This is what engenders hope in the coming Savior (1 Cor. 1:7; 1 Tim. 6:14; 2 Tim. 1:10; Titus 2:11, 13; 3:6; 2 Pet. 1:11). Nor is this merely a hope that awaits an arrival of a visitor from heaven, but one that transforms the earthly into the heavenly. The resurrection hope entails a radical change in the form of human existence—from "the body of our humiliation" to a resplendent form that is like "the body of his glory" (v. 21; cf. 1 Cor. 15:43, 49, 53; Rom. 8:29; 12:2; 2 Cor. 3:18; 1 John 3:2). How is all of this achieved? Through the resurrection power (cf. 1 Cor. 15:27; Eph. 1:19–22).

With these two options clearly sketched, we stand at the fork in the road, and Paul's final appeal is to "stand firm in the Lord" (4:1; cf. 1 Cor. 16:13). It is couched in tender language reminiscent of the letter as a whole (1:4; 2:2, 17; 4:10). It is, after all, "in the Lord" where our lives are lifted to heavenly heights as we share in the resurrection hope. It is from this position that we are able to transcend "earthly things" (v. 19).

Numerous themes appropriate to Lent are sounded in this passage. First, the theme of imitation obviously provides one way of thinking about Lent, whether it is Christ's own suffering that serves as the focal example or that of the faithful people of God. In either case, this can become a time for conforming our own ways and wills to a form of life whose enduring feature is the capacity to appropriate the cross of Christ rather than become its enemy through radical self-indulgence.

Second, the "earthly" life-style is seen as one that gives in to our own desires without any capacity for restraint or self-denial. Even though the portrait here is stereotypical, it etches the outlines of a style of life avidly pursued by many, even many of us.

Third, heavenly citizenship is that which transforms us, even as we live "below," and eventually enables us to move from an ordinary to a resplendent existence.

Luke 13:31–35

Luke 13:31–35 is especially appropriate for the Lenten Season in that this text looks toward Jerusalem and the passion of Jesus. And if Lent be understood as a pilgrimage to Good Friday and Easter, this passage is doubly appropriate, for it falls within Luke's lengthy "journey narrative" (9:51–19:27). This large section begins with the declaration "he set his face to go to Jerusalem" (9:51). That controlling image of Jesus had been repeated as recently as 13:22: "Jesus went through one town and village after another . . . as he made his way to Jerusalem." Luke is fond of the journey format not only for presenting Jesus' ministry in the Gospel and Paul's in Acts, but also for characterizing the Christians as pilgrims, those of "the Way" (Acts 9:2; 19:9, 23; 22:4; 24:14, 22). When the travel narrative is understood as Luke's way of giving a frame to a number of sayings and events in Jesus' life, then the extremely difficult task of reconstructing a chronology for the journey to Jerusalem ceases to be of primary importance.

Luke 13:31–35 consists of two distinct subunits: verses 31–33 and verses 34–35. The latter part is found in Matthew 23:37–39, but with one noticeable difference in what otherwise is an almost word-for-word parallel. The former part, verses 31–33, is in Luke alone.

Perhaps most striking here is the favorable picture of the Pharisees, especially for those of us who had been given the impression that the Pharisees were always and everywhere the villains in the story of Jesus. Herod Antipas, son of Herod the Great, was tetrarch of Galilee (Luke 3:1) during Jesus' ministry. He had beheaded John the Baptist and now was perplexed about Jesus, especially because there was a rumor that Jesus was John raised from the dead (Luke 9:7–9). Apparently Herod now wants to cure his perplexity by killing Jesus also (13:32). Jesus is neither intimidated nor deterred in his ministry, for he lives and works under the divine necessity: "I must be on my way" (v. 33). This means that even though death for Jesus is near ("the third day" is surely intended here to refer to what is impending and not to the exact time frame), he will continue to exorcize demons and heal the sick, he will bring his ministry to its consummation (v. 32), and he will die in Jerusalem (v. 33). This reaffirms the divine imperative with which this entire section began (9:51). That the Pharisees, in an act of friendship, would warn Jesus about Herod should not surprise the reader of Luke. Whereas Mark 3:6 states that Pharisees and Herodians joined in the design to kill Jesus, Luke's parallel to that omits the Herodians and offers the more moderate description of the Pharisees discussing "what they might do to Jesus" (6:11). In Luke, many Pharisees seem open to Jesus (7:36; 11:37; 14:1), even though they do differ strongly with him on certain interpretations of the law. A Pharisee, Gamaliel, was a moderating voice in the Jewish council when dealing with the followers of Jesus (Acts 5:34), and some of the early Christians were, according to Luke, Pharisees (15:5), including, by his own admission, Paul (23:6). But even so, Luke wants us to understand that both friends (Pharisees) and foes (Herod) could not alter Jesus' sure obedience to the will of God.

Very likely it is the attention on Jerusalem that prompts Luke to place here the lament over that city (vv. 34–35). Jerusalem is central in Luke's narrative, not only about Jesus but also about the early church. Luke mentions Jerusalem ninety times; in the remainder of the new Testament, it is mentioned only forty-nine. But the fact that verse 33 ends with the word "Jerusalem" is hardly sufficient reason for Luke to locate here a passage that seems so clearly out of place. "How often have I desired to gather your children" (v. 34) implies a Judean ministry that has yet to occur. Matthew places the saying near the close of Jesus' ministry in Jerusalem (23:37–39), a natural setting for it. Hence, when Jesus says in Matthew, "you will not see me *again* until" (v. 39, italics added), the reference is to the final crisis. In Luke, however, Jesus is on his way to the city; therefore, when he says "you will not see me until," the reference is to his arrival at Jerusalem when the people shout, "Blessed is the king who comes in the name of the Lord!" (19:38), almost the exact words of 13:35.

By locating this apostrophe to Jerusalem earlier, Luke is saying that there is yet time to repent, yet time to receive the Christ, yet time to avoid the final catastrophe. With repentance comes forgiveness—an offer to the world, beginning with Jerusalem (24:47).

Luke 9:28–36

Luke 9:28–36 is offered as an alternate lesson for today, with no suggestion that it be tied to 13:31–35. Interestingly enough, a connection could easily be made, for in Luke's account of the Transfiguration, Jesus, Moses, and Elijah are talking of Jesus' coming departure (exodus) in Jerusalem (v. 31), the very theme of 13:31–35. However, Luke 9:28–36 is offered here (the parallels in Matthew and Mark appear as alternate lections the other two years) to honor a long-standing tradition in some churches to consider the Transfiguration on the Second Sunday of Lent. If such a text seems unusual for the Lenten Season, consider two facts: (1) none of the Sundays in Lent are fast days but preserve the Easter joy even in repentance; and (2) the Gospels themselves set their Transfiguration stories in the context of passion predictions and the turn toward Jerusalem. In fact, the immediately preceding verses (9:23–27) deal with discipleship and cross bearing, themes certainly fitting for Lent.

As recently as the Last Sunday After the Epiphany, the Transfiguration text was the Gospel lesson, as it always is on that Sunday. The preacher may not want to return so soon to Luke 9:28–36; but if so, it would seem wise to focus on the elements of the story appropriate for Lent. Four comments may be suggestive:

1. Luke places the event "about eight days" after the preceding sayings (v. 28), departing from Mark 9:2, which follows closely the Moses story of Exodus 24:16. Because "eight days" was a way of referring to Sunday, perhaps Luke is conveying the message and mood of resurrection.

2. Unlike Matthew 17:1–8 and Mark 9:2–8, Luke inserts the content of the conversation among Jesus, Moses, and Elijah (v. 31) and the response of the disciples (v. 32). The discussion of Jesus' approaching death was for Jesus, not the disciples; therefore sleep kept them from hearing. They did see the glory and that was enough. In fact, it was too much; they did not understand. However, some experiences, though not comprehended, still leave their lasting marks on us.

3. What the disciples do hear is addressed to them (v. 35). Although Jesus' death had its confirmation in the law (Moses) and the prophets (Elijah), Jesus alone is the Son of God and is to be obeyed.

4. Whereas Matthew 17:9–13 and Mark 9:9–13 conclude the story with conversation between Jesus and the disciples, including a command not to tell anyone until after the resurrection, Luke simply offers a closing comment on their silence "in those days" (v. 36). Perhaps like Luke's Mary, they pondered these things in their hearts. When words of witness finally break such silence, they command attention and are worth hearing.

Third Sunday in Lent

Isaiah 55:1–9;
Psalm 63:1–8;
1 Corinthians 10:1–13;
Luke 13:1–9

At the heart of today's Old Testament reading is God's call for sinners to forsake the ways of evil and turn to the Lord, fully assured that God's pardon is freely available. With its emphasis on complete confidence and trust in God, Psalm 63 forms a fitting response. In the epistolary text, Paul recalls Israel's experience in the wilderness as a caution against false confidence and a reminder to flee the sins of idolatry and self-indulgence. In the Gospel text we have an urgent call to repentance, one of the most compelling in the New Testament.

Isaiah 55:1–9

This lesson (extending through v. 11) is one of the readings for the Easter Vigil in all three years of the lectionary cycle. This text comes from Second Isaiah from just before the end of the Babylonian Exile. It was and continues to be a call for hope and trust and a promise of salvation to the hearers. It is an appropriate reading as the church looks more and more toward Easter.

The passage as a whole has two distinct parts, verses 1–5 and 6–11, that are similar in both form and content. In the first section God is the speaker throughout, addressing the people of Israel as a whole. God begins with a series of imperatives (vv. 1–3a) that resemble on the one hand Lady Wisdom's invitation to a banquet (Prov. 9:5), and on the other hand the calls of street vendors. The invitations to come for what the Lord has to offer are both literal and metaphorical: God offers actual food, "food" that enables one to live the abundant life ("that you may live," v. 3a). What the people are invited to "come, buy and eat" is the proclamation of salvation that follows in verses 3b–5. God announces that the ancient covenant with David (2 Samuel 7) now applies to the people as a whole. Again, as is so often the case in the proclamations of Second Isaiah, Israel has in no sense earned this new covenant; it is a free act of God's grace. Moreover, just as the Lord made David a witness to the nations, now all nations will come to the people of Israel. The proclamation of salvation, then, is ultimately directed toward all peoples.

The second section (vv. 6–11) also begins with imperatives—calls to "seek the LORD" and to "call upon him." The "wicked" and "unrighteous" are invited to change their ways and "return to the LORD." These invitations, although addressed to the human heart, are quite concrete. To "seek" and "call upon" the Lord refer not simply to feelings or attitudes but to acts of prayer and worship. For the wicked to "forsake his way" is to change behavior. The foundation for the imperatives is stated at the end of verse 7, "for he will abundantly pardon." The remainder of the section (vv. 8–11) gives the basis for responding to God's call. God's plan for the world ("ways," "thoughts") is in sharp contrast to human designs. That plan is the announcement of salvation that the prophet has presented throughout the book—the redemption and renewal of the people of God. The will of God is effected by the word of God, another theme found throughout Isaiah 40–55. That divine word is the one uttered at creation (Gen. 1:3ff.), and it is God's announcement of the future through the prophets. In its emphasis on the word of God and its contrast between human and divine wisdom, this concluding section of Second Isaiah alludes to the beginning of the work (Isa. 40:1–11).

This second section of the reading is particularly helpful in advancing the theme of Lent: Sinners are urged to confess and repent for their sins, and are encouraged to do so by the assurance that God's pardon is freely available.

Psalm 63:1–8

This psalm contains some features of a lament, but a lament that expresses great trust and confidence in God. Some of its imagery correlates with that of the Samuel narrative. Verse 2 reminds one of Samuel's service in the sanctuary (1 Sam. 3:3), and the references to his thinking of God when he was in bed and his meditating on God in the watches of the night (v. 6) recall the nocturnal character of Samuel's call (1 Sam. 3:15).

The lament character of the psalm is indicated by its consistent address to the Deity and by the strong expression of longing for God (see the opening verse especially). The worshiper desires most of all a compassionate communion and fellowship with God or the continuation of such a relationship. The images of seeking, thirsting, and fainting for God may be compared to the eagerness with which Samuel responded to the word of God. The dry and weary land without God recalls the Israel of Samuel's day when the infrequent presence of God was an accepted and common phenomenon (1 Sam. 3:1).

Like most laments, this psalm contains a vow, or promise, of future action. In verses 3–4, the psalmist promises that his or her lips will praise God and that God will be the object of the petitioner's worship for the rest of life.

The final four verses of the lection are a statement of absolute trust and confidence probably based on the experience of worship noted in verse 2. Numerous images are detailed to express this trust and confidence. The soul is satisfied like one who has feasted on bone marrow and fat. Even when lying upon the bed and thinking of God through the watches of the night, when one is most apt to be aware of life's true relationships and tormented by troubles and conscience, there is still confidence. God has been so much of a help that the petitioner, now turned thanksgiver, can describe the human-divine relationship as being under protective wings like a baby bird protected by its mother.

Finally, the psalmist emphasizes the mutuality of the divine-human relationship. The worshiper clings to God, and God's right hand, the hand of strength, upholds the worshiper.

1 Corinthians 10:1–13

This passage should be read in the overall context of 1 Corinthians 8–10, where Paul discusses the question of eating meat that had been sacrificed to idols. The underlying ethical issue that emerges has to do with what form individual freedom should take within the community of believers. Is it qualified or unqualified? Does individual freedom have limits? What is the relationship between individual freedom and corporate responsibility? How does one's freedom to act relate to one's responsibility to others? From the sound of things, some within the church were insisting on their right to behave as they pleased. Apparently they resisted the idea that their individual freedom might be limited by circumstances or the needs of others.

Responding to this attitude, Paul first offers his own apostolic behavior as a positive example of self-restraint (chap. 9, esp. v. 25). He then turns to Israel as a negative example (10:1–13). Rather than exercising restraint, Israel had been indulgent, giving in to their own desires and following their own will. In addition, they had become self-confident and arrogant. Israel epitomized what some in the Corinthian church were becoming—indulgent, self-willed, overconfident.

Paul's remarks exhibit a fairly clear structure. After elaborating on the biblical theme of Israel's exodus (10:1–5), Paul draws several lessons from this midrashic exposition (10:6–13).

We may consider these in turn. In the opening section he begins by noting that Israel's passage through the Red Sea was a baptism into Moses. After Israel entered the wilderness, they ate and drank supernatural provisions. Here we find an Old Testament theme being Christianized. As the Old Testament story is read, it is interpreted in light of Christian experience. Paul saw in Israel's experience a form of baptismal initiation and eucharistic eating. Indeed, the rock from which they drank is said to be Christ.

Apparently, some of the Corinthians had concluded that their baptism and participation in the Eucharist somehow guaranteed their position before God. They possessed what one scholar has called a "robust sacramentalism." By receiving the sacraments, they felt confident— probably too confident. As a way of cautioning against such false confidence, Paul stresses that even though all of Israel had shared the same saving experience of the Exodus and had received the same spiritual nourishment, they still remained vulnerable. Note the way Paul contrasts "all" and "most"—*all* were under the cloud, *all* passed through the sea, *all* were baptized, *all* ate the same supernatural food, *all* ate the same supernatural drink. They *all* experienced a common deliverance and received the same nourishment. Yet, with *most* of them, God was displeased! Even though they all experienced divine deliverance and were sustained by divine nourishment, the majority of them buckled.

In the remarks that follow, Paul warns against four vices: (1) idolatry (v. 7), (2) immorality (v. 8), (3) tempting God (v. 9), and (4) grumbling (v. 10). In at least two cases, these are vices of indulgence that result from being unable to practice restraint. After reminding us that Israel's experience serves as a warning to us (v. 11), he warns against false confidence (v. 12). Yet the passage ends on a note of reassurance. We are reminded that the temptations we face everyone faces. But besides the universality of temptation, there is the fidelity of God. Just as Israel was provided a way of escape, so can we be confident that God will not tempt us beyond what we are able to bear.

This passage has several features that relate to Lenten observance.

First, the baptismal metaphor in verse 2 reminds us that historically the season of Lent served as a period for preparing candidates for baptism. It serves as a sober reminder that our initiation into the faith in no way insures us against the vices of indulgence. In fact, it may lead to false confidence. Similarly, we may assume that partaking of the Eucharist somehow makes us immune to the evils of selfishness and fleshly desires. Here Paul is calling us to reflect soberly on our baptism and participation in the Lord's Supper and not to develop a false sense of security.

Second, because Lent serves as a time for penitence and prayer, we are prompted to think both of the temptations that beset all of us and of the confident hope from God that strengthens us and enables us to stand firm. In one sense, the passage is a warning; but before it ends it becomes a solid reassurance, inviting us to trust in a God who is faithful. Even if Israel was unfaithful, God was not.

Third, the overarching theme of Paul's "lessons" in verses 6–10 is not to desire evil. The common denominator of the vices he mentions is that they all grow out of inordinate desire, which itself is the basis of evil. It is this sense of craving, setting our hearts on what we want, indeed on what we feel compelled to possess, that the sober reflection of Lent helps us curb.

Luke 13:1–9

One could hardly find a Gospel lection more appropriately Lenten or more characteristically Lukan than our text for today. The entire passage is an urgent call to repentance, a turning from sin and a reformation of action and attitude. The theme of repentance occurs more in Luke than in other New Testament writers. In fact, the Gospel for Luke is the proclamation of repentance and forgiveness of sins (24:47). Also typically Lukan is the parable of the fig tree (vv. 6–9), with its accent on the appeal for mercy that stays the hand of judgment. The reader is reminded of the grace that spared wicked Nineveh, even though that city was also under the judgment of God (Jonah is a favorite of Luke). Furthermore, the design of 13:1–9 is common to Luke—a parable that is interpreted at the beginning rather than at the end (10:29; 12:15; 15:1–2; 18:1, 9). And finally, Luke again includes in the travel narrative (9:51–19:27) materials selected thematically rather than chronologically or geographically, all pointing to the approaching crisis in Jerusalem.

This passage consists of two statements by Jesus (vv. 1–5) that serve as an introduction to and commentary on a parable about a barren fig tree (vv. 6–9). In form, the two sayings are exactly parallel, each ending with the pronouncement, "but unless you repent, you will all perish as they did." But the differences in the two sayings combine to make them inclusive in their application. The first has to do with Galileans, the second with Jerusalemites. Jesus is speaking to all. The first has to do with tragedy caused by a human being, the second with tragedy caused by natural calamity. Jesus is including all the violence and suffering that strikes without reason or meaning.

The question, Why this to these particular people? is as old as the human race. The Book of Job, Psalm 37, and Psalm 73 ask the question. The disciples asked Jesus, "Rabbi, who sinned, this man or his parents, that he was born blind?" (John 9:2). The question assumed that there was direct correlation between sin and suffering. To those disciples (John 9:3) and in today's lection Jesus denied that direct correlation. But still the idea persists: illness, poverty, disease, loneliness, and death are the punishment for sins known or unknown. For Christians, the fatal blow to the idea that suffering and death are the lot of the guilty came at

Golgotha. The One without sin suffered and died on the cross; some present took that as proof he was not the Son of God (Matt. 27:39–43). But Jesus' disciples are forever freed from the ancient notion that prosperity and good health are evidence of divine favor, whereas poverty and suffering are clear signs of divine wrath. Even so, the idea persists. Thornton Wilder's novel *The Bridge of San Luis Rey* (Harper & Row, 1967) is the account of a priest's effort to prove that the reason a bridge collapsed with certain persons on it was to be found in the moral flaws in the lives of those persons. Of course, the priest's efforts, and all such efforts, fail. Jesus rejects such attempts at calculation, not simply because they are futile, but because they direct attention from the primary issue—the obligation of every person to live in penitence and trust before God without linking one's loyalty to God to life's sorrows or joys. *All* are to repent or perish.

Luke's parable of the barren fig tree may be a recasting of the story of the cursing of the barren fig tree (Mark 11:12–14; Matt. 21:18–19), or perhaps Mark and Matthew recast the parable. In either case, Luke's story leaves open the possibility of fruitfulness, and at least a temporary triumph of mercy over judgment. The delay of God's judgment because of the intercession of a prophet or Moses is not uncommon in the Old Testament. In Christian circles, one explanation for the delay of the day of the Lord was that God, for the sake of mercy, was giving more people a chance to avoid the terror of that day (2 Pet. 3:8–9). Luke's message here is similar: there is still time for Israel to repent and to bear fruit as evidence of that repentance. In other words, God's mercy is still talking to God's judgment, and on that conversation hangs our salvation.

Fourth Sunday in Lent

Joshua 5:9–12;
Psalm 32;
2 Corinthians 5:16–21;
Luke 15:1–3, 11b–32

All the readings converge on the theme of God's actions to save the lost or sinful. The key phrase in the Old Testament reading affirms that the Lord has "rolled away from you the disgrace of Egypt" (Josh. 5:9). The psalm pronounces as happy those whose sins are forgiven, and urges that sin be acknowledged. It expresses confidence and joy in the God who forgives. The Epistle proclaims the good news in cosmic terms: "In Christ God was reconciling the world to himself" (2 Cor. 5:19). In the Gospel lection, through the parable of the prodigal son Jesus proclaims forgiveness.

Joshua 5:9–12

The events reported in our reading occur when there is a lull in the narrative of Israel's entrance into the land, but at the point of a key transition. The people of Israel have entered the land, miraculously crossing the Jordan under the leadership of Joshua as they had the Sea under the leadership of Moses. But they have not yet begun the battles for possession of the land. The transition has great significance, for it marks the move from life in the wilderness to life in the land promised to the ancestors.

The immediate context of the reading is the account of three events between the entrance and the battles. All are, in different ways, ritual events of preparation. The first (5:2–9) reports a ceremony of circumcision at Gilgal; the second (5:10–12) is the account of the first Passover in the land of Canaan; and the third (5:13–15) is the story of Joshua's encounter with the mysterious captain of Yahweh's army. The reading for the day encompasses the last verse of the first incident and all of the second.

Ancient traditions stand behind this material, which must reflect ritual practices from the premonarchical period in Gilgal, certainly an important cultic center in Israel's early days. However, the text has passed through the hands of the deuteronomistic editors who were responsible for the long history that begins in the Book of Deuteronomy and is concluded in 2 Kings. Such editors were still working on the history as late as the period of the Babylonian Exile (ca. 560 BC).

Joshua 5:9 concludes the report of the circumcision of all the males who had been born during the wandering in the wilderness, all the generation of the Exodus having died (5:4).

The account comes at this point because circumcision is a prerequisite for participation in the Passover (Exod. 12:43–49). Although there are other reports of adult circumcision (Genesis 34), and it is likely that originally it was a puberty rite, in Israel it was done in infancy. Moreover, although the practice was not limited to Israel, it came to be a physical sign and symbol of membership in the covenant community (Genesis 17).

The account of the circumcision ritual is concluded with a pronouncement from the Lord to Joshua and an etiology of the name of the place. The etymology is not linguistically accurate, but is based on similarity of sounds. The place is called "Gilgal"—that is, "rolling"—because there the Lord "rolled away" the reproach of the Egyptians. Unfortunately, the text does not tell us what it means by "the disgrace of Egypt." Is it assumed—incorrectly—that the Egyptians did not practice circumcision? Does it concern the separation from the religiously unclean practices of the foreigners? Does it refer to the shame and humiliation of slavery? There seems to be no way to know. It is clear, however, that now the Lord has declared the people to be "right," either ritually or otherwise, in a way that had not been the case before.

The celebration reported in 5:10–12, which in historic times was a single occasion, originally had been two, Passover and Unleavened Bread. Passover, a one-day festival, must have begun as a part of pastoral practice, marking the movement from winter to summer pasture. Unleavened Bread, on the other hand, was a seven-day celebration of the spring harvest, in which Israel would not have participated before arriving in Canaan. As Exodus 12 indicates, Passover was a family festival, celebrated in the home, although here it seems to have been a corporate affair held outside.

Significantly, the festival marks both the change of Israel's diet and the transition from wilderness to holy land. The "unleavened cakes and parched grain" were of "the produce of the land" (v. 11). On that very day the manna ceased and the people "ate the produce of the land." God substitutes for one miracle another, equally marvelous. This note might serve to remind us that the series of events that follow in the Book of Joshua do not amount to "conquest." The Lord gives the land to the people; they do not take it through their own strength. Moreover, the appropriate response to such gifts, says the Book of Deuteronomy, is that "you shall eat your fill and bless the LORD your God for the good land that he has given you" (Deut. 8:10). Such rituals of thanksgiving and identification should always mark important transitions, for individuals and for communities.

Psalm 32

One of the traditional seven penitential psalms, Psalm 32 is a prayer of thanksgiving offered by individuals after the forgiveness of sin and the experience of healing.

Prayers of thanksgiving, like this psalm, were offered in ancient Israelite worship after the passage of trouble and the alleviation of distress. They reflect the people's tendency to look back upon the time of trouble and to celebrate the joy of salvation that had made the trouble a matter of the past (though certainly not something to be lost from memory). This helps explain two factors about thanksgiving psalms: (1) they have the character of a testimonial that bears witness to a prior condition that no longer exists but from which the worshiper has been delivered, and (2) much of the psalm is addressed to a human audience, inviting them to participate in the joy and new condition of the redeemed.

The following is the form-critical structure of the psalm: (a) pronouncements of blessedness spoken about or to the one offering thanksgiving, probably spoken by the priest to the worshiper or to the worshiper and the attending congregation (vv. 1–2); (b) the description, in the form of a thanksgiving prayer to the Deity, of the condition from which the worshiper was saved (vv. 3–5); (c) a prayer to the Deity formulated as an indirect call to prayer by those in attendance (v. 6); (d) the prayer response (v. 7); and (e) instruction by the one offering thanksgiving to those in attendance at the service (vv. 8–11).

The two opening verses proclaim the blessed condition or happy estate of the one whose sins have been forgiven. The psalm does not assume the existence of life without sin. It presupposes the existence of sinful persons and proclaims as blessed or happy those whose sin has become a matter of the past. The state of real happiness lies, for the psalmist, not prior to, but beyond, on the other side of, sin.

In verses 1–2 and elsewhere (see v. 5), the psalmist uses three different words for sin: (a) transgression (*pesha'*), or an act reflecting overt rebellion against God, (b) sin (*chattâth*), or an offense by which one deviates from the correct path or true course, and (c) iniquity (*'âwon*), or criminal distortion of life without regard for the Deity. The term "deceit," or "slackness," (*remiyah*) also appears in verse 2, and the claim of its absence can probably be seen as referring to the state of honesty that had to prevail when one confessed various sins. Note also that three descriptions are given with regard to the removal of sin: forgiven, covered, not imputed. Such terminological features can provide the bases for structuring a sermon on this psalm.

In the description of the earlier distress, in verses 3–5, the psalmist coordinates four factors: (1) lack of repentance followed by (2) sickness and strain, and (3) confession followed by (4) forgiveness. In ancient Israel, acknowledgment and confession of sin, as well as restitution to injured parties, were essential ingredients in the repentance process (see Num. 5:5–10). From a therapeutic or psychological point of view, one can say that the psalm writer was fully aware of the need for the sinner to tell his or her story as a form of self-identity and self-enlightenment and thus to claim responsibility for wrongdoing. In 2 Samuel 12:1–14, Nathan tells the "confessional" story with which David then identifies. In ancient Israelite theology, without confession there was no forgiveness of sin.

The association of sickness and unconfessed sin, noted in verses 3–4, illustrates the close psychosomatic connection between physical and mental health—a connection that is being recognized more and more in contemporary culture. Although the physical consequences are described as the result of unconfessed sins, they are also spoken of as the result of divine action as well ("your hand was heavy upon me"). This suggests that the understanding of human sentiments and feelings and the understanding of divine actions are closely interrelated.

Verse 5 expresses something of the exuberance that comes after long-seething and secret sin is allowed to surface and be exposed to the light of day. The articulation, the coming to expression, of the nagging problem is the first step toward healing. Note that three expressions are used for this unveiling of the suppressed sin—acknowledged, did not hide, will confess. The close connection between confession and forgiveness is affirmed in the recognition that following confession "you forgave the guilt of my sin."

This section of the psalm (vv. 3–5) can be an ideal text for the minister to use in addressing the issues of human sinfulness, confession, and forgiveness. The sentiments and conditions described in the psalm are certainly appropriate for contemporary people. The latter, however, frequently assume that what one does with wrongdoing is to "stuff" it or keep it under wraps—the exact sentiments seen as so destructive in the psalm.

Verses 6–11 are to be seen in the context of the thanksgiving ritual in which the worshiper calls upon those attending the service (friends, family, associates) to join in the celebration and to learn from the experience that the worshiper has gone through. The forgiven sinner pleads with the others not to be stupid and hardheaded like a mule or a horse that must be controlled with bit and bridle. That is, they are not to be like the worshiper was before the acknowledgment and confession of sin (see vv. 3–4).

2 Corinthians 5:16–21

So popular is this famous Pauline text that it is used more than once in the lectionary. Part of this passage is the standard epistolary reading for Ash Wednesday every year (2 Cor. 5:20b–6:10), and the reader may want to consult our remarks for this day earlier in this volume, or those for Year A or B. Also, in our remarks on the epistolary readings for Propers 6 [11] and 7 [12] for Year B, which treat 2 Cor. 5:6–10 (11–13) 14–17 and 6:1–13, respectively, we have treated certain aspects of this text that will not be repeated here. For introductory remarks to Second Corinthians, which provides the epistolary readings for Propers 4–9 [9–14] after Pentecost in Year B, consult Proper 4 [9] for Year B.

Apart from the fact that Paul calls for a complete reorientation of our outlook on life and the world, which transcends the "human point of view," or looking at life or Christ "according to the flesh" (*kata sarka*, v. 16), today's text is a classic statement of Paul's theology of the "new creation." To understand this fully, we must remember that Paul saw the Christ-event as the event that triggered a new creation. It was as if the events of Genesis 1–2 were reenacted. As he says in 2 Corinthians 4:6, the God who had spoken so dramatically in bringing the created order into being by saying, "Let light shine out of darkness," has once again broken through the chaos of human darkness. This time the light of life and order now shines through "the face of Jesus Christ."

We should try to grasp the implication of Paul's theology of new creation. He calls us to see the Christ-event as a new beginning, when the universe is quite literally remade, reordered, reconstituted. This is what is meant when the Christ-event is referred to as the "turn of the ages." It becomes the moment when "all things," including time, history, and all that goes to make up life and the world as we know it, are created over again. That he saw the Christ-event as having this hinge quality is seen in his opening words "From now on . . ." (v. 16). A new age has dawned. Time has shifted its course. A new order has begun.

But new creation has not merely occurred "out there." Christ not only served as the triggering device for the reordering of all things; he also becomes the means through which we participate in the reordering. This is what is signified by the pregnant Pauline notion of being "in Christ." It has a local connotation. We are incorporated into the risen Christ, but it is not merely a union of our person with his. It involves our stepping into this process of new creation begun with Christ—becoming a participant in this newly created order, where the old is gone and the new has come. To be "in Christ" means that the new creation God effected in Christ is reenacted within us. So, "if anyone is *in* Christ, there is a new creation" (v. 17, italics added). The reordering of the cosmos that began in Christ now begins in us.

It is in this context that we should understand Paul's various remarks (as well as other New Testament remarks) about "newness." Clearly, being part of the new creation entails personal transformation, or "newness of life" (Rom. 6:4). No longer is it a matter of outward rite but inward transformation (Gal. 6:15). What is more, it is the beginning of a process of renewal that continues as our "minds"—that is, our thoughts, attitudes, and overall outlook—begin to be made over (Rom. 12:2). On a broad scale, what emerges is a "new humanity"

(Eph. 2:15). Even our ways of conceiving the future and life in the future are oriented toward the new (Rev. 21:5).

We should also notice that "all this is from God" (v. 18). Accustomed as we are to thinking that personal transformation results from our own capacity to improve ourselves and our world, Paul issues this stern reminder that the new creation is not our own doing. God tipped the first domino. God is the Prime Mover. The initiative lay with, and lies with, God (cf. 1 Cor. 1:30).

But what form does this "new order" take? One where alienation gives way to reconciliation. The essence of the new creation is the work of God in bringing humanity, indeed all things, back into covenantal relationship with God. The distinguishing mark of the new creation is reconciliation—bringing together. If the old order saw the collapse of God's relationship with humanity, the new saw its restoration. Where God and humanity were once at a standoff, through Christ we now stand together with God, even becoming God's co-workers (2 Cor. 6:1). The new creation may be regarded as the fulfillment of the prophetic hope that depicts Yahweh as "doing a new thing" (Isa. 43:18–19).

None of this was, or is, possible apart from Christ (cf. Col. 1:19–20), and through Christ we are now able to become the "righteousness of God" (v. 21; cf. Rom. 1:17; 3:5, 21–26; 10:3; Phil. 3:9; also Matt. 6:33). Such a relationship becomes a state of blessedness (Rom. 4:8).

If we come to share in God's reconciling work through Christ, it is a natural corollary that we ourselves become ministers of reconciliation, extending God's reconciling love throughout the world. The new creation that God began in Christ, that was reenacted within us, is now continued through the world, through time and history—and continues until the ultimate and complete renewal of all things.

Luke 15:1–3, 11b–32

Even a surface reading of the lections for today reveals their common theme, reconciliation, presented as covenant in Joshua, a theological statement in Paul, and a parable in Luke. Luke's parable of the loving father, more commonly referred to as the parable of the prodigal son, is set in a large section of teaching dominated by many of the parables found only in Luke. Most of these parables—the unjust steward, the rich man and Lazarus, the widow and the judge, and the Pharisee and the publican—are characterized by more narrative quality and more human interest than the briefer parables about seed, leaven, nets, and weeds. Especially is this true of the story before us.

As we observed last week, Luke typically offers a word of interpretation at the beginning rather than at the end of a parable. In 15:1–3 the brief interpretation is in the form of a setting for the story. The setting consists of three statements: Jesus attracts tax collectors and sinners (v. 1); Pharisees and scribes criticize his receiving and eating with such persons (v. 2); Jesus responds to his critics with a parable (v. 3). Actually, Luke offers this setting as an introduction to a trilogy of parables: the lost sheep (vv. 4–7), the lost coin (vv. 8–10), and the loving father (vv. 11–32). The first two are very similar in length, form, content, and concluding comment about joy over the return of the penitent. However, the comment hardly fits a sheep and a coin, both of which are found, not by a return, but by the diligent search of caring owners. The return of the penitent as a theme more properly anticipates the third parable. In fact, the setting (vv. 1–3) and the parable in verses 11–32 fit so naturally that the opinion to the effect that Luke inserted the other two parables seems most plausible.

Certainly, the lectionary has violated nothing in the omission of verses 4–10 for today's Gospel lesson.

The judgment of a few scholars that the parable in verses 11–32 was originally two parables, the younger son (vv. 11–24) and the older son (vv. 25–32), misses both the point of this parable and a literary feature common to many parables. The focus of this story is the father: "There was a man who had two sons." Calling this story the parable of the prodigal son moves the focal point off center. And the apparent conclusion in verse 24, found again in verse 32, does not mark out two stories, for repetition of lines is common in parables (e.g., Matt. 25:14–30).

Without question, this story was offensive to its first hearers, and the preacher should not assume that time has removed that offense. The edge of Jesus' message will remain sharp and effective if at least three radicalities in the story are not blurred. The first lies in the contrast between Jesus' behavior and that of his critics (vv. 1–3). Tax collectors and sinners are not simply friendly folk who have been misunderstood. Publicans had taken jobs with the foreign government occupying Israel and made good money collecting taxes from their own people. Sinners were persons so designated because their offenses had gotten them thrown out of the synagogues. That Jesus ate with them was the clear evidence of his acceptance of them. The Pharisees, guardians of law and high standards of behavior, sensed the erosive force in not distinguishing between good people and bad people. "Birds of a feather flock together." After all, does not forgiving look very much like condoning? To cartoon Jesus' critics as villains is not only unfair; it weakens the story.

Second, notice the radical difference between the younger son's decline to the status of a Gentile, a nobody (Lev. 11:7; Isa. 65:4; 66:17), and the extravagant welcome home. It is that party which is so offensive. The older brother has a point: of course, let the penitent come home. Both Judaism and Christianity provide for the return of sinners, but to bread and water, not fatted calf; to sackcloth, not a new robe; to ashes, not jewelry; to kneeling, not dancing; to tears, not merriment. Who in the church today would have attended that party?

Finally, and perhaps most radically, the father must be presented as one who had two sons, loved two sons, went out to both (vv. 20, 28), and was generous to both. The embrace of publicans and sinners does not mean a rejection of the Pharisees; the reception of sinners is not a rejection of saints. Ours is a "both/and," not an "either/or," God.

Fifth Sunday in Lent

Isaiah 43:16–21;
Psalm 126;
Philippians 3:4*b***–14;**
John 12:1–8

As the season of Lent takes us closer to the commemoration of the death and resurrection of Jesus, the assigned texts sound different and distinctive notes. The Old Testament reading and the psalm proclaim, look forward to, and pray for God's salvation of the people. The mood is joyful. The New Testament lections are not so unambiguous. The epistolary text has Paul announcing the surpassing worth of knowing Jesus Christ, affirming his faith in the resurrection, and—not without a note of warning—calling for his readers to press on with him and hold true. In the Gospel lesson we see Mary's love for her Lord, but also recognize foreshadowings of Judas' treachery and the death of Jesus.

Isaiah 43:16–21

Texts from Isaiah 40–55 provide more Old Testament readings for the lectionary than any other body of literature of comparable length. They are especially prominent during Holy Week and the Sundays just preceding, and for good reason. In addition to including the Servant Songs, the work of Second Isaiah is filled with proclamations of salvation and celebrations of the Lord's redemptive work. Christian readers have always seen the similarity of this prophet's message to the New Testament's good news.

The central message of this prophetic poet, who was active in Babylon shortly before the fall of that empire to Cyrus in 539 BC, is that the captive exiles will be set free and the Lord will lead them home to Jerusalem. As we hear the soaring and joyful words of Second Isaiah, we must remind ourselves that they were uttered to a community not yet set free, and far from hopeful. The fact that the prophetic poet so often argues the case for a God both willing and able to redeem his people suggests that the opposite view was held by many of his contemporaries.

Isaiah 43:16–21 is a self-contained and coherent unit of prophetic poetry, although in the final form of the book verses 14–15 have been attached to its beginning. In terms of literary genre, the passage is a proclamation of salvation, a type well known in Second Isaiah and perfectly suited to his central message. The form of poetic speech is like that of Second Isaiah's prophetic predecessors in that it begins with the messenger formula ("Thus says the LORD," v. 16) and then quotes the words of God concerning a future that he will bring about. Such proclamations appear to be addressed to a people complaining or lamenting about their past or present situations, either directly to God or in an argument with the prophet. Thus there is an argumentative tone to the speech, an attempt to convince the audience that the news is good.

There is a movement in the address from past events through the (assumed) present situation to the immediate future and on to a more distant goal. Formally, the unit consists of two distinct parts, the prophetic introduction in verses 16–17 and the speech of Yahweh in verses 18–21.

In the introduction, the messenger formula is elaborated by means of relative clauses that define the Lord in terms of past actions: "who makes a way in the sea . . . who brings out chariot and horse" (vv. 16–17). The style is not unlike that of hymns of praise, or doxologies. The contents refer to the heart of ancient Israel's confession of faith, the fundamental salvation event of the exodus from Egypt. This is traditional confessional language that enables Israel to affirm not only who God is, but also who they are. For Second Isaiah, the old saving events, especially those of the Exodus, are types of the new ones to come.

The divine speech includes injunctions (v. 18), proclamations concerning the future (vv. 19–21a), and a statement of purpose (v. 21b). There seems to be an abrupt shift from the recollection of the past to injunctions to forget "the former things . . . the things of old." This could be hyperbole: Even the great saving events of the past will pale into insignificance in comparison with the "new thing" the Lord will do. Or the "former things" could refer to the past troubles and complaints of the people.

In any case, the center of the divine speech is the proclamation of the "new thing" that the Lord will do, first stated generally and then more and more concretely. (The rhetorical question in verse 19 suggests the sense of dialogue with an audience.) The actual "new thing" itself is, as it were, offstage. It is the release of Israel from Babylon and their return to Jerusalem. Attention here is focused upon the miraculous transformation of the desert through which the people will travel. The imagery echoes the stories of the Exodus and the wandering in the wilderness. As Yahweh had brought the people through the Sea, so he will bring them through the desert. As Yahweh had fed them with manna and provided water from the rock, so he will make rivers in the desert, give them drink, and even turn the wild beasts into a choir to praise the Lord.

Second Isaiah's announcements and proclamations of salvation seldom give the reasons for God's intervention. When they do, it is either that Israel has paid for its sins (40:2), that the reason lies in the Lord's grace and love for a chosen people (54:8), or in order for them to be God's witnesses among the nations (42:6; 43:12). The concluding line of this passage seems consistent with that last understanding. The new saving event in behalf of the people—whom, God says, "I formed for myself"—is "that they might declare my praise" (v. 21). Thus the new event will open up into more, for God's salvation will be made known to others in the form of songs of praise.

The scope of Second Isaiah's vision is both cosmic and eschatological. The cosmic dimensions are visible in the allusions to creation ("I formed you") and the transformation of the desert with its "wild animals." The eschatological vision encompasses all of history under the saving will of the God who acted, acts, and will act. The future is open, open to the declaration of God's praise.

Psalm 126

Like the text from Isaiah 43, this psalm has a forward-looking orientation that befits the Lenten Season. In addition, it looks backward at the past as a means of giving confidence about the future.

As part of the collection of pilgrim psalms (Psalms 120–134), Psalm 126 would have been sung as the pilgrims moved toward Jerusalem for festival celebrations. In going on pilgrimage, the people assembled at the main town in their district. They spent the night outside in the open, to avoid any contamination or contact with uncleanness. (For example, persons became unclean if they were in the house where someone died.) Under the leadership of a pilgrim director (see Ps. 42:4), the people set out for Jerusalem in the early morning. The trip might take several days. As the people made their way to the Holy City, they sang and recited the material in Psalms 120–134.

Several things about this psalm can be applied to the Lenten Season and the Lenten pilgrimage.

1. A pilgrimage is a movement away from ordinary time, everyday life, to the more sacred, the more holy. For the ancient Hebrew, pilgrimage took one to the sacred city of Jerusalem and to the most sacred spot in Judaism, the temple in the sacred city. As the pilgrims moved toward Jerusalem, they were moving toward the sacred center to observe the festivals that gave meaning and direction to life. Lent, too, is a pilgrimage, a movement to the most significant, the central, celebration of the Christian year.

2. The psalm, like Lent, looks backward and forward: backward to the last festival, "when the LORD restored the fortunes of Zion" (v. 1); and forward to the new time (v. 4). Thus the psalm blends together thanksgiving for the past and requests for the future.

3. The poles of human sentiments are found in the psalm—weeping and rejoicing. Lent is a season of weeping, but weeping in anticipation of the joy and singing to come.

4. The psalm assumes that the upcoming celebration, the holy events of the festival, will be life changing, life refreshing, like the transformation that comes in the desert when rain falls (v. 4). The sense of expectation in the psalm should be the expectation of the Lenten Season.

Philippians 3:4b–14

With its stress on "giving up" what is regarded as gain, and "leaving behind" a past way of life and point of view, this text clearly echoes Lenten themes. It addresses us directly as an autobiographical text depicting Paul's own experience. It is both a confession and a diary. Here we are able to see inside the mind and heart of one for whom the suffering of Christ had become life shaping. In every respect, this epistolary lection is a suitable Lenten text.

First, a word about its context. It occurs within a polemical setting, as seen by the opening words (Phil. 3:1–3). As the chapter draws to a close, Paul singles out the "enemies of the cross of Christ" (3:18–19). It is difficult to tell much about the opponents against whom these remarks are directed. From the sound of things, they are Jewish Christians who perhaps insist on keeping the laws of the Torah, especially the law of circumcision. When Paul contrasts human righteousness based on law with God's righteousness that comes in response to faith (v. 9), we hear echoes of themes played out much more fully in Romans and Galatians.

The one thing that is clear is Paul's insistence of having suffered loss. On this note today's lection begins. What is in view are the privileges implied by his pedigree sketched in verses 5–6. If we establish our identity and find our security in such things as family background, social and religious status, and legal rectitude, Paul insists that we are trying to establish our confidence "in the flesh" (v. 4b). In this context, he is doubtless referring to the rights and privileges he enjoyed as a circumcised Jew. In many ways, he gained much by virtue of who he was. Yet, for all the advantages his position offered him, they finally became of no consequence. At one time they were gain; now he counted them as loss.

His scale of values shifted through his encounter with Christ. The superlative value now became "the surpassing value of knowing Christ Jesus my Lord" (v. 8). We see unfolded here a spiritual consciousness turned inside out by the Christ-event. The aim of his intellectual quest is now Christ. The object of his pursuit is Christ, the existential locus defining both who and where he is. He reaches out to seize Christ just as a sprinter reaches forward to seize the tape at the finish line. Yet he knows all the while that he seeks to possess Christ only because Christ has already possessed him (v. 12).

It may seem odd that our text still presents Paul as one who is driven to possess a goal. Was not his religious crisis caused by the mistaken notion that he could finally attain perfection through the law? Surely he should have learned the futility of religious compulsion.

But our text suggests that his pursuit of Christ differed from his pursuit of the law. For one thing, he now realizes that the righteousness he pursues is not his but God's (v. 9). It is not "my own"; it comes from God. It is no longer his human pursuit of God but God's pursuit of him in which he is involved. In addition, the way to the righteousness he formerly pursued was "from the law" (v. 9). It involved "legal rectitude" (v. 9, NEB). The way to the new righteousness is through faith: "the righteousness which comes from faith in Christ, given by God in response to faith" (v. 9, NEB). At the heart of his new quest was absolute trust in Christ. Even though such faith was neither as reliable nor as predictable as law in terms of measuring progress, it was far more compelling.

We should note especially the futurity of Paul's expressed hope. What unfolds is an unrealized vision of faith. He repeatedly stresses that his quest is partial and incomplete (vv. 12–13). This may be because his opponents were already claiming eschatological perfection, or even moral perfection (cf. 1 Cor. 4:8–9; 2 Tim. 2:18). Perhaps theirs was a "gnostic" outlook that saw their resurrection with Christ, and thus their perfection, as already realized. In any case, the clear thrust of Paul's remarks is that his knowledge of Christ, his empowerment through the resurrection of Christ, and his participation in the resurrection of the dead still lay in the future. Indeed, what impels him is the "prize of the heavenly call of God in Christ Jesus" (v. 14; cf. Heb. 3:1).

As we read these words closely, we see the nature of Paul's exchange: it was an exchange of something he actually possessed for something he might finally possess, the past for the future, past certainty for future hope. And this is what is especially instructive. As we experience loss, it is usually loss of the known, of what we own and have, whether it is our past or our possessions. As we lay all this aside for the superlative worth of Christ, we engage in a cardinal act of faith, for what we gain is a vision that is not ever fully ours until Christ makes us fully his own in the resurrection.

John 12:1–8

The pilgrimage toward Easter has taken us almost to Passion/Palm Sunday. The Fourth Gospel prepares us for that occasion by placing immediately before Jesus' entry into Jerusalem the story of Jesus' being anointed for burial.

In order properly to hear John 12:1–8, it is essential that the story here not be blended into the similar accounts in the Synoptics (Mark 14:1–9; Matt. 26:6–13; Luke 7:36–39). It is likely that all four have a common source, but they come to us bearing the clear intentions of the different writers.

The anointing of Jesus is more vividly a part of the passion narrative in this Gospel than in Matthew or Mark. (In Luke, the anointing is earlier, in Galilee, and with a different message.) John makes this clear in several ways.

First, its literary context is between the raising of Lazarus (11:1–44), the event that precipitated the decision to kill Jesus (11:45–57), and the entry into Jerusalem (12:9–19), the occasion on which Jesus announced that the hour of his death had come (12:20–36).

Second, the place of the anointing is Bethany, where Jesus had raised Lazarus from the dead. According to the Evangelist, Jesus knew that calling Lazarus out of the tomb meant that the Son of God would have to enter the tomb so that life would be given not to Lazarus alone but to the world. In the language of this Gospel, the Son of God would be glorified as a result of the event in Bethany (11:4; 12:23, 32–33). It is important to keep in mind that in John, Jesus' entry into Jerusalem was from Bethany, not Galilee. The crowds were already in the city and were not followers from Galilee, and the excitement had been generated by the reports of raising Lazarus and the resultant plots on Jesus' life (11:55–57; 12:9–19). Bethany, the city of Lazarus' life, figures now in the death of Jesus.

The third signal that the anointing is a passion story is its location at Passover time (11:55; 12:1). Passover is, for this Evangelist, death time: the cleansing of the temple, with its prophecy of Jesus' death, is a Passover story (2:13–22); the feeding of the five thousand, with its message of Jesus' life-giving death (6:52–58), is a Passover story (6:4); and, of course, Jesus died as the Passover lamb (19:31–37).

The fourth indicator that the anointing points to Jesus' death is at the banquet table itself. Not only is Lazarus there, the one whose life sets in motion the forces against Jesus, but also Judas (v. 4). This dark intruder upon this scene of life and joy in the home of a grateful family casts across the table the shadow of approaching death for Jesus.

And finally there is the statement of Jesus himself to the effect that what Mary did was for "the day of my burial" (v. 7)—not that it was Mary's intention to anoint Jesus for burial. Here was an act of hospitality, love, and gratitude to Jesus. However, for many biblical writers, and for this Evangelist in particular, words and deeds have meaning beyond the intentions of those who speak and act. When Caiaphas said, "It is better for you to have one man die for the people" (11:50), he spoke politically, not realizing the greater truth of his words. When the Pharisees said, "Look, the world has gone after him!" (12:19), they were unaware of the irony in a remark that anticipated Jesus' own words shortly thereafter: "And I, when I am lifted up from the earth, will draw all people to myself" (12:32). We speak and act in ways we think most appropriate for the occasion. We may never know, however, what lives are influenced, what differences are made because God takes a word spoken, a gift given, a hand extended, an effort expended, and gives it a life and a power far beyond the intention and expectation that prompted it. As Mark said of this act in Bethany, "Wherever the good news is proclaimed in the whole world, what she has done will be told in remembrance of her" (14:9).

Sixth Sunday in Lent
(Passion/Palm Sunday)

Liturgy of the Palms:
Luke 19:28–40;
Psalm 118:1–2, 19–29

Liturgy of the Passion:
Isaiah 50:4–9*a*;
Psalm 31:9–16;
Philippians 2:5–11;
Luke 22:14–23:56 or Luke 23:1–49

In various communions, the Sixth Sunday in Lent may be celebrated either as Palm Sunday, or Passion Sunday, or both. In the traditions that celebrate both, the Palm Sunday lections provide the readings for the beginning processional or for an earlier "said" service of worship.

In the Liturgy of the Palms for Year C, the Lucan account of Jesus' triumphal entry into Jerusalem serves as the Gospel text. The responsorial psalm, a liturgy for entrance into the temple precincts, is the same in all three years of the lectionary cycle.

In the Liturgy of the Passion, the third Servant Song of Isaiah, which focuses attention on both the suffering and triumph of God's servant, serves as the Old Testament reading. Psalm 31, with its emphasis on misery and suffering, provides an appropriate response. The early Christian hymn cited by Paul in the epistolary reading is notable for its addition "even death on a cross" (v. 8), which underscores the centrality of Christ's suffering within early Christian worship. The Passion Sunday Gospel lection in its long form takes us from the Last Supper to the death of Jesus.

Luke 19:28–40

In sharp contrast to the observance of the Sunday before Easter as Passion Sunday, the celebration of this day as Palm Sunday focuses on Jesus' entry into Jerusalem as an occasion of triumph and praise. In fact, some feel the mood of victory and joy is premature, stealing its message from Easter yet to come, and hence not an appropriate way to worship prior to Good Friday and Easter. In favor of such an observance, however, is the Gospels' own record of the event as the beginning of the final days of Jesus. Traditionally, Palm Sunday services draw from all the Gospels: John contributes the palm branches (12:13); Matthew contributes the prophecy in Zechariah 9:9 (21:5); and Mark, along with Matthew and John, contributes the shouting throng (11:8–10). Luke, although following Mark 11:1–10 rather closely, tells the story his own way, providing the reader with a slightly different understanding of the occasion.

In general, it would be fair to say that Luke's account of Jesus' entry into Jerusalem is more subdued, less crowded and less noisy, than those of the other Evangelists. Notice several features of Luke's story.

First, verse 28 not only ties this event to what precedes but reminds the reader that this episode is a part of the larger narrative begun at 9:51, Jesus' journey to Jerusalem. And the account of Jesus' arrival in Jerusalem is followed by Jesus' weeping over the city and his prophecy of its destruction (19:41–44). Such a context prevents the story before us from becoming autonomous, having a life of its own.

Second, Luke's record makes no mention of hosannas or branches cut from trees. Because those belonged commonly to nationalistic demonstrations and parades, perhaps Luke wants this event to carry no such implication. Jesus is called "King," to be sure (v. 38), but Luke makes it clear very soon that the term is in no sense political or military (23:2–5).

Third, and very important, the entry into Jerusalem is very much a disciple event rather than a burst of enthusiasm on the part of a large crowd surrounding Jesus, as in Matthew 21:8–10 and Mark 11:8–10. Notice: the disciples set Jesus on the colt (v. 35); the disciples spread their garments on the road (v. 36); the disciples rejoice and praise God (v. 37). That the ovation is not by a general multitude in the city for the festival (Matt. 21:9) or gathered as a result of reports about the raising of Lazarus (John 12:12) is an important detail. Christ is praised and hailed as king by his followers, says Luke, and not by the general public. And this is not the group, says Luke, that later called for Jesus' crucifixion. To be sure, Jesus' followers did not understand him or the nature of his messiahship, but neither are they persons who sing praise and scream death within the same week. Such a portrait of a fickle crowd must be drawn from accounts other than Luke's.

Fourth, the expressions of praise in Luke make no reference to David or to Davidic images of the messiah. "King" is used (v. 38), but as stated above, Luke does not permit that word to carry political force. Actually, the praise on this occasion (v. 38) echoes the praise in the announcement to the shepherds of the birth of Jesus (2:10, 13–14).

But even the rather modest parade offered by Luke evokes an objection by some Pharisees (v. 39). We are not told whether their objection was due to disagreement, envy, fear of political repercussions, or some other motive, and therefore honesty demands that the preacher not read into the story information unavailable to us. Nor does Jesus identify the problem the scene generates for the Pharisees; he simply states in a vivid image the clear and certain appropriateness of his disciples' praise. "If these were silent, the stones would shout out" (v. 40) is a statement conveying one or more of several messages: Some things simply must be said; the disciples are expressing ultimate truth; truth cannot be silenced; God will provide a witness though every mouth be stopped; opposition to Christian witness cannot succeed. With all these interpretations of the expressions Luke would agree.

And so Jesus comes to *the* city—the city where God dwells (Ps. 84:1); the city where all go to worship (Psalm 122); the city where all nations shall gather (Isa. 2:1–5). Here Jesus will die, but in this city his disciples will tarry, because from Jerusalem the gospel will be carried to the nations (Luke 24:47; Acts 1:4–8).

Psalm 118:1–2, 19–29

Portions of this psalm are used as the psalm reading for Easter Day. The entire psalm was probably composed initially for use in a thanksgiving service when the Jerusalemite king returned from a victory in battle and participated in a service of thanksgiving in the temple.

The selection and association of this psalm and these verses for Palm Sunday, celebrating Jesus' entry into Jerusalem just before Passover, are based on several considerations. (1) It contains the words said to have been sung as Jesus rode into Jerusalem (v. 26). (2) The psalm was used in the Passover celebrations of Jesus' day. Psalms 113–118, the so-called Egyptian Hallel, were sung by the Levites in the temple as the Passover lambs were slaughtered in the afternoon before the Passover meal. The same psalms were again sung in the homes as part of the Passover Seder, or service, in conjunction with eating the Passover meal. (3) The psalm celebrates the victorious entry of a royal figure, which may be seen as paralleling Jesus' entry into the city. (4) The theme of the psalm—which moves from depicting the ruler as oppressed, attacked, and humiliated to being triumphant, victorious, and celebrated—parallels the fundamental shape of New Testament Christology.

Verses 14–24 are analyzed in the treatment of the psalm in the Easter lection and will not be discussed here. Verses 1–2 call upon the congregation to offer thanks by declaring that God's mercy endures forever. Verse 25 is a congregational or priestly prayer appealing to God for divine favor (see Matt. 21:9). The next verses constitute some of the most difficult textual problems in the Old Testament. Verse 27*b* defies a fully intelligible translation. Compare the NRSV ("Bind the festal procession with branches . . .") with the NEB ("the ordered line of pilgrims . . ."). The following is one suggested interpretation. The priests or a choir blesses the one who has entered the sanctuary (v. 26). A theological affirmation or confession is made in verse 27*a*. (The opening portion reads "Yahweh is El.") The second half of the verse seems to refer to the animals, brought for the sacrifice and celebration, being tied to the altar. The sacrificial meal with its attendant celebration would have climaxed the festive occasion. Verse 28 is the prayer of the ruler, and verse 29 is an admonition or call to thanksgiving addressed to the community.

If one applies Psalm 118 to Jesus' entry into Jerusalem, it must be remembered that for the original supplicant, the valley of anguish lay in the past, on the fields of war; for Jesus, the valley lay ahead, within the walls of Jerusalem.

Isaiah 50:4–9*a*

The Servant Songs of Second Isaiah take us from Passion Sunday to Good Friday. This is the third of the songs. The first (Isa. 42:1–9) and second (Isa. 49:1–7) are read on Monday and Tuesday of Holy Week. This one is repeated on Wednesday, and the fourth (Isa. 52:13–53:12), the song of the Suffering Servant, is the Old Testament reading for Good Friday. Read in the context of Christian worship on these occasions, the texts help interpret the life and death of Jesus for us, just as they did for the earliest church.

The text, of course, did not arise in the church, but in ancient Israel. Although there has been some debate on the point, it is generally accepted that the Servant Songs come from the same figure responsible for their literary context, Isaiah 40–55. That dates this as well as the other poems to a time immediately before the end of the Babylonian Exile in 538 BC. Second

Isaiah, who almost certainly was one of the exiles, announced the good news of release and return to Jerusalem. The prophet's understanding of suffering as part of the servant's role must be indebted in important ways to the experience of Israel in exile.

Who was Second Isaiah's servant of the Lord? No convincing consensus has emerged on the question, and answers vary, to a great extent depending upon which of the songs one emphasizes. If Isaiah 50:4–9 is viewed alone, then an individual rather than a corporate interpretation suggests itself. The text is in the first person singular, as if the prophet were speaking, and the images are personal and physical. Notice the references to the parts of the body: "tongue" and "ear" (vv. 4–5); "back," "cheeks," "beard," and "face" (vv. 6–7). But a specific individual social role is indicated by the references to hearing and speaking, that of the prophet. This is not to conclude that the servant was necessarily a particular prophet—either Second Isaiah himself, one of his contemporaries, or a prophet from the past such as Jeremiah. It indicates, however, that among the roles of the servant was that of the prophet, namely, the hearing and communication of the word of God.

There are two main parts to the song, verses 4–6 and 7–9. In both of them an individual speaks, at first reflecting the language of the individual lament psalm, such as the responsorial psalm for this text (Ps. 31:9–16). Verses 4–5 allude to the prophetic vocation and reception of revelation. There are close parallels to some of the so-called confessions of Jeremiah, which also reflect the individual lament psalms. Both the servant and Jeremiah have suffered because of faithfulness to their callings (Jer. 20:7–16). The second part of the song becomes an affirmation of confidence that borrows language and ideas from the Israelite law court.

Several expressions in the poem call for some explanation. The Hebrew word translated "those who are taught" (v. 4) is rare and is best understood as "disciples" (see Isa. 8:16), indicating faithfulness to the teacher and that which is taught. The imagery of verse 6 suggests violent and hostile opposition to the servant, endured without complaint or reaction. Pulling out the beard was a particularly humiliating action (2 Sam. 10:4; Neh. 13:25). In verse 8, the speaker issues a formal summons of an adversary to a lawsuit, in which he expects the Lord to be a trustworthy judge who will not find him guilty.

The passage has a distinctly autobiographical tone and content. It moves from allusions to the vocation of the servant as a disciple (v. 4), through his faithful execution of his duty (v. 5); it gives an account of his patient endurance of suffering (v. 6) and then affirms his confidence that God will in the end vindicate him (vv. 7–8). The Lord God is with him to help, making him resolute (v. 7) and enabling him to contend against his adversaries. His confidence is not in his own strength, but in the Lord who helps.

Psalm 31:9–16

The misery and suffering that flow through Psalm 31 make it a fitting piece for Passiontide. Although only verses 9–16 are set aside for this lection, one needs to see the complex structure of the whole in order to place these verses in perspective. The following is an outline of the components in the composition: opening address and appeal (vv. 1–2), statement of confidence (vv. 3–6), anticipatory thanksgiving (vv. 7–8), description of the distress and trouble (vv. 9–13), plea for help interspersed with statements of confidence (vv. 14–18), statement of confidence (vv. 19–20), blessing of God (v. 21), thanksgiving (v. 22), and admonition to a human audience (vv. 23–24). Only verses 21 and 23–24 are addressed to a human audience; the remainder of the psalm is prayer addressed to God. Thus the psalm is similar to other laments in that laments are fundamentally human speech addressed to the Divine. The optimism and confidence manifest throughout this psalm indicate that the worshiper had faith in receiving a favorable response from the Divine or that a favorable divine response had already been received (though note the reference to having been heard in v. 22).

The similarity between verse 5a—"Into your hand I commit my spirit"—and Jesus' cry from the cross (Luke 23:46) has helped anchor this psalm to the passion of Jesus. The psalm and its contents also have many linguistic parallels to the Book of Jeremiah (in which the prophet frequently laments his condition) and the Book of Lamentations, both of which come out of conditions of suffering and duress.

The lection includes the worshiper's description of distress, the person's tale of trouble (vv. 9–13), and part of the plea for help (vv. 14–16). If the terms of the lament are taken literally, then the worshiper is suffering from physical illness and social ostracism. Bodily illness and approaching death (vv. 9–10) and harsh treatment by neighbors and friends make the worshiper feel like someone who is already dead and forgotten (vv. 11–12). Social opponents and gossip mongers suggest that enmity and persecution are everywhere (vv. 13, 15). If the expressions of personal distress and anguish are merely metaphorical, they, at least, must have been intended to congeal and to shape the worshipers' sense of alienation.

Physical torment, in verses 9–10, is depicted in terms of the erosion and failure of the body. Over against the nouns denoting physical factors—eye, soul, body, strength, bones—are those denoting psychic factors—distress, grief, sorrow, sighing, misery. Along with such nouns march a string of verbs, all negative in their connotation—wastes, spent, fails, waste away. The person experiences the body (and thus life and years) as degenerating. What should be a source of joy and happiness has become a spring of pain and misery.

The sense of physical suffering is conjoined with the feeling of social alienation in verses 11–13. Note the terms referring to "those out there" who have ostracized the person— adversaries, neighbors, acquaintances, faces in the street, enemies, and persecutors. All are said to hold the person in scorn, ridicule, or dread. One would expect adversaries to treat one badly. One would hope for sympathy from neighbors and acquaintances, but one's sickness may make one a burden and a drag. Even those unacquainted with the sufferer, even by-passers on the street, are horrified. On every hand there is terror. Such a depiction of human life may sound a bit paranoid, and may be. The minister ought to struggle with how sermons can be preached that take seriously a person's feeling of being overwhelmed by opponents, misunderstood and neglected by family, shunned by the healthy and the well-off. Perhaps the psalms allowed worshipers in ancient Israel the occasion to get their feelings off their chests even if the depiction produced a picture with image and reality distorted. Perhaps, at the same time, such expressions aided people to live in a world where altruism is the exception, not the expected.

The plea for help that begins in verse 14 contains many elements of confidence, many statements that are God and life affirming. (The lection omits the negative wishes of verses 17–18, with their desire to see opponents Sheol-bound and put to shame. Such expressions of vengeance demonstrate that even the worshiper was not altruistic!) The plea affirms the worshiper's willingness to place the ultimate destiny of life in the Deity's hands and thus reiterates the theme "into your hand I commit my spirit."

Philippians 2:5–11

Because this is the well-established epistolary lection for the Sixth Sunday in Lent, whether observed as Passion or Palm Sunday, the reader may want to consult our remarks on the passage in this liturgical setting in Years A and B. Also, semicontinuous readings from Philippians occur in Propers 20–23 [25–28] of Year A, and Philippians 2:1–13 is the epistolary text for Proper 21 [26]. This passage also serves as the epistolary lection for all three years for the day celebrating the Holy Name of Jesus: Solemnity of Mary, Mother of God. Treatment of this passage occurs earlier in this volume in connection with January 1.

On the eve of Holy Week, the part of the passage that seizes us is verse 8: "[He] became obedient to the point of death—even death on a cross." This surely sets the tone for the intense observance of Christ's passion that is to follow. Already we hear themes that will be played and replayed as we approach Good Friday and Easter.

In dealing with today's lections, we face an embarrassment of riches. The Gospel texts themselves are quite lengthy and will be difficult to appropriate fully within the service. The problem is compounded by the choice of Philippians 2:5–11 as the epistolary lection, because it is without doubt one of the most influential texts in Christian history and is literally packed with homiletical possibilities.

If it becomes the basis for the homily, we should recognize that even in its compact form it rehearses the Christ drama from preexistence to heavenly exaltation. The story begins with Christ "in the form of God" and concludes with his exaltation to God's right hand.

Scholars have long noted its rhythmical structure, and for this reason, among others, it is believed to be an early Christian hymn unfolding the drama of Christ's descent to earth and ascent to heaven. It has been suggested that the hymn unfolds in six stanzas, each unfolding a different stage in the Christ drama. The following arrangement uses the text of the New Jerusalem Bible:

Stanza I: The Preexistent Christ

(6)   Who, being in the form of God,
did not count equality with God
something to be grasped.

Stanza II: Christ Becomes a Human Slave

(7)   But he emptied himself,
taking the form of a slave,
becoming as human beings are;

Stanza III: Christ's Humiliating Death

and being in every way like a human being,
(8)   he was humbler yet,
even to accepting death, death on a cross.

Stanza IV: God's Exaltation of Christ

(9)   And for this God raised him high,
       and gave him the name
       which is above all other names;

Stanza V: Universal Recognition of Christ

(10)   so that all beings
       in the heavens, on earth and in the underworld,
       should bend the knee at the name of Jesus

Stanza VI: Universal Confession of Christ as Lord

(11)   and that every tongue should acknowledge
       Jesus Christ as Lord,
       to the glory of God the Father.

There is some dispute about whether the hymn should be arranged in six stanzas, as above, or in four stanzas. In either case, there is a clear break at verse 9, and at the very least we can conceive of two parts: the one (vv. 6–8) relating Christ's descent from heaven; the other (vv. 9–11) relating his ascent to heaven. This two-part arrangement is adopted by the NRSV.

Stanza I: Being "in the form of God" attributes to Jesus a divine status that was his from the beginning (John 1:1–16; 17:5; Col. 1:15–20; Heb. 1:3). That "he did not cling to his equality with God" (JB) is a highly controversial phrase that probably implies a level of status fully comparable to that of God.

Stanza II: Becoming human required Christ's self-emptying, or literally making himself nothing (cf. 2 Cor. 8:9). Specifically, it meant entering human form as a servant (Gal. 4:1; Col. 3:22–23; cf. Matt. 20:28). The language doubtless recalls the Servant Songs of Isaiah (53:13–53:12; 42:1). His identity with humanity was complete (Rom. 8:3; Gal. 4:4; Heb. 2:17).

Stanza III: Here we have depicted yet another step downward. Entering human existence was one form of humiliation. It was an even deeper level of humiliation to be subjected to crucifixion. That he "accepted" death may recall Gethsemane (Matt. 26:39–46). In any case, his acceptance constituted full obedience (Rom. 5:19; Heb. 5:8; 12:2).

Stanza IV: At the very nadir of humiliation—the cross—God turned the tables of history and exalted Christ by raising him from the dead. Even though he was humbled, he became ex-alted (Matt. 23:12; John 10:17; Eph. 1:20–23). Here resurrection and being exalted are seen as one "exaltation." In his exalted status, he received the name "Lord" (Acts 2:21; 3:16), a title far surpassing that of any other heavenly being, including the angels (Eph. 1:21; Heb. 1:4; 1 Pet. 3:22).

Stanza V: In his exalted position, Christ is recognized as Lord by the whole cosmos, here conceived as having three tiers—heaven, earth, and underworld (cf. Isa. 45:23; Rom. 14:11; Rev. 5:3, 13).

Stanza VI: In this final stanza, recognition gives way to confession. Finally, all the hosts of heaven acknowledge the basic Christian confession: Jesus Christ is Lord (Rom. 1:4; 10:9; 1 Cor. 12:3; Col. 2:6).

In this early Christian hymn, we are confronted with the dual focus of the Christ-story—humiliation and death along with exaltation and life. As such, it is a text that propels us toward Easter, but it takes us through Good Friday. It embodies the essential paradox of Christian faith—exaltation through humiliation.

Luke 22:14–23:56 or Luke 23:1–49

For the observance of Passion Sunday, the preacher has a choice between the longer narrative (Luke 22:14–23:56) or a segment of that narrative (23:1–49). Even this briefer selection may seem prohibitively long for a sermon, not to mention the entire narrative. Of course, the preacher is free to focus upon only a portion of the story or to base the message primarily on the Epistle or Old Testament lections. However, because passion and resurrection form the center of the Christian proclamation, and because about one-third of the Gospel records concerns the events and teachings of the final days of Jesus' life, the minister is encouraged to use the passion narrative as fully as possible, even if the sermon contains little more than the recitation of the Evangelist's story.

Luke 22:14–23:56 opens with the Last Supper and concludes with the burial of Jesus. Because the narrative is Luke's, it is important that the preacher not presume to tell "what happened" by a general blending of all four Gospels but let the church hear and understand the story as Luke tells it. Although the passion narrative is remarkably the same in all the Gospels, indicating how early this material became a sacred tradition, still each Evangelist made certain emphases appropriate to the overall purpose and understanding of the event of Jesus Christ. The following is a broad outline of the lection with notes pointing out Lucan accents:

The Last Supper—22:14–20. Whereas Matthew and Mark introduce early the subject of betrayal, Luke delays it, so primary attention is on the Passover and the institution of the Lord's Supper. The preacher needs to decide whether verses 19b–20 are part of the text. Without it, the order of cup and then bread recalls 1 Corinthians 10:16.

Farewell Instruction—22:21–38. The announcement of approaching death and what the followers are to do at that time and afterward provides a dramatic and sobering context for Jesus' words. Notice that Luke places here the dispute about greatness, found earlier in Matthew (20:25–28) and Mark (10:42–45). Luke shows his customary respect for Peter's leadership, even in Jesus' prophecy of denial. The enigmatic saying about swords dramatizes the critical nature of the times but does not condone violence (v. 51).

At the Mount of Olives—22:39–46. In this familiar place (vv. 39–46) called Gethsemane by Matthew and Mark, Jesus prays alone, not with Peter, James, and John. Even with heaven's help, the agony is extreme.

Jesus Taken Captive—22:47–53. The question of use of the sword is asked, and Jesus answers with a word and with healing.

The Hearings and Trials—22:54–23:16. Jesus is taken that night to the home of the high priest, and in the morning to the council. (Notice that much of this section is devoted to Peter's denial. Luke adds a moving line in verse 61.) On several matters Luke is very emphatic: the council determined Jesus' death; Pilate never believed the threefold charge against Jesus (23:2); neither did Herod Antipas find Jesus deserving of death (only Luke includes Herod); at the hands of the Jews Jesus was beaten and mocked (22:63–65), but not by Pilate's soldiers (as in Matt. 27:27–31; Mark 15:16–20).

The Sentencing—23:17–25. After Pilate's efforts to release Jesus failed, he delivered Jesus "as they wished" (v. 25), not "to be crucified."

The Road to Golgotha—23:26–32. Characteristically, women are present, and Luke's Jesus ministers to them.

The Crucifixion—23:33–43. Lukan themes of forgiveness and ministering to the penitent sinner are present to the last.

The Death—23:44–49. At his death, Jesus is again declared innocent by Rome (v. 47). Luke's church and state have no quarrel, and Israel's crime against Jesus was in ignorance (v. 34; Acts 3:17).

The Burial—23:50–56. The women of Galilee wait to prepare the body because it is the sabbath. From birth to death, Jesus' story is always, says Luke, according to the Scriptures.

Were the preacher to choose to use the shorter passage (23:1–49), the same procedure could be followed, but with more detailed attention to events from the appearance before Pilate until the death on the cross. Of special importance in this section is Luke's repeated insistence to Theophilus, his reader (1:1–4), that the government is not antichurch nor is the church antigovernment. We do not know if Luke is reflecting the condition of his time or trying to create a better church-state climate.

Monday in Holy Week

Isaiah 42:1–9;
Psalm 36:5–11;
Hebrews 9:11–15;
John 12:1–11

The mood of the texts for this day is one of hope and celebration, already beginning to look beyond the death of Jesus. There are particularly strong connections between the Old Testament text and the reading from Hebrews, for both expect a covenant that will bring salvation to all peoples. The psalm is a song of praise to God for his steadfast love. The tone and message of the Gospel lection are mixed, from a celebration with Martha and Mary, to grumbling by Judas, to a foreshadowing of the death of Jesus, to a foreshadowing of his resurrection.

Isaiah 42:1–9

This reading includes the first of the Servant Songs (see the comments on Isaiah 50:4–9a for Passion/Palm Sunday in this volume), and more. There are two originally independent units—the song itself in verses 1–4, and a distinct prophetic speech in verses 5–9. Both stem from Second Isaiah shortly before the end of the Exile in 538 BC. This literary juxtaposition of the two units addresses one of the perennial problems in the interpretation of the Servant Songs, namely, the identity of the servant. Although the answer to that question is unclear within the song, the subsequent verses interpret the servant as the people of Israel (vv. 6–7). At the same time, the poetic description of the servant's call and role becomes an interpretation of the experience of Israel in and beyond the Babylonian Exile.

The Servant Song itself, 42:1–4, has the form of a public proclamation in which the speaker is the Lord, introducing the servant to an unspecified audience. The proclamation has the force of ordination, indicating first, that God has chosen this particular one, and second, the purpose for which the Lord has chosen him. Thus the form and the contents make it explicit that the servant's role is an extension of—one could say metaphorically, incarnation of—the divine intention. What the servant does and how he accomplishes it have the divine blessing and will accomplish God's purposes.

The only reason given for the election of this servant is God's love: "in whom my soul delights" (v. 1). The Hebrew word for "soul" here refers simply to the self, so NEB accurately translates, "in whom I delight." The ordination with the Spirit of God parallels the understanding of the selection of kings and other leaders as well as the empowerment of prophets.

The central term in the song is "justice" (vv. 1, 3, 4). The understanding of "justice" in ancient Israel must begin with the law court, but not end there. It refers to the establishment of the right, including what we would call procedural justice (due process), as well as what we would call distributive justice—the equitable distribution of rights, resources, and responsibilities. To establish justice was to maintain balance and to correct deviations from fairness, sometimes in the form of retribution. Not only prophets but also the legal traditions were particularly concerned about the protection of the rights—the justice due—the weak and the poor. Underlying procedural and distributive justice for Israel was the substance of this justice, known and maintained in the covenant. Justice among human beings was based upon the conviction that the God of Israel was just, and intended for divine justice to be reflected in the world.

Another key term for understanding the role of the servant is "teaching" (v. 4, NRSV, NEB). The Hebrew word is *torah*, more traditionally translated "law." The concept was deeply ingrained in Israel's view of its relationship to its God. In one sense it is the instruction in covenant responsibilities given by the priests—thus the translation in the NRSV and the NEB. Eventually it came to mean the whole body of divine revelation embodied in the first five books of the Bible.

Especially important here are the extent and manner of the promulgation of justice and *torah*, which promulgation was the servant's role. Its extent is to be universal: "to the nations" (v. 1); "in the earth" (v. 4). Justice and law, which were to characterize the relationships between Israel and her God and among Israelites, now are proclaimed to all. As remarkable as the extent is the manner by which this will be accomplished. The text presents this point only indirectly. It is to be accomplished not by force of arms, nor by power, but by gentleness, concern (vv. 2–3), and persistence to the completion of the task (v. 4).

Verses 5–9 are not simply an interpretation of the servant as the people of Israel, but a summary of the message of the prophet. Following the introductory messenger formula ("Thus says God, the LORD") is a divine speech to Israel. God identifies himself as creator of the earth and all life in it (v. 5) and is not to be compared with images (v. 8). Next, God affirms the election and, implicitly, the redemption of Israel (v. 6*a*), and then proclaims the purpose for which God chose and redeemed Israel; namely, to be "a covenant to the people, a light to the nations," and to set the prisoners free (vv. 6*b*–7). Israel's role thus parallels that of the servant—to mediate God's justice to the world.

With such powerful theological texts as this, it is easy to become carried away with the general and the abstract. To do so would be to miss the point. Both in its ancient Israelite and its early Christian contexts, the force of the text is its specific and concrete focus. God chooses particular human beings or particular peoples to carry out the divine will. Although the text has an unmistakable eschatological direction, it also has in view the establishment of God's will for justice in the midst of concrete human realities and conditions, including all forms of blindness and in prisons of all kinds. Moreover, God's purposes are not fulfilled until all the redeemed see themselves as "a covenant to the people, a light to the nations."

Psalm 36:5–11

The first two sections of this lament differ radically from each other. The first, verses 1–4, describes the wicked in human-to-human speech. (Verse 1 has probably suffered from textual corruption; the opening line makes little sense in Hebrew.) The character and activity of the wicked are described in several ways: life is lived as if it were self-explanatory without reference to the Deity (v. 1b); self-deceit and self-flattery have convinced the wicked of their self-security (v. 2); their words (and actions) are the source of mischief and deceit, threats, denunciations, and accusations, probably because they want to force the world to march to their tune (v. 3); and even in the private confines of the house while waiting for sleep to come, evil machination and plotting are present setting the course for the next day's behavior (v. 4).

Over against this first section stands the second, verses 5–9, which comprises the bulk of the present lection, verses 5–11. The tone, the content, and addressees have all shifted. Verses 5–9 are hymnic praise, addressed directly to the Deity, spoken in worship perhaps by the one making the requests and pleas in verse 11 (but note the "we" in verse 9).

The hymn praises God for steadfast love and righteousness—divine fidelity or faithfulness and equity, we might say. Unlike the wicked, God is consistent and equitable and loving.

Verses 5 and 6 compare the divine attributes to natural phenomena. The heavens and the clouds, the mountains of God (or "lofty mountains" if we take the word God as the means of expressing a superlative), and the great deep are ways of saying that they reach everywhere. The great deep lay underneath the earth, and the base of the mountains extended into the deep (see Jon. 2:5–6). The same inclusiveness is denoted in the expression "you save humans and animals alike."

The security of refuge and the abundance of sacrificial celebrations is extolled in verses 7–9. In this, these celebrations they may be employed metaphorically, but their imagery is that of the temple service. (Jesus' cleansing of the temple, by the way, was on Monday of Holy Week, according to Mark 11:15–19.)

The plea, or request, in verses 10–11 asks that God's steadfast love continue, but hedges that continuity by referring to "those who know you" and the "upright of heart." There is, in other words, a conditionality with regard to God's love. After the general petition in verse 10 on behalf of the general class of those loyal to Yahweh and the divine will, a special personalized request appears in verse 11: don't let me be trampled by the arrogant nor forced to flee because of the wicked.

Hebrews 9:11–15

The central image Hebrews uses to interpret the work of Christ is that of high priest (2:17; 3:1; 4:14; 5:5, 10; 6:20; 7:26; 8:1; 10:21). But it was not as if Jesus were a high priest who simply outperformed the Levitical high priests, doing his work better, or longer, or more efficiently. What distinguished him was that he had been raised from the dead and "passed through the heavens" (4:14) to receive an exalted position with God (7:26).

This is the overarching image unfolded in Hebrews—the risen Christ, exalted to the heavens, marching triumphantly into God's Holy Place, the heavenly sanctuary. There he performs the priestly rites. Lest we think that this is an ordinary sanctuary, we are reminded that Christ carries out his high priestly service in a "greater and perfect tent (not made with hands)" (v. 11; cf. 8:2; 9:24). What happens in this heavenly service far surpasses anything that ever occurred "below," in the earthly tabernacle.

What was different? The sacrifices offered below were animals. The Levitical priests dealt with "the blood of goats and bulls, with the sprinkling of the ashes of a heifer" (v. 13; 9:19; 10:1–4; cf. Num. 19:2–10). Such animal sacrifices were offered as purification rites. In this way, the worshiper obtained ritual purity so that "their flesh is purified" (v. 13). Hebrews sees such sacrifices as inherently deficient. The very fact that they had to be offered repeatedly showed that they were inadequate (10:1–4). But they were most seriously deficient because they failed to deal adequately with the conscience of the one who made the offering. Purification of the flesh is one thing, purification of the conscience quite another.

What was needed was a way for the human conscience to be genuinely and truly forgiven—in other words, a way of experiencing "eternal redemption" (v. 12). And this is what was achieved by the sacrifice of Christ, "who through the eternal Spirit offered himself without blemish to God" (v. 14). Unlike the animal sacrifices offered by the Levitical priests, this was a human sacrifice. It was a sacrifice "without defect or blemish" (1 Pet. 1:19). Not only was it an unblemished life, but a sacrifice willingly made by Christ himself: He "offered himself" (v. 14; 9:25; John 10:18). In a word, it was a self-sacrifice.

But why does the sacrifice of Christ resolve the problem of human sin any better than animal sacrifices? It may be human instead of animal, unblemished instead of blemished, willingly made instead of forced, but it addresses the heart instead of the flesh because it is made not only in behalf of us but instead of us (cf. Rom. 3:24–25; 5:9; 1 John 1:7). Our text also reminds us that Christ offered himself "through the eternal Spirit" (v. 14). The human will can be brought into the service of the living God only as it is prompted by the Spirit of God. Through Christ's self-offering we see the ultimate conquest of the human will as it lives in response to the call of God. It is at this level that our consciences can become purified "from dead works to worship the living God" (v. 14).

Because Christ is officiating in the heavenly sanctuary, having become our high priest through the sacrifice of himself, he now serves as "mediator of a new covenant" (v. 15; 8:6–10; 10:29; 12:24; 13:20; also 1 Tim. 2:5; Gal. 3:19). It is new not only because it invites us into a lasting relationship with God, but also because it makes our entry into the heavenly sanctuary possible. It is also new in the sense that Jeremiah foresees the future covenant between Yahweh and Israel (31:31–34; cf. Heb. 8:6–12). It envisions a time when the law of God is written on the heart, when sins are finally and fully forgiven.

As a text for Holy Week, today's epistolary lection confronts us squarely with the Christ who willingly offered himself for the sins of humanity. As we reflect on this self-sacrifice that was made in the service of the living God, we are urged to consider the nature of our own service and how it is made possible through the sacrifice of Christ. Our text also speaks of promise, reassuring us that "those who are called [will] receive the promised eternal inheritance" (v. 15).

John 12:1–11

From Passion/Palm Sunday through Easter, the Gospel lections will be drawn from the passion narratives. Because these accounts have always been regarded as containing the heart of the gospel, it is likely that the narrative of Jesus' final days—his arrest, trial, and death—hardened quite early into a fixed tradition among the churches. Some scholars believe that this may account for the fact that all four Evangelists relate the story with basically the same outline and with strikingly similar details. However, each Evangelist has his own purpose in writing, and each church addressed has its own needs; therefore, episodes from a common tradition are related from different perspectives. The preacher will want to be alert to this fact in order to avoid preaching from a composite of four accounts rather than from the particular text for the day.

The Gospel for today is John 12:1–11 and not the general topic, "the anointing of Jesus." All four Gospels record the event (Matt. 26:6–13; Mark 14:3–9; Luke 7:36–39) but with important differences. Matthew and Mark place the story in Bethany in the home of Simon the leper, where "a woman" anoints Jesus' head. Anointing the head was in the biblical tradition the ceremony for the coronation of a king. Luke locates the act in Galilee in the home of Simon the Pharisee, where a sinful woman anoints Jesus' feet with tears and with ointment. Luke, like John, knows of Jesus' visits to the home of Martha and Mary, but Luke 10:38–42 and John 12:1–11 are otherwise quite different. For this message, we give our attention solely to the text before us. What would John have us hear?

First, in this Gospel the anointing at Bethany is a passion story; that is, it focuses on the death of Jesus. In this regard John is like Matthew and Mark but unlike Luke, whose anointing story is early, unrelated to Jesus' death, and is told to dramatize the nature of forgiveness. John not only locates the anointing within the passion narrative but weaves into the brief account all the dark forebodings of death. The scene is Bethany, where there waits an empty and available tomb (11:38–44); at the table is Lazarus to whom Jesus gave life, an act that will now cost Jesus his (11:4; 12:9–11); the time is Passover (12:1), which in this Gospel is death time; into this pleasant circle of friends comes Judas, the dark intruder, who, in the time and place of this Gospel, was viewed as betrayer and as thief (12:46); and finally there is Mary's act, an anointing for Jesus' burial. The approaching death of Jesus is clearly the governing theme of the story.

Second, this Evangelist repeats a conviction common to the entire Gospel: in relation to Jesus Christ, the words and acts of others have meanings and effects far beyond what may have been intended at the time. Caiaphas, the high priest, unwittingly prophesied that Jesus' death would save the world (11:49–52); the Pharisees unwittingly acknowledged that the whole world was going to Jesus (12:19). So here, Mary performs an act of hospitality, friendship, and gratitude for a brother restored; but in that act she unwittingly prepares Jesus for burial. However, this is a message not only in John, but in the entire Bible: God uses our acts beyond our intent or capacity. Abraham was hospitable to strangers and entertained angels unawares; two disciples from Emmaus invited a fellow traveler to rest and eat, and a supper became a sacrament; Paul wrote letters to the churches, and a New Testament canon had its beginnings. We never know; our task is to speak and act in a way appropriate to faith's response to the occasion and to leave the conclusions to God.

Third, Mary's act will bless and plague every minister who has to counsel and evaluate similar acts of devotion and gratitude. Three hundred poinsettias announce Christmas; five hundred lilies embellish Easter; and then there are the memorial chimes, the memorial silver Communion ware, and the memorial window. "A gift in gratitude," says the donor; "a sinful waste," says not only Judas but everyone who has looked into hollow eyes and heard the cries of a hungry child. Sound sense and Christian duty know the need is for potatoes, not perfume, and yet checking the shopping list even of the poor reveals that among flour, beans, and pork there will be candy and cologne. The appropriate word is not easily found or easily spoken.

Tuesday in Holy Week

Isaiah 49:1–7;
Psalm 71:1–14;
1 Corinthians 1:18–31;
John 12:20–36

The readings for today take us a step closer to the commemoration of the crucifixion of Jesus, enabling us to reflect seriously upon the last days of his life and upon God's intentions through his life and death. The Old Testament lection, the second Servant Song of Second Isaiah, in this liturgical context is seen to parallel the experience of Jesus—empowered by God, challenged by others, yet expressing confidence in God. The psalm is a prayer for help as well as an expression of confidence, picking up the Old Testament reading's references to selection before birth and to the mouth of the one who responds to God's call. The passage from 1 Corinthians is an interpretation of the cross as human foolishness but divine wisdom, human weakness but divine strength. The Gospel lesson anticipates the cross as God's glorification of Jesus and includes calls for faith in the one to be crucified.

Isaiah 49:1–7

The reading consists of the second Servant Song (49:1–6) plus one additional verse (49:7) that actually begins a new and distinct unit. In the Book of Isaiah as a whole, and Deutero-Isaiah in particular, this passage begins a distinct section of material. Most of the speeches in Isaiah 40–48 are addressed quite explicitly to the Israelites in Babylonian exile, whereas those in chapters 49–55 seem directed more to Jerusalem and the Israelites there. In any case, the passage comes from the unnamed prophet in Babylon in approximately 539 BC, immediately before the end of the Exile.

Like the third Servant Song (Isa. 50:4–9) and unlike the first and fourth (Isa. 42:1–9; 52:13–53:12), this one is presented as a speech by the servant himself. The address to the "coastlands" and the "peoples from far away" is international in scope, already hinting at the message of the poem. Although it is the servant who speaks, in two instances he is heard to quote the words of Yahweh. The substance of the address concerns the servant's call, his response to it, and his mission.

The elements of the poem are easily recognizable on the basis of the shifts in speaker, from the servant's own addresses to his quotations of the Lord. After calling for attention (v. 1a), he gives an account of his vocation (vv. 1b–3). Then the servant reports his frustration and sense of failure, which were overcome by his confidence that his life and work were

179

grounded in the Lord (v. 4). Then an elaborate messenger formula (v. 5) introduces a divine speech in which the Lord is heard to spell out the servant's mission.

The question of the identity of the servant as the nation would appear to be solved in verse 3 ("my servant, Israel, . . ."), until one reads in verse 6 that the servant has a mission *to* Israel. This fact has led some who favor a collective interpretation to see the servant as a group within Israel, or even an ideal Israel.

The servant's vocation certainly is identified here with the prophetic role in ancient Israel, and the language is especially dependent upon Jeremiah. Like that prophet (Jer. 1:5), the servant was called "from the womb"; that is, God designated him even before he was born, choosing him by naming him (cf. Isa. 43:1). His "mouth" in particular was prepared for the task ahead. Like Jeremiah, the servant had doubts and frustrations (v. 4; cf. Jer. 20:7–11). As in the prophet's accounts of their calls, the servant goes on to report the specific task for which he was called.

It is not immediately obvious how the account of the servant's task is related to the prophetic vocation. The duties are two: (1) The Lord expects the servant to bring Israel back to him (vv. 5*a*, 6*a*). This return is quite specific and concrete, referring to the return of the exiles from Babylon and the restoration of the people on their land, and especially in the Holy City, Jerusalem. (2) The servant—as the call to the nations hinted at the beginning—is to be "a light to the nations" in order that God's salvation may "reach to the end of the earth" (v. 6*b*). Thus the restoration of Israel is no end in itself, but a step on the way toward the inclusion of all peoples in the reign of God. The completion of that task is prophetic insofar as it entails the proclamation of the word of God. That word, as the prophets have believed all along, has the power to change the future. It is one of the ways that God intervenes in human affairs.

Psalm 71:1–14

Psalm 71, a lament and supplication in time of trouble, is characterized by a high level of trust and confidence. The trouble appears to have been old age, as verses 9 and 18 suggest. The pleas in these two verses—not to be forsaken—speak of "the time of old age" and "old age and gray hairs." Thus we can imagine this psalm initially being used by the elderly who still hoped to be revived and reinvigorated in spite of old age (v. 20) and who had confidence that there was still a future and still a time of life ahead (note the vows regarding the future in vv. 14–16, 22–24).

This psalm may have originally been written for use by Judean kings rather than for just average people. The fact that the psalm speaks of God's having taken the person from the womb of the mother could imply that the person occupied some position of prominence (see Jer. 1:5). The average person probably would not have made such a claim.

The placement of Psalm 71 to precede Psalm 72 may not be purely accidental. Psalm 72 is one of only two psalms (see Psalm 127) associated with Solomon, who became king in his father's old age (see 1 Kings 1), when David, like the "psalmist" in Psalm 71 was facing death and the end of life. Thus the two psalms could be seen as speaking of David (Psalm 71) and Solomon (Psalm 72).

The passage selected for this lection contains an opening address to the Deity (v. 1), an appeal pleading for help (vv. 2–4), a statement of the worshiper's confidence in God (vv. 5–8), a description of the distress (vv. 9–11), a second appeal (vv. 12–13), and a statement of the worshiper's future action (v. 14).

We can examine the salient features of this psalm in terms of (1) the nature of the distress, (2) the worshiper's statements of confidence, and (3) the nature of the help requested from God.

1. The troubles undergone by the worshiper are related primarily to the opposition of enemies. The gallery of opponents is described as "the wicked," "the unjust and cruel" person, and "enemies" who seek the worshiper's life. The bitterest opponents appear to be those enemies who consider the person forsaken by God and thus without help and support (vv. 10–11). One might assume that the person had some malady or problem that was taken as the sign that God had forsaken or was no longer supporting the one praying.

2. This psalm is permeated by a strong sense of trust and confidence. As the person looks back to the past, there is the affirmation that God has been his or her trust from youth. God is even seen as the one who like a midwife took him or her from the mother's womb (v. 6). Looking to the future, the psalmist prays that the trust in and association with God that was begun as a child will continue into the days of old age and gray hairs (vv. 9, 18). A common theme throughout the psalm is that of God as refuge. The worshiper can confess that God is a refuge and at the same time pray that God will be a refuge (compare vv. 1 and 7 with v. 3). The concept of a refuge is further explicated with reference to God as a strong fortress and a rock—all expressive of both stability and protection. An interesting feature of the psalm's statements of confidence is the reference to the special role the person has for making known or proclaiming God not only to the contemporaries of the day but also to generations yet to come (vv. 7–8, 18). This would suggest that this psalm was not originally composed for use by an ordinary Israelite but was probably written for use by the king, who had a special responsibility for proclaiming the nation's God.

3. The petitions and appeals made to God for help primarily focus on the requests that God not forsake the worshiper (vv. 9–10) or let the person be put to shame (v. 1). Shame plays both a positive and a negative function in the psalm. The worshiper asks to be preserved from shame (v. 1) and at the same time prays that the accusers be put to shame and consumed (v. 13). Shame, of course, would have involved being put into a humiliating situation and at the same time being made to accept the identity that the situation imposed.

This psalm can be exegeted and preached in the context of Holy Week, because it expresses many of the factors that we think of in terms of Jesus' suffering: the opposition of enemies who doubt that God is his supporter, the trust and confidence of the worshiper, and the sense of possessing a message that must be proclaimed and made known to generations yet to come.

1 Corinthians 1:18–31

At the heart of the Christian gospel is the paradox of the cross. As a symbol, the cross expresses the sum and substance of Paul's gospel: Jesus Christ, and him crucified (1 Cor. 2:2). To think of the cross is to think of suffering, as the passion narratives of the Gospels attest. It can scarcely be thought of apart from weakness and impotence. How odd it is, then, that God should choose this, the most fragile of symbols, to express the divine will!

As Paul insists in today's epistolary lection, when viewed rationally the cross is a stumbling block, something the mind trips over. Both Jews and Greeks (Paul's way of saying everyone) saw the doctrine of the cross as quite incredible, if not bordering on the absurd. And so it is when measured in the scale of human judgment. If we want proof of divinity, we normally expect some show of force—thunder, lightning, waters dividing, heavens opening. The last thing we expect is for God to be manifested in a moment of sheer helplessness and abandon. And yet God has chosen to be revealed in this riddle we call the cross.

But Paul has little use for human wisdom as the standard for measuring God's ways. In this, he stands squarely in the Old Testament tradition, which often ridicules the presumed wisdom of human beings (Isa. 19:11–12; 33:18; 44:25; Job 12:17). Moreover, he insists that the human point of view is the short view, limited as it is "to this passing age" (v. 20, NEB).

Even more important, perhaps, is to notice the limits of human wisdom. It can take us only so far. It can bring us to the edge, perhaps allow us to peer over, but in Paul's view, it cannot reveal God to us. This can happen only when God calls us. To put it simply, "The world failed to find [God] by its wisdom" (v. 21, REB). It led the quest, but the quest was unfulfilled. Alas, it was a matter of God's choosing us, not of our finding God.

For Paul, this was a crucial difference, for had human wisdom succeeded in finding God, it could have been justifiably proud. It could openly say, "Eureka! I have found it!" The natural result would have been arrogance, or human pride (v. 29).

As it is, however, God has chosen to confound the wisest of the wise, and in doing so has undercut human boasting. God has worked the divine will according to the divine way, and in doing so has succeeded in demonstrating both divine power and wisdom. This way is wiser because it keeps humans human. In no way can we lay claim to God's saving power because we have solved the riddle of the cross. It is also more powerful because it gives God room to work.

We do well to admit that divine folly is wiser than human wisdom, and divine weakness is stronger than human strength (v. 25). If we need further proof of this, we need only look as close as our own calling and consider "what sort of people [we] are" (v. 26, REB). If we paint honest self-portraits, like the Corinthians we actually have very little to commend us. Neither our wisdom, nor our position, nor our pedigree takes us very far. With very little to offer, then, we are summoned by God, and through this divine calling we become transformed from nothing into something. What we are, we are by God's act, not our own (v. 30). The initiative lay with God in calling us, and the change that occurred in us was wrought by God's power. Ours was divine generation, not human reproduction.

The cross will always be a symbol that divides. For some, it can only be seen as "sheer folly" (v. 18, REB). Others will be able to see in it "the power of God" (v. 18, REB). The latter will always be in the minority, for it requires special perception to conceive of a God who works this way—demonstrating wisdom in folly, strength in weakness.

To be able to see only power through power and wisdom through wisdom is for Paul a sure sign of ruin. Those whose world is put together this way are "those who are perishing" (v. 18). By contrast, if we want to experience the power of God, we must begin at the place where all boasting is excluded—at the intersection of human weakness and ignorance—the cross of Christ.

John 12:20–36

We continue throughout Holy Week with texts from the fourth Gospel. Today's lesson follows John's account of Jesus' entry into Jerusalem (vv. 12–19). The preacher may want to reread John 11:4–12:19, not only to locate our text in Jerusalem at Passover time, but also to capture the atmosphere of death and betrayal that surrounds the festivities of the high sabbath of Passover. The reader will also be reminded that in the midst of the celebrating and plotting, Jesus stands clear and firm as to "the hour" of God's purpose for his life.

"The hour has come for the Son of Man to be glorified" (v. 23). This statement of Jesus was prompted by the coming of Greeks to see Jesus (v. 20), which in turn was prompted by a statement of the Pharisees, "Look, the world has gone after him" (v. 19). In other words, the unwitting comment by some Pharisees that the whole world was drawn to Jesus is a prophecy fulfilled in preview by the coming of Greeks. Who these Greeks are, what their origin is, and what happens to them are not primary concerns of the Evangelist. One would guess them to be Greeks who practice Judaism. Some commentators understand them symbolically as representing through Philip and Andrew (v. 22) a subsequent mission to Gentiles. For the writer, they serve to prompt from Jesus a series of statements about his death, his return to God, and the meaning of that glorification (John's word for Jesus' death and exaltation) for the life of the world. Once Jesus' comments begin, the Greeks vanish from the story.

Apparently, the line of thought prompted by the request of the Greeks to see Jesus is as follows: in order to be available to the Greeks, that is, to the world, Jesus must die and be exalted to God's presence. The earthly career of the historical Jesus must now continue in the ministry of the dead and risen Christ, who will be present and available to the church everywhere. The presence and availability of the living Christ will be the primary subject matter of the farewell discourses of chapters 14–16. The extensive and repeated treatment of this theme testifies to its importance for the Johannine church, and for us. Whether stated in terms of the living Christ or the Holy Spirit, the divine presence is essential for the life of the church.

The line of thought continues. Jesus reflects upon death in a threefold soliloquy: (1) there is a law of nature that death is a necessary precondition for the increase of more life (v. 24); (2) there is a law of discipleship that demands hating, or releasing, or giving one's life in order to have life (v. 25); and (3) the question arises immediately, But is the lord of nature and the master of disciples exempt from the law of death as essential for life? (v. 27). The answer is clearly a no. Instead of the Synoptics' "remove this cup," Jesus says, "Father, save me from this hour? No, it is for this reason that I have come to this hour" (v. 27). Instead of the cry of dereliction from the cross (Mark 15:34), Jesus here receives heaven's confirmation (v. 28). Even though Jesus' soul is troubled (v. 27), very little of Gethsemane's painful struggle appears in John's Gospel. In fact, Jesus did not actually need the confirming voice of heaven; it was, he said, for the benefit of those nearby (v. 30). Not all heard the voice, of course (v. 29); Scripture and experience teach us that events that are for some people occasions of God's self-disclosure are for others natural occurrences.

The time has come; Jesus will be lifted up, both in the sense of being put on a cross and of being elevated to God (v. 32). From this point through verse 36, Jesus speaks of his death in two ways. His death is judgment in that light is judgment upon those who prefer darkness and in that life is judgment upon those who prefer death. And Jesus' death is victory over the ruler of this world (v. 31), for in Christ's presence in word and in the Holy Spirit, persons of all nations and of all times will be drawn again to God (v. 32).

But even the clear word of judgment is softened a bit. "The light is with you for a little longer" (v. 35). For the sake of those of Jesus' time, of John's time, and of ours, the grace of God has stayed the end of all things.

Wednesday in Holy Week

Isaiah 50:4–9*a*;
Psalm 70;
Hebrews 12:1–3;
John 13:21–32

The readings for this occasion are somber reminders of persecution and suffering. The Old Testament lection is the third of the Servant Songs of Second Isaiah, in which the servant reports how he suffered humiliation at the hand of enemies because of his faithfulness to his vocation. The responsorial psalm is an individual lament that asks for deliverance from enemies. The reading from Hebrews provides relief from the somber mood as it looks beyond the suffering and death of Jesus to his exaltation. In the Gospel reading, Jesus discloses that Judas will betray him.

Isaiah 50:4–9*a*

This text, the third of the Servant Songs in Second Isaiah, is also assigned for reading on Passion/Palm Sunday. See the commentary at that point in this volume.

Psalm 70

For all practical purposes, Psalm 70 is identical with Psalm 40:13–17. In the latter psalm, this material forms one of the pleas in the psalm (see also Ps. 40:11) for deliverance and salvation in a time of trouble. The content of Psalm 70 would suggest that the psalm was composed for use by persons who were under attack and threatened by opponents, perhaps false accusers bringing charges of wrongdoing (as was the case with Jesus at his trial) or, on the basis of Psalm 40, perhaps national enemies attacking the Judean king.

Psalm 70:1–3 provides a good example of what has been called the double wish of the lament psalms, because the request to be saved is balanced by a request for the destruction of one's enemies or opponents. Frequently, the calamity that is requested to befall one's enemy is very similar to the condition that the one praying faced. Thus numerous psalms reflect something of that attitude, so widely felt, namely, that those who plan evil should have a corresponding evil beset them. Christians often shy away in horror from the prayers in the psalms that request a destruction or a calamity to fall on one's enemies. Such sentiments seem contrary to the teaching and life of Jesus. We must, however, understand that the psalms sought to give full and appropriate outlets for people to express their true feelings and sentiments. It may be that only by verbalizing such sentiments and expressions can they be overcome or transcended. Expressions of one's truest and deepest feelings may be necessary before one can release them and replace them with better feelings. In many ways, some of the psalms probably allowed persons to vent their anger and hostility to such a degree of animosity and with such a degree of revenge that the mere recital of such cursing wishes relieved the anxiety and pent-up emotions of the worshiper (e.g., Psalm 109).

The opening verse of Psalm 70, with its plea for God to hasten and to deliver, is followed by two verses asking that the enemies be put to shame and turned back; that is, that their plans go awry, so they will end up being shamed. If the prayer was originally offered by the king, then the adversaries could be foreign powers or nations who were threatening hostile military action.

Verse 4 is an intercessory prayer, although the worshiper is included in the group being prayed for. The intercessor requests that all those who seek God and love God's salvation rejoice and proclaim forever that God is great. This is obviously a prayer asking that the king and his subjects be victorious over the enemy or that they be spared a possible impending conflict.

In the final verse, the worshiper reverts to an appeal on his or her own behalf. The fact that the one praying is described as poor and needy does not mean that the person was destitute and poverty-stricken. Such expressions are metaphorical statements characterizing the person in the most sharply drawn and the humblest terms in order to evoke God's aid.

The association of this psalm with Holy Week can be made in two ways: (1) like Jesus, the psalmist was challenged by enemies who sought the person's death and destruction; and (2) like Jesus, the psalmist prayed and made intercessory requests on behalf of others.

Hebrews 12:1–3

Every one of us, athlete or not, knows how difficult and painful it is to hold out to the very end. It may be making a dress, wallpapering a room, plowing a field, writing a book, or finishing a report; the temptation is always the same. We grow weary at the end and find it difficult to maintain the same level of quality, commitment, and enthusiasm we began with. Almost inevitably, the job is more than we bargained for. Had we known how hard it would be, how long it would take, how many fresh starts would be required, we would never have begun. Looking back, we were naive. Yet we have invested too much in the project to quit. How can we hold out?

Today's epistolary text addresses this fundamental human tendency "to lose heart and grow faint" (v. 3, REB; cf. Gal. 6:9; Deut. 20:3). At issue, however, is no everyday project, but the life of faith we have embarked on. For the author of Hebrews, this is most appropriately envisioned as a race, a rather common metaphor for the life of faith in the New Testament, especially for Paul (cf. 1 Cor. 9:24–26; Gal. 5:7; Phil. 2:16; 3:12–14; 2 Tim. 4:7–8; cf. also Gal. 2:2; Phil. 1:27–28). The other athletic metaphor commonly used is the fight, such as a boxing or wrestling match (cf. 1 Cor. 9:26–27; 1 Tim. 6:12; Jude 3).

To think of the Christian life as running a race introduces several images. We lay aside the warm-up suit and anything else that will slow us down. We look around at the crowds whose eyes are staring at us (we think). But we are especially mindful of the other athletes, perhaps old-timers in the stands or those who have just finished their heats in earlier races, for we know they know as others cannot know. Yet this "cloud of witnesses" reassures us because we know others have run and won. So can we. Then there is the final lap, the final turn, the stretch. Here is where cramps can set in, someone can step in front of us, or we simply run out of steam. We call up Olympic images of other runners whose fondest dreams evaporated in this final struggle with weakness, fatigue, and opposition.

When all of these images begin to merge or vanish, it becomes clear that the real test is one of endurance and patience. The one who can hold out—with patience—finally wins.

At first, it may seem remarkable how much the New Testament urges us to endure. The seeds sown in good soil, Jesus reminds us, are those who "hold it fast" in their heart and "bear fruit with patient endurance" (Luke 8:15). Or, in the face of apocalyptic threats, Jesus reminds the disciples, "By your endurance you will gain your souls" (Luke 21:19). It becomes something of an axiom: to be faithful is to endure (Heb. 10:36; Rev. 3:10; 13:10; 14:12).

Nor is this the mindless endurance that simply clings for the sake of clinging or presses on with no clear vision of the destination. In our case, "our eyes [are] fixed on Jesus, on whom faith depends from start to finish" (v. 2, NEB). Ours is a faith that rests in the One who, given a choice between giving up and holding up, held up: he "endured the cross," as disgraceful as it was (v. 2).

At the middle of Holy Week, this Wednesday meditation draws us into the middle of Christ's own suffering, urging us to endure it with him. It is a struggle against rank opposition from sinners (v. 3). Not only was it an inward struggle with his own self-doubts and fears in the face of death, but it was a struggle to muster the power to resist face-to-face those bent on destroying him, whether Judas (as in today's Gospel text) or Satan's other minions. Endurance, then, requires us to fight against ourselves as well as others who conspire, perhaps with us, against the life of faith.

In a word, our text today calls for clear, focused vision on a solitary goal—the life of obedient faith relentlessly pursued. We should know that others—many others—have preceded us in this race and have run well. To them we look for confidence and assurance. We should also know that the One in whom we trust and for whom we live both "leads us in our faith and brings it to perfection" (v. 2, NJB; cf. Acts 3:15; 5:31; Heb. 2:10).

John 13:21–32

Because the Gospel lections for today and tomorrow are from John 13, let us take a moment to familiarize ourselves with this portion of the Gospel.

In John's Gospel the ministry of Jesus as the revealer of God on earth is presented in chapters 1–12. That ministry is one of signs and speeches in the presence of the disciples, the crowds, and the opponents. Although the writer is quite aware of the reader and the reader's situation, as evidenced by the way the story is told, still these twelve chapters are *about* Jesus in *his* historical context. The reader overhears and observes. However, beginning in chapter 13, the reader (that is, the church) is more directly addressed. The crowds, the opponents, and the public scenes are gone, and Jesus turns to prepare the church for betrayal, death, departure, and the coming of the Spirit as "another Advocate" (14:16). Chapters 13–20 could well be entitled "Farewell." These chapters contain the account of the farewell of Jesus (chaps. 18–20) and a rather lengthy preparation for that farewell (chaps. 13–17). By prediction, promise, warning, charge, encouragement, and exemplary act, Jesus prepares his followers for the first major crisis of the church, his departure and absence. It is vital that, following his return to God, Jesus' disciples remain in continuity with the historical Jesus. That continuity will be maintained by remembrance of Jesus' words, apostolic tradition, and the Holy Spirit. These chapters (chaps. 13–17) make that abundantly clear.

Chapter 13 begins this section with an account of Jesus' farewell meal with his disciples. During that meal Jesus indicates his betrayer, and Judas leaves the table to attend to his dark business. The writer closes the scene (vv. 21–30) with a statement more symbolic and dramatic than informative: "And it was night" (v. 30). However, it is interesting that "night" is preserved in the earliest of our traditions about the Last Supper: "The Lord Jesus on the night when he was betrayed took a loaf of bread" (1 Cor. 11:23).

The scene and drama presented in John 13:21–32 center on the roles of three persons: Jesus, the disciple Jesus loved, and Judas. Jesus, in the characteristic Johannine portrait, knows what is to happen (v. 21) and who will do it (v. 26). He also is totally in charge, commanding Judas to do quickly what he has to do (v. 27). After all, no one takes the life of the Johannine Christ; he lays it down and he takes it up again (10:18). However, the description of Jesus as "troubled in spirit" (v. 21) seems to portray a Christ more like ourselves. What does it mean? It could be in the same vein as 11:33; that is, Jesus is emotionally disturbed by the events before him, in this case betrayal by a friend. But "troubled in spirit, and *declared*" (v. 21, italics added) can also be a description of the prophetic state immediately preceding a prophecy. The preacher will have to make an exegetical decision here, setting this paragraph within the portrayal of Jesus throughout this Gospel.

The second significant figure in this text is the disciple whom Jesus loved (v. 23). The commentaries will aid in attempts to guess the name of this disciple traditionally identified as John the son of Zebedee. This unnamed disciple appears in six scenes in John 13–21 (13:21–30; 18:15–18; 19:25–27; 20:1–9; 21:7; 21:20–24); and except for the scene at the cross with Jesus' mother (19:25–27), he is in the company of Simon Peter. This person, obviously very close to Jesus, provides the Johannine church with continuity with Jesus and gives it apostolic authority. This disciple also precedes Simon Peter in knowledge, in faith, and in relation to Jesus. If there were Johannine and Petrine circles of Christianity, then this writer is certain who lies closest to the heart and truth of the tradition about Jesus.

The third important character in 13:21–32 is Judas Iscariot (vv. 26–30). Other than Jesus, Judas receives more attention in 13:1–30 than any other person. Why? Perhaps because the treason by a close associate put the heaviest burden upon those who interpreted the story for the church. Perhaps it was to assure Christians that even in betrayal and death Jesus was not a victim but the one who orchestrated the redemptive drama. Or perhaps it was a warning to that church or to any church of the real possibilities of loss of affection, of unbelief, of self-serving departures from Jesus. After all, the writer says that none of the disciples knew themselves or one another well enough to be sure. "The disciples looked at one another, uncertain of whom he was speaking" (v. 22). Rather than speculating on what social, political, economic, or psychological forces created a Judas, perhaps it would be better for the church to respond as Mark says the original disciples did: "They began to be distressed and to say to him one after another, 'Surely, not I?'" (Mark 14:19).

In verses 31–32, Jesus is again speaking, but not to say to the remaining eleven, "It is all over." On the contrary, Jesus sets the painful events lying before them in the larger context of God's purpose. In what is about to happen, God will be glorified, and the Son will be glorified. The disciples could not at that time understand what the reader understands: God is glorified in the death and resurrection of Jesus in that God's gracious purpose for the world is fulfilled; Jesus is glorified in that his being lifted on the cross means, in this Gospel, his being exalted again to the presence of God.

Holy Thursday

Exodus 12:1–4 (5–10) 11–14;
Psalm 116:1–2, 12–19;
1 Corinthians 11:23–26;
John 13:1–17, 31b–35

Given the formative role the Jewish observance of Passover played in early Christian thought, today's Old Testament reading appropriately recalls the origin of this important festival. Because Psalm 116 was traditionally used in connection with Passover observance, it forms a fitting response. Paul's account of the institution of the Lord's Supper serves as today's epistolary reading. He recalls this tradition as a way of reminding the Corinthians of the need to be responsive to each other's needs. This theme of humble service occupies a central role in the Gospel text, John's account of Jesus' washing his disciples' feet.

Exodus 12:1–4 (5–10) 11–14

The account of the institution of the Passover, the most appropriate Old Testament lesson for Holy Thursday, stands very close to the heart of the Old Testament story and ancient Israel's faith. Nothing was more central to that faith than the confession that Yahweh brought Israel out of Egypt. The Passover, believed to have been instituted on the very night that Israel was set free from Egypt, takes its meaning from the connection with the Exodus. Thus each time the Passover was celebrated, including in the time of Jesus, the people of God remembered that they were slaves set free by their God.

Although the section before us is relatively straightforward, it is part of a very complex section in the Book of Exodus. Because it is the climax of the Exodus traditions, it has attracted a great many diverse elements. The larger unit, which reports the events immediately surrounding the departure from Egypt, begins in Exodus 11:1 and does not end until Exodus 13:16. One can identify four distinct motifs within this section. The most important is, of course, the departure from Egypt itself. Although this is noted quite briefly (12:37–39), it is the focal point of all other motifs. Second is the report of the final plague, the killing of the firstborn children of the Egyptians. This plague is quite distinct from those that preceded it, both in the fact that it was effective and in the extensive preparations for it. The third and fourth motifs are the religious ceremonies connected with the Exodus, the celebration of Passover and the Feast of Unleavened Bread. Passover is linked to the final plague because it entailed a procedure for ensuring that the Israelite firstborn would not be killed, and it is connected in very direct ways with the immediate departure from Egypt. The final plague is what motivated the pharaoh to release Israel, and the Passover was to have taken place just before they left.

Within this section of the Book of Exodus there are duplicates, repetitions, and inconsistencies that reveal the presence of at least two sources, the Priestly Writer and the Yahwist. The style and technical terminology of Exodus 12:1–13 reveal that it comes from the Priestly Writer and thus would date from the postexilic period, approximately 500 BC. Exodus 12:14 begins a section that probably comes from the J source, perhaps as early as 900 BC.

It is important to keep in mind that this passage is part of a narrative, a story more of divine actions than human events. Its setting is the history of salvation, the account of Yahweh's intervention to set his people free. In that context, Exodus 12:1–14 is a report of divine instructions to Moses and Aaron concerning the celebration of the Passover. Thus everything except verse 1 is in the form of a speech of Yahweh, a direct address to Moses and Aaron. These instructions have the tone and contents of rules established for perpetuity and thus reflect the perspective of Israelites centuries after the events.

The instructions are precise and detailed with regard to both time and actions. The month in which the Exodus takes place is to become the first month of the year, and the preparations for the Passover begin on the tenth day of the month (vv. 2–3a). It is a family ceremony, with a lamb chosen for each household—that is, unless the household is too small for a lamb, in which case neighboring families are to join together to make up the right number to consume the lamb (vv. 3b–4). A lamb without blemish is to be selected and then killed on the fourteenth day of the month (vv. 5–6). Blood is to be smeared on the lintels and doorposts of the houses; the meat is to be roasted and eaten with unleavened bread and bitter herbs (vv. 7–9). The meal is to be eaten in haste, and anything not consumed by morning is to be burned (vv. 10–11).

After the instructions comes an explanation of the meaning of the meal and of the practices associated with it. The Lord will pass through the land of Egypt to destroy the firstborn, but will see the blood and "pass over" the Israelites (vv. 12–13). Verse 14, which comes from another writer, stresses that the day is a "day of remembrance," and forever, whereby later generations will remember the Exodus.

In both the present text and later practice, Passover was combined with the Feast of Unleavened Bread. The former was a one-night communal meal, and the latter was a seven-day festival. The combination was quite ancient, but the two originally were distinct. It seems likely that the Feast of Unleavened Bread was a pre-Israelite festival related to the agricultural year in Canaan. Passover, on the other hand, probably originated among seminomadic groups, such as the Israelites, as a festival related to the movement of their flocks from winter to summer pasture. The feast certainly was a family ceremony during the early history of Israel. In later generations, Passover was one of the three major annual pilgrimage festivals for which the people were to come to Jerusalem (Deut. 16:2–7).

The word "passover" (Hebrew *pesach*) is explained in this passage by connecting it with a verb for "to skip" or "hop over," but the actual etymology of the word is uncertain. Throughout the Old Testament it refers either to the festival described here or to the animal that is killed and eaten. Many passages use the word in both senses (e.g., 2 Chron. 35:1–19). The ceremony had both sacrificial and communal dimensions in that the animal was ceremonially slaughtered but then consumed as a family meal.

No ceremony was more important in ancient Israel or early Judaism than Passover. It was the festival in which the people acknowledged and celebrated who they were and who their God was. In remembering the day as the memorial day for the Exodus (Exod. 12:14), they acknowledged that God is the one who sets people free and makes them his own. They knew thereby that they were God's people. Moreover, in the gathering of family and friends for a communal meal in which the story of release from slavery was told, they bound themselves together and to that God who acted to make them who they were.

Psalm 116:1–2, 12–19

Psalm 116 was composed as a thanksgiving psalm to be offered by someone who had escaped the clutches of death, who had stood at the doors of Sheol, but who had recovered from sickness and could again worship and celebrate in thanksgiving at the temple.

In early Judaism, at the time of Jesus, this psalm, along with Psalms 113–115 and Psalms 117–118, was sung in the temple by the Levites at the time of the slaughter of the Passover lambs and again at dinner when the Passover meal was eaten in a family celebration.

Three features have made this psalm especially appropriate to Holy Week, in addition to the tradition of the psalm's association with the Passover season in Jewish ritual.

1. First, the reference to the cup in verse 13 has closely tied this psalm to services of the Eucharist on Holy Thursday. At the Passover celebration, the participants drank four cups of wine in the course of eating the evening meal, which was completed by midnight. (The Jewish Mishnah stipulates that a person too poor to buy this much wine for the ritual could get the money from the temple welfare fund.) This psalm was recited probably at the drinking of the third or fourth cup.

2. Verse 15 speaks of the death of one of God's saints or pious ones. This text should not be interpreted as saying that death can be a good thing in the sight of God (in spite of the tradition in the NRSV or the NEB, which reads: "A precious thing in the LORD's sight is the death of those who die faithful to him"). The sense of the Hebrew seems to be: "A weighty (or serious) matter in the sight of the Lord is the death of his pious ones." God too suffers in the death of the righteous, in the death of God's worshipers. For ancient Israel, this would have been seen as referring to the fact that there would have been one less worshiper of God around.

3. The psalm refers to the sacrifice that the worshiper brings (v. 17). In the earliest use of the psalm, the sacrifice would have been part of a meal eaten in the temple as a service of celebration for renewed health. When the psalm came to be associated with Passover, the sacrifice was re-understood as the sacrificial lamb killed and eaten as part of the national holiday. In Christian tradition, the sacrifice can be seen in relationship to Jesus, who offers himself as the sacrifice on behalf of others.

1 Corinthians 11:23–26

Today's epistolary lection is an abbreviated version of the tradition of Jesus' last supper that is narrated more fully in the Gospels. It is introduced with language ("receiving" and "handing on") typically used to describe the transmission of sacred traditions. The succinct, even formulaic, wording reinforces the impression that we have before us a liturgical tradition honed and refined through repeated recitations in early Christian worship. It was utterly familiar language.

But this move to the familiar occurs as a response to Christian abuses of worship. As the preceding verses show, some church members were behaving in ways that compromised the sacred character of the Eucharist. Paul's response has many elements, ranging from censure to command. But at the heart of his response is this recitation of a well-known, perhaps even well-worn, sacred text.

This move is in itself instructive within the context of Holy Week, for this is a time when the same texts are read every year. The time of the year sets the mood, and we read and hear these texts with certain expectations. We may even grow weary of listening to these familiar texts. We may even long for substitute texts, something different to stretch our minds in another direction.

But there is a time for recalling the familiar, even the utterly familiar. Especially is this the case when the familiar is what has formed us so decisively. This text calls us to remember—no, it requires us to remember: "Do this in remembrance of me" (v. 24). And in doing so, we must go through a sorting-out process, distinguishing between historical and historic events. Many events from the past flood through our minds, but they have not been arranged haphazardly. They have acquired a certain configuration in our minds because some events have become pivotal, enabling us to make sense of others.

In this text, Paul insists that Jesus' last supper—and its counterpart, the Eucharist—is one such event. It has ordering, norming power, at least when properly recalled and duly understood. But when it becomes a blurred image, abuses are liable to set in. When the clear profile of such a formative event loses its focus, something begins to happen to our identity. We begin to forget who we are, and we begin to behave as someone else. As our memory goes, so goes our identity. And as our identity goes, so goes our behavior.

Reliving the events of Holy Week helps to reestablish our identity. By recalling Jesus' last supper and the words he spoke there, we are brought to sober reflection about a body that was broken and blood that was shed. Yet as we reflect, we recall once more that it is not simply "a broken body" or "shed blood," but the "Lord's death" (v. 26) that we gather to honor. And somehow, regaining this single focus serves to sacralize our gathering and helps keep the Lord's Supper from becoming just another meal.

John 13:1–17, 31b–35

"Now before the festival of the Passover" (13:1), says this Evangelist, alerting the reader that the account that follows will be different from the Synoptic records of the last meal. In the Synoptics, Jesus eats the Passover meal with the Twelve (Matt. 26:17–19; Mark 14:12–16; Luke 22:7–13, and especially Luke 22:15) and, following the meal, institutes the Lord's Supper (Matt. 26:26–29; Mark 14:22–25; Luke 22:15–20). In John, the last meal is before Passover, and there is no account here of the institution of the Eucharist. For this Evangelist, Jesus does not *eat* the Passover; he *is* the Passover, bleeding and dying as the Passover lamb (19:31–37). In chapter 6, John presents the feeding of the five thousand as a Passover meal with a eucharistic interpretation. The commentaries will discuss whether John is to be taken as a correction of the Synoptics, as exhibiting evidence of a different source, or as the writer's willingness to sacrifice chronology for theology.

For this Evangelist, therefore, the last meal is the occasion, the setting, for particular words and acts of Jesus. The central act of Jesus in this text is the washing of the disciples' feet (vv. 2–5). The act is not understood (v. 7), even though it is followed by two interpretations

(vv. 6–11, 12–20). It is very important, however, for the reader to understand that Jesus knows exactly what he is doing and what it means. Notice: "Jesus, knowing that the Father had given all things into his hands" (v. 3); "for he knew who was to betray him" (v. 11); and, "I know whom I have chosen" (v. 18). This portrayal of Jesus is consistent with the way John presents him from the prologue through the entire Gospel. Whatever clashes with other portraits of Jesus this may create for the reader, it should be appreciated that John is giving confidence and engendering faith (v. 19) in Christians who might otherwise look upon the events of betrayal, arrest, and death as defeat. After all, John's readers were experiencing betrayal, arrest, and death (15:20–16:3), and to understand these events in Jesus' life as part of a divine plan of redemption would help them interpret their own experiences as having purpose. In other words, Jesus was not really a victim, and, even in death, neither are they victims.

The scene, then, is a powerful and moving one. Jesus is fully aware of his origin in glory; he is fully aware that he is soon to return to that glory; he is further aware that while on earth, all authority from God is his (vv. 1–3). The stage is set by verses 1–3 for Jesus to act in a dazzling way. Will he be transfigured before their eyes? Will he command the disciples to bow in adoration? No; instead, he rose from the table, replaced his robe with a towel, poured water in a basin, washed the disciples' feet, and dried them with the towel (vv. 4–5).

Following the foot washing, two interpretations of the act are offered. Whether the fact that there are two represents two traditions about the meaning of Jesus' act or whether both were from the beginning associated with the event is a matter debated in the commentaries. As we will see, the two interpretations are not unrelated. The first (vv. 6–11) insists that the church is in the posture of recipient, having its identity and character in the self-giving act of the servant Jesus. The church exists by the cleansing act of Jesus. (Some ecclesiastical traditions therefore associate the washing with baptism.) It is this understanding that Simon Peter resists (vv. 6–9). The church in the person of Simon Peter does not want its Lord and Savior to wash its feet.

The second interpretation (vv. 12–17, but it actually extends through v. 20) understands Jesus' act as a model of humility and service that the church is to emulate. The servant is not greater than the master; and the posture of washing feet, whether understood literally or figuratively, vividly holds that truth before the church's eyes. This has been the more widely embraced interpretation, both by the few churches that have accorded foot washing sacramental status and the many that have not. The lesson is not lost even among those who do not continue the practice of foot washing. Perhaps one reason this second interpretation is more widely embraced than the first is that giving service is easier for the ego than receiving it. However, the two interpretations are not necessarily independent of each other. In fact, the church in a state of spiritual health and with a clear sense of its own nature and calling would practice the second because it had embraced the first.

In verses 31b–35 the writer turns up the lights to their brightest, and the dark of Judas' betrayal is scattered by the declaration of God's purpose. (See comments at the end of the previous lesson.) Jesus' prediction of his passion is almost gentle: "Little children, I am with you only a little longer" (v. 33). But whether soft or harsh (as in Mark), the disciples must deal with the absence of Jesus, and they will be able to do so if their relationship with each other is informed and determined by his relationship to them. "As I have loved you" (v. 34) is the key. In fact, this is probably the sense in which the command to love is new. If referring to love as a command is a problem, it most likely is due to thinking of love as a feeling. However, if love is the way God acts toward the world and the way Jesus acts toward his disciples, then love means telling the truth, being faithful in one's witness, and caring for others, even to the point of death.

This commandment, joined to the instructions about foot washing (in this Gospel) and to the Eucharist (in the others and in 1 Corinthians 11), gives to Holy Thursday the ancient designation "Maundy," a form of the word *mandate*.

Good Friday

Isaiah 52:13–53:12;
Psalm 22;
Hebrews 10:16–25 or Hebrews 4:14–16; 5:7–9;
John 18:1–19:42

The first lesson is the most appropriate of Old Testament texts for this day. The mood and tone of the fourth Servant Song as well as its contents enable the church to fix its attention on the suffering of the Servant of God. Psalm 22 is an equally obvious text for the occasion, because Jesus called out its initial words from the cross. Moreover, it is an account of personal suffering and distress, and it is cited (v. 18) in the Gospel lection (John 19:24). The readings from Hebrews are interpretations of the obedient suffering of Jesus as high priest, and one who was fully human. The Gospel lesson goes far beyond Good Friday in that it reports the events from the arrest of Jesus to his burial.

Isaiah 52:13–53:12

In the context of Second Isaiah (Isaiah 40–55), within the Old Testament as a whole and even among the four Servant Songs (Isa. 42:1–4; 49:1–6; 50:4–9), this text is exceptional. Although there is no reason to doubt that it was composed by Second Isaiah just before the end of the Babylonian Exile, it is remarkable for both its style and contents. The poetic language is rich, even extravagant, complicating the problems of interpretation. When is the language to be taken literally and when metaphorically? How much is intentionally vague or hidden? Who is, was, or will be the servant?

When the Servant Songs are considered together and in their context, the most likely candidate for the servant is Israel. Among the roles of the servant, those of the prophet stand out. The servant is the one who—through word and life—proclaims the word of God to the nations. The corporate interpretation is most difficult to sustain with the song before us because its poetic account of the suffering of an individual is so personal. However, the corporate understanding is possible if one sees the language as metaphorical, taking the humiliation of the servant as the suffering of Israel through the Exile.

We may fruitfully explore the meaning of the poem in terms of the different voices that speak and the one of whom they speak. The first of these is the Lord, who speaks at the beginning (52:13–15) and the end (53:11b–12). The point of these addresses that bracket the account of the servant's suffering is to make the divine intention clear. From the very first it is affirmed that God will "exalt" and "lift up" his servant. Although this exaltation is in the future, it is to take place before "nations" and "kings" who will be startled that one whose appearance was "so marred . . . beyond human semblance" (52:14) is exalted by God. Those in highest authority will bow to him. The concluding divine speech strikes the same note and gives the reason for the triumph of the servant—his obedience to death through which he bore the sin of many. The divine purpose, then, is to reverse the expectations of the world.

The second voice is that of the members of the community who speak in the body of the poem (53:1–11a). They seem to address themselves ("Who has believed what we have heard?" 53:1) in patterns that are reminiscent of the complaint or lament psalms (such as Psalm 22), but the language is even more similar to the dirge, or funeral song (2 Sam. 1:17–27). The community mourns the suffering of the servant, giving an account of his life, his unfair trial, his suffering and death. They are in awe of his innocence (53:9), his quiet acceptance of his fate (53:7), and the fact that his suffering was on their behalf (53:4, 5, 10). Another aspect of the community's response is extremely important: In the presence of the suffering of this innocent one they are confronted by and confess their own sins (53:3, 4–6, 8). They recognize that, although they have now come to acknowledge him, during his suffering they did not stand with him.

Finally, there is the Suffering Servant himself. Throughout the entire poem he is not heard to speak a single word. This servant is described at every turn as a human being, exceptional in the breadth and depth of his unmerited suffering. That suffering was both emotional and physical, including deformity or disfigurement (52:14), rejection by the community (53:1–3), and corporal punishment (53:4–7). What is special about the suffering of the servant is that it is vicarious, on behalf of others ("He was wounded for our transgressions, crushed for our iniquities"), and efficacious ("and by his bruises we are healed," 53:5). No wonder the text has been cited so frequently in the New Testament as an explanation of the meaning of the passion and death of Jesus (Acts 8:34; Rom. 5:21; 1 Cor. 15:4).

Thus, on Good Friday this text helps us to encounter human suffering, especially of those who are innocent, and in particular the genuinely human suffering of Jesus. After all, before one can hear the good news of Easter, one must hear the suffering—and the good news—of the cross.

Psalm 22

Since the days of the early church, if not already in the life of Jesus himself, this passionate lament imbued with the pathos of human suffering has been interpreted as the prayer of the suffering Messiah. This secondary reading of the psalm, its christianization, has been encouraged by the assertion that Jesus intoned it upon the cross (Mark 15:34) and by the similarity of details spoken of in the psalm with incidents reported about the trial and crucifixion of Jesus.

Like the story of the Messiah, the psalm moves from misery and suffering to assurance and thanksgiving, from abandonment and isolation to fulfillment and acknowledgment. The psalm falls into two natural divisions: the first (vv. 1–18) focuses on suffering and humiliation; the second (vv. 21b–31 in the NRSV) centers on salvation and praise. Verses 19–21a, an appeal for help, function as a transition text. The first (vv. 1–18), the most appropriate for Good Friday, stops on the downward movement, on the dark side of the equation, on the bewildered and disoriented aspects of existence.

In the first eighteen verses, we encounter an opening address shot through with a complaint against God (vv. 1–2), a statement of confidence (vv. 3–5), a description of distress (vv. 6–8), a second statement of confidence (vv. 9–10), a plea for help (v. 11), and a second description of distress (vv. 12–18). One way of viewing the content of this portion of the psalm is to analyze the trouble in terms of its theological, anthropological, and sociological statements.

Many laments, like this one, allowed the worshiper not only to describe the distress of a bad situation but also to lodge a complaint against God and even to accuse the Deity. The psalm opens this way in verses 1–2, which lament the unaccountable absence of God, and raises the suspicion about whether the Divine is acting responsibly. The worshiper declares that, if prayer is the means, the fault lies with God. The forsakenness by God (v. 1) is contrasted with the persistence of the worshiper (v. 2). Suffering and endurance in the presence of the Deity are one thing; the two in the absence of God are another thing. The first statement of the distress may then be seen as a theological issue.

The anthropological description is found in verses 6–8. Here the depiction speaks of the worshiper as a worm, scorned and despised. Compared with the ancestors of the past who were aided in their endeavors and strengthened by the Divine (vv. 3–5), the worshiper is a nobody, a subhuman. Again the theme of being God-forsaken appears, even calling into question the divine reputation as well.

The sociological dimensions of the distress are developed in verses 12–18. Enemies are described as everywhere; life has no refuge; no safe place remains; even the one living is treated as the dead. Fear (v. 14) and weakness (v. 15) are described as the petitioner's condition—confronted with enemies spoken of as bulls, lions, dogs, and evildoers. One could compare the imagery of the text with that of the accounts of creation in Genesis 1–2. The person in the psalm is a worm, hardly the upright image of God—a potsherd, a piece of broken pottery—not a special creation of God sustained by divine spirit but at the mercy of the animals—not one who rules with dominion over creation. Life has become chaos; cosmos is called into question. Darkness awaits the dawn; the *tohu wavohu* (the formless and the void) await the dawn.

In spite of the dismal picture that the descriptions of distress paint, the psalm is shot through with statements and confessions of great confidence in the Deity. Verses 3–5 affirm that God is holy and that in the past the faith and trust of the fathers were rewarded with divine favor. Such confidence on the part of the worshiper was based on both the nature of God and the experience of the past; that is, the paradigm of the past functions as a source of hope for the future. The confidence in God, expressed in verses 9–10, stresses the prior intimacy that existed between the one praying and God. The psalmist seems to be implying that previously God had been his or her "father," his or her caretaker from the days of birth and youth.

The confidence in God displayed throughout the psalm moves in verses 22–31 to pride of place and suggests that the worshiper received from God some oracle or sign affirming that a reversal of fate was in store, that tears and pains would be replaced by songs and celebration. Perhaps the lection for Good Friday, however, should end with the pain and tribulation, not with victory and triumph.

In relating Psalm 22 to the passion of Jesus, one should not expound it as a prophetic prediction of his suffering and death in spite of the fact that the early Christians used this psalm as one of the primary Old Testament texts for understanding the passion and suffering of the Messiah. Its lines and view of the suffering righteous raised to triumph and praise helped Christians overcome the scandalous execution and suffering of Christ the deliverer.

Hebrews 10:16–25

This first epistolary text for Good Friday combines reassurance and admonition.

Reassurance. Two motifs from the Jeremiah 31 citation are prominent here: a new covenant where God's laws are inscribed on the hearts and minds of God's people, and assurance that the "sins and lawless deeds" of the people of God are no longer remembered.

We do well to reflect on the connection between these two ideas. We know, of course, that the more we inscribe God's will on our hearts the less likely we are to sin. Remembering what God intends for us through God's "laws," we orient our lives accordingly. Recalling what God desires, we respond in turn.

Yet our text is realistic. Even though we know God's laws by heart, we can still perform "lawless deeds." We may have the covenant memorized, yet our wills may be resistant to what the covenant requires. Sin we may, yet God is willing to forgive.

For all this, the arena where the new covenant is played out is in our hearts and minds. God's laws may be etched in stone, even written on a page, but they finally must be rendered operative within the human heart. Here is where divine will and human will encounter each other, struggling to become one, yet all too often at odds with each other. When we are at odds with God, we need forgiveness. And as much as we need it, and as often as we need it, God provides it.

When sin and disobedience are understood as actions within our inner selves, forgiveness is experienced accordingly. This is why the cult is rendered inoperative; it is inappropriate for this level of human experience. When forgiveness is understood this way, sacrificial offerings become obsolete.

Admonition. It is out of this profound sense of forgiveness that the exhortations of verses 19–25 emerge. Because Jesus has provided us direct access to God's inner sanctuary, we are urged to be faithful. Confident that our sins are forgiven, we can approach God "with a true heart in full assurance of faith" (v. 22). We are further encouraged to "hold fast . . . without wavering" (v. 23). We are also urged to be faithful members of the community of faith—to attend its meetings, to encourage each other, and "provoke one another to love and good deeds" (v. 24).

The lines of this text bolster us. Between the lines we see persons who are not fully assured in their faith, who are apt to give up their "confession of hope." And in doing so, they are also apt to turn away and turn inward. Not surprisingly, our text offers a strong, wholesome sense of community as a remedy. It knows that we often need to prod each other both to be good and to do good. It also knows the connection between a sense of forgiveness and the capacity for confident living, and the way both can be experienced within communities of faith where God is not only an article of faith but a living presence.

Hebrews 4:14–16; 5:7–9

On Good Friday, as on no other day of the year, our attention is riveted on Jesus "in the days of his flesh" (5:7). On this day we confront the inescapable fact that Jesus died. For some, it would have been a sure sign of his divinity had he been able to bypass death. After all, the Old Testament had known figures, such as Enoch and Elijah, who had bypassed this event. And when those we know who have loomed larger than life finally die, we realize once again that death is the event that establishes our common link with all humanity.

Both of today's texts honor Christ as our great high priest, neither self-appointed nor self-exalted, but so designated by God (5:10; cf. 2:17; 3:1; 5:5; 7:26; 8:1; 9:11; 10:21). His was not an ordinary Levitical priestly appointment, but unprecedented and unparalleled— "according to the order of Melchizedek" (5:10; cf. 6:20). It was through exaltation that he acquired this position, having "passed through the heavens" (4:14). To be sure, the great high priesthood of Jesus, as envisioned in Hebrews, is an exalted position far "above the heavens" (7:26; cf. Eph. 4:10).

Our text boldly states that the "faith we profess" (4:14, REB) is grounded in this triumphant exaltation of the risen Lord. But there seems to be the awareness that exaltation can be understood as distance, that the exalted Lord can easily become an inaccessible Lord. As we multiply our images of a triumphant Lord penetrating the very regions of heaven itself, we can find ourselves confessing faith in a heavenly Christ remote and far away.

As a way of counterbalancing this portrait of an elevated high priest, officiating in the heavenly temple, our text firmly anchors our thoughts on earth and calls us to think of Jesus "in the days of his flesh" (5:7). We are first reminded of Christ's capacity to sympathize with our human weakness (2:17; 5:2). As one who became fully human, it was his lot to experience temptation of every kind and at every level (4:15). This may recall the Synoptic tradition of his temptation by Satan (Matt. 4:1–11 and parallels) and perhaps the Gethsemane experience as well (Matt. 26:41; cf. also Luke 22:28).

Yet it is the firm Christian conviction that tempted though he was, he endured "without sin" (4:15; 7:26; John 7:18; 8:46; 2 Cor. 5:21; 1 Pet. 2:22). His was the capacity to confront temptation squarely yet remain steadfastly obedient to the divine will—and to do so as no one else had done or could do. As one who was genuinely in touch with human temptation, he becomes one who is genuinely sympathetic. Even though he sits enthroned, we are bold to approach him to "receive mercy and find grace to give us timely help" (4:16, REB). Our text insists that we should do so with confidence (cf. 3:6; 10:19, 22, 35). Our approach should be neither timid nor hesitant, but forthright and direct. We should know that whatever our struggle, it is not beyond his own experience.

Our second text is even more vivid in its depiction of the human agony of Christ. We are told that Jesus "offered up prayers and supplications, with loud cries and tears" (5:7). Most likely, this is a reminiscence of the Gethsemane tradition (Matt. 26:36–46 and parallels; cf. also John 12:27–28). Also possible is a reference to the cry of dereliction in the Synoptic tradition (Mark 15:33–39 and parallels). There could hardly be a more human image than that of Jesus crying aloud, shedding tears, praying to God for deliverance.

As the psalmist was promised, God hears the cries of the afflicted when they cry out to him (Ps. 22:24). It was finally through his suffering on the cross that his obedience was fully tested (5:8; Phil. 2:8). Through his obedience, he became perfected (7:28). As a result, he became the mediator of eternal salvation (9:12; Isa. 45:17).

It is impossible to read today's epistolary text in the context of Good Friday without squarely confronting the humanity of Christ. To be sure, exaltation is a central theme, but it is exaltation through obedience. It also speaks of salvation: God reaches out "to save him from death" (5:7), but only in the sense that God finally raised him from the dead. He was not saved from suffering, nor was he saved from death on the cross. The temptations that he resisted in life were of a piece with his final temptation—to escape suffering and death. But this, as with the others, he resisted, so that his death finally became more than a testimony to his full humanity. It also certified him as the true Son of God.

John 18:1–19:42

On those days when the lectionary offers a longer reading, choices within the passage may be made by the preacher. For Good Friday, the choice may be determined largely by the kind of services provided. If there is but one service of usual length, one may well choose to deal only with the crucifixion (19:17–30). However, if the three-hour afternoon services are scheduled, then the entirety of John 18:1–19:42 could be used.

A text of this size and significance can hardly be treated in one sermon, but it can be approached, even if not too closely. One way of approaching this body of materials is to see it as a narrative in five episodes: arrest (18:1–12); interrogation by religious leaders (18:13–27); interrogation by Pilate (18:28–19:16); crucifixion (19:17–30); and burial (19:31–42). Telling the story as John tells it has its own appropriateness and power. Another approach would be to draw from the narrative the accents, the emphases that the Evangelist makes. In other words, be especially sensitive to overhear what this Gospel writer understands as the meaning of Jesus' passion. Here we will try to combine the two approaches in a necessarily brief sketch.

The arrest of Jesus (18:1–12) is related with drama, with more details than in the Synoptics, but without the emotion of the other accounts. There is no crying or beating the breast here, for John's Jesus does not agonize, neither here nor on the cross. Gethsemane is "a garden" (v. 1). This Evangelist alone says that Roman soldiers (vv. 3, 12) were involved in the arrest. A "detachment of soldiers" (vv. 3, 12) was a "cohort," about six hundred men, and an "officer" was a "chiliarch" (v. 12), an officer over a thousand soldiers. By mentioning their presence, along with officers of Judaism (v. 3), John says that the whole unbelieving world, political and religious, joined in opposition to the Word of God. Through it all Jesus is in charge. Judas, Peter, the soldiers—all receive their directions from Jesus. Because his hour has come, he allows those who could not arrest him earlier (7:30, 44; 8:20, 59; 10:39; 12:36) to do so now. The interrogation by religious leaders (18:13–24) is minimally related by John, the only official action being the questioning before Annas (vv. 13, 19), who does not appear at all in the Synoptics. Caiaphas is mentioned four times, but with sarcasm ("the high priest *that year*," v. 13, italics added), and was disregarded as a factor in the story. Jesus' hour had come; what power did they have in the case? Significantly, more attention is given to Peter than to Jesus' trial. After all, the trial of Jesus has been settled since verse 12:18, but the trial of Peter, of the disciples, and of the church continues. The writer again shows himself more preacher than historian.

The interrogation by Pontius Pilate (18:28–19:16) is, compared with the Synoptics, quite lengthy. There are seven episodes, alternating between Pilate questioning Jesus inside the praetorium and dealing with the Jews outside. The account is full of irony: Jesus the prisoner is in charge; Pilate the governor shuttles back and forth indecisively like a frightened lieutenant; the Jews, in this Gospel the epitome of "the world," have death in their hearts but refuse to enter a Gentile building lest they be ceremonially defiled (v. 28). Pilate's only success is in getting the religious leaders to make what is their real confession of faith, "Caesar is king." At Passover, on the anniversary of freedom from the pharaoh, the pharaoh is embraced. Contemporary parallels flood the mind of every preacher.

The crucifixion (19:17–30) is briefly recorded. Even Mark is more extended here. Jesus is still in control, carrying his own cross (there is no Simon of Cyrene), acting and speaking so as to fulfill Scriptures and bring the intention of Judaism to completion (vv. 24, 28), making arrangements for his mother's care (vv. 26–27), and giving up his spirit (v. 30). He dies as Good Shepherd and as King. As Good Shepherd he cared for his own to the end and gave his life for the sheep (10:11–18); as King, he was unwittingly enthroned by those who mocked, who unwittingly called him King of the Jews. "And I, when I am lifted up from the earth, will draw all people to myself" (12:32). Even human wrath serves to praise God.

The burial (19:31–42) receives as much attention as the crucifixion itself even though the story of Jesus and his disciples is now the record of a corpse and its caretakers. This passage contains two stories about the body of Jesus, verses 31–37 and 38–42. The second provides closure to the preceding events, prepares for the resurrection story, and tells how two hesitant and uncertain believers, Joseph and Nicodemus, found courage in Jesus' death that they could not find during his lifetime. The first, verses 31–37, interweaves two interpretations of Jesus' death. Jesus died as the Passover Lamb, and his body was so treated (Exod. 12:2, 46; Num. 9:12). The Evangelist describes the Passover to end all Passovers, thereby proclaiming a new exodus, not from the slavery of Egypt but from bondage to sin and death (chap. 8). Related to the Passover theme is the sacramental interpretation. The church has understood the water and blood to which John calls special attention (vv. 34–35) as symbolic of baptism and the Eucharist. See also 1 John 5:6: "This is the one who came by water and blood." The writer is thereby telling the reader that the subject is not really the corpse of Jesus but the body of Christ.

Holy Saturday

Job 14:1–14 or Lamentations 3:1–9, 19–24;
Psalm 31:1–4, 15–16;
1 Peter 4:1–8;
Matthew 27:57–66 or John 19:38–42

"If mortals die, will they live again?" is the plaintive cry of today's Job text (14:14). Some form of this question Jesus' followers must have pondered in the aftermath of his crucifixion, and it serves to focus Christian reflection during the hiatus between his death and resurrection. The alternate Old Testament reading sounds a similar note, but there is also a note of confidence present. In Psalm 31 we hear reassurances that God will deliver the afflicted from enemies and persecutors. Suffering sounds the dominant note of the epistolary reading, which assures Christians that the life of discipleship, seriously pursued, will entail suffering. The transfer of Jesus' body to Joseph of Arimathea is treated in both the Matthean and Johannine Gospel texts for today.

Job 14:1–14

The Old Testament texts for Holy Saturday reflect the awareness that it is the lowest and saddest day of the Christian year. Certainly the themes of Job 14:1–14 focus the issues for the day that recalls the time between the death and resurrection of Jesus: "If mortals die, will they live again?" (14:14). But it is not just the contents of this text that are appropriate for Holy Saturday. The tone of profound sadness in the face of death and the mood of anger in light of the brevity of human life in Job 14:1–14 enable the church to focus its reflections on this day.

This reading occupies a key location in the Book of Job. The book consists of a prose prologue (1:1–13) and an epilogue (42:7–17) that frame a poetic dialogue or debate between Job and his friends, concluding with a confrontation between Job and God. The prologue establishes the circumstances that occasion the debate—Job's suffering and grief. The debate itself consists of series or cycles of speeches by the three friends, each speech followed by a response from Job. Our lesson is the concluding section of Job's speech at the end of the first cycle. The poetic dialogues had begun with Job cursing the day of his birth; at the end of the first cycle he considers the day of his death. At the outset he insisted that no life at all would have been better than his suffering. Here he asks about the possibility of life beyond death.

In chapter 14 Job is no longer responding directly to the words of his friends. The section that began in 13:20 often is recognized as a prayer, but the perspective is not maintained consistently. Rather, in this discourse Job alternates between what sounds like a soliloquy in which he is wondering out loud, using words addressed directly to God ("you," vv. 3, 5, 13, 15–17, 20). This ambivalence of address corresponds to Job's passionate requests that God hear and respond to him (13:20–22), and his sense of the distance if not the absence of God (13:24).

In verses 1–6, Job's reflections on the brevity and sadness of human life are provoked by the very question of the possibility of God's response to Job's plea for a fair hearing. Would God condescend to enter into court ("bring me into judgment with you," v. 3) with a mere mortal? But the burden of these verses falls upon human life as short and far from sweet. The point is expressed with powerful and memorable poetry filled with rich metaphors:

> "A mortal, born of woman, few of days and full of trouble,
> comes up like a flower and withers,
>   flees like a shadow and does not last." (v. 1)

Human days are numbered, known only to God. And God is the one who set the limits between birth and death, limits that human beings cannot exceed (v. 5). So Job's prayer changes from a plea that he have a fair hearing before God to a general request that God simply leave human beings alone "that they may enjoy, like laborers, their days" (v. 6). In other words, if God will not deal openly and fairly with these creatures, God should at least not make their lives worse than they are.

Verses 7–14 turn to consider explicitly the question of the possibility of life beyond death. The discourse begins (vv. 7–9) with the extended example of the tree, for which there is "hope." Even though it is cut down, it will live again through its sprouts; even if its root grows old and the stump dies, "at the scent of water it will bud" (v. 9). But then (vv. 10–12), the life and death of human beings is contrasted with that of the tree. The finality of death for mortals is expressed in three distinct verbs: they "die," "are laid low," "expire" (v. 10). Picking up the allusion to water in the revival of the tree, the end for human beings is compared to the disappearance of water when a lake dries up or a river runs dry. Nothing is left. The poet has Job expressly deny the possibility of any kind of revival from the dead, again with three distinct expressions. When mortals "lie down," they "do not rise again," "will not awake," or "be roused out of their sleep" (v. 12). And that—with the exception of two or three texts (Dan. 12:2; Isa. 26:19)—is the consistent view of the Old Testament on the matter.

But Job does not stop there. With both a plea to God and a question, he boldly considers the alternative. He turns first with a petition to God that God "hide" him in the underworld where the shades of the living go (Sheol) and then set a time to remember him (v. 13). Thus Job returns to a theme that he pursues tenaciously in his discourses, the request for a hearing before God. What would be the point of revival after death? For Job it could mean a further opportunity for a fair hearing before God. Thus death for Job signals and underlines the absence of God. Death could be endured, if eventually God would remember him. So Job wants divine justice, but he also does not want to be abandoned.

That is the context for the question that is so dramatic in the ancient Israelite context: "If mortals die, will they live again?" (v. 14). The Old Testament answer is just as clearly negative as the answer of Easter Day is positive. But Christians would do well to live for a while with Job's question and ancient Israel's answer. Indeed, even the Christian faith in resurrection affirms the reality of death, including the death of Jesus. Facing death, we know the actuality—the vitality—of life. Moreover, the particular shape of Job's suffering—being abandoned by God and not taken seriously by friends—should enable us to understand and identify with all who grieve, including grief for themselves: "they are brought low, and it goes unnoticed" (v. 21). It is not just death that saddens Job, but dying alone and abandoned.

Lamentations 3:1–9, 19–24

Framed in the Book of Lamentations by four complaints of the community, chapter 3 is the complaint of an individual, the unnamed "one" (NRSV, "man" REB) of verse 1. The identity of the community in the other poems in the book is clear: it is the people of Israel. But for whom does the complainant of chapter 3 stand? In the liturgical context of the Christian church on Holy Saturday, the words of the sufferer will be heard as the voice of Jesus, very much in the sense of the words of Psalm 22 (another individual complaint) uttered from the cross: "My God, my God, why have you forsaken me?" But because Jesus in his suffering and death stands with all who suffer and die, these words may express their feelings as well.

The background and the theme of the Book of Lamentations is the destruction of the city of Jerusalem by the Babylonians in 587 BC. During and after the Exile, these poems functioned in liturgical settings—quite possibly on fast days—to help the survivors and their descendants come to terms with that national disaster and the crisis of faith it produced. The laments are similar in mood, tone, and function to dirges, or funeral songs. By recounting and bewailing the destruction, and even acknowledging that God had become the enemy, the people expressed and hoped to come to terms with their sense of loss, their grief, and their anger. Moreover, by understanding the destruction as punishment for sin, those people confessed their corporate sins.

Like the four other poems in the book, chapter 3 is an alphabetic acrostic; that is, successive lines begin with successive letters of the Hebrew alphabet. But chapter 3 stands out from the others as the voice of an individual. It would not have been surprising if this individual were a woman, because the other complaints often personify the destroyed city of Jerusalem as a woman. But the individual clearly is male, and that fact has led to many attempts to identify the speaker. Because the prophet Jeremiah often uttered similar complaints, he has been proposed as this individual. Others have argued that he is the servant in Isaiah 40–55, at times an individual but also identified as Israel. But within the literary and liturgical context of the book, chapter 3 most likely views the national disaster and disgrace from the perspective of an individual who experienced it.

Our reading encompasses two parts of the fuller lament. In the first section (vv. 1–9, 19–20), the unidentified individual utters his complaints against God. The leading image is darkness (vv. 2, 6), contrasted with living in the light of God's presence. The tone of the complaint is similar to that of the Book of Job, seen in the other Old Testament reading for Holy Saturday. But whereas Job objected to unfair or unmerited suffering, in this prayer the sufferer is struggling for a way to live with suffering that is justified, that is punishment for sins. God has turned God's hand against this person, and even refuses to answer his prayers (v. 8); God has put him in chains and boxed him in (vv. 7, 9). The particulars of the suffering are not detailed and could fit any number of circumstances, including physical illness. But the petitioner makes it abundantly clear just how much he has suffered. This account of suffering continues through verse 20.

The second part of our reading (vv. 21–24) begins a longer unit in which the mood, tone, and contents are dramatically different. Now the petitioner expresses his hope (vv. 21, 24) and confesses his confidence in the Lord. He knows that the "steadfast love" and the "mercies" of the Lord never cease (v. 22), that God is faithful; therefore, the one in trouble can turn to him.

This poem, including the shift of mood and contents, is parallel in many ways to the individual complaint songs of the Book of Psalms. The central element of these songs is a petition, a request that God help the one in trouble. They also contain complaints about the suffering and about God's failure to help or God's absence, as well as confessions of sin or of innocence. There will be expressions of confidence in God's capacity and willingness to help. Parallel to verses 21–24 are the affirmations that God has heard and will act (e.g., Ps. 6:8–10). It is very likely that in the liturgical use of such songs another voice, that of a priest, would have been heard just before these affirmations. The priest would have pronounced a salvation oracle, a message from God to the petitioner; for example, "Fear not, the Lord has heard your prayer."

Songs such as this one, and the liturgical patterns they reflect, may provide guidance for our meditations, our words, and our actions. This poem moves toward the affirmation of faith in the gracious and merciful God who hears prayers, but it begins with vigorous complaints against God. Ancient Israel clearly believed that all feelings could be brought before God. Can prayers—even those that confess the experience of divine punishment or the absence of God—be answered unless they are expressed?

Psalm 31:1–4, 15–16

Few psalms use such graphic descriptions to depict human misery and affliction as does Psalm 31. The descriptions are very graphic although reasonably nonspecific. Thus, when persons used this psalm in worship to describe their state of being, they could vent true feelings yet do so in highly stylized terms.

Praying this psalm allowed persons to verbalize and express the deep-seated sense of alienation and hurt that they were feeling. The language appears to be highly metaphorical, probably using stereotypical and formulaic expressions that were highly graphic in content and emotional in nature. The labeling of one's troubles in such graphic fashion was probably therapeutic in and of itself because it allowed one to express sorrow and grief.

The overall structure of the psalm is as follows: (1) a general opening address to God, which already contains an initial plea for help (vv. 1–2); (2) a statement of confidence and trust in God (vv. 3–6); (3) a future-oriented statement of confidence (vv. 7–8); (4) a description of the trouble and distress (vv. 9–13); (5) a third statement of confidence (vv. 14–15a); (6) a second plea for help (vv. 15b–18); (7) a fourth assertion of confidence (vv. 19–20); (8) proclamation (v. 21); (9) thanksgiving (v. 22); and (10) admonition (vv. 23–24).

The relevance of this psalm for Holy Saturday lies in its use of the imagery of death to describe a human situation. The psalmist declares that he or she is like one already dead—passed out of life and even out of memory; cast aside like the shattered pieces of a broken pot; unwanted, useless, fit only for the garbage heap of the city dump (v. 12).

In fact, the psalmist describes the many out there who not only dislike him or her but who even scheme and plot to take his or her life (v. 13). Such language as this may sound like the ravings of a paranoid but should be seen as therapeutic language that allowed distressed persons to objectify their suffering to its most graphic, even exaggerated, level.

This psalm is not simply a recitation of a vale of sorrows. Throughout the text there are frequent statements of a calm confidence in the Deity. Such is to be found in verses 14–15, in which the worshiper confesses trust in God and affirms that come what may the times of one's life are in the hand of God, who can deliver one from the hand of enemies and persecutors.

Confidence in the Deity fades naturally into plea and petition for salvation (vv. 15b–16). In spite of the description of the supplicant's condition in such sorrow-drawn and affliction-etched contours, confidence and calm flow through the psalm like a soothing stream. The crucified, dead, and buried awaits the resurrection, life in the morning.

1 Peter 4:1–8

The bulk of today's epistolary text deals with how believers should behave. It concludes with a sober reminder that history will end, perhaps soon. It thus calls for a life of serious, disciplined prayer carried out with loving concern for fellow believers.

Envisioned here is life that has undergone dramatic change. Unrelieved self-indulgence has given way to focus and direction, but conversion has come with a price. Those who once served as companions of pleasure and dissipation have become taunting critics. The new convert is now the object of ridicule, enduring grief because of a decision to "go straight." The old life had its own form of suffering, usually in the form of hangovers and mornings after. But as it turns out, the new life has its own form of suffering too.

Even though the suffering and death of Christ had its own unique form, there is a close correlation between the experience of the believer and that of Christ. In each case, the moral dilemma is identified as the conflict between living "by human desires" and living "by the will of God" (v. 2). In keeping with the Synoptic tradition, the death of Christ is seen as an instance of obedience to the divine will and a victory over self-will.

With this intention to be radically committed to the will of God, we are asked "to live for the rest of [our] earthly life" (v. 2). Being able to overcome our human desires is envisioned as a way of living that is both continuous and habitual. This is not as novel as it looks, for the life of self-indulgence described in verses 3–4 is seen to be just as habitual. What is called for here is a shift from one set of habits to another, yet the overall form of life has a radically different profile.

There is no illusion, however, that such a change is simple and straightforward. Besides the grief caused by our erstwhile drinking companions, there is the hard reality of making the new life work. The example of Christ will provide powerful incentive, to be sure. But as powerful as anything else will be the enduring love of fellow believers. Thus we are charged to "maintain constant love for one another" (v. 8). We all know the breadth and depth of love required to effect a meaningful change of life-style. Such dramatic change is never simply a matter of making good on a vow. It is rather vowing again and again, among people of like mind and purpose, to stay on course.

It is above all within the community of faith where our failed attempts become clearly visible. Here also is where we experience the paradox of faith: we think that sins, once numerous, will diminish, but instead they continue, even multiply. What is different is that they are now drowned in a sea of love, for we are now among companions who know sin, but who also know love.

Matthew 27:57–66 or John 19:38–42

For those churches providing Holy Saturday services, alternate readings are available. Both are accounts of the burial of Jesus.

Three observations may be in order here. First, these are alternate readings and are not to be conflated or harmonized. Matthew and John do have a number of common elements

(Joseph of Arimathea, request for the body from Pilate, Friday evening, new tomb, etc.), but one needs to respect the different purposes and audiences of the Evangelists. Second, the burial of Jesus is not an insignificant item in Christian theology. Perhaps proof of the resurrection of the body is involved here. Or the writers may be addressing those Christians found in some early churches who had no place for the physical in their views of Jesus Christ. Persons who denied that Jesus Christ had come in the flesh were certainly known in the Johannine community (1 John 4:2–3). But whatever the reasons, the burial of Jesus came to be stated explicitly in Christian confessions as early as 1 Corinthians 15:4 and as officially as the Apostles' Creed. And finally, restraint on the part of both preacher and liturgist is essential for the worship to be truly a Holy Saturday service. It is, of course, tempting and easy to steal from tomorrow, to break the seal on the tomb, and to have a pre-Easter Easter service. Admittedly, it is difficult for the church to say, even for two days, "Jesus is dead."

Matthew devotes two paragraphs to the burial of Jesus (vv. 57–61, 62–66). There needs to be a conclusion to the crucifixion story. After all, closure demands answers to basic questions: What happened to the body? Who prepared it? Where was it entombed? But Matthew has more in mind; he is concerned to argue for, to provide proofs for, the resurrection of Jesus. Therefore, he tells the reader that the body was released to Joseph by Pilate's order; Joseph placed the body in a new tomb hewn out of the rock; a huge stone was placed over the opening to the tomb; two women witnessed all this; religious authorities secured the support of Pilate to prevent a theft of the body and a claim of resurrection; the tomb was governmentally sealed (a stronger safeguard than a police cordon today); Roman guards kept sentinel watch. Matthew is not simply witnessing to the resurrection, as was the case with early Christian preaching (Acts 2:32; 3:15; 4:33), but he is already involved in what later became quite common, attempts to *prove* that Jesus was raised from the dead. Such an approach to the resurrection, and to other doctrines, assumes that faith is the response of the mind to the evidence presented. Such faith is not without merit, but it is *belief that*, not *trust in*.

John also devotes two paragraphs to the corpse of Jesus (vv. 31–37, 38–42), but only the second is our concern here. The former is an extraordinary theological treatise relating the body of Jesus to fulfilled prophecy, the Jewish Passover, the Eucharist, and baptism. In verses 38–42 it seems important to this Evangelist to point out that two disciples who had been private, secretive, and fearful in their relation to Jesus now act openly, with courage and at great expense. Some readers of this account are quite critical of Joseph and Nicodemus, observing that the two come out of hiding now that the battle is over. Jesus needed disciples, they say, not caretakers. Other readers are more positive, finding in this burial scene the consistency of John's theology. Even in his death, they say, Jesus continues to draw the hesitant and unbelieving. Jesus had said as much: in death I will draw all people to myself (12:32).

Easter Vigil

Genesis 1:1–2:4*a*
  Psalm 136:1–9, 23–26
Genesis 7:1–5, 11–18; 8:6–18; 9:8–13
  Psalm 46
Genesis 22:1–18
  Psalm 16
Exodus 14:10–31; 15:20–21
  Exodus 15:1*b*–13, 17–18
Isaiah 55:1–11
  Isaiah 12:2–6
Baruch 3:9–15, 32–4:4 or
Proverbs 8:1–8, 19–21; 9:4*b*–6
  Psalm 19
Ezekiel 36:24–28
  Psalm 42 and 43
Ezekiel 37:1–14
  Psalm 143
Zephaniah 3:14–20
  Psalm 98
Romans 6:3–11
  Psalm 114
Luke 24:1–12

With a selection of readings drawn from throughout the Old Testament, the Easter Vigil service takes the worshiper through memorable events and texts that have formatively shaped Christian understanding of the Christ-story. An air or expectation is created as the story moves inexorably forward, and Christ is seen as the embodiment of Israel's fondest hopes. In the epistolary text, Paul links Christ's death and resurrection with the baptismal experience of Christians and draws some of the ethical implications of dying and rising with Christ. Today's Gospel text is supplied by the Lucan account of Easter morning.

Genesis 1:1–2:4a

Ordinarily, the Old Testament lessons for the Easter Vigil are simply read, not preached, taking the worshiping community through a summary of ancient Israel's history. Read in this order and on this occasion, these texts present a history of salvation in preparation for the death and resurrection of Jesus. The story begins with the first chapter of the Bible.

This reading contains the Priestly Writer's account of creation. The mood of the story is solemn and measured; the repetition of phrases lends a liturgical dignity to the recital. If the account was not actually put into this form for worship, it certainly was shaped by persons with a deep interest in liturgy.

In terms of structure, the report consists of two uneven parts, Genesis 1:1–31 and Genesis 2:1–3; that is, the six days of creation and the seventh day of rest. One of the purposes of the story in its present form is to account for the sabbath rest. It was divinely ordained from the very first and thus is taken by our writer as the most universal of laws.

Creation is not *ex nihilo,* out of nothing, but out of chaos. Before creation there were the primeval waters, within which God established the world, and—as the NRSV translation indicates—those waters were troubled by a mighty wind ("wind from God," or "mighty wind"). Moreover, as the Priestly account of the Flood indicates (Gen. 7:11), the waters of chaos stand as the alternative to creation. If God withdraws his hand, the waters can return. In that sense, then, this chapter actually understands God as both creator and sustainer of the world.

In sharp contrast to the other account of creation, which begins in Genesis 2:4b, God is transcendent and distant. The only actor or speaker in this chapter is God, by whose word or act all things that are come into being. Human beings certainly occupy an important place. They are created last of all and are given stewardship over the creation. If this moving and majestic account can be said to have a major point, it is in the divine pronouncement that recurs throughout: "And God saw that it was good." The natural order is good not only because God created it, but also because God determined that it was so.

Psalm 136:1–9, 23–26

Psalm 136 is a communal psalm of thanksgiving recalling the great activities of God in the past. In its structure it parallels much of the first six books of the Bible—the Hexateuch, Genesis to Joshua. The following is the structure of the psalm: (1) the community is called to offer thanksgiving (vv. 1–3); (2) God is praised as creator (vv. 4–9); (3) as the one who brought Israel out of Egypt (vv. 10–15); (4) as the one who led them in the wilderness (v. 16); (5) as the one who granted the people the land of promise (vv. 17–22); and (6) as the one who continues the divine action of providing for the people (vv. 23–26). The constantly repeated refrain "for his steadfast love [or mercy] endures forever" indicates that this psalm was sung or chanted antiphonally.

The verses selected for the Easter Vigil are those concerned with God's acts in creation (vv. 4–9), the personal affirmation of divine care (vv. 23–25), and the call upon all to give thanks (vv. 1–3, 26). The account of creation given in the psalm is far more poetic than the creation account in Genesis 1:1–2:4a.

Genesis 7:1–5, 11–18; 8:6–18; 9:8–13

Like Genesis 1:1–2:4a, the account of the Flood is part of the primeval history. That is, this is the story of the ancestors of the entire human race and not just of Israel. Between that initial chapter and Genesis 7 a great deal transpired. There was the second account of creation coupled with the story of the Fall, ending with the expulsion of the original pair from the garden. Next came the story of Cain and Abel, when a brother kills a brother. Then follow genealogies, along with short reports of events in the lives of the earliest generations. The immediate background of the flood story is the short account in Genesis 6:1–4 of how the "sons of God" took the "daughters of humans" and gave birth to a race of giants. From the accounts of creation to the time of Noah, the story is basically one of human sin and disorder, culminating in God's decision to put an end to the race, with the exception of Noah and his family.

The Flood marks an important turning point in biblical history; but as the Book of Genesis is organized, it is not the most decisive division of time. Following the Flood, the history of human sinfulness continues, with the story of the Tower of Babel. The critical event is reported in Genesis 12:1ff., the call of Abraham. To be sure, sin continues, but now, with the promise to Abraham, the direction of history is known. It becomes a history of salvation.

The verses chosen for this reading comprise a rather full account of the Flood, with the exception of the report of God's decision to set the disaster into motion and God's instructions to Noah. The assigned text comes mainly from the hand of the Priestly Writer, but some of it is from the Yahwist, whose name for God in most translations is LORD. It is also the Yahwist who reports that seven pairs of clean and one pair of unclean animals went into the ark; the Priestly Writer reports one pair of every kind. Moreover, according to the Priestly Writer, the water comes when the floodgates of heaven are opened; the Yahwist speaks of rain. But according to both writers, God put an end to all human beings except that one family, and afterward vowed not to do it again. The reading appropriately ends with the good news that the natural order will abide and the rainbow will be a sign of God's promise.

Psalm 46

This psalm praises God for the divine care of the people and especially for Jerusalem, the City of God. With its emphasis on security in the midst of great turmoil and disruptions in the earth, it provides a proper response to the narrative of the Flood. The worshipers confess, as Noah and his family may have, that they have nothing to fear should the mountains quake and the whole of the cosmos become chaos again.

Genesis 22:1–18

If one does not keep in mind the framework in which this reading appears—both in the Book of Genesis and in the Old Testament—important aspects of it will be missed. The context is the narrative of the patriarchs—Abraham, Isaac, Jacob, and the sons of Jacob—the leading theme of which is the promise that their descendants will become a great nation, will own their land, and will be a blessing to all the peoples of the earth (Gen. 12:1–3).

The fulfillment of those promises comes beyond the Book of Genesis, first with the Exodus and then with the occupation of the land of Canaan as reported in the Book of Joshua.

The immediate prelude to this story is the report in Genesis 21:1–7 of the birth of Isaac. The promise of descendants had been repeated to Abraham and Sarah over and over. Just when it appeared that all hope was lost, they are given a son in their old age. Isaac is not merely symbolic testimony that the divine promise is trustworthy; he is also quite literally the first step in the fulfillment of that promise.

And then comes the account in Genesis 22:1–18 of God testing Abraham by means of a command that threatened to take away the child of the promise. It is certainly one of the most poignant and moving stories in the Bible, and all the more so because of its restraint. Emotions are not described or analyzed, but the reader or hearer will sense with horror the patriarch's dread and grief. Even though we know how the story comes out, each time we read it we can experience the rising tension, feeling that the results may still be in doubt. Will Abraham go through with the sacrifice of Isaac? Will the angel speak up before it is too late?

The story is so meaningful and fruitful and has been told in so many ways over the centuries that it would be a serious mistake to reduce it to a single point. At one level, in the old oral tradition, it probably dealt with the question of child sacrifice. Living among cultures where child sacrifice was a genuine possibility, some early Israelites could well have asked, "Does our God require that we sacrifice our children?" The answer, through this account, is a resounding no. Our ancestor was willing, but God did not require it. The sacrifice of a ram was sufficient. In the framework of the Easter Vigil, one is reminded that God gave his Son.

The leading theme of the story, as recognized through centuries of interpretation, is faith. It is, as the initial verse says, the test of Abraham's faith. What is faith? The biblical tradition answers not with a theological statement, nor with a set of propositions, nor with admonitions to be faithful, but with a story. It is the story of Abraham, who trusted in God even when God appeared to be acting against God's promise. Faith is like that. Faith in this sense is commitment, the directing of one's trust toward God. And it entails great risk, not in the sense of accepting a set of beliefs, but by acting in trust. Did Abraham know that the God he worshiped would not require the life of Isaac? We cannot know, for the story leaves this question unanswered. We are told only how the patriarch acted, and how God acted.

Psalm 16

This psalm, probably originally used as a lament by an individual during a time of sickness, contains a strong statement of devotion of God and thus can be read as a theological counterpart to the narrative of Abraham, whose faithfulness led him to the point of sacrificing his son, Isaac. Like Abraham, the psalmist shows confidence in whatever fate or lot God might assign. This psalm came to be understood in the early church as a prediction of the resurrection, especially Christ's resurrection, and was quoted in this regard by Peter in his sermon at Pentecost (see Acts 2:22–28).

Exodus 14:10–31; 15:20–21

With this reading we come close to the heart of the Old Testament story and the Old Testament faith. In ancient Israel's faith, no affirmation is more central than the confession that the Lord is the one who brought them out of Egypt. Traditions concerning the Exodus provide the fundamental language by which Israel understood both herself and her God. The basic focus of most of those traditions is upon the saving activity of the Lord; the history is a story of salvation.

The account in Exodus 14 actually follows the Exodus itself. The departure from Egypt had been reported in chapters 12 and 13; the rescue of the people at the sea happens when they are already in the wilderness. The two themes that mark the stories of the wandering in the wilderness are already present in this chapter; namely, Israel's complaints against Moses and the Lord (14:10–12), and the Lord's miraculous care (14:13–18, 30–31). The report does mark, however, Israel's final escape from the Egyptian danger, and this relates directly to the theme of the Exodus itself.

This reading, like the flood story, is the combination of at least two of the sources of the Pentateuch, those of the Priestly Writer and of the Yahwist. In the full story of the rescue at the sea, two virtually complete accounts have been combined. The writers tell the story differently, with P reporting a dramatic crossing of the sea between walls of water (v. 22), and J speaking of a "strong east wind" (v. 21) and the chariots clogged in the mud as the water returns (v. 25). But a more important implication of the source division for our use of the text in the context of worship is the recognition that the sources place very different theological interpretations upon what happened. For the Priestly Writer, the emphasis is on revelation. The Lord "hardened the heart of Pharaoh" (vv. 8, 17) to pursue the Israelites in order to "get gain glory for myself over Pharaoh and all his army" (v. 17). That is, the Lord's purpose is for the Egyptians to "know that I am the LORD" (v. 18). For the Yahwist, the purpose is the salvation of the people (v. 13) and their consequent faith, not only in the Lord, but also in Moses (vv. 30–31). In the combined report, both themes are important. God acts in order to reveal who he is and also to save his people.

The reading appropriately concludes with 15:20–21, the account of the Song of Miriam, identified as a prophet and the sister of Aaron. The two-line couplet in verse 21 is the typical beginning of a hymn or song of praise, calling upon the people to sing and giving the reasons why the Lord is praiseworthy. These lines, generally taken to be among the most ancient material in the Hebrew Scriptures, parallel the opening of the Song of Moses in 15:1–17. The difference is that Miriam's song is a call to sing ("Sing"), and Moses' is a first person expression of the song ("I will sing"). Thus there are few occasions in the lectionary when the responsorial psalm follows more directly and naturally from the Old Testament reading than here.

Exodus 15:1b–13, 17–18

The psalm text overlaps with the Old Testament reading and continues it. Moses, having led the Israelites in their escape from the Egyptians at the sea, now leads them in worship. The expression of praise is generally identified as the Song of Moses, and much of it is in the first person singular, "I will sing to the Lord." But the introduction points out that it was sung by Moses and the people, and its communal, congregational character is evident throughout. Although the song is not in the Psalter, it is a psalm nonetheless and probably was used in worship by faithful Israelites through the centuries. The initial lines are placed in the mouth of Miriam in Exodus 15:21, except that they are in the second person instead of the first; she calls for the people to sing to the Lord.

The song is a hymn of praise, specifically praise of the Lord for saving the people at the sea. The hymn is, for the most part, narrative in form; that is, it praises God by recounting the story of God's mighty deeds. In one sense, what emerges is another interpretation of the rescue at the sea, different in some respects from the accounts in Exodus 14. But the language is at points highly metaphorical and rich in imagery that goes beyond the immediate events.

Recollection of the Lord's saving activity at the sea evokes two leading themes in the hymn. The first concerns God's awesome power over events and nature. The specific form of that theme here emphasizes the image of the Lord as a warrior who triumphs over his enemies. But it also asserts that the God praised here is incomparable; there is none like this one (vv. 11, 18). The second theme of the hymn concerns God's love and care for the people whom he has redeemed. God is strength, song, salvation (v. 2), the one who cares for these people out of steadfast love (v. 13). Moreover, God's past care for the people gives rise to the hope that he will continue to act in their behalf in the future (v. 17) and will reign forever (v. 18).

Isaiah 55:1–11

This text is the Old Testament lesson assigned for the Third Sunday in Lent for Year C and was discussed at that point in this volume.

Isaiah 12:2–6

This text has been discussed with the readings for the Third Sunday of Advent.

Baruch 3:9–15, 32–4:4

This passage, often characterized as a hymn to wisdom, is not actually a song of praise such as those in the Book of Psalms. Although it does characterize and praise wisdom, it is basically an admonition to the people of Israel that they listen to and learn from wisdom.

The Book of Baruch is attributed to Jeremiah's scribe and placed in the Babylonian Exile, but it actually stems from a later time. The section from which this reading comes is like other late wisdom literature such as the Wisdom of Solomon and Ecclesiasticus. It identifies wisdom with the law of Moses, "the commandments of life" (3:9), and "the way of God" (3:13; see also 4:1). Behind that answer stands a question that became prominent in the so-called intertestamental period: Is there a conflict between the truth that can be discerned by human reflection or wisdom and that which is revealed in the law?

Our text alludes to the Babylonian Exile (3:10–13), but it is characterized as a spiritual situation of separation from God rather than the actual Babylonian captivity. The verses not included in the reading (3:16–31) also contain somewhat spiritualized allusions to the history of Israel. The lection finds its place in the Easter Vigil, first because of the references to death and its alternative. Israel, growing old in a foreign land, is as good as dead (3:10–11) because the people have forsaken "the fountain of wisdom" (3:12). If they will attend to wisdom, they will gain strength, understanding, life, and peace (3:14). All who hold fast to wisdom will live, and those who forsake her will die (4:1). The second reason for the use of this passage in the Easter Vigil is its theme of wisdom as the gift of God that reveals the divine will to human beings. This is quite explicit in 3:37, which is echoed in John 1:14 and has been taken as a reference to the coming of Jesus.

Proverbs 8:1–8, 19–21; 9:4b–6

The reading from Proverbs 8 is part of a unit that is among a series of twelve extended addresses, or speeches, in Proverbs 1–9. All of them are instructions concerning wisdom or speeches by Wisdom herself. Each one is comprised of reflections upon the nature of wisdom as well as admonitions and exhortations to follow wisdom. Each is a carefully crafted composition that probably arose among Israel's sages for the purpose of teaching their students.

Chapter 8 is the eleventh address. Following an introduction of the speaker in verses 1–3, the remainder is an address by Wisdom herself. Beginning with rhetorical questions (v. 1), the writer sets the stage for the speech by Wisdom, personified as a female figure. As in the NJPSV, one can appropriately capitalize her names: Wisdom and Understanding. Her speech will be in all kinds of public places: "On the heights," "beside the way," "at the crossroads," "the gates," "the entrance of the portals." These lines indicate that wisdom is easy to find and eager to be heard by all.

In verses 4–8 Wisdom speaks in the first person, urging all to pay attention, but she particularly urges the "simple ones" to listen to her. Then she gives the reasons why people should attend to her words: She speaks only "noble things," "what is right," "truth," and straight words that are "righteous."

Verses 19–21 continue to present reasons for following the words of Wisdom. First, the fruit of wisdom is better than gold and silver (8:19). Second, Wisdom walks in and therefore leads her followers in the paths of justice and righteousness (8:20). Here we see that the sages were concerned with the same values as were the prophets. Third, it is prudent to follow Wisdom because the one who does so prospers (8:21).

Wisdom, understood as present in the world, describes herself as the first of God's creations, the principle that guided God's formation of all that is (8:22–31). Certainly, those who wrote and those who read wisdom literature were concerned about the relationship between wisdom and the revealed law, between knowledge gained by experience on the one hand and piety on the other. They concluded that, in the final analysis, there was no conflict between the two: "The fear of the LORD [genuine piety] is the beginning of wisdom, and the knowledge of the Holy One is insight" (9:10).

The verses from chapter 9 come from the twelfth and final address in this initial section of the Book of Proverbs. They may serve as a fitting conclusion to the reading for the day, for Wisdom urges "those without sense" (9:4b) to set out on a path of growth by eating and drinking what she has to offer.

Psalm 19

This psalm of hymnic praise of God declares that God has communicated the divine will and knowledge of the Divine through nature—verses 1–6—and through the law, or Torah—verses 7–13. Without speech, God's voice is heard in the world of nature, and divine communication, like the light of the sun, falls everywhere and nothing can hide from it. In the Torah, God's will is embodied in commandment and precept, and offers its blessings to those whose ways it directs and guards.

Ezekiel 36:24–28

This reading is the central section of a passage in which Ezekiel presents the divine announcement of a new Israel. God, through the prophet (see vv. 22, 32), is the speaker. This dramatic announcement of good news presupposes that the people of God are in trouble. The description of that trouble is given in the context (vv. 16–21) and alluded to in our reading. Israel is in exile, away from the sacred land, but the trouble is even deeper. Separation from the land corresponds to separation from their God. They are in exile because of their sin, their disobedience that led to uncleanness. Now God is about to act, not because Israel deserves it, but for the sake of his "holy name" (v. 22).

There are two aspects to God's expected work of salvation, one external and one internal, corresponding to Israel's present plight. First, the Lord will gather up the people and return them to their land (v. 24). But if they are to remain there (v. 26), a major transformation must occur. That is the second aspect of the good news, the establishment of a new covenant (see Isa. 54:10; 55:3) with a new Israel. This transformation is spelled out in terms of three distinct steps: (1) the Lord will sprinkle (cf. Exod. 24:6) the people with water, purifying them from their uncleanness; (2) the Lord will give them a new heart and a new spirit, replacing their heart of stone with one of flesh (cf. Jer. 31:31); and (3) God will put his own "spirit" within them. "Spirit" here represents both the willingness and the ability to act in obedience. The promise is summarized by the reiteration of the ancient covenant formula, "You shall be my people, and I will be your God" (v. 28). The radical difference between this new covenant and the old one is that the Lord himself will enable the people to be faithful.

Psalm 42 and 43

Although divided into two psalms in the course of transmission, Psalms 42 and 43 were probably originally one psalm. This is indicated by the repeated refrain in 42:5, 11 and 43:5.

It is possible that we overpersonalize such a psalm as this and try too hard to discover some individual's face beneath the poetic mask. It is entirely possible that this psalm was written to be used by worshipers and sung antiphonally as pilgrims set out on their way to some pilgrimage in Jerusalem. The portrayal of the present discontent with life thus forms the backdrop for the expectations of coming worship (see Pss. 84 and 120).

This psalm can be closely associated with the sentiments of Ezekiel 36:24–28, the Old Testament lesson to which it is a response. Ezekiel predicts the coming rescue of God's people from exile and the transformation of the human personality and will. The psalm, originally used as an individual lament, early became associated with the Easter Vigil because it expressed the people's longing for redemption and their lamenting over being absent from the sanctuary. The psalm presupposes that the speaker is living away from the Sacred City. The psalmist's thought about former days when the worshiper went on a pilgrimage to Jerusalem only intensifies the depression and despair that accompany living in a foreign and hostile land, and heightens the desire to be at home again in the temple.

Ezekiel 37:1–14

Ezekiel's vision of the valley of dry bones, like so many other Old Testament readings for this season, stems from the era of the Babylonian Exile. That it is a vision report is indicated by the introductory formula "The hand of the LORD was upon me," which the prophet uses elsewhere to begin reports of ecstatic experiences (Ezek. 3:22). The narration is in the first person and, like most prophetic vision reports, consists of two parts: the description of what was revealed (vv. 1–10) and the interpretation (vv. 11–14). Throughout there is dialogue between Yahweh and the prophet.

The message from the Lord communicated through the report is the response to the problem stated in verse 11. The people of Israel are saying, "Our bones are dried up, and our hope is lost; we are cut off completely." In the vision Ezekiel sees himself carried by the spirit of Yahweh to a valley full of bones, like the scene of an ancient battle. When the Lord asks if the bones can live again, Ezekiel gives the only possible answer, "O Lord GOD, you know" (v. 3). Although the meaning of this response is not immediately plain, it becomes clear in the context: The God of Israel can indeed bring life in the midst of death. When the prophet obeys the command to prophesy to the bones, a distinct sequence of events transpires: bones to bones, sinews to bones, flesh on the bones, and then skin covering them. The importance of the next step is emphasized by the interjection of a further divine instruction. The prophet calls for breath to come into the corpses, and they live. The view of human life as physical matter animated by the breath that comes from God is found throughout the Old Testament (cf. Gen. 2:7).

The interpretation of what has transpired (vv. 11–14) emphasizes that the vision is a promise of national resurrection addressed to the hopeless exiles. In no sense is the seriousness of their plight denied. They are indeed as good as dead, and death in all possible forms is acknowledged as a reality. But the word of God in the face of and in the midst of death brings to the people of God a new reality, life. It is a free, unconditional, and unmerited gift. When read on the eve of Easter, this text is a strong reminder that God is the Lord of all realms, including that of death. Moreover, the promise of life is addressed to the people of God, and resurrection is a symbol not only for a life beyond the grave but also for the abundant life of the community of faith this side of physical death.

Psalm 143

Originally used as an individual lament by worshipers suffering from illness, this psalm prays for God's intervention and rescue. The condition of the worshiper's distress is described in terms of death, of going down to the pit. Such depictions fit well with the description in Ezekiel 37 of the Exile as a graveyard. Like those awaiting Easter morning, the psalmist asks to "hear in the morning of [God's] steadfast love" (v. 8).

Zephaniah 3:14–20

The last of the Old Testament readings for the Easter Vigil is a shout of joy and an announcement of salvation to Jerusalem. The passage begins with a series of imperatives addressed to the Holy City, calling for celebration (v. 14). The remainder of the unit in effect gives the reasons for celebration. These reasons include (1) the announcement that the Lord has acted in behalf of the city and is now in its midst as king (v. 15) and (2) a series of promises concerning the renewal of the city and the return of its people (vv. 16–20). Both the mood and contents of the text anticipate the Easter celebration.

Our unit is the fourth and last section in the Book of Zephaniah and stands in sharp contrast to the remainder of the book. The section that immediately precedes this one (Zeph. 3:1–13) had announced a purging punishment upon the city and its people. But now darkness has become light; fear and terror have become hope and celebration.

The prophet Zephaniah was active in the seventh century, not long before 621 BC. He was concerned with the coming judgment upon his people, particularly because of their pagan religious practices. It is possible that this concluding section of the book was added in a later age, perhaps during the Babylonian Exile (cf. 3:19–20), by those who actually had been through the fires of destruction and who looked forward to celebrating God's forgiveness, which the return from exile represented. But in any case, the theological interpretation presented by the structure of the book in its final form is quite clear: The celebration of God's salvation follows the dark night of judgment and suffering.

Psalm 98

Like Zephaniah 3:14–20, this psalm is an exuberant affirmation of divine triumph and success. This affirmation is noted by the word "victory" in each of the first three verses. The psalm proclaims the victory of God and calls upon the whole world to break forth into song with the sound of musical instruments. As part of the Easter Vigil, this psalm contributes its call for a celebration of salvation and for the recognition of God as king.

Romans 6:3–11

This text serves as the epistolary reading for the Easter Vigil in all three years. Psalm 114 serves as the response to this text, where Paul discusses Christian baptism as the sacramental act of dying and rising with Christ.

It is a most appropriate text to be read in this liturgical setting. The community gathers either on Easter Eve or Easter morning. In either case, the text straddles the death and resurrection of Christ. Like the Roman god Janus, this liturgical moment looks in both directions: back to his death, forward to his life. In one case, the tomb serves as the focus of our attention; in the other, it is the stone rolled away. As we visualize the closed door, our mood is somber, for we can think only of the entombed, lifeless body. As we visualize the open door, we are amazed, if not buoyant, for we feel despair giving way to resurrection hope.

As our thoughts oscillate between death and life in this service, so does today's epistolary text. It is interesting to note that these remarks from Paul are prompted by a question of ethics. One of the objections raised against his theology of justification by faith was that it failed to provide an adequate moral imperative. In fact, some critics apparently charged that it encouraged a form of moral relativism. If we are saved by grace through faith, and not by keeping laws or the Law, what then is the motivation to be good?

Paul's response is to interpret for his readers their own initiation rite into the Christian faith and to press its implications to the full. The place to begin is to realize that baptism actually plunges us into the death of Christ not merely as a symbolic reenactment but as an act of sacramental entry and participation. Jesus had asked his disciples whether they, like he, would actually be willing to undergo a baptism of death. Would they, he wondered, be willing to plunge themselves headlong into violent death (Mark 10:38; Luke 12:50)?

As a way of underscoring the completeness of our reenactment of the death of Christ, Paul repeatedly uses the language of participation: "buried . . . *with* him" (v. 4); "united *with* him" (v. 5); "crucified *with* him" (v. 6); "died *with* Christ . . . live *with* him" (v. 8) (italics added in each case). We miss the point if we see our baptism as an event symbolically analogous to the historical event of Christ's death and resurrection. It is not that we die as he did, are buried as he was, and are raised as he was. It is rather that we are coparticipants with him in that event where death gave way to life.

Only when our union with Christ is seen in such starkly realistic terms, when the deepest part of our selves has actually undergone death, do we experience and enter a new form of existence. There is no other way to describe it than resurrection life. Its radical newness marks it off from every other mode of existence. It is not the old redirected or retreaded but transformed—a new creation (2 Cor. 5:17; Gal. 6:15). It is the creation of what did not exist before—service in the new life of the Spirit (Rom. 7:6; cf. 12:2; Eph. 2:15; also Isa. 43:18–19).

So radical is this redefinition of our selves that our form of living is transformed. Quite literally, who we are changes. And consequently, what we do changes as well. The "old personality" dies (Eph. 4:22; Col. 3:9) as the sinful self is destroyed (Gal. 2:19–21; 5:24). With the destruction of the self comes liberation from the hold of sin (v. 7; cf. Acts 13:39; 1 Pet. 4:1).

What is born in the new creation is a living hope (1 Pet. 1:3). Infused with the Spirit of new life, we begin to experience moral renewal, knowing all the while that full participation in resurrection life lies ahead in the future (v. 8; cf. 1 Thess. 4:17; 2 Tim. 2:11).

For all this, the implications of dying and rising with Christ are not merely postponed to the future. Both death and life are present realities. Christ's death was final, "once for all," and just as final is the life he lives to God (v. 10). It is final, but ongoing. Even so are we to regard ourselves as "dead to sin and alive to God in Christ Jesus" (v. 11; cf. 2 Cor. 5:15; 1 Pet. 2:24; also Gal. 2:19).

So it is, then, that the death and resurrection of Christ is not only ours to ponder but to enter—and having entered, there to live.

Psalm 114

This psalm, read as a response to Paul's discussion of the association of Christian baptism with the death of Jesus, is a celebration of the Exodus from Egyptian bondage and of the entry into the promised land. Typologically, one might say that the Exodus, like Christ's death, symbolizes the end of an old state of life and the dawning of a new state. The entry into the promised land, like Christian baptism, was a time when the benefits of redemption became real. In this psalm, exodus from Egypt and entrance into the promised land are closely joined, so that parallel events are seen as characteristic of the two episodes. At the Exodus, the sea fled and the "mountains skipped like rams"; at the Jordan, the river rolled back and the hills skipped like lambs (vv. 3–4). The address to the sea and river, the mountains and hills in verses 5–6, which is continued in the address to the earth in verses 7–8, serves as the means for making contemporary the Exodus and entrance events. Thus the users of the psalm, which was always read at the celebration of Passover, "became" participants in the past events of salvation just as the Christian in baptism becomes contemporary with the death of Jesus.

Luke 24:1–12

Luke 24:1–12 will appear as an alternate lesson for Easter Sunday. If used here for the Easter Vigil, it is important that the sermon, in fact, the entire service, be one of restraint and anticipation, resisting the temptation to borrow the joyful proclamation from the next day.

It is evident that both Luke and Matthew had access to Mark 16:1–8, although both made changes in substance and form in contouring the empty-tomb story to their own theologies and their readers' needs. Luke introduces the women as "they" (v. 1), delaying until the end to give their names (v. 10). What is important for Luke is that these women witnessed the crucifixion (23:49), the burial (23:55), and the empty tomb (24:3). Only after they enter the tomb and discover the body missing does Luke introduce the messengers in dazzling apparel (v. 4). Luke's simple reference to "two men" (instead of Mark's one, 16:5) joins this passage to the Transfiguration (9:30) and to the Ascension (Acts 1:10), and may indicate how Luke wants the reader to classify and understand this story. Even though our earliest tradition of the resurrection (1 Corinthians 15) centers entirely on appearances of the risen Christ and does not include the empty tomb as part of that tradition, it is clear from Luke's account here and the repetition of it in 24:22–24 that he regarded it as part of the Easter story. The witness of an empty tomb, taken alone, is hardly persuasive; but joined to appearance narratives, it both strengthens and heightens the dramatic force of the church's proclamation.

Luke's account of the message of the two men to the women differs from Mark at four important points.

First, Luke makes Galilee the place where Jesus instructed his followers concerning his death and resurrection (v. 6), whereas in Mark (16:7) Galilee was to be the site of an appearance to his disciples. For Luke, Galilee is now past, and Jerusalem is the center for Christ's appearances (24:13–43) and for the subsequent mission of the church (24:44–53).

Second, the women are reminded of Christ's words, which in Luke constitute a brief formula or creedal statement about betrayal, crucifixion, and resurrection (v. 7). Essentially the same statement is repeated in verses 26 and 46.

Third, the women are not treated simply as messengers. They are reminded of what Christ had taught them, and they recalled the teaching. This is to say, they are treated as disciples in and of themselves and are not told to go tell the disciples.

And finally, the women do go and tell the eleven (v. 9; "apostles" in v. 10), but Luke also includes "all the rest" (v. 9). The group of believers from Galilee is, Luke says later, about one hundred twenty persons (Acts 1:15).

It is now that Luke names some but not all the women who report their experience (v. 10). Among those named, Joanna (8:3) replaces Mark's Salome (16:1). "The other women" had followed Jesus from Galilee and would be present at the beginning of the church in Jerusalem (Acts 1:14). That the apostles did not believe the women (v. 11; repeated at v. 41) may be understood in one of two ways: either as a dramatizing of the burden that the resurrection placed upon faith even among those closest to Jesus, or as Luke's way of minimizing the empty-tomb story as generative of faith. Both interpretations are reasonable and appropriate to Luke's message.

In many translations, verse 12 is omitted from the text and placed in the footnotes. The reasons do not lie in the lack of support in the Greek manuscripts; the weight of evidence is strongly in its favor. Its questionable status is due rather to the widespread judgment that verse 12 is an interpolation from John 20:3–10, and its presence here creates a contradiction with verse 34. However, it could reasonably be expected that the various resurrection traditions would quite early intermingle and influence one another.

The preacher is on solid ground to include verse 12 in this lection and will find in this verse a most fitting close to the Easter Vigil. Simon Peter, who was later to see the risen Christ in a special appearance (1 Cor. 15:5), at this point goes home, "amazed at what had happened." With him the whole church waits until tomorrow.

Easter Day

Acts 10:34–43 or Isaiah 65:17–25;
Psalm 118:1–2, 14–24;
1 Corinthians 15:19–26 or Acts 10:34–43;
John 20:1–18 or Luke 24:1–12

*(If the first lesson is from the Old Testament, the
reading from Acts should be the second lesson.)*

The *Revised Common Lectionary* provides the passage from Isaiah 65 for those churches that use an Old Testament reading on Easter Day and do not celebrate the Easter Vigil with its long list of Old Testament readings. Isaiah 65:17–25 still anticipates the eschatological rejoicing that Easter inaugurates. The responsorial psalm, the same for all three years of the cycle, is a song of thanksgiving for deliverance. In it death is the vanquished enemy. The New Testament readings include instances of all types of early Christian literature concerning the resurrection. The passage from Acts is the proclamation of the gospel—the life, death, and resurrection of Jesus—in almost creedal form. The epistolary text includes a critically important section of Paul's extensive discussion of the resurrection. Luke 24:1–12 and John 20:1–12 are accounts of the discovery of the empty tomb.

Acts 10:34–43

If there is any day of the Christian year when the message of the universal love of God is heralded to the whole world, it is Easter. It is all the more fitting, then, that this sermon summary from Acts be read. It is the first clear instance in Acts of the gospel heralded to a Gentile. It occurs on the lips of Peter, one of the earliest witnesses of the Easter faith (cf. 1 Cor. 15:5). In a few broad strokes, it gives us the essence of the Christ-story (vv. 37–41).

We should note first that our text begins with a bold proclamation of God's impartiality: "I now really understand . . . that God has no favourites" (v. 34, NJB). It is an axiom of Judeo-Christian faith that God shows no partiality (Deut. 10:17; 2 Chron. 19:7; Sir. 35:12–13; Gal. 2:6; Rom. 2:11; Eph. 6:9; Col. 3:25; 1 Pet. 1:17; cf. also 1 Clement 1:3; Epistle of Barnabas 4:12; Polycarp to the Philippians 6:1). Among other things, this means that God cannot be bought, either with money or human favor.

If God is impartial, it follows that the love of God is unbounded, universal in its scope. Thus the terms of God's acceptance are for "anyone who fears [God] . . . and does what is right"

(v. 35; Acts 10:2, 22; 13:16, 26; Ps. 15:2, 4). The language here is sacrificial (cf. Lev. 1:3; 19:5; 22:17–30). Those who live in the fear of God and do what is right become an acceptable offering, even if they are Gentiles (Isa. 56:6–7; Mal. 1:10–11; Rom. 15:16; Phil. 4:18; 1 Pet. 2:5).

True enough, God's word was sent first to Israel (Acts 13:26; Ps. 107:20; 147:18–19), and in keeping with the prophetic promise it was an announcement of peace (Isa. 52:7; Nah. 1:15; cf. Eph. 2:17; 6:15). But it was not as if Jesus were the Messiah of one nation of people. He is rather "Lord of all" (v. 36; Matt. 28:18; Rom. 10:12; cf. Wisd. of Sol. 6:7; 8:3).

We can see, then, how our text confronts the question of God's impartiality: if God shows no favorites, why did the gospel first come to Israel? Peter's concern is to show that the Easter faith is truly universal in scope.

At this point, we have a concise summary of the Christ-story.

1. John the Baptist represents the beginning point (v. 37). This conforms to the way the Gospel of Mark begins, and scholars have noted the similarity of this summary with the overall outline of the Gospel of Mark. Given the importance of John's prophetic preaching, it is little wonder that in some traditions Christians drove down the first peg here (Acts 1:22; 13:23–24; Luke 3:21–22 and parallels; 16:16).

2. The baptism of Jesus (v. 38a). The various strands of the gospel tradition agree in seeing Jesus' baptism by John as his "chrism," the time when God poured out the Holy Spirit on him as an expression of divine favor and approval (Matt. 3:13–17 and parallels; also Luke 4:18; Acts 4:27). It was both a prophetic fulfillment (Isa. 61:1) and a reminiscence of God's appointment of earlier messiahs, such as David (1 Sam. 16:13). Whatever else it signified, it was an expression of power.

3. The healing ministry of Jesus (v. 38b). One of the least contestable aspects of Jesus' life on earth is that he went about healing the sick and exorcising demons (cf. Matt. 4:23–25 and parallels). The name of Jesus itself conveyed healing power (Acts 9:34). His power to perform deeds of kindness toward the afflicted only attested the presence of God within him: "for God was with him" (cf. Isa. 58:11; John 3:2; 8:29).

4. His death by hanging on a tree (v. 39). All the Gospel passion narratives echo this brief statement. "Death by hanging" was no more honorable then than now, and it carried with it the curse of the law (Gal. 3:13; Deut. 21:23).

5. Raised by God on the third day (v. 40). Here we shift to the central focus of our celebration on Easter Day. We should see it as the day God acted decisively not only in behalf of Jesus but in behalf of all humanity (Acts 2:24, 32; 3:15; 4:10; 5:30; 13:30, 34, 37; 17:31). The "third day" is part of the very substructure of Christian faith (cf. 1. Cor. 15:4–7; Hos. 6:2).

6. Made manifest to select witnesses (vv. 40b–41). Part and parcel of the Easter faith is the conviction that the risen Lord appeared, or was made visibly manifest, to a circle of disciples on Easter morning. As those who had "seen," they became his witnesses (Luke 24:48; John 14:19–22; 15:26–27; Acts 1:8, 22; 5:32; also 1 Pet. 5:1). That true recognition occurred in the context of eating and drinking with the risen Lord gives all the more meaning to a eucharistic service celebrated on Easter Day (Luke 24:30, 43; John 21:13).

And what are the implications for those who are privy to this Easter revelation? An irresistible urge to proclaim it abroad (v. 42; Acts 1:8; 4:20). But ours is not simply the message "He is risen!" As victor of both death and life, the risen Lord now becomes the one who is to judge both the living and the dead (Rom. 2:16; 14:9–10; 2 Tim. 4:1; 1 Pet. 4:5). He has been appointed to this special task by God (v. 42; also Acts 17:31).

But there is more. The risen Lord is everything the prophets expected and hoped for (v. 43). Through him forgiveness is now universalized (Isa. 33:24). Faith in Christ becomes the means through which all humanity is able to share in the unbounded, universal love of God. He is indeed "Lord of all."

Isaiah 65:17–25

These are hopeful words from a difficult and troubled time. They are associated with the anonymous prophetic figure or figures who were active in the early postexilic period and were responsible for most of Isaiah 55–66. Many Judeans had returned from Babylon to their homeland. The temple almost certainly had been rebuilt, but the future of the people was by no means secure. In addition, there is evidence of sectarian conflict within the community.

In the context of which our reading is a part there is a somewhat liturgical pattern. Isaiah 63:7–64:12 gives a series of prayers, mainly of complaint and petition, and then Isaiah 65:1–25 records the response. This movement, however, is probably the work of an editor who organized earlier materials.

Isaiah 65:17–25 is a prophetic address, an announcement of salvation. God is the speaker throughout, and the contents concern the future. There are two opening or introductory formulas, in verses 17a and 18b, obvious in the RSV: "For behold, I create. . . ." First the prophet hears God announce the new era (vv. 17–19a) and then present a description of the circumstances of life in that time (vv. 19b–25). The description of the new age is crafted in a pattern that alternates negative and positive, what will not be and what will be. Verses 19b–20a report that there will be no weeping and no early death; then verses 20b–21 describe the positive side—long life and fruitful labor. Verses 22–25 continue such an alternation of negative and positive descriptions.

To characterize this passage as a prophetic address is to observe that the vision of the future is not yet an apocalyptic one. Our writer—or speaker—knew himself to be in the tradition of Second Isaiah as well as Isaiah of Jerusalem from the eighth century BC. He quotes and alludes to both of them. The style of address is especially similar to that of Second Isaiah, and the expression "former things" (v. 17) comes from him. Most important, the announcement of a "new heavens and a new earth" is quite different from the vision that will appear several centuries later in apocalyptic literature, such as Daniel, Isaiah 24–27, and—still later—Revelation 21:1 and 2 Peter 3:13. As the subsequent description makes quite clear, the announcement in Isaiah 65:17 has in view a transformation of circumstances on this earth, and within history, not beyond them.

The vision here concerns a new age of salvation, specifically focused upon Jerusalem. It will be inaugurated with rejoicing, a celebration in which even God participates (v. 19). "Weeping" and "distress" will be ended (v. 19), but death itself will not. Rather, infant mortality and other forms of premature death will be ended (v. 20). It is only death that comes too soon that is perceived as the enemy. Obviously, even in the age of salvation, people will work at construction and agriculture (vv. 21–23), but it will be productive and fruitful labor in which efforts and results coincide (see Amos 9:14; Ezek. 28:11). There will be no need to fear enemies who would take over the fruits of one's labors. Moreover, women will not labor to bring children into a world full of "sudden terror" (v. 23, NRSV footnote). With regard to death, work, and child-birth, the vision of the future appears to reverse some of the curses of Genesis 3:16–19.

But there is more. The very foundation of the situation in which peace prevails is the blessing of the Lord. There is no talk of the new age as a reward for righteousness or the like. Rather, it is a gift of God, who promises to answer prayers even before they are expressed out loud. Finally, the concluding verse anticipates an even more dramatic transformation of the natural order, with natural enemies living in peace with one another—the lion eating straw and the snake eating dust. These lines, which certainly depend upon Isaiah 11:6–9, stress again that the center of the new age will be the holy city Jerusalem on God's "holy mountain."

To be sure, the future envisioned here is far short of the Easter kerygma. Nevertheless, it deserves to be heard. In Isaiah 65:17–25, death is present, but it does not ruin life. People will still work, but in a situation in which justice is present. And it would be good news indeed if women everywhere could bring children into a world that did not present them with the sud-den terrors of war or famine.

Psalm 118:1–2, 14–24

Portions of Psalm 118 formed one of the lections of Passion/Palm Sunday, and at that point in the lectionary commentary we sought to show how the ancient psalm, used on the occasion of a king's triumphal reentry into Jerusalem for a service of thanksgiving, parallels the experience of Jesus' entry into the Holy City. As part of the Scripture readings for Easter Day, the verses selected for today's reading focus on victory and triumph, God's redemption of the one threatened.

Verses 1–2 form part of the call to offer thanksgiving to God; verses 14–18 are hymnic praise of God for the victory given the ruler in battle (see vv. 10–13), and verses 19–24 are part of the litany of entry into the temple.

Psalm 118 is a community psalm of thanksgiving, and the call to offer thanks in verses 1–4 includes all of ancient Israel—the lay and the clergy. Thanksgiving is to be offered by declaring that God's steadfast love endures forever. Thus the opening words of the psalm clearly proclaim and anticipate the note of victory that follows, a victory already anticipated in the reference to the character and love of God.

In verses 14–18, the triumphant leader returning from victorious battle affirms and pro-claims the deliverance worked by God, even deliverance from death itself. The description of the struggle and battle in the field has given way to praise and thanksgiving. Like Moses of old, the ruler and the victorious proclaim a triumph wrought by the right hand of God (see Exodus 15).

In verses 17–18 the experience of battle and the triumph of victory are described in terms of a life and death struggle. The distress and trouble of battle are declared to be the chastening of God, yet God does not surrender the king to the power of death. These verses are thus very similar or analogous to what Christians proclaimed about Jesus: both his suffering and his triumph over death were the work of God. In both, misfortune and humiliation as well as victory and triumph are seen as components in divine activity.

With verse 19, we move to the entry litany itself, which was discussed in conjunction with the lesson for Passion/Palm Sunday. Insofar as Easter Sunday is concerned, the choral response in verses 23–24 (following the royal thanksgiving in vv. 21–22) is the text to be highlighted. The choir proclaims that what has taken place and is now celebrated has been the work of God, and thus it is marvelous (beyond belief, transcending the normal). It is the day in which God has acted and made the rejected stone the cornerstone (v. 22). The response to such activity should be rejoicing and celebration, because the sound of battle and the presence of death have been replaced with songs of victory and the gift of life.

In early Judaism, at the time of the origin of the church, Psalm 118 formed the concluding psalm sung in the Passover celebration. It was used both in the temple and in home observances. As such, it marked and celebrated the triumph of God that had brought the Hebrews out of slavery and bondage in Egypt and toward freedom and service of God in the promised land. Thus it is fitting that such a psalm play a role in the Christian celebration of Easter, which affirms the triumph of God in Christ as the triumph of life over death.

1 Corinthians 15:19–26

The notion of resurrection has never been easy to accept, even for Christians. Clearly, some within the Corinthian church found it an incredible notion (15:12). Apparently, they found it easier to believe that Christ was raised from the dead than that they themselves would undergo a similar experience.

Today's epistolary text occurs in the middle of Paul's discussion of the resurrection, where he responds to the doubts of the Corinthian Christians.

The first verse of our lection actually concludes the thought begun in verse 12. It is generally treated as the final thought of the previous paragraph. It is Paul's final stroke against the desperate thought of life that ends with our last breath. The faith that impelled him to preach was not for hope in this life only, though that might be an improvement. Nor was the Easter faith laced with an element of uncertainty, as if we had to wonder and waver about the hope to which we have committed ourselves and our lives. To proclaim Christ apart from the Easter faith is to proclaim no Christ at all. Such would be a most unfortunate message, and ours would be a pitiable state of self-contradiction undermined by doubt.

The linchpin of Christian faith and identity is the single proclamation that Christ has in fact been raised from the dead (v. 20; 15:4; Rom. 6:4; 8:11; cf. Matt. 16:21 and parallels). This is not only the essence of Easter; it is the essence of Christian existence. How this is conceived may be, and has been, furiously debated. What happened we do not know. That it happened we firmly believe.

Paul insists that Christ's resurrection was not an isolated instance, an event "back there." It is rather an event whose rippling effect has reached all humanity. The metaphor he uses is that of "first fruits," an image drawn from the Old Testament where that which was first harvested symbolized the full harvest that was to come later (Lev. 23:10). It was as if he was the first full plant to spring forth from the ground, the sure sign that others would spring to life in due course (15:23; Col. 1:15, 18; Rev. 1:5; 3:14; also Rom. 8:29; Heb. 1:6). When we see the first daffodil of spring, we know that eventually others will follow.

But how can an event in the life of one person typify the destiny of all persons? We might grant that Christ was raised, but does it follow that we too will be raised? Is it possible for the act of a particular individual to have universal significance—for all time? Genesis 1–3 provided Paul the solution to the problem of Christ's particularity. Its message is clear: through the deed of one man, Adam, death came to all humanity. Through one individual, the destiny of us all was affected (Gen. 3:1–24; Wisd. of Sol. 2:24; Sir. 25:24).

If we can conceive that death passed to us all through the first Adam, we can also imagine that life is ours through the last Adam (1 Cor. 15:45–49). If death came to us through one man, so can life.

The order is clear: first Christ, then "those who belong to Christ" (v. 23), literally "those who are of Christ" (Gal. 5:24). Through our participation with him in his death and resurrection, we become sharers in his destiny (Rom. 6:3–11). This occurs not now, but at his coming (Matt. 24:3; 1 Cor. 1:8; 1 Thess. 2:19; 3:13; 4:15–16; 5:23; 2 Thess. 2:1; James 5:7–8; 2 Pet. 1:16; 3:4, 12; 1 John 2:28).

At the end, Christ hands over to God the reign that has been his (Dan. 2:44; Eph. 1:21–22), but only after vanquishing all hostile forces and powers (1 Cor. 2:6; Eph. 1:21; Col. 1:16; 2:15; 1 Pet. 3:22). In the words of Psalm 110:1, he reigns until every enemy has been put under foot (cf. Matt. 22:44 and parallels; Luke 19:27). The final enemy to be destroyed is death itself (v. 26; Rev. 20:14; 21:4).

The force of this text read on Easter Day is to confront us and reassure us that our destiny—those who are "of Christ"—is indissolubly linked with Christ's own destiny. Death is an enemy. It can be viewed no other way. But what we lost in Adam we have gained in Christ. Our vision of the future can be none other than that of the risen Christ, Conqueror of Death and Bringer of Life.

John 20:1–18 or Luke 24:1–12

Because Luke 24:1–12 was the Gospel for Easter Vigil, we will here attend only to John 20:1–18. One may, of course, use Luke 24:1–12 for this service; if so, comments on that reading can be found in the Vigil lessons.

John 20:1–18 belongs to that body of New Testament material referred to as resurrection narratives. Like Matthew 28 and Luke 24, John joins both elements of those narratives, the empty tomb and the appearance of the risen Christ. Mark 16 has only the empty-tomb portion (if the text ends at verse 8), and 1 Corinthians 15:3–8, our earliest resurrection narrative, has only the appearances, but none, strangely enough, to women. Unlike the Synoptics, this Evangelist speaks of only one woman at the tomb (20:1), but she is the one common to all the Gospels, Mary Magdalene (of Magdala). Luke says (8:2) that seven demons had been exorcized from her; legend portrays her as a beautiful woman redeemed by Jesus from a life of illicit love.

If chapter 21 is regarded as an epilogue, then 20:1–18 is one of two resurrection narratives in this Gospel, the other being 20:19–31 (the Gospel lection for next Sunday). In each of the two, the writer has interwoven a story of an appearance to an individual in the presence of some of the Twelve, the former involving two disciples and Mary; the latter, ten disciples and Thomas. The structure of today's lection is the split story, a form quite common in Mark: the account opens with Mary Magdalene at the tomb, shifts to the two disciples, then returns to Mary.

Verses 1–10 preserve the empty-tomb tradition. This tradition, although containing variations among the four Gospels, seems to have been fixed quite early. Its principal components are these: (1) it is early on the first day of the week; (2) women (woman in John) come to the tomb; (3) the stone has been removed; (4) a messenger appears (two messengers in Luke 24:4 and John 20:12; this element is delayed in John and made a part of the appearance story); and (5) confusion, doubt, fear, and joy follow.

And what is the testimony of the empty tomb? For Mary, it means the body of Jesus has been moved. Stolen? Matthew (28:11–15) develops this substory. Taken to a more permanent burial site? Perhaps. Removed by the gardener for some reason? Mary surmises as much (v. 15). For Simon Peter, who arrives after the other disciple but enters the tomb first (vv. 4–7), the tomb contains burial cloths but no body. No response from him is recorded except that he returned home (v. 10). For the disciple whom Jesus loved (13:22–25; 18:15–16; 19:26–27), the same evidence was more persuasive: he believed (v. 8). This favorable word about this anonymous disciple is consistent with the other references to him (see above), especially in scenes in which he is paired with Simon Peter. Chapter 21 records another such scene. Here is a case of the empty tomb alone, without any other witnesses, angelic or human, generating faith. It is important to keep in mind, however, that such belief, needing very little evidence or support, is congenial to the portrait of a disciple who lay against Jesus' breast at the Last Supper and to whom Jesus committed the care of his mother. But even so, the disciple did not know what to do with this faith, and he, too, went home. Obviously, he has at this point only added another line to his creed: "raised on the third day."

The appearance story (vv. 11–18) is quite different. In the account before us the components are these: (1) Mary hesitates, even resists belief; (2) Jesus appears to her; this did not produce faith immediately; (3) Jesus speaks her name; this promptly renews their former relationship (Jesus knows his own, calls them by name, and they know his voice, 10:34); (4) Jesus informs her that the old relationship can no longer be the same, because he is glorified and available, not to the former circle of friends alone, but to the world (12:20–31); (5) Mary is commissioned to tell the disciples; and (6) Mary obeys the command. The story is complete.

That which Mary is to tell Jesus' brethren is the message of the ascension, not simply of the resurrection (v. 17). For this Evangelist, the death, resurrection, and ascension constitute the glorification of the Son, the return to God, the triumph over evil forces, and the gift of the Holy Spirit to his followers (12:20–32; 14:16–17; 15:26; 16:7–15). Easter is completed at Pentecost.

Easter Evening

Isaiah 25:6–9;
Psalm 114;
1 Corinthians 5:6b–8;
Luke 24:13–49

The notes sounded in the readings for the Easter Evening service are those of hope, joy, and triumph. The First Lesson is one of the rare Old Testament passages that envisions an end of death. Psalm 114, one of a group of psalms associated with the observance of Passover, celebrates the theme of deliverance. First Corinthians 5:6b–8 calls for the celebration of the sacrifice of Christ as the paschal lamb, while the Gospel lection relates the account of the appearance of Jesus to the disciples on the road to Emmaus and his evening meal with them. In this event, we are told that he was "known to them in the breaking of the bread" (Luke 24:35).

Isaiah 25:6–9

This passage from Isaiah, one of the very rare Old Testament texts containing an explicit promise of the abolition of death (v. 8), is placed on Easter Day among the classical New Testament resurrection texts.

But Isaiah 25:6–9 should also be viewed in its own literary and historical context. It appears in the collection of mainly eschatologically oriented materials generally called the Isaiah Apocalypse (Isaiah 24–27), generally and reliably considered to be much later than the time of the prophet Isaiah. Although this section is not apocalyptic in the narrow sense of the term, it contains numerous motifs and ideas that appear in apocalyptic literature. Above all, these chapters express the confident view that, beyond a day of judgment, the reign of God will be established.

In terms of form, Isaiah 25:6–9 is an announcement of salvation with strong eschatological overtones. That is, unlike earlier prophetic announcements that saw the intervention of God in terms of historical events such as military defeat or return from exile, this one sees a radical transformation of the human situation. Its main focus is a banquet that the Lord will prepare on Mt. Zion ("this mountain," v. 6). The meal will include the richest possible food, and "all peoples" will participate. In the background of this promise stand cultic meals (Exodus 19; 24:9–11) that symbolize the intimate relationship between Yahweh and Israel, and perhaps also the sharing of sacrifices. One day, the visionary says, all peoples will come to the holy place for communion with one another and with the one God.

But there is more. With the eschatological banquet, God will inaugurate a new age of joy and peace. The "shroud that is cast over all peoples, the sheet that is spread over all nations" (v. 7) must refer to the attire for mourning, for God "will wipe away the tears from all faces" (v. 8). Mourning cannot be ended as long as there is death; consequently, "he will swallow up death forever" (v. 7). This language seems to be indebted to Canaanite mythology, which tells of the defeat of the god Mot (Death); but it has a very different construction here. Death is not another deity, but a human reality; and its defeat does not recur each year in the spring, but is a single act of God when the new age begins. The apostle Paul cites the verse in his account of the nature of the resurrection (1 Cor. 15:54).

One of the most important features of this passage should not be overlooked on Easter Day. The announcement of the new age of joy and peace extends to all peoples.

Psalm 114

In Jewish worship, Psalms 113–118 came to be associated closely with the festival of Passover. This collection of six psalms came to be called the "Egyptian Hallel" because they were seen as praise for the redemption from Egypt. How early this use of these psalms developed cannot be determined, but it was certainly already a custom at the time of Jesus.

The lambs designated for Passover were slaughtered and dressed in the temple in the afternoon to be cooked for the Passover dinner eaten in the evening. (Additional lambs were often cooked if the size of the Passover party required it. But at least one lamb, from which all observers ate a portion, had to be so designated and slaughtered and cleaned in the temple.) The people with their lambs were admitted to the temple in three different shifts. As the lambs were slaughtered on each of the shifts, the Levites sang Psalms 113–118 in the main courtyard of the temple. These psalms were again sung as part of the Passover meal. Psalms 113–114 were sung at the beginning of the meal and Psalms 115–118 at the conclusion.

Psalm 114 was clearly written for the celebration of Passover. Some of these psalms were originally composed for other celebrations and secondarily adopted for Passover usage.

The psalm opens with general summarizing statements about the Exodus from Egypt and the occupation of the land of Canaan (vv. 1–2). Egypt is described as the land of a people of strange language. The Egyptian language belongs to a completely different language family (Hamitic) from Hebrew (Semitic) and was written, of course, in a strange, nonalphabetic hieroglyphic form. In verse 1, "Israel" and "house of Jacob" refer to the larger inclusive Hebrew people (both Israel and Judah). In verse 2, "Israel" and "Judah" denote the Northern and Southern Kingdoms after the death of Solomon. That Judah is claimed to be God's sanctuary suggests that Judah is considered more special than Israel, which is spoken of as God's dominion. It also suggests that this psalm originated in Judah. The reference to sanctuary is no doubt an allusion to Jerusalem and the temple.

In verses 3–6, four entities are noted—the sea, the Jordan River, the mountains, and the hills. The references to the (Red) sea and the Jordan River hark back to the stories of the crossing of the sea in the Exodus from Egypt (see Exodus 14) and the crossing of the Jordan River to move into the promised land (see Joshua 3, especially vv. 14–17). In both cases, the water parted, fled, or turned back to allow the Hebrews to cross. It is interesting to note, and certainly appropriate for the setting of this psalm in the Passover observance, that the Passover preceded the Exodus from Egypt (see Exodus 12) and was the first celebration of the Hebrews in the land of Canaan (see Josh. 5:10–12). The Passover was thus celebrated as the last taste of Egypt and as the first taste of the promised land. The Passover recalls not only the scars of Egypt but also the first fruits of the land of promise.

The mountains and hills that skipped like rams and lambs (vv. 4 and 6) are not mentioned in the Exodus and Joshua stories. That they are mentioned as skipping around suggests that the language is metaphorical. The same might be said for the action of the sea and the Jordan River, although the final editors of the Hexateuch took both crossings as miraculous but actual events. Verses 5–6 are a taunt so formulated to heighten the action described. The one responsible for such actions does not get mentioned until verse 7, which refers to the presence of Yahweh.

The psalm concludes (vv. 7–8) with a call to the earth to "dance" (probably a better translation than the NRSV's "tremble"). Whether one should read "earth" (= the world) or "land" (= the promised land) remains unknown, although the latter seems more likely. The land is called on to break out in celebration at the presence of God, who worked wonders in the wilderness.

1 Corinthians 5:6b–8

In 1 Corinthians 5, Paul responds to an anonymous report that he had received. Word had it that one of the Corinthian members was living with his father's wife, or stepmother (5:1). Such a relationship was strictly forbidden by Jewish law (Lev. 18:8; 20:11). Roman law also prohibited such a union.

The actions of the offenders themselves are of less immediate concern to Paul than the church's actions—or lack of action! The man and woman remained unnamed, and Paul does not address them directly. Rather, he addresses the church. Theirs was not merely an attitude of tolerance and liberality, but one of arrogance (v. 2). Apparently, they actually boasted of their tolerant spirit, and perhaps even of their ability to devote their time and energy to matters more spiritual than mere physical relationships.

Paul, of course, is shocked and immediately calls for the removal of the offender from the congregation (v. 2). Such acts of excommunication from the community of faith had firm precedent in the Old Testament (Num. 5:3; Deut. 17:2–7). Similar procedures existed among the Qumran separatists. It is in the context of Paul's dealing with this problem of sexual immorality within the Corinthian church that he introduces the subject of leaven. After reminding them once again that their smugness little befits them (cf. 5:2; also 4:6), he reminds them of an everyday truism: "A little leaven leavens all the dough" (v. 6, REB; also Gal. 5:9). This commonplace of popular wisdom has been repeated in many forms, such as, "One bad apple spoils the barrel." The point is always the same: give rot a start, and soon it will ruin everything.

It is the Old Testament that provides the background of the imagery here. The Israelites were instructed to remove all leaven from their homes as they prepared for the celebration of Passover (Exod. 12:19; 13:7; Deut. 16:3–4). The fermenting power of yeast rendered it unclean and unsuitable for the celebration of a holy event. Only bread that was devoid of yeast was to be eaten.

Paul reminds the Corinthians that it is out of character for them to harbor such gross immorality in their midst, much less to boast of it! Christ, the Passover lamb, has been sacrificed (v. 7; John 1:29; 1 Pet. 1:19; Rev. 5:6–14). In effect, the Christian Passover has begun, and the appropriate manner of life for Christian observers is one from which all forms of corruption (leaven) have been removed. It is presupposed that observers of the Christian Passover have "unleavened" character, one that is sincere and true (v. 8).

In the context of Easter Evening, today's epistolary text calls us to recognize the moral implications of the paschal mystery. Above all, we are required to leave behind "malice and evil" and pursue "sincerity and truth" (v. 8). We are likewise cautioned against the bane of arrogance and human presumption. If nothing else, our own arrogance often blinds us to the simplest truths of life that even everyday wisdom knows and teaches. We may scoff at established conventions and mores, and even ridicule the popular proverbs of the masses, but first we should be sure that our own morality and wisdom exceed theirs. It seldom does.

Luke 24:13–49

Blessed is the church that has an Easter Evening service! Of course, everyone is tired. To accommodate the large crowd of worshipers in the morning, preachers, readers, singers, liturgists, and many others pressed into service have done double and triple duty. Some have even participated in sunrise services. But the very conditions that argue against an evening worship argue more persuasively in favor of it. Especially those who have spent the day serving others need now to sit down and be fed. The day needs to be reflected on, gathered up, appropriated. It is a fine evening for a walk; why not to Emmaus?

The resurrection narratives in the four Gospels are similar enough to lose their distinctive traits; they are different enough to demand that their distinctiveness be recognized and preserved. The preacher's first task is to come to clarity about the components of the narrative in the Gospel before us. Luke 24 falls broadly into five parts: (1) verses 1–12, the women at the tomb; (2) verses 13–35, the Emmaus story; (3) verses 36–43, Jesus' appearance to the eleven and others; (4) verses 44–49, instruction and commission; and (5) verses 50–53, the departure of Jesus. Within this material, one can see how the various resurrection narratives had begun to influence one another. For example, verse 12 reflects John 20:6–10; verse 34 confirms 1 Corinthians 15:5; verse 40 seems to be a borrowing from John 20:20; and to verse 51 some manuscripts add a line from Acts 1:9–10. Because verses 1–12 were discussed as the Gospel lesson for Easter Vigil, and because verses 44(46)–53 will be the reading for Ascension Day, we will here consider the second (vv. 13–35) and third (vv. 36–43) components of Luke's resurrection narrative.

Luke 24:13–35, like other stories told by Luke (the prodigal son and the sea voyage of Paul, among others), bears the marks of skill and artistry in narration. The beauty and completeness of such stories do not invite interrupting comments, but their significance in the church's faith demands some discussion. The appearance to the two disciples on the way to Emmaus is not in the list of Jesus' appearances in 1 Corinthians 15:3–8, nor does the story have a parallel in the other Gospels. As it is Luke's style to echo Old Testament stories in his accounts about Jesus (e.g., 1 Samuel 2 lies behind Luke 2:41–52), very likely Genesis 18:1–15 was in Luke's mind here. In this appearance of the risen Christ, as in the others, faith comes slowly. In fact, Luke says, "But their eyes were kept from recognizing him" (v. 16) until faith was born in response to witnessing that included explaining the meaning of Scriptures. At the Transfiguration, the disciples' eyes were dulled with sleep (9:32), and at the Ascension, their vision was blocked by a cloud (Acts 1:9–11). Faith is not coerced or overwhelmed by revelations to the unprepared.

Here the disciples are prepared by the opening up of appropriate Scriptures (v. 25). The role of Scripture in the removal of ignorance and the generation of faith is a strong theme in

Luke (16:31; 24:44–47; Acts 2:14–36). And joined to Christ's "opening the Scriptures" is his self-revelation in the breaking of bread (vv. 31, 35). The meal is clearly described in the language of the Lord's Supper (v. 30), making the story one of experiencing the risen Christ in word (interpreting the Scriptures) and sacrament ("he had been made known to them in the breaking of the bread," v. 35). It is quite possible that the story in verses 13–35 was shaped with Christian worship in mind.

The return of the two disciples from Emmaus to Jerusalem links verses 13–35 to verses 36–43, which record Jesus' appearance to the eleven and others with them (v. 33). Even though the two narratives are in many ways different, they are framed on the same pattern: the risen Christ appears, the disciples do not recognize him, they are scolded for doubting, food is shared, Jesus enables them to understand the Scriptures, and they respond in amazed joy. In verses 36–43, however, a new theme emerges—the corporeality of the resurrected Christ. The offering of hands and feet for examination and the eating of fish are the writer's insistence that Christian faith in the resurrection of Christ cannot be reduced to a vague Greek notion of the immortality of the soul. Neither can the risen Christ be separated as a different being from the historical Jesus: the one raised is the one crucified. "Look at my hands and my feet" (v. 39) is Christ's word to the church. Easter is forever joined to Good Friday, and to follow the risen Christ is to follow the One who bore the cross. Those whom Luke addressed with this clear affirmation are still among us, preferring a Christ without scars.

Second Sunday of Easter

Acts 5:27–32;
Psalm 118:14–29 or Psalm 150;
Revelation 1:4–8;
John 20:19–31

I n the seven-week period following the celebration of Easter, the church has an occasion to reflect on the impact of Jesus' death and resurrection. Quite appropriately, the First Lessons for the next seven Sundays are taken from the Book of Acts, providing the church an opportunity to recall some of the critical events that occurred during this formative period. By doing so, we are able to get a renewed sense of how Easter relates to the church's mission, impelling the church to faithful witness as it moves out into the world.

The Second Lessons for this period are supplied by First Peter, First John, and the Book of Revelation for Years A, B, and C respectively. For this year, we are introduced to some of the memorable passages from the Johannine apocalypse that have given hope to the church throughout the ages.

For the Second and Third Sundays of Easter, the Gospel Lessons focus on post-Easter events. Subsequent Gospel Lessons in the Fourth through the Seventh Sundays are taken from John 10–17.

In today's First Lesson, we have an instance of dramatic, powerful witness as the apostles confront the Jewish Sanhedrin. The first option for a psalm of response shows us the king returning from battle as victor, offering prayers of thanksgiving; the second option echoes the First Lesson with its emphasis on praising God in the temple. Today's Second Lesson is the salutation of the Book of Revelation, John's doxological greeting in the name of Jesus Christ, "the firstborn of the dead, and the ruler of the kings of the earth" (Rev. 1:5). The Gospel lection is the Johannine account of the appearance of Jesus on the evening of resurrection day and the encounter with Thomas.

Acts 5:27–32

T he setting for today's text is the confrontation between the apostles and the Jewish Sanhedrin. It records one episode in a series of events occurring within the precincts of the temple (5:12–42). After the incident involving Ananias and Sapphira, the apostles continued their ministry of signs and wonders (5:12; cf. 2:19, 22, 43; 4:30; 6:8; 7:36; 8:13; 14:3; 15:12). In doing so, they were continuing the healing ministry of Jesus (cf. Luke 4:16–19; 7:21–23). So astonishing were the results of their ministry that increasing numbers joined the faith.

In response to this outburst of messianic mercy, the authorities took the appropriate measures, even more severe than when they had previously resisted the work of Peter and John (4:5–23). Yet as hostility and resistance increase, so does God's capacity to vindicate the cause of the gospel, and the apostles are miraculously freed (5:17–21). It is a matter of sheer wonderment to the authorities that the apostles could have escaped (5:21–26). Once again, they are accosted and brought before the Sanhedrin (5:27–33). As before, the case is decided in their favor, this time through the words of Gamaliel, who cautions his colleagues against obstructing what might possibly be the will of God (5:38–39). Even so, the apostles are punished, but this only serves as an occasion for intensifying their efforts (5:41–42).

Here we see a pattern of events typical of Luke-Acts. First, there is a powerful display of the gospel, either in prophetic word or miraculous deed. Inevitably, this is met with resistance, usually by the authorities. But with the resistance comes divine vindication visibly displayed: the case is thrown out; the disciples are miraculously released. This then serves as an occasion for an even more powerful display of the gospel. We see this pattern begin to unfold in chapter 4, and as the story progresses, the level of resistance and vindication gradually intensifies. By the end of Acts, it becomes clear that the gospel is irrepressible. Nothing is really able to obstruct the progress of God's word.

In today's text, we are first presented with the standoff between the Sanhedrin and Peter and the apostles. Earlier they had been warned (4:18), and they will be warned again (5:40). At issue, as the Sanhedrin saw it, was where to place the responsibility for Jesus' death (v. 28; cf. Matt. 27:25).

In response, the apostles insist that theirs is a higher loyalty: "We must obey God rather than any human authority" (v. 29). A similar display of courage before the authorities is seen earlier (4:19), and many others will follow (Stephen, 6:8–8:3; Peter, 12:1–19; Paul, 16:25–40; 18:12–17; 19:23–41; 21:27–26:32). It is a classic confrontation with many precedents (cf. Dan. 3:16–18) and successors (Martyrdom of Polycarp 14).

There follows a succinct summary of the Christian message: Christ was "put to death by hanging him on a tree" (10:39; 13:29; Gal. 3:13; 1 Pet. 2:24; cf. Deut. 21:23); God raised and exalted him to a right-hand position of preeminence (Acts 2:33; cf. Ps. 110:1; 118:15–16). As exalted Leader and Savior, he extends repentance and forgiveness of sins (2:38; cf. 4:12). To this there is a double witness—the apostles themselves (1:8) and the Holy Spirit, whom God bestows on the obedient (v. 32; cf. John 15:26–27).

In this episode, the gospel clearly wins, as it does throughout Acts. It is all too easy to read these accounts and become triumphalist in our thinking. In this liturgical setting, we may forget that the Easter faith can require defense as well as celebration. The scene Luke sketches is drama no doubt, but episodes like this could and did occur. What we have is an account of courageous witnesses digging in their heels against the intimidating threats of those in power. Even if we celebrate Easter in peace, others may do so at high cost. And so ultimately may we.

Psalm 118:14–29

Portions of this psalm are used in the lectionary for Palm Sunday and Easter Day throughout the three cycles. As was noted earlier, the psalm seems to have been composed for and used as the litany in a public thanksgiving ceremony. As is typical of thanksgiving psalms, much of the wording is human-to-human address.

In this psalm, the king has returned victoriously from battle. He reports to the human audience on his triumph, enters the temple amid acclaim and jubilation, and offers a prayer of thanksgiving and sacrifice.

Verse 14 begins with the description of the sufferer's triumph and the lessons learned from that (vv. 14–18). The returning victor, in verse 19, requests the opening of the gates (to the temple, probably); is responded to by the priests (v. 20); offers a prayer of thanksgiving addressed to the Deity (v. 21); is answered/responded to by the assembly of people or a choir (vv. 22–24), who then ask God for salvation (v. 25). The priest (v. 26a) and people (v. 26b) proclaim blessing on the returning hero and offer a confession (v. 27, which is textually very difficult). The rescued monarch offers a short prayer of thanksgiving (v. 28), and the people are called upon to praise God (v. 29).

The king's description of his distress and redemption begins in verse 5 and extends through verse 18. The monarch describes his suffering as being surrounded by the nations and attacked by fierce enemies. It is uncertain whether the psalm describes an actual battle or whether this description was a standard version that could be used from time to time; that is, on those occasions when the king returned from battle as a winner, not a loser. The battle can, of course, be seen as one of the representative battles of good/God's elect against the bad/the enemies/the nations. In some Near Eastern cultic dramas, the king and his god fought the powers of evil and chaos at the New Year celebration. In Christian tradition, Jesus is said, according to the old form of the Apostles' Creed, to have "descended into hell." Jesus' "harrowing of hell" involved his invasion of Satan's domain and thus was a struggle with hostile powers. In this psalm there are parallels to this harrowing of hell and the king's fight against his enemies.

Verse 14 summarizes the confessional point of the previous verses, affirming that God is the origin of the ruler's strength and the source of his song. Verses 15–16 note the victory songs sung by the king's forces following their triumph, which is ascribed to the right hand (the clean hand, the strong hand) of Yahweh. After an actual battle, one can imagine the troops feasting, dancing, and celebrating at the site of their triumph.

The struggle of the king—like the struggle of Jesus—is depicted in verses 17–18 as a struggle with death. The real enemy, the final annihilator, is death. Thus the king can explain his success in battle as God's not letting him fall into the power of death. Again, the parallels with Easter should be obvious.

The litany of entering the temple gates (vv. 19–20) can be compared with similar entry liturgies in Psalms 15 and 24. Inside the temple precincts, the monarch offers thanks (v. 21). Verse 22 may be seen either as part of the king's thanksgiving and thus a continuation of verse 21, or else as part of the community's response and proclamation and thus a link with verses 23–24. At any rate, the theme of verse 22, like the Easter theme, emphasizes the movement from humiliation/rejection to exaltation/glorification. A stone (= the king = Jesus) that has been rejected by the builders (= the nations = the Jews/Romans) as unworthy and a possible structural defect has been elevated to a place of prominence (= the corner of the building = the king's victory in battle = Jesus' resurrection).

Psalm 150

This final psalm in the Psalter concludes the book with a great and universal call to praise God. As such, it may be seen not only as the fitting conclusion to the book as a whole but also as a statement of faith and confidence in the future. How different the Book of Psalms would have been had it concluded with a moaning and depressing lament!

The tenfold repetition of the call to praise in the body of the psalm is the most characteristic feature of this psalm. Like other examples of the number ten in the Bible, it was probably chosen deliberately both as a memory device (note that we have ten fingers) and as an affirmation of completion or fullness. The two hallelujahs ("Praise the Lord") at the beginning and end are opening and closing liturgical statements that bring the number to twelve.

Three factors in the praise of God are noted: the places of praising (v. 1), the reasons for praising (v. 2), and the means of praise (vv. 3–5).

The places of praising are the temple, which was considered the center point of the universe in late Jewish thought, and the firmament, which was considered the dome or heavens encircling the universe. Praise should thus extend from the center outward to the whole of creation and include every living thing (see v. 6).

The reasons for praise are God's "mighty deeds" and "his surpassing greatness." Thus both divine action and divine being are stressed.

The means of praise are multiple musical instruments of all types. This call to orchestrated adulation suggests something of what went on in festive worship services in the temple. The one medium of praising God that is noted, which is not a musical instrument, is the dance. Throughout the Bible, dancing is associated with celebration and joy (see Exod. 15:19–21; Ps. 30:11), and it probably played a significant role in Israelite worship.

Revelation 1:4–8

In the cycle of Sundays of Easter, the epistolary readings for Years A, B, and C are taken from First Peter, First John, and Revelation respectively. In keeping with the buoyant mood celebrated in the great Easter octave, the fifty-day period that extends from Easter to Pentecost, they are intended to elicit emotions of confidence, joy, and hope.

We should also note that this text serves as the epistolary reading in Year B for Proper 29 [34], which celebrates Christ the King, or Reign of Christ. The reader may want to consult our remarks on this text in Volume B.

As a text for the Second Sunday of Easter, this highly stylized lection from the first chapter of the Johannine apocalypse exudes a feeling of triumph and confident hope. We should first note its structure. It is in the form of an epistolary greeting: "John to the seven churches that are in Asia" (v. 4). To these churches, grace and peace are extended from a threefold source: God, the seven spirits, and Jesus Christ (vv. 4–5). Then follows an acclamation to Christ for what he has done in our behalf (vv. 5b–6). At this point, there is a shift from his past work to his eschatological work. In words reminiscent of the vision of the coming Son of Man in Daniel 7, our eyes are directed toward the future when Christ will appear on the clouds, visible to all. His will be the last word. Finally, in verse 8, our text concludes with the note on which it began: a declaration of the Lord God, the Alpha and Omega, the One who encompasses all of time.

Clearly, the Spirit plays only a minor role in this magnificent text. We receive greetings from "the seven spirits who are before [God's] throne" (v. 4; cf. 3:1; 4:5; 5:6). This is most likely a way of underscoring the fullness of God's Spirit as it is variously manifested.

The God who greets us is defined with respect to time. The present, past, and future are God's in an absolute sense. The formulation here represents an extension of the declaration in Exodus 3:14, "I AM WHO I AM." At the end of the passage, this is amplified with God's own confession as the "Alpha and Omega" (v. 8). Just as these letters respectively begin and end the Greek alphabet, so does God stand at both the beginning and end of time. As such, God is to be understood as both the source from which time and history derive, and its *telos*, the polestar toward which all history moves.

But the setting in the ring is provided by Christ. He is first proclaimed, or confessed, in a threefold manner: (1) as faithful witness, (2) firstborn of the dead, and (3) ruler of kings on earth (v. 5). The progression of thought here seems to be chronological. In his earthly life, he demonstrated complete fidelity even as he died as a witness, or martyr, of the faith (5:9). The second stage points to his resurrection. As one raised from the dead, he became the first to experience resurrected life. Among all the dead, his "birth" to new life made him the first child of life. The third stage points to the dominion that is his as exalted Lord. It is one where he reigns preeminently over every earthly ruler as King of kings, Lord of lords (17:14; 19:16).

Our text does not merely attest the preeminence of Christ; it also unfolds the ways he has benefited us. He is the one "who loves us and has freed us from our sins by his blood" (v. 5). Indeed, his own reign he has transferred to us (cf. Col. 1:13–14), and we have become his own priests officiating on his behalf (cf. 1 Pet. 2:5). Because of this, we ascribe to him eternal glory and dominion.

The text does not end, however, until we are confronted with the future. It is a time of both promise and threat, but especially of threat to those who conspired against him. His judgment will be universal: "All the peoples of the world shall lament in remorse" (v. 7, REB).

The language of today's text is confessional through and through. We are hearing the early church at worship as it acclaims God as Alpha and Omega and Christ as faithful witness, firstborn of the dead, and ruler of all the kings of the earth. But these words are addressed to churches in crisis that are under threat, who are assured that the enemies of Christ will eventually be confronted by him in judgment. Those who are being threatened with extinction must be reminded that God stands both at the beginning and end, else their hope vanishes.

John 20:19–31

The Easter Season provides opportunities for the church to reflect on the biblical witness concerning the disciples' experiences of the risen Christ and to appropriate anew the blessing upon those who have not seen and yet who believe (v. 29). As stated in comments on the Gospel for Easter Day (John 20:1–18), the Fourth Evangelist provides testimony to the resurrection in the form of parallel "double-stories": two disciples and Mary Magdalene (vv. 1–18) and ten disciples and Thomas (vv. 19–29). Each double-story speaks of faith (the beloved disciple, v. 8; the ten disciples, v. 20) and of doubt overcome by a special appearance of Christ (Mary Magdalene, vv. 11–18; Thomas, vv. 24–29). These four experiences of the Risen Christ are certainly not random examples by the writer; they are recounted as further testimony to a central conviction in this Gospel that there are different types and levels of faith. Throughout the book, the Evangelist has shown that there is faith based on signs and there is faith that needs none; there is faith weak and faith strong; faith shallow and faith deep; faith growing and faith faltering. In this Gospel, faith is not a decision made once but a decision made anew in every situation. As a case in point, notice that the last "convert" in this Gospel is Thomas, already a disciple, even one of the Twelve. This understanding of faith should encourage as well as instruct members of the church who are made to feel guilty that their faith was not born full grown in one dramatic experience.

We focus now on John 20:19–31 with four observations that grow out of the text. The first concerns Thomas. Even though this Gospel elsewhere portrays him as courageously devoted to Jesus (11:16) and theologically alert (14:5); even though a noncanonical Gospel bears his name; even though tradition associates him with a mission to India, Thomas has been, because of this text, tagged "Doubting Thomas." But see him in the Johannine context. The beloved disciple believed with no evidence but an empty tomb, Mary Magdalene believed because of a word, and the ten disciples believed because they saw the Lord (v. 20). But for the absent Thomas, faith could come only with difficulty; too much was at stake. He could be sure only after physical contact (v. 25), but whether he actually touched Jesus is not clear (vv. 27–29). For some, faith is as gentle as a child on grandmother's lap, but for others, it is continual wrestling with doubt.

Our second observation concerns Jesus' response to Thomas (v. 29): "Blessed are those who have not seen and yet have come to believe." This statement is most important, for the Evangelist has been concerned throughout the Gospel to assure his readers that faith is no less a possibility for them than for the original disciples. Faith is available to all persons in all places and times with no loss of efficacy due to distance from Jesus of Nazareth. Therefore, having recited different ways faith was generated in the earliest Christian community, the writer pronounces upon the readers the blessing of Jesus Christ. This blessing complements the prayer of Jesus in 17:20: "I ask not only on behalf of these, but also on behalf of those who will believe in me through their word."

The third observation has to do with the gift of the Holy Spirit. The promise of the Spirit, so repeatedly given by Jesus in the farewell discourses (chaps 14–16), is here fulfilled: "He breathed on them, and said to them, 'Receive the Holy Spirit'" (v. 22). Brief as it is, this is the Johannine Pentecost. Whereas many functions and benefits of the Spirit are stated in chapters 14–16, only here are the apostles given authority to grant or refuse to grant forgiveness of sin (v. 23; Matt. 16:19; 18:18). Through the apostles the church is joined in continuity of mission, authority, and benefit to Jesus Christ.

Finally, verses 30–31 obviously are a conclusion, not to the preceding narrative alone but to the entire Gospel. There may have been a time when the Gospel closed here, before chapter 21 was added as an epilogue. If so, the Evangelist's last word was to state as the purpose of the gospel the generation of faith. Because the book assumes that the readers already have some faith in Jesus Christ, this purpose is clearly to clarify, inform, and deepen faith to the end that it be full and life-giving. The last word to the world that crucified Jesus is not a judging but a gracious word: "That through believing you may have life in his name" (v. 31). The assurance of 3:16 has not been forgotten: "For God so loved the world."

Third Sunday of Easter

Acts 9:1–6 (7–20);
Psalm 30;
Revelation 5:11–14;
John 21:1–19

The texts for this season help us recall the beginnings of the church. In that context, the readings for today concern the call and commissioning of two apostles by means of encounters with the risen Lord. The First Lesson gives us the account of the conversion of Saul of Tarsus and his designation as a "chosen instrument" of the Lord (Acts 9:15). The psalm, with its emphasis on healing and recovering from life-threatening illness, is especially related thematically to Saul's blindness and healing. The Second Lesson is part of the vision of angels around the throne of God, singing praises to the Lamb who was slain. The Gospel reading reports the appearances of the risen Lord to Peter, whom he commissions to feed his sheep.

Acts 9:1–6 (7–20)

In today's text, Luke presents us with a narrative account of the conversion of Saul of Tarsus. It is the first of three tellings of this dramatic confrontation with the risen Lord. The other two occur as part of Paul's defense speeches (22:3–21; 26:9–23). Paul himself does not give us such a detailed, full-blown account, but he does insist that his prophetic call to be God's messenger to the Gentiles was a dramatic reversal in his life (Gal. 1:12–17).

As the opening text for the Third Sunday of Easter, this account of Paul's conversion serves as Luke's reminder to us that the appearances of the risen Lord were not confined to Easter Day. Not only does the Lord appear to Saul, but to Ananias as well (v. 10), and this is only one of many such dramatic visions in Acts (10:3, 17, 19; 11:5; 12:9; 16:9–10; 18:9; 22:17–21; 23:11; 27:23). In Luke's view, Easter is not confined to a single day. Instead, the risen Lord continues to be the energizing force in the church.

There is some question whether this lesson is best read as an account of Paul's "conversion" or as his prophetic call. Certainly, Paul interprets this experience in terms reminiscent of Old Testament call narratives (Gal. 1:15; cf. Isa. 49:1; Jer. 1:4–5). Luke's accounts also exhibit similar features. The risen Lord employs the double address "Saul, Saul" (v. 4; also 26:14), which recalls similar instances in the Old Testament where Yahweh issues a summons to Jacob (Gen. 46:2), Moses (Exod. 3:4), and Samuel (1 Sam. 3:4). In a later account, Paul relates that he was divinely commissioned while praying in a trance in the temple (Acts 22:17–21). This bears close resemblance to the famous prophetic call of Isaiah (6:1–13). It is also profitable to compare Saul's conversion with that of Heliodorus recorded in 2 Maccabees 3:22–40 (cf. also 4 Macc. 4:1–14).

In any event, Paul's record as a persecutor of the church is well established, both by his own testimony and that of Acts (1 Cor. 15:9; Gal. 1:13, 23; Phil. 3:6; Acts 8:3; 22:4, 19; 26:10–11). We are on firm historical ground at this point.

The basic elements of the story are well known. Saul is introduced as the archenemy of the church, described here as "the Way" (cf. 18:26; 19:9, 23; 22:4; 24:14, 22). Raging with fury, he searches out Christian men and women, and drags them tied and bound before the authorities in Jerusalem (cf. 1 Macc. 15:21). En route to Damascus, he is knocked to the ground by a lightning bolt from heaven and out of the dazzling light hears the voice of the risen Lord. The text makes it clear that Saul alone experienced this "appearance" (v. 7; cf. 1 Cor. 15:8).

Blinded and dazed, Saul is led to Damascus where he encounters Ananias, God's appointed messenger, who trembles at the thought of meeting this persecutor whose reputation has preceded him. Ever obedient (v. 10; cf. 1 Sam. 3:1–9), Ananias listens to God's charge, which serves as a cameo portrait of the Paul who is presented in Acts 13–28. He is a "chosen vessel" (v. 15, KJV) destined to be God's witness before Gentiles (13:47; 26:17; 28:28; cf. Rom. 1:5, 13–14, 16; 11:13; 15:15–19; Gal. 1:16; 2:2, 8, 9; Eph. 3:8; Col. 1:27; 1 Tim. 2:7), kings (25:13, 23; 26:1; 27:24), and Israel (13:16–43; passim). His will also be a mission of suffering (v. 16), which is elaborately attested in Luke's story of Paul (e.g., 14:19–23).

Ananias finds Saul, lays his hands on him (cf. 6:6; 8:17–19; 13:3; 19:6; 28:8), and bestows on him the Holy Spirit (cf. Luke 1:15, 41, 67; Acts 2:4; 4:8, 31; 9:17; 13:9, 52; 19:6). In response, Saul submits to baptism for the forgiveness of his sins (cf. 22:16) and, after regaining his strength, begins immediately to proclaim in the synagogues of Damascus Jesus as the Son of God (13:33; Luke 22:70).

Even though Luke clearly regards Paul's conversion as a special case and describes it as a way of underscoring his unique role as the apostle to the Gentiles, beyond that it is also instructive. Luke sketches for us a portrait of one prepared by God for a special mission. Thus Paul emerges as another in a long line of divinely commissioned designees who moves out in obedient response, even when it means radically departing from his past and being plunged into suffering as a way of life.

Psalm 30

This psalm of thanksgiving was originally composed for use in a worship service celebrating a worshiper's being healed from some life-threatening illness. As a thanksgiving song, it calls upon the audience accompanying the worshiper (family, friends, fellow villagers) to join in the celebration (v. 4) and to listen to the testimony and preaching of the one healed (vv. 5–6).

Verses 1–3 spell out part of the experience undergone by the worshiper. As usual, the sickness and healing are described in very general categories, for the psalm would have been employed on numerous occasions for different persons with different conditions of illness involved. Sheol and Pit in verse 3 refer to the realm of the dead. Here they do not mean that the individual died; rather, they are used metaphorically. To be subject to any form of sickness was already to be in the grip of Sheol, to be under the power of death. Weakness in life could be spoken of as being under the power of death. The verbs speaking of the rescue—"drawn me up," "healed," "brought up," "restored"—also use spatial images. These factors allowed such psalms as Psalm 30 to be used in the early church when talking about the resurrection (note the use of Ps. 16:8–11 in Acts 2:25–28).

Verse 4 is a call to fellow participants to join in the festivities of the thanksgiving celebration. Verse 6 seems to imply that the worshiper had earlier gone through a phase of life unconcerned with the Deity. This would have been in a period when things were prospering well and before the onset of trouble (see Deut. 8:11–20). If this is the case, one may assume that this attitude was one the worshiper was warning against. "Don't be as I was"—assuming that nothing could threaten life's prosperity. This may be said to be the anthropological lesson, what the case shows about human nature. The second lesson is theological, having to do with the character of God (v. 5). God's anger may be bitter and the reality of divine punishment strong, but these are transitory. It is divine favor and goodwill that are lasting. Tomorrow and the dawn can bring a new day. (This last description is probably based on the fact that worshipers spent the night in the temple and were given divine oracles in conjunction with the morning sacrifice.) This same imagery has impressed itself indelibly in the Christian vocabulary as a consequence of the Easter story.

Verses 7–12 of the psalm are a direct address to the Deity—a thanksgiving prayer perhaps offered in conjunction with a thanksgiving sacrifice. As in most thanksgiving psalms, the speaker or psalm-user rehearses the "before" conditions and then what happened. That is, the psalm contains a statement of the distress from which one was saved and sometimes, as in verses 8–10, a summary of the prayer offered at the time of the sickness. The substance of these verses reflects something of a plea bargaining. The worshiper suggests that nothing is to be gained by death; in fact, it would result in a loss to the Deity—namely, the loss of a faithful worshiper who could no longer offer praise to God in the dust of death.

The "after" vocabulary dominates in verses 11–12. Sackcloth and mourning have been replaced with dancing and gladness. The tears of nightfall have been replaced with the joy that comes in the morning.

Revelation 5:11–14

In today's epistolary reading, we hear the angelic hosts of heaven singing praise to God and the Lamb. It occurs as the last panel of the grand heavenly vision that stretches through two chapters (4:1–5:14). This is the first of several such visions depicted in Revelation. It occurs after the letters to the seven churches of Asia (2:1–3:22). At the outset, we get a glimpse of what is to come as John unfolds his vision of the Son of Man (1:9–20). But the scope of the vision in chapter 1 is far more narrow than the vision of chapters 4–5.

We are introduced to the vision through a door opening into heaven itself (4:1). We are first shown the magnificent heavenly throne splendidly furnished (cf. 4:2, 9–10; 5:1; 6:16; 7:10, 15; 19:4; 20:11; 21:5; also 1 Kings 22:19; 2 Chron. 18:18; Ps. 47:8; Isa. 6:1; Sir. 1:8). Surrounding this central throne are twenty-four other thrones where twenty-four elders are seated clad in priestly attire (4:4, 10; 5:5–8, 14; 7:11, 13; 11:16; 14:3; 19:4; cf. Isa. 24:23). Flashes of lightning and peals of thunder around the throne interrupt the quiet tranquillity we might expect. It is clear that we are in the presence of the Divine before whom all the elements quiver and shake.

The heavenly court includes more than the twenty-four elders. Encircling the throne are the four living creatures, presumably animals (4:6; 5:6, 8, 11, 14; 6:1; 7:11; 14:3; 15:7; 19:4). They resemble a lion, a bull, a human, and an eagle respectively. Each has six wings and is literally covered with eyes. They pour out unceasing praise to God who sits enthroned, and as they sing the twenty-four elders bow down in unison. We see an elaborate, lavishly furnished heavenly court genuflecting in unison as they honor the One at their center—the eternal God who made the universe.

Next our eyes are drawn to the right hand of the enthroned God (5:1–5). It holds a scroll written on both sides and sealed with seven seals. A book so thoroughly sealed can contain only the deepest of mysteries, but alas there is no one in the entire heavenly court who is able to break the seals. Then, out of the misty background there emerges the figure of the Lamb with all the signs of having been slaughtered. It has seven horns and seven eyes. As he moves toward center stage to take the scroll, those in the heavenly court pay him the homage they had previously given to God. Their song expresses their confidence in his ability and worthiness to break the seals (5:9–10). Because he bled as he died, his sacrificial slaughter has qualified him to break the seals and open the book.

It is at this point that today's text begins. First, the heavenly court has lavished praise on God who sits enthroned. Then it directs its attention to the slain Lamb of God. Now the chorus of voices widens to include thousands upon thousands of angels, heavenly figures who are not included in the immediate heavenly court (cf. Dan. 7:10; 1 Enoch 14:22; 40:1; Heb. 12:22). This host of angels is seen as an endless host circling the throne, the animals, and the elders. It is, as it were, a never-ending set of adoring heavenly beings arranged in concentric circles with their attention riveted toward the center.

The angels' song simply echoes that of the twenty-four elders and the four animals—praise to the slaughtered Lamb who is now ascribed every imaginable accolade: "power and wealth and wisdom and might and honor and glory and blessing!" (v. 12; cf. 7:12; 11:17; 12:10; 19:1–2; also 1 Chron. 29:11).

But the circle widens even farther to include not only the twenty-four elders, the four animals, and the angelic hosts, but every living creature "in heaven and on earth and under the earth and in the sea" (v. 13). The language used here is intended to suggest every imaginable region (cf. Exod. 20:4; Deut. 5:8; Ps. 146:6; also Phil. 2:10).

As this breathtaking, opening vision reaches its conclusion and we are prepared for the scene in which the Lamb breaks open the seven seals (chap. 6), the combined chorus of voices that includes every species of aerial, terrestrial, subterranean, and aquatic animal pays honor both to the God who sits enthroned and the slaughtered Lamb. This serves as a means of calling our attention, in closing, to the two chief figures of the vision—God and the Lamb. As a final gesture, the four animals say, "Amen!" and the twenty-four elders bow down.

If we allow ourselves to resonate with the imagery of this vision, we find that we are truly overwhelmed. This attests the immense power of apocalyptic language to engage us. If we allow it to work the way it was intended to work, as we move through the vision we find that we too are being "taken up" into heaven to peer through the open door along with John the Seer. Before long, we find ourselves singing the song of the heavenly host and bowing down in reverence and awe before the eternal God and Christ, the slain Lamb of God whose cause has finally been vindicated. We soon see ourselves among those of "every tribe and language and people and nation" who are made "a line of kings and priests" destined to serve God and rule the world (vv. 9–10, NJB). The Seer's vision, in other words, becomes our own vision.

John 21:1–19

First, a few words need to be said about John 21 as a whole.

John 21 is often referred to as an epilogue. To do so is not to imply lesser quality or authority but to indicate its literary relationship to the remainder of the Gospel. Clearly, the writer drew the Gospel to a conclusion at 20:30–31. In 21:1, "After these things" only loosely joins what follows to what precedes. In addition, verses 24–25 can be taken as the signature of a later hand, perhaps a disciple of the writer of chapters 1–20. But whether by the same or a later writer, a more pressing question has to do with the purpose of this chapter. What does it seek to achieve? Some commentators say that it corrects a rumor in the early church that the beloved disciple would never die. Verses 20–23 certainly explain the origin of the notion and set the record straight, but there is much in the chapter unrelated to that matter. Others say, to rehabilitate Simon Peter. Perhaps, for the one who denied Jesus three times here is given an opportunity to affirm his love three times (vv. 15–19). Simon Peter is certainly a prominent figure in most of the scenes in the chapter. The story confirms 1 Corinthians 15:5 and Luke 24:34, which speak of a resurrection appearance to Simon, and verses 4–8 have a parallel in Luke 5:3–7, in which attention focuses on Peter. In addition, the shepherd imagery of verses 15–19 is echoed in 1 Peter 5:1–5, a text associated with Simon Peter. However, this theory hardly fits the less than complimentary portrait of Simon, especially in verses 4–8 and 20–23, and the more favorable view of the beloved disciple (vv. 7, 20). Another common theory is that this chapter was added by someone favorable to Galilean Christianity who wanted to end the Gospel with a resurrection appearance in Galilee (21:1), as do Mark and Matthew, rather than in Jerusalem. Again, the theory is not adequate for all the material in the epilogue. Perhaps multiple purposes rather than a single one best fit the chapter.

The portion of chapter 21 providing today's lesson may be divided as follows: the setting (vv. 1–3); Jesus' appearance to the disciples (vv. 4–8); breakfast with Jesus (vv. 9–14); Jesus and Simon Peter (vv. 15–19). The scene at the Sea of Tiberias (Galilee) is more Synoptic than Johannine. In Mark 1:16–20, Jesus calls his first disciples from a life of fishing; according to John 1:35–42, the first disciples came to Jesus from following John the Baptist. John 1:43–45 agrees, however, that they were Galileans. The return to fishing implies that the disciples were unable to sustain Easter beyond resurrection appearances. Belief in the resurrection was an item of faith, but it had not been translated into life and mission in the world. The radical decline in church attendance and activity after Easter Sunday indicates that the problem is still with us. When Jesus appeared again (v. 4), it is as though the disciples had not seen the risen Christ before, even though this is the third appearance (v. 14). That which stirs them to faith is Jesus' supernatural knowledge (1:47–49; Luke 5:3–7) concerning the fish. As one has come to expect by now, the beloved disciple is the first to recognize Jesus (v. 7), just as he was the first to believe in the resurrection (20:8).

The breakfast by the sea (vv. 9–14) not only confirms that the risen Lord is the historical Jesus (he eats bread and fish), but recalls some of the most meaningful moments shared during Jesus' ministry. Although not a major theme in John, the other Gospels frequently portray Jesus at table. Early in the thinking and practice of the early church, eating together was an occasion for experiencing the presence of Christ (1 Cor. 11:23–24; Luke 24:28–35, 41–43). Fish and bread quickly came to have symbolic significance far beyond their value as staples of the common diet. Eating together confirmed and encouraged faith for living in the face of immense obstacles.

If the meal with Christ reflects early Christian worship, then worship was also a time of being confronted with Christ's penetrating question "Do you love me?" (vv. 15–19). The exchanges between Simon and Jesus reveal several strong accents in the theology of this Evangelist: faith is a personal relationship with Christ (15:1–8); this relationship has its expression not only in words but in obedience (14:15); one particular form of this obedience is caring for others as Christ did (10:1–17; 20:21); for some, such as Simon Peter, this obedience will result in martyrdom (16:2); but to all, wherever it may lead, the word by which discipleship began is the final word: "Follow me" (v. 19).

Fourth Sunday of Easter

Acts 9:36–43;
Psalm 23;
Revelation 7:9–17;
John 10:22–30

I t is the season of the beginning of the church, and one of the things that accompanied the growth of the early church was witness through the form of "good works and acts of charity" (Acts 9:36). Thus, the commendable example of Dorcas serves as the topic in today's First Lesson, reminding the church that mission often takes the form of responding to the needs of others. The psalmist's theme of the Lord as shepherd anticipates the Gospel reading, where Jesus responds to a challenge by asserting that his sheep hear his voice, he knows them, and they follow him. The Second Lesson is a portion of that vision of the redeemed before the throne of God.

Acts 9:36–43

T oday's First Lesson is the story of Peter's healing the celebrated woman from Joppa, known both by her Aramaic name Tabitha and her Greek name Dorcas, which means gazelle. Because her reputation in the tradition stems from her devotion to "good works and acts of charity" (v. 36), this text is rightfully given prominence in the Easter Season.

Actually, this story is one of a pair of healing stories that occur together at this point in Acts where Peter is reintroduced into the narrative. In Acts 9:32–43 we see him healing a paralytic and restoring to life a Christian woman renowned for her generosity.

As we read today's text, as well as the previous episode, we are expected to recall similar events in the life of Jesus: his healing a paralytic (Luke 5:17–26), raising a widow's son at Nain (Luke 7:11–17), and raising Jairus' daughter (Luke 8:40–56). This is Luke's way of emphasizing that Jesus' prophetic ministry did not end when he died; instead, it continues through the prophetic ministries of Peter, John, and others described in Acts. Peter thus continues the work that Jesus began.

But our minds are also expected to go back even further to recall similar episodes in the Old Testament. Today's text also echoes Elijah's raising the widow's son (1 Kings 17:17–24) and Elisha's raising the Shunammite woman's son (2 Kings 4:8–37). This has the effect of casting Peter more firmly in an Old Testament prophetic mold (cf. Luke 7:17–30). Later, Paul is similarly portrayed as having power to heal (Acts 14:8–11; 28:7–9) and raise the dead

(20:9–10). This second level of reminiscence enables us to see Peter standing in the same tradition as the Old Testament prophets.

Today's episode, then, underscores the continuing effects of the power of God within the messianic community. Luke is careful to note the dramatic impact of these events within the life of the church. In both instances, the effects of Jesus' power are visible: many people come to faith (vv. 35, 42).

This story is powerful at many levels. The portrait of Dorcas is all too familiar: she is a Christian disciple whose life has been devoted to the service of others and whose death leaves an enormous gap. When such folks die, loud laments occur, for there is always the chance that the good work they did will cease. Their death really makes a difference, because their life made such a difference. In Dorcas we are expected to see a concrete example—a named human example—of someone whose life bears witness to the power of the Easter faith.

But power of the Easter faith is seen not only through Dorcas, but through Peter as well. Through his prophetic ministry of word and deed—his healing of Aeneas and his raising of Dorcas—we are also shown the continuing effects of the risen Lord.

Today's text and the previous episode are especially poignant reminders of the way powerful witness occurs through the church's healing ministry. In neither case does Peter preach a sermon, yet in both cases dramatically powerful witness results. Outsiders can discern the Lord's presence through acts of mercy as well as through acts of speech, perhaps even more so.

Psalm 23

The choice of this psalm to accompany the reading from the Gospel of John is based on the psalm's use of imagery drawn from shepherding and on the sense of confidence that permeates the entire composition.

In spite of the fact that Psalm 23 is perhaps the best known of the psalms and that its overall thrust is quite clear, many questions still puzzle scholars about the original considerations that went into its writing. Was it a song of confidence and assurance for general use by the people? Or originally only by the king? Or by someone who had taken asylum and sought protection in the sanctuary because of some accident (perhaps manslaughter)? How is God described in the psalm? Only as a shepherd? Or as a shepherd and a dinner host? Is the psalmist described only as a sheep or also as a dinner guest?

In spite of such uncertainties, the psalm's emphasis on the nature of God and divine actions as the source of human trust is quite clear. The psalmist faces the future unafraid because of confidence based on trust in Yahweh.

Two sets of images can be seen running throughout the psalm: images of trouble and danger and images of assurance and tranquillity. The psalm does not assume a Pollyanna attitude that reads all of life optimistically and expects good everywhere. The writer takes no sunshine, everything-will-be-okay attitude toward existence.

The following are the terms and images used to speak of the negative aspects, the troubles of life: (1) the "shadow of death," (see NRSV footnote) or "the darkest valley"; (2) evil; and (3) enemies. The very fact that troubles are given such a place in the psalm has contributed to its appeal. It rings true to life.

The positive images of protection and assurance predominate in the psalm. Note the following: "green pastures" and "still waters," which provide food and drink to restore one's physical vitality and life (NRSV: "restores my soul"); leads along right paths (RSV: "paths of righteousness") so as to avoid danger; a rod and staff offer protection against predators and direction to the would-be prey; "a table" spread with all the accompanying accoutrements like oil for the body and wine for the spirit; and finally a dwelling in the house of Yahweh (the temple) to the length of a person's days (not "for ever" as in the RSV). To dwell in the temple might be taken literally and understood to refer to a manslayer claiming asylum (see Deut. 19:1–10), to some cultic personnel who served continuously in the temple (see 1 Chron. 9:33), or it might be a metaphorical way of expressing the opportunity to visit the temple (see Pss. 15:1; 24:3).

Revelation 7:9–17

B efore we look at today's text, perhaps we should fill in the gap between this and last week's epistolary reading. After the panoramic vision of God enthroned amid the heavenly court is completed (4:1–5:14), the Lamb proceeds with his appointed task of opening the seven seals of the scroll (5:1). The opening of the first six seals is described in chapter 6. But before the opening of the seventh seal, which is related in 8:1–5, there is an interlude (chap. 7).

The interlude comprises two visions. The first is that of the 144,000 redeemed who enjoy divine protection (vv. 1–8). The second is that of a vast multitude of people who are gathered around the throne of God (vv. 9–17). It is this second vision that serves as today's epistolary lection.

The scene is the same as that depicted in the earlier vision described in chapters 4–5: God sitting enthroned, encircled by the heavenly court of the twenty-four elders, the four living beasts, and the angelic hosts (v. 11). As before, they praise God and the Lamb as those to whom full and final salvation belongs (v. 10; cf. 5:13; 11:15, 17; 12:10; 15:3–4; 19:1–2, 5, 6–8).

What is different this time is that the host of worshipers is now extended even further. The earlier vision ended with all living creatures, probably animals, ascribing worship to God (5:13). But now there is a vast, innumerable multitude drawn from all the peoples of the earth (v. 9; 5:9; 10:11; 11:9; 13:7; 14:6; 17:15). They are standing before the Lamb clothed in white robes (v. 9; cf. 3:4–5, 18; 4:4; 6:11; 19:14). They are also holding palm branches in their hands (cf. Lev. 23:40, 43; also 2 Macc. 10:7). Their white clothing symbolizes purity and righteousness; the branches, victory. As they ascribe salvation to God and the Lamb, the rest of the heavenly court bows in honorific response and pays similar tribute (vv. 11–12).

Because the members of this vast multitude are still unidentified, one of the elders asks the Seer who these white-clad persons are and where they have come from (v. 13). We are told that they are those who have endured the "great ordeal" (v. 14; cf. Dan. 12:1; Matt. 24:21 and parallels). Their robes have been purified through the blood of the Lamb (cf. Rev. 22:14; Gen. 49:11; Exod. 19:10, 14; also 1 John 1:7; Rev. 1:5; Heb. 9:14). They are, in other words, the martyred saints who have been vindicated by God and now form part of the heavenly company.

Their lot is now described (vv. 15–17). This eschatological vision has three features:

1. *Unceasing worship of God in the heavenly temple (v. 15).* They now center their attention around the heavenly throne, serving in the temple night and day (cf. 3:12; 11:1–2, 19; 14:15, 17; 15:5–6, 8; 16:1, 17; 21:22). They now enjoy the divine protection of God's own presence (cf. Ezek. 37:27).

2. *The absence of physical deprivation (v. 16).* Life with God in the heavenly court excludes hunger, thirst, and scorching heat. The description here is a direct quotation of Isaiah 49:10. Also excluded are tears (v. 17b; cf. Rev. 21:4; Isa. 25:8; Jer. 31:16).

3. *The presence of the Lamb in their midst as their shepherd (v. 17).* The Lamb is now envisioned as the Shepherd who lives and walks among his sheep (5:6; Ezek. 34:23). In language reminiscent of Psalm 23, the Shepherd guides the saints to springs of living water (Ps. 23:1–3; cf. also Rev. 21:6; Isa. 49:10).

One of the most obvious features of this text is its thematic connection with Psalm 23 and the Gospel reading (John 10:22–30). All three of these texts speak of shepherds, each in its distinctive way; but the epistolary text, as well as the Gospel text, shows the way in which the imagery of Psalm 23 was appropriated by the early church.

For some, depictions of the eschatological age such as we have here are too distant, too far removed from the world we know and live in. In this text, however, the people of God are central. The martyred saints have moved beyond this life and have begun to participate in the triumph of the heavenly court. The life sketched for them in verses 15–17 may be an eschatological ideal, but it is one to which we have all aspired at one time or another, in one way or another. One of the preacher's tasks in treating this text is to establish some link of continuity between life as depicted here and life as we know it—or wish it to be.

John 10:22–30

It is still Easter, but even Easter does not relieve the church of the task of engaging opposition and unbelief. Hence our lection for today. John 10:22–30 lies within the long section on controversies between Jesus and various opponents (5:1–10:42). Several times in this section Jesus is threatened with death on the charge of blasphemy. Even if that word is not mentioned, that is the issue because Jesus made himself equal with God (5:18; 8:58–59; 10:30–31). This death talk, though real, is ineffective, because in this Gospel, no one takes Jesus' life; he gives it (10:18) when his hour comes (12:23).

Some scholars speak of 10:22–30 as a duplicate passage because it repeats events and conversations centering in the Feast of Tabernacles (chaps. 7, 8). Here at the Feast of Dedication (v. 22), as during the Feast of Tabernacles, Jesus is in the vicinity of the temple. Jesus is pressed to declare openly who he is; Jesus refuses on the grounds that the people would not believe if he did; Jesus declares his unity with God; an attempt is made on Jesus' life. The lines of repetition are evident, but the time, place, and issue at stake still deserve attention.

The controversy in 10:22–30 occurs in Jerusalem, in Solomon's portico, during the Feast of Dedication. This feast is the Feast of Hanukkah, observed in the winter (v. 22), near the time of the Christian celebration of Christmas. Hanukkah commemorated the Maccabean victory over the Syrians about 160 BC, the recovery of the temple, and the consecration of the altar, which had been profaned by the Syrians. Already in this Gospel, Jesus' signs, speeches, and controversies have been presented as occurring on other feast days: Sabbath, Passover, and Tabernacles. In this Evangelist's theology, Jesus fulfills and brings to an end Judaism with all its festivals and traditions. Although the follower of Jesus celebrates this understanding, opposition to it and to Jesus by those who hold dear these traditions is to be expected. And it is important to keep in mind that in this Gospel, the Jews are not only the Jews, but they represent "the world" that does not believe. Church history makes it abundantly clear that "the world" is inside as well as outside the circle of disciples. Our text addresses conditions within the church in which customs, places, traditions, and rituals are held so firmly that the total adequacy of Christ is obscured, if not denied.

Again Jesus is pressed to state clearly if he is the Christ (v. 24). He refuses to answer for two reasons. First, his questioners would not believe even if he told them (vv. 25–26). They have the witness of Jesus' works, but they are unconvinced. In 5:30–47 the testimonies to Christ are listed—John the Baptist, the Scriptures, God, and Jesus' works—and yet the controversy continues. As Chrysostom put it, they do not believe, not because Jesus is not a shepherd but because they are not sheep. The second reason Jesus does not tell them he is the Christ is that "Christ," or "Messiah," is not an adequate term to identify who Jesus is. He is the Messiah, but the term had been so shaped by the expectations and wishes of the people that it was hardly possible to say yes to the question without creating false hopes. When an expectation is distorted, the fulfillment of that expectation gets distorted. The first task of a messiah is to get people to quit looking for a messiah. Jesus moves his auditors beyond the idea of "messiah" to "son of God." The crucial claim is stated in verse 30: "The Father and I are one." It is for this claim that attempts are made on Jesus' life (5:18; 8:58–59; 10:30–31, 36–39).

The line of thought in verses 26–29 seems to be circular: my sheep are the ones who believe, and those who believe are my sheep. Some light may be shed by two comments on Johannine theology. First, faith is a possibility for those who will to do the will of God (7:17). Although faith is a complex theme in this Gospel, one theme is consistent: for those who stand back, arms folded, waiting to be convinced, final proof is never enough. Those who enter the flock hear the shepherd's voice. Second, in this Gospel, Jesus is the revelation—of God, from above, whose ministry is not contingent on any human act or word or request. Even toward his mother (2:3–4), his brothers (7:3–9), and his friends (11:3–6), Jesus behaves according to "his hour"; that is, all directives are from above. So complete is this initiative from above that even Jesus' disciples are those chosen, given of God. In our language, this is a radical understanding of grace: all is of God, not of our choosing. It is inevitable that strong statements of grace sound very much like determinism. Alongside such affirmations, however, are others that announce freely that whoever believes has life eternal (3:16–17). Christian faith lives by and witnesses to both statements: all is of God, and yet whosoever will.

Fifth Sunday of Easter

Acts 11:1–18;
Psalm 148;
Revelation 21:1–6;
John 13:31–35

The readings for this day are rich in their diversity. The First Lesson provides a summary account of one of the most pivotal moments in the life of the early church—Peter's preaching to Cornelius and the latter's subsequent conversion. As a psalm of praise, Psalm 148 picks up the theme of praise from the first reading. Once the Jerusalem Christians recognized that God had been at work in Cornelius's conversion, they broke out in praise of God. John's vision of a new heaven and a new earth, with all things new, supplies the second reading, and it challenges us to think of what might be rather than what is. In the Gospel lection, a great deal is presented in a few verses: Jesus' assertion that God is glorified in the glorification of the Son of Man, his assertion that no one can go where he is going, his gift of the new commandment "that you love one another," and the message that his disciples are known by their love for one another.

Acts 11:1–18

Because these verses aptly summarize the more extended description of Peter's encounter with Cornelius recorded in Acts 10, they appropriately serve as today's first reading. Any event this important deserves our attention during the period after Easter.

What makes this set of events so crucially important in the life of the early church, of course, is its watershed character. As the first bonafide non-Jew to join the Christian movement, Cornelius becomes a symbolic figure. His conversion raises all the natural questions that occur when something truly innovative occurs. Who should be included within the circle of the people of God? Are the traditional boundary markers still to be observed? If tradition prevents Jews and Gentiles from associating with each other, what happens when the old social distinctions no longer exist? How are they to relate to each other within a newly configured people of God?

We are hardly surprised to hear that Peter's mission initiative with Cornelius was criticized by the "circumcised believers" (v. 2; REB: "those who were of Jewish birth"). Their objection appears to have been twofold: Peter not only took the initiative to launch a mission to "uncircumcised men"; he engaged in table fellowship with them. He thus broke two taboos: he dared to redefine who should be included in God's fellowship; and having done so, he sealed his decision with an overt social action that symbolized full acceptance.

It is little wonder, then, that Luke uses valuable space to allow Peter to rehearse his actions "step by step" (v. 4). Those familiar with the Old Testament would know that dreams can be events of great import, especially when the dreamer and God are in conversation. And as this dream unfolds, we hear God challenging some of Peter's most deeply held convictions. Every bit of his past had reinforced the distinction between clean and unclean. He had been brought up learning to ask whether the food he was about to eat was kosher. Was it beef or pork? Where did it come from? How was it slaughtered? All this was done to ensure that nothing "profane or unclean" would ever cross his lips (v. 8).

And yet the very God who was presumably responsible for having invented these distinctions was commanding him to ignore them. Peter is instructed by God, "kill and eat" (v. 7). Even further, Peter is told, "What God has made clean, you must not call profane" (v. 9). Peter is being told by God that the distinctions he is used to no longer hold. His universe of meaning is being challenged to the core.

The reader knows all too tell that the animal vision symbolizes the vast diversity of humankind. We are being told in the most vividly memorable terms that the distinctions traditionally made between Jews and Gentiles do not hold. And to reinforce the point, at every stage God is the prime mover in these events. The vision comes to Peter in a dream—from without, not within. God's Spirit instructs Peter to accompany the three men to Caesarea (v. 12). From the start of Peter's sermon, the Holy Spirit was present, pouring out its power (v. 15). As he preaches, something clicks in his own mind as he recalls that Jesus himself had given his sanction to all of this in advance (v. 16). It was not a human decision to extend the Spirit to these outsiders; it was rather God who "gave them the same gift that he gave us when we believed in the Lord Jesus" (v. 17). Peter realizes that he and Cornelius are experientially equal: they have both tasted the good things of God, and they have done so at God's choosing, not their own. Peter knows God well enough to know that he was not about to try to thwart God's plans (v. 17).

Peter's summary is vivid and overwhelming enough to convince these tough critics. In fact, they are speechless (v. 18). But silence gives way to praise, and even they finally admit that "God has given even to the Gentiles the repentance that leads to life" (v. 18). Note the wording *"even to the Gentiles"*! We hear a note of incredulity. Perhaps it is incredulity that stems from a deep-seated sense of religious superiority that has now been severely challenged. But it is incredulity that gives way to praise of God. Better this than nothing.

In the aftermath of Easter, we do well to remind ourselves of the ongoing power of the Easter faith, and that even its truth is revealed in stages. Luke knows full well that not one, but two conversions occurred in these events: that of Cornelius and that of Peter. Peter's world was reconfigured every bit as much as was Cornelius's world, perhaps even more so. Redefining boundaries always generates controversy, especially when they mark off groups of people from each other. And there is always cause for rejoicing when they are erased with such dramatic effect.

Psalm 148

Psalms 146–150 constitute a small collection of hymns of praise. All begin and conclude with the cultic shout "Hallelujah" that calls upon the community to "praise Yahweh," "praise the Lord."

Psalm 148 consists of two types of genres: two extended calls to praise (vv. 1–4, 7–12) and two statements giving the reason or rationale for praise (vv. 5–6, 13–14).

The psalm is an exuberant summons for the whole of creation to join in shouting out and celebrating the name and glory of Yahweh. Practically no aspect of creation is omitted in the call to praise: angels, heavenly hosts, sun and moon, shining stars, highest heavens, waters above the heavens, sea monsters and all deeps, fire and hail, snow and frost, stormy wind, mountains and hills, fruit trees and all cedars, wild animals and all cattle, creeping things and flying birds, kings, princes, rulers, young men and women, old and young. What a chorus!

In spite of its tone, Psalm 148 should not be faulted for a Pollyanna perspective on life. There are times when unbounded jubilation should reign and carry us to the limits of celebration, to the borders of insanity, and to the heights of self-transcendence. Few are the times when the whole world is a chorus and the music of the spheres invades every nook and cranny of existence. Their scarcity should only endear their occurrence. It is only in such moments that we can spiritually and sensually realize the truth that modern ecology has taught us. We are all—from shining star to slithering snake—in this together, and we need to sing, at least occasionally, the same song and join in a common medley.

The psalm offers two reasons undergirding such praise. The first (in vv. 5–6) declares that Yahweh is the creator of all, who has established everything and set a law that cannot pass away (NRSV margin). The created order is divine handiwork in which every part serves its function within a created natural order (see Jer. 5:22–24; 31:35–36). The second (in vv. 13–14) alludes to the rule of the Davidic monarch, the horn raised up for the people of Israel. (On the horn as the symbol of strength and royalty, see 1 Sam. 2:10; Pss. 75:4–5; 89:17, 24; 92:10; 112:9; 132:17; Lam. 2:3, 17.) The psalm thus anchors praise in the divine rule in the universe and the messianic rule over the chosen people.

Revelation 21:1–6

As we move through the epistolary lessons in the Sundays of Easter, we gradually progress toward the final vision of the last things, including the vision of the New Jerusalem. Today's epistolary lection consists of one part of that final, grand vision that stretches from 21:1–22:5.

Obviously, its liturgical setting is the season between Easter and Pentecost, and this will cause us to see certain themes more than others. But we should remember that this well-known text also figures in other parts of the lectionary, most notably as the First Lesson for the observance of All Saints' Day in Year B and as the Second Lesson for the observance of January 1 when observed as New Year's Eve or Day in Years A, B, and C. The reader may want to consult our remarks in these other settings.

We should begin by noting that this is an apocalyptic vision. We are invited by the Seer to share his vision of "a new heaven and a new earth" (v. 1). As such, it is the fulfillment of the prophetic promise (Isa. 65:17, 19–20; 66:22) toward which early Christian hope was directed (2 Pet. 3:13). To the apocalyptic mind, cosmic scenery could change with one stroke of the brush. Mountains could be moved, rivers redirected. The earth, sky, and sea could vanish before one's very eyes (cf. 6:14; 16:20; 20:11; also Ps. 114:3–4, 7–8; 2 Pet. 3:7, 10, 12). The point is that the world we once knew is no more. All is new.

Our eyes are next lifted up to the open heavens from which we see "the holy city, the new Jerusalem" descending (v. 2). It had become proverbial to think of Jerusalem as the "holy city" (11:2; 21:10; 22:19; cf. Neh. 11:1, 18; Isa. 48:2; 52:1; Dan. 9:24; Matt. 4:5; 27:53). When Christians envisioned heaven, it became natural to do so as the heavenly Jerusalem (Gal. 4:26; Heb. 11:16, 12:22; also Rev. 3:12). The picture is enhanced even further with the introduction of bridal imagery, already used earlier (19:7, 9) and influenced by the Old Testament (Isa. 61:10; cf. Matt. 22:2).

We have already been introduced to the great white throne on which God is seated (20:11). From this throne comes a loud voice that utters an oracle that interprets the vision (vv. 3–4). Two elements are worth noting:

1. God's presence is really meant to be within the people of God. Literally, God's tabernacle is with human beings (13:6; cf. John 1:14). This represents the fulfillment of the fondest prophetic hope that God and the people of God would find their mutual home in and with each other (Lev. 26:12; Ps. 95:7; Jer. 31:1, 33; Ezek. 37:27; Zech. 2:10–11; cf. 2 Cor. 6:16).

2. The presence of God among the people of God means the removal of all human hurt. Everything that once pained us and brought us to tears is now gone, again as the prophets had always hoped (Isa. 25:8; 43:18; 65:17–18; Jer. 31:16, cf. Rev. 7:17). In particular, there is no more death, the most painful of human realities (Isa. 35:10; 51:11; Rev. 20:4; 1 Cor. 15:26).

As if it were not clear how radically different this view of life is, the enthroned God continues the interpretation, proclaiming, "See, I am making all things new" (v. 5). It had been an old promise (Isa. 43:19) now made possible through the Christ-event (2 Cor. 5:17).

The Seer is instructed to write all this down and is assured that it is an absolutely reliable vision (v. 5). With a word of finality he further asserts, "It is done!" (v. 6; cf. 16:17) and is identified as the "Alpha and the Omega" (cf. 1:8; 22:13). The final words of reassurance in today's lection (which breaks off with verse 6, but could easily be extended through verse 8) are that God stands at the fountain of living water, dispensing water free of charge to the thirsty (cf. 7:16–17; 22:1, 17; John 7:37; Isa. 55:1; Jer. 2:13; Zech. 14:8).

Only those with anemic imaginations can fail to be gripped by this vision of the new heaven and new earth. There has never been a human soul steeped in the human condition who has not pined for a radically new world. Whether it is Marx sketching the ideal economic state or Lennon crying for us to "imagine" a peaceful world, the hope is always for something different—and better. What is striking about the Seer's vision in today's text is that in this new world God is the central figure. Whatever else may be hoped for, the Seer sees no chance apart from the mutual indwelling of God and the people of God. The faith of Easter is that this is now possible through the risen Christ in a way otherwise unimaginable.

John 13:31–35

Our Gospel for today falls within that portion of John's Gospel generally referred to as the farewell materials. The public ministry of Jesus ended at 12:50; 13:1–30 records the farewell meal; and 13:31–17:26 consists of farewell discourses and prayer. This entire section is presented as occurring on a single evening, concluding in the garden where Jesus was arrested (18:1). As farewell material, it is both the preparation of Jesus' disciples for his coming death and the message of the glorified Christ to the church preparing them for life in the world following his departure. No other Gospel so extensively deals with the absence of Jesus, the first major crisis for the disciples.

Today's lection consists of Jesus' words spoken at table following the last meal he had with the Twelve. According to John 13:1, the meal is before the Passover (Jesus dies on the day of preparation as the Passover lamb, 19:31–37) and is not the Passover meal as in the Synoptics (Mark 14:12 and parallels). John alone records the foot washing (13:1–20) and joins the Synoptics in recording Jesus' indication of his betrayer (vv. 21–30). Judas leaves the room (v. 30), and our lesson begins, "When he had gone out, Jesus said . . . ."

Brief as it is, 13:31–35 consists of three parts: Jesus' announcement of his glorification (vv. 31–32); Jesus' statement of his glorification in terms of departure from the disciples (v. 33); Jesus' instruction for their life together after his departure (vv. 34–35).

Because the glorification of the Son in this Gospel refers to the death, resurrection, and return to God, verses 31–32 are John's equivalent of a passion prediction. Here as in the Synoptics the announcement meets with confusion among the disciples (13:36–14:11; Mark 8:27–33; 9:30–37; 10:32–35), but there the parallels end. In the Synoptics, the predictions are in private; here Jesus has already told the Jews (v. 33). In the Synoptics, the predictions are followed by instructions on cross bearing, service, and childlikeness; here the disciples are commanded to love one another (vv. 34–35). Also unique to this Gospel is Jesus' translation of his announcement of glorification into terms that are personal and relational. "Little children, I am with you only a little longer. You will look for me . . . . 'Where I am going, you cannot come'" (v. 33). This is family talk; a group is about to lose the one who is their reason to be together. The key to their understanding what is happening and to their future is their relationship to Christ and to one another. The burden of Jesus' word to them is that their relation to him inform and determine their relation to one another. The "one another" here clearly refers to the members of the community of faith. There are, of course, texts urging love for all people, but that is not the thrust of this text. Here and in the prayer in chapter 17 the concern is for Christians relating to one another. The immediate need in the Johannine church was internal harmony. As is clear in 1 John 2–4, doctrinal disputes and differences in response to outside pressures were eroding the unity of the Johannine church. Love for one another was essential for the continued life of the community.

But in what sense is the command to love "new"? Certainly there is no implication that love was absent from their lives in the tradition of Judaism. Perhaps it was new in that the disciples were entering a new time of life in the world after Jesus' departure. Perhaps it was new in that only now had Jesus begun to talk this way to them. Or perhaps the nature of their love for one another was to be new: they were to love as he had loved them (v. 34). And what was the nature of that love? It was, according to this Gospel, a matter of telling the truth, being faithful in sharing the word of God, continuing to act *for* those who may not be responsive, and, if need be, to give one's life. If love is understood as acting toward one another as God has acted toward the world and as Christ has acted toward his disciples, then love is not simply a feeling. If love is a way of speaking and doing and being for one another, then it is not strange to speak of love for one another as a "commandment."

Sixth Sunday of Easter

Acts 16:9–15;
Psalm 67;
Revelation 21:10, 22–22:5;
John 14:23–29 or John 5:1–9

In today's first reading, we see the Macedonian call result in the conversion of Lydia, the seller of purple from Thyatira. Her conversion is a notable example of how the gospel can appeal to an eager inquirer. The responsorial psalm is a song of thanksgiving, including a call for all peoples and nations to praise God. The second reading is the magnificent vision of the New Jerusalem whose gates are always open, but entered only by "those who are written in the Lamb's book of life" (Rev. 21:27). In the first Gospel reading, Jesus promises that the Father will love those who love him and keep his word. The alternative Gospel reading concerns an invalid who experiences the healing grace of Jesus.

Acts 16:9–15

There is hardly a better text to illustrate the way the power of the Easter faith gives rise to a sense of mission than today's First Lesson, the story of the Macedonian call.

As is well known, at this point in the story line in Acts, the Pauline mission is making its way northwestward through Asia Minor. Paul, whose inclination is to move westward to the region of Asia, is probably beckoned by the swirling activity of Ephesus. But the spirit of Jesus has other plans, as Paul and his companions are gently guided northward to Troas, where he sees the vision of the man from Macedonia.

The call comes in a vision (v. 9), Luke's way of reminding the reader of its extraordinary nature (cf. Acts 10:3; 18:9). When visions come in Luke's story, it is a sure sign that God's impulse is being felt, and the characters know that such divine prods are not to be resisted. Accordingly, Paul and his companions comply, "convinced that God had called us to proclaim the good news to them" (v. 10).

With this dramatic event, the mission to Europe begins. This is Luke's way of signifying to the reader that an important transition is occurring. The gospel is now moving out of the familiar territory where the Pauline gospel has been established well enough. It is now moving into uncharted waters. We see this quite vividly in the way Luke sketches the scene at Philippi. He reminds us of the importance of the city: it is a "leading city of the district of Macedonia and a Roman colony" (v. 12). And the events narrated in this city are selected to show the gospel effectively penetrating a number of barriers, both social and religious. Three episodes receive attention: the conversion of Lydia (vv. 14–15), the encounter concerning the demon-possessed slave girl (vv. 16–18), and the imprisonment of Paul and Silas (vv. 19–40). Each in its own way contributes to the overall portrait of an effective Pauline mission in a setting dominated by pagan culture and institutions.

The subject of today's text is Lydia, the Thyatiran native who was a "dealer in purple cloth" (v. 14). From Luke's description, we get the clear impression that she was a woman of means, thus of social standing. Because she is called "a worshiper of God" (v. 14), we know that she was strongly attracted to Judaism. She encounters Paul and his companions at a "place of prayer" (v. 13) outside the city near a river, and we are told that "the Lord opened her heart to listen eagerly to what was said by Paul" (v. 14). From Luke's portrait of her, we know that she is devoted enough to attend a Jewish "place of prayer," perhaps a synagogue. She is inclined to things religious and thus is a ready listener to Paul's message.

The authenticity of her response is indicated by the eagerness with which she responded to Paul's preaching. Both she and her household were converted, and the genuineness of her conversion is reflected in her hospitality. Not surprisingly, at the end of chapter 16, after Paul and Silas are released from prison, they return to Lydia's house where their fellow Christians had gathered. Her home had already become a house-church.

What we have in this episode is a case of genuine conversion in an essentially Gentile setting. Luke's description implies that the Jewish community was neither large nor strong in Philippi. Yet it was sufficiently visible to attract Lydia and her household, and subsequently Paul and his companions. Luke does not use this as an occasion to provide a sermon summary, for he has already done this frequently enough. We can thus imagine that the content of Paul's sermon was similar to those earlier recorded (cf. chap. 13).

The episode doubtless functions to show the way the gospel is able to penetrate to a relatively high socio-economic level in a Roman setting. Lydia's importance is reflected by the fact that her name is given, as well as her hometown. She is the only person so identified in this narrative. Even though she is not mentioned in Paul's Epistle to the Philippians, that letter shows us a strong church deeply committed to Paul and his mission. And there is the strong likelihood that Lydia and her household, and probably others like her, constituted the nucleus of that important Pauline church.

In this instance, the Easter faith is seen to take root in a setting without all of the support and substructure of a strong Jewish synagogue. It does take hold, however, as a well-to-do merchant woman follows her religious longings in the midst of carrying on her business career. It appears to be a case of simple, uncomplicated conversion: a woman most likely decisive in other respects is also decisive in responding to a good thing when she sees it.

Psalm 67

This psalm appears to look in two directions and to express two sentiments. Offering thanks, it makes request; celebrating the harvest, it looks forward to divine favor (vv. 6, 1). One might assume that the psalm, like Psalm 65, was once used in a national ritual or communal thanksgiving. (Note the close connection of thanksgiving and confession in Deuteronomy 26.)

Verse 1 with its threefold indirect request to the Deity—"be gracious," "bless," "make his face to shine"—is reminiscent of the Aaronic priestly blessing in Numbers 6:24–26. The rationale for the threefold petition in verse 1 is given in verse 2. The rationale for Israel's (the "us" in v. 1) blessing is the consequence that it would have in the world of the nations. God's blessing on Israel makes known God's way (or "domain, manner") and saving power among the nations, among the goyim. This may sound like a bit of special pleading—in fact, a form of special greed; namely, to request one's own well-being for the impact it will have on others. Yet we must remember that the ancients were not ashamed to call attention to their god's reputation and to associate that reputation with the well-being of the god's worshipers.

The prayer for the nations (note the refrain in vv. 3 and 5) gives expression to something of a universalistic outlook. (Verse 7 perhaps should be translated "May God bless us; let . . . ," which would give it also a petitionary form.) The psalm certainly contains no narrow, nationalistic sentiment but confesses that God judges and guides the peoples of the world (v. 4), and thus they are God's responsibility.

In the Christian scheme of things, the Easter experience and the exaltation of Jesus celebrated in the Ascension affirm the divine blessings poured out upon the church, blessings that radiate outward to the nations of the world. In addition, like the psalm, the Christian gives thanks for blessings received ("the already" of Christian faith) but looks forward to blessings to come ("the not yet").

Revelation 21:10, 22–22:5

In this epistolary reading, we are still in the midst of the final vision of the New Jerusalem (21:1–22:5). For discussion of the broader literary context, see our remarks on last Sunday's epistolary lesson.

One of the seven angels beckons the Seer, "Come, I will show you the bride, the wife of the Lamb" (v. 9; cf. 19:7–8). With this, the Seer is carried away in the Spirit (1:10; 17:3) and taken to a high mountain. His vantage point is comparable to that from which Ezekiel sketches his vision of the restored temple (cf. Ezek. 40:1–2). But what he sees is the "holy city, the new Jerusalem" descending from God out of heaven (21:2; 22:19; cf. Matt. 4:5; 27:53; Neh. 11:1, 18; Isa. 48:2; 52:1; Dan. 9:24). There follows a magnificent description of the city's structure and measurements (vv. 11–21).

Then begins the major section of today's reading. We are struck by the fact that the New Jerusalem has no temple, especially since such prominence was given to the temple in earlier visions (cf. 3:12; 11:1–2, 19; 14:15, 17; 15:5–6, 8; 16:1, 17). This may in fact be an allusion to the destruction of the Jerusalem temple in AD 70. In response to this, Christians had already interpreted the body of Jesus as the "new temple" (John 2:19–21). Thus, in this vision the temple is replaced by the very presence of the Lord God Almighty (cf. 1:8; 4:8; 11:17; 15:3; 16:7, 14; 19:6, 15; also 2 Cor. 6:18; 2 Sam. 7:8; Amos 3:13) and the Lamb.

The city is lit up in dazzling light, but it is not light provided by the sun, moon, and stars. It was expected that in the eschatological age the heavenly lights would be rendered obsolete, and that the radiant glory of God would alone be needed (Isa. 60:19–20; also vv. 1–3; cf. 24:23; 2 Cor. 3:18; Rev. 22:5). It is thus a city that knows no night (v. 25b; cf. 22:5; Zech. 14:7). In similar fashion, Jesus had come to be identified with light and glory (John 1:1–18; 8:12; also 2 Cor. 4:6).

The city's population includes the "nations"; that is, the Gentiles (v. 24) as well as the kings of the earth. This too was part of the prophetic eschatological vision: God's light would extend to include the Gentiles (Isa. 49:6; 60:3, 11; Ps. 72:10–11). It is a city with an open door, with gates that would never be shut (Isa. 60:3, 11).

Everything unclean is excluded from the heavenly city, especially those whose ways are "foul or false" (v. 27, REB; also, cf. 21:8; 22:15; cf. Ezek. 33:29; Zech. 13:1–2; 2 Pet. 3:13). Membership is limited to those whose names are in the "Lamb's book of life" (21:27; 3:5; 13:8; 17:8; 20:12, 15; also Luke 10:20; Exod. 32:32–33; 1 Sam. 25:29; Ps. 69:28; Isa. 4:3; Dan. 12:1; Mal. 3:16).

This vision of the heavenly city should not be viewed in isolation from the rest of chapters 21–22. In last week's epistolary text, we saw certain features that are not here, and this part of the vision has distinctive elements. We should also note that the vision continues on into chapter 22, with the description of the river of life and the tree of life.

Some of the elements here are continuous with the vision as a whole, most notably the insistence that it is the place where the divine presence is fully and finally realized. No place of worship, no temple, synagogue, or church building is needed any longer. To be this close to the center of God makes the temple redundant.

Also worth noting is its universal population; it is a place for all nations and peoples. Finally, all racial and ethnic barriers are broken, and the new humanity exists in its undifferentiated fullness.

Especially prominent is the stress on moral purity. Revelation makes no mistake about what constitutes good and evil. The line between virtue and vice is sharply etched here (21:8; 22:11, 15). But every utopian vision recognizes that evil in all its forms obstructs the way to true life together. However, if we have to live with it, and even have it live within us here, at least we can look toward a time when it is no more and to a place where it is finally out of place.

John 14:23–29

John 14:23–29 belongs to the section of this Gospel devoted to Jesus' departure from his disciples and his return to God (13:1–17:26). The comments on this material introducing last Sunday's Gospel (13:31–35) may be reviewed to get a sense of the larger context. The immediate context is the farewell discourse in which Jesus is elaborating on the meaning of his departure on the ongoing lives of his followers. It is difficult within these discourses to isolate a distinct unit of material having its own center because of the repetition and the absence of the usual literary clues that signal the beginning and ending of a unit. Verse 23 is in response to a question by Judas (not Iscariot), but verse 24 seems to begin a new line of thought. In order to isolate verses 23–29 as a distinct lection, one needs to focus on the subject matter and not on the literary form. Such an examination yields three themes: love as the bond joining God, Christ, and the disciples (vv. 23–24); the promise of the Holy Spirit (vv. 25–26); peace and joy appropriate to the return of Christ to God (vv. 27–29). Because the three themes do not depend on one another or relate directly to one another, the preacher may want to choose one of them for the sermon. The approach of Pentecost makes the second theme attractive, but verses 25–27 will reappear on Pentecost Sunday, so the preacher will want to plan accordingly. We will discuss the three in the order of their appearance in the text.

Verses 23–24 continue the discussion of love from last Sunday but enlarge the arena of its activity. In response to the question concerning Christ's revealing himself to his disciples (v. 22), Christ speaks of love as the identifying condition existing among himself, God, and the disciples. The love of God for us and the love of Christ for us are common New Testament themes, but our loving Christ and loving God are relatively rare outside the Gospel. The Shema (Deut. 6:4) is repeated in Mark 12:29–30, but most often our relation to God and to Christ is characterized as faith and hope. In John, however, Jesus presses the question "Do you love me?" (21:15–19). God is love, and all relationships derived from that understanding are characterized as love. Fundamental to the union of God, Christ, and the disciples is love. As far as the disciples are concerned, love is formed and sealed by the word Christ has spoken to them, and holding to that word, obeying that word, is the evidence that the relationship of love pertains. When that is the case, God and Christ come and make their home with the disciples (v. 23). The expression "make our home" is the same as that of verse 2; in God's house are many "rooms" or "dwelling places." Hence, just as the disciples are promised a room or home with God in the future, so in verse 23 they are promised that God and Christ will make rooms or dwell with them here and now. "I will not leave you orphaned; I am coming to you" (v. 18). The eschatology of John is both future and present, and both should be claimed by the church. Pentecost and Parousia join and at times blend as both promise and presence.

Verses 25–26 contain the second of five statements in the farewell speeches in which the Holy Spirit is promised (14:16–17, 25–26; 15:25; 16:7–11, 13–15). Peculiar to this Gospel is the designation of the Spirit as Paraclete, that is, as Counselor, Comforter, Helper. In that the Spirit is *another* Advocate (v. 16), the Spirit is to the church what Jesus was to the disciples. In verse 26, four statements are made about the Holy Spirit: (1) God will send the Spirit (we do not have to do something to *get* the Spirit); (2) the Spirit is in Jesus' name (the experience of the Spirit does not permit the disregard or rejection of the historical Jesus); (3) the Spirit will teach the church, for Jesus had not yet fully said all that the church needs to understand (16:12); and (4) the Spirit will bring to remembrance the words of Jesus. The Spirit does not provide direct and unmediated experiences of God that contradict or render useless the tradition or the continuity of the faith community. The Christian faith is authorized by the line of continuity from God, to Christ, to the apostles, to the church (17:1–26). The Holy Spirit confirms and informs that tradition and enrolls disciples in the story of God's word in the world.

Verses 27–29 assure the disciples that peace and joy are appropriate to the events soon to transpire. Jesus' arrest and death are not a triumph of the world but are rather the operation of God's will in all things and the confirmation of the Son's love. The peace given is the confidence that God is God, that God loves the world, that God is for us, and that God makes that love real in acts of self-giving. Therefore, neither our pains nor our pleasures, neither our gains nor our losses are ultimate; they do not create nor do they annul the peace of God. To understand this is to rejoice (v. 28), as Paul would say, "Always" (1 Thess. 5:16).

John 5:1–9

The preacher who chooses to use the alternate text will want to fix in mind that this is a Johannine story with all the traits of a healing account in that Gospel. John 5:1–9 records a sign act followed by a discourse on the issue aroused by that act (vv. 10–18). The invalid is like others we meet in this Gospel (Jesus' mother, Nicodemus, the Samaritan woman, Martha and Mary, the Twelve) in that expectation of something from Jesus is at one level (aid in entering the pool), whereas Jesus responds in a way different from and greater than that expectation. Also as a sign act the story is designed to reveal truth about God, in this instance regarding sabbath activity (vv. 9*b*–18). And because it is a sign act, all the initiative is with Jesus; the attention is on him and not on the invalid or his situation. One will want to avoid, therefore, finding the causes for the healing in the circumstances. Calling the man a hypochondriac is a modern psychological imposition on the story. Neither do we know the invalid's character. And this is certainly not a "Your faith has made you well" story. The man did not even know who healed him (v. 13), and when he learned it was Jesus, he testified against him as a sabbath breaker (v. 15).

The story is about Jesus revealing a God who continues to act for human good, even on the sabbath. There is no wrong day to relieve human misery (v. 17). In this case Jesus acts to heal a man who is a threefold victim. he is a victim of paralysis. He is a victim of a cruel tradition that offers healing only to the first one in the pool. And who would that be? Not the severely crippled but someone able to move quickly, perhaps suffering from chapped lips or a hangnail. And he is a victim of a kind of religion that honors its rules over human need.

When Jesus acts favorably toward one in whom no reasons for the favor can be found, we call it grace, radical grace.

Ascension of the Lord

Acts 1:1–11;
Psalm 47 or Psalm 110;
Ephesians 1:15–23;
Luke 24:44–53

On the day that commemorates the Ascension of the Lord, the paragraphs that begin the Book of Acts will hold center stage. Psalm 47 responds to this account of the Ascension as an exultant hymn of praise of the Lord's coronation as king over all the earth. A similar note is struck in the well-known alternate psalm. The text from Ephesians is chosen for this occasion because it affirms that God has "seated [Christ] at his right hand in the heavenly places" (Eph. 1:20). The Lucan passage, an account of the final commissioning of the disciples by the risen Lord, immediately precedes the Acts passage in Luke's two-volume work.

Acts 1:1–11

For the first few centuries, the church included the celebration of Ascension as part of Pentecost. According to Tertullian, Christ's Ascension took place at Pentecost. But by the late fourth century, the celebration of Ascension and Pentecost had developed as two separate events.

The custom of celebrating the Ascension of Christ forty days after Easter, or on the Sixth Thursday during the fifty-day period from Easter to Pentecost, is largely attributable to the mention of "forty days" in today's First Lesson (v. 3). Strictly speaking, the observance of Ascension will be held on the Sixth Thursday, but as a matter of convenience can be observed the following Sunday, the Seventh Sunday of Easter.

In *The Revised Common Lectionary* the same four texts are employed for Ascension Day in all three years. But as we treat this First Lesson, we might note that in other lectionaries other passages have served as the First Lesson: Year A—Daniel 7:9–14; Year B—Ezekiel 1:3–5, 15–22, 26–28; and Year C—2 Kings 2:1–15. All these appropriately bear on the theme of Ascension and may be consulted for additional perspective. The reader may also want to consult our remarks on the texts for this day in Years A and B.

The first chapter of Acts is most appropriate as an opening lesson, for Christ's ascension is specifically mentioned three times (vv. 2, 9, 22). In the second part of today's opening lection (vv. 6–11), we have Luke's narrative description of this event—the only such description in the New Testament (cf. Luke 24:50–53). Of course, the tradition of Jesus' ascension is known elsewhere, but it is usually referred to only briefly (cf. Mark 16:19; John 3:13; 6:62; 20:17; also 1 Tim. 3:16).

At the outset, we should note that quite often the New Testament does not clearly distinguish Jesus' ascension from his resurrection. Rather, we are often told simply that after his death, he was "exalted," or "taken up," as if his resurrection is itself his ascension (cf. Rom. 1:4; 10:6; Phil. 2:9; Eph. 4:8–10; 1 Pet. 3:22; Heb. 4:14; 7:26). By contrast, Luke sees the resurrection of Jesus and his ascension into heaven as two separate events, separated in time by forty days.

Several features of today's text are worth noting in the context of our celebration of Ascension.

First, it is a time of recollection. We are told that during the forty days, the risen Lord presented himself to the disciples as alive and spoke to them concerning the kingdom of God (v. 3). Not only had this been one of the major themes of the preaching of John the Baptist (Matt. 3:2 and parallels) but of Jesus as well (Matt. 4:23 and parallels). This involved the announcement that the sovereign reign of God had now set in—a time of hope for the poor, the captive, the sick, and the oppressed (Luke 4:18–19).

But in spite of the abundant teaching of Jesus concerning the kingdom of God, especially through the form of parables, confusion still abounded. Those who heard his preaching found it next to impossible to disentangle God's promise of a new era of divine sovereignty from their own notions of nationalism. And the discussion almost inevitably turned to when (v. 6). They have to be told, once again, that establishing times and dates is God's exclusive prerogative (v. 7; also Matt. 24:36 and parallels; also Rom. 16:25; 1 Cor. 2:7; Eph. 1:4; 3:9, 11; Col. 1:26; 2 Tim. 1:9). Their task is not to predict but to wait.

Second, it is a time of anticipation. The disciples are instructed to "wait there for the promise of the Father" (v. 4). The time when the Holy Spirit would be poured out in abundance is not far off, and when it occurs it would be a great outburst of power. In fact, the Spirit and power are always closely linked (cf. Luke 1:35; 24:49; Acts 10:38; Rom. 15:13, 19; 1 Cor. 2:4–5; 1 Thess. 1:5; Heb. 2:4). The Book of Acts provides thorough documentation of the powerful energy unleashed by the Spirit beginning with the Day of Pentecost.

Our text moves beyond the expectation of the pouring out of the Spirit and also points to the ultimate return of Christ. The disciples are assured that his coming will be in a manner similar to that of his departure (v. 11).

In both cases, the cast of the eye is forward. The disciples are now with the risen Lord, but their attention is directed toward a time when he will no longer be with them in the same way. He will be absent, but present with them through the Spirit. The power they now feel in his presence they will experience even when he is absent. They are thus instructed to stop gazing into heaven and be about the business at hand—waiting for the renewal that will begin in Jerusalem.

It is precisely this tension between recollection and anticipation that is felt in the celebration of Ascension. On the one hand, we want to hold on to Easter and the risen Lord, yet we are being beckoned to let go and look to the coming Spirit as the One who will lead us into the future.

Psalm 47

This psalm has long been associated with the Ascension celebration in the Christian church, a celebration that commemorates Jesus' exaltation to the heavenly world. In its original usage, Psalm 47 probably celebrated the "return" of God and the divine ascension in the annual enthronement ritual.

The features in the enthronement ritual, as reconstructed by scholars, involved the removal of the ark (representing Yahweh, the Israelite God) from the temple, the cleansing of the temple and people (the Yom Kuppur, or Day of Atonement, ritual), and the return of the ark to the temple (see Ps. 24:7–10). The return of the ark and its placement back in the Holy of Holies was understood as Yahweh's reenthronement, his ascension back to the throne and assumption of authority as king. Psalm 47 would have functioned in the liturgy as part of the celebration of Yahweh's reenthronement.

The psalm divides into three units, with verse 5 as the fulcrum balancing verses 1–4 and 6–9. Verse 5 affirms the cultic reality ("God has gone up"; that is, Yahweh has ascended with the ark into the Holy of Holies) and notes some aspects of the people's cultic reaction ("with a shout"; "with the sound of a trumpet").

The two units sandwiched around verse 5 are calls to worship with statements giving the reason or motivation for such praise. The first summons—"clap your hands"; "shout to God"— is addressed to the peoples, or foreign Gentile nations (v. 1). The motivation for clapping and shouting is twofold. First, Yahweh, a terrible (in the sense of awesome) God, is the great king who rules over all the earth. (Note the claims made for the ascended Jesus; Phil. 2:10.) Second, this universal claim, however, is counterbalanced in verses 3–4 by the more nationalistic, particularistic claim of the elect people. Jacob is the chosen, the elect, and thus nations are "under their feet"; that is, subordinate to the special people of God. This tension between universalism and election runs throughout the Scriptures and is still today an issue in terms of the relationship of denominations to one another and in terms of Christianity and the church's relationship to other religious communities, not to mention the issue of nationalism versus internationalism. The psalm sees this tension overarched if not overcome in the fact that God reigns as king over both.

The second call to praise, in verse 6, is simply a fourfold "sing praises." The opening line of this verse can best be translated "sing praises, O gods." The sense of this reading would suggest that the gods of the nations are called on to offer praise to the Israelite Deity (see Ps. 82:1 for a similar concept). The motivation for such praise again notes that Yahweh is king over all the earth and reigns over the nations, enthroned on God's holy throne (in the Jerusalem temple).

Verse 9 contains two parallel lines with no connective (the "as" in the NRSV has been added by the translators). The two parallel lines refer to the foreigners—"the princes of the peoples"—and to the Jewish community—"the people of the God of Abraham." The expression "the shields of the earth" appears to be another way of saying "the princes of the peoples"; that is, the rulers of the world are said to belong to the God of Israel.

Psalm 110

New Testament writers quoted Psalm 110 more frequently than practically any other text. Three different uses of Psalm 110:1 can be seen in the New Testament. One usage is related to the question of whether the messiah was a son of David or David's lord (Matt. 22:41–46; Mark 12:35–37; Luke 20:41–44). A second employment of the psalm was its utilization in speaking of the exaltation/ascension of the Son of Man/Jesus (Matt. 26:63–65; Acts 2:32–36; 7:56; Rom. 8:34; Eph. 1:20; Col. 3:1; Heb. 1:3, 13; 8:1; 10:12). A final usage of this verse was in speaking about the ultimate universal rule of Christ (1 Cor. 15:25; Eph. 1:20) when he would put all things under his feet. In addition, the reference to Melchizedek in Psalm 110:4 is used in the Letter to the Hebrews to argue that the priesthood of Christ is superior to that of the Jewish levitical priesthood (Heb. 5:6; 7:17, 21).

The second usage of verse 1 noted above has led to the association of this psalm with the Ascension. The original referents in the psalm differ widely from these secondary New Testament usages. The latter represents a stage of interpretation in which the imagery of the psalm was understood messianically and its metaphors had been spiritualized and universalized.

Psalm 110 was a royal psalm extolling the Davidic king and was probably used in the coronation ritual. The psalm appears to contain two divine oracles addressed to the king (vv. 1 and 4) and two choral or congregational responses (vv. 2–3 and 5–7).

Psalm 110, like Psalm 2, stresses the dominance of the Davidic king over his enemies and foreign nations. The oracle addressed to the king in verse 1 assigns the monarch a position of prominence at the right hand of God. In such a position, the king reigns along with God over the affairs of men. Such a statement as "sitting at the right hand of God" raises the question of how this was understood. In Jerusalem, the royal palace and the temple were part of a large royal complex. God was enthroned as king over the cosmos in the Holy of Holies of the temple. The king upon his throne in the royal palace thus sat enthroned at the right hand of God.

The reference to the enemies being the footstool of the king is best understood in terms of the royal throne furniture. We have no description of the footstool used by Davidic kings, but practically all the art of the ancient Near East shows the use of footstools. Among the royal furniture discovered in the tomb of the Egyptian Pharaoh Tutankhamen were two footstools with stylized representations of the traditional enemies of Egypt worked into the wood as inlay. Thus, when the pharaoh sat upon his throne, his enemies were his footstool. Such a concept surely lies behind the reference in Psalm 110:1.

Psalm 110:2–3 refers to the king's rule from Zion in the midst of his foes, where he was supported freely by his subjects. The latter half of verse 3 seems to refer to the promise of youthful vitality for the king, but the full meaning of the metaphorical imagery eludes us.

The king, in verse 4, is declared to be a priest forever, after the order of Melchizedek. The figure of Melchizedek appears in one other Old Testament passage. In Genesis 14:18, he is described as the king of Salem (Jerusalem?) and as priest of God Most High. Abraham is shown presenting a tithe to this priest-king after having been blessed (Gen. 14:19–20). If Melchizedek was a member or the founder of a pre-Israelite dynasty that ruled in Jerusalem prior to David's capture of the city, then Psalm 110:4 would suggest that the Davidic kings were understood as the successors to this priestly-royal line of monarchs.

The remainder of Psalm 110 stresses the divine intervention of God on behalf of his chosen king and promises the monarch that he, the Lord, will subject nations to the king's rule and will annihilate his enemies.

Ephesians 1:15–23

This text, at least portions of it, is also employed elsewhere in *The Revised Common Lectionary*. The same text serves as the epistolary reading for Proper 29 [34], Christ the King or Reign of Christ in Year A. Ephesians 1:11–23 serves as the epistolary reading for All Saints' Day (November 1) for Year C. The reader may want to consult additional remarks made in connection with those days.

Today's epistolary text should be read as a rich theological reflection on the exalted status of Christ. Throughout the text, Christ's absolute supremacy is assumed, and we may regard it as a fitting text to stimulate our thinking about the theological significance of Christ's ascension.

No clear distinction is made in the text between Christ's resurrection and his ascension. It may be, however, that we have the beginning of a two-stage distinction when we are told that God "raised [Christ] from the dead and seated him at his right hand in the heavenly places" (v. 20; cf. 1 Pet. 1:21). The language is supplied partially by Psalm 110:1, which speaks of the elevation of the king to God's right hand. What is new is his location "in the heavenly places," an important phrase in Ephesians. But in Ephesians it is no longer the exalted Lord himself who shares this place of preeminent position. We who are "in Christ" are also envisioned as being elevated to the heavenly sphere where we will enjoy the numerous spiritual blessings mentioned in this opening prayer (1:3; 2:6). Our text, then, reports on ascension in two senses: Christ's and our own.

From this elevated position, we are in a unique position to receive the spiritual blessings God offers us in Christ. Among these is the capacity for spiritual discernment (vv. 17–18). We are assured that the eyes of our understanding will be opened in the sense that our spiritual wisdom is deepened and our knowledge of God is enriched (cf. Col. 1:9–10; also 1 John 5:20; Isa. 11:2; Wisd. of Sol. 7:7). In particular, we are enabled to grasp the size and shape of the hope to which we have been called (v. 18; cf. 4:4; also Col. 1:5, 27; Heb. 3:1). As elusive as the notion of hope is, this should be especially reassuring to us. Moreover, we are made increasingly aware that ours is a legacy of wealth (v. 18; cf. 3:16; Col. 1:27; Rom. 9:23; 10:12; 11:33; Phil. 4:19).

Besides the gift of spiritual enlightenment that we come to possess in Christ, there is also access to unlimited sources of power and strength (vv. 19–20). This power is not to be understood in the abstract, nor is it to be understood merely as the divine power exhibited in the creation. It is rather the power unleashed by God in raising Christ from the dead— resurrection power. We are assured that it is truly "immeasurable" (v. 19; cf. 3:20; Col. 1:11; 2:12; 2 Cor. 13:4; 1 Pet. 1:5; also Isa. 40:26).

The extent of God's power is seen in the way Christ's ascension made him supreme over "every principality, ruling force, power, or sovereignty" (v. 21, NJB; cf. 2:2; 3:10; 6:12; Rom. 8:38; 1 Cor. 15:24; Col. 1:13, 16; 2:10, 15; 1 Pet. 3:22; 2 Pet. 2:10–11; Heb. 2:5). Everything has finally been put in subjection under his feet (cf. Ps. 8:6; Matt. 28:18; 1 Cor. 15:24–25), and he is now the supreme head of the church, which literally fills the universe (cf. Col. 1:19). In view here is the cosmic body of Christ that extends throughout the universe (cf. 4:12; Rom. 12:5; Col. 1:18, 24; 2:17).

We can see, then, that Christ's ascension has impact on us in at least these two respects: our spiritual understanding is sharpened and our sources of strength are deepened. The theological view of Christian existence expressed here is triumphalist to be sure, and taken alone could easily cause us to see ourselves as exalted to the heavens. Unchecked, it might make us Gnostic.

But in this text we are hearing the language of prayer and praise. Every once in a while, perhaps especially in moments of worship, from our view below we should allow ourselves to participate in Christ's ascension. We should sit with him in the heavenly places and view the universe from the vantage point of the One who is over all.

Ascension Day is not as widely observed as a Christian holiday in America as in Europe. But whether or not the day is celebrated, the Ascension is a vital theme in Christian faith, as its statement in the Apostles' Creed made clear quite early. The Ascension provides closure to the ministry of Jesus, declares his enthronement at the right hand of God, and proclaims Christ's lordship over the church and over all powers in the created order.

Luke 24:44–53

That Jesus Christ is Lord, seated at the right hand of God, is an affirmation found frequently in the New Testament and is often framed on the declaration of Psalm 110:1: "The LORD says to my lord, 'Sit at my right hand until I make your enemies your footstool.'" Less frequent, however, is the expression of the lordship of Christ in the form of an ascension story. The narrative in Acts 1:1–11 is the most complete, but in the Gospel lection for today, reference to Christ's ascension is made.

Luke 24:44–53 continues the Lucan resurrection narrative (24:1–53). A review of the comments on Luke 24:13–49 for Easter Evening will set our verses for today in context. The two parts to verses 44–53 are instruction, commission, and promise (vv. 44–49), and blessing, departure, and waiting (vv. 50–53). In verses 44–49 several Lucan themes are stated and are central to the entire Luke-Acts presentation of Christ and the church. One such theme is the continuity of Jesus' mission with that of Israel. What the risen Jesus is saying is what the pre-resurrection Jesus said, and these teachings are totally congruous with the Old Testament (v. 44). Luke has repeatedly stressed this point (2:21–40; 4:16–30; 24:25–27, 44–45). The death and resurrection of Jesus and the proclamation of the gospel to all peoples were in the plan of God revealed in the Hebrew Scriptures and do not constitute a new departure following the failure of previous efforts. However, it is the risen Christ who enables this understanding of Scripture (v. 45; see also at vv. 25–27). Given this perspective, Luke insists that the Scriptures are sufficient to generate and to sustain faith (16:27–31). A second theme is the universality of God's offer of repentance and forgiveness of sins (v. 47). Luke made this point as early as the presentation of the infant Jesus in the temple (2:29–32), and Jesus placed it on his agenda at the opening of his ministry in Nazareth (4:16–30). Of course, both the commission (Acts 1:8) and its fulfillment in the proclamation to the nations (Act 2:1–36) are central to Luke's second volume. And just as justification by grace through faith is the gospel for Paul, for Luke it is repentance and forgiveness of sins.

A final theme in verses 44–49 lies in the command to the disciples to stay in Jerusalem until they receive "power from on high" (v. 49). Jerusalem is the center from which the word of the Lord is to go to the nations (Isa. 2:3), whereas Mark 16:1–18 and Matthew 28:10, 16–20 focus upon Galilee as the place of the risen Christ's reunion with the disciples. For Luke, here and throughout Acts, Jerusalem is the center of Christian mission. However, that activity has to wait on the outpouring of the Holy Spirit (v. 49; Acts 1:48). Without the Holy Spirit they would not be able to take the gospel beyond the comfort zone of Israel to all the nations of the world.

The second portion of our lection, verses 50–53, relates very briefly the departure of Jesus from the disciples on whom he has pronounced his blessing. The manuscript evidence for the phrase "and was carried up into heaven" (v. 51) is mixed and debated, but if it is absent here, the account appears quite fully in Acts 1:9–11. The disciples return to Jerusalem and to the temple in particular. For Luke's story both of Jesus and of the church the temple in Jerusalem is important (Luke 2:22–38, 41–51; Acts 2:46–3:1; 22:17). The disciples' waiting for the Holy Spirit was in joy, praise (vv. 52–53), and constant prayer (Acts 1:14). The reader of Luke is now ready for volume two, Acts.

Seventh Sunday of Easter

Acts 16:16–34;
Psalm 97;
Revelation 22:12–14, 16–17, 20–21;
John 17:20–26

The long reading from Acts is the account of the imprisonment of Paul and Silas for driving a spirit out of a slave girl. The account of the conversion of the jailer shows how the faith is spread through the deeds as well as the words of the disciples. Part of the psalm responds to the kind of trouble experienced by Paul and Silas; the psalm affirms that God preserves the saints and delivers them from the wicked (v. 10). As a whole, it is a song celebrating the enthronement of the Lord and continues the theme of Ascension Day. The second reading, an anticipation of the return of Jesus, likewise continues the motif of Jesus enthroned on high. The Gospel lection is the last part of the so-called High Priestly Prayer of Jesus, his petition for all who will come to believe, "that they may all be one" (John 17:21).

Acts 16:16–34

In today's First Lesson, we are presented with two incidents that occurred during Paul's mission in Philippi: an encounter with a demon-possessed girl and the conversion of the Philippian jailer.

At this point in Acts, we have moved into another major phase of the Pauline mission. After the Jerusalem conference, Paul and Silas launch a fresh mission into western Asia Minor. In response to the Macedonian call (16:9–10), they cross the Hellespont into Greece and come to Philippi as the first major stop. Luke gives a fairly lengthy description of Paul's preaching in Philippi (16:12–40). After leaving Philippi, Paul and his company move on to Thessalonica (17:1–9) and eventually come to Athens (17:16–34). Here Luke uses the occasion to give us an example of Pauline preaching before a sophisticated pagan audience, hence the sermon before the Areopagus court (17:22–31). Then Paul's successful mission in Corinth follows (18:1–18), and this stage of preaching in Greece ends.

Within this overall literary context, there are four significant sections: (1) preaching the gospel in Philippi; (2) the opposition to the gospel in Thessalonica; (3) the sermon in Athens; and (4) the successful period in Corinth. With each of these major sections, Luke is portraying a significant feature of the Pauline mission among the Gentiles. With the extensive treatment of Philippi, he shows how the gospel takes root in a Gentile setting. The events of Thessalonica are recorded to illustrate the type of resistance the gospel typically met in Gentile settings, especially from the Jewish synagogue. Athens provides an occasion for giving us a typical Pauline sermon to Gentiles in a more sophisticated setting. The description of Paul's preaching in Corinth shows us an instance of Paul's successful missionary work when he stayed for a period of time.

Even though the events in Philippi span several days, Luke's sketch reads like "a day in the life" of Paul, the missionary to the Gentiles. Luke chooses to relate three incidents: (1) the conversion of Lydia and her household (vv. 13–15); (2) the encounter with the demon-possessed girl (vv. 16–24); and (3) the imprisonment of Paul and Silas, the resulting conversion of the Philippian jailer, and Paul's vindication before the civil magistrates (vv. 25–40). This careful selection of incidents shows us how the gospel is received by a well-to-do woman inclined toward Judaism. Further, it shows us how the gospel, in conflict with popular pagan religion, wins out. Finally, it moves to the other end of the social spectrum and shows us how the gospel reaches into the house of a jail-keeper to save his life and soul. In the process, it also demonstrates again that the messengers of the gospel live and work under divine protection and that their cause is vindicated before pagan officials.

As we look at the two incidents comprising today's first lection, we notice first how similar Paul's encounter with the pagan girl is to incidents recorded in the Gospels (cf. Matt. 8:28–34 and parallels; Matt. 15:21–28 and parallels; Mark 1:21–38 and parallels). In once sense, the incident merely serves as the setup for the imprisonment scene. It provides an occasion for stating the charges against Paul and Silas that will be cleared up later (vv. 20–21). We are not told that the pagan girl is converted, but through the well-known technique of placing a confessional statement on the lips of a pagan, Luke clearly places her on the side of faith (v. 17).

As we move to the imprisonment scene, we recall similar imprisonments earlier in Acts (4:3; 5:17–26; 12:1–11). As we noted earlier in our remarks on the First Lesson for the Second Sunday of Easter, a recurrent pattern emerges in Luke-Acts. Whenever the gospel meets resistance, such as imprisonment by the authorities, it is vindicated. The more severe the resistance, the more spectacular the vindication. In today's text, even the inner prison and leg stocks are inadequate to hold God's messengers. The divine rescue comes this time in the form of an earthquake (v. 26; cf. 4:31).

As it turns out, an event that was potentially catastrophic becomes an occasion for experiencing God's salvation. The jailer knows the escape of the prisoners will require his life (v. 30; cf. 12:19; 27:42). Hence, his question operates at two levels. In the context, he is asking what to do to save his skin. But the reader knows that similar questions have been asked earlier (2:37; cf. 22:10; Luke 3:10) and that the real request is for salvation offered by the gospel. It thus becomes an occasion for preaching the word of the Lord (v. 32). What began as an ominous jailing ends as a joyous celebration of faith (v. 34; cf. Matt. 9:22).

Luke's imprint is seen throughout this narrative. The theological points that are scored are thoroughly Lucan: the power of the gospel to penetrate every social level, its capacity to attract converts away from Judaism to Christianity, the conquest of pagan superstition, the divine protection of God's messengers, and the vindication of the gospel in Roman eyes.

The story of the jailer's conversion is especially inviting to the homiletician as an instance of Luke's literary artistry. At one level, it is the story of an imprisonment and a miraculous release, or "salvation," of God's messengers. At another level, it is the story of the miraculous release, or "salvation," of a jailer imprisoned in his own prison. The irony is surely there: those who are imprisoned, God's apostles, are really free, whereas those who are the keepers of the prisoners are really imprisoned. Through role reversal, Paul and Silas become the jailer's deliverers.

Psalm 97

An enthronement psalm, Psalm 97 (see also Christmas, Second Proper) celebrates the exaltation/ascension of Yahweh and the consequences of this for the world and human existence. This psalm is fundamentally a hymn about Yahweh. The single exception is verse 9, which is prayer or speech addressed to God.

The psalm opens with a central affirmation: "Yahweh has become king." (This appears a better translation than the NRSV's "The LORD is king.") Everything else in the psalm tends to radiate outward from this point. Joy and gladness are the responsive tones that should greet such an affirmation.

Verses 2–8 are a cantata describing the universe's reaction to divine kingship; they reach a crescendo in the asseration that Zion hears and the daughters (cities) of Judah rejoice.

The metaphorical descriptions in verses 1–5 borrow from the imagery of thunderstorms—clouds, darkness, fire, lightning—which assault the earth and devour the divine enemies (see Psalm 29). Tucked away amid this assortment of meteorological metaphors is a calming voice among the thundering sounds—"righteousness and justice are the foundation of his throne" (v. 2b). In spite of the violence and apparent irrationality of the characteristics of God, the Divine is consistent, just, and righteous.

God's voice and presence, heard and seen throughout the cosmos (v. 6), are bad news and a destroying presence to those who worship any deity other than Yahweh; even the other gods worshiped with idols bow down to (= "worship") the God of Israel (v. 7).

What others hear in fear and trembling, Zion and Judah, Jerusalem and the Judean towns, hear with rejoicing (v. 8). The two responses of the world (the worshipers of idols) and Zion manifest three reactions to the Divine: being awestruck at the divine might, being humiliated and shamed by discovering the silliness of other worship, and being gladdened by the judgments that come as affirmations.

The psalm concludes with what might be called a moral lesson or a theological homily (vv. 10–11) and then an altar call (v. 12). If we take the marginal reading of the NRSV in verse 10, which provides a literal translation of the Hebrew "You who love Yahweh hate evil," the "altar call" begins earlier. Probably the regular reading in the NRSV is correct, because it merely presupposes that the same Hebrew letter was wrongly repeated. This then gives three affirmations about God, in verse 10, which produces two qualities for humans—light and joy (v. 11).

Psalm 97, with its assurances of divine rule and of the value of righteousness, even righteous hatred, leaves the reader with a sense of calmness that all is well with the world after all, because Yahweh reigns.

Revelation 22:12–14, 16–17, 20–21

The vision of the New Jerusalem is now completed (21:1–22:5), and the Book of Revelation concludes with a series of miscellaneous oracles, exhortations, blessings, and warnings. Today's epistolary lection represents a selection from this epilogue.

The lection begins and ends with the declaration "See, I am coming soon" (vv. 12 and 20). This is a recurrent theme of the book (2:16, 25; 3:11; 22:7). In the context of apocalyptic, this promise serves as a word of reassurance to those who are being oppressed. Within the

Johannine Apocalypse, it may be read as an answer to the martyrs crying out, "How long?" (6:10). Certainly those who were suffering persecution under the Roman emperor Domitian (A.D. 81–96) would find this a reassuring hope, and this was doubtless the intention of the author.

Prior to the final benediction (v. 21), the lection concludes with the early Christian prayer, "Come, Lord Jesus!" (v. 20). It is preserved in its original Aramaic form by Paul (1 Cor. 16:22; cf. 11:26). As it stands here, it should be read as the early Christian prayer of hope uttered in response to the promise of the risen Lord. Thus, the Lord proclaims, "Surely I am coming soon," and the people respond by saying, "Amen. Come, Lord Jesus!" (v. 20).

In today's text, we are assured that the Lord's coming will be a time when we receive judgment according to our works (v. 12). This need not be seen as the harsher side of justice, but simply as a reminder that the Lord will recompense us based on our record. As is typical of apocalyptic, there are only two classes: those who are blessed because of their good deeds (v. 14) and those who are cursed because of their vile deeds (v. 15). The principle of receiving judgment according to what we have done has a long history running from the Old Testament through the various strata of the New Testament (Isa. 40:10; Jer. 17:10; Ps. 28:4; 62:12; Prov. 24:12; Matt. 16:27; Rom. 2:6; 2 Cor. 11:15; 2 Tim. 4:14; 1 Pet. 1:17).

We again meet the familiar refrain that Jesus is "the Alpha and the Omega, the first and the last, the beginning and the end" (v. 13; cf. 1:8; 21:6; also Isa. 44:2, 6; 48:12). In this setting, we should understand it as a way of underscoring the fact that he stands at the end of history.

The final verse of the first section of the lection is a blessing on the vindicated saints whose robes have been washed in the blood of the Lamb (v. 14; cf. 7:14; also Gen. 49:11; Exod. 19:10, 14; 1 John 1:7). Omitting the next verse (v. 15), which lists those who are excluded, certainly produces a more positive reading, but it breaks the pattern established in the preceding verses: the Lord comes to judge according to our deeds, both the good (v. 14) and evil (v. 15).

The blessed saints have the right to the paradisal tree of life that was lost in the Fall (2:7; 22:2, 19; also Gen. 2:9, 3:22, 24). Theirs is also the privilege of entry into the gates of the Holy City (v. 14; cf. Ps. 118:19–20). This is one of several makarisms (pronouncements of blessedness) that occur in the book (1:3; 14:13; 16:15; 19:9; 20:6; 22:7, 18). (This in itself might easily form the basis of a sermon as the preacher examines the various grounds for being blessed according to the Book of Revelation.)

Verse 16 reaffirms the identity of Jesus as the "root and the descendant of David" (Isa. 11:1, 10; Matt. 1:1; John 7:42; Rom. 1:3; 2 Tim. 2:8) and the "bright morning star" (cf. 2:28; Num. 24:17).

Verse 17 should be read as an invitation of the Spirit and the church (the bride) to the reader as an invitation to the messianic banquet. The hearers, in turn, respond by saying, "Come." Their response should be understood as addressing Jesus, as is the case in verse 20. It is their way of imploring the risen Christ to come quickly. Finally, the invitation for the thirsty to come and drink the water of life free of charge should be construed as an invitation to the eschatological feast (cf. 7:16–17; 21:6; 22:1; Isa. 55:1; Jer. 2:13; John 7:37).

The concluding benediction (v. 21), which extends grace to all the saints, is reminiscent of an epistolary conclusion (cf. 1:4–5; 1 Thess. 5:28).

As today's text unfolds, we are struck by the pervasive eschatological character of these various oracles. This element is not entirely foreign to the Easter Season, especially as we approach Pentecost and remember that the outpouring of the Holy Spirit was originally conceived as the breaking in of the New Age.

John 17:20–26

Luke says that before Pentecost the followers of Jesus devoted themselves to prayer (Acts 1:14). Who could fault that preparation? John says that before Jesus' glorification and the giving of the Spirit, Jesus prayed for his followers. Who could fault that preparation? Our Gospel for today is a portion of that prayer.

The question has been raised as to whether John 17 is really a prayer. This question exists only where address to God and address to the congregation has been sharply divided into prayer and proclamation. However, in the Bible such distinctions are not always drawn. In many of the psalms (Psalm 23, for example), the writer moves easily from words about God to words to God. In Deuteronomy 32–33, Moses' farewell speech addresses both the people and God. Paul often speaks to God in the course of speaking to a church (Rom. 1:25; 9:1–5; 11:33–36). Earlier in the Fourth Gospel, one encounters prayers that are also proclamations (11:41–42; 12:27–30). To remember that the audience for both prayer and sermon is God is to become less concerned about the proclamatory nature of Jesus' farewell prayers. The important consideration here is for the reader of John 17 to assume the posture of one being prayed for. It is as though we were in the congregation overhearing Jesus' pastoral prayer for us.

The prayer is that of the historical Jesus (v. 13: "Now I am coming to you") and also of the glorified Lord of the church (v. 11: "I am no longer in the world"). One does not distinguish between pre- and postresurrection materials in John. For example, a postresurrection statement occurs in the conversation of Jesus with Nicodemus (3:13). The point is, the risen Christ and the historical Jesus are the same.

John 17:1–26 may be divided into three parts: Jesus' return to glory (vv. 1–5); Jesus' prayer for his disciples (vv. 6–19); and Jesus' prayer for all who believe through the word of the disciples (vv. 20–26). This last unit is our lesson for today. Every generation of believers can read verses 20–26 with the assurance that the prayer of Jesus is in their behalf. In fact, all distinctions between first generation and subsequent generations of believers are here erased; there are only believers. This, then, is a prayer of Jesus for us.

The central petition of the prayer is for the unity of all who believe. There is nothing here of unity as political expediency, or as mutual accommodation to error, or as agreement on the level of the lowest common denominator. None of the machinery of unity is mentioned. The unity spoken of here is that which is informed and empowered by the unity of God and Christ (vv. 20–23). The line of continuity that authorizes the word by which faith is generated (v. 20) is clear: from God to Christ; from Christ to his apostles; from the apostles to the church. Add to this authorization the gift of the Holy Spirit (20:22) and the church as this Evangelist understood it is both apostolic and charismatic. The unity that prevails when God, Christ, and believers abide each in the other has as its primary purpose the evangelization of the world (v. 21). In unity the witness to the world can be made effectively; without it confusion and division disrupt and erode the witness of the church. If First John is addressed to the same church, perhaps shortly after the Gospel was written, then that letter may reveal some of the tensions, doctrinal disputes, and perhaps personality clashes that disturbed the Johannine church and made this prayer so pressingly important. Present church conditions make it abun-dantly clear that the prayer is as yet unanswered.

The prayer concludes with the twofold promise already familiar to the reader from 14:1–23. The first is that all who believe may share the glory of Christ and abide with him forever (v. 24; 14:1–3). The second promise is for the church's present, just as the first is for the future. Here, as in 14:23, the assurance is that the love that characterizes the relationship between God and Christ will be in all Christ's followers, and Christ himself will be within and among them (vv. 25–26). The church in every generation, in every place, and in every circumstance that embraces this word in faith will abide in peace, in joy, and in full confi-dence that the world will finally be drawn to God (16:33; 12:31–32).

Pentecost

Acts 2:1–21 or Genesis 11:1–9;
Psalm 104:24–34, 35b;
Romans 8:14–17 or Acts 2:1–21;
John 14:8–17 (25–27)

The focal text is the one that serves as the basis for the celebration of the Day of Pentecost, the account in Acts 2:1–21 of the outpouring of the Spirit on those gathered for the festival. The alternate first reading, the story of the Tower of Babel, provides the backdrop for one aspect of the Acts account, the miracle of understanding foreign languages. The psalm praises the power of God's Spirit to create and renew. Both the alternate second reading from Romans and the Gospel lection focus on the Spirit of God.

Acts 2:1–21

In the Christian year, Pentecost marks the day on which we celebrate the coming of the Holy Spirit. It marks the conclusion of the fifty days of Easter and the beginning of the period when the church carries forward the ministries it has received from the Spirit.

It is this text from Acts on which the Christian Pentecost is based. Luke has provided this narrative account of the birthday of the church, when the nucleus of the messianic community is formed. The disciples have been instructed by the risen Lord to wait in Jerusalem for the power from on high (Luke 24:47; Acts 1:8). Meanwhile, they have been receiving instructions from the risen Lord concerning the kingdom of God (Acts 1:2). The apostolic circle has been reconstituted with the appointment of Matthias as Judas' replacement (Acts 1:15–26). All is set for the New Age to begin.

The way Luke tells the story shows it to be a programmatic event. The sermon by Peter provides the centerpiece (2:14–36), but it is duly introduced and concluded. Today's First Lesson consists of Luke's narrative introduction to the sermon and the first main section of the sermon. But we should note that the sermon has an appropriate conclusion. The promise of salvation is offered and accepted. Three thousand souls are added on the first day (2:41), and the church immediately becomes the ideal messianic community (2:42–47). Just as Jesus' sermon in Nazareth served to inaugurate his ministry (Luke 4:16–30), so this Pentecost event and sermon serve to inaugurate the newly constituted people of God.

Ever attentive to matters of time and place, Luke dates the beginning of the church on the Jewish Feast of Pentecost and locates its origin in Jerusalem. Also known as the Feast of

Weeks, the Feast of Unleavened Bread, or the Feast of Harvest, this festival was celebrated fifty days after Passover; hence its name Pentecost (based on the Greek word for "fifty"). As a Jewish observance, it marked the end of the wheat harvest. Its importance and significance in Jewish life is well attested (cf. Exod. 12:14–17; 34:18–23; Lev. 23:15–21; Numbers 28–29; Deut. 16:1–17). In some traditions, it had become a time for celebrating the giving of the law on Sinai, and thus was seen as marking the beginning of a new period in Israel's history. For Luke, this particular celebration of Pentecost clearly marked a new beginning—the arrival of the "last days" (v. 17).

It is also important to note that Jerusalem is the place where the messianic community is reconstituted and begins. For Luke, Jerusalem was more than a geographical place; it was the place where the continuation of God's story had begun (Luke 1) and to which Jesus had been inexorably drawn as God's eschatological prophet (Luke 9:51; 13:33). Here the Christ had been martyred, but here also his cause had been vindicated (Luke 24). It was from here that God's message of repentance and forgiveness of sins would begin to be proclaimed again (Luke 24:47). It was more than the city of Jerusalem; it was Zion, the city of God, to which all the nations would stream when God eventually reestablished the universal kingdom (Isa. 2:2–4; Mic. 4:1–4). We are not surprised to find a roster of the nations represented at this inaugural event (vv. 9–11).

Both the time and place are right for the New Age to begin. And it does begin as the prophets had promised—with the pouring out of the Spirit (v. 4; cf. 2:33; 10:45; Rom. 5:5; Titus 3:6). This is the first of many such events in the life of the new messianic community (4:8, 31; 9:17; 10:44; 11:15; 13:9, 52). As the story unfolds in the rest of Acts, the church becomes both the witness and bearer of God's Spirit. It is the Spirit who impels the church to mission (8:29; 10:47; 13:2; 16:6) and assists it in resolving its controversies (15:28). Just as Jesus had been the bearer of God's Spirit (Luke 4:18–21), so now his successors—the apostles, teachers, and evangelists—bear witness through the Spirit, as the prophets had promised (vv. 4 and 17).

From the way Luke tells the story, we are left in no doubt that his is an inaugural event. The coming of the Spirit is both audible ("a sound like the rush of a violent wind," v. 2) and visible ("divided tongues, as of fire," v. 3). Perhaps the chief sign is the speaking in other tongues (vv. 4 and 11; cf. 10:46; 19:6; also Mark 16:17; 1 Cor. 14:21). This is only the first of many "wonders and signs" that are to accompany the breaking in of the New Age (cf. v. 19; also 2:22, 43; 4:30; 5:12; 6:8; 7:36; 8:13; 14:3; 15:12). All the confusion of Babel (Gen. 11:1–9) is now resolved as each nation hears the Word of God in its own language, that is, understands it (v. 11).

Today's text closes on a universal note: "Then everyone who calls on the name of the Lord shall be saved" (v. 21; cf. Joel 2:32). As Peter later says, God's promise is now "for you, for your children [Jews], and for all who are far away [Gentiles], everyone whom the Lord our God calls to him" (v. 39). If the celebration of Pentecost means anything, it calls the church to a universal witness, to extend the hope of forgiveness to all the nations, even as it has been extended to us (Luke 24:47). The story begins in Jerusalem, but it ends in Rome!

Genesis 11:1–9

It is a complete and self-contained story, this account of the building of the tower of Babel. While it has its place in the primeval history (Gen. 1–11), the pre-patriarchal time, it could easily stand alone. Evidence that it once did is seen in the fact that it contradicts points in the chapter that immediately precedes. While Genesis 11:1 affirms that all people on the earth had "one language," Genesis 10:5, 20, and 31 already accounted for different peoples, "each with his own language." Moreover, Babel had already been mentioned in Genesis 10:10. In spite of these tensions, both the table of nations in Genesis 10 and the story of the tower in Genesis 11:1–9 are, at one level, attempts to account for the same fact, namely, the multiplicity of nations and languages.

In order to be worth telling, any story must have tension, often between protagonists and antagonists. In this case the tension is between human and divine intentions. The account easily divides itself into three parts. The first movement (vs. 1–4) concerns the plans and actions of the human race. After setting the scene—the earth had only one language—the narrator reports that the people settled in the plain of Shinar and then set out to build a city and a tower. The only purposes stated are their desire to make a name for themselves and to avoid being scattered all over the earth (verse 4). In the second part of the story (vs. 5–8) all attention is given to the Lord's reaction. Coming down to see what the human beings are doing, the Lord is concerned about what they may do next, so he decides to confuse their language and to scatter them abroad. The account concludes (verse 9) with an explanation of the name Babel.

A number of points in the story require some explanation. The "plain in the land of Shinar" (v. 2) certainly is the flat river valley of lower Mesopotamia, known in ancient times first as Sumer and then as Babylon. The narrator seems to be a bit surprised at the building materials, but baked mud brick and bitumen for mortar were typical for monumental buildings in Mesopotamia, where other materials were scarce. The "tower" (v. 4) certainly reflects the common Mesopotamian temple-tower, the ziggurat. Such buildings were artificial sacred mountains, where communication between the divine and human worlds took place.

At one level, the story is an etiological saga, as its conclusion makes explicit. One purpose is to explain the name of the city "Babel" as the place where the Lord confused (*balal*) human language. But even that etiology bears a note of polemic, for the Babylonians explained the meaning of their city's name as "gate of God." Other etiological purposes concern the origin of diverse languages from a supposed original unity and the dispersion of people all over the earth from the single place of their origin.

On another level the account seems to view urbanization and civilization to be in some way contrary to the will of God. The tension between sedentary, inevitable bureaucratic, and sophisticated culture—including monumental architecture—and nomadic, seminomadic, or rural cultures is well known.

But what is the fundamental point of tension in the story? Why does the Lord disapprove of the plans for the city and the tower? The answer is not at all obvious; there are only hints that the building of the tower is an expression of human pride and arrogance. Certainly in the literary context the plans to build the city and tower are viewed as sinful. The Yahwist, who is responsible for this story, views the history of the race from the first pair in Genesis 2 through this episode, as a history of sin, rebellion against Yahweh. The turning point to a history of salvation will come for him in Genesis 12:1 ff. with the call of Abraham.

Is it ironic that in Genesis 11:1–9 God disperses and confuses the language of the human race and that the Spirit of God reverses that in Acts 2:1–21? In the texts taken together, separation and confusion are viewed as the results of human arrogance—sin—while union and understanding are signs that the kingdom of God is breaking in.

Psalm 104:24–34, 35b

The two foci of this psalm—the world of creation as the work of God and the universal character of God's rule—make it appropriate for inclusion in the lectionary for Pentecost. A minor but still a significant feature in the psalm, apropos Pentecost, is the association of the Spirit of God with the re-creation and renewal of world orders.

The various stanzas in the psalm, excluding the summarizing depiction and the conclusion in verses 27–35, focus on the various wonders of creation: the sky (2–4), the earth (5–9), the water (10–13), the vegetation (14–18), the moon and sun (19–23), and the sea (24–26). (It is instructive to compare these with the structure and characterization of the six days of creation in Genesis 1.)

The selection for this lectionary picks up with the depiction of the sixth wonder. Verses 24–35 may be divided into three units: verses 24–26 center on the sea in the world of creation; verses 27–30 offer a reflection on creation's dependence upon God; and verses 31–35 (which are no longer addressed to the Deity) marvel at the grandeur and awesomeness of the Lord of creation.

For the psalmist, the sea (vv. 24–26) is God's pond, not some murky, mysterious, monster-laden source of chaos. From the ships and Leviathans (see Ps. 74:14; Job 41:1; Isa. 27:1) that ply its waves to the innumerable creatures small and great that scurry through its waters, they all have been made in the wisdom of God.

Verses 27–30 speak of what might be called "vertical universality." All living things are seen as dependent upon God—for food that fuels and sustains the living and for the breath of life that creates new being. That is, every part of life from top to bottom is the gift of God, not the possessor of that life. When God turns away, the creatures (including humans; note v. 23) become dismayed; when God withdraws the life spirit, the creatures succumb and return to dust. For all the world's greatness, for all its wonder and amazement, for the psalmist, the world is no independent entity. Without divine sustenance it would not survive. Creation is depicted so that, in the words of the Heidelberg Catechism, God "rules in such a way that waves and grass, rain and drought, fruitful and unfruitful years, food and drink, death and sickness, riches and poverty and everything else come to us not by chance, but by his fatherly hand."

The psalm concludes with a confessional statement addressed to a human audience (vv. 31–35). These verses affirm gratitude and praise for the grandeur of the cosmos and its creatures and above all for the God who creates and sustains.

The reference to the "spirit" (or "breath") of God (v. 30), which creates and calls into being, ties this psalm thematically with the account of Pentecost in Acts.

Romans 8:14–17

If Acts 2:1–21 speaks of the Spirit as the possession of the church, Romans 8:14–17 speaks of the Spirit as the possession of us as individuals. With this Pauline text, Luke's narrative account becomes personalized.

Who is a Christian? This question is asked and answered in many ways. For some, being Christian is adhering to the creed. It is a test of orthodoxy. We must ask what one believes and confesses before we can determine whether that person is a Christian. For others, being

Christian is exhibiting a certain form of behavior. We are Christian if we behave like Christians. It is a test of orthopraxy. We must ask whether one's "praxy," or practice, conforms to Christian standards. Still others locate the answer in liturgy. We can tell if we are Christian by whom we worship and how. And so it goes.

The answer of today's text is simple and straightforward: to be a Christian is to be led by the Spirit of God (v. 14). In fact, everyone who is so led is a child of God. The term "led" may not be strong enough to convey Paul's meaning. The New Jerusalem Bible prefers "guided": "All who are guided by the Spirit of God are sons of God" (v. 14). The import of the statement seems to be that if the motivating force, the guiding principle, the central impulse of our life is God's Spirit, then we can claim to be God's children (cf. Gal. 5:18). For Paul, being God's children and having God's Spirit belong together; as God's children, we have received God's Spirit (Gal. 4:6). Just as a child receives the life of the parent, so we receive the life force of God—God's Spirit.

How can we measure the quality of our "sonship" (or, to be more generic, our "childhood")? By whether ours is a life of enslavement or freedom. If we live in fear, either of ourselves, others, unknown forces, or whatever, we are *de facto* slaves. When children are disoriented from their parents, separated from them, disowned or abused by them, they become afraid; but when the relationship is cemented with love, fear is removed (cf. 1 John 4:18; also 2 Tim. 1:7; Matt. 8:26 and parallels; John 14:27). Before we became God's children, we may have been tyrannized by fear, but this is no longer our lot (cf. Gal. 4:8–9).

The metaphor of "slavery" versus "sonship" is made even more precise by Paul's use of "adoption" to explain our changed status. In one sense, God had only one Son—Jesus Christ—but all those in Christ are adopted children, brought into a full filial relationship (Gal. 4:5–6; Eph. 1:5; also, cf. Rom. 8:23).

It may be objected that adoption is not the same as natural childhood. Thus Paul insists that as children of God, we address God in exactly the same way Jesus did, as "Abba! Father!" (v. 15; cf. Mark 14:36). This Aramaic expression captured so effectively the nature of Jesus' relationship with God that the early church apparently chose to preserve it in its original form. Through extensive study done on the use of this form of address, we now know that if it was not a unique way of addressing God, it was at least distinctive. It became a shorthand way of expressing Jesus' complete obedience, as seen in the Gethsemane experience. As we use this form of address in our prayers, we enter a relationship with God similarly close and intimate.

Our text stresses, however, that it is not just a matter of praying the same prayer Jesus did. It is rather that when we verbally express our relationship this way as God's children, then God's Spirit joins with us in our testimony (cf. 1 John 5:10; also 3:1). It is as if our inner spirit and God's own Spirit "bear united witness that we are children of God" (v. 16, JB). It becomes a question of reaffirming our own true identity. We are reminded once again of who we really are—children of God in an absolutely unqualified sense.

The implications of this are that we enjoy all the rights and privileges of heirs (v. 17). Having been admitted to a status comparable to that of Christ, we are Christ's fellow heirs (cf. Gal. 3:16, 26, 29; 4:7; Rev. 21:7; also Mark 12:7; Heb. 1:2).

There is one qualification, however: we must enter with Christ into his suffering. Elsewhere, Paul speaks of the "sharing of his sufferings" (Phil. 3:10–11; cf. 2 Cor. 4:10; Rom. 6:8; also 2 Tim. 2:3, 12; 1 Pet. 4:13; 5:1; Luke 22:28–30). For Christ, the way to glory was through suffering (cf. Luke 24:26), and this is our lot and privilege as Christ's fellow heirs.

John 14:8–17 (25–27)

Easter is completed at Pentecost. Without Pentecost, Easter means the departure of Christ, leaving behind the confused and uncertain disciples who can do no better than return to fishing (21:1–3). With Pentecost, Jesus' promise not to leave his disciples orphaned in the world is kept (14:18).

Pentecost was a Jewish festival celebrating the early harvest, but it came in time to be the commemoration of God's giving Israel the law at Sinai. The festival came fifty days after Passover. Luke, who historicizes the events of the Christian faith, says Jesus revealed himself to his disciples for forty days after the resurrection (Acts 1:3). Following Jesus' ascension (Acts 1:9–11), his followers continued in prayer and expectation (Acts 1:12–14). At Pentecost, the promise of power from on high was fulfilled (Acts 2:1–21). This festival, for the Jews a celebration of the giving of the law, became for the Christians a celebration of the giving of the Holy Spirit. Beyond that, the word does not specify a date or season but symbolizes the coming of the Spirit, which gathers, constitutes, and empowers the church, whether that story is told by Luke or Paul or John.

It is important for the preacher to keep these three New Testament writers distinct and separate when speaking of the Holy Spirit in the life of the church. Each emphasizes a dimension of the Holy Spirit's presence and work in the church in addressing conditions in different congregations. It would be confusing and unfair to Luke and John, for example, to take Paul's discussion of gifts of the Spirit in First Corinthians 12 as the normative definition of the Spirit's manifestation and then interpret Luke and John so as to make them support and elaborate that text, and vice versa. Our lection for today, then, is not "what the Bible says about the Holy Spirit" but a portion of John's teaching on the subject.

The Holy Spirit is, according to this Gospel, associated with Jesus. Upon Jesus the Spirit came at baptism, and Jesus is the one who baptizes with the Holy Spirit (1:33). However, the gift of the Spirit to Jesus' followers had to wait upon Jesus' passion and ascension back to God (7:39; 16:7). Even Jesus' word to Nicodemus about being born of the Spirit assumes the Ascension as a precondition for this work of the Spirit (3:13). In other words, the resurrected, glorified Jesus sends the Holy Spirit upon the church.

What has just been said, however, should not be thought of simply as John's "doctrine" of the Holy Spirit. Our lection occurs in the context of Jesus' parting words to the group he is leaving behind. The confused and saddened disciples are asking questions such as: Where are you going? Can we go? Will we ever be together again? (13:36–14:7). Finally, Philip requests, "Lord, show us the Father, and we will be satisfied" (v. 8). This request lies at the heart of this Gospel in two ways. First, it states a fundamental presupposition of this Evangelist: the basic human hunger is for the God whom no one has seen (1:18), but whom to know is life eternal (17:3). Second, this request looks to Jesus for a revelation of God, which is this Gospel's portrait of Jesus, the revealer of God (1:18). This is the substance of Jesus' response to Philip (vv. 9–11).

At this point, Jesus makes a series of promises to his followers that, if believed, should not only relieve some of their pain at his departure, but also equip them for a fruitful life after his leaving. In fact, his departure, his ascension, is the precondition of their receiving these blessings (v. 12). In verses 12–17, the promises are three: (1) they will be enabled not only to continue Jesus' work, but also to do greater works (v. 12); (2) they will be heard and their prayers answered to meet the needs involved in their life and mission (vv. 13–14); (3) they will be accompanied in their life and mission in the world by another Counselor or

Helper, the Spirit of truth (vv. 16–17). Unlike Jesus, who is now departing, the Spirit will be with them forever.

Verses 16–17 constitute the first of five Holy Spirit promises in the farewell speeches (14:16–17; 14:26; 15:26–27; 16:7–11; 16:13–15). The second of the five is also a part of today's reading even though verses 25–27 are marked as optional. Whereas the first promises the continual abiding presence of the Spirit as Helper and Counselor, the second promises the Spirit as Teacher and Reminder (14:26). This Evangelist wants no one to misunderstand: if the Spirit in the church is of God (and the spirits must be tested: 1 John 4:1), it will not lead the church away from the historical Jesus but will tie the church by instruction and memory to Jesus. The Christian faith has a memory, and to be a Christian is to be enrolled in a tradition as well as to be set free for the future.

Trinity Sunday

Proverbs 8:1–4, 22–31;
Psalm 8;
Romans 5:1–5;
John 16:12–15

I n the early church, this Sunday was observed as the Octave of Whitsun; that is, as the eighth day of Pentecost. The day assumed its character as a celebration in honor of the Trinity in the later Middle Ages. As such, it concludes the commemorations of the life of Christ and the descent of the Spirit and thus brings together the three persons of the Godhead.

All four of today's texts are classical biblical pericopes used in expounding Trinitarian doctrine. In the passage from Proverbs, playful Wisdom delights in the self-proclamation of herself as the first product of God's actions, as one who reveled in the presence of the Maker at creation. The psalm praises God, who created the world for the sake of humanity and assigned humans a place of dominance in that creation. The Gospel reading announces the coming of the Spirit, and the Epistle speaks in Trinitarian terms of God, Jesus Christ, and Holy Spirit.

Proverbs 8:1–4, 22–31

T rinity Sunday is a time for theological reflection, and that is what the Old Testament reading presents for us. It contains serious and sophisticated reflection on issues closely related to the questions that finally led to the doctrine of the Trinity. The text does not contain doctrine in anything like the formal sense, but its affirmations respond to the questions of the relationship of a transcendent God to the world, and the means of divine revelation.

The passage is part of a larger literary context, the collection of poems in Proverbs 1–9. These chapters contain some twelve units, most of them wisdom instructions generally regarded as examples of late Israelite wisdom thought. They are quite different from the remainder of the Book of Proverbs, which is mainly a series of short proverbial sayings, admonitions, and exhortations. Most of the poems in Proverbs 1–9 begin with the address "My son" (RSV; "my child" in NRSV), reflecting the situation of a teacher addressing students.

Our lectionary text is part of a distinct poem (8:1–31), a wisdom speech. Following a brief introduction characterizing her appearance in public places (vv. 1–3), Wisdom herself speaks, mainly to give the reasons why people should listen to her voice and attend to her ways. Wisdom recommends herself because her words are true and valuable (vv. 6–11), she has qualities to be desired (vv. 12–16), and she can be trusted to reward those who follow her (vv. 17–21). In this context, verses 22–31 give the final reason for attending to Wisdom: she was the first of God's creations.

Throughout the passage, Wisdom is personified as an attractive woman. In the light of the parallels with the other instructions in Proverbs 1–9, it appears that Lady Wisdom assumes the role of the teacher. She stands in sharp contrast to that other woman of these chapters, variously described as the "loose woman" (5:3, 20), "the wife of another, . . . the adulteress" (6:24), the woman "decked out like a prostitute" (7:10), or "the foolish woman" (9:13). The last of these is the personification of folly, the antithesis of Lady Wisdom. On the surface, most of the others seem to involve practical moral advice to young men, to avoid certain kinds of women. In the context, however, they reflect another dimension as well, suggesting that same personification of folly one sees in 9:13.

Central to the reflections on Trinity Sunday are verses 22–31. Unifying this section is Wisdom's assertion that she was the first of God's creations and present with God during the creation and ordering of the cosmos. This theme is developed in three distinct movements. First (vv. 22–23), wisdom proclaims that she was the first of all creation. Second (vv. 24–29), Wisdom describes the stages of God's creative activity. Each sentence begins with a temporal clause ("When . . . ," "Before . . . ,"), and most include the reaffirmation that Wisdom was present when God was creating all things. Third (vv. 30–31), Wisdom reports the manner of her presence with God at the beginning.

In pointing out that Wisdom was created first, and stressing the creative power of God, the poem dwells at length, and with genuine joy, on the wonders of the created world. These include the earth itself (v. 23), the waters of both oceans and springs (v. 24), mountains and hills (v. 25), land (v. 26), the heavens and their circular limits (v. 27), the heavenly vault and the primeval waters (v. 28), and the boundaries for the waters and the earth's foundations (v. 29). The cosmos thus described includes facets visible to the human eye, but also those features (such as the heavenly vault, primeval waters, foundations of the earth) only assumed to exist in the ancient Near Eastern world view. In a skillful and subtle way, the poet both marvels at the wonders of the world and reminds the hearers that it is, after all, created by God, and thus has its limits.

Remarkably, human beings are not mentioned until the very end (v. 31), probably for emphasis. As Wisdom is the first of God's creations, human beings are the last.

In the concluding verses (vv. 30–31), Wisdom describes her presence with God during creation. There is no explicit sense that God created the world through or by means of Wisdom, as one sees in Proverbs 3:19–20: "The LORD by wisdom founded the earth; by understanding he established the heavens." Instead, these lines stress Wisdom's playful presence: "playing in his presence continually" (v. 30, NEB), "playing on the earth" and "delighting in mankind" (v. 31, NEB). We are reminded that Israelite wisdom literature has its playful side, using even riddles to discover and communicate truth. Moreover, if wisdom is in any sense a characteristic of God, according to our poet, it must be also God's playful and joyful side.

Although such reflections as this one stand behind the Prologue to John, wisdom here, although personified, is not in any sense an incarnation or extension of God's person. Other wisdom literature goes further. Wisdom of Solomon 7:24–25 sees wisdom as a virtual hypostasis of God ("a pure emanation of the glory of the Almighty," RSV).

Nevertheless, this passage—like the doctrine of the Trinity—is a way of coming to terms with the deep awareness of God as both almighty and transcendent on the one hand, and present in and with creation on the other. If God is distinct from the world—it is an act of divine creation—then how is God active and how is God known? According to the historical and prophetic literature of the Old Testament, this God is known through acts of revelation and intervention in history. The wisdom teachers take another direction that leads to poems such as the one before us. God's will and ways are known in the created order and through wisdom. Wisdom—both as the one who was created first and as a characteristic of human thought and behavior—is the link between God and all who inhabit the earth.

Psalm 8

This psalm was discussed earlier as one of the lections for January 1.

Romans 5:1–5

This is one of those passages that is Trinitarian in the sense that God, Christ, and the Holy Spirit are mentioned, but not in the sense that it presents a fully developed picture of the Triune God (cf. 2 Cor. 13:13; also Matt. 28:19). Even so, read within the context of Trinity Sunday the passage will echo Trinitarian themes as it speaks (1) of the God who bestows peace on those who are justified by faith (v. 1), who lavishes us with love (v. 5), and who invites us to share in the eschatological glory (v. 2); (2) of the Lord Jesus Christ as the one through whom God's shalom becomes a reality and continues to remain a reality because of his mediating role in granting us access to the divine grace (vv. 1–2); and (3) of the Holy Spirit given to us as the means of experiencing the love of God (v. 5).

We should notice that the central focus of the passage is what results for those who are justified by faith (cf. 4:5; Gal. 3:8, 24; Eph. 2:8–9; Phil. 3:9). That we are "rightwised" before God by faith, and not by religious works, provides the premise of the passage (cf. Gal. 2:16; 3:2; Rom. 3:28) and is the point toward which the argument of the letter has moved through chapters 1–4. Given this, certain things follow, the first of which is peace, or a state of reconciliation with God (cf. Isa. 32:17; John 16:33; 1 John 3:21). This emphatic affirmation is based on the reading "we have peace" as opposed to the alternative reading "let us have peace." The former is indicative and implies a present possession, whereas the latter is a hortatory subjunctive and suggests the goal toward which justification directs us.

It is Christ through whom peace is accomplished (Eph. 2:14; Col. 1:22). But he does not merely initiate peace; he sustains it through his role as mediator who grants us access to God's grace (cf. Eph. 2:18; 3:12; 1 Pet. 3:18; Matt. 11:27; John 14:6). Here, as elsewhere, divine grace is presented as that realm in which we position ourselves and find our place to stand (cf. 1 Pet. 5:12).

From this point of existential definition, we already begin to experience eschatological joy—that is, rejoicing anchored in our future hope of participating in God's glory (cf. 8:18, 30; Col. 1:27; Titus 2:13). But not only is the rejoicing future oriented; it is also directed to the present where there occurs the rhythm of suffering giving way to patience, patience giving way to perseverance, and perseverance giving way to hope (cf. James 1:2–4; 1 Pet. 1:6–7; Heb. 6:18–19).

Nor is this a futile quest where we chase a fragile hope. It was already an axiom of Old Testament thought that Yahweh could be trusted, and that those who place their trust in

Yahweh would not be disappointed (Pss. 22:5; 25:20). Further assurance of this is provided because the Holy Spirit, the earmark of the eschatological age, has already been unleashed, ushered into our lives as a gift providing tangible evidence of God's love (cf. Acts 2:18, 33; 5:32; 10:45; Titus 3:5; 1 John 4:13).

In reflecting homiletically on this epistolary reading for Trinity Sunday, we note the way the work of God brackets salvation history: it is the love of God that stands at the beginning and the glory of God toward which all things move, with the reconciling peace of God serving as the ongoing relationship in which we are able to deal with God. The role of Christ throughout the passage is one of active agent, the one through whom we are able to experience God's salvation. This reminds us of the early Christian confession of the "one Lord, Jesus Christ, through whom are all things and through whom we exist" (1 Cor. 8:6). Finally, the Holy Spirit is envisioned here as the one through whom and in whom we actually experience the love of God. It is the Spirit who gives concrete form to divine love and does so within us where God's self converges with our own selves.

John 16:12–15

We linger one more Sunday in the Gospel of John, which nourished and informed Pentecost as well as the Sundays immediately preceding that festival. We do so because one further word needs to be said about the Holy Spirit.

John 16:12–15 is the fifth and final Holy Spirit saying in Jesus' farewell discourses to his disciples (14:1–16:33). A careful reading of these discourses reveals that they are both the parting words of Jesus to his followers and the present word of the risen Christ to his church in the world. Therefore the promises, warnings, and instructions are in the future tense because they are spoken prior to Jesus' death and resurrection, but for the readers of John's Gospel (and for us) they are in the present tense because the message of the now risen and exalted Lord is addressed to them. The reader of this Gospel is not to make distinctions between pre- and postresurrection words of Jesus.

Central among the promises of Jesus to his followers is the Holy Spirit, the Spirit of God, the Spirit of truth, the Comforter or Counselor. Before attending to the text for today, the preacher would be helped by a review of the first four Holy Spirit sayings (14:16–17; 14:25–26; 15:26; 16:7–11). Briefly stated, those passages make the following promises and affirmations: Jesus will ask God to send the Spirit of truth as another Counselor to be with the disciples forever; the Holy Spirit will be sent from God in Jesus' name to teach and to remind the disciples of Jesus' words; the Spirit, sent by Jesus but proceeding from God, will bear witness to Jesus; and finally, upon his departure Jesus will send the Counselor to convict the world of sin, righteousness, and judgment.

The fifth saying, John 16:12–15, continues in the same vein making three important statements about the Holy Spirit, the third bearing directly on the meaning of Trinity Sunday. First, the words of the historical Jesus did not touch every human condition or question that might arise. In fact, had Jesus so spoken, his followers would not have been able to comprehend his message (v. 12). For example, Jesus left no instruction covering the case of a Christian convert whose spouse remained an unbeliever. Paul faced such a problem at Corinth and had to interpret the will of God (1 Cor. 7:12–16). He concluded his comments on marriage, divorce, and remarriage with the words, "And I think that I too have the Spirit of God" (1 Cor. 7:40). This leads to the second statement in our text concerning the Holy Spirit: the Spirit "will guide you into all the truth" and "will declare to you the things that are to come" (v. 13). This is in some ways a frightening promise, for it can be quoted to bless every new notion and to footnote with authority all manner of behavior as well as prophesies as to the fate of the world, the time of the Eschaton, and the certain will of God in every crisis. But that danger notwithstanding, that the Spirit continues to guide and enlighten the church is a conviction not to abandon. To do so would be to deny that the present is as surely God's time as was the first or any other century. The preacher is a proclaimer of God's word to each gathered community, not a curator of ancient records of once glorious days. Were this not so, the Gospel of John itself, an interpretation of the meaning of Jesus Christ, could make no claim on us as Word of God because it could not claim the guidance and enlightenment of the Holy Spirit.

The third and final statement of our text brings us directly to the significance of Trinity Sunday. The Holy Spirit will not speak or act independently, but rather will glorify Christ and will reveal only that which comes from Christ and from God (vv. 14–15). Here is offered a canon by which to test if the spirit by which any person or group acts and speaks is really the Holy Spirit: Are the actions and words in accordance with what we know of God and of Jesus Christ? To be sure, this is no simple test to apply, but it does provide the church a measure of defense against spirits not of God and a measure of confidence in affirming the leading of the Holy Spirit in new and changing circumstances. The Holy Spirit is the hallmark of Christianity, but the church affirms the Holy Spirit as from God and from Christ and as witness to that which God has revealed in Jesus of Nazareth. For example, notice how Paul introduced the Trinity to address excesses and confusion related to the Holy Spirit at Corinth (1 Cor. 12:4–6).

A doctrine of the Trinity has seemed to many to be remote, ancient, and irrelevant, but such is far from the truth. The affirmation of God, Christ, and Holy Spirit has been and is essential for the health of the Christian faith.

Proper 4 [9]
(Sunday between May 29 and June 4 inclusive
(if after Trinity Sunday))

1 Kings 18:20–21 (22–29) 30–39;
Psalm 96; or
1 Kings 8:22–23, 41–43;
Psalm 96:1–9;
Galatians 1:1–12;
Luke 7:1–10

Because the season after Pentecost is uninterrupted by special events or observances, it provides opportunity for focused reading of particular portions of Scripture. All lectionaries take advantage of this extended period in their treatment of the Epistle and Gospel readings. As is well known, during this period Matthew, Mark (and John), and Luke supply the Gospel readings in semicontinuous form for Years A, B, and C respectively.

For the Epistle readings, Year A offers selections from Romans, Philippians, and 1 Thessalonians; Year B epistolary readings are taken from 2 Corinthians, Ephesians, James, and Hebrews 1–10; for Year C, epistolary readings are supplied from Galatians, Colossians, Hebrews 11–13, Philemon, 1 and 2 Timothy, and 2 Thessalonians.

In the treatment of Old Testament readings, two principles of selections are represented in the lectionary tradition. *The Revised Common Lectionary* uses the period after Pentecost for systematic selection of Old Testament readings. In Year A, the Old Testament readings come from Genesis through Judges. Year B readings are supplied by several texts from 1 and 2 Samuel and 1 Kings that focus on David; these texts are complemented by other selections from Song of Solomon, Proverbs, Esther, Job, and Ruth. In Year C, the Old Testament readings focus on the prophets. For six weeks, selections from 1 and 2 Kings feature episodes in the lives of Elijah and Elisha. Thereafter, notable prophetic passages ranging over a period of five centuries supply the Old Testament readings.

In other lectionary traditions, the Old Testament readings are not selected in order to treat Scripture systematically or thematically. Rather, they are chosen to fit with the Gospel reading for a particular day. As a result, they are drawn from throughout the Old Testament.

As usual, regardless of the principle of selection for the Old Testament reading, the psalm is chosen in connection with the Old Testament text and serves as a form of meditation or reflection on the first reading.

For today, in *The Revised Common Lectionary* the Old Testament reading is the account of Elijah's confrontation with the prophets of Baal on Mt. Carmel. The responsorial psalm is supplied by Psalm 96, which heralds Yahweh as the one to be praised over all other gods.

In other lectionaries, the Old Testament reading is taken from Solomon's prayer at the dedication of the temple in Jerusalem. The selections from the prayer emphasize the incomparability of Israel's God, and they petition God to hear the prayer of the foreigner who offers up requests in the temple. Psalm 96:1–9 responds by offering praise to God as Creator and Lord of the heavens.

The Epistle reading concerns Paul's affirmation of the distinctiveness of the Gospel he preached, a gospel singular in its meaning yet universal in its appeal.

The Gospel reading contributes its perspectives to the theme of universalism in the report of the healing of the centurion's slave and in the celebration of the foreigner's faith.

1 Kings 18:20–21 (22–29) 30–39

The semicontinuous Old Testament readings for this season focus on prophets, from Elijah to Haggai and Third Isaiah, from one of the earliest prophets to some of the latest ones. Historically, the readings span the period from the ninth century BC to perhaps as late as the fifth or fourth century BC. The readings provide not only a review of the history of Israel but also a summary of the messages of the prophets over time. The lesson for today is not quite in chronological sequence, for next week's reading will return to an earlier event in the life of Elijah. But it is fitting that a series on the prophets begin with Elijah, and with the account of his conflict on Mt. Carmel with the prophets of Baal.

First Kings 18:20–40 is a self-contained and dramatic narrative. The lectionary omits the concluding verse that reports the outcome of the conflict, namely, the slaughter of the prophets of Baal at Elijah's command. But this unit is one episode in several wider contexts. The extended framework of the story is the Deuteronomistic history (Deuteronomy–2 Kings) that reports Israel's story from the time of Moses to the Babylonian Exile. In that context it is important to recall that the events occur in the Northern Kingdom of Israel in the time of Ahab, famous for his apostasy and for his foreign queen Jezebel. Then this story is part of the cycle of tales concerning the prophet Elijah; and more immediately, it is framed by the story of the drought and famine (1 Kings 18:1–19) and the account of the end of the drought (1 Kings 41–46).

In fact, what appears to be a story of fire on the altar turns out to be an account of rain on the earth. The point at issue between Elijah and the prophets of Baal is, Who is responsible for the fertility of the land? Which god can and will end the drought? Or, who is God? This question, focused in terms of the conflict between Yahweh and the gods of Canaan, is a major theme of the Deuteronomistic history, and it echoes throughout the history of the prophets, especially in Hosea and Jeremiah.

The story of the contest proceeds dramatically, building to a climax; but from the point of view of the narrator as well as the readers, the outcome is never seriously in doubt. The setting had already been in 18:17–19, when Elijah ordered the king to assemble the people and the prophets of Baal on Mt. Carmel. In verses 20–21, Elijah challenges the people. The issue is simple: They must follow either Yahweh or Baal, but not "go limping with two different opinions." Then (vv. 22–25) Elijah challenges the prophets of Baal to the contest. Each side is to choose a bull for an offering, lay it on the wood of the altar, and pray for fire. Whoever answers with fire will be recognized as God. The prophets of Baal are allowed to go first. Then (vv. 26–29) follows the report of the prophets' unsuccessful rituals, including prayers, dancing (v. 26), and even mutilation of themselves with swords and lances (v. 28). All the while, Elijah is ridiculing their efforts and laughing at their god. Still they "raved on" (the Hebrew for this expression may also mean "prophesied"). Their failure is underscored: "but there was no voice, no answer, and no response" (v. 29).

Then (vv. 30–35) Elijah calmly steps forward with instructions for the preparation of the altar. It is important that the people "come closer" to observe all that he does. The allusion to the "altar of the LORD that had been thrown down" (v. 30) underscores both the people's apostasy and the violence of the religious conflict that is the background of the story. The twelve stones used in building the altar stand for the twelve tribes of Israel. Once the altar, wood, and offering were set in place, the prophet has the people pour four jars of water over it all, not once but three times. This action likely has a double meaning. On the one hand, it emphasizes the power of Yahweh and his prophet, to burn up what is completely soaked with water. On the other hand, the pouring of the water may be a ritual related to the prayer for rain.

Elijah's rituals and their results (vv. 36–39) are in stark contrast to those of the prophets of Baal. Addressing the Lord—the God of Abraham, Isaac, and Israel—calmly and directly, he asked that he be vindicated as the Lord's servant and that the Lord be revealed as God. The response is immediate. The "fire of the LORD fell" and consumed the burnt offering, the wood, the altar, and even the water (v. 38). This dramatic event had the expected result: the people acclaimed Yahweh as God.

The lesson of the story of Elijah and the prophets of Baal on Mt. Carmel is clear and direct, and consistent with the understanding of "miraculous" events in the Old Testament. The purpose of such occurrences is revelation, the demonstration of divine power to evoke faith and trust in God. In ancient Israel the conflict between those who followed Yahweh and those who followed the gods of Canaan was real and persistent. But, for all the ridicule of the storm god Baal and his prophets, the story does not insist on monotheism, the belief that there is only one God. Rather, the issue is allegiance, and the perspective is that of the First Commandment: "You shall have no other gods before me" (Exod. 20:3).

Psalm 96

This psalm was discussed earlier as one of the lections for Christmas, First Proper.

1 Kings 8:22–23, 41–43

First Kings 8, as the account of Solomon's dedication of the temple in Jerusalem, lies near the heart of what later generations considered most important about Solomon. Foremost among his many building projects was the magnificent temple. The verses assigned for reading on this day come from the king's dedicatory prayer. The prayer had been preceded by the account of the assembly and the installation of the ark of the covenant in the new building (vv. 1–13), and Solomon's address to the assembly (vv. 14–21). After the prayer (vv. 22–53), the king addresses the people again with a sermon (vv. 54–61), and then concludes the ceremony with sacrifices and a feast (vv. 62–66).

Virtually all of the chapter bears the marks of the theology and style of the Book of Deuteronomy, and thus stems from the Deuteronomistic Historian or Historians who were responsible for collecting and editing the account of Israel's history from the time of Moses to the Babylonian Exile (Deuteronomy through 2 Kings). Although there are numerous older written and oral sources in the work, and there likely was a pre-exilic edition of it, the work as a whole was completed shortly after the last event it reports (2 Kings 25:27–30), during the Babylonian Exile (ca. 560 BC). Consequently, the report of the dedication of the temple was composed for a people who had lost their land and holy city, and knew that the temple lay in ruins.

Solomon's prayer of dedication is a series of four prayers of petition. The first (vv. 23–26) is a prayer that God confirm the promise to David that one of his sons would always sit on the throne in Jerusalem. The second (vv. 27–30) and fourth (vv. 52–53) are general requests that God hear and respond; the third (vv. 31–51) contains a series of petitions concerning seven possible future situations.

Our assigned verses contain the narrative beginning and the initial lines of the first prayer (vv. 22–23), and the fifth of the petitions concerning future circumstances (vv. 41–43), the one that expects "foreigners" to come to the temple.

The first verse (v. 22) of the reading, as well as its larger context, invites reflection on prayer, particularly public prayer. Some of the liturgical features are obvious here, and others are not. It is assumed that Israel's kings performed important priestly functions as a special link between Yahweh and the people. As the temple is dedicated, Solomon is said to be before the altar and in the presence of the assembled people, but the precise location is difficult to identify. (The parallel account in 2 Chronicles 6:13 has him in the courtyard of the temple on an elevated platform.) The posture of prayer is standing with hands outstretched "to heaven" (cf. Exod. 9:29; Isa. 1:15). In view of the fact that gods, like kings, in the ancient Near East generally are pictured as sitting on thrones, the posture of supplication is to stand with outstretched arms. Note, however, that when the prayers are concluded, Solomon is said to have been kneeling before the altar (8:54).

The initial lines of the prayer (v. 23) invite reflection on several matters central to the biblical faith. First, Yahweh, God of Israel, is addressed as incomparable ("no God like you . . .). This is not an assertion of monotheism, although it comes close. Rather, it parallels the view of the First Commandment ("You shall have no other gods before me," Exod. 20:3). Devotion to their God, rather than the abstract question of the number of the gods, is the central concern for ancient Israel. Second, Israel's God is trustworthy and loyal, "keeping covenant and steadfast love" to those who are faithful. These two expressions are virtually synonymous, emphasizing the stability of God's relationship with the covenant people.

The petition in verses 41–43 indicates that ancient Israel's concerns reached beyond boundaries of nation and culture. It is an intercessory prayer on behalf of any "foreigner" who comes to pray in the temple. If Yahweh is incomparable, other peoples will hear and come to worship him. Solomon asks that their prayers be heard. Although stressing the importance of the temple, the petition acknowledges that God's true dwelling place is "in heaven" (v. 43). The goal is that the Lord's "name"—who God is and what God has done—be known to all peoples (v. 43). The Lord does not actually dwell in the temple, but it is called by his name and is the place where he chooses to "put his name" (Deut. 12:5).

Psalm 96:1–9

This psalm was discussed earlier as one of the lections for Christmas, First Proper.

Galatians 1:1–12

Because today's epistolary reading begins the semicontinuous reading of the Epistle to the Galatians over the next six weeks, a few introductory remarks are in order.

At least two sets of issues emerge in Galatians—one theological, the other personal. As we will see, they are closely related. Theologically, the fundamental question is soteriological. On what basis are we accepted by God—by faithfully keeping the law or by faithfully hearing the gospel (3:2)? The practical issue had to do with the terms on which Gentiles could be admitted into the membership as people of God—generally, whether they had to live "subject to the law" (4:21; cf. 2:16–21; 3:2–4:7), and specifically, whether they had to undergo circumcision as the required initiation rite (5:2–12; 6:12–15; cf. 2:3, 12). For Paul, it was a question of freedom versus slavery (4:1–11, 21–31; 5:1).

The personal issue centered on the legitimacy of Paul's apostleship. He had been seriously challenged by those who opposed his theological position and argued for salvation through Torah as opposed to salvation apart from Torah. For them, Paul's gospel had unduly relaxed the requirements of God. They saw his message of freedom from the law as mere concession to human weakness. In their eyes, Paul's gospel offered an easy solution to the pain of circumcision by simply doing away with it. Construed one way, this was an approach that sought "human approval" calculated to gain popular appeal (1:10). The decisive question, then, was where and how Paul received the authority to preach a message so radically challenging to a well-established interpretation of Torah and an equally well-established way of being religious based on this interpretation.

The fusion of these two issues within the churches of Galatia prompted one of the most severely polemical letters from the hand of Paul. Not only his gospel but also his personal integrity was on the line, and at every turn we can see the blood vessels in Paul's enraged eyes. The tone of the letter is bombastic (1:6; 3:1, 3), sarcastic (2:2, 6, 9; 5:12, 15), even desperate (4:11, 19–20). Even in those rare moments when he seeks to be pastoral and conciliatory, his encouragement gives way to stern words of warning and rebuke (5:13–15; 6:11–16). It is a letter written in white-hot heat.

In today's epistolary lection we have the opening words of this letter. The text easily divides in two sections, the opening greeting (vv. 1–5) and a solemn warning (vv. 6–12).

The Greeting (vv. 1–5). Compared with other Pauline greetings, this one is colder and more abrupt. Nothing commendable is said of the Galatians. There is, however, the traditional prayer of grace and peace in their behalf (cf. Rom. 1:7; 1 Cor. 1:3; 2 Cor. 1:2; Eph. 1:2; Phil. 1:2; Col. 1:2).

Even in these opening words, the two central issues of the letter emerge: the source of Paul's apostolic authority (v. 1) and the work of Christ as the sole basis of our deliverance (vv. 3–4). Paul insists that his apostleship is neither humanly initiated nor humanly validated; it is not "by human appointment or human commission" (v. 1, NEB). On this note, his defense begins (v. 11). What he preached came "through a revelation of Jesus Christ" (v. 12), and his prophetic call to preach resulted from the divine intervention of God who had raised Christ from the dead (v. 1).

The essence of his gospel is stated in the form of a kerygmatic summary (v. 4), which aligns him with well-established orthodox Christianity. It is a move reminiscent of Romans 1:1–6, where he commends himself to an unknown audience by introducing his theological position in thoroughly acceptable terms. Three important elements should be noted: (1) the vicarious death of Christ "who gave himself for our sins" (cf. 2:20; 2 Cor. 5:15; Eph. 5:2, 25;

Titus 2:14; 1 Tim. 2:6; also Matt. 20:28); (2) our deliverance "from the present evil age," elsewhere seen to be under the dominion of satanic forces (2 Cor. 4:4; Acts 26:18; also Gal. 4:8–9) and a competing threat against Christian existence (Rom. 12:2; Eph. 5:16; 1 John 5:19); and (3) God as the approving agent of the gospel (cf. Heb. 10:10), to whom all glory is due (Rom. 11:36; Eph. 3:21; Phil. 4:20; 1 Tim. 1:17; 2 Tim. 4:18; Heb. 13:21; 1 Pet. 4:11; 2 Pet. 3:18; Jude 25; Rev. 1:6; 4:11).

The Warning (vv. 6–12). Instead of the usual prayer of thanksgiving offered on behalf of his readers (cf. Rom. 1:8–17; 1 Cor. 1:4–9; Phil. 1:3–11), the opening greeting is followed by this stern warning. By the absence of this opening pastoral prayer, we already sense the severely strained relations between Paul and the Galatians. To dispense with prayer marks the extreme urgency of the situation.

The source of Paul's astonishment is not only the Galatians' fickleness in changing loyalties but the speed with which they have deserted the ranks. He can only attribute it to a combination of their stupidity and the beguiling tactics of the competition (3:1–5). He stresses that it is a desertion of their divine vocation—"deserting the one who called you in the grace of Christ" (v. 6; cf. 5:8). It is God whom they have abandoned.

What had seduced them was "a different gospel" (v. 6), which suggests that the competing message was also Christian (cf. 2 Cor. 11:4; cf. 1 Tim. 6:3). On second thought, Paul is only willing to concede that there is one saving gospel, which his opponents are distorting (cf. 5:10; 2 Cor. 11:4; Acts 15:1, 24). So convinced is he that his gospel stands in direct continuity with the apostolic tradition, he issues an anathema against his opponents (cf. 1 Cor. 16:22; also 12:3; Acts 23:14; Rom. 9:3). Indeed, it is a double anathema, repeated for emphasis (cf. 5:3, 21; 2 Cor. 13:2; 1 Thess. 3:4; 4:6). The Galatians are in sharp contrast to other Pauline churches who sought steadfastly to adhere to the apostolic tradition (1 Cor. 11:2, 23; 15:1–3; 1 Thess. 2:13; 4:1–2; 2 Thess. 2:15; 3:6).

This second section concludes on the note on which the opening greeting began—whether Paul's gospel was merely a ploy for human acceptance. Here, as elsewhere, he insists that his motivation is not to curry human favor (1 Thess. 2:4). Had he wanted to play the game of gaining acceptance from his peers and living according to human standards, he would never have forsaken the race for religious one-upmanship to become a slave of Christ (cf. Phil. 3:4–11). Paul stoutly denies having preached with one eye always on the opinion polls and one finger on the popular pulse.

Luke 7:1–10

During the liturgical year (Advent to Pentecost), biblical texts cluster thematically around the great festivals and observances, but following Pentecost the church enters what is sometimes called "ordinary time." This extended period offers the preacher opportunity to follow the texts in continuity, achieving an immersion in the biblical narrative over a period of time. Such series of sermons provide both preacher and listener a refreshing variation from messages governed by theme or season. There is nothing on the calendar to interrupt our attending at length to Luke.

Luke 7:1–10 opens a section in the Gospel (7:1–8:3) sometimes referred to as "the little insertion," which consists of six units inserted into the Markan framework. Today and for the next two Sundays we will consider four of the six units. Some of this material is found also in Matthew. This is true of 7:1–10, the healing of the centurion's slave, which appears not only in

Matthew (8:5–13) but also in John (4:46–53). Both Matthew and Luke place the story after Jesus' great sermon (on the mount in Matthew, on the plain in Luke), and John joins the two of them in locating the incident in Capernaum. The Matthean and Lucan accounts contain more than sixty identical words, but even so, differences are noticeable and significant. The two most important are Luke's use of intermediaries in the centurion's appeal to Jesus, and Matthew's insertion of a saying of Jesus (vv. 11–12) that Luke places elsewhere (13:28–30). The preacher may want to read Matthew's and John's accounts in order to set in sharper focus the accents peculiar to Luke.

The centurion, a Roman military officer, represents the believing Gentile living within Jewish territory. Luke's practice of relating parallel events from the life of Jesus and the life of the church is continued here. Luke 7:1–10 has its parallel in Acts 10: "In Caesarea there was a man named Cornelius, a centurion of the Italian Cohort, as it was called. He was a devout man who feared God with all his household; he gave alms generously to the people and prayed constantly to God" (vv. 1–2). The story in Luke 7:1–10, therefore, not only foreshadows the mission to the Gentiles that unfolds in Acts but also gives authoritative precedent for that mission from the ministry of Jesus himself.

Luke paints a most favorable portrait of the centurion. He is deeply concerned for an ailing slave (v. 2) and believes Jesus can heal him (vv. 3, 7, 10). However, rather than approach Jesus directly, the centurion sends two sets of intermediaries. The first, Jewish elders, appeal to Jesus on the ground that the centurion is worthy, loving the Jews and building a synagogue for them (vv. 3–5). The officer might have been a proselyte-at-the gate, a Gentile who believed in and worshiped Israel's God but who had not submitted to the rites whereby a Gentile became a Jew. The second set of intermediaries, friends of the centurion, brought word to Jesus that the man felt himself unworthy to receive Jesus in his home (vv. 6–7a). Regarded worthy by others, regarded unworthy by himself—not a bad combination of credentials. Joined to this quality was the man's confidence that a word from Jesus had performative power. As a member of the Roman army, he knew the authority of a command given and received (vv. 7b–8). Jesus praises his faith (v. 9), and the slave is healed (v. 10).

Matthew inserts into the story a saying of Jesus that prophesies a mass influx of Gentiles and the rejection of many in Israel (8:11–12). Luke does not. Even though Jesus says the centurion's faith is not matched in Israel (v. 9), still it is important that Jewish elders interceded for a Gentile. Although history forced Luke to recognize the shift from a Jewish to a Gentile majority in the church, his two volumes make it abundantly clear that he understands God to be a "both-and" and not an "either-or" God.

And so begins the story of faith among those afar off, not only geographically or racially but also generationally—those who have not seen Jesus but who have believed his word (Luke 7:7; John 20:29).

Proper 5 [10]
(Sunday between June 5 and 11 inclusive
(if after Trinity Sunday))

1 Kings 17:8–16 (17–24);
Psalm 146; or
1 Kings 17:17–24;
Psalm 30;
Galatians 1:11–24;
Luke 7:11–17

The Old Testament reading for the *Common Lectionary* is the story of Elijah and the widow of Zarephath. In the primary selection, God sustains life by providing the widow food; in the optional selection, God restores her son to life. In both instances, Elijah is God's instrument. Psalm 146 responds by praising God as the one "who gives food to the hungry" and "upholds the orphan and the widow."

Other lectionaries adopt the second part of the 1 Kings 17 text, focusing exclusive attention on the raising of the widow's son. Accordingly, Psalm 30, a psalm of thanksgiving, praises God as the one who heals and restores to life.

In the Epistle reading, we find Paul in an autobiographical mode rehearsing the story of his prophetic calling, thereby insisting on the divine origin of his gospel.

The story of Jesus' raising the son of the widow of Nain supplies the Gospel reading. Luke's telling of the story contains clear echoes of the Elijah story. There is obviously good precedent for juxtaposing these two texts in one liturgical setting.

1 Kings 17:8–16 (17–24)

The full Old Testament reading includes two episodes in the stories of the prophet Elijah, found in 1 Kings 17:1–19:21; 2 Kings 1. The setting of the stories is the Northern Kingdom during the reign of Ahab (874–852 BC) of the dynasty of Omri. The Elijah stories are an old collection doubtless handed down in prophetic circles before they were incorporated by the Deuteronomistic Historians into their account of Israel's past. Such stories were particularly important to the Deuteronomistic writers because of their conviction that history was set on its course by the word of God through prophets.

Elijah had appeared on the scene abruptly and without introduction, announcing to Ahab that there would be "neither dew nor rain these years, except by my word" (1 Kings 17:1). The word of the Lord then led him first to a brook east of the Jordan to be fed by ravens (1 Kings 17:2–7) and then to Zarephath to be fed by a widow.

In the background of the stories in 1 Kings 17:8–24, then, is the conflict between prophet and king, but that is set aside for the moment. More immediately there is the drought. Although they are linked thematically, these two stories are complete and self-contained: first the tale of the prophet and the widow of Zarephath, and then the account of Elijah's miraculous raising of the widow's dead son.

In the first story (vv. 2–7) the drought provides the narrative tension, the uncertainty that creates suspense. That suspense is heightened by Yahweh's command that a widow will feed him, and even more by the revelation that she is so poor that her life and that of her son are threatened (v. 12). It is not the greatness of the man of God that will save them all, but the power of the word of Yahweh through him. "Do not be afraid," he says, and not as simple reassurance but as an oracle of salvation. Then in typically prophetic form he announces the word of God concerning the future: "The jar of meal will not be emptied and the jug of oil will not fail until the day that the LORD sends rain upon the earth" (v. 14). And that is the way it turned out. It is a story of life and death that ends with the promise of continued life.

In the second story (vv. 17–24), the issue of life and death is even more explicit. Illness and accusations provide the narrative tension. The widow's son becomes so ill that he is as good as dead: "there was no breath left in him" (v. 17). That initial diagnosis might leave doubt, but as the narrative moves on it becomes quite explicit that the boy is dead. The woman's reaction is to blame the prophet: "You have come to me to bring my sin to remembrance, and to cause the death of my son!" (v. 18). After taking the boy to his room and placing him on his own bed, Elijah in turn blames Yahweh: "O LORD my God, have you brought calamity even upon the widow with whom I am staying, by killing her son?" (v. 20). After stretching himself upon the child three times, Elijah prays that the Lord revive him. The result is a foregone conclusion: Yahweh heeds the prophet's prayer and revives the child (vv. 21–22). Then Elijah brings the boy to his mother, who affirms that Elijah is indeed a "man of God" who speaks the true word of the Lord (vv. 23–24).

Both episodes are miracle stories with legendary and folkloristic features. One of their goals is stated in the concluding verse—to validate Elijah as a true prophet. They are told, however, not to glorify Elijah, but to show how the power of God, in the form of the prophetic word, was made manifest through him. Although the Bible contains more dramatic miracle stories than this one, we are still meant to be astonished. To provide a rationalistic explanation—for example, the generosity of the widow moved her neighbors to bring meal and oil, or the prophet revived the boy with a primitive form of artificial respiration—may serve only to reduce the astonishment that the divine word could solve such problems.

Especially when this story is considered in connection with Luke 7:11–17, the role of the widow becomes crucial. That the widow was poor is not surprising. In ancient Israelite society, economic well-being generally required a male head of the household. Even all the Old Testament texts that express God's concern for the widow and the fatherless indicate that there was need for such concern. She is not only poor; she is a foreigner. All the more dramatic then is her willingness to be generous with what little she had, trusting that the prophet's word was indeed the word of God.

Psalm 146

This psalm is the first in a small collection (Pss. 146–150) all of which begin and end with a call to praise, hallelujah ("Praise the LORD!"). The psalm praises God, describing the divine character and divine activity, while simultaneously contrasting the Divine with the human. The composition could be aptly described as a theological synopsis summarizing aspects of Israel's belief about God.

The psalm is structured around two opposites. The negative, cast as a warning, in verses 3–4, admonishes the audience not to trust human leadership, princes or mortals, who cannot aid and whose efforts and plans are destined to sleep with them in the same tomb. (The NJPSV translates v. 3 as "Put not your trust in the great, in mortal man who cannot save.") The best laid plans, the highest hopes, the grandest designs die with their architects; they dissipate with their discoverer's demise. The one who trusts and hopes in such is doomed to disappointment because the mortal (adam) always returns to earth (adamah).

The opposite end of the spectrum is viewed in verses 5–8. Over against the human, the transitory, the disappointing, the inadequate, stands the Divine, the eternal, the satisfying, the sufficient.

Verse 5 declares "happy" anyone whose help and hope lie with the Deity. The term happy denotes a state of well-being and contentment but not necessarily a state of extravagance and luxury. Beginning in verse 6, a series of four characteristics of God are presented as supporting the contention that happy is the one whose help and hope is in God. (1) First, appeal is made to God as creator. As the one who made heaven, earth, and sea—that is, the totality of the universe—God is not bound by the structures and limitations of creaturehood. As creator, God is owner and ruler. (2) Second, appeal is made to the fidelity and constancy of the Creator "who keeps faith forever." Unlike humans, whose plans and programs die with them, God and divine help endure forever. Unlike humans, God is not threatened by the possibility of nonbeing. (3) God is the one who is not only concerned for but also executes (guarantees) justice for the oppressed. In this affirmation and throughout verses 7–9, one finds a consistent emphasis of the Old Testament: God takes a special interest in and acts in behalf of the downtrodden, the powerless, and the despairing. (4) The satisfaction of physical needs is also the concern of God, who "gives food to the hungry." As the maker of heaven and earth, God does not will that humans be oppressed or that they should suffer from hunger.

Following these four divine characteristics, the psalmist speaks of seven activities of God in which the Divine acts to alleviate human distress and to defend those without rights. Most of those noted as the object of God's care are persons without full authority and potential to assume responsibility for and to exercise rights for their own welfare: the prisoners (at the mercy of the legal system or perhaps in slavery), the blind (at the mercy of the seeing), those who are bowed down or with bent backs (in debt or oppressed by others, thus carrying burdens not their own), the righteous (the innocent in the legal system who however were at the mercy of the upholders of justice), the sojourners (foreign settlers or visitors, not members of the native culture, and thus aliens), and the widow and fatherless (who were without the support of a male patriarch in a male-dominated culture). God is declared to be committed to the care of all those, while at the same time God sees to it that the wicked come to their just reward—ruin.

The psalmist here obviously presents the basic nature and character of God but does not claim that conditions and circumstances conform to this idealized divine will. In the list of attributes, God is primarily contrasted with human leaders (vv. 3–4 over against 5–9). Verse

10 adds an eschatological note to the text and points to the future as the time when the intervention of God in behalf of society's rejects and subjects will occur.

In preaching from this psalm, attention should be focused on its attempt to define the divine disposition as in favor of the downtrodden and the destitute, the powerless living at the peripheries of society, in the basements of humanity's houses.

1 Kings 17:17–24

For commentary on this lesson, see the discussion of the alternative Old Testament reading for this day.

Psalm 30

This psalm of thanksgiving was originally composed for use in a worship service celebrating a worshiper's having been healed from some life-threatening illness. As a thanksgiving song, it calls upon the audience accompanying the worshiper (family, friends, fellow villagers) to join in the celebration (v. 4) and to listen to the testimony and preaching of the one healed (vv. 5–6).

Verses 1–3 spell out part of the experience undergone by the worshiper. As usual, the sickness/healing are described in very general categories because the psalm would have been employed on numerous occasions for different persons with different conditions of illness involved. Sheol and Pit in verse 3 refer to the realm of the dead. Here they do not mean that the individual died but are used metaphorically. To be subject to any form of sickness was already to be in the grip of Sheol, to be under the power of death. Weakness in life could be spoken of as being under the power of death. The verbs speaking of the rescue—"drawn me up," "healed," "brought up," "restored"—also use spatial images. These factors allowed such psalms as Psalm 30 to be used in the early church when talking about the resurrection (note the use of Ps. 16:8–11 in Acts 2:25–28).

The verses for this lection contain a call to fellow participants to join in the festivities of the thanksgiving celebration. Verse 6 seems to imply that the worshiper had gone through a phase of life unconcerned with the Deity. This would have been in a period when things were prospering well and before the onset of trouble (see Deut. 8:11–20). If this is the case, one may assume that this attitude was one the worshiper was warning against. "Don't be as I was"—assuming that nothing could threaten life's prosperity. This may be said to be the anthropological lesson, what the case shows about human nature. The second lesson is theological, having to do with the character of God (v. 5). God's anger may be bitter and the reality of divine punishment strong, but these are transitory. It is divine favor and goodwill that are lasting. Tomorrow and the dawn can bring a new day. (This last description is probably based on the fact that worshipers spent the night in the temple and were given divine oracles in conjunction with the morning sacrifice.) This same imagery has impressed itself indelibly in the Christian vocabulary as a consequence of the Easter story.

Verses 7–12 of the psalm are direct address to the Deity—a thanksgiving prayer perhaps offered in conjunction with a thanksgiving sacrifice. As in most thanksgiving psalms, the speaker or psalm-user rehearses the "before" conditions and then what happened. That is, the psalm contains a statement of the distress from which one was saved and sometimes, as in verses 8–10, a summary of the prayer offered at the time of the sickness. The substance of these verses reflects something of a plea bargaining—the worshiper suggests that nothing was to be gained by his death; in fact, it would result in a loss to the Deity, namely, the loss of a faithful worshiper who could no longer offer praise to God in the dust of death.

The "after" vocabulary dominates in verses 11–12. Sackcloth and mourning have been replaced with dancing and gladness. The tears of nightfall have been replaced with the joy that comes in the morning.

Galatians 1:11–24

I t is rare for Paul to engage in detailed discussion of his personal circumstances, as he does here. Given a choice, he preferred preaching Christ over explaining himself. But his back was against the wall. His personal integrity as an apostolic witness was being seriously challenged, and what emerges is an extended account of the circumstances that led to his becoming an apostle of Christ. Clearly, he rehearses these events as a personal apologia. He determines that the best defense is to let his own record speak for itself.

Today's epistolary lection comprises the first part of this rather extended personal defense (1:11–2:21). It serves as a rich resource for reconstructing the historical Paul. Its special value lies in its autobiographical character. Unlike the lengthy and detailed account of Paul found in Acts 12–28, these are his own words told under oath (v. 20). With its careful attention to chronological sequence (note v. 18; 2:1), this passage is one of the most useful resources for constructing Pauline chronology. The sequence of events differs substantially from the account in Acts, and one should consult the commentaries for detailed discussion.

The overall effect of Paul's rehearsal of his former life is to underscore his independence of the Jerusalem tradition, or what might be called Judaean Christianity. His apostolic commission was not validated by consulting with others, much less the Jerusalem authorities (vv. 16–17) Even when he did visit Jerusalem, it was a short, fifteen-day visit where he conferred only with Peter and James (vv. 18–19). Consequently, he was virtually unknown to Palestinian churches, and then only by reputation (vv. 22–23). Even when he went up to Jerusalem fourteen years later (2:1), he came away with his independent apostolic mission validated (2:7–10). In the crunch, he finally resisted the conservative position of Peter and Barnabas (2:11–14), both of whom caved in under pressure from the Christian rigorists, the "circumcision faction" (2:12).

Two themes emerge from this defense. First, the radical reversal in Paul's life occurred through divine intervention. Paul's gospel came "through a revelation of Jesus Christ" (v. 12), which is doubtless a reference to the encounter when the risen Lord appeared to him (cf. 1 Cor. 9:1; 15:8; Acts 9:17; 22:14; 26:16). It was in this event, insists Paul, that God "was pleased to reveal his Son to me" (v. 16). Prior to this, he was bent on destroying the church (1 Cor. 15:9; Phil. 3:6; cf. Acts 8:3; 9:1–2; 22:14; 1 Tim. 1:13), motivated by undiluted zeal for "the traditions of my ancestors" (v. 14; cf. Mark 7:3; Acts 22:3; 26:4–5; also Rom. 10:2). Paul could hardly account for this radical reversal in his life on natural grounds. It was not the result of his own intuition and could in no sense be explained as humanly predicated. His own experience attested that the source of his gospel lay with God who raised Christ from the dead (1:1).

Second, in his encounter with the risen Christ he experienced a prophetic call. In words reminiscent of Old Testament prophetic calls, Paul insists that he had been especially delegated by God even before he was born (v. 15; Isa. 49:1; Jer. 1:5; cf. Luke 1:15). His special prophetic vocation was to preach among the Gentiles (v. 16; cf. Acts 9:15; also 1 Tim. 2:7;

Eph. 3:8), and this distinguished him from the other apostles (2:7–8). Because he interprets his commission in such thoroughly prophetic terms, some scholars prefer to speak of Paul's encounter with the risen Lord as a call rather than a conversion. Such a distinction cautions us against interpreting Paul's encounter with the risen Lord in terms of classical conversion experiences, such as those of Augustine or Luther, where a troubled conscience gives way to a more blissful state of forgiveness. It suggests that we interpret Paul's experience as vocational rather than psychological reversal. But even if Paul does view his former life in terms of rectitude (v. 14), the element of regret, perhaps even remorse, is not lacking (cf. 1 Cor. 15:9).

Homiletically, this text has often served as the basis for exploring the profound change that occurred in Paul and the difference a genuine encounter with the grace of God can make. It is a theme that bears further treatment, but the preacher needs to ask whether the experience being described here was unique to Paul—not only his encounter with the risen Lord but his apostolic vocation. Perhaps another tack might be to explore what actually constitutes a "human gospel" (v. 11). What are the criteria for distinguishing between a gospel that truly comes from God and a gospel that mirrors mere human values?

Luke 7:11–17

The story of Jesus raising from the dead the only son of a widow of Nain (Luke 7:11–17), found only in Luke, is the second of six units in 7:1–8:3 that Luke inserts into the framework of Mark. Except for this and one other major insertion, Luke generally follows the Markan order.

In this account Luke tells his story in a manner clearly dependent on the Elijah and Elisha cycles, early established as two of Luke's favorite prophets (4:25–27). Both Elijah (1 Kings 17:17–24) and Elisha (2 Kings 4:18–37) restore life to young men. In the case of Elijah, the mother was a widow whom the prophet met at a city gate (Luke 7:12). After the son's restoration, Elijah "gave him to his mother" (1 Kings 17:23), a statement quoted from the Septuagint by Luke (7:15). Luke's story is, however, much less dramatic than its Old Testament antecedents. The form of Luke 7:11–17 is similar to that of miracle stories from Hellenistic circles, but the details correspond to burial practices in Israel at the time: the use of a bier, the procession of bearers and mourners, and the moving of the corpse outside the city wall for burial.

Three aspects of the story deserve special attention: the act of Jesus, the response of the crowd, and the editorial work of Luke. If the preacher attends to all three in the sermon, the order in which they are treated will be determined by the intent and emphasis of the sermon. As for the act of Jesus, both his words to the mother and his restoration of the young man reveal compassion and mercy (vv. 13–15) toward the mother. Because the man is her only son and she is a widow (v. 12), he very likely was her sole support. From the moment Jesus saw her until he "gave him to his mother" (v. 15), Jesus' total attention was on the woman. In fact, the story is told so simply and in such subdued tones, it is as though there were no disciples with Jesus, no large crowd with Jesus, and no large crowd in the funeral procession; the storyteller focuses completely on Jesus, the mother, and her son. The raising from the dead is without drama, ritual, or even prayer. The same word of Jesus that from a distance had healed the centurion's slave (v. 7) here is powerful to give life to the dead (v. 14).

In response to the act of Jesus, the crowd is seized with fear and glorifies God. Their expressions of praise are two: "A great prophet has risen among us!" and "God has looked favorably on his people!" (v. 16). The reference to Jesus as a prophet is not uncommon in Luke, for

Jesus ministers in a manner reminiscent of the prophets of Israel, especially Elijah and Elisha (4:24; 7:39; 13:33; 24:19). And in Acts Luke refers to Jesus as the prophet like Moses (3:22–23; 7:35–37). The phrase "has risen among us" may be a faint allusion to Jesus' resurrection but more likely is an echo of the language of Deuteronomy 18:15: "The LORD your God will raise up for you a prophet." The expression "God has looked favorably on his people" (v. 16) is also a favorite of Luke (1:68; 9:44; Acts 15:14). Although in the Old Testament, God's visitation may be in wrath (Exod. 20:5) or in mercy (Ps. 106:4), for Luke divine visitation is always an act of grace.

Finally, a word needs to be said about Luke's editorial contribution. Luke's editing appears in two ways.

First, he locates this story of the raising of the dead here in preparation for verses 18–23, which record Jesus' response to the messengers from John the Baptist. That response includes "Go and tell John . . . the dead are raised" (v. 22).

Second, verse 17 of our lection is not part of the story but is an editorial comment tying this event to the next account: "The disciples of John reported all these things to him" (v. 18). That John's ministry was in Judea probably accounts for verse 17 reading, "This word about him spread throughout *Judea*," rather than the natural and expected "Galilee." The disciples of John can without uncertainty report back to him what they saw and heard (v. 22). The lectionary does not move next to verses 18–35, but the comparisons and contrasts between the ministries of John and Jesus are very important to Luke and to this church.

Proper 6 [11]
(Sunday between June 12 and 18 inclusive (if after Trinity Sunday))

1 Kings 21:1–10 (11–14) 15–21a;
Psalm 5:1–8; or
2 Samuel 11:26–12:10, 13–15;
Psalm 32;
Galatians 2:15–21;
Luke 7:36–8:3

The story of Naboth's vineyard, with its account of the framed charges against the victim and Elijah's denunciation of King Ahab for Naboth's murder, provide the Old Testament reading for the *Common Lectionary*. The selection from Psalm 5 could almost be read as a prayer of Naboth—a plea to God for help by someone beset by deceitful, bloodthirsty foes.

The alternate Old Testament reading treats a similar case of monarchical injustice—David's adultery with Bathsheba and his subsequent murder of Uriah. Psalm 32, a penitential psalm, speaks of forgiveness experienced by the truly penitent, yet it does not ignore the distress and torment experienced by the sinner.

In today's epistolary reading we have a classic Pauline text where he wrestles with the issue of how humans experience salvation and live out the reality.

In the Gospel, yearning leads to adoration and adoration to service.

1 Kings 21:1–10 (11–14) 15–21a

The verses to be read include the beginning and part of the conclusion to the story of Naboth's vineyard. The verses are chosen wisely, for they set the scene and then present the resolution of the drama's conflicts, but one could hardly preach on the text without retelling the entire story. It is yet another account of confrontation between Elijah and the royal household. Usually, in the Elijah cycle of stories the confrontation concerns apostasy from the Yahwistic faith because King Ahab and Jezebel the queen support the religion of Baal. Here, however, the issue is justice, at the level of what we would call civil and criminal law.

In 1 Kings 21, a story of conspiracy, perjury, theft, and murder (vv. 1–16) prepares the way for the account of Elijah's encounter with Ahab (vv. 17–29). Verses 1–4 set the scene for the story of the crimes. It appears at first to be a simple matter that could be resolved by negotiations: Naboth's vineyard is adjacent to the king's property, and Ahab makes a generous offer for it. The owner can choose either a better vineyard or the value in money. Naboth's unequivocal refusal sets the story's tension into motion. He does not explain, but the reasons are implicit in his choice of language. "The Lord forbid" is an oath formula, but more. That this land is "my ancestral inheritance" reflects not only the fact that the land has been passed down through the generations, but that the family holds the property as a gift of or in trust for Yahweh. According to the traditional belief, one does not treat such an "inheritance" as capital investment or real estate.

The irony of the story is similar to that of David and Uriah's wife Bathsheba (2 Samuel 11–12). In both cases, a character's fidelity to traditional religious faith contributes to his death. For Uriah, it is the soldier's duty, and for Naboth, it is his responsibility as steward of the land.

Ahab appears childish and weak. He does not quarrel with Naboth or confront him, but returns home and pouts (v. 4). Then the strong character enters the story and plays her part. Jezebel considers Ahab's passivity to be ridiculous (v. 7); after all, he is the king. So she promises to give him what she does not own. Clearly, her words and actions assume a view of kingship that conflicts with Israel's traditional understanding. Her perspective is the political counterpart to her religious faith, devotion to the religion of Baal. Kings, standing in a special relationship to the gods, may do as they wish. So she engineers a plot to have Naboth accused of blasphemy against God and the king, thereby depriving his descendants of right to the land. Two "scoundrels" (v. 10) collaborate in what can only be described as premeditated murder. Once the deed is done, the queen tells Ahab that the vineyard is his, and the king goes to take formal possession of it (vv. 15–16).

Having run its course and reached its resolution, the first story turns out to be only an episode in the more important sequence of events. History moves in response to the word of the Lord through prophets—that is the belief both of ancient tradition and of the editors of the Books of Deuteronomy through 2 Kings. Thus the word of the Lord came—happened—to Elijah. The narrator does not inform us where the prophet is, except that he is not in the capital city of Samaria. The word of the Lord (vv. 18–19) is a commission in two parts: (1) what to do—go meet Ahab in Naboth's vineyard; and (2) what to say to the king. The opening rhetorical question accuses Ahab of murder and theft, and then follows a cryptic announcement of judgment.

Without transition the scene changes. Elijah has, as usual, appeared suddenly, and Ahab greets him as he did in 18:17, with an accusation. Elijah's retort is in the most familiar pattern of prophetic address, both in the prophetic stories in Samuel and Kings and in the early prophetic books. First comes the accusation, in direct address (v. 20b). It is less specific than the indictment in verse 19, but it moves the violations beyond the realm of civil or criminal law into the religious, covenantal stipulations. "You have sold yourself"—that is, for the price of a vineyard— "to do what is evil in the sight of the LORD"—that is, murder and the appropriation of a person's "inheritance" are not simply matters for human courts, but violations of Yahweh's will. Consequently, such offenses lead to divine intervention in the form of judgment (vv. 21ff.). The punishment fits the crime. Not only Ahab but also his entire household will die.

We leave the story on that note, but it goes on to detail a specific judgment against Jezebel, and then to a modification of the punishment when Ahab repents.

At the heart of the story lies the most basic theme of prophetic literature, the Lord's response to injustice. Implicit are concerns with justice considered various ways. Ahab and Jezebel violate procedural justice—due process—in manipulating the judicial system. They violate distributive justice by taking more than they need and by depriving Naboth of his most basic right. But more than that, they violate the substance of justice, which rests on the character of Israel's God as just. Covenantal stipulations—laws, commandments, traditions about land tenure—mean to show how justice will be established among God's people.

Ancient Israel does not concern itself much with lines between religious faith, politics, and the legal system. All these institutions rest on the conviction that Yahweh seeks justice. Consequently, Elijah—like Nathan before him (2 Samuel 11–12)—boldly confronts the head of the government with his sin, with a word that accomplishes what it says because it comes from the Lord.

Psalm 5:1–8

Psalm 5 is best understood as a composition produced for use in special legal processes in the temple. When regular courts could not reach verdicts in certain cases, because of the nature of the alleged crime or lack of evidence, special appeal could be made to God; that is, to a process of trial and/or ordeal in the temple under the supervision of the priests (see Exod. 22:7–8; Deut. 17:8–13; 19:15–21; 1 Kings 8:31–32; Num. 5:5–31).

A feature in the temple ritual was apparently the affirmation of innocence by the one or ones who felt falsely accused, along with a plea to be judged and a request for the opponent or the wicked to be condemned and punished. Along these lines, the following seems an appropriate outline of the psalm: a plea for a hearing and a judgment from God (vv. 1–3), a hymnic, confessional praise of God (vv. 4–6), an affirmation of purpose and a commitment to worship (v. 7), a request for help (v. 8), a charge against the accusers (v. 9–10), a plea for those, including the worshiper, who seek refuge and recourse in God (v. 11), and a statement of confidence and confession (v. 12).

Only the first eight verses of the psalm make up the lection for today. These are primarily concerned with the worshiper's plea for help and affirmation of innocence and fidelity. Verse 3 suggests that the hearing and/or the final adjudication of the legal case occurred in the morning, perhaps after a night's vigil in the sanctuary precincts (see Pss. 3:5; 4:8). The RSV translated part of verse 3b as, "I prepare a sacrifice for thee, and watch." No term for sacrifice occurs in the Hebrew text, which could just as easily be translated, "I prepare [make ready] for thee, and watch." The preparation could be the worshiper's self-preparation for the sacred suit and hearing, or even the preparation of the case itself. Thus one could translate, "I prepare my case [or the arguments for the defense] for you, and watch." The NRSV has translated the text, "I plead my case to you, and watch."

Two further items should be noted, especially with regard to verse 3. First, the morning was probably the time when cases were heard and verdicts rendered (see 2 Sam. 15:1–6, where David holds court early in the morning, and Ps. 101:8, part of the king's oath of office). This explains the frequent references in the Psalms to salvation and redemption coming in the morning (see Pss. 30:5; 46:5; 49:14). Second, the priests probably handed down the verdict of guilt or innocence as if spoken by the Deity (see Deut. 17:8–13). Part of the accused's ordeal may have been to spend the night and sleep in the temple precincts. Here the priests could observe the individual, and the awesomeness and solemnity of the temple's surroundings may have "forced" the guilty to give up any claims of innocence and to confess.

Verses 4–6, spoken as hymnic praise of God, were a way that the composer of the psalm had for making an individual participant face the consequences of deliberately pleading innocent when guilty. That is, these verses forced the participants to preach to themselves and condemn themselves if guilty. "The boastful [of their innocence] will not stand . . . ; you hate all evildoers [me if I am guilty]. . . . You destroy those who speak lies [like I would be were I pretending innocence]." Today's worship should provide the occasion for the community and individuals to confront the reality of who they are, just as this psalm did for the ancient Hebrews.

Verse 7 implies an assurance that the one pleading innocence would be allowed to worship, that is, to offer a sacrifice of thanksgiving for deliverance.

2 Samuel 11:26–12:10, 13–15

Nathan's encounter with David is the direct consequence of the king's adultery with Bathsheba and the murder of her husband Uriah. Thus this lesson should be read in the light of what precedes it in 2 Samuel 11, which finally reports how David's orders for the death of Uriah were carried out. Today's lesson begins with the note that David made Bathsheba his wife after her period of mourning for her husband was over, and that she bore him a son. In one of his significant interpretive asides, the author of the David story points out that "the thing that David had done displeased the LORD" (2 Sam. 11:27). The reading for the day will show just how displeased the Lord was and how David responded to that displeasure.

The body of the lesson consists of a dialogue between the prophet and the king, introduced by the briefest narrative framework: "And the LORD sent Nathan to David" (12:1). Short as it is, the note is not simply incidental; it makes clear at the outset what is confirmed later (vv. 7, 11, 13), namely, that Nathan does not speak for himself but for Yahweh. The prophets understood themselves to be messengers of the Lord.

Nathan tells the king a story (12:1b–4) of crass injustice, apparently asking for a royal judgment and possibly intervention. The contrasts are so sharp between the poor man with his single ewe lamb that was almost a part of the family and the greedy rich man that David readily pronounces the death sentence (vv. 5–6).

The prophet's reaction (vv. 7–12) reveals that the story was not the report of an actual event but a parable. Specifically, it is a juridical parable in which the addressee—in this case David—is moved to pronounce judgment upon himself. Isaiah's parable of the vineyard (Isa. 5:1–7) is a close parallel. Such parables consist of a story and its interpretation or application. The interpretation of the parable begins with one of the most memorable Old Testament lines, "You are the man!" (v. 7a). Although Nathan's speech is not in poetic meter or parallelism, its basic structure is the same as that of the announcements of the prophets of the eighth and following centuries. It includes the messenger formula, "thus says the Lord," at the beginning and as a key transition. The major parts are the indictment, or statement of reasons for punishment (vv. 7–9), and the announcement of judgment or punishment (vv. 10–12).

The statement of reasons for punishment or indictment has two movements. First, Yahweh, through Nathan, reminds David of his gracious care (vv. 7–8). He had anointed him king, delivered him from Saul, given him Saul's house and wives—noteworthy in view of the sin with Bathsheba—and made him king over both Israel and Judah. Furthermore, the Lord was willing to do even more. The recital concerns God's grace toward David himself; there is no mention of the promise of a dynasty (2 Samuel 7). Second, the Lord states the indictment itself (v. 9). David has "despised the word of the LORD" by taking the wife of Uriah as a wife and killing him "with the sword of the Ammonites." At this point there is no mention of the act of adultery.

The announcement of punishment includes the judgments that the sword shall never depart from David's house, that the Lord will raise up evil from his own house, and that David's wives will be given to another who will lie with them openly. All these things, we will see as the story unfolds, come to pass.

David's response is a short but full confession of sin (v. 13a), whereupon the prophet announces that the sin has been "put away," and the death sentence—which David had pronounced upon himself—set aside. Still, there will be punishment; the child of the adulterous union shall die (v. 14).

Encounter with this story generates a wealth of issues for theological and homiletical reflection: (1) in the biblical faith, no one, not even the king anointed by God, stands above the law; (2) to act irresponsibly in society, especially against those who have less power, is to "despise the word of the LORD" (v. 9); (3) that election—in this case as king—is a reason for punishment, indicates that special status entails accountability (see also Amos 3:1–2); and (4) what is the relationship between divine wrath and mercy? The punishment may appear harsh to us, and it is; but to the writer and the original hearers or readers, this was also a story of God's mercy. As far as David was concerned, the death penalty, which applied not only to murder but also to adultery (see Deut. 22:22), had been reduced.

Psalm 32

This psalm was discussed earlier as one of the lections for the Fourth Sunday in Lent.

Galatians 2:15–21

Here we have one of the classic texts summarizing Paul's basic theological position. Yet as important and theologically laden as this passage is, it should not be divorced from its context. It grows directly out of the preceding discussion where Paul has assailed Peter and Barnabas for equivocating on a matter of cardinal importance. In one context, Peter would eat with Gentiles as equals, but in the presence of Jewish Christian rigorists, who were unwilling to accept uncircumcised Gentiles as full-fledged members of the covenant, Peter would not eat with Gentiles. Such an action could only imply that they were in some sense only half-Christian, and thus inferior to Jewish Christians. Paul insists that Peter cannot have it both ways. He cannot behave in one context as if he were a Gentile without any special obligations, yet in another context require Gentiles to conform to Jewish behavior before he will associate with them.

This practical question of what form Christian friendship should take gives rise to the theological exposition in verses 15–21. These remarks are especially directed against Jewish Christians such as Peter and Barnabas. The crucial point being made is that Jews are justified before God in exactly the same way Gentiles are—through faith in Christ. It is not as if there is one way for Jews to be justified and another for Gentiles, with the main task being to find meaningful ways for persons who have come to God in different ways to relate to each other. Rather,

Paul insists, there is only one way of truly being made right with God, and this is through faith in Christ. Because Jews and Gentiles alike come to God on the same terms, there can be no distinction between them. They are all equals.

What Jews must recognize is what Paul himself had come to see, and what Scripture itself had already asserted: no one is justified by works of the law (v. 16; cf. Ps. 143:2; Hab. 2:4; Gen. 15:6). One way of being religious is to meet the requirements imposed by a sacred law, in this case, the law of Moses. Yet the heart of the Pauline gospel was that this was a misguided pursuit (cf. Rom. 3:20). Works of the law may have value in their own right, but they are not the basis for justification (Rom. 3:28). Indeed, Paul argues that it had never been the case. Just as Abraham had received righteousness through his obediential faith, so had everyone else since, including Gentiles (cf. Rom. 4:5; 5:1; Gal. 3:6–9, 24).

Because Christ, and not the law, was the means through which God's grace was revealed, it is through Christ that both Jews and Gentiles experience justification. This could only mean that all previous distinctions between Jews and Gentiles had been obliterated. And yet, when Peter allowed old distinctions to govern his conduct, it was tantamount to breaking the law that forbade Jews from associating with Gentiles (cf. Matt. 9:11). If this were the case, Christ would actually be the occasion for sin (v. 17). Moreover, if one works to eliminate all distinctions, then reverses position by erecting them again (as Peter had done through his conduct), this in itself is a transgression of principle (v. 18).

For Paul, the true solution to this position of continued ambivalence regarding the law was to understand that union with Christ meant death to the law (vv. 19–20). His theology of baptism was to regard it as an event where the initiate actually participated in the crucifixion with Christ (cf. Rom. 6:6–8, 10; 7:4, 6). Because the cross was itself a violation of the law, it in effect sealed the death of the law (cf. 3:12–13). So closely was his own identity linked with that of the crucified Christ, his life ceased to be egocentric and became Christo-centric (v. 20). The only way he could envision life was in terms of the risen Christ living within him (Rom. 14:8; Eph. 3:17). The contours of his life now conformed to the faith of Christ, who had given himself in love (v. 20; cf. John 13:1; 1 Tim. 2:6).

His final word is a categorical either/or: either justification through Christ or justification through the law—not both. Had the latter been possible, the death of Christ would have been unnecessary. To concede this would be to "nullify the grace of God" (v. 21).

The passage echoes themes sounded in Romans (3:9–26) and obviously brings us close to the center of Paul's theology. One exegetical point worth noting is the phrase "faith in Jesus Christ" (v. 16). Some recent commentators have rendered it in its more literal form "faith of Jesus Christ," suggesting a fresh line of interpretation: that rather than being justified by placing our faith and trust in Jesus Christ, we are justified by the faithfulness that Christ himself exhibited before God. This places greater stress on the work of Christ in our behalf than on our faith in our own behalf.

Luke 7:36–8:3

The Gospel for today consists of two distinct parts: a woman who was a sinner anoints Jesus (Luke 7:36–50), and women share in the ministry of Jesus (8:1–3). These are the last two of six units Luke has inserted at this point in the Markan order (Luke 7:1–8:3); and although both concern women, to join them too closely can be misleading, as traditions about Mary Magdalene (8:2) amply illustrate. More later.

To understand 7:36–50, it is necessary to review the preceding unit in which Jesus testifies concerning John the Baptist (vv. 24–35). Luke says that when Jesus praised John (vv. 24–28), all the people and tax collectors justified God, for they had received John's baptism, but the Pharisees and lawyers had not, having rejected the purpose of God (repentance and forgiveness) for themselves (vv. 29–30). The sharp contrast is between those who accept the offer of repentance and baptism and those who do not, and that is precisely the contrast in our lesson, verses 36–50. The difference is that it now will be precipitated by Jesus, "a friend of tax collectors and sinners" (v. 34), and it will be done at a meal because, unlike John, "the Son of Man has come eating and drinking" (v. 34). In other words, the speech of Jesus in 7:24–35 will now be acted out in verses 36–50.

All four Gospels record a woman anointing Jesus (Matt. 26:6–13; Mark 14:3–9; Luke 7:36–50; John 12:1–8). Luke's story varies most noticeably from the others, even though it clearly has points of contact with Mark's account: Jesus is at table, his host is named Simon, a woman enters the dining area and anoints Jesus with an alabaster flask of ointment. Thereafter the similarities cease. In all but Luke, the anointing is in Judea, is associated with the burial of Jesus, and the issue is the waste of the ointment. In the text before us, the issue is the character of the woman who lavishes upon Jesus her affection and, as becomes evident later, her gratitude for forgiveness.

Luke 7:36–50 can be understood as a drama in four parts. First, there is the setting: Jesus and others are dinner guests of Simon, a Pharisee (v. 36). There is no reason to impugn Simon's motives in inviting Jesus, especially in Luke's Gospel in which Jesus' relation to the Pharisees is not so tense (e.g., 13:31). We are led, however, because of verses 29 and 34, to anticipate tension over Jesus' forgiveness of sinners. The second part of the drama is the crisis (vv. 37–39) created by the entrance of the "woman in the city." That Jesus does not expel her is proof enough to Simon that Jesus is no prophet; if he were, he would know the woman was a sinner. Simon thinks this but does not say it, but Jesus knows Simon's thought, proof by Simon's own criterion that Jesus is a prophet. The third movement of the drama is the solution of the crisis (vv. 40–47). By means of a brief parable (vv. 41–42) Jesus leads Simon to reflect on the meaning of the difference between his response to Jesus and that of the woman. Her behavior is that of one who has been forgiven. It is important not to construe the awkward verse 47 as meaning that her love earned her forgiveness. On the contrary, because she was forgiven much she loved much. The REB expresses it quite clearly: "So, I tell you, her great love proves that her many sins have been forgiven." The fourth and final part of the drama is the christological dispute (vv. 48–50). Reminiscent of Mark 2:1–12, the question of Jesus' identity and authority comes into sharp focus and returns the discussion to its beginning in verse 19: "Are you the one who is to come, or are we to wait for another?"

Luke 8:1–3 begins a new phase of Luke's narrative and consists of a summary statement of Jesus' missionary tour through cities and villages. The striking item in the summary is that Jesus was accompanied not only by the Twelve but "some women" as well (v. 2). These were women who had been healed by Jesus, and some of them were women of position and means, helping finance the missionary tours (v. 3). The one most familiar to us is Mary Magdalene, from whom Jesus exorcised seven demons. There is no evidence to warrant identifying her with the unnamed woman of the preceding story. In fact, there is no evidence to justify portraying her as having been a prostitute. Demon possession in the Synoptic accounts caused various maladies but not moral depravity. Music, art, drama, and popular religion have long pictured Mary as "the fallen woman," and the image will be difficult to break. However, the effort should be made; the truth, not what makes for interesting preaching, should be honored in the pulpit.

Proper 7 [12]
(Sunday between June 19 and 25 inclusive (if after Trinity Sunday))

1 Kings 19:1–4 (5–7) 8–15*a*;
Psalm 42 and 43; or
Isaiah 65:1–9;
Psalm 22:19–28;
Galatians 3:23–29;
Luke 8:26–39

Today's Old Testament reading from the *Common Lectionary* reports Elijah's dramatic encounters with Yahweh at Mt. Horeb. Though unsettling in the way they correct his self-understanding, they result in a renewed prophetic commission. Psalms 42 and 43, taken together, express faith in God's ability to vindicate the cause of the righteous against unjust adversaries.

In the alternate Old Testament reading from Isaiah 65, we hear God speaking to a rebellious people, reminding them of their waywardness but offering hope to those who remain faithful. The responsorial psalm consists of the less familiar section of the well-known Psalm 22, where the psalmist's cries for deliverance give way to confident assurance.

In the epistolary reading, Paul argues that one and all are related to God through faith in Christ, not by deeds of achievement but by grace, not by law but by promise.

The Gospel reading is the Lucan account of Jesus' healing of the Gerasene demoniac—a dramatic example of God's merciful action toward someone in dire need of healing and deliverance.

1 Kings 19:1–4 (5–7) 8–15*a*

This passage is the account of Elijah's arrival at Horeb and of Yahweh's appearance to him there. As a prophetic story, its focus is upon the encounter with the divine presence and the resulting message the prophet is to deliver. The reading breaks off, however, with only the very beginning of the Lord's commission to the prophet.

The geographical setting of the story is important. Traveling forty days and forty nights into the wilderness, Elijah has arrived at "Horeb the mount of God" (19:8). What some of the Old Testament sources and traditions call "Horeb"—Deuteronomy in particular—

others identify as "Sinai." Horeb was the location of Moses' call (Exod. 3:1). The mountain was the site of the establishment of the covenant and the revelation of the law through Moses. Historical geography has not been able to locate the place with certainty. The traditional site, Jebel Musa, is deep in the Sinai peninsula and far from any usual route between Egypt and Canaan. Some recent scholarship tends to seek the site near Kadesh-barnea, much further to the north and nearer the boundaries of Israel. For our text, the important point is that the prophet has gone to the holy mountain of divine revelation and takes up residence in a cave.

What transpires is an epiphany of Yahweh to Elijah. The report has two distinct parts, verses 9b–13a and verses 13b–18. The opening formula, "Then the word of the LORD came to him," (v. 9b) introduces the first encounter, but it could just as well stand as the heading for the passage as a whole. We are not to forget that it was the *word* of the Lord that was decisive in the epiphany. Both sections of the account consist of dialogue between Yahweh and the prophet. Yahweh speaks (vv. 9b, 11a, 13b, 15–18) and Elijah responds (vv. 10, 14). The first two exchanges are divine questions and the prophet's responses. Finally, Yahweh's last word (vv. 15–18) is not a question but instructions, which Elijah obeys but does not answer.

The questions and answers are virtually identical. When the Lord asks Elijah what he is doing in this place, the prophet responds with words of self-defense and, perhaps, self-pity. He cites his zeal ("I have been very zealous," vv. 10, 14) for Yahweh, and the apostasy of the people of Israel; he insists that he is the only faithful one left, and he has had to flee for his life. Note that he accuses, not Ahab and Jezebel, but "the people of Israel" of violence against Yahweh's altars and prophets. The plural reference to altars is an accurate historical allusion, for worship was not centralized in Jerusalem and all other sanctuaries torn down until the time of Josiah in the seventh century. The reference to the slaughter of the prophets may allude to the persecution by Jezebel noted in 1 Kings 18:4, 13.

Between the first and second dialogue is the account of the epiphany itself (vv. 11–13a). It is parallel in some respects to the appearance of the Lord to Moses (Exod. 33:17–23). Both take refuge in the mountain (a cave or a "cleft in the rock"), and neither is allowed to see Yahweh directly. The account of the theophany to Elijah is consistent with a widespread Old Testament tradition. When the Lord appears, there are awesome and dangerous natural phenomena. Here it is first "a great wind" (v. 11) that even splits rocks, then earthquake (v. 11), followed by fire (v. 12). In every case there follows the refrain "But the LORD was not in the wind . . . the earthquake . . . the fire." Finally, there was "a sound of sheer silence" (v. 12; RSV has "a still small voice," and NEB reads "a low murmuring sound"). Only then does the prophet come to the mouth of the cave and hear the word of Yahweh. That "he wrapped his face in his mantle" (v. 13) reflects the deep awareness in the Old Testament tradition that no one can see God and live (cf. Exod. 33:21; Isa. 6:2–5).

The major issue in this passage is the nature of divine revelation. Although awesome and destructive natural phenomena (wind, earthquake, fire) may attend the appearance of the Yahweh, the God of Israel is not to be identified with any of these. The story may even contain a polemic against the popular cultic view of the theophany (cf. Ps. 18:12; 68; Hab. 3:3). In any case, the perspective of this prophetic tradition is unmistakable: God reveals himself by means of the word, here the spoken word, and not fundamentally through the manipulation of natural forces, although those forces, to be sure, are set into turmoil by God's appearance. That word is calm, comprehensible, personal, and purposeful. The purpose of the epiphany is to commission the prophet to change history.

Psalm 42 and 43

These psalms are actually two halves of a single composition that was for some reason separated into two in antiquity. The unity of the two psalms can be argued for on a number of points: (1) an identical refrain appears in 42:5; 42:11; and 43:5; (2) the thought, content, and style of the two pieces are identical; (3) 42:9b is repeated in 43:2b; (4) Psalm 43 has no title or superscription as one would expect if it were a separate psalm; and (5) many ancient manuscripts present the two psalms as one.

The central concerns of these psalms are despair over the present situation and a hopeful desire to worship again in the Jerusalem temple. The despair can be seen best in the threefold refrain. In the refrain, the soul of the psalmist is addressed in a form of self-admonition. The soul is questioned ("Why are you cast down, O my soul, and why are you disquieted within me?") and then admonished or encouraged in a personal self-motivating supplication ("Hope in God; for I shall again praise him, my help and my God"). This dialogue of the self with the self may sound a bit peculiar to modern ears, and yet all of us engage, at one time or another, in such self-diagnosis or analysis. In a way, talking to oneself indicates a person's ability or at least desire to objectify oneself and gain some perspective on matters at hand.

The person who produced these psalms longs to be again in the presence of God, in worship at the temple. That the composition is entitled "A Maskil of the Korahites" could indicate that the psalm was used by a member of the clergy, a Levite of the order of the sons of Korah. The Korahites were cultic officials especially associated with the music of the temple as well as with other duties (see 2 Chron. 20:19; 1 Chron. 9:19, 31; 26:1). Use by a Levitical musician or by Levites would explain many features in the psalm.

The material in Psalms 42–43 shows the following outline: (A) address to God (v. 1); (B) address to a human audience (vv. 2–4); (C) self-address (v. 5); (A') address to God (vv. 6–7); (B') address to a human audience (vv. 8–10); (C') self-address (v. 11); (A2) address to God (43:1–4); and (C2) self-address (v. 5).

In the address to the Deity in verse 42:1, the imagery of water plays a significant role. In verse 1, water symbolizes the object of the thirsty deer's desire and is identified with God. Like a thirsty animal in a desert, the worshiper longs for God like the deer for an oasis. Here God is seen as the source of solace and comfort, as refreshment to a person distraught by distress. In verses 6–7, the imagery of water plays the opposite role. Here water represents the overwhelming, flooding aspects of life—the torrents that wash away the little dams we construct to provide dry land on which to "lifestead." Note the destructiveness indicated in the terminology—deep, thunder, cataracts, waves, billows. All come from God, but all threaten our existence.

The references to the land of Jordan, Mt. Hermon, and the otherwise unknown Mt. Mizar are not really clear. Perhaps they are used to symbolize the torrential flow of waters associated with these regions, namely, the sources of the river Jordan. Mount Hermon, over nine thousand feet above sea level, fed the headwaters of the Jordan.

In the addresses to a human audience, the psalmist speaks of adversity and opposition but also recalls the memories of past days. The first address (vv. 2–4) reaffirms the longing for God and the desire to worship (to "behold the face of God" denotes worshiping in the temple). The psalm emphasizes the present despair and discomfort of life, the tears of the pious, and the taunting of the opponents. References to tears occur frequently in the psalms (see Pss. 6:6; 39:12; 56:8; 80:5; 126:5). In the Middle East, tears and weeping were not looked down upon as weakness; perhaps the ancients knew that only the damned don't cry. The worshiper also refers to the memories of the past, good memories that may make the present even more painful and yet simultaneously stimulate expectations about the future. The past memories recall pilgrimages to the temple with their shouts and singing and festival joys. The second address to a human audience reflects on the features of present living—the routines of devotion day and night (v. 8), the sense of being forsaken by God (v. 9a), the oppression of the enemy (v. 9b), and the psychological wounds that opponents inflict by their jesting over the incongruities between faith and actuality (v. 10).

In 43:1–4, the petition addressed to God is quite aggressive, punctuated by a number of imperatives—vindicate (judge), defend, send out, let them lead/bring. There is, in other words, a move away from the character of passivity found in Psalm 42 to a more extroverted, demanding posture. The responsibility, or at least some of it, for the psalmist's welfare and status is shifted to the Deity who is "commanded" or requested to rectify matters. In addition, God is even accused of dereliction of duty, for not being the adequate source of refuge that the Divine should have been or for even casting away the one who would seek solace in God's protection (v. 2).

What the worshiper desires is God's light and truth; that is, for the worshiper and others to see and understand things as they really are (v. 3a) and to move in pilgrimage to the temple where God dwells (v. 3b). The final goal, the ultimate request, is to go to the altar (to offer sacrifice) and there to praise God (v. 4). In spite of life's troubles, worship is seen as the means for confronting and overcoming them.

It is possible that we overpersonalize such a psalm as this and try too hard to discover some individual's face beneath the poetic mask. It is entirely possible that this psalm (Ps. 42–43) was written to be used by worshipers and sung antiphonally as pilgrims set out on their way to some pilgrimage in Jerusalem. The portrayal of the present discontent with life thus forms the backdrop for the expectations of the coming worship (see Pss. 84 and 120, and note the remembrance of leading pilgrims to the temple in 42:4).

Isaiah 65:1–9

These are hopeful words from a difficult and troubled time. They are associated with the anonymous prophetic figure or figures responsible for most of Isaiah 56–66 who were active in the early postexilic period. By the time these words were written, many Judeans had returned from Babylon to their homeland; the temple almost certainly had been rebuilt, but the future of the people was by no means secure. In addition to external threats, there is evidence of sectarian conflict within the community.

In its literary context, our reading is part of a somewhat liturgical pattern. Isaiah 63:7–64:12 gives a series of prayers, mainly of complaint and petition, and then Isaiah 65:1–25 records the response. This movement, however, is probably the work of an editor who organized earlier materials rather than the reflection of an actual service of worship. Nevertheless, like much of the literature in Isaiah 56–66, this lesson reflects the ritual practices of the postexilic community.

In its context, then, Isaiah 65 stands as God's response to the preceding prayers, specifically the complaints and petitions from a people who experience their situation as divine judgment. The prayers conclude with the words "After all this, will you restrain yourself, O LORD? Will you keep silent, and punish us so severely?" (64:12). To these complaints the words of God in Isaiah 65:1–9 come as rebukes of the people whose sins brought about the judgment, as justification of God's ways with God's wayward people, and finally as reassurance, at least for some.

In verses 1–7 the Lord addresses the people with indictments and words of judgment. Replying directly to the charge that God has not responded to prayer, God asserts that the fault lies with the people. God was ready to be sought and found, but the nation "did not call on my name" (v. 1), that is, did not pray. Instead of worship and prayer, the people were walking "in a way that is not good, following their own devices" (v. 2). Verses 3–5 catalogue the sins of those people. Specifically, they were participating in the rituals of other religions. "Sacrificing in gardens" probably alludes to a fertility ritual, and sitting "inside tombs" probably refers to consulting the dead. They even violated the law further by eating swine's flesh and other "abominable things." Verse 5 sounds sarcastic, as God quotes the words of the people who consider themselves too holy for God. Picking up the people's charge that God keeps silent (64:12), God affirms that he will by no means be silent but will repay the people for their—and for their ancestors'—apostasy (vv. 6–7).

But beginning with a prophetic messenger formula ("Thus says the Lord"), the mood and message shift in verses 8–9, as God's face turns to the future. God begins to announce salvation to a remnant, to those left over after the destruction of judgment, after the Babylonian Exile. The announcement of salvation begins with an allusion to the wine found in the cluster of grapes (v. 8) and promises that the people will be revived as descendants of Jacob and as chosen servants of God who will settle again in the land promised to their ancestors (v. 9). The proclamation of good news for those who survived the Exile is expanded and extended in the remainder of chapter 65.

Such announcements of salvation appear frequently in the literature and liturgy of the postexilic period. They signal that the people of God know themselves to be the recipients of God's grace, and express the confidence that God will continue to care for the elect. More remarkable than the good news is that it appears here—and frequently—in the framework of the announcement of judgment upon Israel for her sins. Why would prophetic figures, leaders in worship, and the people as a whole express and take seriously such words? On the one hand, the recollection of the words of judgment from the earlier prophets served as the basis for warnings: Remain faithful to the Lord lest the disaster be repeated. On the other hand, the incorporation of words of judgment into a liturgical framework functioned as confession of sin. Just as later generations such as those of the postexilic period could identify with the ancestors who received the promise, those who were brought out of Egypt and given the land of Canaan, so too could they stand in solidarity with the sins of their predecessors. Corporate responsibility could be taken to extend over the generations.

Psalm 22:19–28

This psalm was discussed earlier as one of the lections for Good Friday.

Galatians 3:23–29

I n this final section of chapter 3, Paul concludes the fairly extended argument for justification by faith begun in verse 1. From their own experience the Galatians should have known that the Spirit came to them through "believing the gospel message" (3:2, REB) and not through keeping the law (vv. 1–5). In addition, the example of Abraham is instructive: he was reckoned as righteous by God because of his faith in God's promise, not because he kept specific legal requirements, such as circumcision (vv. 6–9). All those who similarly believe are Abraham's seed.

In the next section (vv. 10–14), we find that righteousness based on law keeping is ill-founded, primarily because no one can keep the law perfectly. If being accepted by God is a matter of achievement, true acceptance would require flawless performance. Everyone who tries to become religious in this way ultimately finds religion to be a curse. Instead, we are made righteous not by our achievement but through God's gracious gift, which we appropriate through faith.

If Abraham was accepted by God because he believed, justification by faith is the established precedent, antedating the giving of the law by more than four hundred years. This is the way God has always worked—extending a promise to those who act in faith (vv. 15–18).

The obvious question arises, "Why then the law?" (v. 19). It served to "make wrongdoing a legal offence" (v. 19, REB). It was a necessary, yet temporary, measure put in place until the coming of Christ, Abraham's offspring (vv. 21–22).

Life under the law had been a life of constraint, indeed a form of imprisonment (v. 23; cf. 4:5, 21; 5:18). In a sense, the law served as a "disciplinarian," a guardian or custodian whose role was that of temporary caretaker (vv. 24–25; cf. 1 Cor. 4:15). With the coming of Christ, however, the faith-principle was reestablished as the basis for justification. Like Abraham, Christ had demonstrated unqualified faith in God and thus became the one in whom the divine promise was renewed (3:14). Thus it was in Christ that all who live in faith are able to become God's children, the true heirs of the promise (v. 26; cf. 4:5–7).

What results is a new order of existence where all human distinctions are removed—ethnic, gender, and social (v. 28). To be sure, this is an eschatological reality but one that has already begun to be realized within the Pauline churches (1 Cor. 12:13; Rom. 10:12; Col. 3:11). We already see it beginning to be implemented as Paul instructs his churches about practical matters of faith (1 Cor. 7:17–24). And yet, it by no means was fully realized then, nor is it now. The form of the language suggests that this affirmation of oneness in Christ occurred in the context of a baptismal liturgy (cf. 1 Cor. 12:13; Col. 3:11). Baptism into Christ meant putting on Christ, as one would don a new garment (cf. Rom. 13:14; Eph. 4:24). Besides moral renewal, it implied entering a new world whose ordering principle was oneness in Christ. Union with Christ created a new form of social existence that sought to embody unity in Christ (John 17:21).

The implication of this is that God's original promise is firmly established; by being Christ's children, we experience solidarity with Abraham, who was saved by faith.

This text provides one of the clearest statements of Paul's vision of a new humanity where all distinctions are removed. In Paul's own lifetime, as the debate in Galatians and Romans attests, it was the Jew-Gentile question that came to the fore, and Paul became the champion for a form of religious community in which faith was the fundamental prerequisite for all members. In other ways, we begin to see the removal of sexual and social distinctions, but only embryonically. This continues to be an unrealized vision in the church.

Luke 8:26–39

This lection reports the second in a series of four episodes in which Jesus works wonders: stilling the storm, healing a demoniac, healing a sick woman, and raising a dead girl. The location of the event is a question. Matthew (8:28–34) has it in Gadara, six miles southeast of the Sea of Galilee. Luke places it in Gerasa, thirty-three miles southeast of the Sea of Galilee, a grand city from Alexander's time, the impressive remains of which can still be seen. In either case, Jesus is in Gentile territory. The story prefigures the Gentile mission more forcefully than the healing of the centurion's servant (7:1–10) because that occurred within Israel's borders. Jesus is now among Gentiles, among swine keepers (recall the swine in the far country in the parable of the prodigal, 15:11–32). Luke wants us to remember this later when he writes of Christian missionaries going into Gentile territory and confronting evil spirits (Acts 16:16–34; 19:11–20).

The account is of an exorcism, and although the demon possession is an extreme case, the usual pattern for an exorcism is followed: the confrontation, the identifications by name, the command for the demons to leave, the condition of the one freed of the demon, the effect on the observers. The abyss was the netherworld, the abode of spirit powers (Phil. 2:9–11), the dead (Rom. 10:7), imprisoned spirits (1 Pet. 3:19), and the place of Satan's prison (Rev. 20:3). The demons do not want to return to prison, and perhaps they think going into the animals and into the sea will put them beyond Jesus' power. But the previous episode has reported Jesus' power over the sea. The message is clear: there is no place beyond Jesus' power to set free.

However, the story has its negative fallout: the people of the area ask Jesus to leave (vv. 34–37). In Luke's usual way of telling things twice, Acts 16:16–39 records Paul casting out a spirit from a slave girl and as a result being asked to leave the city. In both cases the reasons for the negative responses are two: fear and economic loss. The fear is prompted by the presence of a power greater than that of demonic spirits. The people had isolated the man with the demon and had given time and expense to guarding and controlling him. This is to say, they had met the situation with tolerance and management of the demonic among them. Now the power of God comes to their community and disturbs that way of life. Even when it is for good, power that can neither be calculated nor managed is frightening. What will God do next in our community? One is reminded of the fear created by Easter.

As for economic loss, it remains the case that the impact of Jesus Christ affects a community's economy. The embrace of the gospel influences patterns of getting and spending. The Gerasenes are not praising God that a man is healed; they are counting the cost and find it too much. Such was Paul's experience in Philippi and in Ephesus as well (Acts 19:18–34): powerful economic forces array themselves against the good news. It remains so today, and being asked to leave by persons you seek to help is a pain unlike any other.

The healed man wants, of course, to continue with Jesus, but the behavior of his fellow citizens makes it clear he is needed in that area. Jesus asks him to remain and make his witness: "declare how much God has done for you" (v. 39). The man did so, except he spoke of what *Jesus* had done for him. Given his experience, that is understandable, but Luke wants it clear that God is the source of all power and grace, Jesus being here the means of it.

Proper 8 [13]
(Sunday between June 26 and July 2 inclusive)

2 Kings 2:1–2, 6–14;
Psalm 77:1–2, 11–20; or
1 Kings 19:15–16, 19–21;
Psalm 16;
Galatians 5:1, 13–25;
Luke 9:51–62

Elijah's unforgettable exit and Elisha's taking up his prophetic mantle are the subject of today's *Common Lectionary* Old Testament reading. As a response, Psalm 77 rehearses the mighty acts of God.

An earlier episode from the Elijah cycle provides the Old Testament reading in other lectionaries. Yahweh commissions Elijah to return to Damascus and perform a double anointing: Jehu as king and Elisha as his prophetic successor. In the second part of the text, Elisha becomes Elijah's disciple. Psalm 16 responds by expressing unyielding faith in Yahweh's capacity to give counsel, instruction, guidance, and deliverance.

The Epistle reading finds Paul urging his readers to walk under the banner of freedom in Christ and to live in freedom as slaves to one another.

In the Gospel reading, Jesus sets his face toward Jerusalem, warning those who would follow him that such a pattern of life comes wrapped in the demands of drastic obligations.

2 Kings 2:1–2, 6–14

This reading is a tale of two prophets—the end of one's career and the beginning of the other's. The atmosphere is heavy with the mysterious and miraculous power of God manifest through these two and worked upon them. Elijah was taken up into heaven in a whirlwind, having used his mantle to divide the waters of the Jordan. That places the emphasis upon the older prophet. But the younger prophet loyally followed his master, actually *saw* him taken up, and also divided the waters of the Jordan with the same mantle. That places the emphasis on Elisha. In the broader literary context in the Books of Kings, the chapter makes the transition from one prophet to the next, but it emphasizes the latter, confirming Elisha as Elijah's successor.

Binding the story together is the account of the journey, the itinerary of the prophets from Gilgal to Bethel to Jericho, across the Jordan and then—for one of them—back again.

Elijah had been a remarkably peripatetic prophet all along. These movements heighten the tension and turn what would otherwise be a brief anecdote into a story with a plot, that is, the creation of tension, its resolution, and its results.

The plot does not turn on the question of what will happen to Elijah. From the very beginning we know Elijah's fate, that the old prophet will be taken "up to heaven by a whirlwind" (v. 1). Left in doubt is Elisha's future. The ground is laid for an answer in the account of the journey. At each stopping place, Elijah asks Elisha, "Stay here" (vv. 2, 4, 6), and in every instance the younger prophet vows not to leave him. Were these requests Elijah's way of testing his successor's stamina and devotion? Their effect is to underscore both Elisha's persistence and his unqualified loyalty to his master.

In the background is the "company of prophets" (v. 7; "sons of the prophets" in the RSV), here fifty in number. These were members of the prophetic guild, probably under the leadership of a "father" such as Elijah. The allusion to this group is a clue to the institution that would have been most interested in perpetuating the stories of the miraculous exploits of the great prophets.

But Elisha stands out from all the others. Thematically, there is a link with Elijah's commission on Mt. Horeb and his designation of Elisha as his successor, the one to carry out God's will for the house of Ahab (1 Kings 19:15–21). There, too, Elijah's mantle had played a role. But our text for the day makes no explicit reference to that original encounter between Elijah and his successor. One might think that Elijah has forgotten altogether the Lord's instructions to commission Elisha.

Once the two prophets have crossed the Jordan, a dialogue transpires that is the key to the story (vv. 9–10). Elijah, aware that the end is near, invites Elisha to make a final request of him. The request for "a double share" of Elijah's spirit asks a great deal, as he points out. (Although according to Deuteronomy 21:17 a double inheritance is the rule for the eldest son.) So Elijah sets a condition: "If you see me as I am being taken from you, it will be granted you; if not, it will not" (v. 10). The climax is thus not the description of the manner of Elijah's departure in verse 11—at the same time graphic and elusive—but the affirmation in verse 12 that Elisha did, indeed, see it. In its resolution we see the story's question clearly: Will Elisha be the successor of Elijah, and one fully endowed with "a double share" of his spirit? The presence of that spirit is confirmed when Elisha divides the Jordan with the mantle, just as Elijah had.

Several specific points in the story call for comment. When Elisha cries out to Elijah, "Father, father! The chariots of Israel and its horsemen!" (v. 12), he is using two titles. The first, "father," indicating respect and affection, stems from his role in relation to the prophetic groups. The second, with its reference to military might, also is applied Elisha when he is about to die (2 Kings 13:15). The phenomena that attend the prophet's ascension suggest both disruptions in nature (whirlwind, fire) and military imagery. They recall the theophany to the prophet on Mt. Horeb (1 Kings 19). Some aspects of the story parallel the Moses traditions: the parting of the waters, and the fact that both Moses and Elijah meet their ends beyond the Jordan and leave to their successors the completion of their tasks.

As there is continuity of authority and power between Elijah and Elisha, so there are contrasts. The former is a solitary individual, always at odds with the royal household. The latter will always seem to have others—prophets, kings, soldiers—around him. He will intervene directly in the political arena, bringing the destruction of the house of Ahab that Elijah prophesied. Finally, Elisha, even with a double share of his master's spirit, will die an ordinary death.

Psalm 77:1–2, 11–20

This psalm divides into two major sections: verses 1–10 are characterized by lamenting and descriptions of distress, whereas verses 11–20 are hymnic in character. Unlike most laments, this psalm contains no plea or appeal for God to act, no request for the destruction of enemies. The tension created and the predicaments noted in verses 1–10 are transcended or bypassed in the praise of God in verses 11–20. It is as if the troubles and distresses were accepted and the attention was focused on God and the divine action in the past. Perhaps the psalmist felt that to describe and praise God's past activities was a means of expressing hope for a repeat of such actions in the future.

The description of the distress and trouble in verses 1–10 takes two forms. The first is an address by the worshiper to a human audience that expounds the worshiper's weariness with ever-present (but unspecified) trouble and indirectly accuses God of dereliction of duty and failure to respond to entreaty and request (vv. 1–3). The second section, in verses 4–10, is direct address to the Deity that continues both the lament and the charges against God. Nighttime is described as a very troublesome time for the supplicant, a time when sleep would not come and the hours were spent rehearsing the past and trying to determine when and why things went wrong. The worshiper repeats those haunting thoughts that gnaw at the psyche of religious people when life goes awry: Has God completely rejected me? Am I suffering from some capricious action of the Divine? Were all those promises without foundation? Has God forgotten me? Am I, like Job, the object of some hidden, celestial game whose rules and objectives I may never know? The NEB translation of verse 10, admittedly a difficult verse to interpret, says quite nicely one such sentiment: "Has his [God's] right hand," I said, "lost its grasp? Does it hang powerless, the arm of the Most High?"

The first half of this psalm was obviously composed for use in worship by a person severely depressed. If the latter half is viewed as the manner in which the priests allowed the worshiper to confront that depression, then several things become obvious. (One should recall, even though it goes against the widespread methods of interpreting the psalms, that the psalms were probably written by members of the temple staff for the use of worshipers. In contexts of what we would call pastoral counseling/care, a psalm, the needs of the worshiper, and the form of the cultic service were set so as to minister realistically to particular human and communal needs.)

The remainder of the psalm (vv. 11–20) shifts completely away from the particulars of any individual situation. The worshiper and the psalm shift to transpersonal, almost cosmic and mythological concerns, to conditions and situations at the founding of the world and the origins of Israel. (An interesting parallel from Mesopotamian culture is the fact that the "dentist," when extracting a person's tooth, went through a liturgy that involved reciting a short account of the creation of the world.) Such a move may have been a way of distracting the person from the immediate problem or a means of focusing one's faith on God's past and glorious acts so as to assure the person that God was still and always had been in control. (The minister here should note, however, that even if there was this desire to instill or reawaken faith in the cosmic dimensions of divinity, this did not override the necessity of the person to give expression to depression and hostile feelings toward God.)

The material shifts from lament and protest to hymnic form. In giving help to such a worshiper, the priests must have known that to focus continually on the individual's particular problems and sleepless nights would get nowhere. The person's "little story," that is, the character and quality of the person's particular life, was best dealt with in the hymnic affirmation of God's and Israel's "great story." (The same thing happens in the Book of Job, where God, in answering Job, never points to or responds to Job's particular problems but transposes the issues to a higher, cosmic key.)

No appeals are made; no personal requests are formulated. The worshiper was apparently dismissed to live in the light of the hymn.

Verses 11–20 combine images and perspectives drawn from the creation of Israel, when God led the people out of Egypt (vv. 14–15), and from the creation of the world, when God triumphed over the chaotic waters and chaos monsters and, amid thunder and lightnings and the trembling and shaking of the earth, God established order and led his people like lambs (vv. 16–20). In light of such a vision of divine activity, now what was your problem?

1 Kings 19:15–16, 19–21

Our reading is an account of piety, politics, and prophetic succession. It begins in the middle of a unit, the account of the epiphany of Yahweh to Elijah on Horeb (vv. 9–18). The awesome appearance of the Lord, then, is the immediate context in which the lection should be read and heard. The broader context is the collection of stories concerning the life and times of the prophet. The reading for the day brings us to the issue at the heart of those stories, the conflict between Yahweh and Baal, between Elijah and the followers of Baal—especially those in Israel's royal palace, Ahab and Jezebel.

This conflict between Israelite and Canaanite religions was both an ancient and a continuing one. When Israel began to establish herself in the land, the fertility religions of Baal and numerous other deities had been practiced in Canaan for centuries. From Israel's perspective, the conflict with the native religion may be seen as a crisis of faith and culture. Which Canaanite practices and symbols could Israel accept and still remain faithful to the God who brought them up out of Egypt? Many said, "None," and that was the official and orthodox answer, in keeping with the First Commandment. But Canaanite culture and religion were powerful forces, and as the Israelites became farmers and city dwellers, it is not surprising that they took over many practices and ideas from their predecessors in the land. Even the kingship—like that of the other nations—represented for many a compromise with culture, for "Yahweh is our king." In the ninth century when Elijah appeared on the scene in the Northern Kingdom, the conflict had become an open one because Ahab's wife Jezebel had officially reintroduced the religion of Baal. Elisha is instrumental in putting an end to that problem, but—as the Book of Hosea shows—it is still alive in more subtle forms a century later.

In the story as a whole (vv. 15–21), the first part (vv. 15–18) concerns that conflict between Yahwism and Baalism. It is framed as a speech of Yahweh to Elijah, introduced by the account of the theophany. God's appearance leads to words of commission—similar in some ways to the vocation reports of other prophets—to the fugitive prophet. The prophet's complaints are answered by commands, first to return to the land where his life was in danger. Yahweh instructs him further to anoint two kings, one for Syria and one for Israel, and a prophet as his own successor (vv. 15–16). Then follows a somewhat cryptic, oracular interpretation of the purpose for which these three are to be anointed (v. 17)—bloodshed. The final sentence (v. 18) at once clarifies the death sentence—presumably for all who *have* "bowed the knee to Baal" and kissed him, that is, his image—and rebukes Elijah for his claim that he is the only one left who is faithful to Yahweh (19:10, 14).

There is a poignant note in this commission. Elijah, who has been at the center of the religious and political conflict, is not to see its resolution. That will be for his successor; his duty is to designate the instruments of the Lord's will. Like Moses, who was not allowed to enter the promised land, he lives with the promise and not its fulfillment.

The second part of the reading (vv. 19–21) reports how Elijah responded to the commission by finding Elisha and ordaining him. Elisha was plowing with oxen when Elijah, without a word, threw his mantle over him. When Elisha runs after Elijah, a curious dialogue transpires. Elisha asks to kiss his parents farewell before following Elijah, who seems to deny that the act with the mantle meant anything. But then Elisha returns, kills the oxen and cooks their flesh on a fire made with the yokes, and feeds the people. The goal of the anecdote is reached when we hear that Elisha followed Elijah and "became his servant" (v. 21).

Actions here speak louder than words. Like many other prophets, Elijah performs a symbolic action, but unlike most others, he does not interpret its meaning. The point, however, is obvious both to Elisha and to the hearers and readers—succession. The mantle is a symbol of the authority that is passed on, as also in the final Elijah episode (2 Kings 2:1–14). Note that Elijah does not literally "anoint" Elisha, as instructed in verse 15. There is no Old Testament example of anointing a prophet, and even the designation of a prophetic successor is remarkable. God usually calls prophets directly, but here does so through another prophet. Elisha's action with the oxen is symbolic as well. He signals a break with his previous occupation and hosts a sacrificial meal. That he became Elijah's servant suggests that his role in some ways is parallel to that of Joshua in relation to Moses (Deut. 31:7–8, 14–23; Josh. 1:1).

Along with issues of the prophetic role and vocation, the passage raises but does not resolve for us the relation between faith and politics. Both those who feel that religious leaders should be involved directly in politics and those who feel they should not are likely to find support in this text. On the one hand, Elijah, like all Israel's prophets, was deeply involved in politics, to the point of instigating rebellion. Without such zeal, it is questionable whether the Yahwistic faith would have survived. On the other hand, his fanatically held faith called forth a bloodbath, which at least one later prophet will condemn (Hos. 1:4–5). Today, in a very different culture, where political and religious institutions are more distinct, we are impelled to struggle with the issues of faith and culture, religion and politics.

Psalm 16

The ancient rabbis understood this psalm as David writing about himself. In addition, they understood the text as speaking about actual death, at least in verse 3a. This text, that the rabbis read as "the holy that are in the earth" (and therefore dead), was said to speak about the deceased because "the Holy One (God) does not call the righteous man holy until he is laid away in the earth. Why not? Because the Inclination-to-evil [the evil yetzer of the human personality] keeps pressing him. And so God does not put His trust in him in this world till the day of his death. . . . That the Lord will not call a righteous man holy until he is laid away in the earth is what is meant" (*Midrash on Psalms*).

In spite of the translation difficulties found in verses 2–4, where the worshiper appears to refer to the worship of other gods ("the holy ones" and "the noble" may denote the holy and mighty god mentioned in v. 4), the remainder of the text makes reasonably good sense. (In addition to the NRSV, one should consult the NJPSV.)

Verses 5–11 open with a short confessional statement addressed to a human audience (v. 5a) and is immediately followed by a confessional statement of trust addressed to God (v. 5b). The terminology of this verse, as well as verse 6, speaks of what one has inherited or been given in life—portion, cup, lot, lines, and heritage. The NJPSV translates:

> The Lord is my allotted share and portion;
>   You control my fate.
> Delightful country has fallen to my lot;
>   lovely indeed is my estate.

Instead of being guilty of worshiping false gods, the psalmist is depicted as one who constantly things of God (vv. 7–8). The counsel God gives (v. 7a) is matched by that of the person's own conscience (NRSV: "heart," although literally "the kidneys," denoting the inner self). The term translated "night" in verse 7b is actually the Hebrew plural "nights" ("watches of the night," "every night," or "the dark night"). The human activity and consistency (v. 8a) are matched by God's consistent preservation, with the consequence that the psalmist can confess, "I shall not be moved," that is, threatened or overcome.

The last section (vv. 9–11) returns to direct address to God, confessing assurance that the request made in verse 1 will be granted; that is, the person will live and not die. It was this section that led to the psalm's usage in early Christian preaching and confession. Again, the NJPSV conveys the meaning better than the NRSV:

> So my heart rejoices,
>   my whole being exults,
>   and my body rests secure.
> For You will not abandon me to Sheol,
>   or let Your faithful one see the Pit.

Sheol and Pit refer to the realm of the dead. Probably the psalm was used originally by persons near death as a result of some sickness. Of course, they do not want to die but want to remain alive to enjoy their heritage (vv. 5–6, 11b).

Galatians 5:1, 13–25

Rather than seeing an abrupt shift at 5:1 from the so-called theological section to the practical, hortatory section of the letter, chapters 5–6 should be viewed as being much more integrally related to chapters 1–4. Freedom is one of several thematic links between the two sections (cf., e.g., 2:4; 3:28; 4:22, 23, 26, 30; 5:1, 13).

One way of reading chapter 5 is as a theological exposition of freedom, for which Paul has so strongly argued throughout the letter, and which is indeed one of the hallmarks of Pauline theology (cf. Rom. 6:18, 22; 1 Cor. 7:23; 2 Cor. 3:17; also John 8:32, 36). Especially is this true of today's epistolary lection.

It may seem odd that our text begins with the reminder that Christ has liberated us and that we should be resolute in remaining free. Yet Paul is all too aware of the hazards of being free, and he targets three potential dangers.

First, freedom may turn out to be more difficult than slavery. There is a good chance that, like the long-term prisoner who is finally set free and finds it difficult to shake the habits of servitude, we may actually "submit again to a yoke of slavery" (v. 1). Freedom, after all, poses new responsibilities. Whereas formerly our choices may have been made for us, we now find they are ours—and ours alone—to make. And one advantage of living under law is that our duties and responsibilities can be spelled out in great detail. We may actually be more comfortable having law define our conduct for us instead of exercising our own autonomy in deciding on the responsible course of action to take. Freedom may be attractive initially because we think it will demand less of us, yet we discover that it actually makes greater demands on us. One of the ironies of life is that the life of freedom requires greater effort than the life of servitude. It has to be nurtured, protected, and rigorously pursued. It is not a lifelong afternoon in a hammock.

Like the Israelites after the Exodus who found themselves actually longing for their former life of servitude, we may find freedom in Christ too much to take. Paul's charge is for us to be resolute in our newfound freedom, to be relentless in our pursuit of freedom, to "stand firm" (v. 1). We are often given this charge to be steadfast, and this in itself suggests that our tendency will be to take the easier course and be lured away to the more comfortable life of slavery (4:9; cf. Rom. 11:20; 1 Cor. 10:12; 15:1; 16:13; 2 Cor. 1:24; 1 Thess. 3:8; 2 Thess. 2:15; Phil. 1:27; 4:1).

Second, freedom may destroy a sense of community. We are cautioned not to allow our freedom to become "an opportunity for self-indulgence" (v. 13). This could be thought of as a warning against sexual laxity (cf. Rom. 7:8), but the following verses suggest otherwise. We are called to a life of loving service to each other and reminded that this is the essence of the law (v. 14; cf. Lev. 19:18; Rom. 13:8–10). And verse 15 reminds us of the nursery rhyme: "There once were two cats of Kilkenny; Each thought there was one cat too many; So they fought and they fit, they scratched and they bit; Til, excepting their nails and the tips of their tails; Instead of two cats, there weren't any!"

More likely, our text is warning us against an overly individualistic interpretation of freedom. The tendency of the flesh, in this sense, would be the tendency to pursue our own needs and desires, oblivious to the common good. That this was a real issue is seen in the church at Corinth (1 Cor. 8–10; esp. 1 Cor. 8:9). So defined, freedom becomes the relentless pursuit of the individual with no moral commitment to others, and eventually becomes inhumane and self-destructive. In any case, we are reminded that freedom can easily be abused and become a cover for our own evil desires (cf. 1 Pet. 2:16).

Third, freedom may translate into a form of moral relativism. One objection to Paul's gospel is that it provides an open license to sin (Rom. 6:1–4). In the absence of law(s), how do we develop a responsible ethic?

For one thing, we can recognize the existence of genuine moral conflict within us. Plato portrayed it as the struggle between two horses pulling a chariot. It is sketched in today's text as a war between the Spirit and the flesh (cf. Rom. 7:15, 23; James 4:1, 5; 1 Pet. 2:11). The two are antithetical to each other (v. 17), for they represent two fundamentally opposed ways of construing reality. "Conflict does not mean peaceful co-existence, let alone co-operation. . . . No cooperation, then, between the two! For how can there be co-operation between total freedom and total bondage? How can the Spirit give assistance to the flesh, or the flesh to the Spirit?" (Barth).

At the very least, we can recognize the existence of two fundamental outlooks, one domain where the Spirit lives and reigns (cf. Rom. 8:4), the other dominated by the flesh (cf. Eph. 2:3; 1 John 2:16; 1 Pet. 2:11). For Paul, life under the law belonged squarely within the latter (3:23; 4:4–5, 21; Rom. 6:14). Essentially, two profiles of existence are sketched. The first set of vices represent the various forms of behavior that result from giving in to the impulses of the flesh, or our own desires (cf. Rom. 1:29–31; 13:13; Matt. 15:19; Luke 18:11; 1 Cor. 5:10–11; 6:9–10; 2 Cor. 12:20; Eph. 4:31; 5:3–5; Col. 3:5, 8; 1 Tim. 1:9–10; 6:4–5; 2 Tim. 3:2–4; Titus 3:3; 1 Pet.

4:3; Rev. 9:21; 21:8; 22:15; also 4 Macc. 1:26; 2:15). The set of virtues, or fruits of the Spirit (e.g., Eph. 5:9; Phil. 1:11; Heb. 12:11; James 3:18; Prov. 3:9; 11:30; Amos 6:13), display the results of living in response to God's own Spirit (cf. 2 Cor. 6:6–7; 1 Tim. 4:12; 6:11; 2 Tim. 2:22; 2 Pet. 1:5–11).

Because freedom, in the Pauline sense, exists where the Spirit presides (2 Cor. 3:17) and provides the norm by which we live, Paul's final charge is to "be guided by the Spirit" (v. 25).

Luke 9:51–62

With 9:51, Luke begins a new section of his Gospel, a fact recognized in many English translations by the use of a break in the text between verses 50 and 51. That 9:51 marks a new turn in the narrative is indicated by a time reference ("when the days drew near"), a purpose reference ("he set his face to go to Jerusalem"; cf. a similar expression in the Servant Song of Isa. 50:6–7), and a final departure reference ("to be taken up," an ascension expression in Luke and 1 Timothy 3:16).

Exactly where the section that begins at 9:51 ends is not quite so clear. If Luke is viewed in relation to Mark, then the unit extends sufficiently to include the stories in Luke that are not found in Mark. This means the end would be at 18:14, for at 18:15 Luke resumes following Mark's framework. Others who prefer to call this Luke's "travel narrative" conclude at 19:27, at which point Jesus arrives at Jerusalem. There is a general correctness to calling 9:51–19:27 a travel narrative because the materials in this section are broadly framed as the trip to Jerusalem. However, the place references are such as to make reconstruction of the itinerary impossible. Approximately one half of the material in 9:51–18:14, although having no Markan parallels, has parallels in Matthew; the other one half is in Luke alone.

It is probably helpful to the preacher to see this section in the larger pattern of Luke's Gospel. The first section of Luke's work was preceded by Jesus' baptism, an event bathed in prayer and given divine attestation (3:21–22). This section is prefaced by Jesus' transfiguration, again marked by prayer and the voice from heaven (9:28–36). The first began with a rejection at Nazareth (4:16–30), the second, with a rejection in Samaria (9:51–56). Neither rejection stops Jesus' ministry; in fact, in each in embryo is the prophecy of an even larger mission to the Gentiles. For the next four months the Gospel lessons will be taken from this special section, this travel narrative of Luke. Although the journey itself cannot be reconstructed, we will be able to experience what Luke wanted to convey: the life of discipleship is a pilgrimage, and those who follow can expect to share in the fate of Jesus.

Today's lesson, 9:51–62, consists of two parts: Jesus' rejection by the Samaritans (v. 51–56) and Jesus' terms for discipleship (vv. 57–62). Although the units have their own integrity, they should be treated together because verses 51–56 set the tone for the encounters with Jesus in verses 57–62. Understanding the unswerving intensity, the destiny-oriented sense of Jesus setting his face toward Jerusalem and the cross, enables the reader to grasp the same intense commitment expected of Jesus' followers. This same pattern occurred earlier in the chapter when Luke placed the demands of discipleship immediately after Jesus' prediction of his death (9:18–27).

Verses 51–56 have a double function. They record Jesus' rejection by Samaritans because his face is set to go to Jerusalem, a statement that at one level testifies to racial tension between Samaritans and Jews, but at another level says they are not willing to follow one who is on his way "to be taken up"; that is, to be killed. But these verses also anticipate the mission of the seventy (10:1–12). Jesus' own ministry, the sending out of disciples by twos, the extension of the mission beyond Judaism, the dependence upon the hospitality of others, the response to those who reject the message, and the movement on to other places, all elements in verses 51–56, provide precedence and dominical authorization for the subsequent mission of the church.

Verses 57–62 provide three examples of encounters between Jesus and would-be disciples as Jesus moves toward Jerusalem as one who has set his face like a firm stone. A threefold pattern was common to storytelling at that time, even though these may have existed earlier as independent episodes. Matthew 8:19–22 records the first two. The pattern here is: "I will follow," "follow me," and again, "I will follow." Given the portrayal of Jesus in verse 51, the reader should not expect Jesus to offer easy options. The call for total and primary loyalty is underscored by setting Jesus' demands over against, not the worst or lowest, but the best and the highest loyalties. Anything less would deny his own destiny and the claims of the kingdom of God. There is no reason, then, for the preacher to search for loopholes in Jesus' absolutes. He is on his way to be taken up; shall he deceive his disciples with offers of bargains?

Proper 9 [14]
(Sunday between July 3 and 9 inclusive)

2 Kings 5:1–14;
Psalm 30; or
Isaiah 66:10–14;
Psalm 66:1–9;
Galatians 6:(1–6) 7–16;
Luke 10:1–11, 16–20

The deceptively simple story of Elisha's healing of Naaman the leper serves as today's Old Testament reading for the *Common Lectionary*. Quite fittingly, Psalm 30 praises the God who heals and delivers from death.

In other lectionaries, the Old Testament reading is supplied by one of the most poignant passages from Isaiah, where Zion is portrayed as a nursing mother tenderly caring for her child. In the opening verses of Psalm 66, God is praised for extending continuous goodness to Israel.

Various moral exhortations comprise the epistolary reading from Paul's concluding chapter of his epistle to the Galatians.

The Gospel text is the Lucan account of Jesus' commissioning of the seventy and their triumphant return.

2 Kings 5:1–14

This passage, the account of the prophet's healing of Naaman, is a straightforward story that moves rapidly from beginning to end, but it is by no means simple. Events transpire on several levels. In its characterizations, its allusions to circumstances, and in the unfolding of its plot, at least three distinct motifs present themselves. Moreover, although the text can be read as a more-or-less self-contained unit, it takes on new dimensions when seen in the light of its sequel, the remainder of 2 Kings 5.

First, like the accounts in 2 Kings 4, we have a story of Elisha's miraculous powers, manifest in this case in the healing of a leper. The first scene, which introduces the problem and the main character—other than Elisha, of course—takes place in Syria (vv. 1–5a). Naaman, a powerful commander of the army and highly regarded by his king, is a leper. The person in need does not ask for help, but a third party proposes that the prophet can remedy the situation. In this case it is an Israelite slave girl who serves Naaman's wife. When the commander tells his king what he has heard, the king sends him off to Israel with a letter of introduction. Setting out loaded down with wealth—presumably to pay the prophet—Naaman presents the letter to the king of Israel. The king is fearful and suspicious, thinking that the Syrian king has made an impossible request so that failure to comply will be a pretext for war (vv. 5b–7).

But then Elisha, who only now (v. 8) is identified by name, intervenes. Messages go back and forth. He tells his king to send Naaman to him, and the commander rides up in all his splendor. The prophet does not meet Naaman directly, but sends instructions for him to wash himself seven times in the Jordan. This behavior and these too-simple and unexpected instructions infuriate the leper, who knows what kind of healing ritual to expect from a holy man (v. 11). Moreover, he has rivers in his homeland. When the servant persuades Naaman to do as instructed he is healed immediately (v. 14).

We, like the ancient hearers, are expected to acknowledge that the power of the Lord is manifest in and through a special individual, and that this power works for health. Although the Elisha stories in their eagerness to glorify the prophet sometimes obscure the point, here it is made obvious that the power to heal belongs to God alone (v. 7).

Second, there is the theme of the needy foreigner, the one who—from Israel's perspective—is an outsider. Through much of their history, Israel and Syria were enemies. The allusion to the Israelite slave girl recalls military conflicts, as does the Israelite king's fear when he hears the letter from his counterpart in Damascus (v. 7). Nationalistic pride rears its head when Naaman speaks disdainfully about the Jordan in contrast to the "rivers of Damascus" (v. 12). But the Israelite prophet heals the foreign general, anticipating a point that will recur over and over in the Gospels, when outsiders—tax collectors and sinners—and foreigners—including Roman soldiers—come to Jesus, and he accepts and heals them. Here we have at least a hint that Israel's faith has the capacity to cross boundaries, to be inclusive. The point is even more emphatic when one considers the sequel to the story (2 Kings 5:19–27). Gehazi, Elisha's Israelite servant, extorts money from the generous Naaman and is cursed with leprosy. The "great man" has become genuinely great in bowing before Elisha, and Elisha's follower has been shown to be guilty of greed.

The third, and central, theme concerns faith. At issue throughout is neither the authority of the prophet nor his power to heal, but the human response to the disclosure of that power. The Israelite king's lament in verse 7 begins to introduce the issue of confession, and Naaman is called upon to trust in the power of the God of Elisha (vv. 1–12). Suspense is created while we await his response. Will he return home, taking his leprosy with him, when health is so near? Finally he takes a chance. The high point of the story is not the restoration of his flesh—the hearers had known all along that this would be the result. It is, rather, the confession, "Now I know that there is no God in all the earth except in Israel" (v. 15). That is the story's goal. Miraculous healing is, to be sure, for the health of the sick person, but it is also for the purpose of revelation, to make known even to outsiders who God is.

Psalm 30

This psalm was discussed earlier as one of the lections for Proper 5 [10].

Isaiah 66:10–14

Because the faith of Israel arose in a patriarchal culture, most of the Old Testament's divine imagery and metaphors for God are male or masculine. But rich and deep female metaphors appear as well. That should not be surprising, because the human image of God is seen to be both male and female (Gen. 1:26–27). In the reading for the day we have a metaphor for God that goes beyond the feminine (culturally defined) to the female, for the loving care of the Lord for Israel is likened to that of a mother comforting her child.

The literary and historical context of our lesson is Isaiah 56–66, a collection of materials commonly identified with Third Isaiah from the postexilic period. This literature includes prophetic announcements, mainly of salvation, as well as liturgically shaped prayers and poems. The collection almost certainly did not originate from a single hand but from the community of the Second Temple as it struggled with questions of its identity and its existence as the people of God.

More immediately, this reading is at the center of Isaiah 66:5–16, a prophetic announcement of salvation and comfort for the people of Israel and of their vindication through the Lord's judgment on those who oppose the people of God. The unit is initiated with two calls to hear, first to the people as addressees (v. 5), and then (v. 6) concerning the Lord as the speaker of the words that follow and the substance of those words as "retribution to his enemies." But that announcement of the Lord's appearance to judge the enemies does not come until the very conclusion of the section in verses 15–16. What follows first in verses 7–9 and then in verses 10–14 are promises of salvation and comfort to God's people.

Throughout this announcement of salvation Zion is personified as a woman, and specifically as a mother. Verses 7–9 describe with amazement a woman giving birth before she goes into labor. The mother is Zion, her son is Israel, her children the people of God. That metaphor continues in our assigned reading. The people who love Jerusalem and mourn over her are called to rejoice with the city (v. 10), and then are invited to "nurse . . . from her consoling breast . . . drink deeply . . . from her glorious bosom" (v. 11). The figure continues with the vision of the mother nursing her children, carrying them on her arm, dandling them on her knees (v. 12).

The female personification of Zion is not without precedent. Frequently through the prophetic and other biblical literature Zion is designated "Daughter" or "Virgin." But here the female figure is not a diminutive but a symbol of sustaining strength and comfort. Zion, which in its narrowest sense refers to the hill on which the temple was constructed, can be used interchangeably with and stand for Jerusalem (v. 13).

In verses 13–14 the metaphor shifts dramatically. The nursing mother who had been Zion is now the Lord. In fact, what had been a metaphor becomes an explicit simile, when the Lord is heard to say: "As a mother comforts her child, so I will comfort you" (v. 13). The Lord, who may act as a warrior against Israel's enemies (vv. 14b–16), will care for the suffering and discouraged people as a mother cares for her child.

The obvious theme for homiletical reflection in this text is its good news: The Lord promises to care for and comfort the people of God. But the dramatically distinctive female metaphors in the passage invite consideration on both the nature of God and on the power of language that refers to God. God is neither male nor female, but as soon as we begin to think of and speak about God personally, the vocabulary of gender seems almost inevitable. Here we are reminded that God acts like a mother with her child. But in the same context, God is seen to be a warrior. Thus the male and military language is so familiar in the biblical tradition that it is used metaphorically, whereas with the maternal imagery, the comparison—"as" or "like"—is explicit. The presence of multiple images and diverse means of expression serves to stress that no human language can contain the Deity.

Psalm 66:1–9

Few psalms fall in the category of community or communal thanksgiving. As a rule, ancient Jewish worship probably used general hymns of praise to express thanks on behalf of the whole community rather than psalms of thanksgiving that focused specifically on the particular reason for thanksgiving. (At least, this is one explanation for the almost total absence of psalms of community thanksgiving.) Even in Psalm 66, one of the best candidates for a community thanksgiving, the focus shifts in verses 13–20 to individual speech (note the "I" throughout this section), perhaps suggesting that a community leader or the king representing the community is the speaker.

The psalm appeals to the people (the nations, the earth) to participate in the praise and to behold the works of God (vv. 1, 5, 8, and 16; the opening verbs in these verses are all plural imperatives). The reasons for praise and observance are given in verses 2–4, 5b–7, 9, and 17–19. These include God's awesome deeds (v. 3), mighty works (v. 5), sustenance of life (v. 9), and response to prayerful requests (v. 18).

Different audiences are addressed in the psalm: verses 1–9 call upon the peoples of the world; verses 10–12 are communal speech to God (note the plural pronouns); verses 13–15 are addressed to God (note the singular first person pronouns); and verses 16–20 are individual speech addressed to a plural human audience.

Verses 1–7 emphasize Yahweh's triumph over enemies and the parting of the Red Sea and the Jordan River (see Exodus 14; Joshua 3; Ps. 114:5–6).

Verses 8–9 praise God for having kept the people alive and for protecting their way, suggesting that this psalm may have been employed in some annual thanksgiving ritual.

God as the tester and protector appears in verses 10–12. The NJPSV translates these verses as follows:

> You have tried us, O God,
>   refining us, as one refines silver.
> You have caught us in a net,
>   caught us in trammels.
> You have let men ride over us;
>   we have endured fire and water,
>   and You have brought us through to prosperity.

Neither the nature of the trouble, in spite of the various images (being refined, being caught like a bird or wild animal, being overrun by horsemen, and being forced to endure extremes), nor the goal of such calamities is discussed. The troubles are there as divinely sent phenomena but as phenomena through which divine guidance has carried the community, carried it to prosperity (the harvests of another year?).

In verses 13–15 a worshiper (the king?) speaks of fulfilling the vows made earlier in a time of trouble. Note the extravagance as a token of thanksgiving.

Finally, the psalmist invites people to hear the testimony, the witness, offered about what God has done (vv. 16–20).

Galatians 6:(1–6) 7–16

In these concluding words to the Galatians, Paul makes two moves, one characteristic, the other uncharacteristic. First, in typical fashion he provides concluding instructions consisting of a mixture of scriptural teaching, proverbial wisdom, and concrete moral exhortation (vv. 1–10; cf. 1 Thess. 5:12–22). Second, in untypical fashion, he returns to themes treated earlier in the letter and once again becomes polemical, even caustic, as he summarizes his own position once for all (vv. 11–16; also, v. 17).

Bearing each other's burdens (vv. 1–6). In this first set of exhortations, Paul focuses on our responsibilities toward each other within the context of Christian fellowship. On the one hand, we should make sure of our own fidelity to the gospel and to ourselves. Among other things, this means controlling our own impulses (v. 1b), having realistic self-perceptions (v. 3), critically evaluating ourselves (v. 4), and shouldering our individual responsibilities (v. 5). Yet, Christian duty is not merely duty to ourselves, but duty to others. This entails gently helping those who have erred find their way again (v. 1). But we can do this arrogantly or sympathetically. The call for us to "bear one another's burdens" (v. 2) recognizes that each of us has burdens that can only be borne with the help of others. Because we all have burdens to bear, we can help others bear their burdens.

Exhortation to generosity (vv. 7–10). It should be noted that the verse immediately preceding this section is a call to generosity; students should be generous in sharing their possessions with their teachers (v. 6; cf. 1 Cor. 9:14; Rom. 15:27). Similarly, the final verse of this section urges us to be generous to believers and unbelievers alike (cf. 1 Thess. 5:15). There is ample evidence to suggest that early Christians felt responsible for taking care of the physical needs of one another (cf. Acts 2:44–45; 4:32–35; 1 Tim. 5:8; James 1:27), but here they are urged to look beyond their own circle and extend their generosity to everyone (cf. Rom. 12:20; Gal. 5:14).

We should note that this is the context where Paul reminds us that we reap what we sow. Taking the immediate context seriously may mean that verses 7–8 have an application that is quite specific and are not to be interpreted as if they state a general principle of the religious life. In any case, Paul cautions us not to be naive and blind to fundamental religious truths (1 Cor. 6:9; 15:33; James 1:16; Luke 21:8). One of the most basic of these truths is that God cannot be duped (cf. Job 13:9). One of the principles by which God orders life is that we reap what we sow (cf. Job 4:8; 15:35; Prov. 11:18; 22:8; Hos. 8:7).

We are presented here with a choice of sowing in one of two fields. This metaphor is captured especially well in JB: "If [we sow] in the field of self-indulgence [we] will get a harvest of corruption out of it; if [we sow] in the field of the Spirit [we] will get from it a harvest of eternal life" (v. 8; similarly REB). The options here are as clear and unequivocal as those set before the Israelites—life or death (Deut. 30:15–20). To sow in the field of the flesh is to pursue the path of self-indulgence, answering only to the call of the *self*, and we are assured that the life so lived finally turns in on itself and leads to death (cf. Rom. 8:6, 13; Eph. 4:22–24; 2 Pet. 2:12). By contrast, to sow seed in the field of the Spirit is to pursue the path of self-abandonment, refusing to yield to the call of the *self* but answering instead to the call of the Spirit. It is the Spirit who summons us to reach outward beyond ourselves, indeed to transcend ourselves. To do so is really to live, now and finally (Rom. 8:6, 13).

So we are urged not to "grow weary in doing what is right" (v. 9; cf. 2 Thess. 3:13; also 2 Cor. 4:1, 16). This charge is reminiscent of Jesus' parable of the great judgment (Matt. 25:31–46). Its effect is startling because it holds us accountable for failing to perform ordinary acts of kindness. Similarly, Paul's charge recognizes all too well that those concrete acts of generosity that are most obviously Christian are precisely the ones we tend to ignore. They are so obvious we cease to do them.

Postscript (vv. 11–16). Even as he signs off, Paul returns to earlier themes with a few summary remarks having the same polemical edge as his earlier discussion. To underscore the importance of these final words, he picks up the stenographer's pen and writes in bold print (v. 11; cf. 1 Cor. 16:21; Col. 4:18; 2 Thess. 3:17; Philemon 19).

First, he attacks his opponents for grandstanding (vv. 12–13). Their primary motive is "to make a good impression outwardly" (v. 12, NIV). The implication is that they insist on circumcision because it is the most popular and least hazardous course of action (cf. Gal. 5:11; Phil. 3:18). What is more, their behavior is inconsistent; they enforce minute ritual observances, such as circumcision, but they themselves violate the law. They do this either by violating the spirit of the law or simply by not keeping all the commandments of the law (Rom. 2:21–22). If the latter sense is in view, Paul is assailing them for insisting on perfect obedience to the law when they themselves are unable to deliver in this regard. The final barb Paul tosses at his opponents is that they like to boast in their results. For them, converts are trophies to be waved, not souls to be cared for (v. 13b).

Second, he defends his gospel and his own behavior (vv. 14–16). In these few verses, we have a remarkably compact summary of Pauline theology. The following motifs are worth noticing:

1. The cross is central (v. 14a). The only trophy Paul waved was the crucified Christ (1 Cor. 1:18–25; 2:2; Phil. 3:3). This formed the center of his preaching and the center of his life.

2. His life is cruciform (v. 14b). Paul had not only reenacted the crucifixion; he had become Christ's coparticipant in the crucifixion (Gal. 2:20). In doing so, the world and its human outlook had died in him, even as it had been unable to lay any claim on Christ (cf. Rom. 6:5–11).

3. Outward religious performance is nothing; inward religious transformation is everything (v. 15). Religious rituals, such as circumcision, have no value in and of themselves (1 Cor. 7:19; Gal. 5:6; Rom. 2:25–26). They are nothing. The performance of a religious act, qua religious act, is a meaningless performance, hollow and devoid of significance. What counts is whether it is in any sense transforming, attesting an inner change that results in a new creation (cf. 2 Cor. 5:17; Rom. 6:4; 12:2; also Rev. 21:5).

4. "New creation," or inner transformation, provides the real clue to our identity before God. Those who see and truly understand this constitute the real "Israel of God" (v. 16), and theirs are the eschatological blessings of peace and mercy (cf. Rom. 2:25–29; 9:6–8; also Pss. 125:5; 128:6).

Even though the two verses concluding the epistle fall outside the bounds of today's text, they are worth noting. In v. 17, Paul issues a word of warning, if not a threat: "From now on, let no one make trouble for me." His gospel is authenticated through his own apostolic sufferings (2 Cor. 4:10; 6:4–5; 11:23–24; Phil. 3:10). The real proof of his gospel is the form of life he lives.

To his credit, Paul concludes the letter with a benediction (v. 18; cf. Phil. 4:23; 2 Tim. 4:22; Philemon 25). At least, the letter concludes with a grace note!

Luke 10:1–11, 16–20

Jesus sending out seventy, two by two, into those towns and villages where Jesus would later come (10:1) is a report peculiar to Luke. Both Matthew (9:35–10:16) and Mark (6:7–11) record the sending out of the Twelve, and some of the instructions parallel Luke 10. However, the differences are striking. Primarily, there is the number, seventy (there is almost equally strong manuscript support for seventy-two). We cannot know if Luke is recalling the seventy nations reported in Genesis 10 (seventy in the Hebrew text, seventy-two in the Greek), or the story of the seventy translators who worked for seventy days to give the Gentiles an Old Testament in their own language (Septuagint), or Moses' selection of seventy elders to be his helpers (Num. 11:16–25). Given Luke's fondness for telling his story with echoes and allusions from the Old Testament, it may be safely assumed that Moses' choice of twelve to represent the twelve tribes (Num. 1:4–16) and then his choice of seventy (Num. 11:16–25) lay in the background of Luke's mind. That Luke is also anticipating the mission to the nations and the day of Pentecost when persons gathered "from every nation under heaven" (Acts 2:5) is also clear. In fact, the Gentiles may already be in mind here in the instruction "eat what is set before you" (v. 8). Food was a critical issue in the spread of the gospel (Acts 11:1–18; Gal. 2:11–21).

Omitted from today's Gospel lesson are verses 12–15, the pronouncement of woes upon certain cities. Even though such words of judgment may have been appropriate afterward when Jesus and his message had been rejected, they hardly fit into a commissioning service. Matthew places these pronouncements in other contexts. We have, then, two portions for our lection: the sending (vv. 1–11) and the return (vv. 16–20).

Verse 16 offers not only a summary pronouncement to conclude the commissioning but contains one of many records of Jesus linking the treatment of his followers to himself and to God. See, for example, Matthew 10:40–42 and 25:30–46. Receiving or rejecting the missionaries amounted to receiving or rejecting Christ and, ultimately, God. This was not only an authorizing word but an encouraging word to those who were dependent on the hospitality of their hearers.

The seventy were sent out in teams of two into those places where Jesus would go later. This practice of sending them as emissaries ahead of him began when Jesus set his face toward Jerusalem (9:51–52), continues here, and will appear again at Jesus' entry into the city of Jerusalem (19:28–34). The reader senses not only preparation for Jesus, but also something magisterial or regal about persons running ahead to announce Christ's coming. The instructions to travel light and to take no time for social amenities (v. 4, perhaps an echo of 2 Kings 4:29) could reflect the conviction that the end is near and all their work is under the shadow of the Eschaton. Although that element is not lacking, more likely Luke is continuing consistently the tone of intense singlemindedness begun at 9:51 ("He set his face to go to Jerusalem") and resumed in stating the strict demands of those who would become disciples (9:57–62). The missionaries were to depend on the hospitality of their hosts and were not to go searching about for the best room and board (v. 7). Very likely these instructions reflect the practice of some early Christian groups.

Jesus had been rejected in a Samaritan village, but rather than call down fire upon those villagers, Jesus moved on to other places (9:52–56). So were the missionaries to make brief their rituals of departure, making no pronouncements of doom, but rather letting what had been missed by such persons serve as the judgment (vv. 10–11). There will be judgment, but that is a word Jesus speaks (v. 12), not the missionaries. It is also significant that to both receivers and rejecters the message is the same: "The kingdom of God has come near" (vv. 9–11). The preachers did not wait to see how they would be treated before preparing their sermons, nor did they have different messages for different groups. Relevance and appropriateness are, of course, vital to preaching, but some aspects of the message are noncontingent.

In some ways, the report of the return of the seventy does not seem to fit the sending. The entire unit centers upon exorcisms (vv. 17–20) that were not included in the instructions before the teams went out. Perhaps another problem is being addressed here. Upon hearing the report of the seventy that they were successful exorcists (and according to Luke, Jesus' disciples did exorcise demons, Acts 8:7), Jesus makes three statements. The first (v. 18) confirms that in his and their ministries, the end of Satan's power and the reign of God is present. That Satan dwelt first in heaven is stated elsewhere (Job 1:6; 2:1; John 12:31; Rev. 12:7), and Luke's description of his downfall is probably based on Isaiah 14:12–15. The second statement (v. 19) comes from Psalm 91:13, a reference to the promise to the righteous that they will reign over all the evil and antagonistic powers that seek to destroy. And the third statement (v. 20) warns against overemphasizing their spiritual gifts. Our chief joy should be, not that we have certain gifts and powers, but that God has received and accepted us. Our names are "written in heaven" (Dan. 12:1; Phil. 4:3; Rev. 3:5; 13:8; 20:15). Luke's warning, though softer, is not unlike Matthew's: "Lord, Lord, did we not prophesy in your name, and cast out demons in your name, and. . . ?" . . . "Go away from me . . ." (7:22–23).

Proper 10 [15]
(Sunday between July 10 and 16 inclusive)

Amos 7:7–17;
Psalm 82; or
Deuteronomy 30:9–14;
Psalm 25:1–10;
Colossians 1:1–14;
Luke 10:25–37

In the *Common Lectionary*, today's reading from Amos is the first of six readings from the pre-exilic prophets. Amos's vision of the plumb line and his confrontation with Amaziah the priest concerning the fate of Jeroboam provide the occasion for him to reflect on his prophetic vocation. Psalm 82 portrays Yahweh insisting on justice for the weak, lowly, and destitute.

In other lectionary traditions, the Old Testament reading promises God's blessing on those who are faithful to the covenant. Similar confidence is expressed in Psalm 25, which heralds Yahweh as steadfast and faithful toward those who keep covenant.

Today's epistolary lection, the first of four readings from Colossians, is comprised of the letter's opening greeting and prayer of thanksgiving. This deeply moving prayer sets the stage for the elevated tone of the letter that defends the exalted status of Christ.

Luke's parable of the good Samaritan serves as the Gospel reading for today.

Amos 7:7–17

This reading contains two distinct units of material from the Book of Amos. The first, 7:7–9, is the third in a series of five vision reports (7:1–3, 4–6, 7–9; 8:1–3; 9:1–4). The second, 7:10–17, presents the report of the confrontation between Amos and Amaziah, the priest of Bethel. It seems most likely that, in an earlier stage in the transmission of the Amos traditions, the series of visions would have circulated as a unit. The story of prophetic conflict in 7:10–17 interrupts the series and probably was inserted at this point in the book on the basis of the common catchwords (Jeroboam) in 7:9 and 7:10.

In the first pair of visions, Amos sees threatening things—locusts (7:1) and fire (7:4). He intercedes on behalf of the people, and Yahweh relents (better, repents). In the second pair the vision is not in itself threatening but is the occasion for an announcement of judgment.

Amos does not intercede, and the judgment stands. In the third vision report (7:7–9), Amos sees Yahweh standing by a wall with a plumb line in his hand, and a dialogue transpires. Although there is great uncertainty about the translation of the rare Hebrew word generally understood as "plumb line," the point of the vision is unmistakable. It is the occasion for an uncompromising announcement of judgment on the Northern Kindgom ("my people Israel"). The blast of Yahweh's anger focuses on cultic and political institutions: "the high places of Isaac," "the sanctuaries of Israel," and "the house of Jeroboam." This announcement of the total destruction of the Northern Kingdom is the persistent and leading theme of the Book of Amos.

The account of the confrontation between Amos and Amaziah has two distinct parts. The first (7:10–11) provides the setting and the background for the second (7:12–17), which reports the direct encounter between the priest and the prophet. The first scene takes place offstage, reporting that Amaziah sent a message to the king accusing Amos, an outside agitator, of conspiracy against the royal house. The evidence for the charge is a quotation of Amos's announcement of death to the king and the exile of Israel. Behind the accusation stands the assumption—common to the prophets as well as their audiences—that the word of God through the prophet has the power to set into motion what it announces.

Then the curtain rises on the encounter between the priest and Amos. Reported from the perspective of a third party who identifies with Amos, it proceeds as a dialogue. Amaziah does not directly challenge the right of Amos to speak, although he does imply that Amos has economic reasons for acting as a prophet ("earn your bread," v. 12). The dispute concerns jurisdiction. Amaziah commands Amos to return to his homeland, Judah, and speak there, appealing to royal authority. The king—and he as the king's spokesman—has the authority to determine who speaks in Israel.

Amos first responds directly to Amaziah's speech and its assumptions about his office (vv. 14–15) and then announces judgment on Amaziah for his attempt to stifle the word of God (vv. 16–17). The initial words of this response are among the most debated in scholarship on the Book of Amos. Does the prophet say, "I am no prophet, nor a prophet's son" or, "I was no prophet, nor a prophet's son"? The Hebrew has two noun clauses with no verb. To render them into English—and to determine their sense—requires some form of the verb "to be," but the tense is uncertain. If it is present tense, then he is denying that he is a prophet or a member of a prophetic guild, or possibly the understanding of prophet assumed by his opponent. If it is past tense, then the following lines do not contradict these words: "The LORD said to me, 'Go, prophesy to my people Israel'" (v. 14). The matter cannot be resolved on grammatical grounds but only in the immediate and larger context.

The key to the account is not in verse 14 but in verse 15. Amos makes it clear that he has the authority to act as a prophet, and in the land of Israel, because Yahweh called him and sent him. He does not give a full-blown report of his call but alludes to the central point that he was commissioned by Yahweh. Thus, whether he is not or was not a prophet, he is compelled ("the Lord took me") to act and speak as a prophet, and those who stand in his way stand in the way of the word of God.

It is misleading to interpret this text as an account of the conflict between institution and charisma, between organized cultic religion and the inspired individual. It is rather the struggle between institution and institution, both of them religious. The priest has the authority of established worship tied to the political institutions. The prophet has the authority of his vocation and the words given to him by Yahweh. But this vocation and these words also have institutional foundations, for all Israel's prophets claim the same authority. Amos, like Amaziah, stands in a long tradition concerning his office and role.

Psalm 82

This psalm, even in its present biblical form, reflects an origin in a polytheistic background when other gods or at least heavenly beings shared the rule with Israel's Yahweh. The psalm does not fit into any clearly definable genre, being neither a hymn, a lament, nor a thanksgiving. The opening verse provides a context for the divine speech/oracle in verses 2–7. The final verse is a plea asking the Deity to judge the world.

The opening verse probably originally read something like: "Yahweh stands in the council of El; in the midst of the gods he pronounces judgment." Several factors are presupposed: (1) The world is governed by a consortium of divine beings, a sort of heavenly council (see 1 Kings 22:19–22; Job 1:6–12). (2) The old Canaanite deity El is noted, and the council is said to be his or headed by him. El (note the name IsraEL) was a Palestinian god worshiped by some early Israelites (see Gen. 33:18–20) who came to be identified with and/or assimilated to Yahweh. (3) Yahweh is here assigned pride of place in the heavenly council as the one who takes charge and holds the other deities accountable. (Although the present Hebrew text reads Elohim [= God] as the opening word, Yahweh was probably the earlier reading, for throughout Psalms 42–83 "Yahweh" seems to have been replaced frequently with "Elohim." Later rabbinical exegetes understood Elohim as referring to human judges, but this does not square with verse 7.)

The reference to the "council of El" occurs only here in the Hebrew Bible. The idea that is expressed—namely, that a council of deities presided over by the supreme god El governs worldly affairs—occurs frequently in the so-called Ugaritic texts that date from the Late Bronze Age (about 1400–1200 BC). The idea that Yahweh stands indicates that a pronouncement is to be made (judges in antiquity sat to hear cases and stood to pronounce judgments and verdicts).

In the divine speech in verses 2–7, Yahweh condemns the other divine beings for their failure to judge properly and for their display of partiality to the wicked. In some sense, the psalm deals with the question of why life is like it is and why justice does not seem to prevail. The divine beings show partiality. In Hebrew law, a court and the judge were not to show favoritism or partiality to either rich or poor, to the powerful or the weak (Exod. 23:3; Lev. 19:15). Justice was ideally to be blind.

Verses 3–4 stipulate the requirements placed upon the divine beings (and by extension one can say placed upon humans as well). The divine beings/rulers of the world/human beings must see that certain powerless classes are not taken advantage of. The weak/the fatherless/the afflicted/the destitute/the needy must be defended against the encroachment of the wicked/those who would take advantage of them.

The interpretation of verse 5 is uncertain. Is it a continuation of verse 4 and thus a description of either the weak and needy or the wicked? Or is it a description of the heavenly beings who are being condemned? The NRSV clearly takes it in the latter sense, closing the divine quotation with verse 4. It seems better to see verse 5 as a description of one of the groups, or both groups, mentioned in verses 3–4. Both the powerless and the powerful could be said to walk about in darkness without knowledge or understanding; that is, they have not the insight and ability to rectify matters themselves. The concluding line, "all the foundations of the earth are shaken," probably means that the moral order of the world is completely askew; there is a lack of justice and the presence of anarchy in too many places.

Verses 6–7 have Yahweh condemn the divine beings, here called "Elohims the sons of Elyon," to die like men, to fall like a displaced prince. That is, they will be removed from power and authority.

Finally, the psalm writer has a plea that Yahweh would judge the earth and rule all nations, because they belong to him (v. 8).

In preaching on this psalm, the minister must realize some of the larger issues with which the psalm is concerned: (1) the problem of why life does not measure up to and manifest a just order is still clearly an issue today; (2) the division of humanity into the wealthy/powerful/wicked and the needy/poor/powerless, into classes, is not the way the world should be; at least, one class should not be where it is by taking advantage of the other; (3) a responsibility of the divine world is the establishment of justice and equality (so frequently we have noticed in the psalms how God is held accountable for his responsibility for order and justice in the world and is charged with failure to do this task); and (4) finally, the psalm breathes an air of hope and expectation in its plea for God to take charge and judge the world himself, to take responsibility for its operation.

Deuteronomy 30:9–14

In some respects this is a curious selection. It begins not only in the middle of a paragraph (Deut. 30:6–9), but also in the middle of a sentence. It may be seen to set some foundation for the Gospel reading, because the parable of the Good Samaritan (Luke 10:25–37) arises in a discussion of the law—the central theme of this section of Deuteronomy—and is prefaced with Jesus echoing some of the words of our lesson: "do this, and you will live" (Luke 10:28). Moreover, the language of Deuteronomy—if not the actual sense of the expressions—is reflected in the lesson from Colossians: "bear fruit in every good work" (Col. 1:10).

This passage is itself part of a powerful sermon, tending toward summarizing the message of the Book of Deuteronomy. It contains parts of the last paragraphs of a lengthy speech attributed to Moses on the plains of Moab (Deut. 29:1–30:20), introduced as "the words of the covenant that the LORD commanded Moses to make with the Israelites" (29:1). Immediately following this speech the narrative resumes, leading finally to the report of the death of Moses.

Opinions vary considerably concerning the antiquity of this section of the Book of Deuteronomy. As it now stands, it has been incorporated into the edition of the book prepared by the Deuteronomistic Historian (or Historians) who wrote the account of Israel's past from the time of Moses to the Babylonian Exile (Deuteronomy through 2 Kings). When that work was written about 560 BC, Israel no longer lived in the land, so words such as these provided interpretation of the disaster of the Exile and guidance for a future return. But the lines are characteristic in every respect of the heart of the Book of Deuteronomy, from the seventh century BC, before the Exile, but centuries after the time of Moses. In that context, the words were addressed to a people who had experienced the fulfillment of the promise of the land. Moreover, there are elements of the most ancient covenant tradition itself, going back to Israel's earliest days. Centuries of use and reinterpretation underscore the grave importance of the matters addressed in this text.

The context of the passage is the conclusion of the covenant between Yahweh and Israel. Clearly, it is a conditional covenant, the prosperity of the people being contingent upon their obedience to the stipulations of the agreement. Those stipulations are set out in the "book of the law" (v. 10). This covenantal context means that the speech is addressed to the people of Israel, that the focus of attention is corporate, not only for the sake of the present group, but also for the community that extends through time (v. 9).

The paragraph that immediately follows this reading (vv. 15–20) will stress that obedience to the law is a matter of life and death. In our lesson the emphasis is upon the blessings of obedience as well as the possibility of remaining faithful. The language is repetitious and hortatory, urging obedience upon the audience, placing the law upon the hearts of the hearers. In the framework of Deuteronomy, the law is not perceived as a burden, but a gift, for it leads to life, the good life that the Lord wants for his people. "Life" means the long and abundant life in the good land.

The first part of the reading is the second half of a paragraph concerning the heart (vv. 6–10). It is not simply external behavior that the Lord desires, but an obedience that emerges from a right heart. But the Lord does not ask that the listeners change their hearts. God will accomplish that for them: "the LORD your God will circumcise your heart and the heart of your descendants" (v. 6). Thus the people will be able to "turn to the LORD" their God with all their heart and all their soul (v. 10). This paragraph emphasizes the blessings of obedience, particularly in terms of fertility. If Israel remains obedient, the Lord will make them prosperous in the fruit of their body, in the fruit of their livestock, and in the fruit of the soil (v. 9). And it is clear that this is what the Lord wants, that the people act in a way that leads to life, so that he may "take delight in prospering you" (v. 9).

The second paragraph (vv. 11–14) seems to be a response to an unexpressed but assumed question or objection: But is it possible to understand and to obey the law? Is it not too high or difficult? In homiletical tones and phrases, the writer has Moses arguing that the "commandment" is neither too hard nor too distant—that is, impossible to understand or to attain. The word—the knowledge of what God expects—"is very near to you; it is in your mouth and in your heart for you to observe" (v. 14). "Observe" here fundamentally means to adhere to, to obey. But in the context, it suggests another meaning as well: The commandment is so near that you can see it and hear it.

"Commandments" and "decrees" (v. 10) are used together in Deuteronomy to signify the law as a whole, the stipulations of the covenant (Deut. 4:1; 5:31; 6:1; etc.). We should not be misled by the repeated reference to such requirements in the plural, for although there are many laws, they all rest upon and amount to one prohibition and one commandment. Thus verses 11–14 refer to "this commandment." Viewed as the negative, the one prohibition is not "to bow down to other gods and serve them" (30:17), but to obey the First Commandment (Deut. 5:7). Throughout the centuries during which the Book of Deuteronomy was developed, that was not an abstract or vague possibility, but a concrete and practical temptation. In the land there were the deities of the Canaanites; in Babylon there were the gods of the dominant culture, including the heavenly powers (cf. Deut. 4:19). We may appropriately see this issue as the conflict between faith and culture. To what extent can one acknowledge the authority of the forces that culture considers as "gods," or make use of the culture's symbols of faith? Deuteronomy is clear: Do not bow down to them at all.

The single commandment on which all the individual laws rests is the positive side of the prohibition: Love the Lord your God, and cleave to him (30:20). This love is parallel to that of a child for a parent, entailing respect and obedience (Deut. 6:5; 8:5). It amounts to devotion to a single God (Josh. 22:5; 23:6–8). How can one command an attitude, a feeling? It can only be in response to God's love (Deut. 7:7, 13; cf. Hos. 11:1ff.), expressed in the history of election and salvation.

If there is but one requirement, with a negative and a positive side, then why are there so many statutes and ordinances and laws? Ancient Israel knew, as we do, that in practice the meaning and application of that loyalty to God are complex. Precisely what does it mean to avoid the worship of other gods and to love God in various circumstances? The multitude of laws and their frequent reinterpretation through time testify to the understanding that those who intend to obey the command to love only one God must work at learning and applying the meaning of that love. The rabbinical tradition developed a practical criterion for applying the law that stems from the theology of this passage. The law leads to life. If one interprets the law and finds that it leads to death, then the interpretation is wrong.

Psalm 25:1–10

This psalm was discussed as one of the lections for the First Sunday of Advent.

Colossians 1:1–14

With this text begins the semicontinuous reading of the Epistle to the Colossians. It is the first of four passages to be read over the next four weeks.

This particular pericope overlaps with the epistolary text for Proper 29 [34] (Christ the King or Reign of Christ) in Year C (Col. 1:11–20), treated later in this volume.

Because the Epistle to the Colossians will provide the epistolary readings for the next four weeks, a few introductory remarks are in order here. Even though the Pauline authorship of this letter is disputed, it stands closer in tone and content to the genuine Pauline letters than do the other disputed Pauline letters, such as Ephesians. It addresses a church that Paul had neither established nor visited, but one started and nurtured by Epaphras, a devoted co-worker of Paul (1:7; 4:12).

The letter is written in response to the threat of false teaching that seems to have consisted of syncretistic, speculative, perhaps even Gnostic elements (2:16, 18, 20–23). Even though we do not know the exact details of the heresy, such as where, how, and with whom it originated, its potential threat was clear. It threatened the unique supremacy of Christ and tended to make of him one among several heavenly figures in the angelic hierarchy. In response to this threat to the supremacy of Christ, the letter presents us with a bold statement of the preeminent superiority and uniqueness of Christ (cf. esp. 1:15–20).

Today's epistolary lection represents the opening section of the Epistle to the Colossians and consists of two parts: the greeting (vv. 1–2) and the prayer of thanksgiving (vv. 3–14).

Greeting (vv. 1–2). The greeting is quite typical of other opening salutations in the Pauline letters (cf. Rom. 1:1; 1 Cor. 1:1; 2 Cor. 1:1; also Eph. 1:1; 2 Tim. 1:1). One of the remarkable features is that here, as elsewhere when Paul is facing a situation threatened by competitive teaching, he underscores his status as apostle. Similarly, the twofold prayer of grace and peace (v. 2) is quite typical (cf. Rom. 1:7; 1 Cor. 1:2; 2 Cor. 1:2; Gal. 1:3; Eph. 1:2; Phil. 1:2; Philemon 3; 1 Thess. 1:1; 2 Thess. 1:2).

Prayer of Thanksgiving (vv. 3–14). Typically, the opening prayers of the Pauline letters do two things: (1) set the tone of the letter and (2) telegraph to the reader some of the major concerns to be dealt with in the letter (cf. Rom. 1:8–17; 1 Cor. 1:4–9; 2 Cor. 1:3–7; Phil. 1:3–11; 1 Thess. 1:2–10; 2:13–16; 3:9; 2 Thess. 1:3–12; Philemon 4–7). Here, the tone is hopeful and reassuring, as Paul seeks to shore up the faith of a relatively young church. The reference to knowledge, spiritual wisdom and understanding (v. 9) already anticipates later themes (cf. 2:2–3). Also, the opening prayer concludes by pointing to the work of Christ in our redemption (vv. 13–14), and this too begins to prepare us for the rich christological sections of the letter (cf. 1:15–20, 27–28; 2:2–3).

In this opening prayer, Paul first recalls the Colossians' life in Christ and does so in terms of a triad of Christian experiences: their faith in Christ, that is, their conversion; their love for all their saints, probably their genuine sense of community and willingness to share their possessions; and their eschatological hope, which gave them direction (vv. 4–5). These three foci of Christian experience, in varying orders, are often employed by Paul in teaching his churches (cf. 1 Thess. 1:3; 5:8; 1 Cor. 13:7, 13; Gal. 5:5–6; Rom. 5:1–5; 12:6–12; also Eph. 1:15–19; 4:2–5; 1 Tim. 6:11; Titus 2:2; cf. also Heb. 6:10–12; 10:22–24; 1 Pet. 1:3–9). In other cases, they occur in pairs: faith and love (1 Thess. 3:6; 2 Thess. 1:3; Philemon 5); faith and hope (2 Thess. 1:4); hope and love (2 Thess. 3:5; cf. 2 Cor. 13:13). What is important to notice here is that the manifestation of this Christian triangle among the Colossians is an occasion of ceaseless thanksgiving (vv. 3, 9; cf. Eph. 1:15–16; Philemon 4–5).

Second, he recalls how they only recently came to the faith: "News of this hope reached you not long ago" (v. 5, NJB). But it is important for them to know that the "word of the truth" (cf. Eph. 1:13; 2 Cor. 6:7; James 1:18; 2 Tim. 2:15) sounded in them had also echoed through them, and beyond "in the whole world" (v. 6; cf. 1:23; also 1 Tim. 3:16). The vital link in their faith was provided by Epaphras, from whom they had learned the faith (v. 7), who served as their emissary to Paul (v. 7) and whose love for them continued unabated. He had also endeared himself to other churches in the region (4:12–13; cf. Philemon 23).

Third, he prays for the Colossians to grow in their capacity for spiritual wisdom and discernment, especially as it pertains to the will of God (vv. 9–10; cf. Rom. 2:18; Eph. 5:17; Acts 22:14; James 4:15; 2 Pet. 1:21; also Luke 12:47). Coming to proper knowledge of God and growing in that knowledge are part and parcel of the Christian experience (cf. Phil. 1:9; Philemon 6; 1 Tim. 2:4; 4:3; 2 Tim. 2:25; 3:7; Titus 1:1; Heb. 10:26; 2 John 1). And yet it is not that we seek knowledge for the sake of knowledge, but rather discernment in knowing how "to lead lives worthy of the Lord" (v. 10; cf. 1 Thess. 2:12; Phil. 1:27; Eph. 4:1). This means, among other things, "bearing fruit in every good work" (v. 10; cf. Rom. 7:4; 2 Cor. 9:8; Eph. 2:10; 2 Thess. 2:17; 2 Tim. 3:17; Titus 2:14; also Mark 4:8, 20).

Fourth, he prays for them to receive spiritual strength to be supplied by God (v. 11; Eph. 1:11–19; 3:16; cf. Acts 20:32; 26:18). It is God, after all, who has granted us a share in the eternal inheritance with the saints and has transferred us from the realm of darkness into the realm of light (v. 13; cf. 1 Thess. 5:4–5; also Luke 22:53). The one in whom our redemption and forgiveness is possible is Christ (v. 14; cf. Rom. 3:24; 8:23; 1 Cor. 1:30; Eph. 1:6, 7, 14; 4:30; also Ps. 130:7).

Luke 10:25–37

Again we have a lesson from Luke that has partial parallels in Mark and Matthew but is sufficiently different in form and location (both geographical and literary) to raise the question whether Luke had another source or perhaps had done major editing. Luke's account of the lawyer and his question about eternal life has parallels in Mark 12:28–31 and Matthew 22:34–40. Mark and Luke set their stories in Jerusalem, in the closing days of Jesus' ministry and in a series of controversies between Jesus and various opponents. It is interesting to note that at that point in his Gospel, Luke follows Mark but omits this one episode, for he had placed his version of it here in the travel narrative. In Mark, the questioner is a scribe; in Matthew, a lawyer. In both, the question has to do with the greatest commandment, and in both, Jesus supplies the answer, complete love of God and love of neighbor (Deut. 6:5; Lev. 19:18). Luke's lawyer asks, "What must I do to inherit eternal life?" and Jesus has him supply the answer to his own question.

The preacher will want to notice the symmetry in Luke's combination of the conversation between Jesus and the lawyer (vv. 25–29) and the extension of that conversation to include the parable of the good Samaritan (vv. 29–37). In the first unit, the lawyer asks a question, Jesus responds with a question, the lawyer responds with an answer, and Jesus does likewise. In the second unit, the lawyer asks a question, Jesus responds with a question following the parable, the lawyer answers, and so does Jesus. The questions are important and so are the answers, but Luke's Jesus makes it doubly clear that the kingdom of God is not a discussion, even between two leaders. Twice Jesus says *do* what you know (vv. 28, 37). It was not more information that the lawyer needed; rather, it was action on his own understanding.

It is evident that the conversation between the two is treated by Luke as the occasion to introduce the parable. The parable itself (vv. 30–35) focuses not on both love of God and love of neighbor but on love of neighbor. This is not an isolated instance. Twice Paul said the whole of the law was summed up in the command to love one's neighbor as oneself (Rom. 13:8–9; Gal. 5:14). It is important to notice that the parable and Jesus' question following do not directly answer the lawyer's question. To ask, "Who is my neighbor?" is to ask for a definition of the object and extent of love. Jesus' question as to who proved himself to be a neighbor shifts the attention to the kind of person one is to be rather than to those who are or who are not one's neighbors. This shift need not be understood to mean the parable originally addressed another question and has been set in at this point rather awkwardly by Luke. The question of Jesus lies outside the parable itself (v. 36; the parable ends at v. 35) and is Jesus' corrective to an improper question.

Most likely the parable is one Luke received, and, therefore, one might ask, What was its original purpose? or To whom was it addressed? The story assumes that its hearers know about priests, Levites, and Samaritans. It also assumes that the hearers know the bitter tension between Jews and Samaritans (John 4:9). The Samaritans were descendants of a mixed population occupying the land following conquest by Assyria in 722 BC. In the days of Ezra and Nehemiah, the Samaritans opposed rebuilding Jerusalem and the temple (Ezra 4:2–5; Neh. 2:19).

The Samaritans built their own place of worship on Mt. Gerizim. Against such a background of enmity, to have characterized the Samaritan rather than the priest or Levite as the one who proved to be a neighbor must have been to its first audience a shocking turn in the story, shattering their categories of who are and who are not the people of God. For Luke and Luke's church, it now serves as an example story to the effect that kingdom people are to act in love, love that has no drawn boundaries, and love that expects no recompense.

Proper 11 [16]
(Sunday between July 17 and 23 inclusive)

Amos 8:1–12;
Psalm 52; or
Genesis 18:1–10*a*;
Psalm 15;
Colossians 1:15–28;
Luke 10:38–42

Amos's vision of the basket of summer fruit, the prophet's accusations against Israel's oppression of the poor and needy, and the threat of a coming day of divine judgment constitute the Old Testament reading for the *Common Lectionary*. Threatening notes are also sounded in the responsorial psalm, as lying, plotting to do evil, and a devouring spirit are assailed.

God's promise to provide Abraham and Sarah a child in their old age is the topic of today's Old Testament reading in the other lectionaries. As a responsorial psalm, Psalm 15 profiles the form of upright life required to enter the sanctuary and offer appropriate worship.

The magnificent christological hymn, with its bold claims about Christ's role in creation and unique relationship with God, dominates the epistolary reading. Even so, the latter part of the passage spells out some of the implications of Christ's reconciling work.

In the Gospel reading, Jesus commends Mary for her concentration and devotion and chides Martha for being distracted by the insignificant tasks of life.

Amos 8:1–12

This lection continues directly where the previous Old Testament lesson in the semicontinuos readings for the season had ended. It begins (vv. 1–3) with the fourth of the five vision reports of the prophet that organize Amos 7–9 (for a discussion of the structure of this part of the Book of Amos, see last week's commentary on Amos 7:7–17) and continues with a series of prophetic speeches first accusing Israelites of wrongdoing (vv. 4–6) and then announcing judgment (vv. 7–12). The diversity of the literature and the changes in the subject matter confirm that Amos did not write the book that bears his name. Rather, Amos was a speaker whose words were passed down in the oral tradition and only later were committed to writing.

There is widespread agreement concerning the date and some of the circumstances of the prophet. The superscription (1:1) places Amos in the reigns of two kings, Uzziah of Judah (783–742 BC) and Jeroboam II of Israel (786–746 BC). References elsewhere in the book, especially Amos 7:9–10, are consistent with this date and also confirm that the prophet was a native of the south who came to the Northern Kingdom of Israel to proclaim the word of God.

Historical allusions in the book and the circumstances assumed by the prophet place him in the last decade or so of Jeroboam II, about 760 BC. The reigns of Jeroboam II and Uzziah were long and relatively peaceful. There had been no major threats from the major Near Eastern powers such as Egypt or Assyria, and that peace seems to have led to prosperity, at least for a few, and—according to Amos—at the expense of many. There seems to have been a breakdown in the old tribal and family systems of land ownership, and the emergence of a wealthy class at the top of the society. These themes are particularly important in the reading for today.

The message of the prophet is clear and strong: Because of their social injustice and religious arrogance, the Lord will punish the people of Israel with a total military disaster. That is the burden both of the vision reports and of virtually all the speeches attributed to the prophet.

The fourth vision report (vv. 1–3) parallels the third one (7:7–9) in form and effect. Whereas the first two reports (7:1–3, 4–6) had begun with visions of threatening events and ended with Yahweh withdrawing the disaster, the second two announce Yahweh's judgment upon Israel. What the prophet is shown is not a threatening thing, but provides the occasion for the announcement of judgment. The Hebrew for "basket of summer fruit" (*qayits*) is a pun on the word for "end" (*qets*). The end is described as a time of death and mourning. The fifth vision report (9:1–4) will continue the progression, announcing total and uncompromising disaster.

The remainder of the lesson includes a series of short speeches of accusation and judgment. Verses 4–8 contain a two-part speech that begins with a summons to hear (see also 3:1; 4:1; 5:1). The first part (vv. 4–6) is an accusation against or indictment of certain Israelites for injustice against others. The charge moves from the general address to those who oppress the poor to specific instances of their oppression. Those with economic power are accused of being impatient and eager to sell grain and wheat, and are then charged with deceitful business practices (v. 5). They are further accused of enslaving the poor and needy because of their debts, as well as "selling the sweepings of the wheat" (v. 6). Like so many other prophetic speeches in the Book of Amos, this indictment is followed by the Lord's own words as he swears to punish the people and the land for these deeds (vv. 7–8).

The announcement in verses 9–10 continues the theme of divine judgment, this time in terms of the day of the Lord. The coming day will be a time of darkness (see Amos 5:18–20), mourning, famine, and thirst. The imagery of verse 9 is that of a solar eclipse, a portent of the darkness of death. The prophet does not describe the disaster but its results—mourning for all those who will have died.

In verses 11–12 the prophet presents yet another vision of coming disaster. God will punish Israel by sending a particular kind of famine. God will deprive them not of bread or water, but of the word of God. The people are then seen to wander all over the world seeking that word but not finding it. In effect, God threatens to abandon the people of Israel.

This text provides the occasion for preacher and people to reflect on justice. Amos, like so much of the Old Testament, is very specific: Oppression of the poor and the needy by those with economic power is an abomination to God. And the prophetic voice is very specific about the forms of that oppression. But the lesson does not stop there. It goes on to proclaim that God will punish the people for their crimes against one another. Thus the preacher needs to think long and hard about the ways that message might be true in the contemporary world.

Psalm 52

This psalm has been selected as a complement to the reading from Amos, which speaks of greedy and dishonest merchants eager to take advantage of every opportunity to acquire gain even to the point of fraud and cheating.

The psalm consists primarily of human-to-human address. Only verse 9 has God as the one addressed. The speaker denounces some wicked person: verses 1–4 contain the charge or accusation; verses 5–7 pronounce judgment that involves the downfall of the wicked (v. 5) and the joyful celebration of the accuser (the plaintiff) or the innocent (vv. 6–7); verse 8 is a statement of the plaintiff's confidence; and verse 9 is a vow about the future action of the faithful.

The psalm, especially in verses 1–5, takes the form of direct person-to-person confrontation. The closest parallels elsewhere in the Psalter are Psalms 4 and 11. Psalm 52 has the speaker address the wicked ("O mighty one," "worker of treachery," "O deceitful tongue") in direct confrontation. Several charges are leveled against the opponent: (1) mischief against the mercy of God (*hesed 'el*, see NRSV note *a*) or the godly (reading *hasid 'el*), (2) plotting destruction, (3) having a tongue as sharp as a razor (probably showing disrespect), (4) working treachery (probably gossip, see v. 4), (5) loving strife more than friendship (NRSV "evil more than good"), and (6) lying rather than truth telling. All of this suggests that the user of the psalm considered the defendant to be a gossipy, hateful, disrespectful person. Perhaps the speaker was the object or victim of the defendant's vicious tongue.

In the description of the delight over the wicked one's fall (in v. 7), the person is subject to a second set of charges. The person is described as (1) one who would not take refuge in God (having no faith, irreligious) and (2) one who trusted in riches and wealth. This implies that the person had a social position of power but one based on personal wealth and intrigue rather than respect in the religious community.

The verdict hoped for or declared in advance in verse 5 pictures a reversal of fate for the wicked, all to be accomplished by God. The imagery implies an erosion of the person's self-assurance and arrogance (the person will be broken psychologically), a loss of home and family, and even death ("uproot you from the land of the living"; although v. 5c could be translated "and your root [offspring] from the land of the living," which would imply death of the person's children).

According to verse 6, the consequence of the person's fall would be witnessed by the righteous ones (the term is plural) and would be greeted with fear (awe? respect?) and laughter (rejoicing). The collapse of the wrongdoer would become an object lesson to warn others about following such a life-style.

In verse 8, the psalm allows the speaker to describe oneself in highly positive terms. The worshiper is one "like a green olive tree in the house of God" (in the temple precincts) and as one secure in his or her faith in the mercy of God. Both of these qualities are in direct opposition to the wicked one who took no refuge in God (v. 7).

Finally, the worshiper offers a twofold vow: to thank God for what God has done and to wait on God's name in the assembly of the righteous/faithful ones (v. 9; see NRSV footnote for the actual reading of the Hebrew text).

How is the ancient usage of this psalm to be understood, and why was it written? We should probably think of a situation in which a person felt misused, abused, or criminally mistreated by another. Under circumstances where such a wrong could not be proven, a person could go to the sanctuary and undergo a ritual trial in which the parties could assert their innocence and call upon God to condemn their enemy (see Deut. 17:8–13; 19:15–21). Here the worshipers may have addressed one another in person-to-person speech, and have gotten their hostilities off their chest. The judgment itself was left up to God. This procedure could explain the hostility against the enemy and the statement of confidence in one's innocence reflected in the psalm, and even the anticipated joy over the other's downfall.

When the psalm was read in general services of worship in the synagogue, its content would have served as moral instruction. It could have illustrated the type of person one should not be, with the warning that the life of the person characterized by such behavior was headed for despair and calamity.

Genesis 18:1–10a

The main theme of this reading is the promise of a son to Abraham and Sarah, but that makes specific the earlier promise to Abraham reported in Genesis 12:1–4. If Abraham's descendants are to become a great nation, as Genesis 12:1–4 reported, he and Sarah must have a son. But a great deal has transpired between Genesis 12 and 18. Abraham and Sarah had set out in response to the Lord's command and begun their sojourn in the land promised to their descendants. The Priestly Writer reports in chapter 17 the covenant of God with Abraham and Sarah. According to Genesis 13:18, Abraham had arrived at Mamre, the location of the events of chapter 18, where he built an altar. The setting for the events reported in our text is Mamre, a traditional holy place just north of Hebron.

The story is similar to many other biblical accounts of remarkable, even "miraculous" births (Samson, Judges 13; Samuel, 1 Samuel 1–2). Typically such stories concern the birth of individuals destined to be great, but this one concerns the parents and the promise more than it focuses on the child. The birth of Isaac to the aged parents is a family story that contains more than a little humor, but it is also designed to emphasize God's faithfulness toward the people descended from those ancestors and that child.

This reading has two distinct parts. Genesis 18:1–8 gives the account of the arrival of three guests and of the patriarch's hospitality to them. Genesis 18:9–10a (the narrative unit continues through verse 15) reports the Lord's promise that Sarah would bear a son to Abraham in their old age, and the matriarch's incredulous reaction. The result of that promise, the birth of that promised son, is reported in Genesis 21:1–7.

The main characters in the first scene (18:1–8) are Abraham and the three "men" whom he welcomes and entertains. Verse 1 ("The LORD appeared to Abraham") is a heading that informs the reader of the true identity of the guests, and of the meaning of the encounter. In the narrative itself beginning in verse 2, Abraham knows only that three "men" have arrived. He greets them with traditional and generous hospitality (see also Gen. 23:7). He offers them water to wash their feet and shade to rest their bodies, and then instructs Sarah to make bread for them while he chooses a calf "tender and good" for his servant to prepare for the meal. The three strangers, Abraham learns later, turn out to be Yahweh and two attendants or angels. It is reported in 18:22 that the two continue their journey to Sodom (19:1) while Yahweh remains with Abraham, who wants to negotiate over the fate of Sodom. So if our story concerns God's gracious care and faithfulness, it also has divine judgment in the background.

In the second scene (18:9–15), the central characters are Yahweh and Sarah, but by stopping at verse 10a a great deal is missed. It is a subtle literary touch that Yahweh need not ask but already knows the name of Abraham's wife (v. 9). This should evoke the interest of the hearer or reader, who already knows the identity of the characters. However, there is no indication that Abraham picked up on this point. Then Yahweh reveals that the arrival of the guests at Mamre is not accidental but in order to promise the birth of a son (v. 10). In case the reader had forgotten just how old Abraham and Sarah were, the narrator reminds them in an aside: both were very old, and Sarah was long past menopause (v. 11). Sarah, eavesdropping at the entrance to the tent, is incredulous. Although her laughter and her comments (v. 12) are not out loud but to herself, Yahweh hears. First he responds to her indirectly, to Abraham (vv. 13–14), affirming with a rhetorical question that nothing is impossible for the Lord and reiterating that Sarah will indeed have a son at a specified time. The references to "the set time" and the "due season" are no new promise but are stated to emphasize that the birth is the result of divine intervention and not some normal situation or a human accident. When Sarah fearfully denies that she had laughed, Yahweh for the first time addresses her directly, correcting and reprimanding her (v. 15).

As elsewhere in the Genesis stories, Abraham is presented as the model of faithfulness, both before God and in his relationships with human beings. For all he knows, the three messengers are human travelers, whom he welcomes and treats with generosity. But above all, this is a story of divine care through the promise of descendants. With the birth of Sarah's child, divine grace is incarnate.

Psalm 15

This psalm has been selected to be read in conjunction with the lections from Genesis 18 for this Sunday and the next because it is concerned with the topic of the character and nature of the righteous person.

The text probably reflects the recitation of moral requirements at the time worshipers were preparing to enter the sanctuary for the celebration of a festival.

The psalm opens with a question, perhaps asked by pilgrims as they reached the temple gates: Who can enter the sacred precincts? It is asked here in a graphic and metaphorical form, as if access was to be permanent (v. 1). Admittance to the courts of the temple is the concern of the questions.

The remainder of the psalm is an answer to the question, probably spoken by cultic officials (the Levites? the priests?) inside the precincts. The requirements for entry are given in a series of qualifications. It should be noted that, in antiquity, temples did not operate on the principle "Everyone welcome, all come." Certain persons (cripples and the deformed, those with improper parentage) and persons at certain times (when unclean from contact with some pollutant, women during menstruation, persons with certain skin ailments) were not admitted into the sanctuary (see Deut. 23:1–8).

The characteristics of those who might enter were probably proclaimed to the worshipers as the proper qualities of life; pilgrims could not be checked on an individual basis, and some of the characteristics noted are as much attitudes as action. The requirements articulated all fall into the category of what we would today call moral qualities and interpersonal attitudes. None of the characteristics would fit into the category of purity laws and regulations, such as having recently touched a dead body or eaten unkosher food. (Note how the two are intermingled in Ezekiel 18.) (For a discussion of the ethical requirements as a decalogue, see *Preaching Through the Christian Year: Year A*, pp. 96–98.)

In Jewish rabbinic interpretation of this psalm, the ethical requirements are given as eleven in number. This reading is reflected in the NJPSV:

> LORD, who may sojourn in Your tent,
>   who may dwell on Your holy mountain?
> He who lives without blame,
>   who does what is right,
>   and in his heart acknowledges the truth;
>   whose tongue is not given to evil;
>   who has never done harm to his fellow,
>   or borne reproach for [his acts toward] his neighbor;
>   for whom a contemptible man is abhorrent,
>   but who honors those who fear the LORD;
>   who stands by his oath even to his hurt;
>   who has never lent money at interest,
>   or accepted a bribe against the innocent.
> The man who acts thus shall never be shaken.

According to rabbinic tradition, God, through Moses, gave Israel 613 laws in the Torah (the Pentateuch). Of these, 365 (one for each day) were negative commandments (or prohibitions), and 248 (equal to the number of parts in the human body according to Jewish lore) were positive commandments. In the Babylonian Talmud (*Makkot* 23b–24a), David is said to have summarized and reduced these 613 laws into the 11 of Psalm 15. That is, the basic underlying qualities of the whole law and all its commandments—prescriptive/positive and proscriptive/negative—are viewed as embodied in the moral values of this psalm.

The first three attributes (v. 2) are stated positively. These use active participles ("the one living" [actually "walking"] without blame, "doing" what is right, and "acknowledging" the truth in the heart). The usage of a participle indicates a continuing state, the ongoing exercise of the activity indicated by the verb and thus essential attributes of character.

The second three attributes (v. 3) are stated negatively and use verbs indicating completed action in the past. These three thus refer to specific, concrete actions and not to personality characteristics. The first concerns the use of the tongue (see Prov. 18:21) and thus psychological injury (see Prov. 18:21), the second physical harm, and the third participation in or conviction of actions to deprive or downgrade the neighbor. This set of negatives concerns one's relationship to others in the community.

The third set of three qualities (v. 4) focuses on the nature and character of a person's associates. The contemptible person is judged abhorrent and to be avoided. An ancient rabbinic saying expresses the fact that one's integrity is threatened by one's associates: "Woe to a wicked man, woe to his neighbor." The positive side of the issue is represented by the statement that the morally upright honors those who fear the Lord. The final affirmation in this set of three declares that the righteous stick to their word ("oath") even when it is to one's disadvantage to do so.

The final set of characteristics (v. 5) contains only two elements: the ethical person does not lend money at interest or take a bribe against the innocent. Both of these involve profiting financially while at the same time perverting and diverting the best interests of society. In numerous places in the Old Testament (Exod. 22:24–26; Lev. 25:35–37; Deut. 23:19–20; and Ezek. 18:8; see also Prov. 28:8), one is forbidden to lend money at interest. That is, one is not to profit from those in society who are disadvantaged. Ancient Israel considered loans within one's community to be a humanitarian, not a commercial, transaction. Numerous biblical texts speak against allowing a bribe to pervert justice (Exod. 23:8; Lev. 19:15; Deut. 16:19).

Colossians 1:15–28

Today's epistolary text consists of three parts: (1) the magnificent hymn where Christ is praised as the head of the created order (vv. 15–20); (2) the effect of Christ's work on the Colossians (vv. 21–23); and (3) the effect of Christ's work on Paul's ministry (vv. 24–28).

The Christ-Hymn (vv. 15–20). If these verses are not themselves an early Christian hymn, they appear to be based on one. Accordingly, the NJB prints them strophically, in the form of a two-stanza poem. Even though these verses are not printed strophically in the NRSV and REB, their editorial notes clearly support the view that they should be read poetically or hymnically. The Nestle-Aland 26th edition Greek text prints verses 15–18 strophically.

If we adopt the NJB's two-part outline, the first stanza (vv. 15–18a) focuses on Christ's role in creation, whereas the second stanza (vv. 18b–20) unfolds the redemptive work of Christ.

a. *Christ and creation.* In this section of the hymn, Christ is given a preeminent role in creation. The controversial claim that he is "the firstborn of all creation" (v. 15) probably means that he is "firstborn" in terms of rank rather than being the first thing created by God. In any case, standing at the head of creation, Christ functions as God's agent of creation (cf. 1 Cor. 8:4–6). As the one *through whom* and *for whom* all things were created, Christ is confessed as both the means and end of creation. The created order is understood as being held together through him (v. 17).

b. *Christ's redemptive work.* Because Christ is experienced as the place where God's fullness uniquely dwells, he is seen as God's agent of reconciliation in the world (vv. 19–20). Both the cross and resurrection figure as central events through which he became "the head of the body, the church" (v. 18). As such, Christ's cosmic preeminence becomes embodied within the fellowship of believers. The object of his work is peace making—reconciling the orders of heaven and earth, which obviously means transforming life as it is normally understood.

The Impact of Christ on the Church (vv. 21–23). Here the Colossian church is portrayed as the community of faith where reconciliation has occurred. The focus is congregational: the "you" of these verses refers to the "saints and faithful brothers and sisters in Christ in Colossae" (1:2). This is worth noting, for we often tend to think of God's work in Christ in terms of the church universal instead of the church local. And yet, here we are reminded that the divine drama takes concrete form within local congregations of believers, even though we all know how ordinary congregational life can be. Like Christ's own incarnation, the ordinary serves as the arena where the incarnation of the gospel occurs.

Our text provides one of the most natural ways for us to establish our identity as a church—contrasting what we once were with what we now are, with Christ as the pivot of change. This form of comparison—once you were but now you are—seems to have been one of the standard forms of early Christian teaching and preaching. On the one side, our past predicament is sketched in terms cold and distant: estrangement, alienation, and hostility (cf. Eph. 2:12–13; 4:18–19; Rom. 5:10; 2 Cor. 5:18). It was a life of doing evil (cf. John 3:19; 7:7). Our new status, however, is sketched in cultic and forensic terms: holy, unblemished, and unaccused (v. 22; cf. Eph. 1:4; 5:27; 1 Cor. 1:8; 1 Tim. 3:10; Titus 1:6–7).

And how has this radical change occurred? Through reconciliation made possible "by Christ's physical body through death" (v. 22, NIV). Though the syntax is ambiguous, it is God who is the agent of reconciliation (cf. 2 Cor. 5:18). We should note the stress on Christ's "body of flesh" as the locus of reconciliation. The Gnostic tendency would have been to deemphasize, even deny, that salvation could have been mediated through Jesus' flesh. The emphasis in the letter on the bodily form of Jesus is in keeping with more orthodox Christian teaching (cf. Rom. 1:3; 8:3; 9:5; 2 Cor. 5:16–21; Eph. 2:14–15; Col. 2:9, 11; 1 Tim. 3:16; John 1:14).

Their faith is conditional, however. It requires steadfastness and constant adherence to the gospel (cf. 1 Cor. 15:58; Eph. 3:17). Even though the gospel was experienced locally, it is universal, having "been proclaimed to every creature under heaven" (v. 23). This is the language of hyperbole, but it serves to underscore the far-reaching impact of the gospel, at least in the eyes of its own proponents (cf. 1:6; Rom. 8:19–20; 1 Tim. 3:16; Acts 2:5; Mark 16:15).

The Impact of Christ on Paul (vv. 24–29). This passage would most naturally extend through 2:5, but even so our text provides intriguing insight into Paul's apostolic self-understanding.

We are struck by the way he conceives his apostolic suffering: "In my flesh I am completing what is lacking in Christ's afflictions for the sake of his body" (v. 24). He clearly envisions Christ's own suffering as continuing into the life of the church, not as having ceased with his death on the cross. Moreover, he clearly envisions the suffering he undergoes in behalf of his churches as a continuation, in some sense, of Christ's own suffering (cf. 2:1; 2 Cor. 1:5; Phil. 1:20; Eph. 3:13; also 2 Tim. 2:9; Acts 9:16). We should probably understand this in terms of the way the messianic age was envisioned as a time of tribulation (Matt. 24:8; Acts 14:22). In this sense, the physical suffering of the crucified Christ merely launched a period when the risen Christ would continue to be identified with those who became members of his own body, the church (1:18; Eph. 1:23; 4:12; also Rom. 12:5). Accordingly, the suffering of Christ continues in the suffering experienced by his messengers and the members of his body. It gives us pause to think of Christ so closely identified with his own that his own suffering continues even in his exalted status as Lord.

Christ also becomes the center of Paul's apostolic commission. His call was made through divine appointment (1 Cor. 4:1; 9:17; Rom. 15:15–16; also Eph. 3:2, 7). His special commission was to reveal the "mystery that has been hidden throughout the ages" (v. 26; cf. Rom. 16:25–26; Eph. 1:9; 3:3–4, 9; 1 Pet. 1:20), namely, that the Gentile would have a full share in God's salvation (Eph. 3:1–6). The church has become the community in which this mystery is unfolded (Eph. 3:5, 10) and is to be understood as the locus of the presence of Christ, "which is Christ in you, the hope of glory" (v. 27; cf. Rom. 8:10; Gal. 2:20; 2 Cor. 13:5; John 17:23).

For this reason, Christ forms the center of Paul's apostolic proclamation (v. 28). His hope is that eventually everyone who is "in Christ" will finally become "mature in Christ" (v. 28; 4:12; 1 Cor. 2:6; 3:1, 18; Phil. 3:15; Eph. 4:13). Here we are called to a level of maturation and formation for which Christ serves as the measure. To bring people to this form of identification with Christ, Paul labors and strives, "helped only by his power driving me irresistibly" (v. 29, JB; cf. 2:1; 4:12; Eph. 3:7, 20; Phil. 4:13; 2 Thess. 1:11).

Luke 10:38–42

Practically everyone who reads or hears the story of Jesus as dinner guest in the home of Martha and Mary is drawn to the simplicity, the personal interest, the realism, and the ease of identification with one of the sisters. No wonder preachers love it; in a sense, it preaches itself in the mere telling.

However, preachers must beware of seduction by apparently easy sermons. Some work needs to be done. Only Luke tells this story, but John joins him in knowing Martha and Mary. John knows them as sisters of Lazarus and locates their home in Bethany (11:1; 12:1–3). Upon the death of Lazarus and also at the dinner for Jesus in their home, their behavior is not unlike that described by Luke: Martha first goes out to meet Jesus while Mary sits in the house (11:20); and at the dinner, Martha serves and Mary anoints the feet of Jesus (12:1–3). In Luke, Mary sits at the feet of Jesus (10:39).

The two writers pose a minor geographical problem for the reader, however, in that John locates them in Bethany near Jerusalem, whereas Luke's travel narrative seems to have Jesus on his way to Jerusalem but at this point still in Galilee. Our text also contains a textual problem. Manuscripts are divided on verse 42: "there is need of only one thing" or "few things are necessary, or only one." If the latter is the correct reading, Jesus is probably telling Martha she is preparing too many dishes; if the former, he is saying that the word of God and not food is the one thing needed. Very likely, this is the point: we do not live by bread alone but by every word that proceeds from the mouth of the Lord (Deut. 8:3; Luke 4:4; John 6:27). If Jesus seems a bit harsh with Martha, it should be remembered that this story follows the sharp turn toward Jerusalem in 9:51, after which Jesus' words to the disciples are rigorous and demanding. The cross awaits all of them on down the road.

The story is a radical one if one notices how Jesus breaks through the social barriers of his time. Jesus is received as a guest in the home of women (Luke does not know or, at least, does not mention a brother). And Jesus teaches a woman. Rabbis did not allow women to "sit at their feet," and yet Mary is clearly pictured here as a disciple. In this regard the episode accords well with Luke's earlier statement about women in 8:1–3. In telling the story, the preacher will want to be careful with the details: it is Martha's house, she receives Jesus into her home, and the whole story centers on her and Jesus. She has a sister, Mary, who is described but who never speaks or enters otherwise into the action.

The preacher can easily be drawn into allegorizing the sisters: Martha, the model of the active and busy Christian worker; Mary, the model of the contemplative and reflective Christian. Such portraits can be overdrawn. Perhaps more fruitful might be a consideration of Luke's location of this story. It follows immediately the parable of the Good Samaritan and Jesus' injunction "Go and do likewise" (v. 37). Now Jesus affirms and blesses not going and doing but sitting still and listening. Side by side Luke has placed occasions on which Jesus called for active engagement with human need and being still, listening, and learning. Luke is not making a choice between them, nor is he asking the reader to accept one and reject the other. Both the Samaritan and Mary are examples, and both are to be emulated. The burden lies in discerning when to do the one and when to do the other. The Christian life involves, among other things, a sense of timing.

Proper 12 [17]
(Sunday between July 24 and 30 inclusive)

Hosea 1:2–10;
Psalm 85; or
Genesis 18:20–32;
Psalm 138;
Colossians 2:6–15 (16–19);
Luke 11:1–13

I n the Old Testament reading from the *Common Lectionary*, God commissions Hosea to marry Gomer, bear children, and give them message-names signifying divine disfavor with Israel. Psalm 85, although acknowledging the iniquity of Israel, offers a message of hope by portraying God as faithful, forgiving, and loyal.

Other lectionaries have selected, as the Old Testament reading, God's famous bargain with Abraham where he is challenged to find ten righteous people in Sodom. For a response, a psalm of thanksgiving for deliverance is chosen.

Exhortations to live out the implications of "life in Christ," along with warnings against useless pursuits and needless restrictions, are contained in the Epistle reading from Colossians.

Prayer provides the overall theme of the collection of Jesus' sayings that comprise the Gospel lection. Along with the shorter Lucan version of the Lord's prayer, we have sayings that urge us to pray. We are assured that asking is both appropriate and necessary.

Hosea 1:2–10

H osea is one of the four Israelite prophets who were active in the eighth century BC. (The others are Amos, Isaiah, and Micah.) He is the only prophet from the Northern Kingdom of Israel whose words are recorded in a book by his name. On the basis of both the superscription (1:1) and historical allusions within the book, we can conclude that the prophet began his work before the death of the last king in the dynasty of Jehu, Jeroboam II of Israel (786–746 BC). Otherwise, the particular reference to the dynasty in 1:4 makes little sense. Consequently, Hosea emerged about 750 BC and was active right up to the time of the fall of Samaria, the capital of Israel, in 721 BC. What seems to be one of his latest speeches (13:16) anticipates but does not yet know of the fall of the city to the Assyrian army.

Hosea's time was a period of internal and external political conflict. The state faced persistent threats from Assyria, as well as perils from its more immediate neighbors, including Judah in the south. In addition, internal political conflicts produced instability. Unlike Judah, which saw the almost uninterrupted rule of the Davidic dynasty, Israel's rulers and dynasties seemed always subject to challenge. Between 750 and 721 BC Hosea would have seen no less than seven monarchs come and go.

Moreover, in a territory open to foreign trade and other contacts, and in a relatively rich agricultural region, the culture of Israel saw the cults of the Canaanite gods continue to flourish. The question, as old as the time of Israel's entrance into the land, was: Who makes the land fertile, Yahweh or Baal? The earlier northern prophets, Elijah and Elisha, led the attack on the prophets and priests of Baal. In the tradition reflected in the First Commandment, they insisted that it was not possible to divide one's loyalties. The people of Israel are to worship Yahweh alone.

And that is the main burden of the message of Hosea. The constant theme of his message is that the people of Israel have failed to be faithful to their God. All their specific acts of disobedience stem from that central failure. Thus they deserve judgment. The central metaphor for that unfaithfulness is presented in the first three chapters. Israel in relationship to Yahweh has been like a whore, selling herself to other gods.

In our reading for the day, Israel's unfaithfulness is graphically presented in terms of the relationship of Hosea to his wife Gomer. The unit (1:2–10) is a third person narrative concerning Hosea's wife and children. What may appear on the surface to present autobiographical information is actually the report of prophetic symbolical actions (see also 2 Kings 13:14–19; Isa. 7:14; 8:1–4; Jeremiah 19; 32). And although it begins with a command concerning his marriage, its main focus is upon the children and their names.

The report begins with a general command to the prophet and its reason: "Go, take for yourself a wife of whoredom and have children of whoredom, for the land commits great whoredom by forsaking the LORD" (v. 2). The word translated "whoredom" in the NRSV has evoked a great deal of controversy. The Hebrew is an unusual abstract plural, but the meaning of the root is the ordinary term for prostitution. Some commentators have taken the term to refer more generally to promiscuity, and REB translates "unchaste woman." In any case, the text would have us understand that the woman's unfaithfulness preceded the marriage. It is not that Hosea learned of the capacity of Yahweh to forgive through his marriage to a woman who subsequently became unfaithful. He was commanded to marry a "wife of whoredom" to present the divine message.

This section is a coherent and complete unit that moves from an introduction that gives the relative date (When the LORD first spoke through Hosea, . . . v. 2) and the general instructions to a climax, if not a conclusion. What follows the command is the report of how Hosea fulfilled it. This account is in three parts, corresponding to the births of the three children, each of whom is given a symbolic name. Although the birth and naming of each child is a complete symbolic action, the unit as a whole develops from accusation and threat of punishment (vv. 4–5), to the Lord's withdrawal of forgiveness (v. 6), to the radical proclamation that the ancient covenant between Yahweh and Israel is ended (vv. 8–9). Thus the report as a whole is organized very much like traditional prophecies of punishment. (Verse 7, which emphasizes that the judgment does not apply to Judah, is not original but would have been added relatively early by a Judean editor.)

By identifying Gomer as a "wife of whoredom" and the offspring as "children of whoredom" Hosea accuses Israel of unfaithfulness, doubtless for participating in Canaanite worship in one way or another. Israel has not adhered to the covenant with her God, so that covenant is ended. A distinctive and central note in the message acted out by Hosea—and not missed by the reporter—is the identification of the prophet and his family with the condemned people. Hosea speaks from within, not from without, and knows that he, too, suffers the end of the covenant.

Psalm 85

Verses 1–2 recall an earlier time when God had restored the fortunes of the people, forgiving their sins and withdrawing the divine wrath. What this section talks about specifically remains uncertain. Does it refer to the return from exile proclaimed in glorious terms in Second Isaiah? Or does it revolve around features of Israel's great autumn festival season, when God was annually proclaimed as forgiving the people's sin on the day of atonement and providing for the people a new slate and a new fate for the coming year? Probably the latter should be seen as the context of this psalm's usage and the phenomenon described in verses 1–3. The prayer for God to revive and restore the people in verses 4–7 would thus be a plea that God would again, in the festival, put away divine indignation and anger and display instead his salvation and thus revive the people.

Verses 8–13 would be an oracle spoken in the service of worship by some cultic official (priest? prophet?) who already envisioned and anticipated what God's response would be and what consequences it would produce. (Note that vv. 1–7 are addressed to the Deity and are thus prayers, whereas vv. 8–13 speak about the Deity and are somewhat similar to the preaching and proclamation of a prophet.)

Psalm 85:8–13 anticipates the appearance of God and already perceives its consequences. What God will speak is peace (shalom!). The consequences of Yahweh's speaking are described in a play on a number of terms—faithfulness, righteousness, peace, steadfast love. What these terms describe are all good qualities. They are depicted coming together as if they were two who meet and kiss or as if one springs from the earth and the other looks down from the sky. That is, because God speaks, full harmony and unity result. Here ideal qualities are merged.

Verse 12 returns to more mundane matters; God will give what is good, and the land will yield its increase. This again suggests the use of this psalm in the fall festival, when the old agricultural year ends and a new year begins. In Palestine, the rainy season, from October through April, is followed by a rainless season, from May through September. Thus the new agricultural year in the Bible began after the first rains in the fall, when new crops could be sown. The fall festival was celebrated as the hinge between the ending of the old and the beginning of the new. Thus the oracle of verses 8–13 closes with the promise of a good agricultural year. (Perhaps vv. 4–7 suggest that the previous year's harvest had not been good.)

Genesis 18:20–32

This story, part of the larger narrative concerning the destruction of Sodom and Gomorrah, comes from the Yahwistic source of the Pentateuch. The tale of these two cities—actually, the focus is upon the one, Sodom—is itself tied to the account of the birth of Isaac to Sarah and Abraham by the travels of the three messengers. In 18:2 they had appeared to Abraham and Sarah, conveying the divine promise of a son (see the discussion of 18:1–10a for last week). Before the reading for today begins, they are said to have headed out to Sodom and Gomorrah (18:16), and afterwards, their number reduced to two, they visit the sinful cities (19:1ff.). The broader narrative that surrounds it concerns the fulfillment of Yahweh's promise to the ancestors (see Gen. 12:1ff.), but it is a self-contained story.

Today's lesson is limited to the dialogue between Abraham and Yahweh, but it is inevitable that it will be read and heard against the dark background of the story of wickedness and divine judgment that follows in chapter 19. But in the meantime, the outcome is in doubt. In fact, we are informed that even Yahweh does not know if the report about Sodom's wickedness is accurate (vv. 20–21), so he is determined to "see whether they have done altogether according to the outcry" that has come to him.

Following that introduction, the remainder of the lesson is the account of the dialogue between Abraham and Yahweh. There is no actual account of Yahweh reporting his plans to the patriarch, but Abraham's initial speech presumes that he knows that the Lord has decided to destroy the city. The decision itself had not been mentioned, even in the divine words that Abraham did not hear. But we had been informed that Yahweh had decided to take Abraham into his confidence (18:17–19). The issue then is posed as the determination of a legal case, the determination of the crimes of the city with a view toward establishing justice.

Having been taken into the Lord's confidence, Abraham initiates the dialogue (vv. 23–25) with a plea on behalf of Sodom. Given the wider Old Testament context, Abraham's speech is a remarkable theological discourse. The initial sentence challenges the widely-held view of collective guilt and punishment, frequently articulated and almost universally assumed in the prophetic literature: "Will you indeed sweep away the righteous with the wicked?" (v. 23). The next sentence makes it clear that the patriarch is not pleading that the innocent be allowed to escape. Rather, he is posing the possibility of the forgiveness of the entire city because of the innocent: "will you then sweep away the place and not forgive it for the fifty righteous who are in it?" (v. 24). The corporate view is not abandoned, but a new possibility is introduced—that the majority who are guilty could be forgiven because of the minority who are innocent. Moreover, Abraham poses his petition in terms of divine justice: "Shall not the Judge of all the earth do what is just?" (v. 25). What a bold intercessor, to instruct the Lord on divine justice!

Without qualification, the Lord accedes to Abraham's petition: "If I find at Sodom fifty righteous in the city, I will forgive the whole place for their sake" (v. 26). Indeed, the sinful majority may be forgiven because of the innocent few. Encouraged by this answer, Abraham renews his intercession, lowering the numbers of the righteous from forty-five to forty to thirty to twenty and finally to ten. In each case Yahweh agrees to the request: "For the sake of ten I will not destroy it" (v. 32).

Who has not read this story (and the following chapter) and wondered how it would have turned out had Abraham continued to lower the numbers? Although the destruction of Sodom for the failure to find ten righteous in it allows that question to remain somewhat open, it is clear that the fundamental issue is not a matter of numbers or percentages. Is God willing to forgive the sinful city because of a few who are righteous? The answer here is yes. In the account of divine justice, this dialogue emphasizes divine mercy. At the same time it serves to argue that the subsequent judgment on Sodom was fair.

Thus this lesson encourages us to reflect upon the meaning of divine justice. Without compromising the biblical sense of corporate responsibility and suffering, it opens the door to corporate forgiveness because of a righteous few. The lesson also evokes reflection on intercession and suggests the possibility of bold prayers for mercy.

Psalm 138

This psalm may be subdivided into three parts. Verses 1–3 thank and praise God; verses 4–6 extol the grace and glory of God and their impact on the rulers of the world; and verses 7–8 express trust in God.

The general tone of the psalm clearly identifies it as a thanksgiving. It differs, however, from most thanksgiving psalms in two ways: (1) there is no description of the trouble or the distress from which the person was rescued (see v. 3, which refers to an appeal to God at an earlier time of distress), and (2) the psalm is addressed directly to the Deity throughout (v. 8a is possibly an exception), whereas most thanksgivings are addressed to a human audience.

The person offering thanks in the original usage of this psalm was probably the king. This is suggested by the references to the kings of the earth in verse 4 who hear the words of Yahweh's mouth, perhaps words spoken by the Judean king. Also, the king was especially the one at God's right hand (v. 7; see Ps. 110:1).

Several elements in the psalm call for elucidation:

1. The reference to "before the gods" (v. 1) could mean one of several things. Ancient translations read "before the angels," "before kings," or "before judges." If the reference is to pagan gods, then the worshiper could be saying no more than, "I sing your praise in an alien culture." If the reference is to heavenly beings (see Pss. 29:1; 82:1), then the phrase could denote worship before the heavenly council of God.

2. To bow down toward the temple does not imply that the worshiper is in some foreign land or away from Jerusalem. This could be a reference to worship or activity at the temple gate, near the main altar, or in the temple courtyard.

3. The lowly may not refer to a class—the poor, the downtrodden, or others in similar conditions—but could be a self-designation, even of a king—the lowly over against the Divine.

4. The verb translated "perceives" in verse 6b may mean, on the basis of an Arabic parallel, "to humble." Thus "the haughty he humbles from afar."

The statement of trust in verses 7–8 gives expression to a serene confidence—almost. Verse 8c still resorts to petition even after the statement of assurance. Note that the psalm does not assume that life will be free of distress and problems but only that God will preserve one through them all. Trouble and enemies are the givens in life; grace and preservation to endure and overcome them are the sustaining gifts.

Colossians 2:6–15 (16–19)

It may be obvious to us that Christ should be the ordering principle of our lives, but it was not to the Colossians. If Christ is merely another member of the angelic hierarchy, as the false teachers apparently claimed, we can see why Paul would need to convince the Colossians to make Christ the sole basis for their lives.

We can consider today's lection in two parts: (1) Paul's appeal for his readers to live according to Christ (vv. 6–8) and (2) the basis for the appeal (vv. 9–15). The optional section (vv. 16–19) gives further instructions about how to deal with those who insist on measuring our faith and practice by their own peculiar yardstick.

The Appeal (vv. 6–8). The appeal has two parts, one positive, the other negative. Positively, Paul urges that the Christ whom we have received should be the Christ in whom we establish our complete identity (vv. 6–7). Negatively, he warns against being seduced by systems of thought that are humanly construed and exclude Christ (v. 8).

Before any appeal is made, we are reminded that the fundamental reality is our confession of faith in "Christ Jesus the Lord" (v. 6; Rom. 10:9; 1 Cor. 12:3; 2 Cor. 4:5; Phil. 2:13). In accepting the gospel as more than mere human word, indeed as the summons of God (1 Thess. 2:13), we receive Christ not only because we accept the message about him as true but also because we appropriate him as a living reality (cf. Eph. 4:21).

For this reason, it is possible to "live [our] lives in him" (v. 6). He becomes the prime Reality for establishing our identity, the sphere we live in, the One in whom our lives begin to make sense. Christian existence is existence "in Christ" (2 Cor. 5:17). This is where the new creation occurs. With Christ as the One in whom we live, he becomes the trunk in which we are rooted (Eph. 3:17; cf. John 15:1–11) and the foundation on which we build (Eph. 2:20, 22; Jude 20). This occurs as we grow in our knowledge of the faith (2 Thess. 2:15), and it becomes an occasion of thanksgiving.

But there will always be competing Christs. We are warned against being captivated by "the empty lure of a 'philosophy' of the kind that human beings hand on, based on the principles of this world and not on Christ" (v. 8, NJB). This is doubtless Paul's slap at the false teachers in Colossae. The implication is that their religious system was a loosely connected amalgam of quasi-philosophical ideas mixed with cosmic speculation, which was finally devoid of any serious content (cf. Eph. 4:14; 5:6). It becomes clear from our text that, for Paul, Christ must provide the fundamental reference point for any philosophical position or worldview that attempts to make sense of reality.

The Basis for the Appeal (vv. 9–15). And what is the basis for such an all-encompassing, unequivocal appeal for us to order our lives entirely with reference to Christ?

First, Christ is the full manifestation of deity. "In him, in bodily form, lives divinity in all its fullness" (v. 9, NJB; 1:19; Eph. 1:23; 3:19; 4:10, 13; John 1:14–16). Because Christ is the complete embodiment of God, we are thereby enabled to experience "fullness in him" (v. 10; cf. Eph. 4:15). Because Christ is the fullest possible expression of the reality of God, those who are "in Christ" are able to experience to the fullest the reality of God. Just as Christ is not a partial manifestation of God, neither is our experience of God in Christ partial. Because Christ is the unique embodiment of God, he is preeminent over "every ruler and authority" (v. 10, 1:18; 2:19; cf. Eph. 1:22; 4:15; 5:23; 1 Cor. 11:3).

Second, through sacramental union with Christ we have experienced "a spiritual circumcision," or inner transformation of the heart by experiencing resurrection life. It had long been a hope within Old Testament thought that Israel would experience genuine renewal that was depicted as a circumcision of the heart (Deut. 30:6; Jer. 4:4; 9:25–26; cf. Acts 7:51). In Christian experience, the sacrament of baptism corresponded to the act of circumcision. Here, we are told that in the baptismal act circumcision is now performed by God, not by human hand, and that it is more than mere removal of a small piece of skin. Rather, it involves the "complete stripping" of our lower nature, "the natural self" (v. 11, NJB, REB). This is the "circumcision of Christ" (v. 11, NRSV), or the "circumcision according to Christ" (v. 11, NJB; cf. Rom. 2:25–29).

In the baptismal act, we become a participant with Christ in the cosmic drama of dying and rising (v. 12; cf. 3:1; Rom. 6:4; Eph. 2:6). We should note here that our resurrection with Christ is envisioned as being already realized, whereas in the undisputed Pauline letters it remains a future reality (cf. Rom. 6:4–11; 8:11). The important point to note is that God has "made [us] alive together with him" (v. 13). The resurrection that God effected in Christ has now been effected within us.

Third, Christ has annulled the power of the law through his own death on the cross (vv. 14–15; cf. Rom. 7:4; 1 Pet. 2:24). Precisely what is meant by the "record that stood against us" is not clear. The image may be that of nailing a canceled debt to the cross (v. 14, NJB). This is seen as a victory over heavenly forces, "the rulers and authorities" (v. 15), who are paraded as a public spectacle in the march of triumph (cf. 2 Cor. 2:14).

Luke 11:1–13

L uke has chosen to assemble in 11:1–13 a number of Jesus' teachings on prayer. There is no reason for the reader to assume that Jesus said all these things on one occasion. Collections of materials into sections on controversies, miracles, parables, instructions on conduct, and other themes are common in the Gospels. That these sayings originally had different settings is evidenced by the fact that Matthew parallels Luke 11:1–4 in 6:9–13 and Luke 11:9–13 in 7:7–11. Luke's parable of the friend at midnight (vv. 5–8) is not found elsewhere. The clear breaks in the passage yield three distinct units: verses 1–4, 5–8, and 9–13. The preacher is, therefore, justified in not attempting to treat the entire passage in one message. On the contrary, the wealth of the material and the varieties of literary texture (question and answer, the Lord's Prayer, a parable, simple analogies, direct instruction) encourage using several sermons to cover the passage.

Luke has provided an introduction consisting of two parts: the example of Jesus and a disciple's request (v. 1). Jesus at prayer is an image frequent and important for Luke: at baptism (3:21), before choosing the Twelve (6:12), before the first prediction of his passion (9:18), and at his transfiguration (9:28). Apparently his own prayer life prompted his disciple's request. To be taught "as John taught his disciples" seems to imply that followers of John, perhaps still in Luke's day, were given a certain form for prayer. Such a practice was not unusual for rabbis. It is significant that the text treats prayer as a learned experience and not simply the release of the heart's natural longings.

The form of the Lord's Prayer in Luke (vv. 2–4) is briefer than the more familiar and more liturgically extended version in Matthew (6:9–13). It consists of two brief petitions of praise to God and three petitions for the ones praying. It is a communal, not a private, prayer (us, we) and assumes that the community longs for the final coming of the kingdom. The overall eschatological thrust of the prayer is present in Luke as in Matthew but may be softened a bit in the petition about bread. The difficult word translated either "daily bread" or "bread for tomorrow" (v. 3) is in Luke prefaced with a present tense verb meaning "continue giving us," or "day by day give us," or "each day give us." Apparently, Luke has in mind not the bread from heaven at the kingdom's coming but each day's provision of daily food. This would be appropriate for those who were to take up the cross "daily" (9:23) and to go on missionary journeys with no extra rations (10:4–7). It is interesting to note that the petitioner also asks God to forgive sins (not debts); but in terms of our forgiving others, it is for their debts to us (v. 4). It has been suggested that this reflects Luke's concern that possessions not hinder community relationships (6:30; Acts 5:1–11).

The parable in verses 5–8 is difficult to read because it is framed as one long question with the many clauses joined with conjunctions in Semitic fashion. Added to the difficulty is the fact that the listener is to identify at the outset with the one who asks a neighbor for bread, but the question ends with attention on the neighbor who responds to the late-night request. These unusual features lend support to the idea that the parable may have originally had another context, perhaps concerning preparedness for the end time, similar to Matthew's story of ten maidens (25:1–13). In its present setting, however, the parable makes the point that if our friends respond to persistent appeals, how much more so will God who desires to give us the kingdom (12:32).

The concluding section (vv. 9–13) extends further the line of thought "from the lesser to the greater." This time, however, the analogy is drawn not from one's friends but from one's parents. If earthly parents give good gifts in response to their children's requests, how much more so will God. Luke has egg and scorpion instead of Matthew's loaf and stone (7:9), but with no difference in meaning. Of significance, however, is Luke's "Holy Spirit" (v. 13) instead of Matthew's "good things" (7:11). The gift of the Holy Spirit is vital to Luke's understanding of Jesus (3:21) and of the church (24:49; Acts 1:4, 5, 8; 2:38). The angel's word to Mary that the Holy Spirit would come upon her (1:35) has its completion in Jesus' word to his disciples that the Holy Spirit would come upon them (Acts 1:8). The Holy Spirit creates, sustains, and empowers the church to continue what Jesus began to do and to teach.

Proper 13 [18]
(Sunday between July 31 and August 6 inclusive)

Hosea 11:1–11;
Psalm 107:1–9, 43; or
Ecclesiastes 1:2, 12–14; 2:18–23;
Psalm 49:1–12;
Colossians 3:1–11;
Luke 12:13–21

In today's Old Testament reading for the *Common Lectionary* we have the well-known and quite moving portrait of Yahweh, the ever-patient father, attempting to raise the recalcitrant child Israel. It is a poignant scene as Yahweh withholds his anger and extends compassion to Israel. A similarly moving portrait of the steadfast love of God is sketched in Psalm 107, a psalm of thanksgiving.

Other lectionaries adopt selections from Ecclesiastes that speak to the dominant theme of the book—the vanity and futility of life. From a somewhat different perspective, Psalm 49 reflects on the futility of trusting in riches. Both this Old Testament reading and the psalm provide a coldly realistic appraisal of life.

Our epistolary reading for today from Colossians sketches a profile of behavior that results from our union with Christ. Expectations for a morally responsible life are set forth quite clearly.

The gospel lesson contains Jesus' parable of the rich man whose fields produced abundantly but whose life was focused only on accumulating more.

Hosea 11:1–11

This passage, for good reason one of the best-known chapters in the Old Testament, reflects in extreme form the style of the Book of Hosea and brings us to the heart of what is distinctive in the prophet's message. Like Hosea 11, most of the book is characterized by sudden shifts of speaker, addressee, mood, and content, to the point that it is often difficult to determine where units of speech or literature begin and end. Frequently, the interpretation of a saying will hinge on the answers to such questions. Moreover, the message of the prophet included both judgment and salvation. How are the two related, and what is the last word? In the final structure of the book, due in large measure to the work of those who collected and edited the prophet's words, the relationship is chronological—first comes judgment followed by salvation. In our text for today, however, we find something different.

Hosea 11 is a divine soliloquy in which the prophet hears Yahweh meditating and deliberating on his relationship to the chosen people. Although the mood frequently shifts dramatically, there is continuity of metaphors and images, and progress of thought from beginning to end. The structure consists of three parts: (1) Verses 1–7 amount to a prophecy of punishment, first stating Israel's apostasy in the context of God's saving acts (vv. 1–4), and then announcing military defeat and return to captivity (vv. 5–7). (2) In verses 8–9 we overhear Yahweh questioning himself and changing his heart. (3) Finally, in verses 10–11 there is an announcement of salvation.

From the beginning we are led to expect something different. Yahweh recalls the exodus from Egypt, often mentioned by Hosea (2:15; 12:9; 13:4), but here he employs the metaphor of a parent's care for a child. As a father calls a son, or a mother teaches a daughter to walk or takes her in her arms, so Yahweh cared for Israel. The language of love dominates the recital. But for all of this care and concern, Israel was unfaithful, turning to worship other gods (v. 2). Prophets frequently used the history of salvation to accuse the people of their failure to act responsibly. The deeper the relationship, the more serious is its violation. Consequently, justice calls for punishment (vv. 5–7), such as Hosea frequently proclaims in word and symbolic action (e.g., 1:2–9).

Once the sentence has been pronounced, the divine judge deliberates within his heart (vv. 8–9). Yahweh asks himself how he can "give up" Israel—make an end to the covenant—and bring destruction. Meditating on such a fate tears at his heart—the seat of the will—and evokes his compassion, so the Lord vows not to allow his anger to work itself out in destruction. That is the dramatic high point of the passage—that the Lord's compassion overthrows his wrath, that the will to love overcomes the—to be sure, justified—will to punish. The drama is not acted out on the plane of history but in the very heart of God.

But the theological high point comes in the reason for this change of heart. The turning of the Lord's will is due to no human activity. Typically, prophetic announcements of salvation do not give human works as reasons for the good news. The reason is, "for I am God and no mortal, the Holy One in your midst, and I will not come in wrath" (v. 9). On the highest and most generous scales of human justice, Yahweh was justified in executing punishment, but divine justice transcends human capacities for either justice or love. Indeed, the radical difference between God and human beings lies not in power, but in the capacity to withhold judgment, to love even those who have been unfaithful (cf. Hosea 3). After this, the announcement of salvation in verses 10–11 is anticlimactic.

Hosea simply presents this soliloquy without calling for a response. What is its effect on its hearers? Certainly it reminds them of the history of their God's care for them and confronts them with their own faithlessness. But how can one react to the divine compassion, to God's radical change of heart? That is the question the prophet leaves with all who read or hear this text.

Psalm 107:1–9, 43

Psalm 107 is a thanksgiving psalm, but a thanksgiving psalm with unique features. Neither a communal nor an individual psalm, it was composed for use in a special thanksgiving ritual. Persons who had been involved in various dangers—lost on a caravan journey, imprisoned, sick, or endangered at sea—and had vowed and made promises to God in the midst of their life-threatening experiences were given the occasion to offer thanks and fulfill their vows.

The psalm calls upon these redeemed (v. 2) to celebrate their redemption; namely, to celebrate their being saved from death in the desert, in prison, from sickness, at sea, offering thanksgiving to God and testimony before the congregation (see vv. 22 and 32). Thanksgiving services were times of merriment and indulgence (recall the celebration at the return of the prodigal son in Jesus' parable). Sacrifices made for thanksgiving were primarily eaten by the worshipers; in fact, they had to be consumed on the day of the sacrifice or the day following (see Lev. 7:11–18).

The psalm is composed of an introduction (vv. 1–3), four sections focusing on four different categories of celebrants (vv. 4–9, 10–16, 17–22, 23–32), and a hymnic epilogue (vv. 33–43). Within each of the four central sections, a double refrain occurs. The first (vv. 6, 13, 19, and 28) reports that those in peril cried out to Yahweh and he delivered them from their distress. The second (vv. 8, 15, 21, and 31) calls upon the redeemed to give thanks to God for his love and redemption.

Verses 4–9 concern those who became lost in the desert, unable to find an oasis or settlement, but whose salvation was granted by God, who satisfied their thirst and filled the hungry.

Verse 43 calls upon the community to learn from the lessons of those who were in peril, appealed to God, and were rescued from potential disaster.

Ecclesiastes 1:2, 12–14; 2:18–23

The Book of Ecclesiastes—in Hebrew the title is *Koheleth*—is one of the five books of the Megilloth. It is, with Proverbs and Job, one of the wisdom books, but little is known for sure about its background or the history of its composition. Its author is identified as "the son of David, king in Jerusalem" (1:1), that is, Solomon. This fictitious attribution doubtless stems from the tradition of Solomon as a wise man and collector of wisdom sayings. Although the work lacks the specific historical allusions that would allow us to date it, it must be one of the latest books in the Hebrew canon. Its author probably was a wisdom teacher who addressed his words to more-or-less wealthy men. Most but not all of the book stems from a single hand. The superscription (1:1) and the epilogue (12:9–14) are secondary, and probably as well various optimistic and pious verses within the book (e.g., 11:9; 2:26; 7:18b), although some of these lines may be expressions of traditional views that the author cites either ironically or to refute them.

The verses assigned for reading today, although not continuous with one another, provide an accurate statement of the central theme of the Book of Ecclesiastes. The initial verse of the lesson (1:2) articulates the theme of the book's argument:

> Vanity of vanities, says the Teacher,
> vanity of vanities! All is vanity.

The key word, which occurs frequently in the work, is the Hebrew term *hebel,* and the construction here expresses the superlative. It comes from a root that means "wind," or "breath," or "vapor." Translators have wrestled with the appropriate rendering of the doubtless metaphorical sense of the expression. Its sense is that everything is either ephemeral or futile, or both. The traditional translation "vanity" goes back to the Latin Vulgate. Given the various meanings of "vanity" in English, the NJPSV reading is an improvement:

> Utter futility!—said Koheleth—
> Utter futility! All is futile! (Similarly in the REB)

The author employs a variety of literary genres to argue his case, from the citation of specific proverbs to reflections based on experience. The section that begins with 2:12 is an example of a royal testament speaking in the voice of Solomon, the wise and wealthy king. The author has the king, presumably toward the end of his days, reporting that he had seriously studied all things and come to a sad conclusion, which he reports at the very outset. Like a scholar or scientist, he had used wisdom to study "all that is done under heaven" (1:12), presumably both natural phenomena as well as human activities. It is the latter that particularly concern him and lead to the conclusion that "it is an unhappy business that God has given to human beings to be busy with" (1:13); "all is vanity and a chasing after wind" (1:14).

Clearly, the writer stands in the tradition of the sages as represented by the Book of Proverbs, and challenges its very foundations. The sages, too, had studied all things and had come to the conclusion that both the world and human life make sense. There is a moral order that rewards the righteous and punishes the unrighteous. Hard work and study assure that one will be happy and prosperous. Both Koheleth and the sages applied the same methods—wisdom—to the same data—human experience—and came to opposite conclusions.

The third part of the reading, 2:18–23, continues the first-person royal testament. Here Koheleth affirms that he came to hate his work, because reflecting on what will become of it leads to the conclusion that all is futile. It is futile fundamentally because he cannot control what will become of the fruits of his labor: "I must leave it to those who come after me—and who knows whether they will be wise or foolish?" (2:18b–19a). Is he frustrated because all that he has accomplished or accumulated may come to nothing after he is gone? Certainly he recognizes the unfairness that what he has earned will be left to be enjoyed by another who did not work for it (2:21). Then he focuses on the problem of human labor and struggle itself: "For all their days are full of pain, and their work is a vexation; even at night their minds do not rest" (2:23).

What is the source, the fundamental difficulty that drives Koheleth to his sad conclusion about human life? Certainly experience teaches that work—both intellectual and physical labor—is difficult and full of frustrations, and that life is difficult. Frequently mortals are even denied the restful sleep they need and desire. Moreover, one does not have to study "all that is done under heaven" to realize that the wisdom doctrine of justice is hard to sustain. All these fuel his frustrations. But behind it all is one reality that calls into question the goodness of life. It is hinted at in 2:18: "I must leave it . . ." The dark presence at the root of his sadness is death. Human finitude for him puts the lie to the meaning of life. For him, the awareness of death cripples the will to live. The book is filled with poignant expressions of the sadness of death: "The silver cord is snapped, and the golden bowl is broken, and the pitcher is broken at the fountain, and the wheel broken at the cistern, and the dust returns to the earth as it was, and the breath returns to God who gave it" (12:6–7).

So what is the Christian preacher to do with this preacher's work? If this book and the Book of Job were not in our canon, the powerful but also potentially destructive wisdom doctrine that all is fair could go unchallenged. And that voice of challenge—rather than the positive and pious additions or the attribution of the work to Solomon—probably explains why this book is a part of the Jewish and Christian Scriptures. At least some of our ancestors in the faith did not cringe before Koheleth's strong words. If the preacher finds it impossible to agree with Koheleth's conclusions about the futility of life, he or she can be sure that there are those in the congregation who at least now and then—if not always—experience such profound futility. Those voices deserve to be expressed and understood, even—and especially—in the context of Christian worship.

Psalm 49:1–12

Like the reading from Ecclesiastes, Psalm 49 presents a rather pessimistic reading of human existence. After a general introduction (vv. 1–4), the psalm contains two main sections (vv. 5–12 and 13–20). Both end in what appears to be a refrain (vv. 12, 20) although the two verses are not quite identical (the NRSV gives the same translation of both without any indication that the Hebrew in the verses differs). The "refrain" is best translated in the NJPSV:

> Man does not abide in honor;
>   he is like the beasts that perish. (v. 12)
> Man does not understand honor;
>   he is like the beasts that perish. (v. 20)

The introduction to the psalm (vv. 1–4) declares that it is a universal address to all humans, a speech of wisdom. Eventually the theme is clear: why should I worry about those in life more prosperous than I? The NJPSV catches the essence of the opening:

> Hear this, all you peoples
>   give ear, all inhabitants of the world,
>   men of all estates,
>   rich and poor alike.
> My mouth utters wisdom,
>   my speech is full of insight.
> I will turn my attention to a theme,
>   set forth my lesson to the music of a lyre.

The first main stanza, the heart of today's lection, consists of a meditation on the frailty of human life and the frailty of searching after and trusting in power and property. Although there are textual problems in verses 7–9, the argument there seems to be that no one, regardless of his or her wealth, can avoid dying. There is no ransom which one can pay that will buy unending life. Everyone must see the grave where "they will go to the company of their ancestors, who will never again see the light" (v. 19).

The wise and the dolt all die and go to Sheol, the world of the dead, where the grave is one's home forever. These who have spent their lives accumulating wealth will leave their possessions to others (v. 10); and though they owned extensive lands in this life, the grave plot will be their land inheritance in the region of the dead (v. 11).

Colossians 3:1–11

Today's text unfolds what we are because of our union with Christ and what we should become as a result of that union. The text is constructed along the familiar distinction between the indicative and the imperative. In the first part of our text (vv. 1–4) we are reminded of who we are as a result of our baptism; in the second part of our text (vv. 5–11) is sketched for us a profile of who we ought to be as a result of this new identity (cf. the paragraph division in NRSV, REB, NJB, NIV).

At the outset, we should also note that a portion of this text (Col. 3:1–4) also serves as one option for the epistolary lection for Easter in Year A. The reader may want to consult additional remarks made there in the liturgical context of Easter. The sequel to today's text serves as the epistolary reading for the First Sunday After Christmas Day in Year C (Col. 3:12–17).

Union with Christ (vv. 1–4). We should note the indicative mood in this first section. It is a straightforward declaration. The form of Greek construction used in the opening phrase suggests an accomplished reality: "Since you have been raised up to be with Christ . . ." (v. 1, NJB). Christ was raised, and we have been raised with him. In his resurrection we have become coparticipants (2:12; Eph. 2:6). Just as emphatically, the text states, "you have died" (v. 3; 2:12; Rom. 6:3–4). We do injustice to the concreteness of this language if we think of it symbolically, or even metaphorically, even though in one sense it is both. We are being reminded that through our baptism we have actually experienced death and resurrection—not simply a death and resurrection, but our own death and resurrection.

The actuality of this is seen by the way our new identity is described. Our life now "lies hidden with Christ in God" (v. 3, REB). So closely are we now identified with Christ that it is impossible to think of our existence apart from the Christ-story. Indeed, Christ can be said to be "[our] life" (v. 4; cf. Phil. 1:21). Is this best described as Christ-mysticism, or as our mystical union with Christ? Perhaps. But not in the sense that it plucks us from our ordinary experience and suspends us in some midair, religious moment where past, present, and future merge. To be sure, our text is remarkable for the way it assumes our already having been raised with Christ as a present reality. It stands much closer to later Pauline formulations (e.g., Eph. 2:6) than to earlier formulations where our own resurrection and experience of the exalted Christ is reserved to the future (cf. Rom. 6:4–11; 8:11). Nevertheless, it still retains a future expectation (v. 4). There still remains a form of glorious existence that is not ours until Christ finally appears (cf. Luke 17:30; 1 John 3:2).

It is a form of sacramental union where our own concrete existence is reoriented. Through our appropriation of the death and resurrection of Christ, our line of vision is now directed toward the Christ exalted to God's right hand (v. 1; Pss. 110:1; 118:15–16; Matt. 22:44; 26:64; Acts 2:33; 7:55–56; Rom. 8:34; Eph. 1:20; Heb. 1:3, 13; 8:1; 10:12; 12:2; 1 Pet. 3:22). More than this, the object of our deepest desires is now directed toward "things that are above" and away from "things that are on earth" (v. 2). It is not as if we become oblivious to the world we live in, nor that we live as if there are not earthly realities. It is rather that our ultimate desires and values come to transcend the earthly as our own world and worldview are transformed by our perspective of the risen Lord.

Christ-shaped existence (vv. 5–11). For the most part, this section is a string of imperatives: "put to death" (v. 5); "you must get rid of . . ." (v. 8); "do not lie to one another" (v. 9). A profile of "whatever . . . is earthly" (v. 5) is sketched with a list of vices (vv. 5, 8; cf. Matt. 15:19; Luke 18:11; Rom. 1:29–31; 13:13; 1 Cor. 5:10–11; 6:9–10; 2 Cor. 12:20; Gal. 5:19–21;

Eph. 4:31; 5:3–5; 1 Tim. 1:9–10; 6:4–5; 2 Tim. 3:2–5; Titus 3:3; 1 Pet. 4:3; Rev. 9:21; 21:8; 22:15). If we can make any distinction at all, the first list focuses more on personal vices (v. 5), the second on social vices (v. 8). All such behavior stands under the coming wrath of God, or "makes God angry" (v. 6, JB; cf. Rom. 1:18; Eph. 5:6; also Matt. 3:7). These are also the character traits of the "old nature" (v. 9, RSV, REB), or the "old self" (NRSV, NJB, NIV), literally the "old humanity."

The metaphor of "putting off" and "putting on" suggests a picture of taking off one set of clothes and donning a new wardrobe, which is probably exactly what happened in early Christian baptism. But it is more than a matter of outward attire or outward behavior. Putting on a new self occurs as a process of renewal oriented finally toward the image of the Creator (v. 10; Gen. 1:26–27). It takes the form of "being renewed in knowledge" (v. 10; cf. Rom. 12:2; 2 Cor. 4:16; Titus 3:5). The more we seek the true knowledge of God that transforms us into the divine image, the more the old self gives way to the new self. What actually emerges is a new creation, not only within the individual who experiences this profound change, but within the social order where "Christ is all and in all" (v. 11). Its transforming impact is to remove all distinctions (v. 11; cf. Gal. 3:28; 1 Cor. 12:13).

We do well to note the way our text moves from individual appropriation and transformation to a new social reality, and this may well provide at least one homiletical suggestion. One tendency is to appropriate this text only in terms of individual ethics, especially if we read it as one of the classical expressions of Christ-mysticism. The individual element is there, but the text moves well beyond this as it pushes us to a form of behavior that is both individually and corporately transforming.

Luke 12:13–21

The parable of the rich fool is found in the New Testament only in Luke, but it occurs elsewhere in Near Eastern lore and also in the Gospel of Thomas (Logion 63) in a simpler form. In fact, the Gospel of Thomas also has the conversation of Luke's verses 13–14, but it stands without context or elaboration (Logion 72). In characteristically Lucan fashion, the interpretation of the parable is at the beginning (for other examples, see 18:1 and 18:9).

The parable comes as the beginning of a section on the attitude of disciples toward possessions; here the subject is covetousness (vv. 13–21), followed by teachings on anxiety (vv. 22–34). The section comes rather abruptly as a change of subject. The shift, which amounts to an interruption, is provided by a question from someone in the crowd. The brief exchange between the person with the request and Jesus and Jesus' warning about covetousness constitute a pronouncement story (vv. 13–15). The parable that follows is not inextricably joined to the pronouncement story and could be told effectively in a great number of settings. However, verses 13–15 do influence how one hears the parable.

The parable of the rich fool is a story pointing out the folly of covetousness, the failure to see the distinction between what one has and what one is. Covetousness was a violation of the law of Moses (Exod. 20:17) and the teaching of the prophets (Mic. 2:2) and seems to have been a widespread problem in the early church (Rom. 1:29; Mark 7:22; Col. 3:5; Eph. 5:5; 1 Tim. 6:10). It exists in many forms, sometimes as the desire to possess what belongs to another, and at other times the desire to accumulate when one already has enough to meet one's needs. Some persons, however, seem unable to know what is enough until they reach the point of too much, and often, too late. This inordinate craving to hoard as a guarantee against insecurity is not only an act of disregard for those in need but puts goods in the place of God. Luke calls it not being "rich toward God" (v. 21; Paul calls it worshiping and serving "the creature rather than the Creator," Rom. 1:25); and both Colossians (3:5) and Ephesians (5:5) label covetousness "idolatry."

The preacher will want to be careful not to caricature the farmer in the story. There is nothing here of graft, manipulating the market, theft from neighbors, or mistreatment of workers. The man is not a criminal, and to state or imply as much would be to miss the point. His land produces bountifully; the soil, sun, and rain join in making him a wealthy man. He makes an economic decision and replaces his old barns with larger ones. He is, after all, not wasteful and careless. If, then, he is not unjust, what is he? He is a fool, says the parable. He lives completely in and for himself. He talks neither to others nor to God; he talks to himself, he congratulates himself, he plans for himself. He dies suddenly, and "the things you have prepared, whose will they be?" (v. 20). Luke could well have repeated here an earlier statement of Jesus: "What does it profit them if they gain the whole world, but lose or forfeit themselves?" (9:25). Paul probably would have remarked at the close of the parable, let those who possess things live as though they did not possess things (1 Cor. 7:29–31).

Again and again, Luke will raise the subject of possessions, holding up as the standard for the Christian community the voluntary sharing of one's goods. This, Luke says, was the message of John the Baptist (3:10–14) and of Jesus (6:30; 16:19–31), and was the practice of early Christians (Acts 4:34–37).

Proper 14 [19]
(Sunday between August 7 and 13 inclusive)

Isaiah 1:1, 10–20;
Psalm 50:1–8, 22–23; or
Genesis 15:1–6;
Psalm 33:12–22;
Hebrews 11:1–3, 8–16;
Luke 12:32–40

In the *Common Lectionary*, today's Old Testament reading is the first of two readings from the eighth-century prophet Isaiah. Today's text, comprising the opening superscription of the book that introduces the vision of Isaiah and the second half of God's lawsuit against Israel, boldly confronts Israel with its shortcomings. Some of the same themes concerning what constitutes acceptable sacrifice before God occur in the verses selected from Psalm 50.

Other lectionaries have selected for the Old Testament reading the familiar Genesis text relating God's covenant with Abraham. The portion of Psalm 33 selected for the responsorial psalm praises Yahweh as the ever-watchful provider of the people of God.

Today's epistolary reading is the first of four readings from the Epistle to the Hebrews. Along with the well-known definition of faith, it rehearses some of Israel's exemplars of faith.

The Gospel reading from Luke continues the theme of riches from last week's story of the rich fool with sayings of Jesus dealing explicitly with the use of possessions. It concludes with a call to be vigilant.

Isaiah 1:1, 10–20

Today's lesson contains three distinct units from the first chapter of the Book of Isaiah. The second, 1:10–18, is a distinct and well-known unit of prophetic speech; and the third, 1:19–20, is also self-contained, although it continues the theme of the second. The first, the superscription to the book in verse 1, could easily be overlooked because of its simple listing of Judean kings, but it is equally important.

Most of the prophetic books begin with superscriptions such as the one before us. Most of them, including Isaiah 1:1, were not written by the prophets themselves, for they refer to both the prophet and the book that follows in the third person. Thus the superscription to Isaiah comes from scribes who copied and saved the book, and also supplemented the original prophetic words with later materials. So the superscriptions are important as interpretations of the prophetic messages. Like most of the others, the superscription to Isaiah contains first of all the title to the book, "The vision of Isaiah son of Amoz." Titles are necessary to identify books among collections of books, so the superscription is part of the process by which a canon of sacred Scripture was developed. This superscription, like most of the others to the prophetic books, makes an important theological claim concerning the words that follow: This is the *vision* that Isaiah *saw*. The word translated "saw" is a technical term for divine revelation. Thus, the originally oral discourses now written on a scroll are presented as the word of God.

The other elements of the superscription also make important claims. By identifying the prophet as a particular individual ("the son of Amoz") and specifying his dates in terms of the kings of Judah, the editors insist on the historical particularity of the word of God. Moreover, the words concerned particular places ("Judah and Jerusalem"). But because those words are divinely inspired, they are to be read and attended to by later generations, and in different places, although not without remembering their original horizon.

The historical horizon of Isaiah of Jerusalem, the prophet responsible for much of the material in Isaiah 1–39, was the eighth century BC. According to 6:1, he began his prophetic activity at a major turning point in Near Eastern history, "the year that King Uzziah died," which would have been ca. 742 BC. Historical allusions within the book support the conclusion that he was active at least until 701 BC, and perhaps even longer. The reference to Jerusalem in the superscription is not coincidental, but calls attention to the fact that he was a man of the capital city, active in and around the palace and the temple.

Although a great many of Isaiah's words and actions concern national and international politics, the speech in 1:10–20 pertains to cultic ritual and morality. In terms of genre or literary type, it is a priestly or prophetic torah (or instruction) speech; that is, the prophet poses as a priest answering a question of the laity concerning proper acts of worship or sacrifice. Its closest parallels in terms of both form and content are the famous speeches in Amos 5:21–24 and Micah 6:6–8. Micah includes the question "With what shall I come before the LORD?"

The torah speech of verses 10–17 begins with a summons to hear or a call to attention (cf. Amos 3:1; 4:1; 5:1). An accusation is contained in the way the addressees are identified: "rulers of Sodom . . . people of Gomorrah." The allusions form a catchword with the previous verse, but in verse 9 Sodom and Gomorrah signified the destruction in store, whereas in verse 10 they refer to the wickedness of the addressees. The particular audience is the ruling class of Jerusalem ("rulers"). Isaiah identifies his message as both prophetic ("word of the LORD") and as priestly ("teaching [Hebrew *torah*] of our God").

What follows is organized in two sections: the negative, or what the Lord rejects (vv. 11–15), and the positive, or what the Lord desires (vv. 16–17). Rhetorical questions (vv. 11, 12) initiate and organize the negative section. The prophet first hears the Lord rejecting all kinds of sacrifices (vv. 11–12). The rejection of offerings is then extended to include incense (v. 13a), as well as all forms of religious celebration and assembly (v. 13b). At this point we are given the first hint of the problem with religious observances: "I cannot endure solemn assemblies with iniquity." Verse 14 repeats and underscores the Lord's repudiation of religious festivals: "Your new moons and your appointed festivals my soul hates"; that is, "I hate." Perhaps the most radical announcement of all comes in verse 15 with the rejection of prayer itself ("stretch out your hands" refers to the posture of prayer), and the reason is given: "I will not listen; your hands are full of blood." This certainly is a metaphor for unspecified acts of violence.

The language of verses 16–17 is direct address with a series of instructions or admonitions. This positive section implicitly continues the imagery of verse 15. "Wash yourselves" refers to the literal cleaning of bloody hands, to ritual purification, and to the transformation of one's life: "cease to do evil." The instructions that follow move from the general to the specific, making it perfectly clear that doing "good" and seeking "justice" are not empty abstractions, nor do they refer simply to changing one's attitudes. To seek justice is to care for the powerless members of the society, the oppressed, the orphan and the widow.

The speech in verses 18–20 continues the metaphor of the trial or lawsuit begun in 1:2. It functions as a call to the people to repent of their sins and change their ways. The Lord pleads the case with the people, arguing for an outcome other than judgment. God holds out the possibility that the sins of the people can be washed away (v. 18), spells out the blessings for them if they are obedient (v. 19) and their judgment if they continue to rebel.

It is tempting to take verses 10–17 in particular as a total rejection of cultic activity and a call for social justice. But it would be a mistake to use this text to drive a wedge between piety and social action, between the life of prayer and worship on the one hand and intervention in behalf of the oppressed on the other. It seems unlikely that Isaiah himself ever put aside ritual. He was in the temple when he had the vision of the Lord of justice (chap. 6). Moreover, Israel's songs of worship constantly emphasize the link between piety and concern for equity in society. The liturgies for entrance into the temple make this explicit: "O LORD, who may abide in your tent? . . . Those who walk blamelessly, and do what is right" (Ps. 15:1–2; see also Psalm 24). Fundamental to coming into the presence of the Lord is living a life of obedience to that Lord's will for justice.

Psalm 50:1–8, 22–23

The opening verses of this psalm (vv. 1–6) form part of a call to worship that constitutes an affirmation of the coming of Yahweh to judge the people. The remainder of the psalm is composed of speeches of Yahweh to the worshipers placing them under judgment and condemnation. This psalm thus appears clearly to have been part of a liturgy of judgment carried out in the context of worship, perhaps a service of covenant renewal or of national lamentation. Some officiating priest perhaps spoke verses 1–6, and a prophet proclaimed the judgment of God in the remainder of the psalm. This psalm speaks of the presence of awesome phenomena as attendant upon the coming of God—devouring fire and mighty tempest. Such descriptions were at home in speech about Yahweh's appearance in theophanies, especially about the theophany at Sinai (Exod. 19:16–19). Just as God appeared at Sinai when the law was given with the accompaniment of unusual phenomena, so in similar terminology Psalm 50 describes the appearance of the Deity to judge the people.

The psalm opens with a piling up of divine names—El ("Mighty One"), Elohim ("God"), Yahweh ("the LORD"). This threefold ascription of names, which stresses the honorific power of the Divine, is followed by a threefold summons to assemble for judgment. God summons the earth (v. 1), then the heavens and the earth (v. 4), and finally "my faithful ones" (v. 5), the members of the covenant community. The heavens and the earth are to appear as witnesses to the proclamation of judgment that follows, for they, as permanent features of the world, are also witnesses to the initial giving of the law and the demands for obedience.

Verses 7–8 are included in this lection because of their similarity to the material from Isaiah. Verse 8 has Yahweh declare, "I censure you not for your sacrifices, and your burnt offerings, made to me daily" (NJPSV), unlike the Isaiah text, which condemns the outpouring of sacrifice following Jerusalem's threat by an earthquake. Verses 9–13 deny that Yahweh has any need for sacrifices and that God consumes the flesh and blood of offerings.

Verses 14–15 and 22–23 offer the positive requirements of God, but the texts are ambiguous. It can be translated as "bring thanksgiving as their sacrifice" (NRSV) or whoever "sacrifices a thank offering" (NJPSV), for the words for thanksgiving and thanksgiving sacrifice were the same.

Genesis 15:1–6

For a discussion of this lesson, see the commentary on Genesis 15:1–12, 17–18, the Old Testament lesson for the Second Sunday in Lent in this volume.

Psalm 33:12–22

The following is an outline of the entire psalm: communal call to praise (vv. 1–3), hymnic praise of the Deity (vv. 4–19), communal response expressing confidence in God (vv. 20–21), and a communal appeal addressed to the Deity (v. 22).

The psalm opens with calls to the community to join in celebration. Five imperative verbs are employed: "rejoice" (a better translation is "shout out"), "praise," "make melody," "sing," and "play skillfully." All are terms denoting making music or singing loudly.

Israelite worship differed drastically from that of most modern church services. Nothing comparable to our sitting and listening to a sermon expounding Scripture actually existed, or if so, it was the unusual rather than the normal. (The structure of worship centering on Scripture reading and preaching was borrowed by Christians from the later synagogue.) Cultic celebrations in the Jerusalem temple were characterized by throngs of pilgrims, processions, chanting, singing, dancing, and so forth. Even acrobatic and simulated games were performed. (See the activities noted in 2 Sam. 6:2–19.) Theological affirmations were carried by the rituals and the singing.

In such worship, the congregation that assembled for worship often joined in the singing/chanting of hymns. These hymns performed two functions for the participants. On the one hand, they allowed the congregation to give expression to their feelings. On the other hand, they served to indoctrinate the community in proper theology. (The hymns, probably like all the psalms, were written by religious professionals associated with members of the temple staff.)

Hymns generally offer reasons stating why God should be praised, or they give the motivations for praise. These warrants for praise generally speak about the qualities or acts of Yahweh that evoke doxology and commendation. Two groups of these reasons are found in today's lection.

A pivotal verse in Psalm 33 is verse 12, which, like the vision of Abraham, focuses on the particularity and peculiarity of the chosen people. This verse contains two affirmations. The first declares that the nation that has Yahweh as its God is blessed. One might expound this half of the verse as a view of sacred history from the "inside." That is, it affirms Israel's special status on the basis of the nation's worship of Yahweh. What gave Israel its uniqueness was its worship of Yahweh. Other nations had their gods or god, but Israel served Yahweh whom they, of course, understood as the real Deity. As worshipers of the true divinity, Israel could thus rest confident in the superiority of its religion.

The second half of this verse—"Happy is . . . the people whom he has chosen as his heritage"—makes the same affirmation but attributes Israel's special status to divine initiative rather than to the correctness of the nation's religion. (Although the term "happy" occurs only once, it governs both halves of the verse.) The election theme, of course, is given its fullest expression in the narratives about Abraham.

Verses 13–22 play on two themes: the might and greatness of God, on one hand, and the attitudes and sentiments of the people, on the other. In exegeting and preaching this text, these two issues can form the poles for discussion and proclamation.

What is said of the Deity?

1. God is first of all depicted as the sovereign of the universe who, from an exalted position, looks over and oversees the affairs of all the humans on earth (vv. 13–14). This is no longer a Deity who shares in the governance of the world but one who is the governor of the world. All the human world is under his supervision and observance.

2. Yahweh is the one who has shaped the hearts of people (who therefore should have an innate knowledge of God and the divine will) and observes all their deeds; that is, God assesses what they do in terms of what they should do (v. 15). Here the Deity is depicted as the author of the human instincts (the heart) and the judge of what is done on the basis of that knowledge of the heart (their deeds).

3. In comparison to the Deity, a king with his army, a warrior with his strength, and a horse with its might are really nothing (vv. 16–17).

Human attitudes that are noted in the text as the proper posture before the Deity are referred to in the terms "fear," "waits for," "trust in," and "hope in." Fearing, waiting, trusting, and hoping are what humans, and especially the chosen people, must do and what they confess they are doing (vv. 18–22). These attitudes, which certainly can be related to the picture of Abraham the migrant, are seen as the basis of the human-divine relationship, especially in times of need and want (v. 19).

Hebrews 11:1–3, 8–16

For this and the next three Sundays, the epistolary readings are taken from Hebrews 11–13. The first ten chapters of the Epistle to the Hebrews provided the semicontinuous epistolary readings for Propers 22–28 [27–33] in Year B, and the reader may want to consult our introductory remarks to the epistle made in connection with Proper 22 [27] in Year B. Because the Epistle to the Hebrews is used extensively in various liturgical settings, the reader may profitably consult the Index for additional material.

Today's text is taken from the first part of the well-known eleventh chapter of the Epistle to the Hebrews, which provides an impressive list of faith exemplars. Our selection brackets the examples of Abel, Enoch, and Noah (11:4–7), and highlights the faithful examples of Abraham and Sarah. It opens, however, with the classic definition of faith that has come to be identified with this epistle.

Faith Defined (vv. 1–3). For the author of Hebrews, "faith is being sure of what we hope for and certain of what we do not see" (v. 1, NIV). Or, stated in a slightly different fashion,

"Faith gives substance to our hopes and convinces us of realities we do not see" (REB). The two parts of this definition may very well serve to encompass the two dimensions of the present and the future. On the one hand, faith gives us a grasp of the future that renders it as hope (cf. Rom. 8:24–25). We are thereby able to look forward expectantly, firmly assured that the future to which we are summoned has genuine substance. On the other hand, faith also enables us to interpret the present in terms of realities we cannot see (cf. 2 Cor. 4:18).

To sharpen the definition, we might compare this understanding of faith with that of Paul, but we should not distinguish too sharply between the two. For both, faith is obedient response (cf. Rom. 1:5). But Paul seems to lay greater stress on the element of trust and utter dependence, whereas Hebrews stresses the element of steadfast commitment to the divine promise. In Hebrews, faith is the faithfulness "which one shows to God and [God's] promise by holding fast to what was once seized, and by allowing it to be normative for one's behavior. The concept contains both aspects: assent to the divine promise, and the persistence with which this assent is maintained in assurance of the future. Marked stress on this second aspect alongside the first characterizes the uniqueness of Hebrews' conception of faith" (Strathmann). As the author of Hebrews views faith, it is this constancy in clinging to the divine promise, even when it became dim, that consistently characterized our ancestors (v. 2).

Also important to note is the insistence that our understanding of faith is reflected in our theology of creation (v. 3). Drawing on the biblical account of creation (cf. Genesis 1; Ps. 33:6, 9), our author stresses that the universe came into being through an act of divine speech. Out of this spoken word of God sprang the visible from the invisible (Rom. 1:20). To account for what we see in the world of creation, faith looks to God as the one in whom unseen reality became visible reality. In this view, the origin of all we know and see cannot be conceived, known, or explained apart from the creative act of God. We begin, then, with the way we construe the created order as a clue to whether we can make sense of what we see in terms of what we cannot see, whether in fact we have the capacity for faith.

Faith Exemplified (vv. 8–19). Abraham and Sarah became the paradigms of faith in a variety of New Testament witnesses (cf. Rom. 4:3–25; 9:9; Gal. 3:6–9, 15–18; James 2:21–24; cf. 1 Pet. 3:6). Singled out in today's text are Abraham and Sarah's capacity to shape a vision of the future informed by the promise of God and to project themselves forward into that future. We should note the number of times the word "promise" occurs in our text (cf. vv. 9, 11, 13). For Abraham, it was his singular response to the call of God (Gen. 12:1–4), the promise to possess a land (Gen. 15:7), and his willingness to become a foreigner in another land (Gen. 23:4, 12; 26:3; 35:27). But more than this, he followed the promise as an itinerant, a pilgrim living in tents (Gen. 12:8; 13:12). But in this transitory mode of life, his faith pushed ahead toward a more permanent dwelling—the city of God with lasting foundations (cf. 12:22; 13:14; Rev. 21:10–27; also Wisd. of Sol. 13:1). What emerges is an assured promise sustained by hope.

Sarah also lived in response to the divine promise and was able to become pregnant even though she was well beyond age (Gen. 17:19; 21:2; also Rom. 4:19–21). This miracle of birth is explained by her conviction that God is a faithful God (v. 11; cf. 1 Cor. 1:9; 10:13; 2 Cor. 1:18; 1 Thess. 5:24; 2 Thess. 3:3; 2 Tim. 2:13; Heb. 10:23; 1 John 1:9; Rev. 1:5). Consequently, from one person an innumerable host of descendants came (v. 12; cf. Gen. 22:17; 32:12; Exod. 32:13; Deut. 1:10; 10:22).

In retrospect, what Abraham and Sarah (and Abel, Enoch, and Noah as well) exemplified was faith that responded to promise without seeing it come to full fruition (vv. 13–15). Living in hope, but not in fulfillment, they became strangers and exiles (cf. Gen. 23:4;

1 Chron. 29:15; Pss. 39:12; 119:19; 1 Pet. 1:1; 2:11; Eph. 2:19). Theirs was a pilgrim existence that moved where it was led by God.

In no sense is the vision of faith in today's text a static vision, as if steadfastness means clinging to a stake driven in the ground. It is rather a steadfast clinging to a divine promise that moves us through time and history. Even if we stay in one place, the promise of God calls us to leave and move on to new horizons. "Faith thus becomes a confident wandering" (Käsemann). We move in response to the summons of God, and in so doing move from one alien existence to another. As we move, what was once invisible to us becomes visible, even as we move into another world that is new to us. Initially, we find ourselves returning to the land we left, but in the venture of faith it lays less and less claim on us. What we finally find most compelling is a sure vision of what we hope for and a firm conviction of what we cannot see.

Luke 12:32–40

The preacher has been served such neat, well-defined units from Luke (the Good Samaritan, Martha and Mary, the rich fool) that it may have been forgotten that one of the early tasks in studying a biblical text for preaching is to ascertain the limits of the passage. Where does it begin and end, does it have a center, and can it be lifted out for study and proclamation without tearing it? Today's Gospel lesson invites the preacher back to that discipline. English translations tend to make two paragraphs of our text: verses 32–34 and 35–40. Commentaries discuss verses 32–34 along with verses 22–31. An unaided reading of the text leads to a preliminary judgment that verse 32 belongs with verse 31, verses 33–34 continue the discussion of possessions but move in a new direction, and verses 35–40 provide a new focus for reflection. Looking to the parallels in Matthew offers little help. Matthew parallels Luke's verses 32–34 at 6:29–31, does not have Luke's verses 35–38 at all (instead he has the parable in 25:1–13), and parallels verses 39–40 at 24:43–44. Mark 13:35–36 is similar.

The decision by the preacher can perhaps best be made thematically. Verses 32–34 deal with possessions, and verses 35–40 concern being prepared for the Lord's coming. Although the two themes could be joined in a single message, the preacher may prefer to treat only one. Either path taken is valid, and Luke's message need not be violated in the process.

Our lection offers first the conclusion to the section on possessions (12:13–34). Within that section Jesus deals with covetousness (vv. 13–21) and with anxiety (vv. 22–32). As the teaching on anxiety comes to a close, the reader is urged to trust God who knows our needs and, instead of seeking things, to seek God's kingdom (vv. 30–31). And then, as if to quiet any anxieties created by these teachings against anxiety, Jesus says, "Do not be afraid, little flock, for it is your Father's good pleasure to give you the kingdom" (v. 32). In other words, seeking the kingdom is not a futile search for that which is being withheld. On the contrary, seek the kingdom with confidence that God desires to give it to you.

With verses 33–34 the discussion of possessions comes to a close on a positive note. No longer warning about covetousness and anxiety, Jesus calls for a demonstration of freedom from both in the generous giving of alms. Like Judaism before it, the Christian community assumed responsibility for the needy (16:9; 18:22; 19:8; Acts 2:44–45; 4:32–37; 9:36; 11:27–30). Concern for the poor was a priority in both Jewish and Gentile Christianity (Gal. 2:10). There is no reason those who traveled light on missionary tours (10:4) should be burdened with surpluses when at home.

Verses 35–40 turn the reader's attention to the matter of preparedness for the Lord's coming. All the teachings we have now considered for several weeks are not forgetful of 9:51: Jesus' time to be taken up was at hand, and he set his face toward Jerusalem. Neither, says Jesus, are they to be forgetful of the Lord's return. Actually, teaching concerning the Parousia continues through verse 48; but verses 41–48, prompted by Peter's question in verse 41, are addressed to Christian leaders. Verses 35–40 pertain to all. They consist of two brief parables (vv. 35–38, 39–40) in which the Lord is portrayed as a master returning home from a wedding feast and as a thief entering the house at an unpredictable hour. The first parable is a very positive picture with servants ready and waiting. Their lamps are burning and their loins are girded (the long outer garment is gathered up at the waist), the very image of readiness for work or for a journey (Exod. 12:11). Upon them is pronounced the Lord's beatitude, for even after the passing of a great deal of time (until Luke's own day), they remain prepared. The second parable offers a picture more frustrating than positive. The householder is unable, of course, to stay awake all the time, but he is also unable to know when the thief will come. But readiness in the kingdom cannot be based on calculations. Rather, readiness is being busy at one's Christian duties; when that is the case, the uncertainty of days and hours is no cause for anxiety.

Proper 15 [20]
(Sunday between August 14 and 20 inclusive)

Isaiah 5:1–7;
Psalm 80:1–2, 8–19; or
Jeremiah 23:23–29;
Psalm 82;
Hebrews 11:29–12:2;
Luke 12:49–56

Isaiah's famous parable of the vineyard, whose message of judgment is couched in memorable poetic form, serves as the Old Testament reading for today in the *Common Lectionary*. The image of Israel as a vine, once flourishing but now ravaged, is elaborated in the verses selected from Psalm 80.

In other lectionaries, the Old Testament lesson from Jeremiah deals with false prophets and the slippery question of distinguishing between true and false prophets. Psalm 82 presents God as siding with victims of oppression.

In the epistolary reading from Hebrews, exemplars of faith from Israel's later history are presented as forerunners to Christ, the chief exemplar of faithful obedience.

Some sharp-edged sayings of Jesus concerning judgment are found in today's Gospel reading from Luke.

Isaiah 5:1–7

This famous passage, the song of the vineyard, is a self-contained unit, quite distinct from what precedes and what follows in terms of both form and content. It begins with a distinct introduction, moves to a clear conclusion, and is followed in 5:8ff. by a series of indictments.

Although the fundamental point of this unit is clear and relatively simple, the route to that point is circuitous and complicated. Initially, the speaker announces that he will sing a song; but when one examines the unit as a whole, it becomes clear that the song is limited to verses 1b–2. If it is not a song, then what is it, and how does the prophet reach that powerful conclusion? In order to understand just what kind of literature this is, we have to note the shifts of speaker or role and the outline of the poem.

The speaker who issues the call obviously is the prophet Isaiah of Jerusalem in the eighth century BC. But what role does he assume? In verses 1 and 2 Isaiah speaks as the friend of the bridegroom. Decisive here is the translation of *dodi* ("beloved" in the NRSV) as "friend," as well as the realization that in the song he is not speaking of his own "vineyard" but about that of another. As is common in Hebrew love poetry, the vineyard represents the beloved. In verses 3–6 the prophet assumes another role, that of the owner of the vineyard, who now speaks for himself. That owner brings charges against his vineyard, reporting as if in court that he had done everything necessary to promote growth. The vineyard had failed him, so he announces the punishment. In verse 7 Isaiah speaks as prophet, indicting Israel on behalf of Yahweh. This application makes transparent what had only been hinted at in verse 6 ("I will also command the clouds . . ."), that the owner is Yahweh and the vineyard is Israel. Thus, in the initial love song Isaiah has spoken as friend of Yahweh.

Once he has the attention of the audience, the prophet begins a love song, perhaps even singing one already known in Israel. But already in verse 2 the tone and contents of the song have changed to suit his purpose, ending in an accusation against the "vineyard": "he expected it to yield grapes, but it yielded wild grapes" (v. 2). Then, in the role of the owner of the vineyard, the prophet addresses the audience directly. First (vv. 3–4) he asks that they "judge between me and my vineyard" (v. 3), that is, determine which of the two is guilty of failure. Second (vv. 5–6), the owner, assuming that the verdict is against the vineyard, pronounces judgment on the vineyard. He himself will execute that judgment, returning the land to a waste and even prohibiting the clouds from raining on it.

It appears, then, that what began as a song, and a love song at that, has now become a trial in which Isaiah, on behalf of and even speaking for the owner of the "vineyard," argues a case before an Israelite audience. The closest parallel to this passage, 2 Samuel 12:1–15, is the prophet Nathan's confrontation of David with the parable of the poor man's lamb. After David has taken Bathsheba and had her husband Uriah killed, Nathan comes to David with the tale of a rich man who stole a poor man's favorite lamb. David responds in anger against the criminal, and when he pronounces judgment on him, Nathan says, "You are the man!" (2 Sam. 12:7). Likewise, in Isaiah 5:1–7 the accused hear a parallel that leads them to pronounce judgment upon themselves. Both texts are juridical parables.

Isaiah 5:1–7 thus has two uneven parts. Verses 1–6 contain the parable of the vineyard, and verse 7 gives the conclusion. In that conclusion the identity of the partners is revealed: the vineyard is Israel and the "owner" is the Lord of hosts. Then the indictment implied in the parable is made explicit: "he expected justice, but saw bloodshed; righteousness, but heard a cry!" These concluding lines contain plays on words, determined by the Hebrew words for "justice" and "righteousness." He expected *mishpat* ("justice") but saw *mispah* ("bloodshed"), *sedeqah* ("righteousness") but heard *seaqah* ("a cry"). The conclusion does not go as far as the parable did. In the parable the owner moved on from indictment to the pronouncement of judgment, but the conclusion stops with the indictment. That leaves the final emphasis on the accusation, but the implications are not forgotten. The hearers are left, like David in 2 Samuel 12, to apply the judgment upon themselves.

The indictment is against the people of Israel and Judah. It is a sweeping accusation, but it lacks details. The failure of justice and righteousness is a frequent theme in the early prophets in particular (Amos 5:21–24; Mic. 6:6–8; Isa. 1:10–17, 21–22). "Justice," particularly in Isaiah, refers to fair and equitable relationships within society grounded in the justice of the Lord and established through honest procedures. When such justice fails, it is because the economically and/or politically powerful have taken advantage of the weak. "Righteousness" refers to that relationship with the Lord from which springs loyalty to the Lord's expectations of justice. Isaiah implies that the failure of justice and righteousness will lead to disaster for the Lord's elect people.

Psalm 80:1–2, 8–19

This psalm is a communal lament. Such prayers were offered by the community in the context of a national fast after some calamity had threatened its existence or dissipated its life. On such occasions, the people broke with the normal routine of life, assembled at sanctuaries, offered sacrifice, lamented their distress, and entreated the Deity to intervene in their behalf.

The integral relationship of the entire psalm, which is addressed to the Deity, is substantiated by the threefold repetition of the refrain in verses 3, 7, and 19, which is almost identical in all three. Perhaps in the service of communal lamentation, these refrains represent the part of the liturgy spoken by the entire congregation, whereas the rest of the psalm was voiced by the priest or person in charge.

An outline of the entire psalm makes for a better understanding of the opening verses. The following are the component parts: (a) address to the Deity with an initial plea (vv. 1–2); (b) the initial refrain (v. 3); (c) a description of the distress (vv. 4–6); (d) the second refrain (v. 7); (e) a second description of the distress (vv. 8–13); (f) a plea for God's help (vv. 14–17); (g) a vow or promise of loyalty to the Deity if salvation is forthcoming (v. 18); and (h) the concluding refrain (v. 19).

Two primary images of the Deity appear in the psalm. At the beginning, God is addressed as the Shepherd of Israel (v. 1), a very common way of speaking of the Deity in the ancient Near East, where sheep raising and the importance of shepherds were widely understood. In verses 8–13, God is portrayed as the viticulturist, or vineyard keeper. Both images imply a God who must oversee the items under divine supervision—the sheep and the vineyard—with great care, concern, and tenderness.

The opening address to the Deity would suggest that the psalm originated in the Northern Kingdom of Israel. The use of the name Joseph for the people as well as the reference to the northern tribes of Benjamin, Ephraim, and Manasseh (the last two were names of the sons of Joseph; see Gen. 48:1) point in this direction. Also the reference to God as "You who are enthroned upon the cherubim" was a divine epithet used of God's sitting enthroned upon the ark, which contained cherub decorations. (Cherubs were considered semidivine figures probably depicted with an animal body, human head, and bird wings; in the ancient world, they were not depicted, as in medieval times, as fat little winged angels!) This epithet was used at the old ark shrine in Shiloh (see 1 Sam. 4:4). All of this implies that the distressful situation requiring a lament had to do with a calamity involving the northern state of Israel. What the calamity was is unknown, perhaps defeat in some military campaign.

The theme of God as the keeper of the vineyard and Israel as the vine dominates verses 8–19 and thematically connects this psalm with the Isaianic text of the so-called "song of the vineyard" (Isa. 5:1–7). The psalm describes God's bringing a vine out of Egypt (see also Hos. 9:10) and preparing a vineyard. The vine grew far and wide, covering the mountains, and even extending its shoots to the Euphrates River (probably in the reign of David). Now the vine lies trampled, and the people lament their state (vv. 12–13).

Verse 17a petitions God to remember and support the "one at your right hand"; that is, Israel the elect, which occupies the place of honor at the right hand of the Divine. God is reminded in verse 17b that Israel is, after all, Yahweh's creation and thus a responsibility of the Divine. On its behalf, the community vows to offer fidelity and worship as thankful response (v. 18).

Jeremiah 23:23–29

Today's lesson is part of a larger collection of sayings in the Book of Jeremiah (23:9–40) concerning false prophets. It even begins with a superscription, or heading, that indicates the topic "Concerning the prophets" (23:9). The section consists of at least five distinct units, verses 9–12, 13–15, 16–22, 23–32, and 33–40. Our reading contains most of the fourth unit. It is likely that this unit reflects the secondary or editorial combination of at least two originally independent prophetic sayings, verses 23–24 and 25–32.

As verse 23 makes abundantly clear, the speaker of these words is Yahweh, the God of Israel and of all the world. Of course, this word of God comes through the words of the prophet, as the oracle formula ("says the Lord") indicates. The section is disputational in form, doubtless reflecting actual encounters between Jeremiah and others who claim to have received divine revelations. If taken alone, the first section (vv. 23–24) would not necessarily comment directly on the issue at hand, the authenticity or veracity of those alternative claims to know the divine will. It is the Lord's assertion concerning God's proximity and omniscience. In the form of rhetorical questions, the Lord asserts that he is not distant but near, and that none can hide from him. But in the context, "them" (v. 24) certainly refers to Jeremiah's opponents, and the assertions about the Lord form the basis for the case that follows.

In verse 25 the image turns from what the Lord can "see" to what the Lord can hear. This cannot be coincidental, for the issue of revelation turns on that very point. Yahweh asserts that he has "heard what the prophets have said who prophesy lies in my name." They are said to say, "I have dreamed, I have dreamed!" In the disputational and accusatory context, this quotation will have dripped with sarcasm. But it also sets the fundamental issue of the source of the divine message, sight rather than hearing. In some Old Testament traditions, dreams were understood as legitimate means of revelation (Gen. 28:12; 37:1–9; 40; 41) but not to Jeremiah.

The argument then alternates between the means of revelation and the content of the messages of the dreaming prophets. They prophesy lies, "the deceit of their own heart" (v. 26), and they are making the people forget the name of the Lord just as their ancestors forgot and turned to the Canaanite god Baal (v. 27). So Jeremiah hears the Lord posing a test. Let these prophets tell their dreams—and, presumably, the interpretation of the dreams—but let "the one who has my word speak my word faithfully" (v. 28). The power of that word is expressed in two images. It is like a fire and like a hammer that breaks rocks. Thus the word of the Lord through the genuine prophets has the power to accomplish what it says (see Amos 1:2).

The issue raised by this text is not only a theoretical and theological one but practical and concrete. Nor is it just one for antiquity, but it is one faced daily in our time as well. It begins as the question of distinguishing between true and false prophets, but it is even broader than that: Whose word is the word of God, and how can one know? More than any other prophet, Jeremiah addresses this issue and develops more than one response. In the immediate context of this lesson he suggests that one way to recognize false prophets is by their immoral behavior: they commit adultery (23:14; cf. also 23:10–11). Or they do not tell the truth, telling the people the good news that they want to hear (23:16–17). At points Jeremiah seems to suggest that the only true prophet is the one who announces judgment. Or, as in this unit, the means of their revelation is wrong because they either tell their dreams as if they were the word of God, or they "speak visions of their own minds" (23:16). So even ecstatic experience does not guarantee validity. The emphasis upon the word of God, spoken by one who has "stood in the council of the LORD" (23:18), is a central emphasis of Jeremiah. Moreover, the true prophet is one who is called by the Lord (see Jer. 1:4–9) and not one who speaks when the Lord did not speak to him (23:21).

It seems clear that the question of distinguishing between true and false prophecy was a major issue for ancient Israel, as it is for us. In that debate two major criteria emerged. First, one will know the true prophet when what he announces comes to pass. That, along with the assertion that the true prophet announces judgment, is the criterion Jeremiah employed in his confrontation with another prophet of the word, Hananiah (Jer. 28:1–17). Deuteronomy spells this out plainly: "If a prophet speaks in the name of the LORD but the thing does not take place or prove true, it is a word that the LORD has not spoken" (Deut. 18:22). Of course, this measure is useful only after the fact.

The other criterion is a theological yardstick, suggested in the passage before us: No true prophet leads the people away from faith in the one God to whom they owe their allegiance. This also is spelled out in the Book of Deuteronomy: "If prophets or those who divine by dreams appear among you . . . and they say, 'Let us follow other gods . . .' you must not heed the words of those prophets" (Deut. 13:1–3). Thus the test becomes the First Commandment. Any word that would lead to compromise with the command to worship only the Lord is a false word. This criterion provides no easy means for testing the spirits, but it does suggest that all claims to speak the truth be examined in the terms of the heart of the biblical faith.

Psalm 82

This psalm was discussed earlier as one of the lections for Proper 10 [15].

Hebrews 11:29–12:2

Today's epistolary lesson overlaps the text used on Wednesday in Holy Week in Years A, B, and C (Heb. 12:1–3). Even though the liturgical context is quite different, the reader may want to consult our remarks on this text made in that connection.

Today's lection comprises two parts: (1) a catalogue of Israelite heroes who exemplified faith (11:29–40), and (2) an exhortation to follow the example of Jesus, the supreme exemplar of faith (12:1–2).

Exemplars of Faith from Israel's Past (11:29–40). The latter part of chapter 11 continues the list of Israel's ancestors who exemplified unusual measures of faith. Having just focused on Moses in 11:23–28, the author now acknowledges the faith of Israel itself in being willing to pass through the Red Sea "as if it were dry land" (v. 29). Then follows, in fairly rapid succession, a summary review of Israel's history from the conquest onward with moments of remarkable faith highlighted. So well known are the figures or events mentioned here that little elaboration is needed.

The compressed account of Israel's later history is rehearsed with vivid images and unforgettable phrases. In some cases, the referent seems quite clear. "Shutting the mouths of lions" likely recalls daring deeds of Samson (Judg. 14:6) or perhaps David (1 Sam. 17:34–35). Other phrases are more cryptic. The identity of those who "won strength out of weakness" is left to our imagination, although we think of numerous figures who stuck with the cause of God against great odds, for example, Gideon (Judg. 6:15), Samson (Judg. 16:17), Esther. The mention of women who "received their dead by resurrection" and those who were tortured, "refusing to accept release, in order to obtain a better resurrection" (v. 35) appears to bring the story line forward into the Maccabean period (cf. 2 Macc. 6:18–31; also 2 Maccabees 7).

Even though it may not be possible to identify every image precisely, what is important is to let the powerful effect of each image register on us. Even if we allow for a certain amount of rhetorical flourish in this description of the vicissitudes of the faithful, we should not be blasé about the conditions under which some of our ancestors have exhibited tenacious faith. And this list is intended to remind us of the horrific price at which faithfulness has sometimes been purchased. Hence the reminder: of them "the world was not worthy" (v. 38).

What they all had in common, according to today's text, was their ability to exhibit faith even in the midst of unfulfilled promise. They both lived—and died—with their promises unfulfilled. And yet for all their unrealized hopes, somehow they grasped the future as belonging uniquely to a faithful God. What is remarkable, then, is their capacity to live, and die, with no clear hold on the future, and yet do both as if the future were already theirs. This is the essence of faith, as Hebrews sees it—that which gives substance to our hopes and convinces us of things unseen.

Jesus as Exemplar (12:1–2). This part of today's lection draws on the race metaphor, which is frequently used in the New Testament to illustrate aspects of the life of faith (cf. 1 Cor. 9:24–26; Phil. 3:14; 2 Tim. 2:5; 4:7; also Phil. 1:27–28; 1 Tim. 6:12; Jude 3). The image of the athletic contest, or more specifically the foot race, provides an effective metaphor for including the host of examples cited in the previous chapter. They are envisioned as "so great a cloud of witnesses" who have completed the race and now watch as we run the same course of faith. As every runner knows, what is required, above all, is the ability to hold out till the end—endurance, or perseverance (*hypomone*, cf. 10:36; Luke 8:15; 21:19; Rev. 2:2–3, 19; 3:10; 13:10; 14:12). We should look to Jesus "who leads us in our faith and brings it to perfection" (v. 2, NJB). If the race metaphor is still in view in this exhortation to focus our attention on Jesus, perhaps we should think of Jesus as "pioneer and perfecter" in athletic terms as faithful starter and finisher.

The race metaphor is continued in the latter part of the chapter, where we are urged to lift our drooping arms, strengthen our weak knees, and find a straight and level course so as not to inflict further injury on ourselves (vv. 12–13). The language is supplied by Isaiah 35:3–4, where the image seems to be that of tired, exhausted POWs rather than fatigued athletes (cf. also Job 4:3; Sir. 25:23). It is a universal image—the person "bone tired," weary to the point of collapse, walking with arms drooping by the side, legs ready to give way at the knees. It may be fatigue from hoeing cotton all day, fighting fires all day, standing at the operating table all day, or assembling parts all day, but it is fatigue all the same. The last thing we want is another hill to climb (cf. Prov. 4:26–27).

What is being combatted here, however, is not general fatigue, but fatigue that besets the life of faith. Struggle is part and parcel of this contest (v. 4), and it inevitably entails discipline (vv. 5–11). For all sorts of reasons, we can be tempted to forsake the life of faith. We may grow weary through sheer boredom, or we may find ourselves fighting enemies and battles that take their toll on us physically and mentally. The resistance may be open assault and physical abuse we experience at the hands of demonic archenemies. As long as faith is genuine, it meets resistance both from without and within, and such resistance can become debilitating. In the face of the enervating effects of living in faith for the faith, our text summons us to react in strength.

But how is this to be done concretely? The answer is supplied later in the chapter in verses 12–17.

First, there is a general exhortation for us to strive for peace and purity of life. It is one thing to be troubled, quite another to be a troublemaker. If we live in faith, we will make enemies, but we need not try to make them. At the heart of Christian faith should be the insatiable appetite for God's shalom (cf. Matt. 5:9; Mark 9:50; Rom. 12:18; 14:19; 2 Cor. 13:11; 1 Thess. 5:13; 2 Tim. 2:22; 1 Pet. 3:11 = Ps. 34:12–16). The true vision of God must also include the pursuit of holiness, the quest for a character shaped by God's own otherness (cf. Matt. 5:8; 1 John 3:2).

Second, we are called to implement the peaceful and pure life by being watchful. The text enjoins us to "see to" certain things. This is a call to collective sensitivity, to a form of community discipline where we are actively urged to seek some things and avoid others. The community of faith is here being summoned to be self-conscious in shaping its identity and retaining that identity. Three things are called for specifically:

1. We should see to it that "no one fails to obtain the grace of God" (v. 15). The community of faith should not be oblivious to the needs of its own members, but should have enough active concern for one another so that no one slips away (10:24–25).

2. We should see to it that no internal evil is allowed to destroy the community. No "root of bitterness" should be allowed to take root and become noxious poison that kills everything and everyone. For Israel, this poisonous weed was idolatry, the failure to maintain unalloyed allegiance to the one God, Yahweh (cf. Deut. 29:17–19).

3. We should see to it that no one forsakes the life of faith and becomes "an immoral and godless person" (v. 16). Esau provides the classic example of someone who is unable to see that his birthright ties him to the divine promise; thus he sells it for a bowl of soup (Gen. 25:33–34; 26:34–35; 27:30–40). As Esau shows, only in retrospect do we realize what we lost by jettisoning our religious heritage.

Luke 12:49–56

Let us remind ourselves that the time between Pentecost and Advent provides the opportunity to treat continuous readings that give the preacher and the listeners a sense of the narrative and the overall impact of a writing. During this time one also becomes impressed with the structure and movement of the document and the unusual patterns to the material. It is certainly a time for a church to disabuse itself of any notion that a Gospel is written as a biography in chronological order.

Luke 12:49–56 is a clear illustration of unusual patterns in the text. Verses 49–53 are spoken to disciples; verses 54–56 to the multitudes. For verses 49–50, the other Gospels have no parallel, but for verses 51–56 Matthew does. Matthew's version of verses 51–53 is found in 10:34–36, and verses 54–56 are paralleled in 16:2–3. However, Matthew seems to have been aware of Luke's verses 49–50, because Luke's unusual phrase "to cast fire" (v. 49) echoes in Matthew's "to cast peace" (10:34), translated "to bring fire" and "to bring peace" in the NRSV. For our purposes here, we will consider the word to the disciples (vv. 49–53) and the word to the crowd (vv. 54–56). This is not to separate entirely the two units. Even a casual reading gives one a sense of Luke's reason for joining them: both reflect a disturbed and disturbing present with even more unsettling events on the horizon.

Verses 49–50 express the burden of the one who has set his face toward Jerusalem because the hour of his death, resurrection, and ascension is at hand (9:51). Jesus is ready to enter that dark hour and have it accomplished. Referring to his passion as a baptism is found elsewhere

(Mark 10:38). The apocryphal Gospel of Thomas contains two interesting expressions about the "fire" of Jesus' ministry. "Jesus said, 'I have cast fire upon the world, and see, I keep it until it burns up'" (Logion 10), and "He that is near me is near the fire; and he that is far from me is far from the kingdom" (Logion 82). The joining of baptism and fire in our text may be a reflection of the preaching of John the Baptist concerning Jesus: "He will baptize you with the Holy Spirit and fire" (3:16). Luke later joins the symbols of Spirit (wind) and fire on the occasion of his followers' being baptized with the Holy Spirit (Acts 1:5; 2:1–4). But all that waited upon Jesus' "baptism" of a different kind—suffering and death. Then the fire he would cast on the earth would judge, cleanse, and inspire (Zech. 13:9; Mal. 3:2–3).

Jesus' words in verses 51–53 remind the reader of old Simeon's prophecy when the child was being dedicated at the temple: "This child is destined for the falling and the rising of many in Israel" (2:34). The decision to follow Jesus, as we have already seen, can disrupt even family obligations (9:57–62). Here it is stated more sharply: taking on a primary loyalty to Jesus creates a breakup of old loyalties, even those as close as family ties. The picture of family tensions here is taken from Micah 7:6, but unlike Micah and Matthew's version (10:34–36), the division is not a case of the younger against the older. There is in Luke no sense of social revolt but of Jesus "making a difference" in the sharpest meaning of that phrase. How the reader understands this and similar passages depends to a large extent on how one understands the condition of the church addressed by Luke. If it were somewhat accommodated to the culture, placing loyalty to Jesus somewhere among its other loyalties, then verses 51–53 are very confronting. But if that church were already experiencing the price being paid, even in the home, for following Jesus, then these words are comforting. The church could find some peace in the knowledge that Jesus himself had said it would be this way.

In verses 54–56 Jesus chastises the crowds for being expert at predicting the weather on the basis of signs and yet being blind to what is really going on among them. It is not fully clear to what Jesus refers in the phrase "interpret the present time." He could be referring to the social and political unrest fomenting. Pilate had already violently crushed a small threat of revolt (13:1–3). The rebellion that would eventually become war, destroying Jerusalem and the temple, was already afoot. More likely, however, Jesus is referring to his own ministry as, in Matthew's wording, the sign of the times. But the two were related in the mind of Luke and other Christian writers. The rejection of Jesus' offer of the way of the kingdom was understood as bearing directly on the calamities to befall the nation politically. Luke's picture of Jesus weeping over Jerusalem "because you did not recognize the time of your visitation from God" (19:41–44) says it all most vividly.

Proper 16 [21]
(Sunday between August 21 and 27 inclusive)

Jeremiah 1:4–10;
Psalm 71:1–6; or
Isaiah 58:9*b*–14;
Psalm 103:1–8;
Hebrews 12:18–29;
Luke 13:10–17

Today's Old Testament reading in the *Common Lectionary* begins a nine-week cycle of readings from Jeremiah and Lamentations. Quite naturally, the first selection is the account of the prophet's call and commission. Given the challenge Yahweh set before Jeremiah, welcome reassurance is given in Psalm 71, which expresses confidence in Yahweh's ability to provide assistance and stability in times of trouble.

The conditions for experiencing the nourishing guidance of God are poetically depicted in the Old Testament reading from Isaiah 58 in other lectionaries. Continuing in the same vein, the opening part of Psalm 103 enumerates the benefits of faithful service to God, who is praised as merciful, gracious, and slow to anger.

Sinai and Zion provide the reflective images of today's epistolary text from Hebrews, which invites us to join the pilgrimage that ultimately leads to the heavenly Jerusalem.

In today's Gospel text, Jesus' healing of a crippled woman serves as the occasion for exposing the hypocrisy of biblical interpretation that insists on literal observance at the expense of human need.

Jeremiah 1:4–10

This reading is also the Old Testament lesson for the Fourth Sunday After the Epiphany in Year C. For commentary, see the discussion at that point in this volume.

Psalm 71:1–6

The following elements go to make up the psalm's content: description of trouble (vv. 7–11), appeals for help (vv. 2–4, 12–13, 17–18), statements of trust and confidence (vv. 1, 5–6, 16, 19–21), and vows to perform certain actions in the future (vv. 14–15, 22–24).

The selection of this psalm to accompany the text on the call of Jeremiah is based on the parallelism in vocabulary and imagery between the two passages.

We can examine the salient features of this psalm in terms of (1) the nature of the distress, (2) the worshiper's statements of confidence, and (3) the nature of the help requested from God.

1. The troubles undergone by the worshiper are related primarily to enemies. The gallery of opponents are described as "the wicked," "the unjust and cruel," and "enemies" who seek the worshiper's life. (Reference is made to "accusers" in v. 13.) The bitterest opponents appear to be those enemies who consider the person forsaken by God and thus without help and support (vv. 10–11). One might assume that the malady or problem the person had was taken as a sign that God has forsaken or is no longer supporting the one praying.

2. The psalm is permeated by a strong sense of trust and confidence. As the person looks back to the past, he or she affirms that God has been his or her trust from youth. God is even seen as the one who like a midwife took him or her from the mother's womb (v. 6). Looking to the future, the psalmist prays that the trust in and association with God, which was begun as a child, will continue into "old age and gray hairs" (vv. 9, 18). A common theme throughout the psalm is that God is a refuge. The worshiper confesses that God is a refuge and at the same time prays that God will be a refuge (cf. vv. 1 and 7 with v. 3). The concept of a refuge is further explicated with reference to God as a strong fortress and a rock—all expressive of both stability and protection.

An interesting feature of the psalm's statement of confidence is the reference to the special role the person has for making known or proclaiming God not only to the contemporaries of the day but also to generations yet to come (vv. 7–8, 18). This would suggest that the psalm was not originally composed for an ordinary Israelite but was probably written for the king who had a special responsibility for proclaiming the nation's God.

3. The petitions and appeals made to God for help focus primarily on the request that God not forsake the worshiper (vv. 9–10) or let the person be put to shame (v. 1). Shame plays both a positive and a negative function in the psalm. The worshiper asks to be preserved from shame (v. 1) and at the same time prays that the accusers be put to shame and consumed (v. 13). Shame, of course, meant being put in a humiliating situation and at the same time having to accept the identity that the situation imposed.

Isaiah 58:9b–14

O
ur passage is part of the so-called Third Isaiah (Isaiah 56–66) and very likely stems from the years soon after the return of the exiles from Babylon. The reading reflects some of the religious practices that developed during the Exile and afterwards, and also indicates some of the divisions that were emerging in the newly reconstituted community of faith in Judah. The mood of disappointment and frustration with the new life in Jerusalem is similar to that reported in Haggai 2:1–9 and Zechariah 7.

The reading is part of a composite unit of literature (Isaiah 58) concerned with the general topic of cultic activity. Verses 1–12 concern fasts; verses 13–15 turn to the issue of proper observance of the sabbath.

In some ways, the form of the larger passage is similar to the prophetic torah, or instruction, in Micah 6:6–8 (see also Amos 5:21–24 and Isa. 1:10–17), with a question from the laity answered by a religious specialist. But the dialogue here is more like a dispute than a request and an answer. It is clear that the addressees are the people in general, but the role of the speaker is not so obvious. Generally, he speaks with prophetic authority, on behalf of God. It is quite possible that the setting for such a discourse was the sort of community of worship and teaching that later became the synagogue.

Although Isaiah 58:9b–14 is a quite distinct unit, its meaning is clearer when seen in the context of the verses that precede it. In 58:1–2 Yahweh speaks to instruct the unidentified speaker in what he is to say to the people. He is told to be bold and direct, proclaiming to the people their "rebellion" and "sin." Those violations are not specifically identified, and it is presumed in verse 2 that those same people have regularly inquired of the Lord and his will.

Next (v. 3a–b), this speaker responds to the divine instructions by quoting the words of the people. They complain to God because their fasts have not been effective. The assumption is that fasts are a form of prayer, probably of penitence. Fasts in ancient Israel, along with the use of sackcloth and ashes (v. 5), generally were associated with rituals of mourning, but they were also used as part of petition and intercession (2 Sam. 12:16, 22). Public fasts became important in the exilic and postexilic periods, and several such days were known (Zechariah 7). The rituals for the Day of Atonement must have included fasts (Lev. 16:29–31; 23:27–32; Num. 29:7).

Then (vv. 3c–4) our speaker responds with an indictment of the people for their attitudes and their behavior on fast days. Business as usual, and oppressive business at that, continues on such days (v. 3c). People are contentious when—verse 4 implies—the public fast should be a reverent expression of solidarity before God.

To this point the author has said, in effect, that fasts are not effective because the participants do not take them seriously, do not devote themselves reverently to fasting. In verses 5–7, however, he begins to question the very idea of fasts (v. 5), and then to state what kind of "fast" would evoke the desired response from God (vv. 6–7). In a series of rhetorical questions, each expecting the answer "yes," an answer is spelled out in four points: "loose the bonds of injustice," "undo the thongs of the yoke," "let the oppressed go free," "break every yoke" (v. 6).

It turns out that these four metaphors refer to one activity—to care for the poor, to set them free from oppression, from the bonds of their poverty. Verse 7 states the point in very practical terms. Those complaining should see that the ones in need have food ("share your bread"), housing ("bring the homeless poor into your house"), and clothing ("when you see the naked, to cover them"). The final line of the verse is best read, "And not to ignore your own kin" (NJPSV), that is, your fellow Judeans. This catalogue of social responsibilities is similar to that in Zechariah 7:8–10 and is an echo of Isaiah 1:10–17, which advocates justice and righteousness (especially for widows and orphans) as the necessary prerequisite for genuine worship.

Verses 8–9a promise that when these conditions are fulfilled, the people will live in the light of God's presence, and God will hear their prayers.

That point is extended in detail in today's lesson, verses 9b–14. The voice that utters these words presumably is the one originally called to proclaim (58:1). The language is hortatory, urging right behavior and genuine worship. Each of its two parts (vv. 9b–12 and 13–14) is introduced by the conditional "if." Each of the conditions is stated as a lengthy sentence with a series of parts (vv. 9b–10 and 13) followed by promises of divine favor (vv. 11–12 and 14). The first part concerns fasts. If the people will abide by that "fast" described in verses 6–7, then God will indeed be their guide, they will be like "a spring of water, whose waters never fail" (v. 11), and the ruins will be rebuilt (v. 12). It is possible to take this promise as a form of works righteousness, that good works will earn salvation. Good works would then only replace fasting as a means of earning God's favor. Doubtless many heard—and many will continue to hear—these words in that way. However, the more fundamental meaning is that those who attend to justice and righteousness thereby live in the presence of the just and righteous God; they are part of God's people. Moreover, when the people attend to the needs of the hungry, the homeless, and the naked, they have their own reward: the solidarity of the community is strengthened, their "light" breaks forth, their "healing" springs up, and their "vindication" (v. 8, NRSV footnote) goes before them.

The second part (vv. 13–14) concerns the sabbath in particular. It should be remembered that in ancient Israel the sabbath was fundamentally a day of rest, of cessation from labor, more than a day for worship. So the condition for blessings is that the people of God refrain from pursuing their own interests, enjoy (!) that holy day, and honor it by not serving their own interests. The promised reward is hardly material blessings, although it is implied. Rather, those who enjoy the sabbath "shall take delight in the LORD" (v. 14), and that Lord will feed them with the heritage of their ancestor Jacob. This last probably refers to the continued possession of the land, but in the context it also suggests that they will be the Lord's own people Israel.

Psalm 103:1–8

This hymnic psalm of thanksgiving comes very close to being a theological catechism enumerating the personal qualities and behavioral characteristics of the Deity. In expounding this psalm, the ancient rabbis, however, were interested in what it had to say about the human, that is, its anthropological dimensions. In speaking about "all that is within me," the Midrash (rabbinic commentary) on Psalms notes ten things within a person: "the windpipe for voice, the gullet for [swallowing] food, the liver for anger, the lungs for drink [to absorb liquids], the gall for jealousy, the maw [when full] for sleep, the stomach to grind the food, the spleen for laughter, the kidneys for counsel, and the heart for decision." Of interest here is the way various organs are associated with particular human emotions.

In speaking of the expression "bless the Lord," one ancient rabbi noted the following as the distinction between God as artisan and all other artisans: "A sculptor makes a statue; the sculptor dies, but his sculpture endures. But with the Holy One, it is not so. For the Holy One made man, and man dies, but the Holy One lives and endures. This neither the sculptor nor the silversmith can do. The silversmith casts an image; the silversmith dies; the casting endures. But the Holy One made man, and it is man who dies; it is the Holy One who lives and endures for ever and ever."

Although a thanksgiving, this psalm contains no direct address to the Deity; thus it is not a prayer of thanksgiving. In fact, the composition begins as a self addressing the self (v. 1). In the final stanza, the range of vision is greatly expanded, arching out to include the angels, the heavenly hosts, and all the works of creation.

If we include verse 6 with verses 1–5, and this is a possible although not an obvious division, then the first six verses speak of seven deeds of the Deity:

> forgives iniquity
> > heals diseases
> redeems from the Pit
> > crowns with steadfast love and mercy
> satisfies with good as long as one lives
> > renews youthful vigor like that of an eagle
> works vindication and justice for all oppressed

All of these actions are expressed through participial forms of the verbs. One might take such formulations, like participles in English, as describing states as being. Thus the actions denoted are taken as descriptions characteristic of the Deity.

Verses 8–13 have a second series, containing this time six items that describe the character of Yahweh, particularly with regard to the divine reaction to human error, wrongdoing, and re-bellion. Verse 14 should be considered in conjunction with these verses, for it offers anthropo-logical insight and rationale for divine behavior, offering reasons anchored in human existence for God's grace and mercy.

Hebrews 12:18–29

Today's text divides into two halves. In the first part, the two covenants are contrasted (vv. 18–24), and in the second part we are urged to pay heed to the God who has instituted the new covenant (vv. 25–29).

The two covenants contrasted (vv. 18–24). We are actually presented here with two routes for our pilgrimage, each with a different destination: Mt. Sinai and Mt. Zion. We should note the language used to introduce each way: "You have not come to . . ." (v. 18) is clearly con-trasted with "but you have come to . . ." (v. 22). The language of coming, or journeying, suggests a pilgrimage and probably continues the race metaphor introduced in verses 1–2 and continued in verses 12–13.

First, we have sketched for us the way that has been, or should have been, abandoned, from which we have turned away (vv. 18–21). It is the way of Mt. Sinai, understood here as "something that can be touched" (v. 18). This emphasis on the palpable recalls the earlier con-trast between the earthly and the heavenly tabernacle (8:1–6; 9:11–12; 10:19–22). Sinai is thus identified with the earthly reality of the tabernacle that was experienced with the senses, for the Israelites were warned against touching the holy mountain (Exod. 19:9b–15).

But more than this, we are reminded that the giving of the law on Sinai was a terrifying moment. The sights ranged from blazing fire to total darkness. Dark clouds were accompanied by bolts of lightning and peals of thunder. With the wind and storm, there was the divine voice that filled the heavens, accompanied by the blast of trumpets (Exod. 19:12–22; 20:18–21; Deut. 4:11–12; 5:22). So overwhelming was this divine epiphany that Israel was petrified (v. 20; Exod. 20:18–21). Even Moses himself experienced this encounter with God as a moment of ter-ror (v. 21; cf. Deut. 9:19). All this is by way of saying that Sinai is an unnerving experience that sends shivers through the soul.

Second, we have sketched for us the way of Mt. Zion, the destination to which the pil-grimage of the new covenant leads us (vv. 22–24). It is sharply contrasted with Sinai because it links us with heavenly realities, notably the "heavenly Jerusalem" (v. 22; cf. Gal. 4:24–26). Here we have presented the eschatological vision expected by the prophets (Joel 2:32; Isa. 4:5) and embodied in apocalyptic hopes (Rev. 14:1–2; 21:1–22:5).

What we find here is Paradise in every sense: the city inhabited by the living God (11:10; 13:14; Rev. 21:2); the heavenly Jerusalem (Gal. 4:26; Phil. 3:20; Rev. 21:10); the heavenly court of angels (Rev. 5:11; Dan. 7:10); "the assembly of the firstborn who are enrolled in heaven" (v. 23; cf. Luke 10:20; Phil. 4:3; Rev. 3:5; cf. Exod. 32:32; 1 Sam. 15:29; Isa. 4:3); God the uni-versal judge (Rom. 2:6; 2 Tim. 4:8; James 4:12; 5:9); the spirits of the righteous who have been perfected, perhaps through martyrdom; Jesus the high priest and mediator of the new covenant (cf. 7:22; 8:6–10; 9:15–22; 10:29; 13:20; also Luke 22:20); and the sacrificial blood of Christ that surpasses the blood of Abel, that is, the blood of forgiveness not the blood of revenge (9:13–14; 1 Pet. 1:1–2; cf. Heb. 11:4; Gen. 4:10).

An appeal in the form of a threat (vv. 25–29). In the second part of our text, we hear both an appeal and a warning—or rather an appeal made as a warning. The tone may surprise us in light of the fearful picture painted in verses 18–21, but the tone is stern. We are warned not to refuse the voice of God. Israel may have heard the divine voice on earth; but we hear it echo through the heavenly city, and we do well not to ignore it (v. 25; cf. Heb. 2:2–4; 10:28–29). Ultimately, the divine voice will shake both earth and heaven. This is a clear reference to the final dissolution of the cosmos, and this eschatological upheaval will supersede all previous moments when God's voice shook the earth (cf. Judg. 5:4–5; Pss. 68:7–10; 77:19; 114:7; Hag. 2:6, 21; also Matt. 24:29).

In the face of this cosmic shaking, the only secure way is to be a part of the unshakable kingdom (v. 28; cf. Isa. 66:22; Dan. 7:14–18). The proper response is to worship God (9:14; Rom. 1:9; cf. Deut. 11:13) in a way that is pleasing (11:5–6; 13:16, 21; 2 Cor. 5:9). The final note is a sober reminder of God's destructive power (v. 28; 10:31; Deut. 4:24; 9:3; Isa. 33:14; 2 Thess. 1:6–8).

Within the context of Hebrews, this sharply etched contrast between earthly Sinai and heavenly Zion is understandable, but the preacher will think carefully about this terrifying portrait of Sinai and ask whether it does full justice to the Old Testament. An additional tension is the rejection of the way of fear, as symbolized by Sinai, in the first part of our lection, and the threatening note on which our passage ends. What cannot be denied, of course, is the truly captivating, paradisal vision of the new covenant sketched in verses 22–24. It is every bit as powerful as the much grander version in the Book of Revelation and lends itself equally well to preaching.

Luke 13:10–17

The preacher who has been following the Gospel lessons from Luke, especially since 9:51 about two months ago, may by this time begin to feel what the listeners are feeling: these demands of discipleship are heavy. Recall some phrases from those texts: set his face to go to Jerusalem; leave the dead to bury the dead; whoever puts the hand to the plow and looks back; carry no purse, no bag, no sandals; shake the dust off your feet; go and do likewise; one thing is necessary; beware of all covetousness; sell your possessions and give alms; be ready, for the Son of Man is coming at an unexpected hour; I came to cast fire upon the earth, not peace but division. If there is a sense of an accumulated burden, then let the preacher welcome this story of a healing. However, for all its refreshing promise, it, too, is not without strong tension and controversy. In fact, this is Luke's last reference to Jesus teaching in a synagogue, and the scene is prophetic of what awaits Jesus in Jerusalem. To alert the reader further about dark days ahead, Luke again mentions Jerusalem (v. 22) and has Herod Antipas reappear in the story (v. 31), this time threatening Jesus' life.

We cannot locate this healing geographically; it has already become clear that Jesus' journey to Jerusalem, beginning at 9:51, is theological and pedagogical, not geographical. The story recalls a similar incident at 6:6–11 as well as the tension in the synagogue at Nazareth (4:16–30). It was Jesus' custom to attend the synagogue on the sabbath (4:16); his ministry was inside, not outside, the worship and common life of Israel. To be in the synagogue on the sabbath was to be at the heart of Judaism in its most prevalent and in many ways its strongest form.

Apparently the stooped woman came to worship, although the synagogue leader spoke to the crowd about coming on the sabbath for healing (v. 14). Notice that the woman does not approach Jesus, makes no request of him, and reveals no faith in him. Once healed, she praises God (v. 13), but the initiative for the healing belongs totally to Jesus. In this respect, her recovery is through an act of radical grace. The leader's reprimand is directed to the people as accessories in sabbath violation, but it indirectly is an attack on Jesus. Jesus' response is not to the people but directly to the leader and to his associates, whose application of sabbath law is hypocritical. The key words are "bound" and "set free." The leaders permit a bound (tethered) animal to be loosed for watering on the sabbath, but they forbid this woman, a daughter of Abraham and not an animal, who has been bound by Satan eighteen years, from being set free from her infirmity on the sabbath.

Jesus' argument, from the lesser to the greater, is incontrovertible. The house is divided: the adversaries are put to shame; the crowd rejoices. Such is the effect of the presence of Jesus and the inbreaking of God's reign over satanic forces. A crisis is created; but if setting a woman free shatters an unhealthy peace, then crisis it has to be.

Proper 17 [22]
(Sunday between August 28 and September 3 inclusive)

Jeremiah 2:4–13;
Psalm 81:1, 10–16; or
Sirach 10:12–18 or Proverbs 25:6–7;
Psalm 112;
Hebrews 13:1–8, 15–16;
Luke 14:1, 7–14

Today's Old Testament lesson in the *Common Lectionary* presents us with a prophetic oracle taking Israel to task for its infidelity and ambivalent loyalty to Yahweh. The theme of Israel's stubborn resistance is continued in the response of Psalm 81.

In other lectionaries, we have two options for Old Testament readings—both wisdom texts. The first text from Sirach assails pride as the enemy of faithful obedience to God. The brief text from Proverbs cautions against a self-promoting spirit. A richly textured portrait of the righteous and the benefits of righteous living are described in Psalm 112.

The final epistolary reading from Hebrews consists of miscellaneous exhortations that spell out the obligations of responsible discipleship.

The ways our attitudes about ourselves and others surface in the context of dining are seen in Jesus' teachings from today's Gospel reading from Luke.

Jeremiah 2:4–13

With this reading we continue a series of eight lessons from the Book of Jeremiah, interrupted or supplemented by one reading from the Book of Lamentations, traditionally associated with that prophet. The semicontinuous readings from the prophetic literature for the season are arranged more or less chronologically. Beginning last week, we have moved from the eighth-century prophet Isaiah to the seventh-century prophet Jeremiah.

Jeremiah was the prophet of the end of the Judean kingdom. According to the superscription (Jer. 1:2), Jeremiah received his call and began his work in the thirteenth year of King Josiah, that is, 626 BC. In recent years, doubts have arisen that Jeremiah was active so early, because few if any historical allusions to Josiah, and above all to his reform in 621 BC, are to be found in the book. But the international as well as internal Judean conflicts that led up to the final destruction of Jerusalem by the Babylonians in 587 BC provide the context for the work and message of Jeremiah.

In the time of Josiah, the main international threats to Judah's survival were Assyria in the north and Egypt in the south. In 609 BC, Josiah, the favorite king of the Deuteronomistic Historians responsible for Deuteronomy through 2 Kings, was killed at Megiddo by the Egyptian army as it marched through the region to support Assyria against the rising threat of the Neo-Babylonians. But by that time, the Babylonians had put an end to the Assyrian Empire. In 605 BC the Babylonian king Nebuchadnezzar moved through the small Palestinian states against the Egyptians, and soon thereafter Josiah's successor, Jehoiachim, became a vassal of the Babylonians. But within two or three years he revolted. In 597 BC Jerusalem was besieged and then captured by the Babylonian army, and the first wave of exiles carried off to Babylon. In the meantime, Jehoiachim had died and was succeeded by Jehoiachin, who was taken to Babylon, along with booty from Jerusalem. The Babylonians set up Zedekiah, another member of the royal family, as their puppet ruler in Jerusalem. However, he soon rebelled, and in 588 BC the Babylonian army again surrounded Judah's capital city. When the city fell in 587 BC, the Babylonians leveled its wall and buildings, including the temple of Solomon, and carried off another wave of exiles to the shores of the Euphrates. This time the Babylonians named Gedaliah, the governor of the province, but he too rebelled, eventually fleeing to Egypt in 582 BC. Tradition has it that Jeremiah was forced to accompany the rebels (cf. Jeremiah 43–44). In any case, there is clear evidence that Jeremiah was active through the second destruction of Jerusalem in 587 BC.

The intensity of international threats was matched throughout Jeremiah's time by internal conflicts within Judah and Jerusalem. The divisions—if not parties—were both religious and political. Josiah's reformation was on the one hand an assertion of political independence from the Assyrians and on the other a series of sweeping changes in religious practices. Most dramatically, Jerusalem was decreed to be the only legitimate place of worship, and all other sanctuaries were destroyed. All this was in the interest of the worship of Yahweh alone. Obviously, groups that favored Judah's independence of foreign domination influenced every successive ruler. But on the other hand, there were those, including the prophet Jeremiah, who argued against rebellion against Babylon on various grounds.

It is not easy to locate today's lesson in this historical horizon with confidence, for historical allusions are vague at best. It seems likely, however, that these are some of the earliest lines from Jeremiah. If he was active in the time of Josiah, the themes of these verses fit that period reasonably well. The major issue concerns apostasy from Yahweh and thus parallels the concerns that motivated Josiah's religious reforms.

The literary context of our lection is the collection of accusations in Jeremiah 2:1–4:4. In that context, the apostasy of the people's leaders is equated with the establishment of foreign alliances (2:14–19), but it is quite possible that this is a subsequent interpretation by the editors of the collection.

Jeremiah 2:4–13 is a prophetic address with some of the characteristics of a prophetic lawsuit. Except for the introductory summons (v. 4) and the messenger formulas (vv. 5, 9, 12), the entire speech is attributed to Yahweh, who speaks directly to the "house of Jacob" and "all the families of the house of Israel" (v. 4). This latter identification is unusual in Jeremiah. It could refer to the Northern Kingdom; but in view of the references to the history of the Lord's saving acts, it more likely is the traditional title for the people as a whole.

Following the call to hear, the accusations are set into motion by a rhetorical question (v. 5), establishing an argumentative tone. In the first part of the speech (vv. 5–8), Yahweh argues that the ancestors turned away from him to "worthless things" (v. 5). On the other hand, Yahweh had brought Israel out of Egypt, led them in the terrifying wilderness, and brought them into "a plentiful land" and fed them (v. 7). By contrast, the people had failed to approach their Lord in prayer or inquiry ("Where is the LORD?" v. 6) and had defiled the land (v. 7). The accusations are addressed most concretely against groups of responsible leaders: priests did not formally inquire of the Lord; those responsible for the law—perhaps a particular class of priests of scribes—did not know the Lord; the rulers sinned against the Lord; and the prophets "prophesied by Baal, and went after things that do not profit," that is, false gods (v. 8).

At this point in the typical prophetic address, we would expect a turn from accusation or indictment to announcement of punishment, and the "Therefore" of verse 9 would mark that turn. Instead, the accusations of past sins become the foundation for further accusations, this time of contemporary apostasy. Jeremiah has Yahweh inviting the people to look at other nations and see if anything so incredible has ever happened—that a people changed its gods, "even though they are no gods" (v. 11). Then comes the heart of the accusation: Israel has traded its glory (its God) for "something that does not profit" (false gods). The point is reiterated metaphorically as a twofold accusation: Israel has forsaken the Lord, "the fountain of living water," and dug out for themselves cisterns "that can hold no water" (v. 13). It is a powerful contrast between an undying spring and a leaking pit that can at best collect rainwater.

The fundamental issue of this unit is the fidelity of the people—and even more directly of their leaders—to Yahweh alone. On this point, Jeremiah, like Deuteronomy, sees no room for compromise. It has not come to the point of monotheism, explicitly arguing that there is only one God, although the alternatives to Yahweh are considered "no gods" (v. 11). Nor is the issue posed mainly in terms of propositional theology, or orthodoxy. Rather, the issues at stake are religious practice: Whom will you worship, to whom will you turn in prayer, and in whose name will you prophesy? The passage could be viewed as an application of the First Commandment: "I am the LORD your God, who brought you out of the land of Egypt, out of the house of slavery; you shall have no other gods before me" (Exod. 20:2–3).

Psalm 81:1, 10–16

Psalm 81 was a frequently used psalm in worship during the Second Temple period. Seven psalms were selected for singing in the temple during the course of a week. These were Psalm 24 (Sunday), 48 (Monday), 82 (Tuesday), 94 (Wednesday), 81 (Thursday), 93 (Friday), and 92 (Saturday). Thus this psalm was used throughout the year. Its choice for such usage was probably based on the psalm's call for obedience.

Psalm 81 has frequently been interpreted as a prophetic liturgy used in worship to remind the people of the necessity to obey the law or even as part of a covenant renewal ceremony. In such an analysis, verses 1–3 call for the assembly to offer praise and worship to God; verses 4–5b provide the reasons for worship; and verses 5c–16 contain the prophetic sermon spoken as a direct address of the Deity to the people, as was common in prophetic speech.

Verse 3 connects the psalm's original usage with a festival or feast day. The new moon was the first day of the month in a lunar calendar. The full moon, or the fifteenth day of the month, is here stipulated as the feast day. The soundings of the trumpets to mark the first day of the seventh month is commanded by Leviticus 23:23–25. This is the day that was and still is celebrated as Rosh Hashanah, or New Year's day. (The term actually means "the head of the year.")

The fifteenth day of the month marked the beginning of the Feast of Tabernacles, or Booths (Succoth), which lasted for seven days (Lev. 23:33–36).

One of the features associated with the Feast of Tabernacles, according to the legislation in Deuteronomy, was the reading of the Book of Deuteronomy. According to Deuteronomy 31:10–13 (RSV), Moses commanded, "At the end of every seven years, at the set time of the year of release, at the feast of booths, when all Israel comes to appear before the LORD your God at the place which he will choose, you shall read this law before all Israel in their hearing." Psalm 81 may be seen as part of the admonition to observe the law that formed a part of the great autumn feast.

The opening verses of this psalm call for various forms of praise: singing, shouting, and the playing of various musical instruments. (See 2 Sam. 6:12–19 for some of the celebration that went on at festival times.) The rabbis noted that verse 1 refers to the God of Jacob, and they questioned why none of the other patriarchs are mentioned. The answer they arrived at was in terms of Balaam's statement in Numbers 23:21. "Why did Balaam choose to mention Jacob—not Abraham and not Isaac—only Jacob? Because Balaam saw that out of Abraham had come base metal—Ishmael and all the children of Keturah; and he also saw that out of Isaac there had come Esau and his princes. But Jacob was all holiness" (*Midrash on the Psalms*).

The motivation for celebrating the festival is given in verses 4–5; namely, God commanded it and established it as a statute, ordinance, and decree.

The divine oracle consists of two types of material: reviews of the past (vv. 6–7, 10a, 11–12) and admonitions to obedience (vv. 8–9, 10b, 13–16). The reviews of the past, on the one hand, stress the redemptive action of Yahweh by emphasizing the deliverance from Egypt and the testing in the wilderness. On the other hand, the reviews highlight the people's unfaithfulness to which God responded by giving them over to their stubborn hearts and allowing them to follow their own counsels (v. 12: a good sermon topic!). The admonitions call upon Israel to hear, to listen, to have no other gods (see Exod. 20:3; Deut. 5:7), to be receptive to divine blessings—all with the promise that such responses will be rewarded abundantly.

Sirach 10:12–18

Because readings from the Book of Sirach, also called Ecclesiasticus, appear so infrequently in the lectionary, some introductory remarks concerning the work may be useful at this point. The name of the book, The Wisdom of Jesus ben Sirach, or simply Sirach, indicates the author. Jesus ben Sirach was a Jewish scribe and teacher who conducted a school in Jerusalem in the second century BC. He wrote the book that bears his name ca. 180 BC, during the Hellenistic period and before military conflict had broken out between the Maccabees and the Seleucids. The book was written both to pass on the teacher's wisdom to later generations and to present the Jewish faith as reasonable in a Greek context. The author wrote in Hebrew; but except for some fragments found among the Dead Sea Scrolls, no copies in the original language exist. The book has come down to us through the Christian canon, primarily because it was translated into Greek (ca. 132 BC in Alexandria) by the author's grandson (see the Prologue).

The Book of Ecclesiasticus and its author stand near the end of a long tradition that reaches back at least to the time of Solomon. The work is wisdom literature, the type of material that was either created or collected by Israel's "sages," teachers, and scribes. Such literature includes collections of individual sayings and proverbs (as in Proverbs 10–30), collections of poems (as in Proverbs 1–9), and longer compositions (such as Job, Ecclesiastes, and The Wisdom of Solomon). The Book of Sirach is a composition; but although material is arranged topically, its overall plan is difficult to discern.

The thought of wisdom literature is distinctive in the Old Testament in its reliance on understanding-based experience and traditions of such experience. It is practical, prudent, often occupied with the best advice for success in the world, and tends to support the status quo. Nonetheless, like the prophetic tradition, it is concerned with justice; and like the priestly perspective, it respects the law and worship. In later wisdom literature, the perceived tension between revelation and rational understanding is resolved through the affirmation that "the fear of the Lord [that is, genuine piety] is the beginning of knowledge" (Prov. 1:7; see Sirach 1:11–20), and the recognition that wisdom is a divine attribute and divine gift to human beings. A persistent assumption of the wisdom literature, visible also in the passage before us, is the view that there is a direct relationship between righteousness and rewards, unrighteousness and punishment.

Generally speaking, the first section of Sirach (1:1–10:3) concerns wisdom and wisdom's ways. Our reading comes near the beginning of the second large section (10:4–18:29) that deals with human life under and in relationship to divine providence. The particular focus in the immediate context (10:4–18) is human pride as sinful. Human pride, however, is considered in the context of fundamental convictions about divine authority: "The government of the earth is in the hand of the Lord. . . . Human success is in the hand of the Lord" (10:4–5). On the other hand, human life is fleeting: "How can dust and ashes be proud?" (10:9); even "the king of today will die tomorrow" (10:10).

So our lesson concerning human pride begins with assertions and definitions. The "beginning," or the essence, of pride "is to forsake the Lord" (v. 12). Pride is equated with sin that leads to further abominations and then to divine punishment (v. 13). Verses 14–17 present the works of divine providence as arguments against human pride. In effect, through historical events the Lord humbles humanity. The Lord overthrows powerful rulers and "enthrones the lowly in their place" (v. 14), plucks up nations and "plants the humble in their place" (v. 15). The Lord destroys nations and even "erases the memory of them from the earth" (vv. 16–17), showing that even national fame is fleeting. The discourse concludes with a negative assertion about the source of the sin of human pride: "Pride was not created [better, "intended"] for human beings" (v. 18). That is, human pride, and the violence it engenders, was not part of the divine intention for humanity. Rather, pride is rebellion against that very intention. Those who look at history will know that human beings have no justification for standing proudly in the face of God.

Proverbs 25:6–7

With the exception of the concluding poem on the ideal wife, Proverbs 10–31 is a large collection of short wisdom sayings. There is little systematic organization in the collection, although some sayings are grouped according to content and others according to form or simply linked by catchwords. Most are quite brief, consisting of a single two-part sentence.

There is no way of determining the date and authorship of the individual sayings. The attribution of the book as a whole and of the collection in Proverbs 10:1–22:16 is based on the tradition of Solomon's legendary wisdom. The final form of the book is relatively late, reflecting the literary activity of the wisdom teachers such as ben Sirach (Sirach 51:23). But in the collections, old and newer sayings stand side by side. Some of the forms of the proverbs and doubtless many of the individual sayings come from folk wisdom, but others would have been composed as the teachers and sages reflected on the meaning of life and sought the most apt and memorable way of expressing their conclusions.

The sayings come in various forms and styles, and serve different ends. They are different from the formal instructions, such as the ones in Proverbs 1–9. Some simply draw a conclusion from experience and state it as a general truth. The purpose is to make sense of reality, especially of human relationships in society. Others express a value judgment about some aspect of experience and indicate directions for conduct: "Whoever loves pleasure will suffer want; whoever loves wine and oil will not be rich" (Prov. 21:17). Typical themes of such sayings are the differences between wisdom and foolishness, the values of hard work, and the merits of prudent behavior. Still other sayings go a step further and give explicit directions for conduct in the form of commands, prohibitions, exhortations, or admonitions: "Do not rob the poor because they are poor, or crush the afflicted at the gate" (Prov. 22:22). Although they are similar to the Old Testament laws, their force is different because their authority rests not upon divine revelation but on the persuasiveness of the directions themselves.

The saying in Proverbs 25:6–7 presents instructions directly and expresses value judgments ("it is better . . ."). The two verses comprise a single long sentence. The first half (v. 6) states the admonition in a twofold manner, but there is a single point: Do not put yourself in the higher or more honorable position. The reference to "the king's presence" and to "the place of the great" indicates the awareness of distinctions of class and political power, and reflects the concerns of the royal court. The second half of the sentence gives the reason for following the advice of the first half: "It is better to be told, 'Come up here,' than to be put lower in the presence of a noble." That is, if you elevate yourself above your position, you risk the embarrassment of being put in your place, and in public. Another reason is implied: If you show proper deference, you might then be raised to a higher position.

Fundamentally, this saying concerns deference and knowing one's place among the powerful more than it concerns genuine humility. Like many other verses in the Book of Proverbs, it gives advice to the ambitious about how to succeed, particularly in a governmental bureaucracy. The advice may be good, if one's goal is to avoid embarrassment and to advance in the bureaucracy. But are those goals worthy of the biblical faith at its best?

These two verses from the Book of Proverbs doubtless have been selected to function as commentary on the Gospel lesson for the day, with the saying of Jesus, "For all who exalt themselves will be humbled, and those who humble themselves will be exalted" (Luke 14:11). This Old Testament lesson is useful commentary in so far as it points out the danger of misusing the Gospel lesson. The reading from Luke concerns humility. It is not to be turned into advice about how to be exalted.

Psalm 112

This psalm consists of human-to-human address that seeks to instruct and offer advice about the art of living. This text is an alphabetic psalm having twenty-two lines (omitting the opening, "Praise the Lord"), each beginning with a successive letter of the alphabet.

The symmetry and order of the psalm, reflected in its alphabetic structure, are also characteristic of its thought. It assumes a morally oriented and governed world in which the righteous and blessed enjoy well-being and in which the wicked (noted only in v. 10) receive the opposite.

Verses 2–3 promise great and elevated status to those who delight in God's commandments. They will possess status in life as well as wealth and riches in their houses.

In the central section of the psalm, the righteous (see v. 1) are described. Three characteristics of the righteous are expounded. (Verse 4 is difficult to translate. It could read: "He [the righteous] rises in darkness like a light for the upright ones, gracious, merciful, and righteous.")

1. The righteous deals equitably and generously, lending money and giving to the poor (vv. 5, 9). In ancient Israel, it was forbidden to charge interest on a loan to one's countryman. This prohibition against lending money at interest is found in all sections of the Hebrew Scriptures (Exod. 22:25; Lev. 25:35–38; Ps. 15:5; Ezek. 18:8). One should not make a profit by trafficking on the misery of others' problems. At the same time, goodness is relational; it is what one does to and with others.

2. The righteous life can withstand adversity and can confront existence with serenity (vv. 6–8). The righteous is not shaken (not a reed blown back and forth by every wind), can withstand evil tidings or bad news, is stronghearted and firmly planted, unafraid. Constancy in life is the principle advocated and the personality trait being praised.

3. The righteous are remembered (v. 6b). Not only the person but the acts of righteousness are lasting. Verse 9b can be translated "an act of charity endures for ever," because the word for righteousness also meant charity.

Hebrews 13:1–8, 15–16

In this final reading from the Epistle to the Hebrews, we have a set of concluding admonitions. This miscellany of Christian advice, which actually extends through verse 21, reminds us of similar lists of exhortations we find at the end of other New Testament letters (cf. 1 Thess. 5:12–22; also 1 Cor. 16:13–14; 2 Cor. 13:11–13; Gal. 6:1–10; Phil. 4:4–13; Col. 4:1–6). The recommendations here follow no set order, nor do they explore a common theme. Rather, they move from one topic to another. Let us consider them in turn.

Love for fellow Christians (vv. 1–3). The first call is for "mutual love" (*philadelphia*, v. 1), sharply stated in REB: "Never cease to love your fellow-Christians." Earlier, the readers are urged to cultivate a genuine sense of community among themselves (10:24). This was a regular concern within early Christian communities (cf. Rom. 12:10; 1 Thess. 4:9; 1 Pet. 1:22; 2 Pet. 1:7). At times, it was advice that was especially needed, for Christian communities sometimes found themselves threatened by internal strife ranging from minor disputes (Phil. 4:2; also 2:1–4, 14–15; 1 Cor. 1:10–11) to more searing dissensions (2 Cor. 10–13; 1 John 4:20–21; also 1 John 4:7–12). These various bits of encouragement at least reflect a sober realism among New Testament writers. They knew only too well the sheer difficulty of living together in community and did not naively assume that Christians would automatically love one another.

Concretely, love for fellow Christians meant extending hospitality to strangers, most likely to fellow Christian travelers (Rom. 12:13; 1 Pet. 4:9). As an incentive, we are reminded of those Old Testament instances where Yahweh appeared in the form of strangers (Genesis 18–19; Judg. 6:11–24; 13:3–23; Tobit 5:4–6:1). Such display of concern for strangers was important enough to become a criterion for leadership in the churches (1 Tim. 3:2; Titus 1:8), as well as for determining who could be assisted financially by the churches (1 Tim. 5:10). It was more than simply accommodating passersby, but specifically had to do with hosting itinerant Christian preachers, teachers, and other faithful workers (Matt. 10:11–15; Luke 10:1–12; Acts 17:5–9; 21:4, 7, 16–17; Rom. 15:28–29; 16:1–2; 1 Cor. 16:10–11; Phil. 2:29; Philemon 22; 3 John 5–8, 10). Even though the practice could be abused (2 John 10; Didache 11–12), it was nevertheless expected that traveling Christian teachers would be well received by other Christians.

Another way of showing love was to visit fellow Christians imprisoned, or ill-treated in other ways, for the sake of the gospel (10:34; 11:36). Doing so is to take seriously the teaching of Christ (Matt. 25:31–46) and to exhibit genuine empathy (1 Cor. 12:26).

Marriage and sexual morality (v. 4). Even though Jesus was celibate, he taught a high view of marriage informed by the biblical account of creation (Matt. 19:3–9; Gen. 1:27; 2:24). This view was sustained in the early church in spite of ascetic tendencies that placed severe strains on marriages (1 Corinthians 7). So well regarded was marriage that it could become an analogy for the relationship between Christ and the church (Eph. 5:21–33). Fidelity to marriage vows excluded fornication and adultery, and our text takes a typical hard line against violators (cf. 1 Cor. 6:9–10; Gal. 5:20–21; Rev. 21:8; 22:15).

Contentment and reliance on God's care (vv. 5–6). We are instructed not to "live for money" (v. 5, REB). Being locked into the love for money is recognized in the New Testament as one of the cardinal vices (1 Tim. 6:10) and serves to disqualify one from a position of leadership (1 Tim. 3:3). The seduction of riches and their debilitating effects become a major theme in Luke-Acts (cf. Luke 12:13–21). To counteract the compulsive desire to acquire possessions and find our sense of security in them, today's text calls for a sense of contentment grounded in reliance on God's fidelity (Phil. 4:12; 1 Tim. 6:8). It is the God who faithfully promised to care for Israel (Gen. 28:15; Deut. 31:6; Josh. 1:5) and to whom the psalmist confidently looked for sustenance (Ps. 118:6; 27:1–3) on whom Christians rely for life and sustenance (Matt. 6:25–34; Rom. 8:31–39).

Loyal respect for Christian leaders (v. 7). Early Christian communities appear to have been organized in a manner similar to Jewish communities, where there were duly appointed or selected leaders to oversee various aspects of community life (cf. Acts 11:30; 14:23; 15:2–3; 20:17; 21:18). These included a body of presbyters, who at the earliest stages were also designated as bishops, and their role of oversight appears to have been limited to single congregations of believers (cf. Acts 14:23; 20:17–38; Phil. 1:1; 1 Tim. 3:1–7; Titus 1:5–9). Other leadership roles also emerged as some became deacons and deaconesses (Acts 6:1–7; Rom. 16:1; Phil. 1:1; 1 Tim. 3:8–13). Whether today's text is in reference to enlisting respect (and obedience, 11:17) for duly-appointed elders is not clear, for this terminology is absent. The leaders who are to be remembered, respected, and imitated are those who "spoke the word of God," thus who have been teachers (cf. Acts 4:29, 31; 8:25; 11:19; 13:46; 14:25; 16:6, 32; Phil. 1:14). Elders had the responsibility to teach (Acts 20:28; 1 Tim. 3:2; 5:17; Titus 1:9) and may very well be in view here. But this just as easily may be a call to respect those whose leadership has been proven through their teaching and service (cf. 1 Cor. 16:15–18; also Luke 22:26). Whoever they are, their manner of life is expected to be exemplary as a model for imitation (6:12; cf. 1 Cor. 4:16; 11:1; Gal. 4:12; Eph. 5:1; Phil. 3:17; 4:9; 1 Thess. 1:6; 2:14; 2 Thess. 3:7, 9).

Reliability of Christ (v. 8). Even though the first part of today's lection ends with this bold declaration of Christ's immutability, the context suggests that it actually belongs with what follows (vv. 9–11). Nevertheless, even in its detached form it provides a strong concluding note for this lection. Reminiscent of an opening motif of the letter (1:12; cf. 7:24), this reassuring claim attributes to Christ what Israel had predicated of God—One who is the same through the ages, unaffected by time (Ps. 102:27).

Responding to God in worship and sacrificial giving (vv. 15–16). In the concluding section of today's lection, we are urged to offer continual "sacrifice of praise to God" and to do so through Christ (cf. Lev. 7:11–18; also Pss. 50:14, 23; 107:22). What is being called for here, of course, are continual prayers of praise.

But along with these "sacrificial offerings" of prayer, we are also reminded that doing good and sharing what we have are also "sacrifices . . . pleasing to God" (v. 16). With this explicit call to generosity, our passage returns to the opening theme of mutual love and showing hospitality to strangers. It is an apt reminder that Christian faith finally reaches fruition when the heart that believes opens itself generously to the needs of others.

Luke 14:1, 7–14

Verse 1 provides the setting for Luke's material through verse 24. "Table talk" was a fairly common literary device for gathering into one place several independent units. In verses 1–24 there are four stories that do not depend on one another for their meaning: verses 1–6, 7–11, 12–14, 15–24. Even if Luke is here using a literary device for joining pieces of tradition, this is not to say the setting of a meal was an unimportant detail for him. On the contrary, meals were of profound theological significance for Luke. Bread was important; in fact, where some eat and some do not eat, the kingdom is not present (16:19–31). Breaking bread was important; in fact, the real test of whether the church included persons who were different was not at the point of baptizing them but of eating with them (Acts 11:1–3). Fellowship meals were central in the church's life together; in fact, the risen Lord "had been made known to them in the breaking of the bread" (24:35). Let no one think, then, that Luke's locating many of Jesus' teachings "at table" was only "a nice little touch."

Both verses 7–11 and 12–14 concern self-seeking, in the one case as guest, in the other as host. Upon observing the scramble for places of honor, Jesus advised choosing the lowest place, far removed from the head table. In so doing, one avoids public embarrassment and may, on occasion, be called up to a higher place, providing one a moment in the spotlight of public admiration. In and of itself, this is of no religious significance but rather is sound practical advice on social behavior. However, Luke says Jesus spoke it as a parable (v. 7), meaning that Jesus is not simply discussing etiquette. That Jesus has in mind kingdom behavior is made explicit in the closing statement: "For all who exalt themselves will be humbled, and those who humble themselves will be exalted" (v. 11). This pronouncement occurs frequently in the Gospels (Matt. 18:4; 23:12; Luke 18:14).

In dealing with this and similar teachings of Jesus, the preacher will be alert to the devious ways in which the ego can convert Jesus' words into a new strategy for self-exaltation. Modesty can be exaggerated, and humility can be a form of pride. It would be too bad if this teaching generated a mad rush for the lowest seats, with the competitors all the while glancing toward the head table, waiting to be called up.

Verses 12–14 address the host, and again Jesus is not giving lessons on social graces. The point is, hosting can be a way of making others feel they are in your debt, so they in turn will reciprocate when preparing their guest lists. The cycle of seeking a return on one's behavior toward others repeats itself, for common sense dictates that self-interest not offer self or goods to persons who cannot repay. In the kingdom, however, God is always host, and we extend God's invitation to those who cannot repay. After all, who can repay God? Jesus, therefore, is calling for behavior that lives out this conviction about the kingdom; that is, inviting to table (quite different from sending food to) those who have neither property nor place in society. Luke's fourfold list (the poor, the maimed, the lame, and the blind; v. 13) is repeated in the next story (beyond our lection). In that passage containing the parable of the banquet (vv. 15–24), these people from the fringes are guests at the banquet, replacing those who failed to attend because they had other things to do. From the Song of Mary (1:46–55) to the end of his Gospel, Luke is careful to remind us that these, too, are kingdom people.

Proper 18 [23]
(Sunday between September 4 and 10 inclusive)

Jeremiah 18:1–11;
Psalm 139:1–6, 13–18; or
Deuteronomy 30:15–20;
Psalm 1;
Philemon 1–21;
Luke 14:25–33

In the Old Testament text from the *Common Lectionary*, the message of the Lord to Jeremiah at the potter's house sets out the alternatives for Israel; obedience and salvation or disobedience and judgment. The selections from Psalm 139 respond by reminding us of God's intimate knowledge of us.

The alternatives of life and death also serve as the axes on which the Old Testament text from Deuteronomy 30 is constructed. Similar clarity of choice between being righteous and wicked is presented by Psalm 1 in its well-known depiction of the two ways.

Paul's brief but moving letter to Philemon, which exposes the tensions created when social relationships are redefined by the demands of the gospel, serves as the epistolary reading for today.

In the cluster of Jesus' sayings collected by Luke in today's Gospel text, the cost of discipleship and the need to calculate that cost thoughtfully are addressed.

Jeremiah 18:1–11

The prophet Jeremiah was active in the seventh century BC, from about 627 BC until the second capture of Jerusalem by the Babylonians in 587 BC. (For further historical background, see the commentary on Jeremiah 2:4–13 for Proper 17 in this volume.) The prophet would have witnessed the deuteronomic religious reform under King Josiah and the last decades of Judah's history before the Exile. Jeremiah was deeply involved in the political affairs of the time, and more than once found himself in trouble with the authorities.

The Book of Jeremiah is a long and complicated one, containing materials of diverse sorts and origins. There are prophetic addresses in poetry, prose speeches, narratives about the prophet, and Jeremiah's complaints, very similar to the psalms of individual complaint. There are announcements of judgment on Judah and on foreign nations, announcements of salvation, and more or less sermonic speeches calling for obedience to the law or repentance. We know already from the story of Jeremiah and Baruch (Jeremiah 36) that the prophet did not write the book, but that it originated as a collection of his speeches dictated to the scribe. Close reading has shown that the book continued to grow long after Jeremiah's time. Much of it was edited—and significant portions added—by deuteronomic writers during the Babylonian exile. Deuteronomic editing may be present in the text for day, especially in verses 7–12.

This report of Jeremiah's revelation in the potter's house is paired in the context with the account of a symbolic action concerning pottery (Jer. 19:1–13). It begins with an introduction that refers to the prophet in the third person. Jeremiah hears the Lord's command to go to the potter's house (v. 2), and he obeys, observing the potter at the wheel reworking a "spoiled" vessel into another one (vv. 3–4). Then he reports, in the first person, the word that the Lord revealed to him. Everything that follows (vv. 6–12) is a divine speech to the prophet, which he would have been expected to transmit to the people.

In terms of both style and contents, there are three parts to the speech. First (v. 6) there is the direct application of the analogy of the potter and the clay to the relationship of Yahweh to the house of Israel. The application is in the form of a rhetorical question, and its point is the Yahweh can do as he will with Israel. Various aspects of the metaphor may be central: the Lord's power, Israel's frustration of the Lord's design, the Lord's judgment, or Yahweh's will to make something worthwhile of the people. The second part of the address (vv. 7–10) sets out a series of alternatives, conditions that will determine the way Yahweh acts in the future—not just toward Israel but toward any nation. The emphasis here is on Yahweh's capacity to "repent" of evil (v. 10, RSV; NRSV has "change my mind") if a people turns from its evil ways, or of good if a nation is disobedient. The third part (vv. 11–12) applies these possibilities directly to Judah and Jerusalem, warning of evil and calling for repentance.

Thus, in its present form the metaphor of the potter and the clay stresses repentance, both divine and human. God, who can shape a people as God wishes, wills to be affected by how they behave toward God. If the analogy itself suggests omnipotence, the remainder of the passage underscores God's responsiveness to human actions and makes human beings fully accountable for what happens to them.

Psalm 139:1–6, 13–18

This psalm appears to be a composition produced for use in legal procedures in the temple when an individual was charged, perhaps falsely, with some particular wrong or crime. In Psalm 139, the wrong appears to be some form of idolatry or turning away from Yahweh, the God of Israel. This is suggested by three factors: (1) there is no indication in the psalm of charges about injury or wrong done to humans; (2) the "wicked way" (v. 24), or, in some readings of the Hebrew text, "idolatrous way," suggests apostasy or false worship as the problem; and (3) the plea for action by God in verses 19–24, especially verses 19–22, focuses attention on those who defy God, lift themselves up against God, and hate God, which demonstrates the concern for the proper relationship to the Deity as the focus of the psalm.

The psalm is best understood as the lament of one who feels unduly and falsely accused of infidelity to God. Verses 1–18 speak about the Deity's knowledge of the worshiper, whereas verses 19–24 are a call for God to judge and slay the wicked. Thus the latter verses would have functioned as one's self-curse if the person praying them fit the category of those upon whom the judgment is requested. At the same time, verses 21–22 are also an affirmation of the worshiper's innocence. The worshiper can claim to hate, with a perfect (or utter) hatred, those who hate God. Although such an expression may shock our sophisticated sensibilities, it was a way of expressing devotion to God, championing the divine cause, and placing oneself squarely in God's camp. Under these circumstances, such extravagance in terminology would have been expected in ancient cultures.

Verses 1–8 all speak or confess the knowledge that God has of the human/individual situation. (Note that the entire psalm is human speech to the Divine, that is, prayer.) Verses 1–6 describe the *insight* God has into the life of the individual. Verses 7–12 describe the divine *oversight* that God has of the individual life. Verses 13–18 speak of the divine *foresight* that God has over the person from conception to death. In a way, all these sections seek to say the same thing by approaching the matter from different perspectives or slightly different angles. The reason for such extensive coverage of the topic of God's knowledge of the individual is that the supplicant in the legal case was claiming innocence, and one way to do this was to point to the omniscience of God. Had anything been amiss, were there any infidelity, then the Deity would surely have known and taken action.

The insight that God is said to have into the person in verses 1–5 is expressed in a number of ways, mostly in the form of opposites: sitting down—rising up (inactive—active); inward thoughts—from afar; my path (where I go, my walking)—my lying down (where I rest, my reclining); behind—before. All these are ways of saying that persons in the totality of their behavior are known to God. Even the thought, before it finds expression on the tongue in words, is known (v. 4). The knowledge of God, the psalmist confesses, is a fathomless mystery (v. 6).

Verses 7–12 affirm that there is no escaping the Deity, whose presence (Spirit) knows no limit and who is not subject to the normal conditions of existence. A number of geographical metaphors, again in opposites, are employed to illustrate the point: heaven—Sheol; winds of the morning (to the east)—uttermost parts of the sea (to the western horizon). In all these places, the psalmist says he or she would find God (see Amos 9:2) or be found by God. The psalm, however, not only affirms the all-pervasive knowledge and oversight of God, but also the universal sustaining quality of the Divine—"Your hand shall lead me, and your right hand shall hold me fast" (v. 10).

For the Divine, according to the psalmist, normal conditions do not prevail. Verse 11 makes this point, a point best expressed in the new NJPSV which, following medieval Jewish exegetes, translates: "If I say, 'Surely darkness will conceal me, night will provide me with cover'"; then darkness does not conceal, because for God light and darkness do not determine or set limits regarding knowledge.

Verses 13–18 affirm that from conception until life's end "all things" are known by God. Verse 16 expresses a rather strong note of predestination. The psalmist claims that one's life was known by God like a book even before the first day was lived; at least, the length of one's life was already determined and recorded by God!

Deuteronomy 30:15–20

This passage is itself a powerful sermon, and appropriately so, for both in terms of its location in the book and its substance it is a summary statement of the message of the Book of Deuteronomy. It contains the final words of a lengthy speech attributed to Moses on the plains of Moab (Deut. 29:1–30:20), introduced as "the words of the covenant that the LORD commanded Moses to make with the Israelites" (29:1). Immediately following our reading the narrative resumes, leading finally to the report of the death of Moses. In substance, these six verses state the major points of the book: obedience to the law, establishment of the covenant, the conditions for life in the promised land, and responsibility laid upon the hearts of the people.

Opinions vary considerably concerning the antiquity of this paragraph. As it now stands, it has been incorporated into the edition of the book prepared by the Deuteronomistic Historian who wrote the account of Israel's past from the time of Moses to the Babylonian Exile (Deuteronomy through 2 Kings). When that work was written about 560 BC, Israel no longer lived in the land, so words such as these provided interpretation of the disaster of the Exile and guidance for a future return. But the lines are characteristic in every respect of the heart of the Book of Deuteronomy, from the seventh century BC, before the Exile, but still centuries after the time of Moses. In that context, the words were addressed to a people who had experienced the fulfillment of the promise of the land. Moreover, there are elements of the most ancient covenant tradition itself, going back to Israel's earliest days. Centuries of use and reinterpretation underscore the grave importance of the matters addressed in this text.

The context of the passage is the conclusion of the covenant between Yahweh and Israel. The reference to "heaven and earth" (v. 19) as witnesses reflects the background of this covenant in the ancient Near Eastern treaty tradition, in which the gods were called upon to witness the agreement and its stipulations, and to verify violations. This covenantal context means that the speech is addressed to the people of Israel, that the focus of attention is corporate, not only for the sake of the present group, but also the community that extends through time (v. 19).

Obedience to the law is a matter of life and death. That is the central point of the address. In language that is repetitious and hortatory, this point is urged upon the audience, laid upon the hearts of the hearers. The law is not perceived as a burden but as a gift, for it leads to life, the good life that the Lord wants for his people. "Life" means the long and abundant life in the good land; "life" parallels well-being or "prosperity," and "death" parallels "adversity" or misfortune (v. 15).

"Statutes" (or "decrees") and "ordinances" are used together in Deuteronomy to signify the law as a whole, the stipulations of the covenant (Deut. 4:1; 5:31; 6:1; etc.). One should not be misled by the repeated reference to such requirements in the plural, for although there are many laws, they all rest upon and amount to one prohibition and one commandment. That one prohibition is not "to bow down to other gods and serve them" (v. 17). During the centuries when the Book of Deuteronomy was being developed, the prospect of serving gods other than Yahweh was not an abstract or vague possibility, but a concrete and practical temptation. In the land there were the deities of the Canaanites; in Babylon there were the gods of the dominant culture, including the heavenly powers (cf. Deut. 4:19). We may appropriately see this issue as the conflict between faith and culture. To what extent can one acknowledge the authority of the forces that the culture considers as "gods" or make use of the culture's symbols of faith? Deuteronomy is clear: Do not bow down to them at all.

The single commandment on which all the individual laws rest is the positive side of the prohibition: Love the Lord your God, and cleave to him (v. 20). This love is parallel to that of a child for a parent; it entails respect and obedience (Deut. 6:5; 8:5). It amounts to devotion to a single God (Josh. 22:5; 23:6–8). How can one command an attitude, a feeling? It can only come in response to God's love for the people (Deut. 7:7, 13; cf. Hos. 11:1ff.), expressed in the history of election and salvation.

If there is but one requirement, with a negative and a positive side, then why are there so many statutes and ordinances and laws? Ancient Israel knew, as we do, that in practice the meaning and application of that loyalty to God are complex. Precisely what does it mean to avoid the worship of other gods and to love God in various circumstances? The multitude of laws and their frequent reinterpretation through time testify to the understanding that those who intend to obey the command to love only one God must work at learning and applying the meaning of that love. The rabbinical tradition developed a practical criterion for applying the law that stems from the theology of this passage. The law leads to life. If one interprets the law and finds that it leads to death, then that interpretation is wrong.

Psalm 1

This psalm was discussed earlier as one of the lections for the Sixth Sunday in Epiphany.

Philemon 1–21

Of all the Pauline Letters, this brief note to Philemon most resembles the personal letters preserved among the papyri from the ancient world. The circumstances that occasioned the letter are well known. Onesimus, the runaway slave of Philemon, had made his way to the city where Paul was imprisoned, probably Rome (vv. 1, 9–10, 13, 23). There he had become a Christian through the direct influence of Paul. As the one who had become his spiritual father (v. 10), Paul assumed responsibility for his welfare and considered it in his best interest to return him to his master Philemon, a resident of Colossae (Col. 4:9). What we have here is a letter of recommendation where Paul appeals to Philemon to receive back his runaway slave "no longer as a slave but more than a slave, a beloved brother" (v. 16).

Even in its brief form, the letter follows the same basic structure as other Pauline Letters: greeting (vv. 1–3), a prayer of thanksgiving (vv. 4–7), the appeal (vv. 8–22), closing greetings (vv. 23–24), benediction (v. 25).

The portrait of Philemon that emerges within the letter is especially revealing. We are told that the church met in his house (v. 2). This level of hospitality distinguished a select group of early Christians (cf. Acts 16:15, 34, 40; 17:6–7; 18:1–11; Rom. 16:5; 1 Cor. 16:19; Col. 4:15). It is also a probable indication of his high social position. Not only did he make his home available for the service of the gospel, but he followed suit with his own life, for he is described in intimate, yet highly respectful, terms as a "dear friend and co-worker" (v. 1).

The extent and quality of his service is also reflected in the prayer of thanksgiving (vv. 4–7), which is unusual compared with other Pauline thanksgivings in that it is couched in the second person singular and is thus addressed directly to Philemon. We are told of his faith in the Lord and love for the saints (v. 5; cf. Col. 1:4; Eph. 1:15; also 1 Cor. 13:13), as well as the joy and encouragement he has brought to Paul (v. 7). He has been a source of refreshment to the saints (v. 7).

In view of the fact that Paul will later ask Philemon a favor, we are not surprised at this laudatory tone. But it need not be interpreted purely as a strategic move to enlist Philemon's favor. The overall tone actually suggests that Philemon is a benefactor of the church. Between the lines we should perhaps see references to his generosity in behalf of the church. If so, his "love for all the saints" (v. 5), the joy and encouragement he has brought Paul (v. 7), and the refreshment he has given the saints (v. 7) may be softly couched expressions for the money he has given to the church. Accordingly, Paul's prayer that the sharing of his faith (v. 6), or "the sharing of your faith," may be a prayer for his continued financial support in making possible the promotion of the knowledge of the gospel. (Note *koinonia*, or "fellowship," in reference to financial contributions in Acts 2:42; Rom. 15:26; 2 Cor. 8:4; 9:13.)

It is conceivable, then, that Philemon has also been a financial supporter of Paul (v. 7), to the point that Paul can consider him a "partner" (*koinonos*) in the gospel (v. 17; cf. Phil. 1:5). There is also the intriguing, cryptic remark in verse 19 that Philemon is indebted to Paul for his "own self." Paul might have been responsible for saving Philemon's life, but more likely it suggests that, like Onesimus, Philemon had been converted by Paul.

What emerges from the letter is the portrait of a well-to-do Christian, a convert of Paul, who has given both himself and his property in the service of the church. Because of Philemon's generous temperament, Paul seems confident that he will accept Onesimus back and thinks it unnecessary to pull rank in making this appeal (vv. 8, 14). His appeal is made to love for love's sake (v. 9). The special appeal that Onesimus be received as a Christian brother (v. 16) also reflects a mood of confidence (v. 21). Even though he would return as a slave, it is to a relationship that has begun to be transformed by the gospel (cf. 1 Tim. 6:2; 1 Cor. 7:22).

An equally informative portrait of Onesimus emerges from the letter. As a young convert, he has endeared himself through his service so that Paul can refer to him as "my own heart" (v. 12). Elsewhere, he is called "faithful and beloved brother" (Col. 4:9). We should also note the well-known pun in verse 11: at one time useless (*achreston*) but now useful (*euchreston*). Here too we have a picture of someone setting out on the road of Christian service, urged on by the encouragement and support of Paul, his father in the gospel, and Philemon, now his brother in the gospel.

As we have seen, one homiletical possibility is to do a character study of Philemon, supplemented perhaps by the portrait of Onesimus. On another level, the letter raises the question of equality in Christ (Gal. 3:26–28; 1 Cor. 12:13) and how this was addressed by Paul and the early church. Although it is a debated question, the letter is not an appeal for Philemon to set Onesimus free, but rather to accept him back as a slave, albeit one who is now a Christian brother. Whether this was Paul's standard practice will depend on how one interprets the controversial phrase in 1 Corinthians 7:21. The preacher will need to consider how the gospel even in the first century began to call into question oppressive social practices, and the way Paul's letter to Philemon is related to this.

Luke 14:25–33

Luke provides a transition from the semiprivate conversation of Jesus in 14:1–24 to Jesus' reentry into the public arena. Verse 25 tells us two things about the teachings that follow: they are addressed to the crowds, and they will be in response to the hearers' enthusiastically joining the company of Jesus and his disciples. Jesus speaks here to those who come to him (v. 26), not to those called out from the crowd to join him. In other words, we have a repeat of the situation in 9:57, where a volunteer comes to Jesus saying, "I will follow you wherever you go." It is important to read what follows as Jesus responding to the enthusiasm of those who seem unaware that he is moving toward the cross and that his disciples are not exempt from their leader's burden.

The structure of our text is as follows: verse 25 is transitional and introductory; verses 26–27 state the demands of discipleship, paralleled in Matthew 10:37–38 as part of the charge to those being sent out; verses 28–32 contain twin parables; and verse 33 repeats in digest verses 26–27. In fact, the unit is built on a refrain: "whoever does not . . . cannot be my disciple" (v. 26), repeated in verse 27, and after the parables repeated again in verse 33. The negative form of this refrain expresses the caution and warning to the hasty volunteers who may be caught up in the movement toward Jerusalem as though it were a march or a parade. To persons already cautious, Jesus has already spoken his word: drop everything and come immediately (9:59–62).

The repeated call to cross bearing (v. 27; earlier at 9:23; Mark 8:34–35) is here joined to the unusual demand that one hate one's family and even one's own life (v. 26). The key to understanding this teaching is the word "hate." It is a Semitic way of expressing detachment, turning away from. It is not the emotion-filled word we experience in the scream, "I hate you." Were that the case, verse 26 alone would shatter all the calls to love, to understand, to forgive, to care for others, especially one's own family (1 Tim. 5:8), found throughout both Testaments. Hating one's own life is not a call to self-loathing, to throw one's body across the doorway and beg the world to trample on it as though it were a doormat. Paul labeled as value-less such "self-imposed piety, humility, and severe treatment of the body" (Col. 2:23). Rather, what Jesus is calling for is that those who follow him understand that loyalty to him can and will create tensions within the self and between oneself and those one loves; and in such a conflict of loyalties, he requires primary allegiance.

The two parables that follow (vv. 28–32) say, in effect, "Now sit down and decide if that price is more than you will pay." The first parable is drawn from rural life and the building of a tower in the vineyard from which to watch for destructive animals and thieves. The second is from the royal capital where decisions of war, peace, and compromise are made. But with peasant or king, the same fear of embarrassment should create caution. No one should take on more than can or will be carried through to completion. The questions are two: Do I have the resources? and, Will I commit them fully to this purpose? For prospective disciples, the willingness to make full commitment *is* the one needed resource. Without that, all other resources are insufficient.

Proper 19 [24]
(Sunday between September 11 and 17 inclusive)

Jeremiah 4:11–12, 22–28;
Psalm 14; or
Exodus 32:7–14;
Psalm 51:1–10;
1 Timothy 1:12–17;
Luke 15:1–10

Sobering words of judgment are heard in today's text from Jeremiah in the *Common Lectionary*, with its vivid depiction of the devastation, chaos, and gloom that result from invading armies. An equally gloomy view of humankind is also presented in Psalm 14, although it holds out hope for the poor and oppressed.

In the alternate Old Testament text from Exodus 32, God's rage against Israel's decision to build the golden calf is successfully met by Moses' plea in their behalf. Psalm 51, a sinner's powerful plea for mercy, serves as the psalm of response.

In the epistolary reading from 1 Timothy, the first of a cycle of semicontinuous readings from First and Second Timothy over the next six weeks, we hear Paul reminiscing about the mistakes of his past and his experience of divine mercy.

The Lucan parables of the lost sheep and the lost coin—both emphasizing the rejoicing that occurs when sinners repent—serve as today's Gospel text.

Jeremiah 4:11–12, 22–28

The Old Testament lesson for today consists of selections from a distinct section of the Book of Jeremiah (4:5–6:30) in which the prophet accuses Judah and Jerusalem of sins against the Lord and announces judgment upon them. This larger unit was shaped by the editors of the book who selected and organized originally independent addresses of the prophet. Both the theme and the tone of the composition are established in 4:5–8: An enemy from the north (v. 6) is about to attack and devastate Jerusalem (Zion) and Judah; moreover, that enemy is the instrument of the "fierce anger" (v. 8) of the Lord. The verses assigned for today are surrounded by prophecies of judgment (4:5–8, 13–18, 27–31; 5:1–31; 6:1–12).

Although it is generally agreed that most of these lines originated with Jeremiah, it is virtually impossible to determine the historical horizon in which they were uttered. Although the historical events of the time of Jeremiah are relatively well known, it is difficult to connect individual prophetic sayings with those events. The verses include historical allusions, but they are vague and could refer to a number of different events. The identity of the enemy from the north is particularly uncertain. These addresses may come from very early in the prophet's career, but most likely they stem from the time just before the first capture of Jerusalem by Nebuchadnezzar in 597 BC. In the present composition, the edited speeches seem to address the situation before the second siege of Jerusalem and its total destruction in 587 BC, and in that context the enemy from the north is seen to be Babylon.

Jeremiah 4:11–12 contains the opening formula for a prophetic address ("At that time it will be said . . ."), the statement of the theme of the address ("a hot wind . . . a wind too strong . . ."), and the prophet's affirmation that he will announce judgment. Although some of the speeches in the Book of Jeremiah are admonitions and warnings, what follows this introduction clearly is not a warning or summons to repent. The hot wind from the desert will not "winnow or cleanse," but bring disaster. Thus the burden of Jeremiah's words is to set that judgment into motion and to give the reasons for it in terms of the people's sins.

In verse 22 the prophet articulates the reasons for the coming judgment with a sweeping accusation that the people of Jerusalem and Judah are "foolish"; they are "stupid children." This is similar to Isaiah's indictment of those same people:

> I reared children and brought them up,
>   but they have rebelled against me. . . .
> but Israel does not know,
>   my people do not understand." (Isa. 1:2–3)

According to Jeremiah, the people do not know what is good for them because they "do not know how to do good" (v. 22). This reference to knowledge recalls Hosea's frequent use of such language: There is "no knowledge of God in the land" (Hos. 4:1). Knowledge can refer to cognition, knowing the stipulations of the covenant. It can also mean acknowledgement, that is, acting in obedience to the Lord. It can also, particularly in Hosea, refer to that deep relationship between Lord and people expressed metaphorically as carnal knowledge.

This broad indictment is followed (vv. 23–26) by a dramatic and powerful vision of devastation. In describing what he has seen, Jeremiah announces what is to come. The imagery is almost, but not quite, apocalyptic in its scope and recalls both the Priestly (Gen. 1:1–2:4a) and the Yahwistic (Gen. 2:4b–25) accounts of creation. The drama is heightened by the four-fold repetition of "I looked" at the beginning of each scene. The first two scenes (vv. 23–24) concern inanimate aspects of the world: the earth, the heavens, the mountains, and the hills. The earth and heavens are seen to have returned to their conditions before creation, for the earth is "waste and void" and the heavens have "no light." The mountains and hills are seen to be in a state of perpetual earthquake. The third and fourth scenes (vv. 25–26) concern all forms of life. No one lives on this arid, dark, and shaking earth; even the birds of the air have disappeared. Moreover, the cultivated and fruitful land has become a desert, and where there were cities there is a wasteland of ruins. To this point the prophet has simply described his horrible vision of destruction, but he concludes by naming the cause of this transformation. All this has been—will be—caused by the Lord exercising his fierce anger (v. 26).

Our reading concludes (vv. 27–28) with an explicit announcement of judgment, introduced with a prophetic messenger formula ("For thus says the LORD . . ."). The land (probably Judah) will be a desolation, the earth will mourn (see Hos. 4:3), and the heavens will be darkened. The judgment will not be total, for the Lord "will not make a full end," but because the Lord has set this judgment into motion he will not turn back.

Whether it was uttered early in Jeremiah's career or as late as the second siege of Jerusalem by the Babylonians, the prophet's announcement of judgment turned out to be correct. Judah and Jerusalem were indeed destroyed. More relevant for our own situation in the modern world, the Book of Jeremiah offers lessons about the continuing use of prophetic indictments and announcements of judgment. On the one hand, they may serve as warnings. The crimes and sins and stupidity of the people of God led to disaster. Beware lest it happen again. On the other hand, such prophetic words, uttered in worship, can function as confession of sin. In hearing the prophet's indictment of the ancient people of Judah and Jerusalem, we may find ways to acknowledge or own sins, our failure to be the people of God.

Psalm 14

A few psalms or portions of psalms appear more than once in the Old Testament. For example, Psalm 18 also appears as 2 Samuel 22. Psalm 14 recurs as Psalm 53, although with a few minor alterations, the most obvious being the use of the divine name Yahweh in Psalm 14 and the use of Elohim in Psalm 53. We really have no explanation as to why some material was repeated in such similar form other than the fact that, for some reason, it fitted well in two places. So far as the psalms are concerned, however, we have little more than conjecture to go on in explaining why any of them appear in the order they do.

Psalm 14 is clearly a lamenting or complaining psalm that protests about the widespread prevalence of evil in the world. Most of the lament psalms in the Psalter are true prayers; that is, they are addressed to the Deity about some particular trouble or general condition, and they request the Deity to rectify matters. Psalm 14, however, has no verses addressed directly to God; the Deity is spoken of throughout in the third person. Thus the psalm is not a prayer. It would be interesting to know how this psalm was used in worship. Who is speaking? the king? the high priest? an ordinary worshiper? someone who has been mistreated by the wicked?

The psalm has something of a didactic, or teaching, flavor about it. There is a descriptive, reflective quality about it, with its pessimistic depiction of the human situation. This descriptive character is further expanded in some copies of the ancient Greek version of the Old Testament, which adds the following between verses 3 and 4:

> Their throat is an open sepulcher:
>   with their tongues they have used deceit;
> the poison of asps is under their lips,
>   whose mouth is full of cursing and bitterness;
> their feet are swift to shed blood:
>   destruction and misery are in their ways;
> and the way of peace they have not known:
>   there is no fear of God before their eyes.

This insertion is paralleled by Romans 3:10–18. Perhaps Paul copied this from the Greek or the Greek translator of the psalms, or a later copyist incorporated the material from Paul's letter.

If we take this psalm as a "homily" on the wicked, what does it say? (1) Verses 2–3 imply that all humans are corrupt, all are bad, all are perverse. No one does what is right. The two expressions "are wise" and "seek after God" are to be understood as synonymous. Thus the psalmist places everyone under a blanket condemnation. (2) The basic human problem as seen by the psalmist seems to be practical atheism, the assumption in the heart that "there is no God" or that God does not care or take human actions into account (v. 1). Such a position makes the person into the sole authority of what is acceptable or permissible. For the author, such behavior was corrupt, resulting in abominable deeds, in failure to do the good. (3) Real knowledge of the way things are should lead one to do the good and worship God (v. 4). Because of this lack of knowledge, people live without respect for one another, consuming one another with the casualness with which one would eat bread. There is wrongdoing; but even worse, there is no guilt or remorse. (4) In spite of all appearances to the contrary, God is still in control and is a refuge to the poor and the oppressed (vv. 5–6). The "poor" and the "righteous" are those opposed by the powerful. (Here the writer denies the absoluteness of the claim that all humans are bad that was expounded in v. 2.) (5) The final two verses are an expression of hopeful eschatology: someday the human condition will be as it should be.

Exodus 32:7–14

This passage must be understood in the context of the covenant between Yahweh and Israel. Hardly had the people agreed to bind themselves in covenant before they violated one of its most fundamental stipulations. Murmuring and complaining about needs both real and imagined were one thing, but the rebellion reported in the story of the golden calf is quite another matter, rupturing the covenant relationship and threatening the life of the community. This account of the making and worshiping of the golden calf is the initial part of a coherent unit of material that includes Exodus 32–34, and leads finally to the renewal of the covenant.

Our assigned reading contains two distinct units of narrative, each one of them dominated by dialogue between the main parties. The reading is preceded by Exodus 32:1–6, which reports a dialogue between the people of Israel and Aaron. While Moses is on Mt. Sinai receiving the revelation of the law, the people become impatient and resentful of their leader's absence, so they demand that Aaron "make gods for us, who shall go before us" (v. 1). Without visible resistance, Aaron calls for all the gold earrings and fashions them into a golden calf, declaring it to be the "gods" (!) who brought Israel out of Egypt (v. 4). When the people worship the image, he builds an altar and proclaims a festival.

In the first unit of our reading (vv. 7–10), the scene shifts to the mountain, and a dialogue between Yahweh and Moses begins with a lengthy divine speech. The Lord tells Moses to go down immediately, for "*your* people, whom *you* brought up out of the land of Egypt, have acted perversely" (v. 7, emphasis added). He then informs Moses of the people's actions and declares his intention to let his wrath "burn hot against them" and destroy them (v. 10).

The second unit (vv. 11–14) consists primarily of Moses' response to the Lord. It is a prayer of intercession on behalf of the rebellious people. Moses pleads the case for forgiveness by pointing out that the Egyptians would consider Yahweh's intentions evil from the outset, and he reminds the Lord of the promise made to the ancestors to multiply their descendants and give them the land of Canaan. The passage concludes with the report that the Lord "changed his mind about the disaster that he planned to bring to his people" (v. 14, or "repented of the evil which he thought to do," RSV).

If one reads no further in chapter 32 than verse 14, the tensions in the story as a whole would not be obvious. When Moses returns down the mountain to the people, he hears the sound of the festival and apparently is surprised to learn firsthand what Yahweh had already told him in verses 7–10. He initiates punishment, having the Levites kill three thousand men, and then tells the people that he will go up to the Lord and attempt to make atonement on their behalf. When he pleads for forgiveness, the Lord assures Moses that his angel will lead the people to the promised land, but the Lord will punish the guilty parties. He does so by sending a plague. The themes of the sin and Moses' intercession continue into the next two chapters. These various perspectives on the events indicate that although there is thematic unity, the section has been composed of more than one source or tradition. The basic story line comes from one of the older Pentateuchal sources, most likely the Yahwist. Verses 7–14 almost certainly are a later deuteronomic addition to the story.

The story of the golden calf probably has been influenced by the memory of the events reported in 1 Kings 12:25–33. When Jeroboam rebelled after the death of Solomon and established the Northern Kingdom, he set up golden calves in Bethel and Dan, saying, "Here are your gods, O Israel, who brought you up out of the land of Egypt" (v. 28; cf. Exod. 32:4). In the deuteronomic tradition of the seventh century and following, if not earlier, one of the functions of the story of the golden calf in the wilderness was as polemic against a concrete problem, the corruption of worship in the Northern Kingdom.

Three important themes for theological and homiletical reflection emerge from this lesson.

The first, the sin of the people, is the one that has received the most attention in the history of Christian interpretation of the text. Note, above all, that in Stephen's speech in Acts, those sinful people are accepted as "our ancestors" (Acts 7:38). Specifically, the making and worship of the golden calf violated the Second Commandment, but in doing so it violated the first one as well. What was the calf, or what did it represent? In Exodus 32:1 the people seem to ask for a replacement for Moses, but in verse 4 the calf clearly is identified with Yahweh. In the Canaanite culture surrounding Israel, the calf must be related to the bull that symbolizes the god Baal. Aaron as religious leader responds to a religious need with a religious solution: a cult object, an altar, and a festival. But especially according to the deuteronomic tradition, less religious activity is better than more of questionable form. Even if people should construct an image only to make their worship of Yahweh more concrete, there is the danger that they will confuse the symbol with the reality that is beyond all symbols. Thus our narrator holds the people up to ridicule for their actions.

And what of the role of Aaron in this affair? At best, his character is weak, for he gives the people what they ask for. It is a wonder that he is not among those punished by death. Compare the report of his construction of the idol in verse 4 with his own explanation in verse 24: "I threw it [the gold] into the fire, and out came this calf!"

The second theme concerns the role of Moses as mediator. He stands between the people and God, and communicates in both directions. His immediate response to the Lord's report of the people's sin and the threat of punishment is to intercede. Although there is no threat to him (v. 11b), he identifies with the people, the same ones who have grumbled about his leadership so many times. As he pleads and argues, he neither offers excuses for the people nor insists that they deserve forgiveness. Rather, he appeals to the faithfulness and mercy of God.

The third theme, the capacity and willingness of God to repent, is noted only briefly, but it runs like a thread through the entire story. It is the foundation for the prayer of intercession and the factor that makes a renewal of the covenant possible. Even as the Lord is announcing his decision to destroy the people, he is leaving room for change by indirectly inviting Moses to interfere (v. 10).

Psalm 51:1–10

This psalm was discussed earlier as one of the lections for Ash Wednesday.

1 Timothy 1:12–17

With today's epistolary text, we begin the semicontinuous reading of the Epistles of First and Second Timothy that extends through the next six Sundays. As a way of introducing these lessons, we provide here some general remarks about the Pastoral Epistles.

These two letters, along with Titus, have been designated "Pastoral Epistles" because of the explicit attention they give to the pastoral care of churches. Even though they are attributed to Paul, their Pauline authorship is widely disputed; consequently, they are generally regarded as pseudonymous letters. Among the reasons for questioning their Pauline authorship is the difference in vocabulary and style reflected in the letters. A number of terms and phrases prominent in the undisputed Pauline Letters are absent here, and a number of terms and phrases absent in the undisputed Pauline Letters are present here.

It has also been noted that the Pastorals demonstrate a different set of concerns. Not only is the mood of the letters different, but the agenda is different as well. There is a more prominent interest in institutional questions, such as the protocol for worship (1 Tim. 2:1–15), the characteristics and responsibilities of church leaders (1 Tim. 3:1–13; 5:22), instructions for ministers (1 Tim. 4:1–16; 6:11–16; 2 Tim. 2:1–3, 20–26; 3:1–17; 4:1–5), and practical concern for administering to the needs of persons (1 Tim. 5:3–16). Also prominent is the attention given to heretical teaching (1 Tim. 4:1–16; 6:3–10; 2 Tim. 1:13–18; 2:16–19) and the corresponding emphasis on preserving the soundness of the apostolic faith.

What all this suggests is that these letters stem from a period when the church is moving from a more fluid form of organization to a more highly structured, institutional form of organization. These are also the kinds of instructions one would expect after the death of someone as prominent and influential as Paul. Here we see the concern to continue the Pauline legacy and to maintain fidelity to Pauline traditions; these letters clearly stand within the Pauline trajectory (2 Tim. 1:3–14). Their viewpoint is one of praise for Paul, and there is a consistent interest in perpetuating a favorable memory of Paul. Most likely, what we have in these letters are some genuine Pauline reminiscences that have been preserved among his disciples and have been written, codified, and applied to their own situation.

In today's epistolary text, we have a Pauline prayer of thanksgiving. It echoes many themes found in the undisputed letters, although there are some new motifs as well.

Paul's apostolic commission (v. 12). To be entrusted with the gospel qualified Paul as a steward in the true sense (1 Cor. 4:1), and consequently he gives instructions to his churches as one who was found trustworthy (1 Cor. 7:25). The source of his strength lay with the risen Lord (Phil. 4:13; 2 Cor. 12:8–10; 2 Tim. 4:17; cf. John 15:5), whom he encountered in the Damascus road experience (Acts 9:15; Rom. 9:21–24; Gal. 1:16; Rom. 1:5).

Paul's former life (v. 13). One of the firm historical features of the Pauline portrait is his conduct prior to his apostolic call. It is attested in both his own writings and the later account of Acts (Gal. 1:13; 1 Cor. 15:9; Phil. 3:6; Acts 8:3; 9:1, 21; 22:4, 19; 26:10–11). Here, the insistence is that he acted in ignorant unbelief (cf. Acts 3:17; 13:27; 17:30; Luke 23:34). The confession that he is the "foremost of sinners" (v. 15) strikes a new note, for he does not speak in such starkly remorseful terms in his undisputed letters. Instead, he prefers the less implicating phrase "the least of the apostles" (1 Cor. 15:9–10). Moreover, his conscience appears to remain quite robust when he recalls his previous conduct (cf. Phil. 3:3–11).

Paul's experience of grace (vv. 14 and 16). By his own account, his apostolic commission was a gift of grace (1 Cor. 15:9–10). the Christ-event could hardly be described in terms other than grace overflowing (Rom. 5:20). In today's text, this comes to be embodied in a "sure saying" (v. 15), a phrase unique to the Pastorals (1 Tim. 3:1; 4:9; 2 Tim. 2:11; Titus 3:8). Its content is perhaps the remnant of a liturgical confession and is thoroughly christological: "Christ Jesus came into the world to save sinners" (cf. Matt. 9:13; Luke 15:2; 19:10; John 3:17; 1 John 4:7).

Paul as an exemplar (v. 16). Here Paul is presented as an instance of the patience of Christ and is held up as an example for others seeking eternal life (2 Tim. 1:13; cf. 2 Thess. 3:7). In the Pastorals, Paul's conduct becomes exemplary (2 Tim. 3:10–11).

The doxology (v. 17). The prayer concludes by offering praise to God as the King of the Ages (Tobit 13:7, 11–12; Ps. 145:8–13), immortal (Rom. 1:23), invisible (Col. 1:15; Heb. 11:27; John 1:18; 5:37; 6:46; 14:9; 1 John 4:12), one (2:5; 6:15; 1 Cor. 8:4–6; John 5:44; cf. 2 Kings 19:15, 19; Isa. 37:20).

Luke 15:1–10

Now that we are halfway through the "ordinary time" between Pentecost and Advent, peculiar advantages to continuous readings through a Gospel become evident to both preacher and listener. The structure, movement, and special accents of a given writer come more clearly into focus. Less and less time is needed to call attention to the structure of a particular lection because patterns have begun to emerge. Such is the case with Luke 15:1–10.

Today's Gospel reading consists of three parts: (1) an introduction (vv. 1–3); (2) a parable (vv. 4–7); (3) a second parable (vv. 8–10). These two parables are the first two of three (vv. 11–32). Offering materials in triplets is fairly common in Luke (9:57–62; 11:42–52; 14:18–20; 20:10–12). The second and third parables are peculiar to Luke, but the first has a parallel in Matthew (18:12–14), even though the differences between Luke and Matthew are significant, as we will see. The two parables in our reading say essentially the same thing, a case of repetition apparently for emphasis. We find such doubling of stories elsewhere at 5:36–39 and 14:28–32.

The introduction (vv. 1–3) provides the setting and the transition to Jesus' response to that situation. Jesus is attracting tax collectors (collaborators with the Roman government in collecting revenue from their own people) and sinners (not simply a moral description but a term for religious and hence social outcasts). Pharisees and scribes murmur: "This fellow welcomes sinners and eats with them" (v. 2). The situation is not an unfamiliar one in the Gospels (Mark 2:15–16; Matt. 9:10–11; Luke 5:29–30). The word translated "welcomes" could actually mean that Jesus is hosting these persons and is not simply present with them at someone else's dinner. But regardless of who is the host, the issue is table fellowship, which demonstrates how fully Jesus welcomes and accepts sinners. Breaking bread together was the act of full embrace and a critical matter for both Jesus and the early church. Earlier (7:31–35) Luke had pinpointed as the key issue in the rejection of John the Baptist and Jesus the table practices of the two men. John ate no bread and drank no wine; that is, he had table fellowship with no one. Jesus, on the other hand, ate and drank, for which he was labeled "a glutton and a drunkard, a friend of tax collectors and sinners" (v. 34). The dinner table was central to that culture.

Before moving to Jesus' response in the two parables, we may well caution ourselves about making broad and hasty judgments against the Pharisees. Their position reflects a warning firmly fixed in the Old Testament (Prov. 1:15; Psalm 1; Isa. 52:11) about associating with evil persons, a warning Paul found useful in dealing with moral issues in the Corinthian church (2 Cor. 6:14–18). In addition, their stance concerning fellowship with sinners has been taken by most parents who do not want their teenagers to be unduly influenced in wrong directions. It is easy enough to sit at a safe distance and cheer on Jesus as he welcomes sinners and socializes with them; it is not so easy to be his disciple in the matter. The point is, the Pharisees stand in a reasonable and long-respected position; Jesus' behavior is radical and disturbing. The church that calls him Lord still finds it so.

The parables of the lost sheep and the lost coin (vv. 4–10) are identical in structure, the second serving to reinforce the first. Matthew tells the parable of the sheep but does so in a context of instructions to disciples about responsibility toward fellow disciples, especially new ones, who may stumble or go astray (18:1–14). The sheep is not lost in Matthew but "has gone astray" and is restored to the fold (vv. 12–13). In Luke the sheep is lost; that is, it represents the sinner (v. 7), such as can be found in Jesus' presence. So strong is the love for the lost sheep that the ninety-nine are left in the wilderness while the lost one is being sought. Such love takes risks in order to find the lost, which would not have been the case if the ninety-nine lay safely sheltered in a fold, as one old gospel song has it. Of course, the sheep and the coin do not repent or return; the precise application of that theme awaits the third parable (vv. 11–32). What is central in these two as well as in the third is the joy of finding, a joy so abundant that it calls on others to share in it. Such is heaven's joy at the coming of sinners, and Jesus calls upon his critics to join him and heaven in celebrating the presence of tax collectors and sinners. That joy, expressed in the next parable as a party for the prodigal, is not only the heart of the gospel, but also its offense. After all, does not forgiveness look very much like condoning when viewed from a distance?

Proper 20 [25]
(Sunday between September 18 and 24 inclusive)

Jeremiah 8:18–9:1;
Psalm 79:1–9; or
Amos 8:4–7;
Psalm 113;
1 Timothy 2:1–7;
Luke 16:1–13

In today's Old Testament reading from the *Common Lectionary*, we hear the mournful cries of Jeremiah as he grieves over the people of Israel. Jerusalem in ruins, defiled by foreign armies, prompts the prayer for help in Psalm 79, where the psalmist implores God for some merciful response.

In the other lectionaries, the Old Testament text from Amos is a loud protest against practices that oppress the poor. Quite fittingly, Psalm 113 offers praise to God, who exalts the poor and needy and answers the prayers of barren women.

Universal concern sets the framework for the summons to prayer found in today's Epistle lesson from 1 Timothy, which urges us to pray for everyone, especially political leaders.

The shrewd businessman whom the tradition has labeled the "dishonest steward" is the focal character in today's Gospel reading, a story reflecting Luke's distinctive interest in the responsible use of possessions.

Jeremiah 8:18–9:1

More than any other prophetic book, Jeremiah abounds in personal and emotional poetry in which the prophet expresses his agony over the fate of the people and over his own vocation. Most of this poetry is in the form of individual complaints, often called the laments of Jeremiah (see 11:18–23; 12:1–6; 15:10–21; 17:14–18; 18:18–23; 20:7–13; 20:14–18). These poems are very similar to the individual complaint psalms in that the prophet expresses himself vigorously to God, complaining of his troubles and—either explicitly or implicitly—asking for divine help. The lesson before us today is not such a complaint, but it is similar in tone. It is not a prayer, nor is it a prophetic address. Rather, it is like a soliloquy in which Jeremiah expresses his own deep and personal distress over the fate of the people.

Although the historical horizon of these lines cannot be determined, their literary context is clear and important to the interpretation of the passage. Although it may have originated independent of that context, this poem is presented as the prophet's reaction to the immediately preceding prophecy of judgment in 8:16–17. In those verses Yahweh is heard to announce disaster upon the whole land and the city, that is, upon Judah and Jerusalem. Because of the poetic language, the precise form of this disaster has been a matter of dispute among commentators. Verse 16 seems to envision the coming of an enemy army into the land through the northernmost tribal territory of Dan. The "horses" and "stallions" would be pulling war chariots. In verse 17 the Lord promises to let snakes loose among the people, "adders that cannot be charmed, and they shall bite you. . . ." Although it is possible that this announcement is to be read literally, given its connection with verse 16, it is more likely that it is to be understood metaphorically. The snakes that cannot be charmed are the enemy from the north, whose advance cannot be stopped.

In Jeremiah 8:18–9:1 the prophet reacts to the impending disaster, a disaster that he himself would have announced. Although he quotes the words of Yahweh as well as the words of the people, the unit is framed as the prophet's address to no one in particular. The poem is framed at the beginning and the end by Jeremiah's direct expressions of grief. In verse 18 the prophet simply affirms that his joy has been replaced with grief and his "heart is sick." The preceding announcement of judgment and the subsequent lines make it clear that the source of this distress is both the impending disaster and the sins of the people that have brought that judgment in the first place. In the concluding verse of the poem (9:1) we hear the prophet wishing that his head were a spring and his eyes a fountain so that he could weep without ceasing for the people. We are left to conclude that he has already literally cried his eyes dry with grief.

Between these two verses the reasons for Jeremiah's grief become plain. He quotes the people crying out for the Lord's help, but foolishly relying on the old tradition of Zion as Yahweh's home (v. 19a). The implication is that because this is so Jerusalem cannot be violated by its enemies. This prayer of the people is followed by the words of Yahweh (v. 19b). Whether this interruption by Yahweh is part of the original poem or a later addition that clarifies the poem's meaning, its point is the same: Yahweh is indeed in Zion, and he is provoked to wrath against the people because of their idols and foreign images. Then (v. 20) the people affirm, in proverbial language, that the time is up, and Jeremiah explains that his suffering and grief are because of "the hurt" of his people.

It is not clear whether the most famous lines in the poem (v. 22) are uttered by the prophet for himself or by the prophet on behalf of the Lord. The "balm in Gilead" would have been a salve to heal wounds. The verse implies that the people have not and will not take advantage of any way of correcting their ways that have led to their judgment.

The most important and distinctive note in this passage is the prophet's identification with and grief over the people whom he himself has condemned. One might hear some prophets—possibly Amos—announcing judgment without any remorse whatsoever. But that is not the case with Jeremiah. He knows that he is included among the condemned people. There will be no separation in which the sinners suffer and the righteous escape. Remarkably, these words that ring such personal and individual emotions are expressions of a corporate perspective, the deep conviction that the people of God stand or fall together.

Psalm 79:1–9

Like the companion text from Jeremiah, Psalm 79 is a lament over the destitute condition of Jerusalem and its people. The psalm contains a description of the distress and trouble (vv. 1–4), appeals for God to act in behalf of the community (vv. 5–12), and a vow to be thankful forever if redemption is granted (v. 13). The description of the distress becomes a bit clearer in the NJPSV:

> O God, heathens have entered Your domain,
>   defiled Your holy temple,
>   and turned Jerusalem into ruins.
> They have left Your servants' corpses
>   as food for the fowl of heaven,
>   and the flesh of Your faithful for the wild beasts.
> Their blood was shed like water around Jerusalem,
>   with none to bury them.
> We have become the butt of our neighbors,
>   the scorn and derision of those around us.

The description of the calamity indicates a major military defeat of the people that involved foreigners forcibly entering the temple precincts. Most interpreters understand this text to be a lament over the capture and destruction of Jerusalem by Nebuchadnezzar. The Babylonians twice captured the city of Jerusalem. The first time was on March 16, 597 BC, a date known from Babylonian sources and the only exact date we know for any event in pre-exilic Judean history. This war against Jerusalem and its capture are noted in 2 Kings 24:10–17. The second time Nebuchadnezzar captured Jerusalem (in 586 BC), the city and temple were looted and burned (see 2 Kings 25:1–21). Whether this psalm was written to lament one of these occasions or some other event cannot be determined absolutely.

The four conditions described in one lament proper are (1) heathens have entered the sacred temple precincts (v. 1a–b), (2) the city of Jerusalem has been laid waste (v. 1c), (3) citizens have been slaughtered, their bodies left unburied to be consumed by beasts and birds (vv. 2–3), and (4) Judeans and Jerusalemites have become the butt of jokes and have lost face among the nations of the world (v. 4). Even if one allows for poetic exaggeration, it is clear that Jerusalem has suffered a major catastrophe wrought by the hands of a foreign army.

Verse 5 indicates that the city's plight was understood as the consequence of Yahweh's wrath. God's anger and wrath against the people are seen as the ultimate cause of calamity rather than the political and military miscalculations of the people or the superior strength of the enemy.

The plea for help in verses 6–12 asks for deliverance and redemption for the city and simultaneously for punishment of the enemy as well as the quieting of the taunting neighboring states (a sevenfold revenge in v. 12!).

The prayer for help appeals to God's reputation—the name—so as to involve the Deity more intimately in the catastrophe (v. 9; note in v. 12 that it is God who is said to be taunted). If the Deity's people are oppressed, then the reputation of God is called into question.

The closest the community comes to acknowledging its guilt in producing the circumstances that brought defeat is in verse 8 where one finds reference to the "iniquities of our ancestors" ("our former iniquities"; so the NJPSV). Nonetheless, the community does not call for salvation based on its uprightness (see Ps. 44:17–22) but appeals to the compassion of God (v. 8b).

Amos 8:4–7

For a discussion of this passage, see the commentary on Amos 8:1–12 for Proper 11 [16] in this volume.

Psalm 113

This psalm is discussed as one of the lections for Visitation, May 31, Years A and B.

1 Timothy 2:1–7

Because this text also serves as the epistolary reading for Thanksgiving Day, Year B, the reader may want to consult our remarks in that connection.

As a part of instructions given concerning worship (2:1–15), these verses focus specifically on prayer. The emphasis, however, is different from other New Testament passages about prayer. The teachings of Jesus, for example, contained in the Sermon on the Mount, not only provide a model prayer but caution us not to pray merely as a form of visible piety (Matt. 6:5–15; Luke 18:10–14). To those less accustomed to religious prayer, he teaches the importance of simply asking, reassuring us that God does in fact answer our requests (Luke 11:1–13). Other passages urge frequency in prayer (Acts 2:42; Rom. 12:12; Eph. 6:18; Col. 4:2; 1 Thess. 5:17).

In today's text, there is a different emphasis. If there is a single theme running through our text, it is universality. The text opens by urging us to pray for everyone (v. 1). This is reinforced by the insistence that God's love is universal and that God wills the salvation of everyone (v. 3; cf. Rom. 11:32; Titus 2:11; 2 Pet. 3:9). In the early Christian creed embodied within our text, Christ's death is seen as a ransom offered for everyone (v. 6; cf. 2 Cor. 5:15; also Matt. 20:28; John 3:16). And finally, the passage ends with a reference to Paul's appointment as a preacher, teacher, and apostle to the Gentiles (v. 7; Acts 9:15; Rom. 1:5; 15:16; Gal. 1:16). His apostolic charge was to extend the good news to everyone (Rom. 1:16–17).

These are words well worth hearing, for it is all too easy for the church to turn in on itself. We can find ourselves praying only for people like ourselves, for those whom we know, even for those whom we love, like, or prefer. Our text challenges us to break through this ecclesiastical parochialism, as does Jesus' injunction "Love your enemies and pray for those who persecute you" (Matt. 5:44; cf. also Lev. 19:34; Rom. 12:14; Luke 23:34; Acts 7:60; 1 Pet. 3:9; Luke 6:35). This is difficult, of course, because our prayers tend to relate to what is close to us—our concerns, our friends, acquaintances, and loved ones, our spaces and places. But as localized as the love of God and the love of Christ are, as directly as they address us in our own needs, they are not confined to who we are and where we are. Neither should our prayers be nearsighted. This is one fundamental point of our text.

There are, of course, other themes as well. There is also a call for us to pray for leaders of government—"kings and all who are in high positions" (v. 2). It is a sentiment in keeping with other New Testament passages that call us to respect civil authorities (Rom. 13:1–7; Titus 3:1; 1 Pet. 2:13–17). A similar tradition of civil respect is also found in the Old Testament (Ezra 6:10; Bar. 1:10–11; Jer. 29:7). The motive here is stability. Peaceful government means peaceful living and being "free to practise our religion with dignity" (v. 2,

REB). Because those in such positions of authority would have been non-Christian, this too should be seen as an extension of the universal impulse of the passage, even though the motive is one of self-interest.

Perhaps we should note that the passage only calls for supplications to be made in behalf of ruling authorities. Unlike other passages (e.g., Rom. 13:1–7), it does not actually enjoin submission. This is a distinction worth making, because it would be naive to assume that Christians will always bow before kings and princes with no questions asked. Being prayerful for political leaders is one thing; being blindly submissive to them is quite another.

Apart from these instructions on prayer, we should also note the theological motifs. As noted earlier, embodied within our text is what appears to be an early Christian confession (vv. 5–6). Similar to other two-part confessions (e.g., 1 Cor. 8:4–6), this one mentions the one God (cf. Rom. 3:30; Eph. 4:5–6; Deut. 6:4–5), but primarily focuses on the redemptive work of Christ, our mediator with God (cf. Heb. 8:6; 9:15; 12:24; Gal. 3:19). Our passage is also unusual in its description of God as "Savior," although this is typical of the Pastorals (1:1; 4:10; Titus 1:3; 2:10; 3:4; cf. Jude 25).

Luke 16:1–13

Except for verses 16–18, the entirety of Luke 16 is devoted to teachings concerning possessions. As we have already seen (12:13–21, 32–34), this is a subject of primary concern to Luke, not only in his record of Jesus' teaching, but as early as the preaching of John the Baptist (3:10–14) and as late as the church subsequent to Jesus (Acts 2:43–6:7). The discussion in Luke 16 consists of two parts, verses 1–13 and 14–31, each part controlled by a parable, and each parable beginning, "There was a rich man" (vv. 1, 19). Both parables are found in Luke alone. In the first part, only verse 13 has a parallel elsewhere; Matthew places this saying in the Sermon on the Mount (6:24).

Vital to the interpretation of parables is the discerning of the limits of the parable itself; that is, exactly where does the parable begin and end? Obviously, such a task is primary when one is seeking to isolate a story as Jesus told it, but it is equally basic to discovering to what use or for what purpose a particular writer preserves the Jesus tradition. By knowing where the "quotation" from Jesus ends (and begins, although beginnings are usually clear), the interpreter then can recognize the comments on the story that are offered by the Gospel writer. These comments reveal how the Evangelist understands and uses Jesus' words. Parable scholars generally agree that the Evangelists do not usually insert comments within a parable but preserve it intact, placing their own interpretations before or after.

All of this is to bring into focus the primary difficulty faced by the preacher-interpreter of Luke 16:1–13: Where does the parable of the shrewd steward end, and what is Luke's point in telling it? That Luke has given us a parable with appended sayings is generally agreed, but there is no common judgment as to where one ends and the other begins. The beginning of verse 9, "And I tell you," seems clearly to be a saying of the Lord and, therefore, is offered by Luke as Jesus' own interpretation of the parable. If that is the case, then the parable means that disciples are to handle material things so as to secure heaven and the future, not here and now. Such instruction would be another way of stating what was said at 12:33: "Sell your possessions, and give alms. Make purses for yourselves that do not wear out, an unfailing treasure in heaven." The same idea is in Mark 10:21 and parallels. A strong case can be made, however, for ending the parable at verse 8a. Verse 8b seems clearly an interpretative generalization and not really a part of the parable. On the basis of this judgment, that verse 8b is a commentary on the story, what does the parable mean? Just as the master of the steward commended him for his shrewdness, so the children of light (1 Thess. 5:4–5) can learn something from the shrewd people of this age. And what is to be learned? Verse 9 answers that: handle possessions so as to gain, not lose, one's eternal habitation.

Given either of these reconstructions, it is evident that Luke has joined to this parable a string of sayings of Jesus concerning possessions that evidently existed in other contexts. When read in isolation, verse 8b is a self-contained thought, as is verse 9. Verse 10 is even more distant from the parable, having nothing to do with being shrewd or prudent in securing one's future, but rather arguing from the lesser to the greater, that one's behavior in small matters prophesies behavior in matters of major importance. Verses 11–12 follow generally the same line of thought, while verse 13 makes an abrupt shift from lesser-to-greater reasoning to an all-or-nothing pronouncement. Luke has done here what was done at 11:1–13. At that point the subject of prayer was introduced, and Luke joined to the topic a collection of Jesus' sayings on prayer. It is so here on the subject of possessions. The preacher obviously has some decisions to make in order to ensure that one sermon is preached, not many, and that the hearer is not overloaded by that sermon.

Two comments about the parable itself. First, that the steward was dishonest is unrelated to the story's focus, but the listeners will probably need some help in being assured that is the case. Second, as to how the steward managed the books to secure his future, two possibilities exist: (1) he subtracted his own commission as a way of reducing the bills, but in which case he would not have been dishonest; and (2) the debtors did not know he had been fired, thought the reductions were legitimate, and praised the owner, who in turn commended the steward. This latter description seems best to fit the story.

Proper 21 [26]
(Sunday between September 25 and October 1 inclusive)

Jeremiah 32:1–3a, 6–15;
Psalm 91:1–6, 14–16; or
Amos 6:1a, 4–7;
Psalm 146;
1 Timothy 6:6–19;
Luke 16:19–31

J eremiah's purchase of a field at Anathoth becomes a symbol of hope for Israel in the *Common Lectionary*'s Old Testament text for today. It concludes with God's assurance that "houses and fields and vineyards shall again be bought in this land." Psalm 91 responds by portraying God as faithful protector.

Those who pursue lives of ease and self-indulgence are targeted in Amos's well-known prophetic oracle, which serves as the Old Testament reading for today in other lectionary traditions. Placing full trust in Yahweh serves as the focal concern of Psalm 146.

The final reading from 1 Timothy, which serves as today's epistolary reading, urges us to set our hopes on God rather than the evanescent uncertainty of riches.

Contrasting images of wealthy self-indulgence and abject need are played out in today's Gospel lection, the Lucan story of the rich man and Lazarus, which has resonances with several of the other texts for today.

Jeremiah 32:1–3a, 6–15

J eremiah 32 marks a dramatic change in the message and ministry of the prophet. Up to this point in his career, his message had been an almost unrelenting announcement of judgment on Judah and Jerusalem. Now that his dire prophecies are on the verge of being fulfilled in the final siege and destruction of Jerusalem by the armies of Babylon, Jeremiah comes forth with an almost puzzling proclamation of good news. And it is not just puzzling to modern readers of the Book of Jeremiah. To judge by the prayer for insight that follows our lesson (32:16–25), Jeremiah himself questioned why God's word of judgment had become a word of hope.

The historical context of the words and events reported in these verses is both clear and significant. Verses 1–3a spell out that historical context both in terms of international events and the circumstances of the prophet Jeremiah, and there is no reason to doubt the accuracy of this report. The time is during the second and final siege of Jerusalem by Nebuchadrezzar, following Judah's revolt against Babylonian authority. The "tenth year of King Zedekiah," the "eighteenth year of Nebuchadrezzar," was 588 BC, not long before the fall of the city in 587 BC. Jeremiah is "confined in the court of the guard" (v. 2) connected to the king's palace, apparently because his persistent announcements of the city's fall and the king's exile (vv. 3–5) were considered by the authorities to be destroying the morale of the people.

What transpires at this time is an almost classic prophetic symbolic action, or sign act, but it is identified as "the word of the LORD" that came to Jeremiah (v. 6). Reports of such symbolic actions are common in the classical prophetic literature (Isa. 7:10–20; 8:1–4; Hos. 1:2–9; 3:1–5; Ezek. 4:1–17; 5:1–17) and may be either third person or first person accounts. Jeremiah 32:6–15 is a first person account. It includes the report of the divine instructions to perform a particular action (vv. 6–8), the report that the prophet did as told (vv. 9–14), and the interpretation of the meaning of the action (v. 15).

By means of the report and interpretation, a simple real estate transaction becomes a message from the Lord. During the siege, and possibly when pressure from the Babylonians had been relieved by the advance of the Egyptian army, Jeremiah, having been informed by the Lord what is about to happen, has a visitor. Hanamel, the son of his uncle Shallum (v. 7), comes to Jeremiah in the court of the guard and asks him to buy his "field that is at Anathoth in the land of Benjamin, for the right of possession and redemption is yours" (v. 8). Behind this allusion is the traditional view of land ownership in ancient Israel; namely, that it is to remain in the family (Lev. 25:25–31; cf. also Ruth 4), and when it is to be sold it is to be offered to the closest relative. Because we are not told why Hanamel wants to sell the field, that point must not be important to the prophet's message.

The details of the transaction are spelled out in meticulous and technical detail (vv. 9–14). These verses give us the clearest picture in the Hebrew Scriptures of such legal transfers (see also Genesis 23 and Ruth 4). Everything was done according to law and tradition. Jeremiah reports that he weighed out the purchase price (seventeen shekels of silver) and handed it over to his cousin, signed and sealed the deed, and had the process witnessed. Then, in the presence of Hanamel and the witnesses, Jeremiah turned over the deed of purchase to Baruch the scribe, instructing him to put the documents "in an earthenware jar, in order that they may last for a long time" (v. 14). The reference to two deeds, one sealed and one open, recalls the use of double documents in Mesopotamia, both containing the same terms and sealed, but one inside the other. But Jeremiah's documents would have been either papyrus or leather. Most likely there was actually only one piece of writing material with the contents written twice. One half would have been rolled up and sealed, leaving the other half open for public inspection. The sealed copy would ensure against altering the contract and could resolve any disputes.

Not only the introduction of the report as the "word of the Lord" but also the particular instructions to Baruch begin to indicate that this transaction is more than a simple purchase of property. That he is to place the deed in a jar so that it will last a long time might not be unusual, but in this context it takes on special significance. This word of the Lord concerns the events in the distant future. The interpretation in verse 15 discloses how Jeremiah's action is a message from God: "Houses and fields and vineyards shall again be bought in this land" (v. 15). This message is secure because the prophetic symbolic actions, like their words from the Lord, were understood not as dramatizations or as ways to make complex messages clear but as actions that set the future into motion.

As the later interpretations (32:16–44) of this message make plain, this symbolic announcement of salvation does not contradict Jeremiah's previous announcements of judgment. He does not share the wishful thinking of his fellow inhabitants of Jerusalem that the city would not fall nor the people be carried off into exile. He was convinced the end for the city was in sight, and it was. The message of the purchase of the field was good news for the more distant future. The Lord would indeed punish Judah and Jerusalem for their sins, but that would not be the end of the Lord's history with the Lord's people. After the Exile the Lord would bring them back and settle them on the land, and fields would again be bought and deeds signed and sealed and witnessed (32:44).

Psalm 91:1–6, 14–16

In some respects, this psalm is an enigma for scholars. In what context did it originate? Who is being spoken to and about in the psalm? A breakdown of the psalm may help answer these questions. Verses 1–8 seem to be a brief sermonette addressed to a "you" but spoken in reasonably general terms. The thrust of these verses is to assure the worshiper of divine care and preservation in the face of a forthcoming situation of grave danger. In verses 9–13, the address to the worshiper becomes a little more personal, a little more directly assuring. Reading these verses, one gets the feeling of a particular "you," an actual human person being spoken to. Verses 14–16 shift from human-human speech to divine-human speech. In God's address, in these verses, the "you" has become a "he" or "she"; the person earlier spoken to has become the person spoken about.

One way of interpreting this psalm is to see it as originally used in a worship service in which the king was the central figure (see Psalms 20–21). The king was perhaps facing the dangers of a forthcoming war. (If not about a king going to war, then perhaps the context was a situation in which an ordinary person was confronting a major but dangerous undertaking—a long journey, a dangerous job, military service. At any rate, the psalm was to launch one forth with confidence and chutzpah.)

The person offered assurance in the psalm is the righteous and faithful (v. 1; "O you who dwell in the shelter of the Most High and abide in the protection of Shaddai," NJPSV) and who trusts in the divine for protection (v. 2). The true worshiper is promised to be protected from any number of perils, some human and some demonic (vv. 3–6). If the imagery in verse 4 draws upon that of a mother bird protecting her young, then this verse presents a maternal protective image of the Deity.

The divine speech that finishes off the psalm uses language that is both calming and consoling. There is no longer reference to snakes, thousands dying on every hand, pestilence in the darkness, and "things that go 'bump' in the night." There is, however, the repetition of the casual relationship, as in verses 1–2 and 9: "Those who love me" (v. 14). These final verses are dominated by a focus on the Divine: in God's speech, the first person pronoun or suffix occurs twelve times in Hebrew. The divine "I" hovers over the sentiments of the psalm and is the source of the promises of protection.

Amos 6:1a, 4–7

This reading doubtless was selected because its themes are closely related to the Gospel lesson for the day. Both concern eating and drinking. More significantly, both presume and disapprove of economic class distinctions in their audiences. Luke reflects on the way masters relate to slaves, and Amos rails against the sins of the rich and powerful.

There is widespread agreement concerning the date and some of the circumstances of the prophet. The superscription (1:1) places Amos in the reigns of two kings, Uzziah of Judah (783–742 BC) and Jeroboam II of Israel (786–746 BC). References elsewhere in the book, especially Amos 7:9–10, are consistent with this date and also confirm that the prophet was a native of the south who came to the Northern Kingdom of Israel to proclaim the word of God.

Historical allusions in the book and the circumstances assumed by the prophet place him in the last decade or so of Jeroboam II, about 760 BC. The reigns of Jeroboam II and Uzziah were long and relatively peaceful. There had been no major threats from the major Near Eastern powers such as Egypt or Assyria, and that peace seems to have led to prosperity, at least for a few, and—according to Amos—at the expense of many. There seems to have been a breakdown in the old tribal and family systems of land ownership, and the emergence of a wealthy class at the top of the society. These themes are particularly important in the reading for today.

The central message of the prophet is straightforward and unequivocal: Because of their social injustice and religious arrogance, the Lord will punish the people of Israel with a total military disaster. That is the burden of virtually all the speeches attributed to the prophet.

Amos 6:1–7 contains two units that are similar in some respects but distinct in others, suggesting the possibility that they were originally independent oral addresses. The first unit (vv. 1–3) begins with the cry "Alas" (Hebrew *hoi*, traditionally translated "woe"), and most translations presume that the second unit (vv. 4–7) begins the same way. Although the actual expression (*hoi*) does not appear in verse 4, many commentators and most translations assume that the word either has fallen out or is taken to resume the expression from verse 1.

Addresses that begin with the cry "woe" frequently appear in the prophetic literature (see Isa. 5:8, 11, 18, 29, 21). What usually follows that expression is a description of the wrong behavior of those addressed. Here Amos directs these two woe speeches to the wealthy and powerful. In the first case (vv. 1–3), he criticizes their self-satisfaction and accuses them of ignoring the dangerous signs of the times. In the second case (vv. 4–7), he paints a picture of the idle rich who are not concerned about "the ruin of Joseph." Amos indicts their self-indulgent activities, including their leisure, their rich diet, their entertainment and diversions, their drinking, and their excessive care for their bodies. Such self-centered lives distract their attention from the decline of the nation and the dangers on the horizon.

The section concludes with an ironic announcement of judgment (v. 7). The leaders of revelry will be the leaders into exile, and "the revelry of the loungers shall pass away." As the prophet presents his message, he neither warns his hearers nor calls for them to change. Rather, he proclaims that the Lord will bring judgment in the form of military defeat and exile. Moreover, although the rich and powerful are particularly responsible for the coming disaster and will lead the way into exile, the whole nation will suffer, including those who have already suffered oppression at the hands of the rich.

Psalm 146

This psalm is the first in a small collection (Psalms 146–150) all of which begin and end with a call to praise, hallelujah ("Praise the Lord!"). The psalm praises God, describing the divine character and divine activity, while simultaneously contrasting the Divine with the human. The composition could be aptly described as a theological synopsis summarizing aspects of Israel's belief about God.

Verses 3–4 warn against placing one's faith in humans even if the humans are extraordinary and exceptional ("princes"). Humans are ultimately helpless; they all die, and with death their planning ceases and their thinking terminates. Such death-oriented creatures are not proper objects of trust.

On the other hand, God is a worthy object of trust and one who brings blessedness and happiness in his train. A series of four characteristics of God are presented as supporting the contention that "happy is the one whose help and hope is in God." First, appeal is made to God as creator. As the one who made heaven, earth, and sea—that is, the totality of the universe—God is not bound by the structures and limitations of creaturehood. As creator, God is owner and ruler. Second, appeal is made to the fidelity and constancy of the Creator "who keeps faith forever" (v. 6). Unlike humans, whose plans and programs die with them, God and divine help endure forever. Unlike humans, God is not threatened by the possibility of nonbeing. Third, God is the one who is not only concerned for but also executes (guarantees) justice for the oppressed. In this affirmation and throughout verses 7–9, one finds a consistent emphasis of the Old Testament: God takes a special interest in and acts in behalf of the downtrodden, the powerless, and the despairing. Fourth, the satisfaction of physical needs is also the concern of God, who "gives food to the hungry." As the maker of heaven and earth, God does not will that humans be oppressed nor that they should suffer from hunger.

Following these four divine characteristics, the psalmist speaks of seven activities of God in which the Divine acts to alleviate human distress and to defend those without rights. Most of those noted as the object of God's care are persons without full authority and potential to assume responsibility for and to exercise rights for their own welfare: the prisoners (at the mercy of the legal system or perhaps in slavery), the blind (at the mercy of the seeing), those who are bowed down or with bent backs (in debt or oppressed by others, thus carrying burdens not their own), the righteous (the innocent in the legal system who however were at the mercy of the upholders of justice), the sojourners (foreign settlers or visitors, not members of the native culture and thus aliens), and the widow and fatherless (who were without the support of a male patriarch in a male-dominated culture). God is declared to be committed to the care of all these while at the same time seeing to it that the wicked come to their just reward—ruin.

The psalmist here obviously presents the basic nature and character of God but does not claim that conditions and circumstances conform to this idealized divine will. In the list of attributes, God is primarily contrasted with human leaders (vv. 3–4 over against vv. 5–9). Verse 10 adds an eschatological note to the text and perhaps points to the future as the time when the intervention of God in behalf of society's rejects and subjects will occur.

In preaching from this psalm, attention should be focused on its attempt to define the divine disposition as in favor of the downtrodden and the destitute, the powerless living at the peripheries of society, in the basements of humanity's houses.

1 Timothy 6:6–19

What would be our last words to a young, aspiring minister? Today's text provides one possibility. It belongs to the last major section of advice Paul gives to Timothy (6:3–21). The note on which it begins is to beware of detractors (vv. 3–5). They are caricatured here as conceited ignoramuses fixated on stupid, meaningless controversies. Their fatal flaw is to believe that religion should turn a profit (v. 5). For them, in pursuing the religious life the chief questions are; What is the bottom line? What is the cash value? It is a common type. First there is the sermon, then the request for money. Peddlers of God's word, Paul calls them (2 Cor. 2:17).

If this is the standard against which the minister's life will be measured, then what are the dividends? What is the gain? On this note, our text begins.

"Of course religion does yield high dividends, but only to those who are content with what they have" (v. 6, REB). This defense of the religious life triggers a set of reflections on riches (vv. 7–10), a theme to which our text returns (vv. 17–19). Our text sketches life that puts wealth on the periphery rather than at the center of things, that sees money as valuable but not as the ultimate value, as a worthwhile means to an end but not an end in itself. Hold a penny at arm's length, and it will appear as a dot against the sun; hold it next to the eye, and it will cover the sun. In our text, life is viewed with the penny held at a distance.

In the first part of our text, riches and wealth are viewed from this radically different perspective. There are four cautions.

First, "godliness combined with contentment" becomes the aim of our life's pursuit. The word for "godliness" is *eusebeia*. Often translated as "piety," it is better rendered as "religion." It suggests a form of life whose ultimate quest is for God. It is to be preferred over athletic discipline because it enables us to live in the present and face the future (4:8). Coupled with this is "contentment"—the capacity to be satisfied with what is ours rather than being driven to possess what is not ours. "Be content with what you have" became a proverb in the Hellenistic-Roman world and was wisely appropriated by Christian teaching (Phil. 4:11; Heb. 13:5).

Second, all the trappings of life fade before the double miracles of birth and death. We neither enter nor leave life with assets (v. 7; cf. Job 1:21; Eccles. 5:14; also Gen. 3:19). Riches and possessions are finally to be viewed as decorations along the way. The only real necessities are food and clothing (v. 8), and the ascetic tenor of our text implies that we need little of either (cf. Matt. 6:25–33).

Third, riches are seductive (v. 9). Like the brambles in the parable of the sower (Matt. 13:22), riches ensnare through suffocation. What begins as the innocent desire to make a fair profit becomes an obsession to own. Before long, we no longer own but are owned. The desires that were once prudent and constructive become senseless and harmful. What began as modest desire has now become ruin and destruction.

Fourth, the insatiable desire for money is at the root of every form of evil (v. 10; cf. Heb. 13:5). This too became a proverb in the Hellenistic-Roman world, although it circulated in various forms. The love of money is the root, mother, and hometown of all other evils. What the proverb recognized is how avarice establishes a network with other forms of vice. For this reason, it is seen as an enemy of the life of faith (cf. Matt. 6:24; Titus 1:11). Not only this, it leaves a trail of tears (v. 10*b*).

In the second part of our text, we have a positive set of instructions for the rich.

First, the rich are charged not to be haughty (v. 17). Popular proverbs recognized the direct correlation between being rich and being conceited, and a humble spirit is seen as the proper corrective (James 1:10; also Rom. 11:20; 12:16).

Second, we are reminded of the uncertainty of riches and urged to rely on the God who is the source of all we have (v. 17). The story of Job depicts, among other things, how evanescent wealth is, as does the parable of the rich fool (Luke 12:17–21). This alone should caution us against setting our heart on them (Ps. 62:10) instead of on the living God (1 Tim. 4:10).

Third, riches can have positive value if they belong to persons who are "generous, and ready to share" (v. 18; e.g., Acts 10:1–2). If we make proper disposition of our possessions, we will find ourselves engaged in doing good deeds. And what is the motive for doing so? To lay "a good foundation for the future" (v. 19; cf. Matt. 6:19–21). This may not be the best of motives, but it is one the rich well understand.

Bracketed by these instructions on riches is the charge to Timothy as a "man of God" (vv. 11–16; cf. 2 Tim. 3:17; also 1 Sam. 2:27; 1 Kings 13:1). In contrast to the opponents (vv. 3–5), he is urged to pursue the several Christian virtues (cf. 2 Tim. 2:22; also Gal. 5:22–23). He is also charged to enter the arena and there "fight the good fight of the faith" (v. 12; 1:18; 2 Tim. 4:7; also 1 Cor. 9:25; Heb. 12:1; Jude 3). The charge that follows (vv. 15–16) appears to embody an early Christian confession where God is praised as the only Sovereign (2 Macc. 12:15; Sir. 46:5), King of Kings (Deut. 10:17; 2 Macc. 13:4; 3 Macc. 5:35; Rev. 17:14; 19:16), Lord of Lords (Col. 4:1; Ps. 136:2–3), immortal and invisible in dazzling, unapproachable light (John 1:18; 5:37; 6:46; 14:9; Rom. 1:20; Col. 1:15; Heb. 11:27; 1 John 4:12; also Exod. 33:20).

The language here is quite formal and possibly derives from a formal ordination service in which the minister is charged to embark on a life based on the good confession (cf. 2 Tim. 4:1).

Luke 16:19–31

Before moving to the story of the rich man and Lazarus, it may be helpful to review the introductory comments on last week's Gospel lesson in which the general theme and structure of Luke 16 were discussed.

The story of the rich man (called Dives in the Vulgate, *dives* meaning "wealthy" in Latin) and Lazarus offers itself to the preacher as both simple and complex, clear and puzzling. The story is well traveled, existing in several cultures and in many versions. At least seven versions of it appear in rabbinical sources. Many scholars trace it back to Egypt, where stories of the dead abounded. In that lore, for example, Osiris offered a cup of cold water to the blessed dead. The version in Luke is a Jewish modification of the story; notice the central place of Father Abraham. If this is properly to be called a parable, it is unusual in that proper names are used. No other parable of Jesus does so. The use of the name Lazarus and the theme of being raised from the dead naturally prompt questions as to the relationship between Luke's story and the account of the raising of Lazarus in John 11. There seems to be more than coincidence here, but questions of sources and influences are still unanswered.

In spite of brevity, the account is rich in detail. The sharp contrast between the rich man and the poor is vivid and evocative. This is true even in death: the rich man died and *was buried*; the poor man died. The contrast continues into the next world. The preacher will want to avoid taking the descriptions of the fates of the two men as providing revealed truths about the hereafter and divine answers to questions about the state of the dead. The story simply conveys popular beliefs of the time and is not given by Jesus or by Luke in response to interest in what happens to people immediately after death.

Stating what is *not* the intention of the story does, however, raise the question of what is its message. An answer is not easy because the story as we have it here has two parts. The first, verses 19–26, is clearly presenting the reversal of fortunes in this world and the next. The rich man's character is reflected in his refusal of charity to the poor, a violation of the law of Moses (Deut. 15:4–11), not to mention common human compassion. We know the other man only as poor, but "poor" had come to be in some circles almost a synonym for "righteous" (Luke 4:18; 6:20). That God would reverse the fortunes of such persons was a widely held belief and a strong conviction of Luke (1:51–53; 6:20–26). Were the story to end at verse 26, therefore, it would be appropriate to the context and to Luke as a whole.

However, the second part of the story, verses 27–31, carries a different theme. Here the reader is told through the conversation between Abraham and the rich man that the Scriptures—that is, Moses and the prophets—are effective and adequate for faith (v. 31). Rejection of the Scriptures means that not even a resurrection from the dead would prove effective. Interestingly enough, this, too, is a strong emphasis in Luke. Not only is Luke careful throughout the Gospel to show that what Jesus does and teaches is according to Scripture, but the risen Christ enables his disciples to understand what Moses, the prophets, and the writings taught about the Messiah's passion and resurrection (24:25–27, 44–47). The preaching of the early church, says Luke, continued to establish the message about Jesus from the Jewish Scripture (Acts 2:16–36).

The preacher may, therefore, use Luke 16:19–31 to deal with knotty problems of possessions or to deal with the role of Scripture, the record of what God *has* done, to generate faith in what God is doing. Either would be quite Lucan. But why a story with two thrusts? Ready answers are unavailable. Some scholars have suggested that Luke has employed this version of the story to develop two themes introduced earlier in verses 14–17. Those two themes address a love of money that distances one from God (vv. 14–15) and the tendency of some enthusiasts to set aside Moses and the prophets as no longer valid (vv. 16–17). With some reflection, the two themes may really become one: the embrace of material goods as the primary interest of one's life is a base and flagrant dismissal of scriptural command and precedent. The end of such a life is fairly predictable.

Proper 22 [27]
(Sunday between October 2 and 8 inclusive)

Lamentations 1:1–6;
Lamentations 3:19–26 or Psalm 137; or
Habakkuk 1:1–4; 2:1–4;
Psalm 37:1–9;
2 Timothy 1:1–14;
Luke 17:5–10

In the *Common Lectionary*, the single exception to the cycle of readings from Jeremiah for the nine-week period that began with Proper 16 [21] is this text from Lamentations, a book traditionally attributed to Jeremiah. Today's Old Testament text, the opening six verses of the book, sketches in eerily unsettling images the desolation of Jerusalem after its destruction. Two options for responses are offered: the hopeful declaration of God's mercy and faithfulness in Lamentations 3:19–26; or Psalm 137, the psalmist's lament, sung by the rivers of Babylon, calling for God to display some form of just response to the destruction of Jerusalem.

In other lectionaries, the Old Testament reading is the opening plaint of Habakkuk, calling for Yahweh to hear his cry for help, followed by his resolute expectation that help would come. Response is offered by the opening section of Psalm 37, with its call for implicit trust in Yahweh's capacity to vindicate the cause of the just.

For the epistolary reading, we have the Pauline reminiscence from the opening chapter of Second Timothy where, among other things, Paul places his complete trust in God.

Faith's leveraging capacity against tremendous odds and a sense of our own inadequacy before God are treated in the sayings of Jesus from today's Gospel text from Luke 17.

Lamentations 1:1–6

In the Christian canon the Book of Lamentations is among the prophetic books, following Jeremiah. This is the result of the traditional attribution of the book to the prophet Jeremiah, as early as the time when the book was translated from Hebrew into Greek. But in the Hebrew canon, Lamentations is included with the writings as one of the *megillot*, five books connected with specific events in the liturgical calendar. Appropriately, the Book of Lamentations is read in Jewish worship on the occasion that commemorates the destruction of the temple by the Romans in AD 70.

Lamentations consists of five carefully crafted poems that arose during or after the Babylonian Exile. Although Jeremiah was not the author, it is fitting to associate the book with that prophet both in terms of mood and historical circumstances. In somber words Jeremiah announced the fall of Jerusalem and the exile of its people; Lamentations bewails the city's destruction and the dispersion of its population into foreign lands.

The first four of the five poems are alphabetic acrostics; that is, lines or verses begin with successive letters of the Hebrew alphabet. For the most part, the poetry is in the *qina* meter, a distinctive rhythm common to dirges. In fact, in some cases the Hebrew word means dirge or lamentation (Amos 5:1). These poems are similar in some ways to the communal complaints or laments in the psalms (Psalms 44; 74; 79; 80). They share with these songs a mood of deep sadness and describe disasters for the community. However, the communal complaints of the Psalter finally are prayers, petitions to God for help in time of national trouble. These poems, on the other hand, hardly address the Lord. The various speakers seem to speak to and for the community that has experienced tragedy. Thus they are formally and functionally more like the dirges or funeral songs that express and thus try to come to terms with grief (2 Sam. 1:17–27).

In many respects Lamentations 1:1–6 sets the tone for the entire book. These verses graphically describe the disaster that has befallen Jerusalem and its people, and mourn over what has happened. Each successive verse paints a different facet of the state of the city after its destruction. Verse 1 contrasts Jerusalem's former status with the present. Once full of people, she is lonely; once great, she is now a widow; once a princess, she is now a vassal. In verse 2 the city, personified as a woman, is heard to weep with none to comfort her; her friends have become her enemies. Verse 3 is a rare instance in the book when the grief is extended beyond Jerusalem to the nation, Judah, who is now in exile. Verse 4 is filled with allusions to the temple and worship there. "Zion" refers specifically to the temple mount, but often is a synonym for Jerusalem. The "festivals" here would have been the great pilgrimage feasts. In verse 5 the description of the disaster of the Exile continues, but now it is interpreted theologically as the Lord's punishment for the people's sins. Verse 6 uses the affectionate title "daughter Zion" for the city, which has lost its majesty and whose princes are pursued like deer before the hunter.

Rituals of mourning and funeral songs are essential for the survival and well-being of both individuals and communities. If grief, whether for death or disaster, is not expressed, it will be repressed and continue to produce pain, depression, and anger. Thus Jewish communities over the centuries have continued to find in these ancient lamentations the means to articulate their own grief. These songs have also functioned as the confession of corporate sin, even over the generations, as verse 5 makes clear. We, too, might find in these sad songs the words to express our own pain over community disasters, whether on the level of the congregation, the neighborhood, the nation, or even the whole world. And in the process we can lift up the community's responsibility for such disaster to one another and to God.

Lamentations 3:19–26

Most of this text has been previously discussed as one of the lections for Holy Saturday. Over against the horrid state of devastated Zion in Lamentations 1:1–9, this text extols waiting and hoping undergirded by faith in God. Verse 25 declares that Yahweh will respond favorably to those who wait and that it is good to wait quietly upon the Lord. Verses 25, 26, and 27 all begin with the word "good" (*tob* in Hebrew) and constitute the stanza devoted to the letter ṭ. Thus verse 27 should be read with verses 25–26 and not with verse 28, as in the NRSV.

Psalm 137

This lection is characterized by two sentiments: the enormous sorrow of being in exile (vv. 1–4) and an unceasing devotion and loyalty to Jerusalem (vv. 5–6). The final portion of the psalm is permeated with a thirst for revenge on the enemies and destroyers of Jerusalem, the Edomites and Babylonians (vv. 7–9).

This psalm was composed by those who had been taken into exile following the destruction of Jerusalem by the Babylonians under King Nebuchadnezzar in 586 BC. From this time until the edict of Cyrus, 583 BC, the city and its temple lay in ruins, and its glory was preserved only in the memory of those who had stood within the gates.

The opening verses, verses 1–4, express the sorrow and heartache felt by the exiles who sat by the irrigation canals in Babylon and remembered Zion, the mount on which the temple was constructed. The time and the memories were so painful they could no longer sing or celebrate but hung their musical instruments on the trees. The captors only increased their grief by taunting the exiles by requesting that they sing one of the songs of Zion. These songs of Zion, such as Psalms 46, 48, 76, and so on, had proclaimed the greatness of Jerusalem and declared that Zion would always be protected and defended by God. Now in exile, the people were forced to recognize that Jerusalem had not been inviolable, so sacred that it could not be captured. With the faith expressed in such songs threatened by the realities of assault by Babylonian troops and overwhelmed by war machines and battering rams, it was no time for song, and especially not in a foreign land.

In these four verses, one can see and feel the sorrow and grief borne by those exiled in a strange land. We can hear the tales of sorrow, the cries of woe and anguish, and the shrieks of suffering souls. A sermon built around these verses could easily make several points.

1. Like the ancient Judeans of old, many, or perhaps all, of us live at times in states of exile. Many are the exiles that can come our way. There is the exile of the divorced who live away from familiar surroundings and separated from family. To the unemployed, there is the exile of being without a job, of facing life without the necessary mooring. To the young adult, there is the exile of leaving home.

2. Sorrow and sadness must be given words so we can face and endure them. Although there may be some value in a stoic acceptance of sorrow—a certain nobility in the acceptance of misery—modern psychology and ageless common sense stress the need to let go with our feelings and to verbalize our pain and grief. Grief and sorrow that go unspoken may break the heart that seals them in and hugs them tight.

3. Tears are as normal a part of life as laughter and joy. When the occasion calls for tears, we should let them flow. The time to sit by the waters of Babylon and weep comes to everyone. Our prayers, when the tears flow, can renew our hope and preserve our faith.

The second part of the reading, verses 5–6, expresses the psalmist's undying loyalty to Jerusalem and the unwillingness to surrender sacred memory even in the midst of a history that seemed to defy every confidence in that loyalty. These verses address Jerusalem directly as if the city were a person. The psalmist declares his or her faithfulness by requesting to come lame and dumb if Jerusalem fades from memory or is crowded out by some other joy. Jerusalem here is, of course, more than just the city. It is also the symbol of better days and the embodiment of cherished memories when life was more as it should be.

Verses 7–9 give vent to the Judeans' desire for revenge against the Edomites who served as cheerleaders at the destruction of Jerusalem (v. 7) and the Babylonians who destroyed the Holy City (v. 8). Verse 9 is the infamous text that declares a blessing on the one who would spread the brains of Babylonian babies on the rocks: "a blessing on him who seizes your babies and dashes them against the rocks!" (NJPSV).

In spite of, or maybe because of, the pathos of such psalms as this one, we can be thankful that the ancient Hebrews faced life and its calamities with an unfettered honesty that could give vent to the depths of affliction and torment. They could still hold to their faith and memories from the past even if that past was separated from the present by ashes of destruction, by miles of desert traversed under duress, and by the scenery of a land foreign and strange.

Habakkuk 1:1–4; 2:1–4

Because prophetic words are so historically concrete and specific, it is always important to know as much as we can about the circumstances in which they arose. But the Book of Habakkuk, unlike most other prophetic books, gives us no date for the prophet. There are historical allusions, but they are uncertain and ambiguous. The most likely historical framework, based on the reference to the rise of the Chaldeans (the Neo-Babylonian Empire, 1:6), is during the last decades of the Assyrian Empire, 625–612 BC. Thus the "wicked" mentioned in the book probably are the Assyrians.

Our texts for the day are best understood in the context of the book's structure. It has two distinct parts, chapters 1–2 and chapter 3. The final section, a hymn or song of praise, celebrates the appearance of God to intervene against the nations and thus bring salvation to the people; God acts in wrath against the wicked. The first two chapters are organized as a visionary dialogue between the prophet and God (1:2–2:4), followed by a series of woes against the wicked (2:5–20).

The superscription to the book (1:1) is similar to the one to the Book of Nahum. There is another superscription or title in 3:1, indicating that the two parts of the book may once have circulated separately. The term translated "oracle" could also be read "burden," appearing frequently as the heading to prophecies against foreign nations (Isa. 13:1; 14:28; 15:1; 17:1; 19:1). The word "saw" (also in Isa. 1:1; Amos 1:1) is used here as a technical term for the reception of divine revelation and indicates that those who passed on the written words of the prophet considered them to be the authoritative word of God. Habakkuk is specifically identified as a "prophet," but the contents of the book strongly suggest that he was a cultic prophet, associated with the temple worship.

Remarkably, the first words that follow the superscription are not an oracle or divine revelation at all, but the words of the prophet to Yahweh (1:2–4). These lines give the first move in the dialogue, Habakkuk's complaint to God. The form of expression and the tone are quite familiar, like those of the individual complaint or lament psalms (e.g., Psalms 5, 6, 17, 22). The prophet complains about the presence of evil and suffering, and the fact that the wicked overpower the righteous. Addressed to God, this is the question of divine justice. Seen in national and historical context, it may be an objection to the oppression of Israel by Assyria and a prayer for relief.

Habakkuk 1:5–11 reports Yahweh's answer to this initial complaint, a promise that he will raise up the Chaldeans to put an end to these wicked oppressors. Then in 1:12–17 the prophet speaks again, reiterating the complaint and basing his plea for help on confidence in the justice of God (2:13). How, he asks, can the suffering of the righteous be reconciled with faith in a just God?

The second part of our reading (2:1–4) gives the Lord's second response. The prophet vows to take his stand to watch and wait for an answer (2:1), recalling the image of Ezekiel as the Lord's sentry (Ezekiel 33). The revelation has three parts. First, the prophet is to "write the vision" plainly, "so that a runner may read it" (2:2). This last expression probably means that the writing must be so legible that a runner can read it without stopping; but it may be metaphorical, suggesting that those who read it will be enabled to go on, to keep in the Lord's path. Second, the Lord cautions patience. The vision may seem slow in coming, but come it will (2:3). Finally, there is the promise concerning the life of the one who is righteous (2:4).

These lines in 2:4, some of the most famous and influential in the Old Testament, call for special comment. We cannot expect that their meaning here will have been exactly the same as their force in the New Testament (Rom. 1:17; Gal. 3:11; Heb. 10:37–38). "But the righteous live by their faith" (or "faithfulness," NRSV footnote) translates three well-known Hebrew words. "The righteous" (*sadiq*; cf. Psalm 1) is the one who is faithful to the law, who is just in all human relationships and pious in religious observances. "Faithfulness" is a more accurate reading of the Hebrew *emunah* and refers to steadfastness, fidelity, trustworthiness, especially in the covenant relationship. References to "life" are found in similar contexts (Ezekiel 33; Amos 5:6–7, 10–15), in which cases it means the full, abundant life before God and in the covenant community. Thus Habakkuk 2:4 means: in fidelity to God the righteous one lives the full life. In effect, the full life is defined by faithfulness. To the prophet's question about the justice of God and the suffering of the righteous, God reminds him that the righteous in their faithfulness have their own reward—life.

Psalm 37:1–9

Psalm 37 reads in many ways like a miniature version of the Book of Proverbs. Several assumptions may be seen as foundational pillars undergirding the teaching of the psalm.

1. The world and life are assumed to be reasonably well ordered and to make sense if understood in proper perspective. This seems reflected in the well-ordered form of the poem itself—an alphabetic composition.

2. A strong and necessary interrelationship is presumed to exist between actions and results, between deeds and consequences. That is, a particular type of pattern of action is assumed to lead to predictable results.

3. What appears to contradict this view of the world and behavior, such as the success of the wicked or the triumph of the unrighteous, is only a temporary state, an illusory condition that will soon pass.

4. When the world and human society do not seem to conform to the pattern, in that temporary disruption of the normal state of affairs one should remain faithful and endure the momentary absence of proper conditions.

5. Ultimately, the good, the right, the proper will be rewarded—"the meek shall inherit the land" (v. 11a)—and prosperity will be the reward of the diligent.

Various ways of speaking of the human situation and of the proper conduct of life are found in these opening verses of the psalm. Verses 1–2 contain two prohibitions followed by the motivation or reason, in this case the reason one should not act a certain way. Verses 8–9 contain two imperatives followed by the reason one should act a particular way. Verses 10–11 contrast two consequences of behavior patterns.

Let us look at some of the practical advice offered in this psalm. First, throughout the psalm one is warned against jealousy and the agitation of life that comes from being obsessed with the success of others. "Do not fret" occurs several times (vv. 1, 7, 8). The resentment of others that underlies jealousy and anger is seen as self-defeating and as ultimately a denial of faith in God's justice. Fretting tends only to produce evil (v. 8b). Second, being jealous, especially of the wicked and wrongdoers, is bad because their success is doomed and their fate foretold. Third, the best attitude in life is one that trusts in God, does good, and waits patiently. Fourth, those who are not given to anger, not overcome by wrath, and not "torn-up" over others' status—that is, the meek—will possess the land and enjoy its fruits.

This psalm must have offered encouragement and provided sound advice to those in ancient Judah who may have doubted the value of their commitments in light of the success of the wrongdoers. At the same time, it held out hope for a change for the better and affirmed the age-old conviction that sowing and harvesting are intimately related in spite of all evidence to the contrary.

2 Timothy 1:1–14

As the opening section of Paul's second letter to Timothy, today's epistolary lection exhibits the formal characteristics of a Pauline Letter: a greeting (vv. 1–2), a thanksgiving (vv. 3–5), an appeal (vv. 6–14).

Greeting (vv. 1–2). The tone of endearment is already set in the opening greeting from Paul the apostle (Rom. 1:1; 1 Cor. 1:1; 2 Cor. 1:1; Eph. 1:1; Col. 1:1) to Timothy, "dear son of mine" (v. 2, NJB). Even though Timothy had not been converted by Paul, he had become Paul's understudy and constant companion (Acts 16:1–3; 17:14–15; 18:5; 19:22; 20:4; Rom. 16:21; 1 Cor. 4:17; 16:10; Phil. 2:19–24; also Heb. 13:23). Were it not for this father-child relationship, the tone would be patronizing. Instead, we have an epistle where paternal instructions and advice are given to a youthful child in the faith who is following in his teacher's footsteps.

Thanksgiving (vv. 3–5). Like the opening thanksgiving in the Epistle to Philemon, this prayer is addressed to an individual. It is similar to other Pauline thanksgivings in its reference to gratitude to God (Rom. 1:8; 1 Cor. 1:4; Phil. 1:3; Col. 1:3; 1 Thess. 1:2; 2:13; 3:9; 2 Thess. 1:3; Philemon 4), unceasing prayer in behalf of the recipient (Rom. 1:9; Phil. 1:4; Col. 1:9; 1 Thess. 1:2; Philemon 4), and eagerness to visit in person (Rom. 1:11; Phil. 1:8; Philemon 22; cf. 2 Tim. 4:9, 21).

What is especially remarkable here, however, is the way in which faith as tradition informs the thanksgiving. First, Paul's own service to God with "a clear conscience" (1 Tim. 1:5, 19; 3:9; Acts 23:1; 24:16; 2 Cor. 1:12) is defined with respect to those who preceded him in the faith, "my ancestors" (v. 3), or "my forefathers" (REB). Second, Timothy's own faith is indebted to those who preceded him, his grandmother Lois and his mother Eunice (Acts 16:1). Faith is what is handed down from mother to daughter to son, but not merely as a package passed from one generation to another, but as "a faith which was alive" in mother and daughter and which now lives in the child of the third generation (v. 5, REB; cf. 3:14–15).

We should note the different set of concerns voiced in this opening prayer. We are already in the third generation, where the concern is for continuity with past tradition and what can be done to transmit faith as a living tradition (cf. 2 Tim. 2:1–2).

The Appeal: an exhortation to courage and endurance (vv. 6–14). The appeal from the veteran apostle has at least three aspects.

First, *a call for a rekindled spirit* (vv. 6–7). Timothy is reminded of his ordination to the ministry when he received God's spirit through the laying on of Paul's hands (v. 6; cf. 1 Tim. 4:14; 5:22; also Acts 6:6; 8:17–19; 9:12, 17; 13:3; 19:6; 28:8; Heb. 6:2; cf. Num. 27:18, 23; Deut. 34:9). Though confirmed by the laying on of human hands, the prophetic ministry is in every sense a gift that comes from God. But as the distance increases between teacher and disciple, what was originally a flame of fire can become an ember. As initial enthusiasm wanes, it may be necessary to "stir into flame the gift from God" (v. 6, REB).

Above all, it should be remembered that the minister should not roll over and play dead. The spirit we have from God is not a "spirit of timidity" (RSV) or a "cowardly spirit" (REB; cf. Acts 4:13, 20–21; Rom. 8:15; John 14:27). It is rather "a spirit of power and of love and of self-discipline" (v. 7). It may seem odd to juxtapose love with power and self-discipline, but it is a useful reminder that love need not be spineless and undisciplined.

Second, *a call for bold witness* (vv. 8–12). Timothy is charged not to be ashamed of bearing witness to the faith (v. 8), even as Paul was unashamed (v. 12; Rom. 1:16–17). The charge is in keeping with Jesus' warning that the disciple who recoils in shame before the gospel is undeserving of the name and is finally excluded (Matt. 10:33; Luke 9:26). There is first the scandal of the gospel itself, which runs against the grain of the world (1 Cor. 1:18–25), and the more we think of its oddity the less we are willing to go to the mat for it. There is the additional burden of living with and defending its exponents and proclaimers, especially when they shame themselves and the gospel through imprisonment (v. 8). Our text suggests that we have reached a point in Christian history where it is not necessarily popular to defend the reputation and memory of Paul.

Apart from the general shame of the gospel is the pressure it brings, and the minister finally has to suffer in its behalf, as Paul did (Phil. 1:7, 12–14; Eph. 3:1; 4:1; Col. 4:18; Philemon 1, 9–13). The call to ministry also becomes a call to suffering (2:3; 4:5).

What should we do when our call is threatened by pressure and suffering? Return to the creed, what we believe and confess. In the center of this call to bold witness we have an early Christian confession (vv. 9–10, printed strophically in Nestle 26th). We are reminded of the God who saved and called us through grace and not through our own merits (cf. Titus 3:5; Eph. 2:8–10) and who was manifested through the "appearing," that is, the coming of Christ into the world (Rom. 16:26; 2 Thess. 2:8; 1 Tim. 6:14; 2 Tim. 4:1, 8; Titus 2:11–13; 1 Pet. 1:20). It was God who finally abolished death by raising Christ from the dead (cf. Heb. 2:14–15; 1 Cor. 15:55; 2 Tim. 2:8) and brought us life and immortality (Acts 26:23; 1 Cor. 15:53–54; John 1:4, 9). This is the God by whom Paul was commissioned and in whom he believes and places his ultimate hopes (v. 12).

Third, *fidelity to the apostolic faith* (vv. 13–14). This final reminder is to follow "the outline of sound teaching" (v. 13, REB). Typical of the Pastorals is this importance given to the orthodox faith (1 Tim. 1:10; 6:3; 2 Tim. 4:3; Titus 1:9; 2:1). The faith is that which must be adhered to, guarded, and protected (1 Tim. 6:20). It is the divine treasure entrusted to us by the Holy Spirit who dwells within us (v. 14; Rom. 8:11).

In one sense, this final reminder strikes us as being hollow. Where is the existential immediacy of the preached Word? Where is the moving encounter with the risen Christ? And yet we all know the power of the inherited faith, embodied in words and phrases that have been etched out in the life and struggles of the church. We also know how the shape of this faith, even in its written form, can also shape us, but only if the words bear witness to a living faith. We are being reminded that faith understood as the repository of the apostolic witness may not only inform us, but form us. In the face of threats, the faith we confess may become the most stabilizing force we know, especially as we remember the lives of our predecessors in whom faith was not only something believed but something lived.

Luke 17:5–10

Luke 17 opens with four independent sayings (vv. 1–2, 3–4, 5–6, 7–10) addressed by Jesus to his disciples (v. 1; apostles, v. 5). Today's lection consists of the last two of these sayings. Variants of verses 5–6 are to be found in both Mark (11:22–23) and Matthew (17:20; 21:21), but the parable in verses 7–10 is in Luke alone. Because all four of these logia address matters of discipleship, it is not difficult for the preacher to find ways to join them with some thematic unity. However, that is not necessary. One may choose to frame the message on verses 5–6 or verses 7–10 as self-standing units of tradition with minimal reference to immediate context. Such would not in this case be a violation of the text. Sayings of Jesus in the Gospels often have a proverblike integrity, carrying their meaning intrinsically rather than contextually.

Verse 5 functions as a transition from the subject of forgiveness (vv. 3–4) to that of faith. If one sees verses 5–6 as having a contextual meaning, then very likely the apostles' request for increased faith is an expression of their sense of inadequacy in the face of the unusual demands of caring for weaker members of the community (vv. 1–2) and forgiving repeatedly the offending brother or sister (vv. 3–4). In other words, "Lord, make us adequate for discipleship." Jesus' response "If you had faith . . ." deserves careful examination. The Greek language has basically two types of "if," or conditional, clauses: those that express a condition contrary to fact ("if I were you"); and those that express a condition according to fact ("if Christ is our Lord"). The conditional clause of verse 6 is the second type. One could translate it, "If you have faith (and you do)." In other words, Jesus' response is not a judgment on an absence of faith but an indirect affirmation of the faith they have and an invitation to live and act in that faith. The apostles request an increase of faith, and Jesus says that even the small faith you have is effective and powerful beyond your present realization. The possibilities opened up by faith cancel out such words as "impossible" (a tree being uprooted) and "absurd" (planting a tree in the sea). The small faith already theirs could put them in touch with the power of God.

Students of the passage have pondered Luke's use of mulberry tree rather than mountain, as appears in the Markan and Matthean parallels. Is Luke's a different saying or a variant? We cannot be sure. Some commentators have taken Luke's mulberry tree as entering the tradition in this way. Mark and Matthew speak of a mountain being moved into the sea in the context of the story of Jesus cursing the fig tree. The words "mulberry" and "fig" have the same Greek stem, and in the process of transmitting the tradition, mulberry came into the story when it was told in some circles. Interesting, and perhaps true. However, whether trees or mountains, the act of faith taps the fundamental resource of both Christian and Jewish communities: nothing is impossible with God.

The parable in verses 7–10 opens in a fashion common in Luke: "Will any one of you?" or "Who among you?" (11:5–7; 14:23, 31; 15:4, 8). This story concerns a slave who does double duty, serving in the fields and in the master's house. The slave-master relationship is without analogy in our employee-employer society, and so the preacher is well advised not to draw social and economic lessons from the parable. The rather simple thrust of the story is that the slave's time and labor belong to the master, and, therefore, the slave has no claim on the master, even after a period of obedient service. There is no point of fulfilled duty beyond which the servant can expect special favors in return. There is no ground for boasting (Rom. 3:27), no work of supererogation, no balance of merit after obligation is paid. Disciples of Jesus live by faith, even if it be as small as a mustard seed, but the life of trust is new each day. Like the manna in the wilderness, there is no surplus for tomorrow, no time in which there is more than enough for today. Disciples of Jesus live in obedience, but that, too, is new each day. One does not ever say, "Now that I have completed all the duties of love, it is my turn to be served." Such calculations are foreign to life in the kingdom of God.

Proper 23 [28]
(Sunday between October 9 and 15 inclusive)

Jeremiah 29:1, 4–7;
Psalm 66:1–12; or
2 Kings 5:1–3, 7–15c;
Psalm 111;
2 Timothy 2:8–15;
Luke 17:11–19

A portion of Jeremiah's letter to the Judean exiles in Babylon, which offers commonsense advice for long-term survival in a foreign land, serves as the *Common Lectionary*'s Old Testament reading for today. Psalm 66 offers praise to God for sustaining Israel throughout its turbulent history.

The account of Elisha's healing of Naaman the leper in 2 Kings 5 serves as the Old Testament reading for today in other lectionaries. Proper response is offered by Psalm 111, a psalm of praise and thanksgiving to God for numerous acts of kindness.

The Epistle lesson from 2 Timothy issues a call for us to anchor our faith in Jesus Christ, with the full recognition that faithful endurance may involve pain and suffering.

Luke's story of Jesus' healing the ten lepers, only to receive a word of thanks from an unlikely Samaritan, provides the Gospel lesson for today.

Jeremiah 29:1, 4–7

The lesson assigned for today gives the heart of Jeremiah's letter—probably the first of several letters—written from Jerusalem to the Judean exiles in Babylon. The historical situation, as indicated in the expanded superscription in 29:2, was soon after the first fall of Jerusalem in 597 BC, when king Jehoiachim (the Jeconiah of v. 2) and the leading citizens of the city were carried off to Babylon. Verse 1 identifies what follows as the prophet's letter to the leaders of the community in that foreign land, significantly listing the addressees as "the remaining elders among the exiles, . . . the priests, the prophets, and all the people."

Obviously there was a vigorous exchange of letters between Jerusalem and the exiles in Babylon. A second letter from Jeremiah concerns the false prophet Shemaiah (29:24–32) and alludes to a letter that Shemaiah had sent to Jerusalem in response to Jeremiah's first message. According to 29:3, Jeremiah's letter was entrusted to envoys from King Zedekiah to

Nebuchadnezzar in Babylon. Presumably along with their official royal correspondence the envoys took Jeremiah's letter and delivered it to the exiles and their leaders. From ancient Near Eastern documents we know a great deal about letters during this era. They were carried from the senders to the addressees by messengers, who then read them—and perhaps explained them—to the hearers. Letters contain, in addition to the body of the message, the names of the addressees, greetings, and the name of the sender; they typically begin with a messenger formula "thus says X to Y." Given this situation of oral delivery, it is unlikely that these verses contain the verbatim message of the prophet.

Remarkably, we have here a message within a message. Jeremiah's letter to the exiles is a message from the Lord, like most of his speeches to the citizens of Jerusalem and Judah. This is clear from the prophetic messenger formula that stands at the beginning of the body of the letter in verse 4.

Like most of the New Testament letters of Paul, this one is occasioned by a problem among the people of God. The problem is set out by the context within which our assigned verses appear. Chapters 27–29 deal with a common problem, in addition to the question of what the Lord has in store for the people of Judah. That problem is the question of distinguishing between true and false prophecy. From the perspective of Jeremiah and the editors of the book, the concern is to identify as false prophets those whose message differs from Jeremiah. We are informed in the verses that immediately follow our lesson (vv. 8–9) that Jeremiah's letter was occasioned by lying and deceiving prophets and diviners. So he writes to give the true word of the Lord and also to announce the Lord's judgment on those false prophets (vv. 21–23).

Usually in the prophetic literature the word of Yahweh through the prophet is an announcement concerning the future, either of judgment or salvation. There is that aspect to this message within a message. Jeremiah gives the bad news that the Exile will not be brief, but is to last seventy years (v. 10), and he announces judgment upon the false prophets. But there is also the good news that eventually the Lord will return the people to the land promised to their ancestors. But the heart of the letter in the verses before us today is unusual for a message from the Lord. The main contents are instructions for the behavior and the attitudes of the people in exile. Jeremiah advises the exiles to settle down in Babylon for the long term. They should "build houses and live in them; plant gardens and eat what they produce" (v. 5). Moreover, they are to ensure the future of the people of God by marrying and having children, and by seeing that their children marry and have children. The purpose of these actions is to "multiply there, and do not decrease" (v. 6), so that there will be a people for the Lord to bless in the distant future. Instead of rebelling against their oppressors, they are to "seek the welfare of the city where I have sent you into exile" (v. 7). The "city" is Babylon, which can stand for the empire of which it is the capital. And remarkably, the exiles are instructed to "pray to the LORD on its behalf, for in its welfare you will find your welfare" (v. 7). The hated enemies are to be lifted up in their prayers to the Lord.

From this letter as well as other exilic books such as Ezekiel we learn a great deal about the circumstances of the captives in Babylon. Obviously they were not sold off into slavery but were allowed to keep their families and communities together. Public gatherings were permitted, and so was communal worship. Away from Jerusalem and the temple, portable religious activities, such as public and private prayer, became more important.

Certainly the prophet's instructions were practical recommendations for long-term survival in difficult circumstances. But Jeremiah does not understand his words as pragmatic guidelines. Rather, like his earlier words and the words of the other classical prophets, he is interpreting historical events theologically and drawing out the implications. What he says is consistent with his earlier messages from the Lord: Do not resist the Babylonians, for they are carrying out the will of the Lord. By submitting to Babylon, the exiles will submit to the will of the Lord.

Psalm 66:1–12

This psalm was discussed earlier as one of the lections for Proper 9 [14].

2 Kings 5:1–3, 7–15c

For a commentary on this lesson, see the discussion of 2 Kings 5:1–4 for Proper 9 [14] in this volume.

Psalm 111

This psalm is a thanksgiving psalm, although its content is primarily a hymn of praise. In ancient Israelite worship, the individual or community offered thanksgiving after some calamity had passed or after a rescue from some state of distress. As a rule, thanksgiving psalms generally contain more material that is addressed to a human audience than is addressed directly to the Deity. Thanksgiving psalms were, therefore, a way of offering one's testimony. This, of course, is the exact opposite of the lament psalms, which fundamentally contain only address to the Deity. Thanksgiving psalms were thus primarily intended for the worshiping audience more than for the Deity. Psalm 111, although setting out to give thanks to the Lord, contains no direct address to God.

That this psalm was used in a context of thanksgiving is clear from the opening verse, as is the fact that the thanksgiving was offered in public worship—"in the company of the upright, in the congregation." The psalm, unlike most thanksgivings, contains no reference to the distress from which the one offering thanks may have been saved or to any special reason for offering thanks.

In fact, what we have in the psalm, following the opening verse, is a hymn of praise extolling the works of God and the divine fidelity to the covenant. That a thanksgiving takes the form of a hymn should not surprise us.

The works of God singled out in the psalm for praise are declared both worthy of study and of remembrance (vv. 2–4). The works, or acts, of God are seen as the deeds of Israel's sacred history. Three special acts are recalled. There is, first, the giving of food for those who fear the Divine (v. 5). This verse seems to allude, although not with absolute certainty, to the protection and care for Israel in the wilderness when the people were fed with quails and manna (see Exod. 16:13–35). Second, God displayed great power in giving the Israelites the land of Canaan as "the heritage of the nations" (v. 6). Finally, there is reference throughout the psalm to the covenant that was given at Sinai (see vv. 5, 7–9). The twofold stress of verse 9 emphasizes both the redemption of God and the commands of the covenant. Or we could say that the psalmist is declaring that in the redemptive acts of the past and in the commands of the covenant, one possesses the means to study and remember in obedience the works and ways of God (vv. 2, 4). Such study should lead to the fear of God, which is the beginning of wisdom (v. 10).

2 Timothy 2:8–15

These words of advice continue the theme of last week's epistolary lection—fidelity to the apostolic tradition. Their force is centripetal, driving Timothy back to the center, to that which motivates, orders, and sustains him in a fruitful ministry. They establish what is peripheral—hairsplitting disputes that go hand-in-glove with teaching that veers away from the apostolic tradition (2:14, 16–19). They are a summons to remember, to engage in *anamnesis* concerning the tradition, not only to recollect but to reenact and reappropriate the tradition just as it happens in celebrating the Lord's Supper.

First, Timothy is told to "remember Jesus Christ" (v. 8). Because Timothy was not a contemporary of Jesus, this is obviously a call to remember the gospel message of Jesus Christ, specifically that which Paul preaches. Hence the wording of NJB: "Remember the gospel that I carry." It is a summons to rehear, reappropriate, even relive the preached Christ.

The content of Paul's gospel is summarized in a two-part formula: "raised from the dead, a descendant of David" (v. 8). The formulation is reminiscent of earlier traditional summaries appropriated by Paul, and with which he aligned himself (Rom. 1:3–4; cf. Acts 13:22–23). The order is unusual; we would expect the Davidic descent to precede the Easter faith. Also striking is the absence of the cross in this summary of the Pauline gospel (cf. 1 Cor. 2:2; Gal. 6:14).

Second, the gospel entails suffering (vv. 9–10). For the gospel, Paul is fettered (Phil. 1:7, 12–13; Eph. 3:1; 4:1; Col. 4:18; Philemon 1, 9–13), but the gospel itself is always unfettered: "God's message cannot be chained up" (v. 9, NJB). Paul did not allow his own circumstances to serve as an obstacle to the progress of the gospel (Phil. 1:12–14). The irrepressibility of the word of God becomes a major theme in Luke-Acts, and the story of Paul concludes on this very note (Acts 28:31). In the end, nothing could finally hinder Paul's proclamation of the gospel.

The suffering he endured was vicarious—for the sake of the elect, those who have been called by the gospel (1 Thess. 2:2; also Matt. 24:22). His apostleship took the form of service for others, in keeping with the essential message of the Christ-event (2 Cor. 5:14–15).

Third, the gospel is remembered and appropriated in worship (vv. 11–13). As part of this exhortation to fidelity, a fragment of an early Christian hymn is cited. This form-critical judgment has achieved a broad consensus, seen by the fact that these verses are printed strophically by RSV, REB, NJB, and NIV. The hymn is introduced as a "sure saying" (v. 11; cf. 1 Tim. 1:15; 3:1; 4:9; Titus 3:8), something we can rely on.

The sentiments of the hymn are resonant with Pauline theology. Dying and rising with Christ recalls his theology of baptism (Rom. 6:5–11; also Gal. 6:14; Col. 2:12). As is the case in the undisputed letters, sharing the resurrection life is a future reality. This sharply contrasts with the overrealized eschatology of the opponents (2:18). Moreover, our sharing in the reign of God, which comes through endurance, is also a future gift (cf. Matt. 10:22; 24:13; Acts 14:22; Rom. 8:17; cf. Dan. 12:12–13).

We are also warned, in words reminiscent of Jesus, that denying our confession will eventually mean that we are denied by Christ (cf. Matt. 10:32–33; Mark 8:38; Luke 12:9; 1 John 2:22–23; Jude 4). However, the pattern is broken in the last verse with the reminder that our faithlessness will not nullify God's faithfulness (cf. Rom. 3:3). The one surety we have is God's absolute fidelity (1 Cor. 1:9; 10:13; 2 Cor. 1:18; 1 Thess. 5:24; 2 Thess. 3:3; Heb. 10:23; 11:11; 1 John 1:9; Rev. 1:5; cf. Deut. 7:9; Ps. 145:13). "[God] cannot deny himself" (v. 13); the integrity of God remains intact (Num. 23:19; Titus 1:2; Heb. 6:18).

Fourth, the centering force is the word of the gospel (vv. 14–15). Timothy is charged to remind his hearers of this "sure saying" in the hope that they will concentrate on the heart of the confession and not be seduced by useless disputes (cf. 1 Tim. 1:4; 6:4). The main task is for Timothy to become exemplary in his own conduct (v. 15). He too must endure, as Paul endured, in order to receive divine approval. Like Paul, he must remain undeterred in his proclamation of the gospel, and thereby become an unashamed workman (1:8; 1 Tim. 4:6–7; also Rom. 1:16–17). And finally, he must deal straight with the message of truth, refusing steadfastly to play fast and loose with the gospel (cf. 2 Cor. 6:7; Eph. 1:13; Col. 1:5–6; James 1:18).

Once again, we are challenged by this text to be faithful to the gospel we have received. In one sense, it is a call "back to the basics," and we should remember that this is a move typically made in the Pastorals when the faith is being threatened by false teaching. But there are times when this is a worthwhile call. The church can lose sight of the center, and when it does the preacher's task is to reduce the Christian message to its barest essentials and ask the church to engage in *anamnesis* of the Christ who is proclaimed, known, and received through the gospel.

Luke 17:11–19

Luke's repetition of the phrase "on the way to Jerusalem" (v. 11) reminds the reader that the story to follow occurs in the travel narrative begun at 9:51 and also serves to note a transition in the material between verses 10 and 11. The preacher need not struggle to connect the account of healing ten lepers with what precedes. This story is found in Luke alone. Although there is some similarity to Mark's account of Jesus healing a leper (1:40–45), common elements are not sufficient to argue for these as variant tellings of one incident.

One is impressed by the realistic detail of the account. Lepers tended to live in groups (2 Kings 7:3); they avoided contact with nonlepers (v. 12; Lev. 13:45–46; Num. 5:2); but they kept close enough to populated areas to receive charity. Jesus' command that they show themselves to the priests (v. 14) was also according to the law of Moses (Lev. 14:2–32). However, one is also struck by elements in the story that raise questions. For example, the location between Samaria and Galilee (v. 11) seems unusual for one going to Jerusalem, especially in view of Jesus' having much earlier gone from Galilee into Samaria (9:52). It is quite possible that Luke here uses the Galilee-Samaria border to introduce a story involving both Jews and a Samaritan (v. 16). Another uncertain element in the text is Jesus' command to show themselves to the priests. Did this apply also to the Samaritan who was outside the rituals of Judaism? Also, why reproach the nine for not returning (vv. 17–18) when they had been told to go and show themselves to the priests? In fact, their healing occurred upon their going— their obedience apparently the expression of faith essential to their healing (v. 14). Some commentators, sensitive to these questions, have taken the account as an idealized story joining faith, obedience, and gratitude.

However, it seems more natural to understand Luke 17:11–19 as a two-part story: verses 11–14 and 15–19. The first part is a healing story with all the elements of a healing: a case of evident need, a cry to Jesus for help; Jesus treats them as already healed, as indicated in his sending them to the priests; their healing occurs in their act of obedient faith. (In Mark 1:40–45, the leper is sent to the priest *after* the healing.) The second part, verses 15–19, is a story of the salvation of a foreigner. It is the foreigner who praises God and gives thanks to Jesus. It is the foreigner to whom Jesus says, "Your faith has made you well" (v. 19). Clearly, the expression "made you well" refers to some blessing other than the cleansing from leprosy that has been given to all, including those who did not give thanks and who did not praise God. That additional blessing we usually term "salvation."

Assuming that the other lepers were Jews, the story makes two points vital to Luke: the faith of foreigners (7:9; 10:25–27; Acts 10–11) and the blindness of Israel (Acts 26:16–18). In a sense this story is a foreshadowing of Acts 28:26–27, the turning of the Christian missionaries from Jews to Gentiles. It is very important to notice that Jesus did not reject the nine Jewish lepers. They were blessed with his healing. Neither did Jesus set aside Jewish law; he sent them to the priests as the law required. But by the time Luke was written, such stories probably were told in abundance: the Gentile responds affirmatively; Jesus' own people do not. Very likely this account was inspired by an Old Testament story to which Jesus had earlier referred (4:27)—the healing of a leper who was a foreigner (2 Kings 5:1–14). That story also had two parts: Naaman was cleansed, and Naaman was converted to Israel's faith.

We cannot suppose that Luke told this story simply to paint a favorable picture of a Gentile and an unfavorable one of the Jews. Quite possibly the church in Luke's day had begun to presume upon God's favor and to take blessings for granted, without gratitude. If so, again it was, and is, the outsider who teaches the people of God what faith is, what praise is, and what thanksgiving is.

Proper 24 [29]
(Sunday between October 16 and 22 inclusive)

Jeremiah 31:27–34;
Psalm 119:97–104; or
Genesis 32:22–31;
Psalm 121;
2 Timothy 3:14–4:5;
Luke 18:1–8

For the final reading in the Jeremiah cycle in the *Common Lectionary*, the classic text expressing the prophetic hope of a new covenant is chosen. As a responsorial psalm, the selection from Psalm 119 celebrates the psalmist's unstinting love for Torah and devotion to its precepts.

For other lectionaries, the Old Testament reading is the story of Jacob's nightlong wrestling match at Peniel recorded in Genesis 32. Unalloyed confidence in God's protective care is expressed in Psalm 121.

In today's epistolary reading, Timothy is urged to be devoted to Scripture in a way reminiscent of the sentiments expressed in Psalm 119:97–104; he is also charged to be true to his calling as a minister.

As our Gospel lesson, we have Jesus' parable of the widow whose persistence penetrates a judge's callous indifference.

Jeremiah 31:27–34

This lesson contains two quite distinct units of prophecy concerning the future, verses 27–30 and 31–34. They have in common the proclamation of the Lord's salvation for "the house of Israel and the house of Judah." But because each of the units emphasizes very different aspects of that good news, either of these well-known passages would be sufficient for homiletical reflection and interpretation.

It is important to be aware of the context of Jeremiah 31:27–34. These two units are part of what has been called the little book of comfort (chaps. 30–31), a collection of announcements of restoration. What follows our lesson in chapter 32 is the report of something Jeremiah did during Nebuchadnezzar's siege of Jerusalem (see the commentary of Jer. 32:1–3a, 6–15 for Proper 21 [26] in this volume). The prophet had been imprisoned in the court of the guard for saying that the Babylonians would be victorious. While he was there, he bought a field in Anathoth from his cousin as an action symbolizing God's future for the people. Even before Jerusalem was destroyed he announced: "Houses and fields and vineyards shall again be bought in this land" (Jer. 32:15). So a powerful spiritual vision of changed lives and obedient hearts is followed by, of all things, a real estate transaction. The point seems clear: So long as they are on this earth, even the people of the new covenant still need a place to live, actual ground for growing food, and a marketplace where things are bought and sold.

Modern interpreters of our first unit, verses 27–30, typically have considered it important in understanding the history of ideas concerning retribution. They tend to see its significance in the expression of a change from a doctrine of corporate responsibility, even over the generations, to an emphasis on individual retribution. The old saying about the parents eating sour grapes and the children's teeth being set on edge is no longer true. Rather, "all shall die for their own sins" (v. 30). Although there is some truth to the view that in the exilic and postexilic periods there was a shift in the direction of individualism, such an interpretation misses the main thrust of the prophetic message.

As verse 27 makes plain, with its formula concerning the future and its attribution of all that follows to the Lord, this is a prophecy, an announcement of the future. The first part (vv. 27–28) should not be lost because the second part is so memorable. Through the prophet, the Lord promises to repopulate the devastated and abandoned land with people and animals. Verse 28 quotes—with slight variations—the words of Jeremiah's vocation report. He was called "to pluck up and to pull down, to destroy and to overthrow, to build and to plant" (1:10) by proclaiming the word of the Lord. In our passage the Lord himself says he has done those things. Now that the disaster is on the horizon, a new horizon of salvation opens up.

The saying concerning retribution (vv. 29–30) does not mean that the traditional interpretation of history in ancient Israel has been overthrown. Repeatedly, both Jeremiah and the editors of his book proclaimed that the Exile was divine punishment for generations of sins. What these verses proclaim is that now the cycle is broken. Once Israel and Judah have suffered their punishments and have taken responsibility for their own actions, they will no longer suffer for the sins of their ancestors. Rather, they will be established again in their land.

Our second unit, verses 31–34, is an unqualified announcement of salvation, containing the only explicit Old Testament reference to the New Testament, that is, new covenant. In Jeremiah's vision of the future, the new covenant comes only through and beyond suffering, in this case that of the Babylonian Exile. Thus these hopeful words come from a time of crisis and transition, when many people would have been asking if God's covenant with the people has come to an end. Jeremiah insists that judgment is not God's final word.

Like so much of the Old Testament, this promise comes from a time of crisis and transition, the disaster of the Babylonian Exile. When the prophet hears the Lord promise to make a new covenant with the house of Israel and the house of Judah, he has in view the situation of the exiles in Babylon. These lines respond to the most serious question on the minds of those people. Has the covenant ended? Is this blow the Lord's final word to us?

One who speaks of a new covenant must also have in mind an old one. Verse 32 spells that out directly by recalling the covenant at Mt. Sinai following the Exodus and by reminding the people that this is the covenant they broke. But there were other old covenants as well, each of them new in its time. Before Mt. Sinai there were the covenants with Noah, Abraham, Isaac, and Jacob. After Sinai, Moses led the people in a renewal of the covenant on the plains of Moab, as did Joshua at Shechem. Later Samuel led the tribes in a covenant when kingship was established. In Jeremiah's time there was the hope of reestablishing the covenant under young King Josiah.

All these covenants were viewed as occurring at critical moments in the life of the community. When transitions and changes brought life and faith into doubt, it was time for a covenant or for the renewal of the old covenant. All were taken as initiated by God and as responses to God's initiative. Moreover, all involved promise.

The language in Jeremiah 31:31–34 is particularly intimate. In recalling the old broken covenant, the prophet hears the Lord saying, "I took them by the hand," like a mother leads a child, and "I was their husband." He has no problem at all with mixing the metaphors, for the message is clear. Even in the past, the Lord was as close to the people as flesh and blood. The way has been prepared for the new level of intimacy of the covenant on the heart.

The word that stands at the center of the passage is "covenant." A covenant is a special kind of relationship in which parties pledge themselves to one another. Old Testament covenants generally had two parts: a promissory oath and the stipulations or contents of what was promised. The fact that the law here is written, even on the heart, suggests that the basic reference is to the stipulations. In that respect the covenant is like the written law. Israel will not forget what they have sworn to do.

This promise of a new covenant contains one of the most ancient and persistent formulations of the covenant vows: "I will be their God, and they shall be my people" (v. 33). Though the stipulations could be spelled out in lists of laws and even books of laws that defined how a covenant people behaved, this simple sentence said it all. All the people had to do to make a covenant was to say, "We will to be God's people."

It should be emphasized that the making of a covenant with God was not an individual, but a communal, act, the work of the community of faith. It was Israel's covenant with God at Mt. Sinai that made them a people, the people of God, binding them not only to God but also to one another.

What then is new about the new covenant? That God initiates the covenant, that he forgives sins, and that Israel will "know" the Lord intimately had been features of older covenants. What is without precedent is the law written on the heart, the covenant at the core of one's being. The newness is a special gift, the capacity to be faithful and obedient. In the Old Testament, the heart is the seat of the will (see Jer. 29:13; 32:39; Ezek. 11:19; 36:26); consequently, the special gift here is a will with the capacity to be faithful. God thus promises to change the people from the inside out, to give them a center. This covenant will overcome the conflict between knowing or wanting one thing and doing another. In the new covenant the people will act as if they are owned by God without even reflecting upon it.

Which laws, then, are written on the heart? All the laws of Moses? Just the Decalogue? The answer is all of these things, and none of them. Just these words will suffice: "I am yours, and you are mine," says the Lord. That is the language of love and faithfulness.

Psalm 119:97–104

The 176 verses of this psalm divide into twenty-two stanzas of eight lines each. In each individual stanza, all eight lines begin with the same Hebrew letter, working through the alphabet in order. In each of the stanzas there is a play on a series of synonyms for the law or the will of the Deity. Generally, there are eight such synonyms per stanza, and generally the same eight are used throughout the entire psalm. In this, the thirteenth stanza of this massive psalm on the law, the terms used are *law, commandment, testimonies, decrees, word, ordinances, words,* and *precepts.*

This psalm has been selected to be read with the new covenant text from Jeremiah because it focuses on the observance of the law and its incorporation into the life of the righteous one. There is an emphasis on the existential appropriation of and meditation on the law. The text allows the speaker (and reader!) to boast of a superior standing because the law is a constant source of study, is obeyed to the fullest, and is even taught to the person by God. Thus there is a claim of being superior to one's enemies, teachers, and the aged.

Observance of the law is understood as involving not only positive obedience but also the negative avoidance of wrongdoing: "I hold back my feet from every evil way" (v. 101). As a result, the words (or promises) of God are sweeter than honey to the palate (v. 103).

Genesis 32:22–31

In terms of context, Genesis 32:22–31 is the counterpart to Genesis 28:10–19a. That story of Jacob at Bethel took place as the patriarch was leaving Canaan for northwest Mesopotamia, and the events in today's reading take place on the boundary of the land as he is returning. Both are at key turning points in the life of the patriarch, and in both instances he is the object of divine revelation at a dangerous time, and at night. Fear stands in the background of both accounts. In the first instance he was fleeing from Esau; here, having escaped the wrath of his father-in-law, he knows he is about to meet his brother. So the immediate context of Jacob's nocturnal struggle at the Jabbok is his conflict with his brother. A story of struggle with superhuman powers is framed by a confrontation between brothers.

Brief as it is, the story of Jacob at the Jabbok is strange and complicated. Some of its strangeness and complexity can be explained in terms of the history of its transmission and development. There is strong evidence that the tradition was passed down in the oral tradition in various forms. We begin to recognize that evidence when we attempt to identify Jacob's opponent. Initially we are told that "a man wrestled with him until daybreak" (v. 24), but later it appears that the opponent has the power both to put Jacob's thigh out of joint with a touch and to bless him. This confusion, along with the facts that the opponent fears the daylight and refuses to divulge his name, suggests a nocturnal demon. In the struggle, the opponent declares ambiguously that Jacob has "striven with God and with humans" (v. 28), and in the end the patriarch says he has "seen God face to face" (v. 30). It seems clear, then, that the narrator has taken over an ancient, pre-Yahwistic tradition that once talked of a nocturnal demon or deity and reinterpreted it as a confrontation between Israel's God and her ancestor.

The complex history of tradition is also revealed in the fact that the story has so many distinct resolutions or conclusions. Some of these points seem almost trivial when compared with the others. There are two distinct etiological conclusions: one explaining the name of the place as Peniel ("face of God") because Jacob saw the face of God there and lived (v. 30); and the other explaining the origin of a ritual practice. The Israelites do not eat "the thigh muscle that is on the hip socket" because the opponent struck the ancestor's hip socket at the thigh muscle (v. 32). This latter point is particularly curious, not simply because the taboo is unattested elsewhere, but because it was a human thigh that was touched and animal muscles that are therefore not to be eaten.

The two other resolutions to the story are more integral to the plot and to one another. One concerns the change of the ancestor's name to Israel or, more likely, the giving of an additional name. This emerges directly from the struggle. On the one hand, Jacob demands to know his opponent's name, but the antagonist refuses to disclose it. In the old oral tradition, to know the name of the nocturnal demon or deity was to obtain a measure of control over it. On the other hand, when the adversary asks, Jacob identifies himself and in turn receives the new name, Israel ("one who strives with God," or "God strives"). The other point concerns the blessing, a direct result of the conflict. The opponent demands to be released because daybreak is approaching, but Jacob refuses to release him until he is blessed (v. 26). This is the hinge upon which the drama turns. Who will win the contest? Jacob received his blessing (v. 29), but he did not escape without injury.

In all levels of the tradition, this is a story of strife and struggle. Our author, the Yahwist, and his audience would not have missed the corporate implications of the story and its results. The people of Israel, like their patronymic ancestor, had striven with powers both human and divine and, in the time of the monarchy, knew that they had prevailed and been blessed. Moreover, although the ancient tradition may have viewed the conflict as one with some demon, our narrator finally knows that behind the hidden visage is the face of God. As the old traditions have been incorporated into a theological interpretation of Israel's past, there is a skillfully developed ambiguity in the identity of the opponent.

Those who know struggle—and who does not?—will find it easy to identify with both the protagonist and the storyteller. Life entails strife, conflict, and struggle. Often we can neither see the face nor know the name of what confronts us in the night. The struggle may even be with the unfathomable mystery of God. The passage, however, goes further than holding up a mirror to life as struggle. By example it says: do not let go, but continue to struggle, even when God is experienced as threatening. Furthermore, by its resolution it concludes that struggle—even with God—may end with a blessing, even though one may limp on afterward with the scars of the battle.

Psalm 121

This psalm forms part of a collection of psalms put together for use by pilgrims as they made their way to Jerusalem to celebrate the various festivals (note the reference to ascents or pilgrimage in the heading). The psalm has a distinct note of departure about it and thus is fitting for use with the Old Testament reading about Abraham's journey to a new land.

The psalm is clearly human address, without any speech addressed to God. Thus the psalm is not a prayer. A particular feature of the psalm is the change of person between verses 2 and 3. The opening verses are spoken in the first person, whereas the remainder of the psalm is addressed to someone in the second person. The reason for this change of person will become clear in our subsequent discussion.

Before leaving on pilgrimage, the worshipers in a region assembled in a centrally located village in order to travel in a group to Jerusalem. After spending the night in the open air, to avoid any possible contact with uncleanness in the houses, the group moved out under the supervision of a director. The trip to Jerusalem, which might take several days, was not blessed with any special amenities (like constantly accessible toilet facilities) and, like all travel in antiquity, was beset with possible hazard and hardship.

Psalm 121 is best understood as a litany of departure recited antiphonally as the pilgrim group departed from the village where they had assembled. Verses 1–2 were sung by the pilgrims, and verses 3–8 were sung by those who remained behind or perhaps by the leader/director of the pilgrim group.

Verses 1–2 are to be understood as a confession (the second half of v. 1 should not be translated as a question but as a statement). The worshiper speaks of looking to the hills (of Jerusalem) from whence help comes. That is, one looks to the God of Jerusalem, who made heaven and earth.

The affirmation of God as creator of heaven and earth, that is, of everything, may seem so obvious to us and may even seem an innocuous statement. To appreciate fully the impact of such a perspective about the world, one has to realize that for most ancients the world was an arena of conflicting powers and beings. In a polytheistic religion, one god controlled one aspect of life or nature and another some other aspect. Often deities were considered in conflict with one another. Thus the world was neither a very hospitable nor a very predictable place. One constantly had to worry if the proper gods had been placated. On the other hand, the belief in one god as the creator of the heaven and the earth allowed one to see things as reflective of a single divine will. Such a worldview provided a sense of cohesion and security about life.

As the pilgrim faced the dangers of the forthcoming journey to Jerusalem, the confession that the creator God was the source of help was reassuring and confidence boosting.

Verses 3–8 are a response offering assurance to the individual pilgrim that God will constantly care for and preserve the worshiper. Note the number of statements with imagery concerning travel: the foot stumbling, the guardian constantly awake, a shade along the way, day and night as one was on the road constantly, going out (leaving) and coming in (returning). Both the moon and the sun, referred to in verse 6, were considered deities in the ancient world and could be objects of dread. Because pilgrims traveled by day and slept in the open at night, the sun and moon were constant features of their journey. Travelers feared sunstroke (see 2 Kings 4:19; Jon. 4:8), and many other disorders such as epilepsy, fever, and lunacy (related to the word *lunar*) were ascribed to the baneful influence of the moon.

A significant emphasis in this psalm is the constant presence and care of the Deity. God, unlike Baal or other deities (see 1 Kings 18:29), is described as one who does not sleep or slumber. That is, God is continuously on the job.

In developing sermonic ideas for using this psalm, the minister can easily move from the imagery of an actual pilgrimage reflected in the psalm to the understanding of life itself as pilgrimage.

2 Timothy 3:14–4:5

It is one thing to be encouraged to learn new things, probe new vistas, push beyond our present boundaries into uncharted territory. It is quite another to be told to "keep to what you have been taught and know to be true" (v. 14, NJB). The one values what is new, untested, and potentially eye-opening and life-changing, whereas the other values what is tried and true. One eyes the future; the other casts a backward eye to the past.

The outlook of today's text, in keeping with the overall perspective of the Pastorals, is traditional. The past is valued and cherished. It provides not only precedent but also stability. We are told to hold on to the tradition, what we have been taught, and to continue in that. Sailing new waters, clearing new paths, forging new vistas—all these are frowned on. The way forward is through the old, not the new. It is an outlook foreign to the spirit of the Enlightenment.

One reason for this cautious conservatism is the threat of false teachers, a constant concern of the Pastorals. New teaching has been given a bad name and is repeatedly dismissed as philosophy, myth, senseless disputing pseudoknowledge (cf. 1 Tim. 6:20).

What, then, is valued in this approach?

First, *past teaching* (vv. 14–15). We are urged to "stand by the truths you have learned and are assured of" (v. 14, REB). The focus here is clearly catechetical. It is the truth of the gospel, and the teaching deriving therefrom, that we have received from faithful witnesses (1:12–14; 2:2; also 1 Tim. 6:20).

As important as what we were taught is the person who taught us: "remember who your teachers were" (v. 14, NJB). For Timothy, of course, they were his grandmother Lois and his mother Eunice (1:5; Acts 16:1), and Paul as well (2:2). He is reminded of the cumulative effect of Christian nurture—becoming acquainted with Scripture through childhood.

Most of our teachers are forgettable, but a few are unforgettable. We remember those who taught us the faith, but especially those who excited us about the faith. Their faces still form fresh images in our minds, and their words still echo within us. What they said blended with who they were, and now their word and character shape what we say and who we are. To say that our teachers have influenced us and shaped the contours of our thinking and living is to acknowledge the power of the tradition. There can be no real doubt of the norming value of what we were taught and who taught us.

Second, *sacred Scripture* (vv. 16–17). The primary referent here is Jewish Scripture, the Old Testament, for the New Testament writings had not yet been collected. It is this sacred text to which the early Christian community looked for guidance and instruction (Rom. 15:4; 1 Cor. 10:11). This repository of worthwhile teaching does two things: it has the "power to make [us] wise and lead [us] to salvation through faith in Christ Jesus" (v. 15, REB). We are told that Scripture is "inspired" (v. 16, NRSV, NJB, REB) or "God-breathed" (NIV), meaning not only that it speaks of God but that God speaks through it. As the collected oracles of the community of faith in whom God has acted and through whom God has spoken, Scripture speaks to us uniquely of God. Because God called the community into existence, and Scripture bears witness to this divine-human dialogue, its ultimate origin is God and may be said to come from God (2 Pet. 1:19–21).

As the repository of the collected wisdom of Israel and the oracles prompted by God, Scripture is uniquely suited to provide instruction in the life of faith. We should note carefully both the extent of the claim being made here for Scripture and the type of value attributed to it. It is said to be "profitable" or "useful" (v. 16), which in itself is a modest claim. It is said to be useful in four respects:

1. Teaching—as a source for positive instruction
2. Reproof—as a source for refuting error
3. Correction—as a source for "guiding people's lives" (NJB)
4. Training in righteousness—as a source to provide "discipline in right living" (REB)

It is most particularly suited for "everyone who belongs to God" (v. 17; cf. 1 Tim. 6:11; also 1 Sam. 2:27; 1 Kings 13:1), in this case, the minister, but more generally for the person committed to the quest of God.

With this orientation to what has been received and to Scripture as the richest source of the tradition, Timothy is now given a solemn charge to continue steadfastly in the work of ministry. It is a charge made in the very presence of God (v. 1; cf. 1 Tim. 5:21; 6:11–13) and Christ, the eschatological judge of "the living and the dead" (v. 1; Acts 10:42; Rom. 2:16; 14:9–10; 1 Pet. 4:5).

The content of the charge is straightforward: " proclaim the message" (v. 2). This is to be done season in and season out: "welcome or unwelcome, insist on it" (v. 2, NJB). The proclamation of the gospel is to be done in all of its aspects: convincing—using argument and persuasion in speaking the message forcefully; rebuking—using stern words to censure and correct; exhorting—using words of encouragement in trying to elicit a response. All the gestures should be employed: the pointed finger to highlight the argument, the slap of the hand to censure, the arm around the shoulder to encourage. All of this is to be done with enduring patience (v. 2).

Coupled with the charge is a warning that students, left to themselves, will take the easy road (vv. 3–5). They will want a dull message whose edge has been sanded off. Their ears will itch for teaching that soothes. The stern demands of the gospel will be interpreted in watered-down form, and the truth will be exchanged for myths. Faced with this prospect, the minister is urged to pursue a steady course of fidelity, even in the face of suffering—to "work to spread the gospel" (v. 5, REB).

Luke 18:1–8

The parable of the unjust judge, found in this Gospel alone, is typically Lucan in structure. The parable itself (vv. 2–5) is prefaced by an introduction stating the purpose for the parable (v. 1) and is followed by interpretive comments (vv. 6–8). Like the parable of the dishonest steward (16:1–13), the lesson to be learned is drawn from the behavior of someone who is less than admirable. The parable is structured on an argument from the lesser to the greater: if an insensitive and hardened judge will hear the pleas of a widow, how much more can we trust that God will hear the prayers of those who day and night cry for vindication. It would be an error, therefore, for the preacher to draw a straight analogy between the judge and God.

In fact, the introduction to the parable can be slightly misleading. That disciples ought always to pray and not lose heart is a valid and important lesson in constancy, but the point in our text concerns not prayer in general but a specific prayer. Discerning the specific problem being addressed demands that we look at the context and at the interpretive comments at the conclusion of the parable.

The context for today's lection begins at 17:20 with the question concerning when the kingdom of God is to come. This question prompts a series of teachings on the day of the Son of Man (vv. 22–37). The closing verse of our text continues to speak of the coming of the Son of Man (v. 8), making it clear that the parable of the unjust judge is to be interpreted in that context. With this understanding, verse 1 should be interpreted as a word to disciples who have been taught to pray "Thy kingdom come," but who now have grown weary and are losing heart. Their discouragement is probably due in part to the passing of time and to what is usually referred to as the delay of the Parousia. By Luke's day, several generations had passed, and time alone can erode enthusiasm and faithfulness (Heb. 6:11–12; 2 Pet. 3:11–14; Rev. 21:7). But verses 7–8 make it clear that the faithful are not only experiencing the passing of time but also are undergoing persecution. They are seeking vindication.

The question, How long will the Lord tarry? was a burden on the faith of Israel as well as the early church. When will the cup of God's wrath be full so that vindication will come for the faithful? Most of the answers offered by prophets and apocalyptists spoke of God's desire that all have opportunity to repent, and this included those from whom the faithful prayed for deliverance. In the text before us, the disciples are told to continue in sustained faithfulness in their prayer for the coming of the kingdom. In addition, they are assured that the time of waiting and of persecution is near an end. God "will quickly grant justice to them" (v. 8).

Verse 8, however, poses a new question for the followers of Jesus. The question, When? posed by the Pharisees is clearly the wrong one (17:20–21). The question, How long shall we continue to pray? is doubly answered in the parable and the comments that follow. But the really crucial question is the one asked by Jesus: The Son of Man is coming to vindicate his people, but who are his people? Will those apparently so interested in the Eschaton and the reversal of the fortunes of the evil and the good be faithfully committed to Christ up until the end? Will the Son of Man actually find faith among us? As stated by Christ elsewhere, "The one who endures to the end will be saved" (Mark 13:13).

Proper 25 [30]
(Sunday between October 23 and 29 inclusive)

Joel 2:23–32;
Psalm 65; or
Sirach 35:12–17 or Jeremiah 14:7–10, 19–22;
Psalm 84:1–7;
2 Timothy 4:6–8, 16–18;
Luke 18:9–14

The bounty of God's love is reflected in the eschatological vision sketched by the prophet Joel in the *Common Lectionary*'s Old Testament reading for today. The text concludes with the promise of the outpouring of God's Spirit. Psalm 65 praises, among other things, God's creative and sustaining power, and does so with richly memorable images drawn from nature.

Other lectionaries provide two options for the Old Testament reading. The text from Sirach 35 honors God as generous and unequivocally just, incapable of being bribed. In the text from Jeremiah 14, forthright confession causes the people to plead for mercy. The first half of Psalm 84, which serves as the psalm of response, expresses the sentiments of a joyful worshiper in the temple.

A mood of somber farewell is expressed in the Epistle lesson from 2 Timothy, yet the passage expresses the words of a soldier who has fought hard, a runner who has run well.

Pharisee and tax collector stand in sharp contrast to each other in today's Gospel text, which Luke uses to illustrate one of his favorite themes—divine reversal.

Joel 2:23–32

Although there is no superscription that dates the Book of Joel, the political and religious references fit the Persian period, probably about 400 BC. Whereas the earlier prophets criticized priests and challenged the validity of rituals, Joel quite likely was a cultic prophet, one who participated directly, and probably in an officially recognized fashion, in the services of worship in the Second Temple. We hear him giving the call to prayer and fasting, ordering the priests to gather the people, giving instructions for prayer, and then proclaiming—as priests do—the divine response to the people's genuine prayers of confession and contrition.

The Book of Joel is a liturgical work in two parts. In the first part (Joel 1:2–2:17), the prophet directs the community to convene a service of complaint and petition to God, initially because of the threat of a plague of locusts (1:4–20) and then because of the terrifying prospect of the day of the Lord. In the second part (Joel 2:18–3:21), the mood has changed dramatically because the people have repented. God promises salvation and over and over again assures the people that their prayers have been heard. The day of the Lord has become a day of salvation because the people trusted in their God.

Both in terms of form and content, the passage before us is a series of announcements of salvation. It had been preceded in verses 21–22 by words of assurance to the natural world, spoken by the prophet. The land itself is called to rejoice. Then (v. 23) the prophet issues similar calls to the people to celebrate because God has given the rain. The rain will bring the harvest, so verses 24–25 announce the reversal of the bad fortune described in the first part of the book. The Lord promises that there will be plenty of grain, wine, and oil, and that he will restore the losses caused by the locusts. In a further announcement of salvation (vv. 26–27), the bounty of nature is related to the joy of worship and the continuing presence of God among the people. When all these things happen, the people will be assured that there is no other God but Yahweh.

The last verses of our reading (vv. 28–32) proclaim the renewal of humankind through the gift of the Lord's spirit. The announcement of salvation has moved beyond the promise of material blessings and looks toward a time when all of the Lord's people will experience divine revelation and will join together on Mt. Zion. The vision is inclusive. There are gifts of the spirit for all, female and male, young and old, free and slave—indeed, it will be for "all flesh." Throughout the Old Testament, the "spirit" of the Lord was understood as that which gives life (Gen. 2:7), the difference between a dead body and a living being. It is also the Lord's spirit that grasps prophets and gives them the divine message. The spirit empowers and reveals. Here, when the Lord pours out his spirit the result is prophecy, dreams, and visions. These three are used here almost synonymously for the experience of divine revelation—specifically, the vision of the reign of God. Verse 30 begins a new unit in the book, one that provides the apocalyptic context in which the vision of the spirit of the Lord should be understood.

Thus the passage moves from celebration of the bounty of nature—the land, animals, pastures, trees, vines, rain—to the promise of the coming reign of God. The first may seem too materialistic and worldly, and the latter too spiritual for modern tastes; the one too bound to the earth and the present, and the other too distant and otherworldly. Would we prefer a vision of the reign of God that is neither one nor the other, but a compromise? Remarkably, the Old Testament tradition insists on both. God will reign fully one day; but for the present, God's grace is known in the good gifts of creation.

Psalm 65

Very few psalms of community thanksgiving are found in the Psalter (see Psalms 67, 92, 107). A hymn may have served as the community's response to specific acts of divine providence, and thus no great need existed for writing special thanksgiving psalms. Psalm 65 is probably one of the exceptional psalms of communal thanksgiving.

All of the psalm is direct address to the Deity, although some scholars see a radical change of tone between verses 1–4 and verse 5 following. Some even argue for three psalms (1–4, 5–8,

9–13). The composition appears, however, to be a unity, and the elements of sin, creation, and divine blessing of the crops/harvests noted in the text are not so unrelated.

Verses 1–4 focus on the human admission and divine forgiveness of sin. Difficulties in translating verses 1–2 make the exact meaning uncertain. For example, in the Hebrew, the opening line says, "To thee praise is silent" or "is waiting." Note the KJV, which reads, "Praise waiteth for thee." Verses 2b and 3a can be translated, "Unto you all flesh shall bring the requirements of iniquity." At any rate, certain factors seem clear.

1. The occasion for the celebration and the praise of God is the fulfillment of vows. These may have been vows made to be carried out if certain conditions were met by God, such as providing a good crop year or forgiving sins, probably the latter. Moderns look judgmentally on vows or deals with God, or at least we publicly express ourselves that way. Ancient Israel was unashamed of such arrangements.

2. A public, communal acknowledgment of sin is made. A basic feature of Israelite religion was a routine day of national repentance (Yom Kippur). Other days of repentance were held when deemed necessary. The minister who preaches on this psalm should imaginatively think about what such days of national repentance might do in contemporary culture, where admitting wrong and guilt is itself considered to be a national sin.

3. Worship in the temple is viewed as an exhilarating source of joy and blessedness. The goodness of the temple (v. 4c) probably refers to the sacrificial feasts eaten in the temple in conjunction with thanksgiving. (The covered dish dinner has a long genealogy and a most sumptuous ancestry!)

In verses 5–8, the psalm shifts to focus on the divine creation of the cosmos and the establishment of order in the world. Chaos is represented by the seas, the waves, the people (and the roaring and tumult). Over against these, God establishes, stills, and pacifies so that the regularity of nature in which the mornings and evenings follow each other provides successive shouts for joy.

The verses in the psalm most reflective of the theme of thanksgiving as an agricultural festival are verses 9–13. The entire cycle of the harvest year is reflected in these verses. There is reference, first, to the autumn rains (called the early rains) that water the ground and make plowing and sowing possible. In Palestine, the summer, from about mid-May until late September or early October, is completely rainless. During this period, the land dries up and vegetation dies. The early fall rains, from "the river of God" in the heavenly world, soften the land and seeding follows. The winter rains make possible the growth of grain. Then in the late spring, harvest occurs. The harvest in verses 11–13 speaks of the bounty of the spring season; God's wagon drips fatness upon the land. Pastures, hills, meadows, and valleys give forth their crops and newborn animals, all considered the blessings of God.

Sirach 35:12–17

For information on the Book of Sirach (or Ecclesiasticus), see the commentary of Sirach 10:12–18 at Proper 17 [22] in this volume.

There are variations among the modern translations in the versification of this passage because translators have made different decisions about the underlying text. The assigned verses correspond to the versification of the NEB and the REB. With some variations, the JB and the NJB give both versifications. In the NRSV the lection is 35:14–20. In our commentary we will list the verses of the NRSV first and those of the NEB and the REB second.

The section before us is part of a larger unit (34:18–35:20) concerning worship, mainly sacrifices and prayers. The immediately preceding passage (35:1–13/1–11) is a poetic discourse on the relationship between obedience to the law and sacrifices. Obedience to and the study of the law—that is, the first five books of the Hebrew Scriptures—are important to ben Sirach, and his book contains a great deal of reflection upon and interpretation of it. In this first section of chapter 35 his fundamental point is that the foundation for proper sacrifice and other forms of worship is obedience to the law in all of one's life: "The sacrifice of the righteous is acceptable" (35:9/7). He encourages his hearers to be generous in their worship because the Lord has been generous to them.

Our assigned lesson was chosen doubtless because of its thematic parallel to the Gospel lesson for the day, Luke's parable of the Pharisee and the tax collector. Their common concern is proper prayer. In both texts it is the unexpected party whose prayer is heard. There is a parallel of social class between Luke's tax collector and ben Sirach's poor and widows.

The basic issue is genuine piety. Ben Sirach focuses both on behavior and attitudes or intentions, counseling first that one should not offer God a bribe (v. 14/12). Is "bribe" here literal or metaphorical? If it is literal, as the parallel lines in this verse suggest ("dishonest sacrifice"), then the verse picks up the concerns of 34:21–31: one should not offer to the Lord what one has taken from the poor. If it is metaphorical, then it concerns one's intentions in making sacrifices: one should not be self-seeking but should act out of gratitude (35:10–12/8–10). It is easy to misunderstand ben Sirach's counsel that with the Lord "there is no partiality" (v. 15/13). In the succeeding verse it seems clear that the Lord will attend particularly to the words of the poor, to those who have been wronged. "He has no favourites at the poor man's expense, but listens to his prayer when he is wronged" (v. 15/13, NEB). The next section of our reading (vv. 17–19/15–16) emphasize the Lord's attentiveness to the prayers of the orphan and the widow, especially when they cry out against "the one who causes them to fall." In the concluding verse the author stresses more generally that it is "the one whose service is pleasing to the Lord" whose prayers will be heard, which will "reach to the clouds" (v. 20/17).

Thus a discourse that begins with advice and instructions concerning worship becomes a lesson about human and divine justice. Ben Sirach shows how thoroughly he has studied not only the Torah but also the psalms and the prophets. This homily on proper sacrifices and prayers is strikingly similar in content to Isaiah 1:10–17, in which the Lord is heard to reject all worship from hands bloody with injustice, and concludes that to do good and to seek justice is to rescue the oppressed, defend the orphan, and plead the widow's case. It also parallels Israel's literature of worship that constantly links the life lived according to the law's justice with acceptable sacrifice and prayer (Pss. 1; 15; 24; 26; 50:16–23; 82). Anyone who would drive a wedge between piety and social justice will seek in vain for biblical warrants.

Jeremiah 14:7–10, 19–22

The verses assigned for reading today are part of a larger collection of material (Jer. 14:1–15:9). Although this unit doubtless contains material that goes back to the prophet Jeremiah, it was edited into its present form by the deuteronomistic editors of the book, probably during the Babylonian Exile. These editors, as well as Jeremiah before them, were concerned with making sense of the disaster that had befallen Judah and Jerusalem. In this collection of material, both the editors and Jeremiah were also concerned with the role of Jeremiah in the events at the end of Judah's history, specifically the role of the prophet as intercessor. Were not prophets supposed to communicate not only the words of Yahweh to the people but also the words of the people to Yahweh? Did Jeremiah intercede, and if he did, why was not his intercession on behalf of the people effective?

Both the larger unit (14:1–15:9) and the portions of it selected for reading today have liturgical shape, and echo with the language of prayer and response. It is that interest in prayer, the question of effective prayers, that accounts for the assignment of this text for reading with the Gospel lesson for the day, Luke's parable of the Pharisee and the tax collector. It is unlikely that Jeremiah 14:1–15:9 contains the actual liturgy for a prayer service; rather, it has been composed and structured according to liturgical patterns that would have been well known—a service of communal complaint or lament.

Such services organized the community's response to actual or impending disasters. Jeremiah 14:1 indicates that the problem is a drought, but later the disaster is more comprehensive: "by the sword, by famine, and by pestilence" (14:12). In the final edited form, the military defeat and exile by the Babylonians seems to be in view. As we see from the communal complaints in the Psalter (Psalms 79; 80; 85), such occasions would have included prayers that describe the trouble, pleas for God to help, confessions of sin, and affirmations of confidence in God's power and mercy. In a complete liturgy, various voices would have spoken, including the people, the priests, sometimes prophets, and perhaps choirs.

Verses 7–9 are a prayer for help, usually the very heart of the individual or communal lament or complaint. In this prayer the people confess their sins, first indirectly ("Although our iniquities testify against us, . . ." v. 7) and then explicitly ("our apostasies indeed are many, and we have sinned against you" v. 7). Their plea to God is to act, to intervene to help. In verses 8–9 the people argue their case, expressing confidence in God ("O hope of Israel, its savior in time of trouble") and suggesting that God, by not responding, is acting contrary to God's nature ("stranger in the land," "traveler turning aside for the night," "like someone confused"). The prayer concludes with another affirmation of confidence ("you, O LORD, are in the midst of us"), a reminder that those in trouble are the Lord's own ("we are called by your name"), and a final plea ("do not forsake us!").

A dramatic shift of speaker and addressee occurs in verse 10. From words *to* God we have words *of* God. This verse would have been uttered by the prophetic voice, for it begins with the messenger formula ("Thus says the LORD") common to Jeremiah and the other prophets. In form the verse is a concise prophecy of punishment. Following the messenger formula there is the indictment or the reasons for punishment ("they have loved to wander"). Then, after the transitional "therefore" comes the announcement of punishment: "the LORD does not accept them, now he will remember their iniquity and punish their sins." In the context, this prophetic word from the Lord functions as the response to the prayer of the people. God's answer is an emphatic "No, I will not help you." Significantly, this prophecy of punishment is not addressed directly to the people but refers to them in the third person. So who is addressed? It can only be the prophet. Thus it is implied that not only did the people pray for help but also Jeremiah interceded on their behalf.

Verses 19–22 contain another prayer of the people for help. Again, the situation is presented to the Lord, who is asked why he has rejected Judah and Zion (v. 19). The people confess their sins (v. 20), plead directly for God to help (v. 21), and affirm their confidence in God, contrasting the Lord's power with that of idols (v. 22). As often in complaint songs of both the individual and of the community, the petitioners appeal to God's honor and to the Lord's special relationship with them (v. 21).

What follows this second prayer of the people is another divine response (15:1–4), which is again directed to the prophet. Here it becomes clear that Jeremiah has performed the traditional prophetic role as intercessor for the people. Even when Moses and Samuel had interceded on behalf of their people, God had refused to intervene to save. Now Jeremiah is informed that the die is cast, and by the history of the people's sins. The people are doomed to pestilence, the sword, famine, and captivity. The prophet's role is to announce judgment and thus set it into motion. This harsh answer to a prayer recalls Isaiah 6:9–13, which also includes prophetic intercession.

In its context, our lesson evokes serious and troubling reflections on prayer and God's answers to prayers. Of course, the editors of this unit of the Book of Jeremiah had the advantage of hindsight, knowing that the national disaster had not been averted, although many among the people prayed for help. We, too, will recall that some of our prayers in the past have not been answered in the affirmative.

Psalm 84:1–7

Two issues dominate this psalm: pilgrimage to Zion and worship in the temple. The psalm can be understood as a composition written for singing as pilgrims journeyed to attend a festival in Jerusalem. (Many scholars, however, understand the psalm as a composition by someone who could not make the trip to Jerusalem. Thus it is a psalm of homesickness for Zion. This interpretation seems unlikely.)

Psalms were no doubt sung by pilgrims on the journey to Jerusalem. Psalm 42:4 speaks of the throng making its way in procession to the house of God "with glad shouts and songs of thanksgiving." Isaiah 30:29, speaking of the good time to come, says: "You shall have a song as in the night when a holy festival is kept; and gladness of heart, as when one sets out to the sound of the flute to go to the mountain of the LORD." Psalms 120–134 are a collection of songs to be sung on pilgrimage.

One might expect that on pilgrimage antiphonal singing might take place. That is, the leader of the pilgrimage group and the pilgrims would engage in singing to lift the spirits, pass the time, and express the "tourist" atmosphere of the occasion as well as genuine religious sentiments. This may help explain some of the variations in address in Psalm 84. The following verses are addressed to the Deity—1, 3–7a, 8–10a, 12—whereas the others speak about the Deity—2, 7b, 10b–11. Perhaps the two types of material in the psalm were sung by two different groups in the pilgrimage party or by the leader, with the pilgrims responding.

Verses 1–2 manifest the temple veneration, almost a mystical devotion to the temple, from two perspectives. Verse 1 appears as an objective assertion, or as an affirmation external to the worshipers: "How lovely is your dwelling place, O LORD of hosts!" The temple was, of course, the "house [home] of God," and here one has the type of accolade that might be made in value-judging a human's place of residence—"What a lovely place you have!" From the external affirmation, the psalm turns to the internal emotion associated with the temple (v. 2). Longing, fainting for, yearning for, singing for joy about are feelings associated with the temple courts. We Christians, and Protestants in particular, may have difficulty sharing or understanding the almost sensual happiness and joy associated with festival observances in the temple. Such observances combined high pageantry, feasting, and dancing, and the sense of the divine presence with the atmosphere of a country fair and community reunion. Old acquaintances were renewed, past experiences shared, and new relationships acquired. At the same time, one participated in the cultic services and sacrifices that were seen as restoring and preserving world order.

Verses 3–4 give expression to this devotion in terms of a fantasied identification. How glorious it must be for the birds who nest in the temple precincts, near the altars! The birds—here sparrows and swallows—did not nest in or even beside the altars (the altar of sacrifice in the courtyard and the altar of incense in the building) but near them. "Those who live in your house" may refer to the birds, but also the phrase could denote the temple servants, some of whom were always in the temple.

Verses 5–7 speak about factors associated with the pilgrimage—finding refuge (strength) in God and contemplating the roadways or pilgrim paths to Jerusalem. The presence of pilgrims in the valley of Baca ("thirst" or "weeping") transforms it into an oasis, just as the early fall rains, which could begin in September before the fall festival, moisten the soil, hot and arid from the rainless summer. As the pilgrims move closer to Jerusalem, their numbers swell ("from strength to strength") as parties from other areas join together.

2 Timothy 4:6–8, 16–18

Faced with death, we tend to say and do certain things. We soberly reflect on our impending death in view of our immediate circumstances. We look at our life in review and then cast a glance into the future that lies beyond death. We also speak of what—or who—ultimately matters to us. And if we are people of faith, our farewell reflections will inevitably speak of God.

In today's text, we have Paul's farewell words, shorn of the human particulars (vv. 9–15, 19–21). In one sense the entire epistle of Second Timothy should be read as a last will and testament of Paul, but the words of today's text represent his concluding sentiments. It is hard to say to what degree they are the words of the historical Paul. To be sure, they echo themes Paul used to describe his own ministry. These include the metaphors of sacrificial libations (Phil. 2:17), fighting either as an athlete or a soldier (1 Cor. 9:24–27; cf. 1 Tim. 1:18; 6:12; also Jude 3), and running the race (1 Cor. 9:24–25; Phil. 3:12–14; cf. Acts 20:24). At the very least, they represent how Paul was remembered by his admirers. They should perhaps be read alongside the Lucan version of Paul's words (Acts 20:17–38) or compared with other testaments (cf. Gen. 49:1–27; Deut. 33:1–29).

The two parts of today's text reflect slightly different concerns and moods. In the first section (vv. 6–8), we have Paul's sober reflections on his impending death, his former life, and his view of the future. The mood is not so much resignation but matter-of-fact realism: "the time of my departure has come" (v. 6). Nothing of the morbid or macabre here, nor the sentimentalizing of death. Paul is facing death as a fact of life. In the second section (vv. 16–18), the mood shifts slightly. There is the sense of abandonment. The old warrior has been forsaken, and we detect a querulous tone as Paul mentions those who deserted him (v. 16; cf. 1:15; 4:10). For the true soldier, the cardinal sin is desertion. But balancing this sense of irritation with the less loyal is the sense of trust in the Lord who never deserts.

Reflections on death, life, and reward (vv. 6–8). At other times Paul had stared death in the face (1 Cor. 15:30–32; 2 Cor. 1:8–11) and in more contemplative moments expressed the desire to "depart and be with Christ" (Phil. 1:23). He could envision himself as a libation being poured over a sacrificial offering (Phil. 2:17; cf. Exod. 29:40; Num. 28:7). But here there is a note of finality, as if the last drop of the libation is being poured on the altar: "my life is already being poured away as a libation" (v. 6, NJB).

Oddly enough, nowhere in the New Testament is the death of Paul recorded, although there are hints (cf. Acts 20:29, 38; cf. 2 Pet. 3:15). It speaks of the death of principal figures in terms that are either brief or allusive (cf. John 21:18–19, 23; Acts 7:54–8:1; 12:2). The notable exception, of course, is Jesus. According to later Christian tradition, Paul was beheaded in Rome during the reign of Nero (AD 54–68).

Looking back, Paul summarizes his life confidently, even triumphantly. He is the fighter who has fought hard, the runner who has run well (v. 7). He has "kept the faith," meaning that he has been faithful to the tradition. Accordingly, he views the future expectantly, looking to receive the victor's crown (v. 8; cf. 1 Cor. 9:25; 2 Tim. 2:5; James 1:12; Rev. 2:10; 3:11; also Wisd. of Sol. 5:16). His eye is fixed on "that day," the day of Yahweh, when the exalted Christ serves as "righteous judge" (4:1; cf. Heb. 12:23; James 4:12; 5:9). Sharing with Paul in the reign of God will be "all who have longed for his appearing" (v. 8); that is, all who regard his incarnation as the welcome manifestation of God (1:10; Titus 2:11), as well as those who welcome his final appearing in the Parousia (cf. 1 Tim. 6:14; Titus 2:13; 2 Thess. 2:8).

Human desertion, divine loyalty (vv. 16–18). At his first hearing, Paul stands alone. It is a picture reminiscent of the trial of Jesus (Matt. 26:56; Mark 14:50; John 16:32). Earlier he mentioned those who have left—Demas, Crescens, Titus (v. 10). Only Luke accompanies him. In the face of human desertion, Paul finds the Lord to be ever present and near (cf. Acts 18:9–10; 23:11; 27:23–24; also Phil. 4:5). He also becomes the source of strength out of which the gospel is proclaimed to the Gentiles (cf. Phil. 4:13; 2 Cor. 12:8–10; John 15:5). Being "rescued from the lion's mouth" (v. 17) recalls the language of Psalm 22:21 (cf. Pss. 7:2; 17:12; Dan. 6:16–24; 1 Macc. 2:60) and suggests deliverance from a violent death. In words reminiscent of the Lord's Prayer, Paul looks to be delivered from every evil (v. 18; cf. Matt. 6:13; John 17:15; 2 Cor. 1:10; 2 Thess. 3:3) and hopes to share in the heavenly reign (2:12). The final word is a Pauline doxology (cf. Rom. 16:27; also textual addition to Matt. 6:13).

When preaching from this text, the minister will need to ask whether, and to what degree, these are the words of the historical Paul. But the historical-critical question need not set the agenda entirely. What we have here is a portrait of Paul's farewell. As we have seen, there are enough echoes and links to the undisputed letters of Paul for it to ring true. Apart from this, however, the text does present us with one way of confronting death, measuring life, and facing the future. For Paul, none of these could be done seriously apart from the life of faith. For that reason, the mood of our text is confident, and the message is one of hope.

Luke 18:9–14

W ith the parable of the Pharisee and the tax collector we conclude the special section of Luke that began at 9:51. This will not conclude Luke's travel narrative, which continues until the entry into Jerusalem (19:40), but 18:14 ends the material in Luke that is a departure from the Markan framework.

As was true of the parable of the unjust judge (18:1–8) immediately preceding, this story is not only unique to Luke but is told in typically Lucan fashion. The format is this: an introduction stating the purpose and thrust of the parable (v. 9); the parable proper (vv. 10–13); and comments on the parable (v. 14). In this case, the closing comments are two: the statement of the justification of the publican and the statement of the reversed roles of the humble and the proud. This second comment is in the form of a pronouncement and as such was used in a variety of contexts (Luke 14:11; Matt. 18:4; 23:12). If one wonders why this parable is located here, the answer may simply be in the fact that it, like the one before it, deals with prayer. In addition, both parables deal with justification, the words "grant justice" in the previous story being a form of the word here translated as "justify." It may be, however, that Luke thought it wise to follow a parable about the prayers of saints with one about the prayers of sinners, lest arrogant claims be made by either group.

The parable of the Pharisee and the tax collector conveys in story form the doctrine of God's justification of sinners and judgment on the efforts of those who try to establish their own righteousness. These twin accents are usually associated with Paul, especially his Roman and Galatian Letters, but they are in fact as old as the Garden of Eden, the tower of Babel, and Jonah's mission to Ninevah. The parable makes its point by means of the reversal of stations so familiar in Luke when dealing with the self-righteous and the humble, the strong and the weak, the haves and the have-nots (1:51; 6:20–26; 16:19–31). It would be difficult for any interpreter of the parable to improve on the clear statement of Luke; it is addressed to those who trust in themselves, thinking they are righteous, and who despise others.

However, few parables have been subjected to more distortion than this one. For example, one common error is painting the Pharisee as a villain and the tax collector as a hero, and in so doing each gets what he deserves. This is exactly the opposite of the parable's message. The Pharisee is not a villain but rather represents complete dedication to observing the law of Moses. In fact, his recitation of his performance is that of a person exceeding the law's demands. His prayer is a common rabbinic expression of thanksgiving prefaced by the claim of the psalmist with reference to personal behavior (Ps. 17:3–5). Nor is the tax collector a hero. In fact, as a tax collector working for Rome collecting taxes from his own people, he is a reprehensible character, religiously unclean and politically a traitor. Although his prayer is according to Psalm 51, his life is offensive. To miss this fact is to rob the parable of its radicality. God justifies the ungodly, a truth blurred by popular caricatures that present the Pharisee as a hollow hypocrite but the tax collector as generous Joe the bartender or honest Albert the atheist, both to be admired for their rejection of organized religion. Cheap novels that play on these themes do not understand that God justifies sinners who confess and rely on grace. The Pharisee trusts in himself; the tax collector trusts in God: that is the difference.

The preacher-interpreter will want to be extremely sensitive to Luke's focus, lest the parable be presented in such a way as to make the tax collector proud and thankful that he is not as others. Nothing is gained if parishioners leave the sanctuary thankful that they are not like the Pharisee.

Proper 26 [31]
(Sunday between October 30 and November 5 inclusive)

Habakkuk 1:1–4; 2:1–4;
Psalm 119:137–144; or
Isaiah 1:10–18;
Psalm 32:1–7;
2 Thessalonians 1:1–4, 11–12;
Luke 19:1–10

In the opening words of today's Old Testament text for the *Common Lectionary*, we hear echoes of our own protest to God against injustice in the world, while in the closing words we are reassured that the righteous will live by faith. The theme of righteousness also pervades the selection from Psalm 119, although the emphasis falls on the righteousness of God. These words serve well as a response to the reading from Habakkuk, for they boldly assert and defend God's justice.

For other lectionaries, the Old Testament reading is the latter half of God's lawsuit against Israel, with which First Isaiah begins. It is a hearty protest against many forms of Israel's infidelity. If the Old Testament reading issues harsh judgment against Israel, Psalm 32, a song of thanksgiving by a forgiven sinner, offers hope.

Paul's opening prayer of thanksgiving in Second Thessalonians serves as today's epistolary reading, concluding with the confident hope that God would make these new converts worthy of their calling.

In the Gospel lesson, we meet the familiar story of Zacchaeus, whose encounter with the Lord results in his conversion and uncommon generosity.

Habakkuk 1:1–4; 2:1–4

For a commentary on this lesson, see the discussion of it with the readings for Proper 22 [27] in this volume.

Psalm 119:137–144

This psalm (see above, Proper 24 [29]) uses the following synonymous terms relating to the Torah: *judgments, decrees, words, promise, precepts, law, commandments.* The theme of righteousness in this eighteenth stanza of the psalm correlates with the reading from

457

Habakkuk. Here the emphasis is on divine righteousness. The law is viewed as a stabilizing and delightful element in life in spite of others' lack of respect for the law and in spite of trouble and distress.

Isaiah 1:10–18

For a commentary on this reading, see the discussion of Isaiah 1:1, 10–20 with the lessons for Proper 14 [19] in this volume.

Psalm 32:1–7

This psalm was discussed as one of the lections for the Fourth Sunday in Lent in this volume.

2 Thessalonians 1:1–4, 11–12

This is the first of three semicontinuous readings from the epistle of Second Thessalonians to be read over the next two weeks. They should perhaps be read along with the closely related set of semicontinuous readings from the epistle of First Thessalonians that serve as the epistolary readings for Propers 24–28 [29–33] in Year A. Nevertheless, a few introductory remarks to Second Thessalonians are in order here.

The church at Thessalonica was established by Paul and his co-workers Silas and Timothy during his mission in the Aegean area (1 Thess. 1:6–10; 2:1–2, 9–12, 17–20; Acts 17:1–9). Predominantly Gentile in its composition (1 Thess. 1:9–10), this fledgling church was born and flourished in a hostile setting (1 Thess. 2:14–16; Acts 17:5). As those who had received the word with "grave suffering" (1 Thess. 1:6, REB), they knew the pressure of religious persecution firsthand. But they had demonstrated remarkable patience and steadfastness in the face of open resistance.

Coming from a Gentile background, they were probably less accustomed to Jewish ways of thinking about the end time and life after death. As a result, eschatology confused them. In the epistle of First Thessalonians, the primary question they asked was whether one of their members who had died would thereby be excluded from the heavenly reign. Was it necessary for one to be alive when the Lord returned? Paul assures them that both those who are alive at Christ's coming and those Christians who have died previously will share in the Lord's coming (1 Thess. 4:13–18). They are also reminded that the date of the Lord's coming is unknown, and the proper response is to be constantly alert (1 Thess. 5:1–11).

The situation envisioned in the epistle of Second Thessalonians is slightly different. There is still eschatological confusion, but this time the worry is not about the future. From some outside source, perhaps a letter forged in the name of Paul, the Thessalonians had been taught that the day of the Lord had already come (2 Thess. 2:1–2). If this had not already been taught, there was the fear that it would be. Paul's response to this is to underscore the futurity of the Lord's Parousia. As he does so, Paul sketches a series of events that are to occur in the interim, thus demonstrating that some things are still to occur before they can say that the Lord has already come (2 Thess. 2:3–12).

Because of the sharp difference between the types of eschatological misunderstanding addressed in each of the Thessalonian epistles, some scholars have questioned the authenticity of the second epistle. They find it difficult to believe that the situation could have changed so much so soon. Others have noted a more radical apocalyptic tone in the second epistle, suggesting that the instructions given there have a sharper, more vindictive edge than we normally find in Paul.

If the epistle of Second Thessalonians does not come directly from Paul's hand, it stands very close to the first epistle, both in time and outlook. More important than the question of authorship, however, is the awareness of how the letter addresses a congregation of believers for whom the price of faith is persecution (1:4).

Today's text includes the salutation and opening prayer of thanksgiving (1:1–4), which concludes by noting the afflictions the church is having to endure. The mention of affliction in verse 4 prompts a rather severe statement concerning God's response to the enemies of the people of God (vv. 5–12). The final two verses of this response serve as the concluding portion of today's epistolary lection. By bracketing verses 5–10, the *New Common Lectionary* omits a troublesome portrait of God, thereby making the overall text less troubling for a liturgical setting. But the preacher is obligated to pay close attention to what has been bracketed, if for no other reason than to appreciate the salutary features of those parts of chapter 1 that have been chosen for today's epistle reading.

The response in verses 5–12 is framed in the clear expectation of the future coming of Christ (cf. 2:3–12). This event is conceived in terms informed by Jewish apocalyptic. The Lord is expected to be "revealed from heaven" (v. 7; Dan. 7:13–14; Mark 9:1; Luke 17:30; 1 Cor. 1:7; 1 Pet. 1:7, 13; 4:13), accompanied by a host of "mighty angels" (v. 7; Matt. 13:39, 41, 49; 16:27; 24:31; 25:31; Luke 12:8–9). In terms reminiscent of Old Testament depictions of the coming day of the Lord, this event is also to be accompanied by "flaming fire" (v. 8; Exod. 13:22; 19:16–18; Isa. 66:15; cf. 1 Cor. 3:13, 15).

Out of this cosmic upheaval comes the exalted Christ "inflicting vengeance" (v. 8; cf. Rev. 19:11–16). It may be an unsettling image to us, this vengeance-bringing Christ, but the notion of a God who vindicates the people of God against their enemies has a long history (cf. Deut. 32:36). It becomes something of an axiom that God can play this role, whereas human beings cannot (Rom. 12:19; 13:4; 1 Thess. 2:16; Heb. 10:30; Luke 18:3).

The objects of the Lord's vengeance are twofold: (1) "those who do not know God," that is, Gentiles (v. 8; cf. Jer. 10:25; Ps. 79:6; 1 Thess. 4:5; Gal. 4:8; 1 Cor. 15:34); and (2) "those who do not obey the gospel of our Lord Jesus," that is, Jews (v. 8; cf. Isa. 66:4; Rom. 10:16; 1 Pet. 4:17). Another interpretation is to see only one group of resisters who are described in two respects: in terms of their ignorance as well as their disobedience. Whether one group or two, they suffer a similar fate. First, the Lord actually visits them with affliction (v. 7; Phil. 1:28; Rev. 14:13). Second, they suffer "the punishment of eternal destruction, separated from the presence of the Lord" (v. 9; cf. Isa. 2:10, 19, 21; Ps. 64:7–9; 1 Thess. 3:13).

In light of this tribulation that is expected to continue, the threat turns to prayer (vv. 11–12), which forms the second part of today's epistolary lection. Paul's prayer is that those under pressure will be strengthened in their resolve and enabled to be worthy of their call (v. 11; also v. 5; cf. 1 Thess. 2:12; Phil. 1:27; Eph. 4:1; Col. 1:10). It is, after all, the kingly reign of God for which they are suffering (v. 5; cf. Acts 14:22; 1 Thess. 2:14; 3:4; Eph. 3:13).

This concluding portion of chapter 1 returns to the theme of prayerful thanksgiving in verse 3. This, of course, is the opening part of the introductory prayer, which typically opens Pauline letters (cf. 1 Thess. 1:2; 2:13; 39). The occasion for his joyful confidence is the Thessalonians' abundant faith and their growing love for one another (v. 3). Their spiritual heartiness is the more remarkable, considering their circumstances (v. 4). Given the start they have made, Paul's prayer in verses 11–12 exudes confidence.

In preaching from this text, we can scarcely ignore the jolting effect of the middle portion of chapter 1. In the plainest terms, we are told that God inflicts punishment on those who afflict God's people. We might well wonder why Christians are instructed not to "repay anyone evil for evil" (Rom. 12:17; cf. Matt. 5:38–42), whereas such behavior at times characterizes God. In trying to account for this form of theological response, we do well to remember that it is a response to persecution. In Revelation, there are times when the church under the threat of annihilation no longer finds meek and gentle images of Jesus appropriate forms of response. In some settings, the only meaningful response to oppression may be aggression, as hard as this is to square with ordinary perceptions of the Christian gospel.

Luke 19:1–10

The episode in Luke 19:1–10 is a Lucan story. This is to say, it is without parallels in the other Gospels. All three Synoptics have Jesus approaching Jerusalem by way of Jericho, and all three record the healing of a blind man (two blind men in Matthew) near Jericho (Matt. 20:29–34; Mark 10:46–52; Luke 18:35–43). However, only Luke tells of Jesus' encounter with Zacchaeus in Jericho. The story does remind the reader of an earlier story in Luke 5:27–32 (Mark 2:13–17; Matt. 9:9–13) concerning Jesus and Levi. Levi was a tax collector; Jesus was a guest in Levi's house; critics murmured against Jesus for this association; Jesus responded with a pronouncement ("I have come to call not the righteous but sinners to repentance," v. 32). The structure of 19:1–10 is much the same, including a very similar closing pronouncement (v. 10).

The episode in Luke 19:1–10 is a human interest story. Luke is well known for his parables that have a narrative plot and include more than the usual amount of interesting detail: the good Samaritan, the rich fool, the rich man and Lazarus, the dishonest steward, the unjust judge, the Pharisee and the tax collector, the prodigal son. It is also the case that Luke evidences conscious literary artistry in narrating nonparabolic stories. The appearance of Jesus to the two disciples on the road to Emmaus (24:13–35) is a classic example of the storyteller's art. The story before us, though briefer, is not without some of the same qualities. In addition to being interesting, Luke 19:1–10 generated some discussion in the early church on the issue of Jesus' stature. The Greek text as well as most English translations permit "because he was short in stature" to refer back to Jesus. An early Jewish critic of Christianity commented on Jesus' short stature as contrary to what one would expect in a son of God.

The episode in Luke 19:1–10 is a conflict story. "All who saw it began to grumble and said, 'He has gone to be the guest of one who is a sinner'" (v. 7). In that day as well as today, the common wisdom was "birds of a feather flock together" and "you can judge a person by the company he keeps." That Jesus rejected such wisdom in his seeking and searching love is a vivid and repeated truth of the Gospels. Loving and forgiving are not condoning, and the behavior of Jesus fulfills rather than abrogates righteousness.

The episode in Luke 19:1–10 is a radical story. Zacchaeus is not only a tax collector; he is a *chief* tax collector. All the criticism that could be hurled against a tax collector (ceremonially unclean, socially ostracized, politically treasonous) could be compounded against Zacchaeus. In a corrupt system, the loftier the position the greater the complicity in that corruption. No one need defend Zacchaeus on the grounds that his private conduct is not revealed. The fact is, one is not privately righteous while participating in a corrupt system that robs and crushes other persons. And Zacchaeus is rich. Given Luke's already stated comments on wealth (1:53; 6:24; 16:19–31), the reader is alerted in verse 2 to the radicality of the act of grace that follows.

Finally, the episode in Luke 19:1–10 is a salvation story. Terms important to Luke tell the story. "Saving the lost," a rare expression, is found here in verse 10 and in 15:6, 24, 32. Zacchaeus *and his house* (v. 9) receive salvation, a concept important to Luke (Acts 10:2; 11:14; 16:15–31; 18:8). Most scholars agree that verse 8, which softens the radicality of the act of grace and which may lead some to think Zacchaeus acted so as to merit forgiveness, was probably a post-Easter church reflection inserted to instruct Christians as to what the fruits of repentance would mean. In the Old Testament, voluntary restitution involved the original amount plus 20 percent (Lev. 6:5; Num. 5:7); compulsory restitution called for doubling the original and in some cases repaying four- or fivefold (Exod. 22:1; 3–4; 2 Sam. 12:6). In Luke's church, forgiveness was not solely a transaction of the heart. Genuine repentance bore fruit. This was made clear as early as the preaching of John the Baptist when crowds and tax collectors and soldiers came asking, "What should we do?" (3:10–14).

Proper 27 [32]
(Sunday between November 6 and 12 inclusive)

Haggai 1:15b–2:9;
Psalm 145:1–5, 17–21 or Psalm 98; or
Job 19:23–27a;
Psalm 17:1–9;
2 Thessalonians 2:1–5, 13–17;
Luke 20:27–38

In contrast to the rather harsh prophetic words from previous Old Testament readings, this text from Haggai, which serves as today's *Common Lectionary* Old Testament reading, speaks of the abiding Spirit of God and the splendor of the new temple. It is a vision of hope propelling us into the future. Two psalms are offered as possible responses. The selections from Psalm 145 extol the greatness and splendor of God, who is depicted as close and responsive to the cries of worshipers. Psalm 98 is also a hymn of celebration to God, the righteous judge of the world.

For other lectionaries, the Old Testament text from Job 19 expressing faith in the living Redeemer sounds a note of triumph. Quite appropriately, in the opening section of Psalm 17 we hear an innocent petitioner supplicate God for help and deliverance.

Today's epistolary text addresses confusion arising from eschatological misunderstanding, yet concludes with the confident expectation that God will bring the salvation of believers to full fruition.

Eschatological themes are also found in today's Gospel reading, Luke's version of Jesus' dispute with the Sadducees about the resurrection and his teaching about what life will be in the age to come.

Haggai 1:15b–2:9

As we approach the end of our series of semicontinuous readings from the prophetic literature, we move into the final period of prophetic activity in ancient Israel, the postexilic period. The captives in Babylon began returning to Judah and Jerusalem in 538 BC following the decree of Cyrus, and the first of them arrived in Jerusalem in 536 BC. Sixteen years later, when Haggai first addressed the returned exiles, they had not yet begun rebuilding the temple. We can be quite precise about these dates because the Book of Haggai is very specific, placing the prophetic addresses in the sixth through the ninth months of the second year of the Persian monarch Darius; that is, 520 BC.

Haggai is a bridge between prophetic and priestly institutions and theologies. He is identified as a prophet (1:1) and, like earlier prophets, addresses the people with words from God, announcing the future. But the content of his message mainly concerns a particular problem, the rebuilding of the temple in Jerusalem. One might say that he brings the authority and fervor of prophetic revelation to bear on what was traditionally a priestly matter. Like a priest, he is deeply concerned not only with the holy place, but also with maintaining the distinction between clean and unclean (2:10–19; cf. Lev. 10:10–11).

The message of Haggai is not without its difficulties in Christian preaching. We look in vain among his words for the passionate concern for justice and righteousness that rings through the messages of the earlier prophets. Moreover, his first revelation urging the people to rebuild the temple (1:1–11) seems almost crass and simplistic in attributing the relative poverty of the returned exiles to the fact that they have not begun work on the temple. Prosperity will follow, he says, if the people will give their energy to the construction.

When the passage assigned for today's reading begins, the work on the temple had started under the leadership of Zerubbabel the governor and Joshua the high priest. But when the people saw the foundations and imagined how the completed building would appear, they were profoundly discouraged. Haggai asks if anyone remembers the old temple in its former glory (v. 3). Few, if any, could possibly remember the first temple, for it had been torn down for sixty-seven years. The comparison they make is between the present reality and the legend of Solomon's glorious temple. But, to judge from the prophet's response, the problem was deeper than disappointment with the building. The temple, along with the monarchy in the line of David, symbolizes for all of them the kingdom of God. Complaints about the building, then, reflect doubts about the presence and power of God.

Haggai responds to these doubts with words of encouragement and reassurance, appealing first to the past and then to the future. Addressing Zerubbabel the governor and Joshua the chief priest, he urges them to be courageous and pronounces the Lord's assurance of his presence, reminding them that they can stand on the promises made during the Exodus (vv. 4–5). Then, in words that reflect a hope similar to that in Isaiah 2:1–4, he promises even more dramatic signs of the coming kingdom of God. The expression "in a little while" (v. 6) has eschatological overtones; Yahweh will "shake" both the created order and all nations, who will bring their treasures to the very temple that the people find disappointing. This promise signals the expectation that all peoples of the earth will recognize and acknowledge through their gifts that Yahweh is God, and Jerusalem is where God is to be worshiped.

What have bricks and mortar to do with the reign of God? Haggai knew that the completion of the temple would not bring in the New Age. God himself will do that. Haggai means to set human work and devotion in the full scheme of God's work—past, present, and future. God acted, acts, and will act, calling for each generation to respond and thus to participate in God's design. Haggai, the practical visionary, calls for his generation to demonstrate its devotion by building the temple, and the God to whom all silver and gold belongs (2:8) will attend to its splendor. The kingdom is that time and place where God's will is done. The temple will be a symbol of God's graceful presence for all the world.

Psalm 145:1–5, 17–21

This acrostic, or alphabetic, psalm interweaves petition and proclamation, prayer and praise, speech to God and speech about God into a well-integrated and articulate composition. Petition/prayer/speech to God is found in verses 1–2, 4–7, 10–13a,

15–16, and proclamation/praise/speech about God is found in verses 3, 8–9, 13b–14, 17–21. Verse 13b belongs with verses 14–21.

Verses 13b–20 may be said to describe the nature of the king who rules over his domain. One of the linguistic features of these verses is the word "all" (Hebrew *kol*), which appears over a dozen times in these verses. The term indicates the inclusiveness and universality of the actions and sentiments of God.

Two things should be noted, in general, about this latter part of the psalm. (1) The author of the psalm, and thus all who used it, speaks about God in a rather detached fashion. Theological speech is present in an almost unique form, but there is little passion, little sense of intense feeling. This fits in with the teaching and didactic quality and alphabetic form of the psalm. (2) The theology of the psalm is one based on extreme confidence, assurance, and certitude. That is, the psalm seems to breathe the air of success in life, to reflect the positive outlook of one secure in the world, confident in the operations of the cosmos and positive in outlook and perspective.

Verses 13b–21 may be viewed (and preached) in terms of two, almost synonymous, propositions that are stated and then further expounded and illustrated. The propositions are found in verses 13b and 17. God is "faithful [loyal] in [to] all his words, and gracious in all his deeds" and "just in all his ways, and kind in all his doings." Two characteristics of the Deity are emphasized: fidelity to justice in actions, and mercy (kindness) as the disposition, the motivating sentiment, behind divine actions.

Verse 14 illustrates the principle that justice is characteristic of divine actions. Such justice is shown in God's rescue of the falling, God's support of those bowed down. Those who suffer and are oppressed needlessly and without cause can find in God a defendant and one who rights the situations. (This is one of the reasons why the Old Testament, especially the psalms, contains so many laments and complaints, so many gripes about the human situation. The expression and articulation of the human hurt is viewed as therapeutic; it also is assumed that ultimate reality, God, is disposed to give justice.) That God upholds the falling and raises the fallen echoes one of the major themes of the Bible—God as the special protector of the weak and oppressed, God as the one who "reverses human fate," who brings to fulfillment and realization the unpromising. (This is the Cinderella theme that can be seen as a dominant motif in so much of the Old Testament: Abraham and Sarah with no children, Moses as a babe afloat in the Nile, the Hebrews in slavery, David as a shepherd lad.)

Verses 15 and 16 illustrate the principle that God is gracious. All living things (good and bad, Israelite and foreigner, human and animal) are dependent on God and are not disappointed. God's providence and care sustain the whole of existence.

In verses 17–20, verse 17a is illustrated in verse 18, and verse 17b is illustrated by verses 19–20. (Verse 21 is a sort of closing benediction.) In verses 17–20, a few modifications and conditions enter the picture and slightly modify the more sweeping claims in verses 13b–16. Note that "in truth" is a condition in verse 18b, and verse 20 claims that God preserves those "who love him" but destroys the wicked. Even in God's providence, moral factors are seen as playing their role.

Psalm 98

This psalm was discussed earlier as one of the lections for Christmas, Third Proper.

Job 19:23–27a

This passage contains the best-known lines in the Book of Job, and Christians can hardly hear them without strains from Handel's *The Messiah* echoing in their ears. In Christian worship and theology, the Redeemer of verse 25 is understood to be Christ, who will come again in the last days ("at the last") to save the faithful. Although this is a legitimate reinterpretation of Job, it is a reading beyond the context of the book, and it presumes only one of the many possible interpretations of this complex and difficult passage.

This reading is part of one of Job's responses to his friends. The book consists of a prose prologue (1:1–13) and epilogue (42:7–17) that frame a poetic dialogue or debate between Job and his friends, concluding with a confrontation between Job and God. The prologue establishes the circumstances that occasion the debate—Job's suffering and grief. The debate itself consists of series or cycles of speeches by the three friends, each speech followed by a response from Job. Our lesson is found in the concluding section of Job's speech at the end of the second cycle (12:1–20:29). The poetic dialogues had begun with Job cursing the day of his birth; at the end of the first cycle he considers the day of his death. At the outset he insisted that no life at all would have been better than his suffering. In the second cycle of Job's responses, the debate focuses on divine justice, with Job arguing for a trial before God in which he would be found to be innocent. Our passage is part of Job's response to Bildad's speech in 18:1–21.

Job's response (19:1–29) begins with complaints against the friends: "How long will you torment me; . . . are you not ashamed to wrong me?" (19:1–3). They do not support him or defend his cause against God, but rather accuse him of deserving his fate. They blame the victim, and we know from the prologue to the book that Job is a victim. Job continues with his appeals for justice and his descriptions of his distress, again turning to the friends for help: "Have pity on me, have pity on me, O you my friends, for the hand of God has touched me!" (19:21).

The words of our assigned text are addressed indirectly to the friends, but they—like so many of Job's speeches—sound like a soliloquy. And why not? The friends simply do not listen. Still insistent that he is innocent and that this fact eventually will be known, Job imagines that his words would be written down, "inscribed in a book" (v. 23). Then, possibly realizing that "a book" might not last long enough, he wishes that his testimony to his innocence could be "engraved on a rock forever!" (v. 24), inscribed with an iron pen and then filled with lead. Job is convinced that eventually he will be found innocent, and he wants it known that although the case was in dispute he would not capitulate to the charges of his guilt.

Then follow the famous words in verse 25, traditionally translated, "For I know that my Redeemer lives, and that at the last he will stand upon the earth." In the Hebrew Scriptures the word translated "Redeemer" (*goel*) has a great many different meanings, including the blood avenger of the killing of a close relative, the next of kin with the right or responsibility to buy family property when it comes up for sale (see the discussion of Jer. 32:1–3a, 6–15 at Proper 21 [26] in this volume), one who defends the accused or the oppressed, and a variety of other possibilities. Given the legal language of the dialogues and Job's defense of his innocence, it is most likely that the term refers to a defense attorney who will argue Job's case and vindicate him. Thus the NRSV footnote gives the alternative reading "Vindicator," the NEB has "vindicator," and the REB reads "defending counsel."

Who is this one who will defend and justify Job? Is it God, a human being, or some other? Translations that capitalize the word clearly suggest that Job believes that God will eventually vindicate him. This decision is supported by the affirmation that the Redeemer "lives," and by the traditional reading of verse 26: "then in my flesh I shall see God." However, the text of verse 26 is so corrupt as to be almost unreadable, and there are other arguments against identifying the vindicator with God. Primarily, throughout the poetic dialogues Job has persistently perceived God not as his defender or redeemer, but his adversary. And that is what God is to the end of the poetic portion of the book. Only in the prose epilogue does God restore the fortunes of this sufferer.

The question of the identity and the function of the Redeemer or defense attorney cannot be resolved with certainty. One thing is clear: Job insists without compromise that his suffering is unjust, and that eventually—perhaps not until the end of time, but eventually—his cause will be demonstrated to be right. If he is not vindicated by God, he will be vindicated before God. But whether these are read as hopeful and confident words or not depends primarily on the horizon within which they are interpreted. In the poetic portion of the book they continue the sad complaint, with confidence only in the justice of Job's case. In the book as a whole, Job could be said to have been redeemed, and before the end of time. In the context of the Christian canon, this Redeemer is seen to be the Son of God.

Psalm 17:1–9

Psalm 17 is a psalm composed for use in legal hearings at the temple when a person felt or was falsely accused of some wrong. Old Testament laws concerned with the administration of justice allowed for cases to be appealed to Yahweh and the temple personnel when it was impossible to decide a case in the normal fashion, that is, when a jury of elders could not reach a verdict (see Exod. 22:7–8; Deut. 17:8–13; 19:15–21; 1 Kings 8:31–32). Failure of the normal process might be the result of a lack of witnesses, the particularity of the case, or other reasons.

In the temple ritual or ordeal, the litigants in a case would appeal to God for a verdict, assert their innocence, and place themselves under an oath or curse. The priests sought to determine guilt and innocence, and where they could not, the participants' self-imprecation was assumed to bring condemnation upon the guilty. Frequently, the litigants spent the night in the sanctuary under the observation of the cultic officials. Apparently, verdicts in a case were declared in the morning.

The following is an outline of the contents of the psalm: (1) an opening appeal to God for a hearing (vv. 1–2), (2) a statement of innocence (vv. 3–5), (3) a second appeal (vv. 6–9), (4) a description of the accusers (vv. 10–12), (5) a final appeal (vv. 13–14), and (6) a statement of confidence (v. 15). Note that the entire psalm consists of prayer addressed to the Deity.

In the initial appeal to Yahweh (vv. 1–2), legal and court terminology prevail: "just cause," "lips free of deceit," "vindication," and "the right." The case of the supplicant is laid at the feet of Yahweh, with an appeal that Yahweh would hear, give heed, and look upon (favor) the right or innocent one in the case. The specifics of the case are not laid out. Such psalms as this one were composed to be used over and over again by different persons as the need arose. Thus the statements about the case are made in general terms in order to cover a particular type of situation rather than a specific situation per se.

In verses 3–5, the worshiper, as defendant, offers to the Deity a statement of innocence. If the psalms were written by temple personnel, then this statement could have served two purposes. On the one hand, it allowed the innocent person to affirm innocence in the strongest of terms. On the other hand, for one who was actually guilty but pretending innocence, this statement forced the litigant to lie in a strong fashion. Such statements of innocence may have forced the guilty into a crisis of conscience and thus confession. At any rate, it would have greatly intensified the sense of guilt and perhaps served to engender a reevaluation of one's status before God. The worshiper, in other words, was forced, in the context of a solemn service in the temple in the presence of Yahweh, to confront the reality of guilt and innocence. The worshiper was confronted with telling the truth or lying with a high hand. The cult was as committed as any other institution to truth telling!

Innocence is asserted in several ways in verses 3–5. References to the heart and testing at night (when asleep) indicate the total commitment of the person and the conscience to truthfulness. Reference to the mouth indicates a claim not to have participated in slanderous gossip or unsubstantiated accusations. Commitment to "the word of your lips" is a claim to have lived by the divine teachings as made known in the community. The supplicant claims that knowledge of God's will has kept him or her from participation in the ways of the violent. The paths of God have been where the supplicant's feet have trod.

In the appeal, the worshiper asks God to incline the ear, hear the words of appeal, and answer (v. 6). The matter, however, is not left at the level of a legal hearing and verdict rendering. There is also a request for divine mercy and love. Verse 15 expresses the worshiper's confidence of divine favor and, in a legal case, a favorable decision given in the morning.

2 Thessalonians 2:1–5, 13–17

Today's epistolary lection consists of the opening and closing sections of chapter 2. In the opening verses (vv. 1–5) we are introduced to the question troubling some of the Thessalonians—whether the "day of the Lord is already here" (v. 2). In the concluding verses (vv. 13–17), we have a twofold prayer: thanksgiving (vv. 13–15) and benediction (vv. 16–17).

When the day of the Lord comes (vv. 1–5). From some source, the Thessalonians have been told that Paul thinks "the day of the Lord is already here" (v. 2). In verses 1–12, he seeks to disabuse them of this notion. Stoutly denying this form of realized eschatology, he insists that a number of events must first occur before the end comes. Among them, he mentions "the rebellion" and the revealing of the "lawless one" (v. 3). What these refer to is not clear. It was a common expectation that some form of political upheaval would precede the Eschaton (cf. Matt. 24:6–14; 1 Tim. 4:1; 2 Tim. 3:1–5; Jude 17–19). Similarly, the appearance of some antichrist figure was a common feature of Jewish apocalyptic (cf. Matt. 24:23–24; 1 John 2:18; Rev. 13). Typically, such figures are portrayed as excessively arrogant, assuming for themselves the role of God (v. 4).

After reminding his readers that this was part of his original teaching, Paul next unfolds a series of events that still must occur (vv. 6–12). The text is full of apocalyptic ambiguities, among the most notable a reference to some "restraining" force or person (vv. 6–7). For an unspecified interval, the restrainer holds the "lawless one" at bay, but eventually the restrainer is removed. This unleashes the uncontrolled force of Satan, which precedes the end.

Thanksgiving (vv. 13–15). One of the unusual features of the Thessalonian letters is the way the typically brief Pauline prayer of thanksgiving becomes extended throughout the letter (cf. 1 Thess. 1:2; 2:13; 3:9; 2 Thess. 1:3). Given the intimate relationship between Paul and the Thessalonian church (cf. 1 Thess. 2:1–12), we are not surprised to learn that this church is a constant source of thanksgiving (v. 13). They are in every sense "beloved by the Lord" (v. 13; 1 Thess. 1:4–5; cf. Deut. 33:12).

The real source of Paul's thanksgiving is in the divine calling they experienced. They were chosen "from the beginning" (v. 13, NJB), which may mean that they were his first converts in Europe. This would be difficult to square with the account in Acts where the church at Philippi is established first as part of Paul's Aegean mission. Earlier, he had reminded them of the unique nature of their calling. They had received the "word of God" not as an ordinary human message, but as "what it really is, God's word, which is also at work in you believers" (1 Thess. 2:13). The preached Word is to be seen as the mediated power and presence of God. It is no mere human voice that is heard through the preaching. As our text suggests, God is actively at work through the gospel, choosing and calling, provoking and evoking (cf. Rom. 8:30).

Through the divine call, the Spirit elicits our response to salvation, purifying us and setting us apart to a life of service (James 1:18; 1 Thess. 5:19). We experience salvation through the sanctifying work of the Spirit (1 Cor. 6:11; 1 Thess. 4:8; 1 Pet. 1:2). But it is also our conviction that the gospel is true, rings true, indeed is the truth, that causes us to respond to God's call. Through this experience of salvation, we are directed to the glory of Christ (cf. 1 Thess. 5:9).

Stemming from the thanksgiving is a solidly based exhortation to stability and fidelity: "Stand firm and hold fast to the traditions" (v. 15). Being loyal to our vocation is difficult enough even in times of relative calm and placidity, but more so in the face of persecution. It is the gospel in which we stand, and there we find our stability (cf. 1 Cor. 15:1–3; also 16:13; Gal. 5:1; Phil. 1:27; 4:1; 1 Thess. 3:6, 8). One way this occurs is through holding fast to the traditions we were taught in connection with the gospel—the stories of Jesus and the stories about Jesus with the interpretations and guidelines related to Christian behavior (cf. 1 Cor. 11:2, 23; 2 Thess. 3:6). What we have been taught forms the beginning of our fidelity (1 Thess. 3:4; 4:2, 6; 5:27; 2 Thess. 2:2, 5).

Benediction (vv. 16–17). Coupled with this exhortation to fidelity in verse 15 is a prayer that Christ himself (cf. 1 Thess. 3:11), along with God the Father, will extend comfort (cf. 1 Thess. 3:13; 2 Cor. 1:3–7) and will establish us on the road to worthwhile words and deeds (cf. 2 Cor. 9:8; Eph. 2:10; Col. 1:10; 2 Tim. 3:17; Titus 2:14).

Luke 20:27–38

Because much has transpired in the career of Jesus since our lection for last Sunday (19:1–10), we need first to set the context. Jesus is in Jerusalem, he has already cleansed the temple, and he is now engaged in a series of controversies with Jewish leaders. Two questions have already been put to Jesus: the source of his authority (20:1–8) and the matter of paying tribute to Caesar (20:20–26). The question about the resurrection of the dead, our text for today, in Luke is the third and final question before Jesus puts to his interrogators a question concerning the Christ as David's son (20:41–44). Matthew (22:34–40) and Mark (12:28–34) have a fourth question put to Jesus before Jesus himself becomes the questioner: Which is the First Commandment? Luke does not include that question here because he dealt with that subject earlier when a lawyer tested Jesus by asking, "Teacher, what must I do to inherit eternal life?" (10:25–28). On the question before us now, that of the resurrection of the dead, Matthew (22:23–33) and Mark (12:18–27) have parallels that agree completely with each other. Luke's account is noticeably different, not so much in the question but in a portion of Jesus' answer, especially verses 34–36.

It is important in understanding Luke 20:27–38 to keep in mind that the question posed about the resurrection came not from bereaved persons seeking hope or from believers searching for more clarity on the doctrine. Rather, Jesus is being interrogated by persons who already were fixed in their position that there was no resurrection of the dead (v. 27; Acts 23:8). The Sadducees (the name may have derived from Zadok, high priest under Solomon) were one of the several parties within Judaism. They were of the priestly class, many of them aristocratic and wealthy; they were theologically conservative; and they regarded as normative in their religion only the five books of Moses. What was not to be found in the first five books of the Old Testament was not authoritative. The Pharisees, on the other hand, believed there was an oral as well as a written tradition from Moses, and within that oral tradition was the basis for belief in the resurrection. It was a subject of heated debate between the two parties (Acts 23:6–10); the Sadducees sometimes baited their opponents with impossible "what if" questions. Such is the game played here with Jesus. Anyone who has been a target for religious questions raised by persons who had no intention of being influenced by the answers can sense the frustration of a no-win situation.

Jesus, however, does not respond to the attitude but to the question. His answer is twofold. The first part (vv. 34–36) simply points to the inappropriateness of the question, given a fundamental difference between life in this age and in the age to come. Marriage is appropriate for this age, because the fact of mortality necessitates a means for perpetuating life. However, those who attain to the resurrection from the dead are children of God and are as the angels. Such a condition does not have need of marriage. It is important to notice that Jesus does not respond in terms of the widespread belief that everyone has an immortal soul. Rather, resurrection from the dead is an act and gift of God for "those who are considered worthy of a place in that age and in the resurrection from the dead" (v. 35). Immortality is based on a doctrine of human nature; resurrection is based on a doctrine of God's nature.

The second part of Jesus' answer is a response in kind. The Sadducees, in keeping with their belief in the Pentateuch as Scripture, based their question on Deuteronomy 25:5–10, the levirate law of marriage that spells out the duty of a man toward a deceased brother. Jesus appeals to the same body of Scripture, Exodus 3:6, to affirm God as a God of the living and not of the dead. The inference is that Abraham, Isaac, and Jacob have or will have continuous life with God. Nothing about intermediate states of the deceased is stated or implied.

It is important for Luke's theology that Jesus' teaching on the resurrection is continuous with Judaism, at least as understood in a major tradition, Pharisaism. It is important for Luke and his church as Christians, and for us, that resurrection from the dead is grounded in both the words and the experience of Jesus.

Proper 28 [33]
(Sunday between November 13 and 19 inclusive)

Isaiah 65:17–25;
Isaiah 12; or
Malachi 4:1–2*a*;
Psalm 98;
2 Thessalonians 3:6–13;
Luke 21:5–19

A vision of a new heaven and a new earth is vividly sketched in the text from Third Isaiah that serves as the Old Testament reading in the *Common Lectionary* for today. The responsive reading is supplied not by the Psalter, but by the song of praise in Isaiah 12, which heralds God as strength, shield, and source of saving power.

In other lectionaries, the text from Malachi announces the coming day of the Lord, which brings with it judgment against the wicked and comfort to the righteous. The theme of God's role as universal judge is continued in Psalm 98.

The epistolary text from Second Thessalonians addresses the problem of idleness as an erroneous response to the preaching of an imminent Parousia.

The Gospel reading is Luke's version of Jesus' apocalyptic discourses concerning the end of Jerusalem and the temple, the coming of the Son of Man, and the Eschaton. In all of today's texts that speak of God's judgment, we are reminded that it will be a time of both distress and joy.

Isaiah 65:17–25

For a discussion of this lesson, see the commentary on the texts assigned for Easter Day in this volume.

Isaiah 12

This chapter is the conclusion of a long speech by the prophet Isaiah that begins at Isaiah 10:27*d*. This speech comes from a very particular historical context which, since the German translation of Martin Luther, has been called the Syro-Ephraimite

War. The circumstances were as follows. (1) Western Syro-Palestinian states had formed a western coalition to end the domination of the region by Assyria under the powerful king Tiglath-pileser III (744–727 BCE). (2) Israel and Judah for years had followed a pro-Assyrian policy and had cooperated with the Assyrians. This policy had brought them under severe pressure from such kingdoms in the region as Damascus and Phoenicians (see Amos 1–2). (3) In the fall of 734 BCE, Pekah seized the throne in Samaria and threw Israel into the power struggle on the side of the anti-Assyrian forces (2 Kings 15:23–31). (4) Ahaz, supported by the prophet Isaiah, declined to break the treaty with Assyria and refused to join the coalition. (5) The forces of the anti-Assyrian coalition, now led by King Rezin of Damascus—thus Syria—and Pekah of Samaria—thus Ephraim in the term Syro-Ephraimite War, attacked Ahaz and Jerusalem to depose Ahaz and to replace him with a king favoring the revolt against Assyria (see 2 Kings 16:5 and Isa. 7:1–9).

In his speech in Isaiah 10:27d–12:6, the prophet describes the movement of the enemy troops against Jerusalem (10:27d–32), announces the intervention of God in behalf of the people and King Ahaz (10:33–34) and predicts a bright and glorious future for the Davidic regime (chapter 11).

In chapter 12, the lection for this Sunday, Isaiah presents two thanksgiving hymns to be sung after victory: the first by the king (vv. 1–2) and the second by the people ("O royal Zion" in v. 6 in NRSV should be read "O inhabitant of Zion" or perhaps "O citizenry of Zion").

The king offers thanks for rescue and confesses faith in God and the congregation is called upon to sing praises to God and to make divine redemption known throughout the world.

The enigmatic reference "With joy you will draw water from the wells of salvation" (v. 3) probably alludes to rituals associated with the Festival of Tabernacles. According to the Mishnah (*Sukkah* 4:9–10), water was brought from the pool of Siloam to the temple in solemn procession during the festival, and a water pouring ritual was carried out in the temple precincts to symbolize the coming rains. If Isaiah is here referring to this ritual, then he was probably assuring the king and the people that the next Festival of Tabernacles would be an exceptional celebration since then they could praise God for deliverance from the anti-Assyrian coalition and for the salvation of Zion.

Malachi 4:1–2a

Because "Malachi" probably is not a proper name but the title "my messenger" (see Mal. 3:1), the Book of Malachi is an anonymous book. Its style is quite distinctive, consisting almost entirely of dialogues between God or the prophetic figure and the addressees.

This style lends a didactic and argumentative character to the work. The topics of the dialogues include God's love for the people (1:2–5), accusations against the priests and people concerning their poor sacrifices (1:6–2:9), marriage to foreign women (2:10–16), questions about the justice of God (2:17–3:5 and 3:13–4:3), tithes and offerings (3:8–12), and admonitions to be faithful for the day of the Lord is coming soon (4:4–5; see also 3:13–4:3).

No date is given for the unnamed prophet, but he surely would have been active in the postexilic period, probably after the dedication of the temple in 515 BC, but before the time of Ezra and Nehemiah (around 400 BC). Like the other prophets of this era, this one is concerned with priestly and cultic matters, such as proper sacrifices, tithes, and offerings. At the same time, however, Malachi is like his prophetic predecessors in his concern for justice (Mal. 3:5) and in his announcement of the coming day of the Lord.

It is important to be aware of the context of today's very brief lesson. The immediate unit of which it is a part is Malachi 4:1–3, which itself is the concluding paragraph in a dispute that began in 3:13. Its theme is the justice of God, specifically directed to those who assert that evildoers prosper. The dispute is not an actual one, but a rhetorical device to present a case and argue a point. The prophet does not directly deny the allegation that evildoers prosper, but looks beyond the present to a time when God's justice will be established. Records are being kept, he argues, in a "book of remembrance" (3:16; see also Dan. 7:10; Rev. 20:12; 21:27), so that God will distinguish between the righteous and the wicked.

Then in 4:1–3 the prophet announces the coming of the day of the Lord (see also 3:2–4). The expectation of a day of the Lord was already a traditional matter by the time of Amos in the eighth century BC. Obviously, his contemporaries anticipated a time of salvation for Israel, but Amos announced that it would be a time of "darkness, not light," a time when the Lord would judge Israel (Amos 5:18–20). The expectation seems to be rooted in the ancient tradition of the holy war, as the time of the Lord's victory over the Lord's enemies. For Amos, there was to be no separation between sinners and righteous, and Israel had become the enemy of Yahweh. By the time of Malachi, "the day" had become a time when the Lord would establish justice, rewarding the righteous and punishing those who work evil. Malachi, like Amos, has in view a day within history and on this earth. In our passage, the expectation takes on almost apocalyptic overtones, moving more and more in the direction of the detailed and extensive visions of the end in Daniel and Revelation. Thus, although the unrighteous may indeed prosper in the present age, God will on that day vindicate those who "revere" God's name; that is, those whose piety is genuine.

The eschatological dimensions of the text are especially appropriate for the end of this season of the Christian year. God will one day make all things right, establishing God's just reign over all. But what does one do in the shadow of that day, at once terrible and glorious? One is faithful to God, obedient to the will of God known through the traditions (the law, 4:4) and open to the possibility of changed hearts (4:5–6).

Psalm 98

This psalm was discussed earlier as one of the lections for Christmas, Third Proper.

2 Thessalonians 3:6–13

One of the side effects of eschatological misunderstanding is that it can upset people's schedules. If the Lord is expected to come soon, one response is to put down the tools, fold the arms, and wait for his return. Perhaps this is the reason both letters to the Thessalonians address those who are idle (vv. 6–7, 10–12; 1 Thess. 5:14). There appear to be instances of idleness unrelated to fixations on the end time, what might be called cases of general shiftlessness (cf. 1 Tim. 5:13). One of the main concerns of today's text is to address this tendency to stop working, for whatever reason.

We should first notice the advice to shun those who are living in idleness. Anytime people form themselves into groups, they eventually formulate rules and guidelines for deciding when persons are no longer members. They also develop procedures for removing members who are no longer full members or who, for some reason, have violated the stated or unstated rules of membership. The Old Testament provides extensive instruction governing membership within Israel and establishes guidelines when persons should be removed from the community. The separatist community at Qumran also developed elaborate rules and guidelines for determining when members should be avoided or excluded.

Thus, when the early Christian communities show evidence of policing their own membership, they are acting in concert with ancient precedent as well as reflecting an established sociological reality. Paul warns his churches to take note of troublemakers and keep a watchful eye on them (Rom. 16:17). In cases where members violate moral codes, there are clear instructions not to associate with them (cf. 1 Cor. 5:5, 9, 11; 2 Tim. 3:5; Titus 3:10–11; cf. Matt. 18:17). In today's text, it is the person who has stopped working who is to be avoided, primarily because such behavior is not in keeping with the teachings Paul had transmitted to the church. Part of these teachings must have been his instructions to "admonish the idlers" (1 Thess. 5:14), but probably there were teachings connected with his eschatology where he spelled out his conviction that preparing for the end time did not mean to stop working (1 Thess. 5:6, 11; cf. 1 Cor. 7:27–31).

As a response to the idlers, Paul adduces his own example (v. 7), a typical method of moral instruction (1 Cor. 4:16; 11:1; Phil. 3:17; 4:9; 1 Thess. 1:6; cf. Heb. 6:12; 13:7; also Eph. 5:1; 1 Thess. 2:14; Gal. 4:12). In his first epistle he had rehearsed with the church the way he had worked night and day in their behalf (1 Thess. 2:9). This seems to have been his normal pattern rather than an isolated instance among the Thessalonians (cf. 1 Cor. 4:12; Acts 18:3; 20:34).

He also stresses that his actions in this respect were exceptional. As an apostle, he had the full right to expect his churches to support him financially (v. 9; cf. 1 Cor. 9:6). On his side was established religious precedent, the law of Moses, and the teaching of Jesus (1 Cor. 9:3–14; cf. Matt. 10:10). But he chose not to exercise this right and instead paid his own way as he worked to establish new churches.

Accordingly, his rule among his churches was: the one who does not work cannot eat (v. 10). In the first letter, one reason given to support this rule is that it will enable the church to command the respect of outsiders (1 Thess. 4:11–12). For Paul, it was important how the church was viewed by pagans (cf. 1 Cor. 10:33; 14:24–25). His view was that a church full of thumb-twiddlers little commended itself to the pagan public. Consequently, he advised the church to take a responsible course of action in this respect. Christians are to "do their work quietly and to earn their own living" (v. 12; cf. 1 Thess. 4:11).

As a final word, he urges his readers not to "be weary in doing what is right" (v. 13; Gal. 6:9; 2 Cor. 4:1, 16).

In the wrong hands, this text can easily become a club used to beat those who are out of work, especially the long-term unemployed. Clearly, if we are idle and remain idle, for no good reason, we come under the censure of this text. Paul's example also serves as a worthwhile corrective to the 9-to-5 view of ministry. As we all know, genuine ministry often involves us in round-the-clock work. People in need do not punch a clock. But perhaps one of the most important dimensions of this text is its insistence that we best prepare for the end time not by being idle but by working and earning our own living.

Luke 21:5–19

It is frequently the case with biblical narratives that descriptions of what is going on are interwoven with descriptions of what is really going on. This is to say, historical events are presented but not with the historian's interest. Rather, these events are set in the larger context of God's purpose being worked out, descriptions of which call not for historical language but for images, symbols, and figures. Such is the nature of today's Gospel.

Luke 21:5–19 joins the prediction of the destruction of the temple (vv. 5–7) with an apocalyptic discourse on the coming of the Son of Man (vv. 8–36), our lection ending at verse 19. In early Christian circles, the destruction of Jerusalem (AD 66–72) was understood as an eschatological event, a sign that the end was near. That the two subjects were joined in all three Gospels (Matt. 24:1–36; Mark 13:1–37) is no surprise. As we will note in the discussion below, it was a question about the former that led into the latter.

Both Matthew and Mark identify the comment about the beauty of the temple as coming from the disciples, whereas Luke more vaguely says "some were speaking about the temple" (v. 5). After Jesus' comment to the effect that not one stone shall be left on another (v. 6), both Matthew (24:3) and Mark (13:3) shift the scene to the Mount of Olives from which Jesus gave the apocalyptic discourse. Luke does not. All three agree on the two questions that follow, even though they disagree on who asked them (Matt. 24:3; Mark 13:4; Luke 21:7). When? and, What will be the sign?

That portion of the apocalyptic discourse that constitutes our lesson falls into two parts: the signs of the end (vv. 8–11) and the time of testimony to precede the end (vv. 12–19). What is said in verses 12–19 chronologically precedes the events of verses 8–11. The signs of the end are threefold: the appearance of false messiahs and false calculators of time and place (v. 8); wars, tumults; and international conflicts (vv. 9–10); and natural disasters with cosmic terror (v. 11). Concerning these signs the disciples are advised that the end is not yet, and therefore they are to be neither led astray nor terrified.

Preceding these signs is the time of testimony (vv. 12–19). The chronology is reversed in the service of the writer's point. The principle of end-stress says to state last that which is of primary importance. In this case it is the call to faithful witness under great duress and pain. Because of their faithful witness, the disciples will be delivered up before synagogues (fulfilled in Acts 4–5) and before governors and kings (fulfilled in Acts 24–26). They are assured, however, that in those crises they will be given "words and a wisdom" (v. 15) that no opponents can withstand (fulfilled in Acts 4:8–13; 6:10). Matthew (24:20) and Mark (13:11) here promise the Holy Spirit as provider of one's speech; Luke had already stated that earlier (12:11–12). Christians are warned that they will be betrayed by relatives and friends (v. 16), that some of them will suffer death, and that all will be hated because of their devotion to Jesus (v. 17). Verse 18 is obscure in view of verse 16. It may be a misplaced saying (Matt. 10:30; Luke 12:7); it may mean that some will die but you will not; it may mean that although the persecutors can kill in a physical sense, in a far more important sense you will be kept safe. In any case, endurance and faithfulness are the keys to life.

The time of Luke's writing and our time fall within verses 12–19—the time of testimony. The end is not yet. During the time of testimony, disciples will experience suffering. They are not exempt. There is nothing here of the arrogance one sometimes sees and hears in modern apocalypticists, an arrogance born of a doctrine of a rapture in which believers are removed from the scenes of persecution and suffering. There are no scenes here of cars crashing into one another on the highways because their drivers have been blissfully raptured. The word of Jesus in our lesson is still forceful: "This will give you an opportunity to testify. . . . By your endurance you will gain your souls."

Proper 29 [34]
(Christ the King or Reign of Christ;
Sunday between November 20 and 26 inclusive)

Jeremiah 23:1–6;
Luke 1:68–79; or
Psalm 46;
Colossians 1:11–20;
Luke 23:33–43

The Old Testament reading for both the *Common Lectionary* and other lectionaries is the opening section of Jeremiah 23, where Yahweh promises to gather a remnant of his people, raise up for them responsible leaders, and provide eventually a wise and just king in the Davidic line. For the *Common Lectionary*, the response is supplied by the Benedictus in Luke 1:68–79, Zechariah's prophecy that envisions God's raising up a Savior from the house of David. For the other lectionaries, Psalm 46, which praises God as the one who provides refuge and strength in time of trouble, serves as the response.

The epistolary reading offers one of the most extraordinary christological hymns in the New Testament, praising Christ as creator and reconciler of the cosmos.

For the Gospel lesson, we have Luke's account of Jesus' crucifixion, with its distinctive emphasis on Jesus' forgiving spirit and merciful remembrance of one of the criminals who was crucified with him. Several motifs in this passage relate to the overall theme of the reign of Christ the King.

Jeremiah 23:1–6

Jeremiah 23:1–6 consists of two distinct paragraphs, as all modern translations indicate. Verses 1–4 contain an announcement of judgment against the "shepherds who destroy and scatter the sheep" and an announcement of salvation to the "flock": the Lord will remove their reasons for fear by giving "shepherds who will shepherd them." The second paragraph (vv. 5–6) is an announcement of salvation: Yahweh will raise up a just and righteous king in the line of David. As they stand in the final form of the Book of Jeremiah, the second unit is both a contrast with and an extension of the first. But there are disjunctions between the units which suggest that they originated independently and perhaps even come from different authors. The first paragraph speaks of "shepherds" (plural), whereas the second has a single king; the first is prose and the second poetry (although not all translations set these verses in poetic lines).

Commentators on this passage have disagreed about its authorship and historical provenance. Certainly verse 3, if not all of the first unit, assumes a situation after the time of Jeremiah, namely, the Babylonian Exile. On the other hand, the bad shepherds could very well be the last kings of Judah during the time of Jeremiah. Authorship of verses 5–6 is likewise an open question, although most recent commentators tend to attribute it to Jeremiah. The problem with that conclusion is that this would be the only point where Jeremiah, unlike Isaiah, expresses his hope for restoration in terms of the Davidic dynasty. However one resolves that question, the entire unit comes either from the era just before or during the Babylonian Exile.

The "shepherds," both good and bad, certainly represent political and religious leaders. Concluding a section of the Book of Jeremiah concerning the last kings of Judah, the reference definitely is to the series of rulers, but it could just as well apply to the officials as a whole. The "shepherds who will shepherd them" (v. 4) could be either the succession of righteous kings or, more broadly, political and religious leaders.

The juxtaposition of the unit about shepherds, with the promise of a king in the line of David, calls attention to the importance of pastoral imagery in the biblical messianic expectations. Surely that imagery is indebted to some extent to the tradition that David himself was a shepherd. (See 1 Sam. 16:19.) When applied to David the image is a rich combination of power and gentle care: the pastoral king, the royal shepherd.

Verses 5–6 provide a concise summary of the major features of the messianic hope in the Old Testament. The one who is to come will be a king in the line of David (2 Samuel 7) and will be raised up by the Lord to prosper in all that he does. Justice and righteousness will characterize his reign (Isa. 9:6–7), bringing salvation to the people of God, in this case the people of Israel and Judah. That he will reign as king means he will be a monarch with real power and autonomy, neither a vassal of a foreign power nor controlled by officials of the royal court. The throne name given to him, "Yahweh is our righteousness" (v. 6), suggests that through him the Lord vindicates the people as righteous.

Although the king is an ideal one, the promise is rooted in flesh and blood and history. This is the promise that the earliest followers of Jesus saw fulfilled in him, the divine will incarnate. Theologically, the Old Testament text enables us to keep our eyes fixed on two points also fundamental to the New Testament witness: the humanity of the Anointed One, and the faith that through him God is at work.

Luke 1:68–79

For comments on this lection, see the Second Sunday of Advent, where this song of Zechariah served as the psalm for the day.

Psalm 46

This psalm affirms God's rule over chaos and gives expression to some of the beliefs held about the city of Jerusalem (or Zion) by the ancient Judeans. This psalm, like Psalms 48 and 76, celebrates Zion as the city of God and proclaims divine protection for the city. The earth and existence may be threatened, but Zion is declared steadfast and divinely protected.

Originally, Psalm 46 was probably used in the great autumn festival, the Feast of Tabernacles, which celebrated the end of the old year and the beginning of the new year. One of the functions of the fall festival was to put the old year behind and to greet the new year. One way in which this was done was through the celebration of God's power to overcome chaos and the forces of disorder. (Note how this is a theme of our political campaigns and part of the promises of each new administration.) As part of the ritual celebration, the world was described as temporarily returning to chaotic conditions (the Good Friday motif). In reaffirming divine rule over the universe, God reenacted the original creation. Thus every new year or autumnal celebration was, as our new year's days are, a new beginning.

Psalm 46 shares in this thinking about chaos and order but presents the city of Zion as so divinely protected that, whatever the chaotic conditions are, Zion will remain an unshaken refuge.

In verses 1–3, the text speaks of chaos in the world of nature. The NJPSV translates verses 2–3 as:

> God is our refuge and stronghold,
>   a help in trouble, very near.
> Therefore we are not afraid
>   though the earth reels,
>   though mountains topple into the sea—
>   its waters rage and foam;
>   in its swell mountains quake.

The second stanza speaks of chaos and uncertainty in the historical realm—"nations rage, the kingdoms totter"—but the people of Yahweh have no need to fear (v. 6). Verse 4 refers to a river whose streams make glad the city of God. Jerusalem, of course, had no major stream nearby. What then does this refer to? Three options suggest themselves:

1. The ancient high gods, such as El in Canaanite thought, were assumed to live on a sacred mountain (like Olympus in Greek mythology). This sacred mountain was also considered the source of one or more rivers. Thus it is possible that language that was originally used to speak of some other deity and some other sacred site has been transferred to Yahweh and to Zion.

2. The Garden of Eden was assumed to be located on a mountaintop in some texts (see Ezekiel 28). Because streams flowed from the garden (see Gen. 2:10–14) and if Zion was identified with the Garden of Eden, then one could expect to talk about streams in regard to the site.

3. Maybe the stream referred to was the spring Gihon, which supplied Jerusalem with its source of water. It is interesting to note that one of the streams flowing from the Garden of Eden was called Gihon (Gen. 2:13).

At any rate, water, the source of life and such a precious commodity in Palestine, is here associated with Jerusalem. The prophet Ezekiel later built on this imagery of water and Zion, and predicted a time to come when a stream would flow from under the temple and water the land of Palestine, transforming it into a paradisaical state (Ezek. 47:1–12).

Verses 8–9 invite people to behold the works of Yahweh; namely, how God works desolation in the earth, brings wars to an end, and destroys the weapons of war—the bow, the spear, and the chariot. Thus we have in the schematic framework of the Zion theology the idea of chaos followed by divine intervention, followed by universal peace or at least the destruction of the weapons of war (see Isa. 2:2–4). War dances, war games, and the symbolic destruction of the enemy may have been a part of the ritual of the fall festival.

In verse 10, a divine oracle occurs, probably spoken in worship by a cultic official. The NRSV translates the opening word as "be still." This assumes that the divine word is addressed to the people of Yahweh. The term basically means "leave off," "abandon," or "stop." Perhaps the oracle is here assumed to be addressed to the enemies, the nations of verse 6. If so, it demands that they recognize Yahweh and halt their aggressive actions, probably against Zion.

Throughout this psalm, the emphasis falls not only on the inviolability of Zion, where to live was considered a special privilege (see Isa. 4:3), but also on God as the protector of the city. The refrain in verses 7 and 11, as well as verse 1, praises God as the source of the city's security. Zion was a secure fortress because Yahweh was a sure refuge.

Colossians 1:11–20

It would be difficult to find a text more fitting to celebrate the kingship of Christ than today's epistolary text. There is wide agreement among scholars that this text embodies an early christological hymn, or poem, although its extent and arrangement are still disputed.

As to the structure, it is widely agreed that the hymn is introduced in verse 15 as part of the opening prayer of thanksgiving and intercession (vv. 9–14). In the twenty-sixth edition of Nestle-Aland, verses 15–18a are printed strophically, whereas the remaining verses 18b–20 are printed as prose. Neither the NRSV, REB, nor NIV print the text strophically, although the notes in the annotated REB treat it as a Pauline redaction of an earlier hymn. The most graphic layout is provided by NJB, which extends the "poem" through verse 20. It is then arranged and analyzed in two parts: (1) verses 15–18a depicting Christ as the supreme head of the created order and (2) verses 18b–20 unfolding Christ as the head of the new creation.

Regardless of where we establish the boundaries of the hymnic section, the form-critical investigation of this passage has generated numerous fascinating possibilities for interpretation and homiletical appropriation.

A few preliminary observations are in order. We should remember that the epistle to the Colossians is written in response to teaching that threatens the supremacy of Christ. There is some evidence that the syncretistic theology of the opposition regarded Christ as a member of the angelic hierarchy (cf. 2:18), thus compromising his preeminent and unique status. It is in this context that this hymn occurs. Most likely, it does represent a Christianized version of an earlier hymn heavily influenced by Jewish wisdom traditions. In its present form, the praise earlier given to Wisdom as the source of all creation, the reflection of God, and that (One) holding the universe together is now transferred to Christ. Apart from the hymnic form, we should notice the nature of the theological response. To combat a competing Christology, Paul draws from the worship experience of the church. The lesson here is that the living experience of the church, its experience of the exalted Christ in worship, is sometimes the best response to an inadequate theology—that is, as long as our hymns are as profound and theologically rich as this early Christian hymn.

Let us look at some of the prominent motifs of this christological hymn.

1. It opens with Christ presented as "the image of the invisible God" (v. 15). In the Jewish wisdom tradition, Wisdom was praised as "a reflection of eternal light, . . . an image of [God's] goodness" (Wisd. of Sol. 7:26). Capitalizing on this development, Christians came to regard Christ similarly (2 Cor. 3:18; 4:4; Heb. 1:3, 6).

2. To speak of Christ as the "firstborn of all creation" does not imply that he was the first thing to be created, as some held in early Christian controversies concerning the nature of Christ. This is rather a claim to preeminent rank (cf. Ps. 89:27; also Rom. 8;29; Rev. 3:14).

3. Christ is also God's agent in creation: "in him all things in heaven and on earth were created" (v. 16). Here again, in the Jewish wisdom tradition, Wisdom was regarded as a crucial actor in creation (Wisd. of Sol. 9:1–2). For Christians, it was the preexistent Christ who played this role (John 1:3, 18; Heb. 1:2; Rev. 3:14), and this became an element of early Christian confession (1 Cor. 8:6). As the hymn later states, "all things have been created through him and for him" (v. 16; cf. Rom. 11:36). We should note the cosmic proportions of Christ's creative influence (v. 16). No conceivable part of the universe or reality as we can envision it can be explained or accounted for apart from the creative work of Christ.

4. Christ's preexistence is asserted in the claim that he is "before all things" (v. 17). Again, Wisdom was seen to have preceded the created order (Prov. 8:22–31). It is the incarnate Logos who now occupies this position (John 1:1).

5. Related to this is the claim that "in him all things hold together" (v. 17). Christ becomes the organizing principle of the universe, but more than that he is actually seen as the One in whom all reality coheres (Heb. 1:3).

6. Besides being head of the created order, Christ stands at the head of the "new creation." As the exalted Lord, "he is the head of the body, the church" (v. 18)—not a local congregation, but the universal one that reaches into the heights and depths of the cosmos (cf. Eph. 1:22–23; 4:15; 5:23; also 1 Cor. 11:3).

7. His status as head of the new creation results from his being "the firstborn from the dead" (v. 18). As the first one to experience resurrected life through the power and agency of God, Christ becomes resurrection's first child (cf. 1 Cor. 15:20; Rev. 13:14; also Rev. 1:5; Rom. 8:29; Heb. 1:6).

8. As the preexistent Christ who stands at the head of the created order, and as the incarnate Christ who is raised from the dead, he becomes the full embodiment of God's own presence: "in him God in all his fullness chose to dwell" (v. 19, REB; cf. 2:9–10; John 1:16; Eph. 1:23; 3:19; 4:10, 13).

9. Because of his unique status, Christ becomes the one through whom reconciliation occurs (v. 20). In his sacrificial death on the cross and the shedding of his blood, peace is made between God and the world (cf. 2 Cor. 5:18–19; also Eph. 1:10; 2:13–16). It is a form of reconciliation that reaches to every conceivable level—personal as well as cosmic (v. 20; cf. Eph. 1:10).

If the Feast of Christ the King is intended to lift our vision of Christ, this hymn can certainly serve to launch our thoughts upward. If our tendency is to impose limits on the work of Christ, today's text forces us to enlarge our horizons. We are taken from creation to new creation, from the beginning of time to the end of time, from microcosm to macrocosm, from alienation to peace; and wherever we are taken, there we find a reflection of God in Christ.

Luke 23:33–43

The passion narrative, the inner sanctum of the Christian faith, is probably the earliest fixed body of tradition about Jesus. In Luke it is found in 22:1–23:56, and within that narrative is our lection for today, the account of the crucifixion. If this seems to be an unusual choice for a Gospel reading on the Sunday of Christ the King, then take a moment to let the irony sink in: Jesus is declared king by mocking Roman soldiers and a cynical governor (vv. 36–38). They spoke more truth than they knew.

One is impressed by the brevity of the account. Luke writes in the straightforward and unadorned manner of a historian, just as he did of the actual birth of Jesus (2:1–7). Both the birth and the death have prompted a continuing flow of emotion among Jesus' followers, expressed in music, art, poem, and song. But Luke understands what we sometimes forget, that the significance of this event does not lie in our flow of tears but in his flow of blood. "Suffered under Pontius Pilate, was crucified, dead, and buried": this the church not only confesses but continues to struggle with to discern its meaning.

Luke provides the essentials. The place was The Skull. He does not use the Aramaic "Golgotha" ("Calvary" in Latin) as do Matthew (27:33) and Mark (15:22). The tradition that the crucifixion took place on a hill probably was prompted by the usual preference for a highly visible place so that Rome could warn the general populace that crimes against the empire would be punished severely. Crucifixion added shame and pain to death itself. Luke assumes that the readers know what a crucifixion is. Literally, it meant to be impaled on a stick. Apparently, the Romans added to this ancient torture the crossbeam. It was usually the crossbeam that the accused carried to the place of execution, where the body was affixed by ropes or nails.

Luke tells us who was in attendance at the execution. The soldiers assigned to crucifixion detail were there, of course. They made sport of Jesus (vv. 36–37). Luke is not as clear as are the other Evangelists that it was the soldiers who cast lots for Jesus' clothes (v. 34; Ps. 22:18). The leaders of the people were there, mocking Jesus with two titles, Messiah and Chosen One (v. 35; recall 9:35). Both they and the soldiers assume that if one has God's favor, a proof of it would be the use of it to end suffering and avoid death. It is the sad truth that many of us still think this way about the uses of God's power for our own relief. The larger truth is, if Jesus is to save others, he cannot save himself. The crowd is there, says Luke. They had been with Jesus all along but now watch in silence (v. 35), apparently feeling helpless before the combined forces of state and religion. Luke will later say (v. 49) that Jesus' acquaintances from Galilee, including the women, watched from a distance.

Twice Luke turns our attention to the ones on the crosses. The first time is to hear from Jesus a word of forgiveness because "they do not know what they are doing" (v. 34). The preacher will note that the NRSV registers some manuscript differences here: some have this statement; others do not. Whatever may be decided by the preacher in handling verse 34a, the content of Jesus' saying is in accord with his teaching on forgiveness (15:4) and love of enemies (6:35). And the ignorance motif ("they do not know what they are doing") is quite common in Luke (19:42; Acts 3:17; 13:27; 17:30). The "they" of the prayer covers all implicated in Jesus' death.

The second time Luke turns our attention to those on the crosses is to let us overhear the conversation among them (vv. 39–43). One criminal joins the mockers; the other does not, acknowledging the justice of his own punishment and the injustice of that of Jesus. The penitent criminal recognizes Jesus' kingly power and is promised a place in Paradise (abode of the righteous dead, 2 Cor. 12:3; Rev. 2:7). In this brief interchange, Luke is able to witness to Christ's exaltation into his glory (24:26; Acts 2:32–36) and to Jesus' power and willingness to save a sinner. Three times Jesus has been mocked, "Save yourself." Here he does save, but not himself. That the one saved is a dying criminal is fully congenial to the types of persons blessed by Jesus throughout his ministry. That ministry continues in Jesus' dying hour, "For the Son of Man came to seek out and to save the lost" (19:10).

All Saints, November 1, or on First Sunday in November

Daniel 7:1–3, 15–18;
Psalm 149;
Ephesians 1:11–23;
Luke 6:20–31

All of the readings for today not only make one appreciatively aware of the saints of God but also remind the reader of the hostile forces with which God's people have always had to contend. Daniel sees not only the saints who possess the kingdom but also the four beasts; the psalmist, surrounded by enemies, nevertheless praises God; the writer of Ephesians praises God who through Christ has formed a cosmic body of the reconciled by subduing the powers of hostility and disobedience; Luke's sermon on the plain offers Christ's blessings on the saints, but follows with woes on those who resist and oppose the way of the kingdom. The Bible is not blind to the immensity of evil in the world.

Daniel 7:1–3, 15–18

The specific link between All Saints' Day and this text is its reference to "the saints of the Most High" (v. 18, RSV). But a reading from the Book of Daniel is highly appropriate for other reasons as well—its apocalyptic vision of a final judgment day, of the resurrection of the dead (Dan. 12:1–3), and of a kingdom of God in which the saints take their rightful place.

Our lection comes from the central chapter in the Book of Daniel, which was written during the Hellenistic period in a time when faithful Jews were experiencing persecution. The one responsible for their trouble was the Seleucid ruler Antiochus Epiphanes. Because so much of the symbolism of the book relates directly to historical persons and events, it can be dated with confidence to 167–164 BC.

Daniel 7 contains the first of four vision reports in the book. Although similar in some ways to earlier prophetic visions, the apocalyptic visions are quite distinctive. Like most prophetic visions, they report what was seen and then give an interpretation. Often the visionary sees himself in the revelation and sometimes in dialogue with God or some intermediary. But apocalyptic visions are much longer, and their symbolism is striking, bizarre, and detailed. The more significant contrast is that prophetic visions, like prophetic speeches, generally concern the immediate future and the continuation of history, whereas apocalyptic visions set the immediate situation of the visionary and his contemporaries into the framework of world history as a whole and its imminent radical transformation. The writer of Daniel was convinced that the wars and persecutions of his time were the last throes of the forces of evil, and that God would soon act to establish his kingdom.

The verses that make up our lesson should be read in the context of Daniel 7 as a whole. The first and last verses of the chapter provide a narrative framework. The remainder contains the report of what Daniel saw (vv. 2–14) and its interpretation (vv. 15–27), which at points reverts to the description of the visionary scene. Everything is recounted in the first person, from the perspective of the visionary. Today's reading thus includes the beginning of the vision and the first part of its interpretation.

Verse 1 is the narrative introduction, indicating the date of Daniel's visionary experience and the fact that he recorded what he saw. As in a great deal of apocalyptic literature, the writer has attributed the vision to a famous figure and has located it almost four hundred years before his own time. Verses 2 and 3 set the scene and summarize the vision. The four winds and the great sea in tumult provide the background for the appearance of four beasts. Then follows the detailed description of the four terrible beasts, each one composite in form and vicious in behavior. Everything leads up to the fourth beast, which has ten horns, and then a little horn. Each beast represents a different world empire, successively the Babylonians, the Medes, the Persians, and the Greeks. The ten horns of the fourth beast are the rulers following Alexander the Great, and the little horn stands for Antiochus Epiphanes. It was common in apocalyptic literature to see the history of the world in terms of four eras, with the last the most terrible of all. Then (v. 9) the scene shifts to the heavenly throne room, with the Ancient One passing judgment on the beasts.

Daniel reports that the visions disturbed him (v. 15), so he approached "one of the attendants" and asked for and was given the interpretation of what he had seen (v. 16). The first two sentences of the interpretation correspond to the two main scenes. The four beasts are four kings who will arise (v. 17), but the vision of the Ancient One contains the promise that "the holy ones of the Most High" ("saints of the Most High" in the RSV will inherit an eternal kingdom. Those "holy ones," or "saints," are the Jews who have remained faithful to their God during the time of persecution.

This text was originally written primarily for just those saints, to encourage them to endure difficult times. The writer means to communicate a divine revelation concerning the course and end of history, which end will be the reign of God in justice. God will put an end to the worldly enemy and will set up a kingdom in which the faithful will take their place. Even suffering under bestial powers has meaning, and it will last only for a short time.

For the writer of the Book of Daniel, and for the early Christians, the New Age was already breaking in. They could see themselves living in the light of that age, which was the reign of God. The details of that future—when, where, how?—have not been revealed to us. But the confidence that God would ultimately triumph and vindicate the saints has enabled generations of the faithful not only to endure, but to live the abundant life.

Psalm 149

This psalm which, like Psalms 146–150, begins and ends with a hallelujah ("Praise Yahweh") consists basically of two extended summons. The first is a summons to praise and concludes with a reason for praise (vv. 1–4). The second is a summons to a very militant type (vv. 5–9) of action.

The opening call is a summons to participate in communal worship ("in the assembly of the faithful"). The call is to diverse forms of action in the context of worship—praise, sing, be glad, rejoice, dance, make melody. The object of the worship is described as Israel's Maker, he who called the nation into being, and as King, he who rules over the community centered in Zion (see Ps. 87:4–6). The reason for the praise is the fact that God takes pleasure (delights) in his people and bestows victory upon the lowly.

In the summons to action, the faithful are called on to exult in their glory (to celebrate their triumph/success) and to sing for joy. A string of other actions are noted in verses 6–9. The reference to couches in verse 5 could refer to the pallets on which people sat to eat the sacrificial meals. A change of two letters in the Hebrew word for "on their couches" would give "by their families" and suggest something like a military organization or rallying. A very militant quality runs through the remainder of the psalm as if the call was to warfare. The people are called upon to subdue nations, chastise people, bind kings, and fetter rulers all to the glory of the faithful.

Ephesians 1:11–23

Portions of this text overlap with the epistolary text (Eph. 1:3–14) used for the Second Sunday After Christmas Day in Years A, B, and C. These verses are included in the text that serves as the epistolary reading for Ascension in Years A, B, and C, as well as the epistle reading for the Proper 29 [34], Christ the King or Reign of Christ in Year A (Eph. 1:15–23). The reader may want to consult our treatment of this passage in these connections.

Set in the context of All Saints' Day, this magisterial text from the opening chapter of the epistle to the Ephesians will highlight the role of the saints in God's overall purpose (vv. 15 and 18). It should be recognized, however, that in the New Testament all Christians are designated as "saints." They are the "holy ones" (*hoi hagioi*) whom God has set apart, or sanctified, in the act of redemption. God's church comes to be identified with "those who are sanctified in Christ Jesus" (1 Cor. 1:2), and there is solidarity between such persons in a given locality and all those everywhere who have been called by God (1 Cor. 1:2). To be designated as God's "holy ones" means that we live in response to God's call. Sanctification and election go hand in hand.

It is quite likely that "God's holy ones" became the most common, and perhaps most distinctive, form of designation for early Christians. Informed by such passages as Daniel 7:22, which speaks of the "holy ones of the Most High," early Christians saw themselves as those in whom God's purpose came to fulfillment, and thus as the embodiment of God's people. In this sense, the designation had a sectarian cast, marking Christians off from other Jewish groups who made similar claims on God's promise. Even with its sectarian focus, the term "saints" nevertheless applied to all Christians, and not to a select few, as the term came to be used in later Christian centuries.

In our text from Ephesians, it is the church as a whole, "all the saints" (v. 15), that represents the culmination of God's eternal purpose (3:7–13). Through this new configuration of humanity, it became possible for Jews and Gentiles alike to share in God's promise, and this is the mystery, "hidden for ages" (3:9), that is finally revealed in Christ.

It is impossible, of course, to separate the destiny of the saints from the destiny of Christ. For, as our text suggests, the divine purpose came to fulfillment in Christ, and through Christ by extension it came to fulfillment in Christ's people. Sharing in God's promise occurs as we appropriate Christ within us and as we live in Christ, but it also projects us toward a future hope, the "glorious inheritance among the saints" (v. 18). This is the promise toward which the Christian gospel looks—sharing in the exaltation of Christ ultimately (vv. 19–23).

Luke 6:20–31

In the service of thanksgiving and remembrance, Luke 6:20–31 may be viewed as a description of the way of life of those who have entered into the "joy of the Lord." Indirectly but clearly, such a treatment of the text would carry a strong imperative for the listeners who would be reflecting on the lives of the departed faithful with a view to imitating their faith (Heb. 13:7).

Our lection falls naturally into two parts: verses 20–26 and 27–31. It is clear that Luke and Matthew are working with the same tradition even though Matthew, by locating Jesus' preaching from the mountain (chaps. 5–7), echoes Moses and Mt. Sinai, whereas Luke has Jesus with the people on a level place (v. 17). This identification with the people was seen earlier in his baptism (3:21). The mountain in Luke is Jesus' place of prayer and critical decisions (vv. 12–16). Matthew's sermon is four times as long as Luke's, but Luke's differences involve more than omissions. Luke has the pronouncement of woes, for example, while Matthew does not, and some of the sayings vary in order as well as in wording. The important thing for the preacher is to stay with Luke lest the more familiar Matthean sayings bleed unconsciously into the message.

Luke's four blessing and four woes are reminiscent of the blessings and curses of Deuteronomy 11:26–29. The blessings are on the deprived: the poor, hungry, weeping, rejected (4:18–19; 14:12–24); and the woes are on their opposites: the rich, full, laughing, accepted. The reversal of fortunes is as sharp here as in Mary's song (1:46–55). When Jesus announced in Nazareth that his ministry was to the deprived (4:16–19), he said, after reading Isaiah 61:1–2, "Today this scripture has been fulfilled in your hearing" (4:21). We can take that to mean that the favor of God upon these people does not have to wait until the Eschaton but is at work now. And to say the blessing of God is "at work" is to be taken literally. Blessings and woes are not suggestions for the good life with a list of problems to be avoided. A blessing or a woe is a divine pronouncement, and it is performative; that is, it does what it says. Such a view of God's word, which accomplishes what it says, is not a familiar one in a society that speaks of words as "only words."

The content of verses 27–31 is tightly packed, indicating that Luke is working with a compilation of sayings of Jesus. These verses deal with the disciples' response to those who victimize others, those who hate, curse, abuse, strike, steal, and beg. Followers of Jesus may be victims, but they are not to see themselves as such; they are not to have a victim mentality, being shaped and determined by the hostilities unleashed on them. Rather, they are to take the initiative, responding not in kind or simply playing dead, whining, or excusing themselves as victims. This initiative means acting not according to principles learned from the oppressor but according to the kingdom principles of love, forgiveness, and generosity. This is not a covert strategy for a soft kill, but a living out of the life one learns from God, who is kind even to the ungrateful and the wicked (v. 35).

Thanksgiving Day

Deuteronomy 26:1–11;
Psalm 100;
Philippians 4:4–9;
John 6:25–35

Because Thanksgiving Day is not an observance growing out of the events of the liturgical year, the readings for the day are unrelated to any of the three cycles of the lectionary. The lections are chosen for their appropriateness to the spirit and purpose of this day: to bring an offering and recall God's mercy (Deuteronomy 26); to reaffirm loyalty to the God of our salvation (Psalm 100); to be grateful in all circumstances (Philippians 4); and to partake of the eucharistic bread of heaven (John 6).

Deuteronomy 26:1–11

There could hardly be a more appropriate Old Testament lesson for Thanksgiving Day than this one, for it contains the liturgical instructions for a thanksgiving ceremony in ancient Israel. The ceremony is the celebration of the festival of the first fruits, or the Feast of Weeks, one of the three great pilgrimage feasts prescribed in the Book of Deuteronomy. The other two are Passover-Unleavened Bread and the Feast of Booths (Deut. 16:16–17).

This text is also the Old Testament reading for the First Sunday in Lent in Year C. For more detailed commentary, consult the discussion at that point in this volume.

With regard to the use of this lesson on Thanksgiving, we may emphasize that ancient Israel knew that life itself brings many reasons for giving thanks and praise to God. If there is food to sustain life, there is cause for celebration. But the call in this passage is not to look so much to the fruitfulness of nature as to the past. One who looks back even a few years or generations, to say nothing of centuries, knows that countless others have helped make life possible. So the main admonition here is to remember, and especially to remember the acts of God in the past. Living in the land is itself proof that God is faithful to God's promises. It is hardly possible to command someone to be thankful, but thankfulness—and with it hospitality to others—will be evoked if one meditates on the history of salvation.

Psalm 100

This psalm is one of only a few in which its use is noted in the superscription (see Psalms 30, 102). The occasion for its usage is said to be the presentation of a "thank offering," a sacrifice offered when an individual or the community wanted to express its appreciation to the Divine (see Lev. 7:11–18). Such sacrifices were consumed—that is, the entire slaughtered animal except for gift portions paid to the priests was cooked and eaten—by the worshipers in a great "religious barbecue" in the temple courtyard. According to the law in Leviticus, the thanksgiving sacrifice had to be consumed completely on the day it was presented (7:15). This meant that extravagance, even gluttony, for the day was a requirement. Thanksgiving was a joyful celebration.

Psalm 100 is a communal psalm. All the imperative verbs are in the plural in the Hebrew, a fact that is not apparent in English translation. The psalm does not contain the full features of a thanksgiving psalm; in fact, it is an extended summons or call to praise and to thank God. Those called upon to make a joyful noise to God were probably only the Israelites in the psalm's ancient usage.

The elements in thanksgiving are noted as "joyful noise," "gladness," "singing," "thanksgiving," "praise." When we think of thanksgiving only as verbal expressions or as cognitive communication, we restrict too greatly its range of meaning and its forms of expression.

Two motivations are given for the praise and thanksgiving. The first stresses God as creator and preserver of human life (v. 3). Thus thanksgiving flows from the dependent humans to the Divine. Here thanksgiving is anchored in a theology of creation, although the creation spoken of may refer to the creation of Israel, its origination in the past (see Isa. 29:23; 41:1, 21). The second, although not as clearly drawn, offers as the reason God's fidelity in history (v. 5). Here the idea is the continuing, recurring love and fidelity of God. Thanksgiving throughout the psalm is associated with public worship; in the temple "come into his presence," "enter his gates . . . and his courts."

Philippians 4:4–9

A portion of this same text occurs earlier in Year C as the epistolary text for the Third Sunday of Advent (Phil. 4:4–7). It also overlaps with the epistolary text (Phil. 4:1–9) for Proper 23 [28] in Year A. The reader may want to consult our remarks in those liturgical settings.

What makes this an appropriate text to be read on the occasion of Thanksgiving is Paul's injunction "in everything by prayer and supplication with thanksgiving let your requests be made known to God" (v. 6). This is in concert with his exhortation to "give thanks in all circumstances" (1 Thess. 5:18; cf. Col. 3:17). This includes giving thanks for the food we eat (Rom. 14:6; 1 Tim. 4:3), for being delivered from the snares of death (2 Cor. 1:11), for being called into the Body of Christ (Col. 3:15), for all humanity, especially those in positions of rule and authority (1 Tim. 2:1–2), for everything God has created (1 Tim. 4:4).

For Paul, one of the sure marks of being pagan is being unable to express thanks to the God we know (Rom. 1:21). One of the realities of Christian existence is that the more we experience the abundant grace of God, the more our thanksgiving to God increases (2 Cor. 4:15). There is a similar correlation between our generosity and our thanksgiving to God: giving of our means to others "overflows with many thanksgivings to God" (2 Cor. 9:12). Expressing gratitude is seen as the most suitable substitute for inappropriate forms of speech (Eph. 5:4). At the very heart of worship is thanksgiving (Eph. 5:20; Col. 3:17).

Paul's instructions to his churches to be thankful in everything also conforms to his typical practice of opening his letters by offering a prayer of thanksgiving (cf. Rom. 1:8; 1 Cor. 1:4; Eph. 1:16; Phil. 1:3; Col. 1:3; 1 Thess. 1:2; 2:13; 3:9; 2 Thess. 1:3; 2:13; Philemon 4), as well as expressing thanks on other occasions (Rom. 16:4; 1 Cor. 14:18; 2 Cor. 9:15).

Our inclination to be thankful is anchored in Christ's own experience of gratitude. Before eating, he gives thanks (Matt. 15:36; Mark 8:6; John 6:11, 23), but especially before instituting the Eucharist he does so (Matt. 26:27; Mark 14:23; Luke 22:17; 1 Cor. 11:24). It becomes his posture in prayer (John 11:41). Jesus' story of the ten lepers who were cleansed, with only one of them—a foreigner—appreciative enough to return and express thanks, points to its importance in his teaching concerning the kingdom of God (Luke 17:11–19). That thanksgiving can be abused is also illustrated in the parable of the Pharisee and tax collector (Luke 18:11). Saying a prayer of thanksgiving to God may be nothing more than a hollow cliché, masking inner distortions of the soul (Luke 18:11).

In today's text, thanksgiving is the counterpart to anxiety (v. 6). The anxious heart may very well result from our inability to make requests of God that are proper expressions of thankful hearts. It is one thing to supplicate God, quite another to do so with a thankful heart. Asking God to fill our needs may become nothing more than the uncontrolled urge toward self-fulfillment. Even our prayers may be narcissistic. But they can hardly become so if they are uttered as expressions of thanksgiving to a God who has broken through the self, both the divine self and the human self.

Properly understood, thanksgiving excludes the excesses of the self, those urges we have for God to satisfy our own needs as if they were the only needs. Thanksgiving, as Paul understood it, is uttered as a response to God's "indescribable gift" (2 Cor. 9:15). It begins when we recognize that God's own giving was an act of consummate self-giving. The most appropriate response is an act in which we see ourselves as recipients of grace and not as petitioners of grace. It is that which we experience best if we receive it without asking. To think that we receive it because we ask is to misunderstand it.

John 6:25–35

The Gospel lection for this Thanksgiving Day service is drawn from one of the most profound, multifaceted, and influential chapters not only in the Fourth Gospel but in the New Testament. Lest the preacher and listeners drown in its complexity, it will be wise to allow the nature and intent of the Thanksgiving Day service to serve as a guide to the one among many perspectives, all justified and supportable, that will be the governing theme for the message. For example, if the worship is to be a eucharistic service, John 6 certainly yields that language and understanding. If the accent is to be on gratitude for God's daily provision, that, too, is in the text in abundance. Or again, if Christ is to be offered as the Bread beyond bread, there is no lack of that emphasis in this chapter. But one best not try to do in one sermon all that the Evangelist accomplishes in chapter 6.

At the risk of oversimplification, John 6 may be divided into three parts in its presentation of Christ: Jesus the provider of bread to the hungry (vv. 1–15); Jesus the bread from heaven, the word of God (vv. 22–50); and Jesus the eucharistic bread that we must eat in order to live (vv. 51–71). The story of walking on water (vv. 16–21) has been omitted even though it was early joined to the feeding of the multitudes (Mark 6:30–52), no doubt based on the Exodus story of God's mastery of the sea and the feeding of Israel. As early as Paul, these two events served as types of baptism and eucharist (1 Cor. 10:1–5). Our lection for today falls within the second portion of the threefold presentation of Christ. Again it should be said that these divisions are not sharp and firm. For example, in the first movement of the narrative, the feeding of the multitude, there are many clues to the second and third. This is not simply a compassion story, because what Jesus is about to do will be a sign; that is, it will point beyond itself (v. 6). The language describing the feeding is eucharistic (vv. 11, 23). The event occurs at Passover, the festival that echoes the death of Jesus. The reader is alerted, then, to look beyond bread to Bread.

It is, however, in verses 25–35 that the meaning of the sign of feeding the crowds begins to develop. It is not enough that Jesus be seen by the people as a prophet like Moses, who fed Israel in the wilderness (v. 14; Deut. 18:18). It is not enough that the people desire to make Jesus king (v. 15). Enthroning those who do things for us has a long and disappointing history. That which Jesus urges is the quest for the Bread that truly satisfies, that does not perish, that gives life eternal (vv. 25–29). Here Jesus begins to draw attention away from the previous day's meal; after all, their ancestors had been given food in the wilderness and they died (vv. 31, 49). Rather, Jesus draws attention to himself as the true bread from God.

Jesus as the bread of life (v. 35) is not yet developed in the eucharistic sense ("unless you eat the flesh of the Son of Man and drink his blood," v. 53). Within our lection Jesus is the bread of life in that he is the bread of God "which comes down from heaven and gives life to the world" (v. 33). Here the manna analogy very likely refers to Jesus as the Logos, the Word of God as presented in the Prologue (1:1–18). Or to put it another way, verses 25–35 are a commentary on Deuteronomy 8:3: "He humbled you by letting you hunger, then by feeding you with manna, with which neither you nor your ancestors were acquainted, in order to make you understand that one does not live by bread alone, but by every word that comes from the mouth of the LORD." Jesus as the true bread from heaven not only speaks but is the Word of God, making God known to us (1:18), whom to know is life eternal (17:3).

Presentation of the Lord, February 2

Malachi 3:1–4;
Psalm 84 or Psalm 24:7–10;
Hebrews 2:14–18;
Luke 2:22–40

This day is the celebration of the event reported in the Gospel reading, the presentation of Jesus in the temple in Jerusalem in accordance with Jewish law. Either of the psalms is highly appropriate, for both enable the church at worship to recreate the scene at the temple. Psalm 84 is a pilgrim hymn in praise of Zion, and Psalm 24:7–10 is an entrance liturgy that praises the king of glory. The christological reflections in Hebrews 2:14–18 show a fully human Lord as high priest in the service of God. Malachi 3:1–4 is the promise of a messenger of the covenant who will come like a "refiner's fire," after which the offerings—such as those mentioned in the Gospel—will be acceptable to God.

Malachi 3:1–4

The Book of Malachi originated in the postexilic period, between 520 BC, when the temple was rebuilt, and 400 BC, when the law was instituted by Ezra. Sacrifices and offerings in the temple seem to have become a regular part of the life of worship. Judah would have been a province of the Persian Empire, with its own "governor" (Mal. 1:8).

Nothing is known about the life of the prophet himself, not even his name. "Malachi" is not a proper name but the title "my messenger," apparently taken from the passage before us (3:1). The person responsible for the book continues the ancient prophetic tradition of speaking in the name of the Lord concerning the immediate future, and he is willing to challenge current beliefs and practices. He was deeply interested in priestly matters and likely was identified with the Levites (Mal. 2:4–9).

The reading for today is part of a unit that begins in 2:17 and concludes with 3:5. It is a disputation between the prophet, speaking on behalf of the Lord, and persons whose words he quotes. They have "wearied" the Lord by saying, "All who do evil are good in the sight of the LORD, and he delights in them," and by asking, "Where is the God of justice?" (2:17). In short, because evildoers prosper, these opponents question the presence of a God of justice.

Malachi 3:1–4 is the prophetic response to such objections. The prophet hears the Lord announcing the arrival of a messenger, the messenger of the covenant, who will prepare for the appearance of the Lord himself in the temple. The day of arrival, elsewhere called the day of the Lord, will be a terrible time, for no one can stand before him. It will be a day of refining and purification, particularly of the Levites, who will then present offerings that "will be pleasing to the LORD" (v. 4).

Next, the Lord himself will appear in judgment, punishing "all who do evil" (2:17), including sorcerers, adulterers, and those who deal unjustly with the weak, such as hirelings, widows, orphans, and resident aliens (3:5). Where is the God of justice? He is sending his messenger to prepare the way, cleansing the priesthood and the temple worship, and then God himself will approach as judge. Sinners may prosper, but not for long.

The passage has reverberated in various ways through Christian tradition. Mark took the messenger to be John the Baptist and quoted the initial line of verse 1 to introduce the account of John's appearance and his baptism of Jesus. On the commemoration of Presentation, read with Luke 2:22–40, the ambiguities of verse 1 take on added significance. Is Jesus the messenger, or the Lord himself, who "will suddenly come to his temple"? The somber, apocalyptic tone of the passage from Malachi underscores the threatening aspects of the presentation of Jesus in the temple (Luke 2:34–35). Behind this serious note, however, the good news of Malachi is unmistakable. God will establish justice, and the arrival of his messenger will restore the means of communion with God (3:4).

Psalm 84

The two psalms selected for reading in celebration of Jesus' presentation at the temple are concerned with devotion to the temple (for a full discussion of Psalm 84, see Proper 16 [21], Year B). Psalm 84 may have been once used in conjunction with pilgrimages made to Jerusalem at festival time, although verse 9 seems to suggest it was used by the king. Psalm 24 contains words spoken at the time when pilgrims entered the sanctuary precincts.

Psalm 84:5–7 probably talks about the route to Zion taken by pilgrims as they made their way along the roads to the city. At the time of the fall festival, some of the early autumn rains may already have fallen, reviving the parched land. "Strength to strength" (v. 7) could be translated "stronghold to stronghold"; that is, the people move from one village outpost to another.

The piety of the worshiper and the psalm composer can be seen in various ways in the text. One way of analyzing the materials is to note the three groups whom the writer declares "blessed" (or "happy," which is a better translation of the Hebrew word used in all three cases).

1. First, happy are the birds that dwell continuously in the temple (vv. 3–4). The sparrows and swallows that nest in the sacred precincts have the advantage of constantly dwelling in the house of God, where they can sing God's praise forever.

2. Happy are those who go on pilgrimage to Jerusalem (vv. 5–7). To visit the temple and Zion is to experience happiness and to see "the God of gods."

3. Happy are those who trust in God (v. 12), who find their confidence in him. Here we have a sort of generalizing pronouncement that moves beyond the specificity of temple piety.

Verse 10 may be taken as embodying the overall sentiment of the psalm: to visit the temple and worship in its courts were some of the supreme experiences for the ancient Hebrews.

Psalm 24:7–10

Of all the psalms, Psalm 24 probably illustrates most clearly the fact that the psalms were used as the spoken part of cultic rituals (see also Proper 10 [15], Year B). Throughout verses 3–10, the material is comprised of a series of questions and answers probably recited by pilgrims and priests.

The psalm opens (vv. 1–2) with a hymnic praise of Yahweh that identifies the God of Israel as the possessor of the world and all that is in it. The ownership of the terrestrial kingdom is Yahweh's by right of creation. Yahweh is the one who anchored the earth in the midst of the seas and established it firmly upon the rivers (or streams) of the deep that ancients believed lay underneath the dry land. (Such a belief is partially based on the presence of springs and wells that suggest that water lies beneath the earth.)

The questions in verse 3 were addressed by the pilgrims to the priests inside the temple as the pilgrims arrived at the gates of the temple. The questions concern the qualifications demanded of those allowed to enter the sacred precincts: "Who shall ascend the hill of the LORD [who can enter the temple precincts]? And who shall stand in his holy place [in the temple in the presence of God]?" The priestly answer in this catechism of admission (vv. 4–5) brings together two types of ethical qualifications: purity of outward deeds (clean hands) and purity of thought or inward truthfulness (pure heart) followed by purity of religious practice or unadulterated faith (not lifting up the soul to what is vain) and purity in speaking (not swearing deceitfully). These four principles in themselves provide a rather comprehensive perspective of ethical demands and requirements. If such demands as these were made as part of the worship, then one surely cannot accuse ancient worship services of being devoid of ethical interests and demands.

Verse 6 provides the worshipers' response to the requirements for entrance: "Those are the kind of people we are." Thus they claim the promises of verse 5—blessing and vindication from God.

With verse 7, the focus shifts from humankind and the moral values of living to God himself. The pilgrims or choir outside the sanctuary address the temple gates demanding that they be lifted up so that the King of glory may come in. But how could God enter the sanctuary? No doubt, the ark, the symbol of God's presence, had been carried out of the temple to reenter with the pilgrims on a high holy festival day. The choir or priests within offer a response in the form of a question. "Who is this King of glory?" (v. 8). God is then described as the one strong and mighty, mighty in battle. Perhaps part of the festival involved the proclamation of God's triumph over the forces of evil.

Hebrews 2:14–18

At one time, especially in the Western church, this feast day was oriented toward Mary, and this was reflected in its name, "Purification of the Blessed Virgin Mary." But because this appeared to threaten the doctrine of the sinlessness of Mary, in modern times the Roman church reverted to the more ancient understanding of the Eastern church that celebrated this day as the "Presentation of the Lord." This more nearly conformed to its various designations in the East: "Coming of the Son of God into the Temple" (Armenian); "Presentation of the Lord in the Temple" (Egyptian); "The Meeting of the Lord" (Byzantine). The shift in title reflects a shift in emphasis: it is intended to be a feast of the Lord and not a feast honoring Mary.

With this focus on the presentation of the Lord, which, according to scriptural prescription, took place forty days after his birth (Lev. 12:2–8), this feast day has an incarnational cast. Celebrated on February 2, the fortieth day after Christmas, it serves to mark the end of the Christmas Season. Although the Gospel reading provides an account of the Lucan story of the presentation of Jesus in the temple (Luke 2:22–40), the epistolary reading serves to anchor the redemptive work of Christ in his incarnation. This text should not be forced in a false harmony with the Gospel reading, for each reflects a different theological interest. Nevertheless, there is a certain irony in the fact that the child who is presented in the temple "according to the law of Moses" finally becomes the merciful and faithful high priest officiating in the heavenly temple, making expiation for the sins of the people.

Several features of today's epistolary lection are worth noting.

First is the solidarity between Christ, "the one who sanctifies," and all humanity, "those who are sanctified" (v. 11). In the previous verses, several Old Testament texts are placed on the lips of Christ to show that he identifies completely with all of God's children (Ps. 22:22; Isa. 8;17–18). As such, he was born a member of the human family, sharing completely in our nature as "flesh and blood" (v. 14; Rom. 8:3, 29; Phil. 2:7). Just as it is the lot of every member of the human family to die, so did he experience death.

The effects of his death, however, were far from ordinary. For one thing, it was God "for whom and by whom all things exist" who made Jesus the "pioneer . . . perfect through suffering" (v. 10). In addition, through death he passed through the heavens and became the exalted Son of God (Heb. 4:14). Because his death was both uniquely exemplary and triumphant, he destroyed death as the stronghold of Satan (v. 14; John 12:31; Rom. 6:9; 1 Cor. 15:55; 2 Tim. 1:10; Rev. 12:10). In his death, he delivered "all those who through fear of death were subject to lifelong bondage" (v. 15). The incarnation of Christ eventually meant the freedom of all humanity from the fear of death.

The second feature of our lection is Christ as the merciful and faithful high priest (3:1; 4:14; 5:5, 10; 6:20; 7:26; 8:1; 9:11; 10:21). Because of his complete obedience, he demonstrated his true fidelity as the Son of God (5:8–9; cf. 1 Sam. 2:35). Because of his complete identification with the entire human family through his becoming "flesh and blood," he can be thoroughly sympathetic with the human condition. His own suffering and testing qualifies him to assist us in our sufferings and testing (v. 18; 5:2; cf. Matt. 4:1–11 and parallels; 26:36–46 and parallels).

In his role as high priest, Christ makes expiation for our sins (v. 17). His unique experience as one of God's earthly children makes it possible for him to plead in our behalf (5:1; Rom. 3:25; 1 John 2:2; 4:10; cf. Exod. 4:16).

Christ as a heavenly high priest, officiating in the heavenly temple and pleading in our behalf, can easily become a lofty image, far removed from the world we know and live in. Oddly enough, Christians have always found it easier to worship such an elevated Christ, enthroned high above the heavens. It is far more difficult for us to envision a Christ who became like us in every respect (v. 17). Yet today's epistolary text makes this unqualified claim about Christ, who was concerned not with angels but with the descendants of Abraham (v. 16). Given a choice between the company of angels and the company of humans, Christ plumps for flesh and blood. Why shouldn't we?

Because Hebrews 2:10–18 serves as the epistolary reading for the First Sunday After Christmas in Year A, the reader may also want to consult our comments in the earlier volume in connection with that day.

Luke 2:22–40

The text that provides a Gospel basis for the service of the presentation of Jesus is found only in Luke (2:22–40). In fact, Luke places between the nativity (2:1–20) and Jesus' beginning his public life at age thirty (3:23) three stories: the circumcision and naming when the child was eight days old (2:21; see the special service for January 1); the presentation in the temple when he was about forty days old (2:22–40; Lev. 12:1–4); and the visit to the temple at age twelve (2:41–52). All this is to say that the Jesus who began his ministry at age thirty was thoroughly grounded and rooted in his tradition, that observance of the law and attendance to temple duties were very important, and that although he was a Galilean, neither he nor his disciples scorned Jerusalem. In fact, says Luke alone, Jesus' disciples were to remain in Jerusalem after his ascension and from Jerusalem were to launch their mission (24:47–48). "And [they] returned to Jerusalem with great joy; and they were continually in the temple blessing God" (24:52–53). It is no wonder that Jesus, the true Israelite, went to the synagogue on the sabbath, "as was his custom" (4:16). Jesus and some of the religious leaders disputed over the tradition, to be sure, but it was a tradition he knew and kept from childhood.

When one looks at the presentation account itself, it is evident that there is the story line (2:22–24, 39–40) into which two substories have been inserted: that of Simeon (vv. 25–35) and that of Anna (vv. 36–38). The principal story line seems to have as its basic purpose the demonstration that in the life of the Christ Child the law of Moses had been meticulously observed (vv. 22, 23, 24, 27, 39). In the course of making that point, Luke has conflated two regulations: a mother was to be ceremonially purified after childbirth (Lev. 12:1–4; in cases of poverty, Lev. 12:6–8 was applied), and a firstborn male was to be dedicated to God (Exod. 13:2, 12–16). Of course, provision was made for parents to redeem their son from the Lord (Num. 18:15–16) so they could keep him as their own. Luke says nothing about the redemption of Jesus; perhaps his silence serves to prepare the reader for the next story in which Jesus in the temple at age twelve said to his parents, "Did you not know that I must be in my Father's house?" (v. 49). That story, along with verses 40 and 52, makes it evident that Luke is echoing the story of the boy Samuel, who was dedicated to God and who lived in the temple (1 Samuel 1–2).

In the persons of Simeon (vv. 25–35) and Anna (vv. 36–38) Luke tells how the Israel that is true, believing, hoping, devout, and temple-attending responded to Jesus. Simeon's acknowledgment of Jesus as "the Lord's Messiah" was inspired by the Holy Spirit (v. 26), and Anna's was that of a true prophet who fasted and prayed continually (vv. 36–37). Simeon longed for "the consolation of Israel" (v. 25), a phrase referring to the messianic age. The Nunc Dimittis (vv. 29–32) may have been a portion of a Christian hymn familiar to Luke and his readers. Simeon's words make it clear that Israel's consolation would not be a time of uninterrupted joy; hostility and death would be aroused by the appearance of the deliverer. Good news always has its enemies. Mary herself would pay a heavy price: "and a sword will pierce your own soul too"

(v. 35). Devout and obedient Israel, as portrayed in the old prophet Anna, also saw in Jesus "the redemption of Jerusalem" (v. 38). Her thanks to God and her witness concerning Jesus provide a model of the Israel that accepted Jesus and saw in him the fulfillment of ancient hopes. Luke will write later of that portion of Israel that rejected Jesus and turned a deaf ear to the preaching of the early church. But in Luke's theology, they are thereby rejecting their own tradition and their own prophets as it was interpreted to them by one who was a true Israelite, Jesus of Nazareth. He kept the law, held Jerusalem in great affection (13:34), and was faithful to the synagogue. Moreover, his teaching was in keeping with all that was written in Moses, the prophets, and the writings (24:44). No prophet is so powerful and so disturbing as the one who arises out of one's own tradition and presents to the people the claims of that tradition.

Annunciation, March 25

Isaiah 7:10–14;
Psalm 45 or Psalm 40:5–10;
Hebrews 10:4–10;
Luke 1:26–38

I n the seasons of the death and resurrection of Jesus, this day calls our attention to the announcement of his birth. The Gospel lesson is central here, for the day celebrates the events reported in Luke 1:26–38, the angel Gabriel's announcement to Mary. The tradition represented in Isaiah 7:10–14—the promise of a birth as a sign of God's salvation—stands in the background. Psalm 45 responds to the messianic promise, and Psalm 40:6–10 to Mary's faithfulness. The second reading concerns the purpose for which Christ came into the world.

Isaiah 7:10–14

T his passage from the Book of Isaiah provides important background for the Lucan account of the Annunciation. Central here is the prophecy of a birth as a sign of God's intentions toward God's people. Moreover, the name of that child, "Immanuel," which means "God is with us," is an interpretation of the Lord's will. Although we now recognize that Isaiah had in view a particular woman and child in his own time, and not Mary and her son Jesus, the ancient promise still has its contribution to make to Christian worship and to the Christian life.

Some of the literary and historical questions concerning our passage can be answered with relative certainty. It is one of a number of reports of encounters in Jerusalem between Isaiah and King Ahaz at a particularly critical moment in the history of Judah. The historical situation is summarized in Isaiah 7:1–2 and spelled out further in 2 Kings 16:1–20. When the Assyrian king Tiglath-pileser III started to move against the small states of Syria and Palestine, the leaders of those states began to form a coalition to oppose him. Apparently because Ahaz of Judah refused to join them, the kings in Damascus and Samaria moved against Jerusalem (about 734 BC) to topple Ahaz and replace him with someone more favorable to their policies. In the passage (7:1–9) that immediately precedes our reading, Isaiah counseled nonresistance based on faith in the ancient promise to David that one of his sons would always occupy the throne in Jerusalem. The fact that our unit begins with the expression "Again the LORD spoke to Ahaz" (v. 10) indicates that it is a continuation of the prophet's actions in the same situation.

Isaiah 7:10–14 is good news in the form of a prophetic symbolic action, especially to the king but also thereby to the people as a whole. Note that the entire section is presented as if the Lord himself is speaking directly to King Ahaz, but it would have been the prophet who conveyed the message. In the previous unit, Ahaz had been afraid; here he refuses even to inquire of the Lord, even when Isaiah instructs him to do so (vv. 11–12). It was common for kings or other leaders to inquire of the Lord, often through prophets, before deciding to go to battle (see 2 Kings 13:14–19). When Ahaz refuses to ask for a sign, the prophet becomes impatient and says that the Lord himself will give a sign: "Look, the young woman is with child and shall bear a son, and shall name him Immanuel" (v. 14). He goes on to interpret the sign, promising that before the child knows how to "refuse the evil and choose the good"—that is, within a short time—the present military threat will have ended. Although the means are not stated, the prophet promises that God will intervene to save his people.

Few textual and translation problems in the Old Testament have generated more controversy than those of Isaiah 7:14. However, there can be little doubt about the meaning or translation of the crucial word. The Hebrew word 'almah is correctly rendered by the NRSV and almost all other modern translations "young woman." The term is neutral with regard to her marital status. It was the Greek translation of the Book of Isaiah, the Septuagint, that read "virgin" (Greek parthenos), thus setting the stage for the particular messianic interpretation of the passage expressed in the New Testament. The bridge between the eighth century and the early church is thus yet another historical and theological context, that of the translation of the Hebrew Scriptures for Jews in a Hellenistic, pre-Christian culture. It is equally clear that the Book of Isaiah originally read here "young woman" and that the Evangelists inherited a translation of Isaiah that read "virgin."

As in most other prophetic announcements or symbolic actions, Isaiah has the immediate future in view, and thus the woman and child are his contemporaries. As the NRSV (see also REB) indicates, he indicates to the king a woman who is already pregnant. But the identity of the woman is difficult if not impossible to establish. In view of a context that stresses the significance of the Davidic dynasty, many commentators have taken the child to be the crown prince, and the woman as the wife of Ahaz. Others, seeing the passage in some ways parallel to Isaiah 8:1–4, have argued that the woman was the wife of the prophet, and the child his son. It is quite likely, however, that the "young woman" was simply a pregnant woman whom Isaiah saw as he was addressing the king.

One of the keys to the meaning of this passage is the word "sign" (Hebrew 'oth). It is the same word used in the tradition about the "signs and wonders" performed in Egypt before the Exodus and thus has come to be associated in our minds with the so-called miraculous. However, such signs may be ordinary events as well as extraordinary ones. The decisive point in the Old Testament view is that a "sign" is revelatory, that it communicates God's word or will or nature. Thus it is not remarkable that in Isaiah 7 something as common—and also as wonderful—as the birth of a baby boy is a message from God, and for the future. The name embodies the promise of God's saving presence.

To be sure, it is hardly possible for Christians to hear this passage and not think of the coming of Jesus. But in addition to directing our attention to the incarnation, Isaiah 7:10–14 has its own good news. It is a message that sees pregnancy and birth—even when not understood as miraculous—as signs of God's concern for God's people. Furthermore, this message is directed to a people living in chaos and fear, faced with such specific problems as international politics and the threat of destruction. Even in such a situation, the word of God offers hope.

Psalm 45

Psalm 45 is clearly a wedding psalm. The references to the king and the bride in the text, however, are the source of differences in interpretation. Four approaches are worthy of note.

1. One line of interpretation is what might be called the metaphorical approach. This assumes that the marriage described is simply a conventional wedding. The normal, everyday groom is described in metaphorical language as a "king" and the bride as a "princess."

2. A second approach can be called the mythological. This assumes that the wedding partners are actually the male deity, played by the king, and the female goddess, played by the queen.

3. A third approach is the allegorical. The king in the text stands for Yahweh, and the bride is his chosen people. What is said in the text is not to be taken literally but allegorically.

4. A fourth interpretation is the historical. This assumes that the text was composed for an actual wedding for an actual ancient Israelite or Judean king. Because the text refers to Tyre, it has sometimes been assumed that the psalm was composed for the marriage of King Ahab of Israel to the Phoenician princess Jezebel, who was from the city of Tyre.

The association of this text with the Annunciation strains any reading of the text unless one wants to understand the king in the text as God and the bride as the virgin Mary. The more common Christian interpretation is to relate the figure of the king to that of Jesus, as is already done in Hebrews 1:8–9. If Jesus is identified with the groom, the bride, however, is best understood as the church, not as Mary. At any rate, any exegesis of the text that Christianizes the interpretation forces the imagery considerably.

Of the four interpretations noted above, the most likely original reading is that which sees the psalm as a composition from an actual wedding of a Hebrew king, though it is doubtful if we can identify which king was the groom.

The following is the outline of the psalm: (1) a statement about the poet and the purpose of the poem (v. 1), (2) the glorification and praise of the king (vv. 2–9), (3) the glorification and praise of the bride (vv. 10–15), and (4) a statement to the king that promises him great and famous progeny (vv. 16–17). The psalm allows us some insight into the opulence of the royal court and a glimpse at some of the flattery of the king that must have characterized court life.

Although the poet praises and flatters the king, he may also have engaged in some "preaching" to the monarch by making frequent reference to the king's responsibilities. The ruler is described as the fairest of men, one blessed with grace. The king, gloriously garbed in regal splendor with girded sword, can be visualized in the imagery of verse 3. The king, whose arrows destroy his enemies, is portrayed as the defender of the right and the cause of truth. The throne of the king is proclaimed as eternal and his rule as one of equity and righteousness. The status and well-being of the king are reflected in the perfumes that scent his royal robes, in the ivory palaces where he is entertained by instrumental music, in the daughters of royalty who inhabit his mansion, and in the golden splendor of his queen.

The bride is addressed and admonished to forget her family and country (Tyre) and to give her affection and attention to her new husband. The bride in her wedding finery and her attendants and ladies-in-waiting are described as being led in procession to the palace of the king.

The psalm concludes, like many modern Near Eastern weddings, with a statement expressing the hope and assurance of numerous offspring. Because fertility—numerous offspring—was considered a blessing from God (see Ps. 127:3–5), such a promise or blessing was especially appropriate for the king, whose offspring would share in the rule of the Davidic dynasty to whom God had promised eternal rulership.

Psalm 40:5–10

This lection is excerpted from the thanksgiving portion of a psalm probably originally used by the king. Verses 5–10 comprise the worshiper's thanksgiving spoken directly to the Deity in response to having been redeemed from some great distress (described in vv. 1–3). The association of this text with and its appropriateness for the Annunciation are its emphasis on willingly submitting to the divine will (see esp. v. 8), as was the case with Mary.

Several statements in the text require explanation. Verse 6 declares that God does not desire sacrifice. Four different types of sacrifice are referred to, some of the freewill type and others mandatory. What the verse intends to emphasize, however, is that what God really requires is a faithful, hearing attitude. The expression "ears thou hast dug for me" probably was a proverbial way of saying, "I am really hearing you."

The book referred to in verse 7 may have been the Book of the Law, especially if this was written for use by the king (see Deut. 17:14–17), perhaps an official record or court document, or maybe a heavenly book in which it was believed were recorded all the activities of a person's life. At least, the book seems to give a favorable opinion of the worshiper (see v. 8).

In verses 9–10, the worshiper testifies to having proclaimed the salvation of God. In these verses, the same point is made with two positive affirmations (vv. 9a, 10b) and three denials (vv. 9b, 10a, 10c). The psalmist declares that the story he or she made known in public worship in the life of the congregation has thus borne testimony to God's salvation.

Hebrews 10:4–10

The phrase from today's epistolary reading that makes it suitable for Annunciation Day occurs in verse 5: "When Christ came into the world." This text occurs as part of a larger argument within the Book of Hebrews in which the death of Christ is presented as a sacrifice eminently superior to the forms of animal sacrifice prescribed by the Mosaic Law. Thus our text is introduced with the claim that the blood of bulls and goats is ineffective in taking away sin (cf. 9:12, 19). One of the main arguments the Book of Hebrews makes against animal sacrifices is that they had to be made repeatedly—"year after year" (10:1). Rather than taking away sin, these sacrifices merely served as annual reminders of sin.

To buttress this point, the author interprets the incarnation of Christ in terms of doing the will of God. To this end, he quotes Psalm 40:6–8, one of the classic Old Testament texts insisting that obedience is better than sacrifice (cf. 1 Sam. 15:22–23; Isa. 1:10–11; 29:13–14; 58:1–9; Jer. 6:20; Hos. 6:6; Joel 2:12–13; Amos 5:23–24; Mic. 6:5–8; Zech. 7:5–7; cf. Matt. 9:13; 12:7). The limitations and abuses of a sacrificial system were well recognized within the Jewish tradition. Anyone who knows religious traditions knows the tendency for worship to become a matter of externals—going through the proper motions at the right times in the right way. There is the constant need to remember that service to the Deity is central and fundamental. Without that, all expressions of worship become empty.

The psalmist recognizes that God has not required him to offer burnt offerings and sin offerings merely for the sake of going through the motions of worship. In these things per se, God takes no pleasure (v. 6). What matters to God is not the rites themselves but the motivation of the heart that offers the rites, that makes the sacrifices. In a word, doing the will of God—this is what gives meaning to these acts of religious observance.

The author of Hebrews actually places the words of Psalm 40 on the lips of Christ. It is introduced with the words "he [Christ] said" (v. 5). These words are then to be understood as actually providing us with Christ's view of sacrifices and the superiority of doing God's will to offering burnt offerings and sin offerings. The author proceeds to explain the text (vv. 8–9). The upshot of his midrashic explanation is that because Christ came to do the will of God, he effectively relegated the system of animal sacrifices to their deserved place of second importance: "He abolishes the first in order to establish the second" (v. 9).

Because of Christ's willingness to do the will of God, his sacrifice counted in a way Levitical sacrifices did not: it made possible genuine sanctification once and for all (v. 10; cf. 10:14, 29; 13:12; also 1 Thess. 4:3; Eph. 5:2).

As a passage for Annunciation Day, this text provides another perspective for understanding the incarnation of Christ. It might be read with other passages that interpret the purpose of Christ's coming to the earth as doing the will of God (cf. John 4:34; 5:30; 6:38). As one of the well-known texts stressing the superiority of inner motivation over outward religious expressions, it might be explored profitably in this direction. The homilist might choose to examine how Christ himself, in his teachings and actions, sought to get at the essence of true religion rather than concern himself with questions of protocol and prescription.

Luke 1:26–38

It would be a mistake to think that the early church's sole interest in the calendar was in various attempts to ascertain the time of the end and the return of Christ. Although such calculations have waxed and waned throughout the life of the church, the calendar has held other interests for Christians. Quite early there was a desire to structure the disciplines of worship and prayer on the significant hours and days in the life of Christ. Christian calendars were developed and framed primarily around the seasons of central importance, Easter and Christmas. Once a date was set for the celebration of Jesus' birth, it was only a matter of time until the day nine months earlier would be observed as the Annunciation, the day of Gabriel's visit to Mary. By thus observing March 25, the church was able to focus upon the beautiful text of Luke 1:26–38 outside the already rich and full season of Advent.

Luke says that Mary received the word of God's favor from the messenger (the meaning of the word "angel") Gabriel. In later Judaism, angels, both in the service of God and in the service of Satan, came to figure prominently in theology and in popular religion. Such beings were common in religions of Persia and may have found a welcome in Jewish thought in a time when the distance between a transcendent God and human beings required mediators. Angels carried messages and performed other functions in God's dealings with creation. In some literature, important angels were given names, Gabriel being one of the most familiar (Dan. 9:21). In the New Testament, Luke's stories are the most populated with angels, with the obvious exception of the heavenly scenes in the Apocalypse. Christians have differed in their ways of appropriating the conversation between Mary and an angel: some literally; others by means of literary, psychological, or sociological categories. The story has survived all interpretations.

Luke apparently has no need to speculate on the choice of Mary as the mother of the Christ. The point is, God has chosen her, and as in any act of divine grace, the reasons are enfolded in God's purposes and not in the recipient. The angel's message that Mary's child will be Son of God and son of David is a composite of phrases and lines from Isaiah, Genesis, 2 Samuel, Micah, Hosea, and Daniel. It is possible that this hymnlike expression of praise (vv. 32–33) came to Luke from an early Christian liturgy. Many scholars believe that the church quite early put together Old Testament verses that were useful in worship, preaching, and teaching new members.

Mary wonders, quite naturally, how she, without a husband, can conceive and bear a son. She is given no answer that approaches biology. Rather, she is given an announcement and a bit of information that functioned as a sign of the truth of the promise. The announcement was that the birth would be the work of the Holy Spirit and the power of the Most High (v. 35). In other words, Jesus of Nazareth is God's act of grace and power. The information that encourages Mary's faith is that her kinswoman Elizabeth, old and barren, is in her sixth month of pregnancy. Echoed in the Elizabeth story is that of Abraham and Sarah (Gen. 18:14). But behind the stories of Mary's, Elizabeth's, and Sarah's conceptions is the creed beneath and behind all other creeds: "For nothing will be impossible with God" (v. 37). It is to this word that Mary responds in trust and in obedience.

Visitation, May 31

1 Samuel 2:1–10;
Psalm 113;
Romans 12:9–16*b*;
Luke 1:39–57

The lections for use in commemorating Mary's visit to Elizabeth (Luke 1) focus on Mary and, through Mary as representative, on all the lowly and humble who serve God. Luke uses the song of Hannah (1 Samuel 12) in the song of Mary, and both Psalm 113 and Romans 12 speak of God as helper of those who do chores for which they get little attention and less praise. By keeping the attention on Mary as God's servant, the preacher will avoid making this a premature Advent service.

1 Samuel 2:1–10

This text has found its place as the Old Testament lesson on Visitation primarily because Hannah, the mother of Samuel, has been seen as a type of Mary, the mother of Jesus. In addition, the occasions of the Song of Hannah and the Magnificat are quite similar. Both concern the birth of babies who are divine gifts, and both of the babies are dedicated by their mothers to the service of God. Moreover, several themes in Hannah's song parallel those of the Magnificat, especially those that focus upon God's care for the lowly.

Hannah's Song, like Mary's comes at a critical point in history. In the lengthy history of Israel from the time of Moses to the Babylonian Exile, Samuel is an extremely important figure who spans two distinct eras, the end of the period of the judges and the beginning of the monarchy. The baby whose birth Hannah celebrates will be the last and most significant judge, but he will be more, serving both priestly and prophetic functions as well. Finally, he will be the one to preside over Israel's debate about whether or not to have a king, and will designate first Saul and then David as kings.

None of this is told in the account of the birth of the boy Samuel, but it is made clear from the outset that he is a child of destiny. In his birth, the devotion of a woman and the graciousness of God work hand in hand. Long past the age of childbearing, Hannah goes to the sanctuary at Shiloh, presided over by Eli the priest, to pray for a son, vowing that he would be dedicated to serve the Lord. The Lord heard her prayer, and when the child was weaned she took him to Shiloh to hand him over to service in the sanctuary.

The Song of Hannah is presented as part of the service for the consecration of Samuel. However, its relationship to the context is quite loose. Within the song there are no specific allusions to the persons or the period, but, on the other hand, an anachronistic allusion to the king (v. 10). It is likely that the song itself is a later addition to the narrative, supplied as an appropriate expression of Hannah's piety, and a typical part of a service of worship.

Hannah's song is similar in many respects to other Old Testament lyrical poetry that arose and was used in worship. In particular, it is a song of thanksgiving that has, like many such songs, features of hymns of praise. The thanksgiving song typically was part of services of worship not found on a liturgical calendar. When an individual or the nation found itself in trouble, a prayer service was held in which the central part was a prayer of complaint. When the individual or the nation was delivered from the distress, a service of thanksgiving was called for. When Hannah first went to the sanctuary at Shiloh, she went to complain about her barrenness and ask the Lord's help. Now, fulfilling the vow made as part of that prayer, she gives thanks.

Songs of thanksgiving and praise spring from the human experience of God as both powerful and caring. Hence they are filled with the mood of joy and confidence. Because that experience takes many forms, the themes of such songs are almost unlimited. They may celebrate the world as God's creation, or particular acts of salvation in history or in one's life. Among the themes of the Song of Hannah are the following: (1) there is joy and rejoicing because of the Lord's help (v. 1); (2) the Lord is incomparable as a sure support (v. 2); (3) the Lord chooses the weak over the powerful (v. 4); (4) the Lord cares for the needy, whether they are hungry or barren (vv. 5, 8a); (5) the Lord's power extends to all things, over life and death and to the foundations of the earth (vv. 6, 8b); (6) the Lord protects the faithful against the wicked, defeating his adversaries, and his reign will extend to the ends of the earth (vv. 9–10).

Psalm 113

This psalm is discussed as one of the lections for Visitation, May 31, Years A and B.

Romans 12:9–16b

This text is also included in the text that serves as the epistolary reading for Proper 17 [22] in Year A (Rom. 12:9–21). Additional comments may be found in that connection. Because the same texts are used for Visitation in Years A, B, and C, the reader might also want to consult our remarks made in connection with Years A and B.

On the occasion celebrating Mary's visit to Elizabeth, it is the Gospel reading from Luke that sets the liturgical agenda (Luke 1:39–57). This tradition of Mary's "visitation" is recorded only in Luke, and it is the Magnificat that sets the tone for the observance of this day. One of the primary notes sounded in this passage is the exaltation of the lowly: Mary the humble handmaiden of God is raised to an exalted position as the one through whom the promise of God will be fulfilled. It is the reversal of roles we come to expect in Luke: God dethroning the mighty and enthroning the lowly in their place.

What makes today's epistolary reading appropriate in this setting is its insistence that we "not be haughty, but associate with the lowly" (v. 16). We miss the full force of this injunction if we read it as an ethic of politeness. It is more than a warning not to be conceited toward those of lowly estate. It is a mandate to identify with them, to be with them in their lowliness. In a similar fashion, the Magnificat is quite revolutionary in its social outlook. It calls for the reversal of the normal social order and reminds us that Yahweh's concern is to feed the hungry and send the rich away empty. In its boldest form, it envisions a radical redistribution of resources.

So does today's epistolary text call for radical identification with the earth's lowly. Only in this way can the charge to "love one another with mutual affection" (v. 10) be carried out seriously. What is being called for here is a level of Christian fellowship that transcends all barriers—social, racial, gender. It is a form of community that expresses itself concretely in displays of genuine hospitality (v. 13), where financial contributions are made as expressions of Christian love. In view here are the "needs of the saints" (v. 13), and the primary focus of this instruction is internal. Yet this urge to transcend self-interest is reaching out to the needs of others extends beyond the Christian circle (cf. Gal. 6:10).

As it turns out, hating "what is evil, [and holding] fast to what is good" (v. 9) may result in self-exposure. That which is evil may very well be our refusal to "associate with the lowly" in any genuine sense of identification and empathy. What it may expose are those subtle forms of discrimination that are masked by other forms of religiosity, even prayer and worship. We may find ourselves being religious in one sense, but discriminatory in another, much more sinister sense. We want to come to God without fully identifying with all of God's creatures: high and low, exalted and humble, franchised and disfranchised, rich and poor.

"Holding fast to what is good" may mean clinging to those from whom all signs of good are ostensibly absent, in whom good no longer appears to reside, for whom there is no more good, who are indeed regarded by us, by the church, and by society as "no good." Only in this way can all signs and expressions of haughtiness and conceit be removed from the Christian fellowship. Only in this way can "love be genuine" (v. 9).

Luke 1:39–57

The service of Visitation recalls Mary's visit to her kinswoman Elizabeth in the hill country of Judah. This celebration provides not only the occasion for the church to anticipate Christmas yet six months away, but also the opportunity to hear Luke sing and expound on that beautiful moment. Before the births of either John or Jesus, the reader of Luke is made privy, through their mothers, to the profound Christian themes yet to be lived out and proclaimed.

Elizabeth and Mary are not nameless and faceless women who are no more than the wombs that carry great sons. They are persons with names, addresses, beliefs, hopes, and joy in service. Such is Luke's treatment of women in the Gospel story. Mary will reappear in trust and devotion (Acts 1:14), as will other women who join in the mission (Luke 8:1–3), and to them is entrusted the one sustained hallelujah of the Christian faith: He is risen (Luke 24:1–12).

Mary's visit to Elizabeth provides the occasion for the two women to celebrate the angel's word to Mary, which was also the angel's word to Abraham and Sarah: "For nothing will be impossible with God" (1:37; Gen. 18:14). As Paul was to express it, God gives life to the dead and calls into existence things that do not exist (Rom. 4:17). It does not matter whether it is a case of an old and barren couple or a virgin without a husband. The Visitation is, therefore, a double celebration of the power of God to give life.

The Visitation is also a study in contrasts. Elizabeth is old, the wife of a priest who was part of an ancient order of things in Israel. Having a child in her old age is a reminder of the past: Abraham and Sarah, Manoah and his wife, Elkanah and Hannah, from whom came Isaac and

Samson and Samuel. The promises of God survived and continued through the unlikely births to the old and barren. But Mary was young, a life new, virgin, and all promise. She and her child do not remind one of the past; in fact, in them begins a new history. Mary's child is continuous with the past, to be sure, the fulfillment of a promise, but in him God is doing a new thing. So radically new is this act of God that the only appropriate means was a woman young, and a virgin.

The Visitation is also a beautiful reflection, through the women, of the futures of their unborn sons. As Elizabeth is humbled by the visit of "the mother of my Lord" (v. 43), so John was witness and servant to Jesus. As John leaped in Elizabeth's womb when Mary entered the house (vv. 41, 44), so John's joy was that of a groomsman when the bridegroom arrived (John 3:29–30). As Elizabeth blessed Mary not only for her child but also because Mary believed the word of God (vv. 42–45), so John would come calling for faith in Jesus as the means of life in the kingdom. There is never any question for Luke that Jesus and not John is the Messiah, but neither is there any question that both Elizabeth and Mary are servants of God's purpose, both their sons are gifts of God, and both sons have appointed ministries in God's plan for the ingathering of the nations.

The Visitation is also a preview of reversals yet to come. The ordinary structures of history, the usual cause and effect sequences of events, could not sustain or contain what God would be doing. The empty will be full and the full, empty; the poor will be rich and the rich, poor; the powerless will reign and the powerful will be dethroned. In a close approximation of the Song of Hannah (1 Sam. 2:1–10), Mary sings of the eschatological reversal of stations and fortunes in the realm where and when God's love and justice rule supreme.

Holy Cross, September 14

Numbers 21:4b–9;
Psalm 98:1–5 or Psalm 78:1–2, 34–38;
1 Corinthians 1:18–24;
John 3:13–17

As is true throughout the liturgical year, the Gospel lection is the magnet that gathers the other readings. The statement in John 3 about Jesus' being lifted up makes use of the bronze serpent story in Numbers 21. The Epistle presents Paul's preaching of the cross as God's weakness and foolishness that is stronger and wiser than all human achievements. Both selections from the Psalms praise God, whose victory lies not only in strength but in goodness that spares the guilty.

Numbers 21:4b–9

Like many other Old Testament readings for special days, this one has been connected with the particular occasion on the basis of typological exegesis. The association of this passage from Numbers with the cross of Jesus comes from New Testament times. "Just as Moses lifted up the serpent in the wilderness, so must the Son of Man be lifted up" (John 3:14). It continues to be instructive to reflect on the ways the story of the serpent in the wilderness is like the story of the cross.

It seems as if Moses had nothing but trouble from the people of Israel in the wilderness. On other occasions in the readings for this season, we have encountered those people complaining against Moses and the Lord, even objecting to the burdens of their election, the fact that they were set free from slavery in Egypt.

Although this story of complaint begins like most of the others, its results are quite different from the previous ones. There is the general observation that the people "became impatient on the way" (v. 4). The reader familiar with the story of Israel's travels from Egypt will already find this remarkable; they had been impatient and dissatisfied almost from the first day! Then follows the grumbling that is a summary of all the things they have complained about from the beginning. They grumble against God and Moses about being in the wilderness, about the lack of food and water, and—inconsistently—about the food they do have. This doubtless is an objection to the manna, never especially appealing, but certainly boring after the traditional forty years in the desert.

Usually what has happened at this point in the stories of Israel's complaints is Moses' intercession with the Lord, who graciously meets the needs of the people, either for food, water, or security. But we hear without explanation that the Lord sent "fiery serpents among the people and they bit the people, so that many people of Israel died" (v. 6). Now the people do two things: they confess their sin of rebellion against the Lord and the leadership of Moses, and they ask Moses to intercede with the Lord to remove the serpents (v. 7).

When Moses prays for the people, the Lord responds but does not "take away the serpents." Instead, the Lord instructs Moses to make a fiery serpent and set it on a pole so that those who are bitten may look at it and live (v. 8). Moses did as instructed, setting up a bronze serpent, and it functioned as promised (v. 9).

The religious background of the traditions in this passage are complex. The belief is widespread that the image of a dangerous animal can function as protection against it, and the image of the snake in particular is associated with healing rituals in various religions. But does not the very fashioning of such an image violate the Second Commandment (Exod. 20:4) and thus threaten to violate the First Commandment (Exod. 20:3)? Perhaps that is why the text mentions cautiously that the people were only to "look at" the bronze serpent. It is not an idol but a gift of the Lord. There must have been such an image in the temple in Jerusalem, for 2 Kings 18:4 reports that when Hezekiah purified the worship, he destroyed "the bronze serpent that Moses had made." Even healing symbols can become objects of idolatry.

Theologically, the most important factor here is the pattern of sin, punishment, and God's means of grace. Once the people sin, experience the punishment, confess their sin, and pray for relief, the Lord responds. On the one hand, it appears that the Lord was eager to respond almost before they asked. On the other hand, the prayer is not granted in the form requested. Sin has—and will continue to have—its effects. The dangers remain, and the people continue to suffer from the potentially death-dealing snakes. However, now there is healing from the Lord, although the scars of the snake bites—the effects of sin—doubtless will remain.

Psalm 98:1–5

One of the enthronement hymns, Psalm 98 praises Yahweh as the sovereign reigning over the world of creation and as the special benefactor of the house of Israel. Thus both the universal and the particular domains of Yahweh are noted.

Much of this psalm consists of calls or summons to praise/worship as well as reasons why God should be worshiped and praised. Those called upon to praise God are the community of Israel (implied; vv. 1–3), all the earth (all humanity; vv. 4–6), and various elements in the world of nature (sea, world, their inhabitants, floods, and hills; vv. 7–9). The ancient rabbis, in commenting on verse 8, noted that there are only three references in Scripture (Old Testament) to the clapping of hands: the peoples clapping hand in hand (Ps. 47:1), the trees of the field clapping branch against branch (Isa. 55:2), and the floods clapping against the banks of the river (Ps. 98:8).

The reasons for praise in the first section (vv. 1–3) are all associated with the word "victory." God has won victory for himself (v. 1), God has made known his victory (v. 2), and the ends of the earth have seen his victory (v. 3). The marvelous things God has done, which are not spelled out, are related to his vindication ("His triumph"; NJPSV) in the sight of the nations and to the manifestation of his steadfast love and faithfulness to Israel. The reason for praise in the second section (vv. 4–9) is the coming of God to judge the world, not simply to judge but to judge with (establish) righteousness and equity (v. 9).

Psalm 78:1-2, 34-38

This psalm is a long composition offering a recital of the historical epochs of Israel's past. The following epochs are covered: (1) the patriarchal period (vv. 5–11), (2) the Exodus and wilderness wanderings (vv. 12–53), (3) the settlement in the land of Canaan (vv. 54–66), and (4) the election of David and Zion (vv. 67–72). These epochs and the events associated with them are used as points of departure for preaching and proclamation. In this psalm, most of the past is interpreted as times of disobedience and is used to engender a sense of guilt and shame from those addressed in the psalm.

The two sections selected for this lection are part of the introduction (vv. 1–2) and a portion of the psalmist's interpretation and preaching on the wilderness theme (vv. 34–38). The opening verses present the historical synopsis and interpretation that follow as a teaching or a parable, that is, not as a pure recital of history but as an interpretative reading of the past intended to speak to the present.

Verses 34–38 are a portion of the homily on Israel's behavior in the wilderness. Although cared for, preserved, and fed in the desert, the Hebrews are described as having constantly sinned. The people are depicted as demurring and demanding, unappreciative and uncooperative. Over and over again, God has to act to reprimand them. Verses 34–38 proclaim two things about the people. First, they were not repentant until they were punished; they did not turn toward God until God had turned against them. Their repentance was the product of divine coercion. Second, their devotion was superficial and temporary. Their mouths and their tongues were committed to religious expression, not their hearts. Flattery and lies, not fidelity and loyalty, were their hallmarks.

In spite of the people's behavior and their transient faith, they depicted God as their refuge and redeemer (v. 35). Long-suffering and forbearing, God forgave and did not destroy; God withheld his anger and did not give vent to his wrath (v. 38).

1 Corinthians 1:18-24

Portions of this text overlap with the epistolary readings in several other liturgical settings. For the Fourth Sunday After the Epiphany in Year A and Tuesday in Holy Week in Years A, B, C, the longer form of the text is used (vv. 18–31). For the Third Sunday in Lent, Year B, a shorter form is used (vv. 18–25). This same text also serves as the epistolary reading for Holy Cross in Years A and B. The reader may want to consult our remarks in these other settings for additional information about this passage.

A special feast day celebrating the cross has origins at least as early as the fourth century, when Constantine's mother, St. Helena, is said (according to one tradition) to have discovered the cross on which Christ was crucified. The date was September 14, 320. Some fifteen years later, in Jerusalem two churches were dedicated: the Church of the Cross and the Church of the Resurrection. In connection with this, the cross discovered by Helena became an object of veneration for the faithful, and out of this arose an annual feast celebrating the cross. An important feature of this celebration was to display a relic of the cross by lifting it up for the faithful to see. Because of this, the feast came to be known as the "Exaltation of the Holy Cross."

Among the epistolary readings that have been used in connection with this feast day are Philippians 2:6–11, 1 Peter 3:17–22, and today's text from First Corinthians. The central theme, of course, is the cross of Christ and its redemptive power in the world.

One of the major themes of today's epistolary text is the paradoxical nature of the cross. Ostensibly, it is a sign of scandal, utterly incomprehensible to everyone (Jews and Greeks) except those of us who experience it as a unique instance of God's love and power. What the cross signifies is the capacity of God to show love through powerlessness, to bring about our redemption through a display of self-giving. Such action on the part of God upsets our normal expectations and the expectations of the world. We would normally expect God to be manifested in great displays of power and strength, not in a moment of utter weakness and powerlessness. And yet the cross becomes one of the chief focal points through which we see God being manifest to us.

One way the cross exercises powerful influence on us is by forcing us to think paradoxically about human existence and divine power. As Barth remarks, "Truth cannot be expected to encounter [us] as a phenomenon which is immediately and directly illuminating, pleasing, acceptable and welcome to [us]. [We] would not be who [we] are if the promise of the Spirit came to [us] easily and smoothly." And so it is that the message of the cross cuts across the grain, repels us before it attracts us, transforms us even as it clutches us. We first encounter it as an act of consummate folly, and even after we have been lured by its curious force we may even still find it nonsensical.

Yet for those "who are being saved" it remains "the power of God" (v. 18). Why is this so? For one thing, it continues to reverse our human values. As Barth suggests, we expect truth to encounter us in ways that conform to who we already are, when in fact it encounters us by challenging who we are and what we know. Otherwise, we would already have and embody truth. Left to ourselves, we develop expectations of God that conform to our own views of deity: exaltation without humiliation, power without suffering, rising without dying. It is the cross that constantly rubs against our human grain, presenting us with a God who astounds us with divine folly. In the end, we discover our own folly in thinking that God would act in human ways, much less that God must act in human ways. The lingering echo of the cross is that "God's foolishness is wiser than human wisdom, and God's weakness is stronger than human strength" (v. 25).

John 3:13–17

As a magnet, the subject of the cross has been held over the text for the day, drawing to itself those verses pertaining directly to that event. Fairness to the subject and to the text demands, however, that verses 13–17 be set back into the context in order to extract them again.

John 3:1–21 is usually regarded as a conversation between Jesus and Nicodemus. However, where the Evangelist ends the conversation and where his own comments begin is not clear. One has but to look at different red-letter editions to see this uncertainty illustrated: Do Jesus' words end at verse 15, at 16, or at 21? The question is, however, a moot one, because the text reveals clearly that John is doing more than reporting a conversation. Such a shift begins at verse 7 with a change from the singular to the plural "you." The message from Jesus, says the writer, is to all and not to Nicodemus alone. The plural continues in verses 11 and 12. In addition, at verse 11 the "conversation" becomes more openly a debate between the church and the synagogue over the subject of life in the kingdom. Note the "we" versus "you" (plural). Furthermore, at verse 13 the passage becomes even more obviously a post-Easter Christian message by the statement in the past tense, "No one has ascended into heaven except the one who descended from heaven, the Son of Man." The earthly sojourn of the Savior is viewed as a completed event. It would be unfair, therefore, to treat this text within the confines of a private conversation at the beginning of Jesus' ministry, and it would be grossly unfair to be critical of Nicodemus for not understanding it. The Evangelist, by means of Nicodemus, is addressing the reader.

And what is the Evangelist saying to the reader? Let us confine ourselves to the bearing of the text on our subject, the cross of Christ. If the cross is not mentioned in verses 13–17, how is it to be discerned here? To be sure, in traditional church art, music, and theology, John 3:16 is associated with Golgotha. It is as though it were to be translated, "For God so loved the world that he gave his only Son *on the cross.*" That the cross is a part of the Johannine understanding of salvation is beyond question. Jesus lays down his life for the sheep (10:11); he lays down his life for his friends (15:13); he dies as the Passover lamb providing the freedom of a new exodus for the people of God (19:31–37). But the cross in this Gospel is the means of glorifying the Son (12:23–28); that is, of returning the Son to the presence of God. Hence the double meaning of being "lifted up" (v. 14; 8:28; 12:34)—up on the cross and up into glory. This being lifted up is as surely an act of God's grace and love as was the provision for salvation in the camp of Israel when they suffered God's judgment and punishment for their unbelief and disobedience (v. 14; Numbers 21). Jesus' being lifted up was an act of love from God toward the world, and to be understood as this Evangelist presents it, that act needs to be seen in the full movement of the descending and the ascending of the Son of Man (v. 13).

In summary fashion, John's message may be stated this way: the Son came into the world to reveal God (1:18), whom to know is life eternal (17:3). That revelation is not only in signs and discourses but also in the cross.

The God revealed in the Son is a God who loves, who loves the whole world, and who desires none to perish but that all have life eternal. God does not simply wish this; God sends the only Son to offer this life as a gift.

However, the cross refers not only to Jesus' death but to his being lifted up to God. This also is a part of the salvation event in that the glorified Christ sends the Holy Spirit to his church (7:39). "Nevertheless I tell you the truth: it is to your advantage that I go away, for if I do not go away, the Advocate will not come to you; but if I go, I will send him to you" (16:7).

Index